THE COLLECTED WORKS OF PAT ROBERTSON

The Collected Works of
PAT ROBERTSON

THE NEW MILLENNIUM

THE NEW WORLD ORDER

THE SECRET KINGDOM

INSPIRATIONAL PRESS
New York

Scripture Quotations

THE NEW MILLENNIUM: Unless otherwise indicated, all scriptures are quoted from The Holy Bible, New International Version, © 1973, 1978, 1984 by the International Bible Society. Used by permission.
THE NEW WORLD ORDER: Unless otherwise noted, Scripture quotations are from the New King James Version. Copyright © 1979, 1980, 1982 Thomas Nelson, Inc., Publisher.
THE SECRET KINGDOM: Unless otherwise indicated, all Scripture quotations are from The New American Standard Bible (NASB), © The Lockman Foundation 1960, 1962, 1963, 1968, 1971, 1972, 1973, 1975, 1977 and are used by permission.

Other Scripture quotations are from the following sources: *The Jerusalem Bible (JB)*. Copyright © 1966 Darton, Longman & Todd, Ltd., and Doubleday & Co., Inc.; *The King James Version (KJV); The Holy Bible, New Century Version (NCV)*. Copyright © 1987, 1988, 1991 Word Publishing. Used by permission; *The Holy Bible, New International Version (NIV)*. Copyright © 1973, 1978, 1984 International Bible Society. Used by permission of Zondervan Bible Publishers; *The New King James Version (NKJV)*. Copyright © 1979, 1980, 1982 Thomas Nelson, Inc., Publisher; *The Living Bible (TLB)*. Copyright © 1971 Tyndale House Publishers, Wheaton, Ill. Used by permission.

Published in 1994 by Inspirational Press, A division of Budget Book Service, Inc., 386 Park Avenue South, New York, NY 10016

Inspirational Press is a registered trademark of Budget Book Service, Inc.
Published by arrangement with Word, Inc., a division of Thomas Nelson.
Library of Congress Catalog Card Number: 94-77190
ISBN: 0-88486-106-6
Text designed by Hanner Lerner.

Printed in the United States of America.

Contents

Volume One
THE NEW
MILLENNIUM
1

Volume Two
THE NEW
WORLD ORDER
281

Volume Three
THE SECRET
KINGDOM
513

Volume One

The New Millennium

This book is dedicated
to those who sincerely are seeking
to learn the truth of the spiritual megatrends
which are shaping the future of our world.

My profound appreciation goes to Dr. James Black whose indefatigable labor, warm good nature, and vast book publishing experience is responsible for the structure of this work.

I also want to thank two superb newsmen, Drew Parkhill and John Waage, for always being available with the hard-to-find research material and the arcane statistics I always seemed to need at the last minute.

My thanks to editor, Al Bryant, who is this year retiring from a long publishing career.

I would be remiss if I did not mention the help of two key executives at WORD, Incorporated, Joey Paul and Kip Jordon, who made the challenge of writing this book so irresistible that I agreed to do it even though my instincts told me that such a project had to be impossible in light of everything else that I was already obligated to do.

Finally, I owe profound thanks to my wife, Dede, who put up with before dawn mornings, books and papers everywhere, and who faithfully read and discussed every chapter with me as it appeared, then encouraged me on.

Contents

Preface   7

Part I
The Clash of Ideologies

1 A New Beginning   13
2 The Fall of Communism   27
3 The Rise and Fall of Secularism   50
4 The Rise of the Supernatural   69

Part II
The Tri-Lateral World

5 The Unification of Europe   97
6 The Rise of the East   116
7 The Undermining of America   139
8 The Assault on the Family   163

Part III
2000 and Beyond

9 Technology and the Environment   187
10 The New Economics   213
11 The Rise of Anti-Semitism   231
12 Looking Ahead   258

Bibliography   278

There can be no new world under present conditions. Something dramatic has to happen to alter man and his world. That leaves us with only one absolute certainty about the future: Christ as the Prince of Peace, with the government upon His shoulders.

—BILLY GRAHAM

Preface

As THE APOSTLE Paul said, "Now we see through a glass, darkly; but then we shall see face to face . . . Now I know in part, but then I shall know fully." God promises that someday all the mysteries of life will be clear to us; someday all the events of our lives will be revealed and everything will make sense.

But today, there are limits to how much we can know about the significance of the happenings in our daily lives, especially with the rapid pace of the changes taking place in the world around us. Consequently, it is incredibly difficult to predict what lies ahead in the next week, let alone the next year, two years, or decade.

Nevertheless, wisdom has taught us that when we can observe certain trends over a period of time, we can believe that certain other effects and events will probably take place. So as we look ahead at the decade of the 1990s, and toward the year 2000, I would like to focus on some of the things that we can see in our world and begin to analyze some of these trends and their potential consequences.

Absent the violent overthrow of government, or severe economic crisis, or the direct intervention of God in our society, or absent a major spiritual revival, what lies ahead for the United States can be understood to some degree in the light of the trends taking place today in this nation and around the world.

From the vantage point of history, and with a respect for the ethical and moral traditions which have provided the foundation for Western society throughout most of our history, we can even begin to speculate on what lies ahead.

So, what we will talk about in this book will be a broad range of analysis of the events of the next decade, and how they will affect each individual and his or her family, and what they will likely mean for the United States and our relations with the rest of the world.

We approach these subjects with humility, recognizing that we are fallible human beings; and we recognize that the sudden changes we have already seen in the international arena are clear evidence of the volatile nature of the forces at work in the political world, and in the spiritual world. There will certainly be changes and reversals in some of these events which may shed new light on the issues I will be discussing here.

In some cases, things may in fact turn out quite differently than we had anticipated. Even so, I trust those changes will not invalidate the focus of this work nor its perspectives. I hope, rather, to confirm the volatility of the world situation and affirm other points of focus in this work with greater clarity.

My essential concern has been to reset the pieces on the chessboard of history, to restore a sense of who we are today and how we have come to be where we are.

In the whirlwind of world upheaval, social change, and cultural and emotional restructuring of such tremendous proportions, it is easy to forget the outlines and the context of our experience. We forget where we've come from and how we got here. We even forget that there are definite and unchangeable benchmarks of the human condition.

It is my hope that this book will help to re-establish some of those factors in such a way that we can find a renewed vision of truth and justice, and that we can step out bravely into the new world and the new millennium that waits just ahead.

When we speak from the Bible, we will say "Thus saith the Lord," but otherwise, most of the observations presented here will be my own considered opinion. While I continue to trust the Lord for His wisdom and insight, and while a lot of research and commentary has been included in this work from various professional and scholarly sources, the responsibility for the use and application of these observations rests with the author.

For a world beginning a period of tumultuous, exciting, and sometimes frightening changes the words of the prophet Daniel ring clear and true:

> Let the name of God be blessed forever and ever
> For wisdom and power belong to Him.
> And it is He who changes the times and epochs;
> He removes kings and establishes kings;
> He gives wisdom to wise men,
> And knowledge to men of understanding.
> It is He who reveals the profound and hidden things;
> He knows what is in the darkness.
>   (Daniel 2:20–22 NASB)

It is my fervent hope that each reader will be challenged and strengthened by what follows.

Part I

THE
CLASH
OF IDEOLOGIES

Nature abhors a vacuum, and secularism has left a spiritual vacuum in the hearts of all those who once turned to it for freedom and hope. To survive, the humanists will either have to decamp or change their ways, and this is the decade in which one of those two will most certainly come to pass.

1

A New
Beginning

This decade will witness "a revolution in the sphere of human consciousness." The Christian church will have an opportunity as great as it experienced at the fall of the Roman Empire.

T HE MEDIA HAVE barely been able to keep up with the rush of world events. Day after day, the headlines of our daily papers and news magazines shout the news of revolutionary changes taking place in every corner of the globe.

Emblazoned across the front page of the *New York Times* Sunday editorial section just a few months ago was a photograph showing a massive portrait of Lenin being erected in Moscow for the fortieth anniversary of the Bolshevik Revolution, in 1957.

After its first forty years, the Revolution still lived in the hearts of the reformers, and the onslaught of communism seemed awesome and relentless to the rest of the world. But by February 1990, the headlines had a very different look. Now they proclaimed the great Lenin "The God That Failed."

After seventy years it is now clear that communism has failed to deliver the great social order and prosperity it promised. Marx and Lenin were wrong, and governments around the world that once pinned their hopes on an idealistic dream—on an economic theory born out of the failures of nineteenth century industrialism—are overthrowing those communist ideologies. As the *New York Times* proclaimed, they are "Renouncing the Revolution's Holy Writ."

Who would have dared imagine over the last forty years that we would live to see the day that the communist empire would fall apart in a single year? Who would have dared to predict that we would see a time when the nightmare of Marxist-Leninist communism would be nothing more than a bad dream?

Would anyone have believed we would see the brutal dictator of East Germany tried for crimes against the state? When the even more repressive and brutal Stalinist head of Romania, Ceausescu, would be executed by a firing squad? Or when millions of people in Poland, Czechoslovakia, Hungary, East Germany, Latvia, Lithuania, Romania, Bulgaria, and the toughest of the lot, Albania, would be demonstrating in the streets for democratic reform?

Communist party after communist party were suddenly dissolving before our eyes—not with revolutionary gunfire, but by demonstrations and public protest, and with remarkably little loss of human life.

We watched stunned as the Berlin Wall crumbled. The nightly news showed us every dramatic detail as the barbed-wire barriers between Hungary and Austria came down. The flow of people and information was suddenly opened up between East and West, and families that had been separated for years by brutal communist tyranny were finally reunited.

Hundreds of thousands of people from East Germany came into West Berlin without restraint. They were shopping, and they were free to stay if they wished. Who would have dared to dream it was possible? And yet it is happening, even now, before our very eyes.

FILLING THE VACUUM

Even more significant than the fall of communism itself is the revival of religious faith in the East Bloc countries. The head of an atheistic system, Mikhail Gorbachev, actually met with the Pope, who is the most visible expression of "theism" and Christianity in the world. And in that historic meeting, the leader of atheism told the world that they needed spiritual truths behind the Iron Curtain. The Kremlin confessed that the Soviet people were perishing from the lack of moral values.

What does this mean for us as we enter into the decade of the 1990s? **Among its many other weaknesses, communism failed to recognize what Pascal called "the God-shaped vacuum" in the human soul.** The spiritual vacuum left by seventy years of communist totalitarianism has created a desperate hunger in the souls of men and women around the world, wherever communism has prevailed. While pockets of Christianity survived by going underground, the majority of these people have been left spiritually and emotionally destitute.

Now they have the freedom to seek nourishment, but what will they find to fill the emptiness? What will satisfy their hunger? In a recent interview, the director of the Center for Strategic Studies at the Free University of Rome, Enrico Jacchia, told the *Wall Street Journal,* "There's a strategic void. Anybody with a concrete design may well succeed."

Beliefs and social structures, both physical and spiritual, are being explored like never before, which means that a "window of opportunity" is open. The need is great. But how will Christians respond?

I believe the 1990s are a "decade of opportunity." There has never been such opportunity in the history of Christianity. As one major belief system crumbles before our very eyes, it is leaving spiritually naked a population of between one and a half and two billion people.

In the process, the crumbling of atheistic communism gives the lie to humanists and atheists and all those who deny the reality of God all over the world, because it says that a system based on atheism, on collectivism, which does not permit people freedom, ultimately will fall. And the reverse of that is also true: "where the Spirit of the Lord is, there is liberty" (2 Corinthians 3:17 NKJV). When you begin to have religious revival in any country, sooner or later that country will move toward freedom.

Who would have dreamed that a television program based on Bible stories, on the discussion of the origin of man, of the fall of man from the garden, of the birth of Jesus Christ, of the crucifixion on the cross, that these very stories would be shown on the communist-run television system? First in Leningrad, then in Latvia and Estonia, then throughout the Soviet Union.

I am proud to report that such a thing did happen because programs we produced at the Christian Broadcasting Network, with the help of our associates in Japan, were available to be shown on those systems at a time when the people were ready to see and hear.

Today our "SuperBook" and "Flying House" animated Bible stories are being broadcast eight times a week inside the Soviet Union, and millions of people are being taught the truths of the Bible on the very vehicle once used for communist, atheistic propaganda inside these communist countries.

That is one small step, but before we take a broader look at the opportunities and the challenges that lie ahead as we approach the new millennium, I think we should look back at our history, to the way these cultures and customs came into being. If we pause to try to understand some of the things that led to this moment in time, we will get a better perspective on what we can expect to happen in the next ten or twenty years.

THE LEGACY OF ROME

At the time of the birth of Jesus Christ, the Roman Empire controlled the then-known world. Through systematic military and political conquest, the Romans conquered all the lands surrounding the Mediterranean and their dominion had grown larger than any previous empire.

The Assyrians, Babylonians, Persians, and the Greeks under Alexander the Great, each created vast and powerful kingdoms in their time. But the Roman Empire surpassed them all. With it had come a universal language, a system of roads, and a stable and orderly government.

The principal religion of Rome at the time of Christ was the Babylonian cult of Ishtar: the so-called "mystery religions" of the erotic goddess known as Astarte among the Canaanites and Ashtoreth among the early Hebrews. These religions were involved with various forms of occult spiritism that had demonic roots. Later the Romans began to worship their emperor as god on earth.

As each emperor died, Roman society began to deify the next emperor and to worship him. By the end of the third century A.D. the corruption and decadence of the rulers made it clear that emperor worship was a fraud. As the people recognized this fraud and the cult gradually disappeared, Christianity emerged as the only logical alternative.

The early apostles had covered all these regions and, despite terrible persecution, the truth of Jesus Christ was spread far and wide. The blood of the martyrs had been the seedbed of the church.

Early civilizations could not have dreamed of the incredible means of communication we take for granted today. Today, thanks to the power of radio, television, jet airplanes, and now satellites, words and ideas can travel across continents and around the world in a split second. But in ancient times, ideas could only move as rapidly as messengers on foot, or in fast chariots, could carry them. By our standards that was not fast at all.

Given the great difficulties of travel and language, and the risks involved in sharing a revolutionary new form of worship, the true scope of what was accomplished by a tiny band of first century Christians is almost inconceivable.

They started out a mere handful, 120 at first, and then a few thousand, and then a few thousand more. But they were valiant and committed even unto death. They burst forth out of Jerusalem, and sailing on creaky old ships or walking torturous journeys, and in constant peril, those men and women turned the world upside down. Within 300 years they had won the Roman Empire for Christ.

THE ASCENDANCY OF THE CHURCH

By the year 320 A.D., the Emperor Constantine had made Christianity the religion of the Empire, and from that point on missionaries began carrying the gospel around the world. Through their efforts, Christianity ultimately replaced the "mystery religions."

The pagan religions also worshiped gods known as the "Baals," which means lords. They had many types of strange gods and goddesses. They worshipped idols of every imaginable sort, which prompted the apostle Paul to say, when he was giving his sermon on Mars Hill, "I see that you are a very religious people." But since they had been created in the minds of men and not in the mind of God, the deities of the Greeks and the Romans were very human-like and fallible creatures.

While the sanctuaries of the Egyptians had been shrines to the ancient pharaohs, their religion was naturalistic and animistic. They worshiped the sun and moon, owls and snakes, and a whole host of imaginary creatures. The pantheons of Greece and Rome, as well as all their temples and shrines, were populated by supernatural beings that resembled human beings much more than gods. They had the same lusts and passions and angers of human beings; they just had a lot more of them.

The priests and scribes credited the various gods with vast powers and with control of the sun, stars and planets; yet Zeus and Apollo and Jupiter behaved like surly, selfish mortals. It was relatively easy by such standards to consider a man, such as the emperor, a god. If no better, he was clearly no worse.

In each of these pagan religions there was always a seed of Satanic root, and even as the various cults failed in the West, those seeds refused to die. As the mysteries began to disappear in the West, they migrated to what is now India, and from there on to China and the Far East.

That particular type of religion which involved the worship of man-kind, and deities like man, of many demonic gods and goddesses, and a belief in reincarnation, began to take root in India even as it was being supplanted by Christianity in the Mediterranean world.

From 320 on, Christianity spread throughout the Roman Empire and moved up into Northern Europe. It displaced some of the more primitive religious systems of the Teutonic tribes, and with the growth of Christianity came education, culture, and the genuine enlightenment that inevitably springs from the faithful worship of Jesus Christ.

When the Roman Empire finally began to collapse under the weight of internal corruption, the only power with the strength and authority to replace it was the Church of Rome. Pope Leo the Great personally saved Rome from attack by Attila the Hun in 452, and from a similar fate at the hands of Genseric, leader of the Vandals, in 455.

The spiritual and temporal power of the Roman Church was complete when, on Christmas Day in the year 800, Pope Leo III crowned Charlemagne as the Holy Roman Emperor. This laid the foundation for the designation of Europe—and subsequently the European colonies in North and South America—as Christendom.

This Christian empire combined the might of Rome and the passionate faith of the Byzantine Empire, which had grown strong in Eastern Europe. The church then unified the authority of the European monarch with the authority of the Pope of Rome in what was called a "holy alliance."

From that moment, and for a period of a thousand years—from about the year 500 to the year 1500—Christianity flourished throughout Europe. The civilizations of Greece and Rome had been replaced by a new emerging civilization based on the Bible and the worship of Jesus Christ.

The Christian faith spread to Russia, where there were mass conversions around the year 1000. It spread into England, Ireland, France, Spain, Italy, Germany, Scandinavia, and all over the continent of Europe. There was one religion, one worship, and Jesus Christ was Lord of all: spiritual and temporal.

When any institution becomes that powerful, it inevitably becomes corrupt. "Power corrupts. Absolute power corrupts absolutely," as Lord Acton put it. The seeds of great corruption began to grow within the papacy, and in the Roman Church, and in the government. To get ahead in the government, as in every area of the political and business life of the times, it was necessary to be well connected in the religious life of the society.

Popes began to be popes not because of their allegiance to Jesus Christ, but because of their desire for temporal power. There were feuds within the church—popes and anti-popes, intrigue and corruption, splendor and excess. Therefore, it was not surprising that, about the year 1500, a major challenge was launched against the corruption of the church. That challenge, which we know as the Protestant Reformation, eventually brought about the formation of the Protestant church.

The first expressions of the Reformation came from the teachings of Martin Luther and what, by the middle of the sixteenth century, would be known as Lutheranism. Secondly, through the teachings of the French theologian, John Calvin, came Calvinism, which led to the Presbyterian and Reformed traditions within the Protestant church.

Over the following decades other expressions emerged, such as the

Baptists in about 1620. During the next 100 to 150 years, Methodists and the various "holiness" churches came into being through the teachings of John Wesley.

DARKNESS AND THE LIGHT

During the period when the Roman Catholic Church was falling from its place of supremacy, and before the Protestant movement could occupy any comparable degree of authority in Western culture, nonreligious, secular movements began to make their way into European thought through the writings of men like Rene Descartes and Baruch Spinoza. The most pernicious came to be known as "rationalism."

People influenced by these new ideas began to believe that the human mind was more important than the supernatural, and that the aim of philosophy and ethics—and all of life for that matter—was the attainment of god-like human perfection. *Reason, not God, was the center of their universe.*

The philosophers began to speak of God as the great Watchmaker who made the universe, created and organized it after a very carefully defined plan, then withdrew. They suggested He wound the universe up like a clock then turned it loose to run according to the laws He had given it. This belief was known as Deism, and out of Deism came the age of "The Enlightenment," during which the "rationalistic" ideas of thinkers such as Descartes, Rousseau, Voltaire, and others had great impact.

Henri Beyle (pronounced baal), who wrote under the name of Voltaire, was essentially an atheist. He loved to poke fun at every type of religious expression. He was a rascal and a lovable rogue with an irreverent and infectious sense of humor. The learned aristocrats of his day found it easy to buy whatever Voltaire was selling.

Jean Jacques Rousseau, though personally a very peculiar and scandalous man, attracted many followers as well. Rousseau did not believe in the original sin of man; instead, he believed that every human being possessed an essential nobility and dignity that needed to be fanned into flame by greater and greater personal freedoms.

Rousseau taught that there was a "noble savage" inside of people who was merely in chains. If the savage in us could be freed, we could have heaven on earth for the enlightened people whose inner deity would come forth without help from (or need of) God, but merely from political freedom.

Out of these new and revolutionary ideas came the horrors of the French Revolution, and the breakup of what was called the *ancien regime,* or the old order. The old order was systematically and brutally dismantled in France through the vehicle of the Revolution, and with it came a turning against the Church.

The Catholic Church had been so closely allied with the old order, with the nobility, with the kings, and with the court, it was discredited in the eyes of the people. The revolutionaries thought that in order to be free politically it was necessary to be free of Christianity. From that time, the central role of the Church in European society was gone forever.

A RAGE OF ANGRY MEN

The rationalist movement swept into the 1800s, an era that brought forth three major figures: Karl Marx, Charles Darwin, and Sigmund Freud. Each of these men—in company with a cadre of German theologians who emerged on the heels of the Revolution—were committed to debunking the Bible, turning against the supernatural, and teaching their own rationalistic theory that man and all the creatures of the animal world are mere products of blind evolution.

Man is *not* made in the image of God, they argued, and if there is to be salvation for mankind it will not be through divine intervention but through scientific discoveries and through the new technologies that were coming about in the Industrial Age. For each of these products of the Age of Reason, the Church was, at best, irrelevant, and Jesus Christ and God were more myth than fact.

It was an age of intellectual rage. The rise of rationalism and the revolutionary spirit led inevitably to the events of 1917. The Bolshevik Revolution of 1917, which came at the height of a horrible, bitter world war (1914–1918), resulted in greater loss of life than any war mankind had ever known. Out of it emerged a country and a government based, not on a religion, but on *atheism.*

So a small band of people, just 17,000 of them, brought forth the tyranny of communism and a new government in the Soviet Union. From the very beginning it was an awesome and terrible force.

The stunned silence in the air during those first years must have seemed very much like what we feel today as we are seeing the evil and the lies of communism exposed.

Who could have dreamed in those days that this atheistic state based on the collective ownership of property, a vicious dictatorship of the proletariat, and the suppression of the desires and the ambitions of every normal person, would sweep the world? But it did, indeed.

First communism was spread by subversive groups in Europe, and then after World War II, by the takeover at the point of the gun in Poland,

Czechoslovakia, Hungary, the Baltic States, Romania, and Bulgaria, and in the enormous nation of China.

Almost half of the population of the earth fell under the heel of a system of atheism. And in the rest of the world, Christianity was on the defensive. In Europe today, less than ten percent of the people attend any kind of church. There are state churches in some of these countries, but hardly anyone attends them, hardly anyone cares about religious values and religious matters, or remembers much about them.

Instead of the world being filled by Christianity, and instead of missionaries going out to evangelize in Africa and in Burma and China and all the nations of the world, and instead of the Western countries holding high the light of God's truth, suddenly we have a world where atheism, based on rationalism, has for decades been holding millions captive.

THE AGE OF UNREASON

In the United States of America, key universities, most of which had been founded by Christians, have been taken over by people who are sympathetic with Marxism, some of whom even believe passionately in communism. While only a few label themselves Marxists, almost all identify themselves as "secular humanists."

Virtually all the great universities—Harvard, Yale, Columbia, Princeton, Brown, Amherst, Dartmouth, Bryn Mawr, the various Wesleyan colleges, and many other private colleges and universities in America—were founded by Christians with strong moral values and absolute faith in God.

The humanists, on the other hand, believed in absolute human potential. As philosophical pragmatists, they subscribed to ideas popularized by William James and C.S. Pierce, which denied the existence of absolute or divine truth and held that the true value of any thing or any idea was merely its usefulness.

The leading spokesmen among the humanists—from John Dewey to Isaac Asimov—claim that there is no God, that the Bible is not the revealed Word of God, that mankind should be free of all sexual restraints, that there should be no question of guilt or sin or salvation or redemption, that man is to live out his life here on earth, that he is simply another part of the world he lives in, and that he is just a rung or two above the apes on the evolutionary ladder.

One of the doctrines of *The Humanist Manifesto,* first published in 1933 and signed by John Dewey and the vanguard of leftist intellectuals at this time, was that all humanists should find common cause with socialists around the world. These humanists did not believe in nationalism, they did not want individual countries, and they did not believe in the private ownership of property.

They wanted men to live in a social environment where the means of production were controlled by the state "for the common good of everyone." They were not avowed communists as such, but they believed in everything the communists believed in.

The signers of the Manifesto agreed, "A socialized and cooperative economic order must be established to the end that the equitable distribution of the means of life be possible. . . . Humanists demand a shared life in a shared world." In the revised Manifesto, published in 1973, the signers proclaimed their commitment to a one-world government. They write,

> We deplore the division of humankind on nationalistic grounds. We have reached a turning point in human history where the best option is to transcend the limits of national sovereignty and to move toward the building of a world community in which all sectors of the human family can participate. Thus we look to the development of a system of world law and a world order based upon transnational federal government.

The document is signed by over 150 intellectuals, scholars, authors, lawyers, planned parenthood activists, social workers, and ministers of the Unitarian church. Notable among them are behaviorist B. F. Skinner, author of *Beyond Freedom and Dignity*; Francis Crick, co-discoverer of the DNA molecule; poet John Ciardi; science fiction writer and virulent atheist Isaac Asimov; Soviet scientist Andrei Sakharov; and Paul Kurtz, editor of *The Humanist* magazine, who drafted the 1973 and 1980 versions of the Manifesto. Most notably, about 40 percent of the original signers were professors and university teachers.

In the universities where they have had so much power, especially during the reign of John Dewey at Teacher's College, Columbia University, the humanists have been teaching what is called "Cultural Relativism." There are no absolutes, there are no rules to follow, they claim, but each society must work out its own rules according to what it feels will be best for "humanity."

This was a very appealing doctrine for the new generation of intellectuals emerging in the 1930s. It looked to science for answers. It put man in charge of his own potential. And while these people were teaching in the schools of America and Britain and other European countries, they believed that the economic and political model to follow was taking shape before their eyes, in the Soviet Union.

Shortly after the Bolshevik Revolution, the American writer, Lincoln Steffens, said on his return from a trip to the Soviet Union, "I have seen the future, and it works!"

Well, the future didn't work and the Soviets were actually failing at everything they tried, but they were being propped up in the public esteem by a press and by an academic elite which was determined that humanism and socialism had to work.

In one of the greatest acts of gall on record, Lenin had the nerve to ask for financial aid from the West to prop up his struggling experimental government even after he had proclaimed the death of capitalism. And to the amazement of everyone, including Lenin, he got it. Such were the times.

A NEW AWAKENING

Today we have come full circle. It has taken us over seventy years to see that bubble burst and the false dream of communism explode. But it has exploded because it is false and it is wrong. People want to marry when they please, they want to travel as they please, they want to work where they please, they want to study what they please, and they want freedom *from* the state.

People want to work out their own destinies as God gives them the wisdom. They want to be accountable to the just laws of an ordered society. They do not want repression. They've learned communism neither works as a framework for economics or government. It never did work, and it never will.

Suddenly the model for the humanistic world view is collapsing before the eyes of the world. In the United States, the educational system founded on humanism is collapsing. Many of the governmental policies founded on humanism are also crumbling.

In an article in *The Humanist* magazine, Isaac Asimov expressed his fear that the construct of liberal humanism based on the socialist worldview has been damaged by the fall of communism. **The death of communist ideology is taking with it the whole facade of liberal, atheistic, humanistic, and deconstructionist thinking, and Asimov is absolutely right. Their side has lost.**

Even though the writer tried to absolve his own fears by attacking Christianity and religious values—saying that religious faith and superstition are the same thing—his point was taken. The mask is off. Communism, humanism, secularism, and atheism have failed, and anyone who can't see that now will find out soon enough.

EXPLODING THE MYTHS OF HUMANISM

The ethics that come from humanism are exploding dramatically before our eyes, with scandal after scandal in politics and business and public life. The free love and unrestrained sexuality they said was to be part of their system has destroyed the lives of young people all over the world.

We have a million teen-agers pregnant out of wedlock each year; we have a million and a half abortions each year; we have a shocking breakup of homes and families; we have as many as two million children running away from home every year.

There has been a continuous decline of our standard of living before the onslaught of more dedicated, more resolute people of Asia. All this is happening at a rapid pace. It is suddenly clear that beneath all the social failures there has been a fundamental flaw in the world's values.

The humanists who are honest (and unfortunately not many of them are yet intellectually honest) are beginning to say, "We were wrong." Today the press of America is pointing to a religious revival in the communist world and saying to the world that it is because of the religious faith of the Russian people, the Hungarian people, the Polish people and others, that this sweeping transformation is taking place.

The new prime minister of Poland, who was elected by the labor movement, Solidarity, was asked what his belief system was. He said very simply, "I am a Christian." Not a communist, but a Christian, and in his case, a devout Roman Catholic. This is the leader of the country that has been in the vanguard of the movement toward freedom.

THE SPIRITUAL CONFLICT

It is only fair that the American press should pose the battle between communism and capitalism in ecclesiastical language. In speaking of Lenin as "The God That Failed" and the doctrines of the revolutionaries as "Holy Writ," the editors of the *New York Times* recognized the essential spiritual nature of the conflict.

From the beginning, the war of ideologies has been a conflict between the verities of God and the vanities of man. First we had the mystery religions based on the worship of men; then the worship of false gods and animistic beings; then there were religious people consulting oracles, and finally a central church which, even while it had been founded on worship of the true and living God, degenerated into an oligarchy based on green, temporal power, and corruption.

In earlier times there were cities absolutely full of temples, but they were false temples dedicated to false gods. The dominion of the true Church fell into disfavor when it allowed false ideologies and faulty teachings to prosper. But today all these failures are being swept away by a fresh vision of Christianity. We are seeing the revealed truth of the living God, and the truth of the Holy Bible.

Eastern Europe, the Soviet Union, Communist China, and many other places where darkness has prevailed, are now being exposed to the Light of the World, to man's essential need for a Savior who came to earth, was born as a man, lived among us, was crucified, dead, buried, and rose again. A Savior who lived among His followers and taught them for forty days before ascending into heaven. Then, by the power of His Holy Spirit, He directed them to preach a gospel that had never been heard before in that form in all the world. Along with that incredible message came miracles and works of mighty power. They swept before them everything that was false and everything that wouldn't stand.

When the emptiness and fraud and shame could not be hidden any longer, the false religions of the old world tumbled like dominoes. Suddenly there was nothing left but Christianity to fill the void that a failing political system, a crumbling economic system, and a collapsing religious system left behind.

A DECADE OF CHANGE

In 1990 we witnessed a similar awakening. In his address to the United States Congress in February, the newly elected president of Czechoslovakia, Vaclav Havel, declared the current revolution in Eastern Europe not a war of invasion or retaliation but a "revolution in the sphere of human consciousness." That this European writer, hardly known in the West until recently, and imprisoned for years for refusing to bow to communist ideologies, should now stand before Congress as the leader of his country was an amazing irony. And the irony of his words could not be ignored.

He told his audience of Americans and foreign diplomats, "We are still incapable of understanding that the only genuine backbone of all our actions, if they are moral, is responsibility—responsibility to something higher than my family, my country, my company, my success." The furnace of adversity had prepared this man for this hour, and the truth of his appeal should be an alarm to every man and woman of faith.

The American press printed portions of Havel's New Year's Day speech to the people of Czechoslovakia; but some of the parts they did not print should not be missed. Havel said, "Our first president wrote, 'Jesus and not Caesar.' . . . This idea has now been reawakened in us. I dare say that perhaps we have even the possibility of spreading it further, thus introducing a new factor in European and world politics. Love, desire for understanding, the strength of the spirit and of ideas can radiate forever from our country, if we want this to happen."

"We are a small country," he said, "but nonetheless we were once the spiritual crossroads of Europe. Is there any reason why we cannot be so again? Would this not be another contribution through which we could pay others back for the help we will need from them?"

What a powerful statement from this remarkable man. I can only concur with George Weigel, of the Ethics and Public Policy Center in Washington, D.C., who says, **"If Vaclav Havel is not the 1990 Nobel Peace laureate, then the prize this year has no meaning."**

But the churches of Eastern Europe are small and inexperienced, not yet fully prepared to deal with the sudden freedom of religion and the frenzy of interest in the gospel. In a recent report in the magazine, *Christianity Today*, Bishop Beredi of Yugoslavia, said, "I don't see that we are ready to use all the privileges we have today." The people are hungry and they are coming by the hundreds, but the churches are scarcely able to cope. "We are so small," Beredi said, "we don't have the resources."

Too few pastors, too little training: these are common concerns. Peter Kuzmic, director of the Evangelical Theological College in Osijek, Yugoslavia, said, "We need quality literature that speaks to the man on the street who has never been inside a church, never read the Bible, doesn't understand religious language." But despite the crying need for aid, Kuzmic believes that the time is right and the door is open. "There is a vacuum here," he adds, "which needs to be filled with the gospel of Jesus Christ."

Christians from the free democratic nations of the West must acknowledge that they have a clear call to reach out to these people. We have a challenge to encourage and support these aspiring churches and to welcome an entire new generation of Christians into the fellowship of Christ. How will we respond? What an incredible hour for the world. What an opportunity.

"He has loosed the fateful lightning of His terrible, swift sword," says the great Battle Hymn of the Republic, "His truth is marching on!" And we, the children of the true and living God, must carry forth His banner into all the world. This could well be the decade of our greatest challenge.

The fall of communism makes the 1990s truly the decade of opportunity for the Christian church. This is an incredible hope for the world.

2

The Fall of Communism

The world has come to the conclusion that freedom works, not a centralized control economy. Marxist communism will cease to exist as a unifying philosophy for any society.

This decade will witness not only freedom in the formerly communist lands but a dangerous death rattle in the Soviet Union as it breaks apart.

IN FEBRUARY 1989 the Soviet Union turned tail and got out of a little country called Afghanistan, and from Riga in the Baltic to Cam Ranh Bay in the South China Sea, the myth of Soviet invincibility was forever shattered.

Who could have dreamed that within a single incredible year we would see the collapse of one communist government after another, and that in Poland, where the democratic revolution actually began, a Christian would be elected prime minister? The collapse of the hard-line government in East Germany and the breaking up of the hated Berlin Wall were object lessons to the world.

The reconstitution of the Communist Party of Hungary into a republican-style Socialist Party; the execution of the brutal dictator, Ceausescu, in Romania; the virtual disintegration of the governmental body, the Communist Party, in Yugoslavia; the declaration by Lithuania that it was an independent state; the Azerbaijan revolt against the central government of Moscow; and all the incredible events that took place in that twelve-month period brought a new vision of hope to men and women all around the world. Suddenly the regime Ronald Reagan had boldly labeled the "Evil Empire" didn't look like much of an empire anymore.

Even as the Soviets continue to arm at a staggering rate, spending upward of 25 percent of their entire GNP on arms, the ideology of communism has been mortally wounded. Someone has compared the Soviet Union to a crippled old man with a howitzer in the closet. He may be weak, but he's not powerless.

There is a genuine, ongoing danger of an armed uprising by separtist militants, or a military adventure by reactionary elements in Moscow. We cannot allow ourselves to be lulled into a false sense of security. But the events of 1989 and 1990 have given us unmistakable evidence that communism, as an ideology to claim men's hearts and minds, can never again be the threat it once was.

Human beings are creatures made in the image of God, and our hearts yearn to know Him. Any system that denies that yearning, and any ideology that attempts to prove that God does not exist, is destined to fail. God will ultimately find a place in the hearts of people, regardless of their ideologies, and regardless of the political system.

THE TYRANT IS DYING

At the height of its terrible reign, communism has gripped more than two billion people on this planet—at least forty percent of the population of the entire world. While we do not have absolute and final evidence that the seventy year reign of terror has been ended once and for all, the handwriting is on the wall. Today there is no question that Marxist-Leninist communism has failed, and with it has come the failure of atheism as a unifying ideology for a society.

Communism fails because it is an economic theory which does not relieve the suffering of the people, let alone provide for their prosperity. Atheism fails because it does not square with the reality of our world, nor does it address itself to the deepest needs of humanity.

The collectivism of socialism also goes contrary to another very fundamental truth: the innate worth of the individual. While a modern society is a vast organism with widespread powers and responsibilities, it is still made up of individuals who do their jobs each day in communication and in union with many others like them.

The decisions of millions of consumers, business people, factory managers, small entrepreneurs, and owners of large corporations, make up an inter-related network of decisions that affect thousands, millions, and sometimes tens of millions of individual transactions.

That is a fact of life in a busy world. However, the communist system supposed that a small elite cadre of leaders could be responsible for all of those decisions and could, in effect, manipulate and control the way business is done. Never can the decision of any twelve men in a central policy council replace the wonderful complexity and inventiveness of an entire society.

Even the attempt to do so is wrong because it claims for the government a God-like authority. The small cadre of *nomenclatura*, as they were called, saw themselves, in effect, as God's substitutes on earth assuming the authority of God in the lives of people. Any society or any group of people which ascribes such power to itself is doomed to fail. The collective cannot assume the responsibility of the individual, for every individual is called by God to his or her own unique responsibility.

The great truth of this was enunciated in the book of Jeremiah when God said to the prophet, "Before I formed you in the womb I knew you, before you were born I set you apart; I appointed you as a prophet to the nations" (Jeremiah 1:5). Before he was born Jeremiah was called to his unique destiny by God.

Every one of us has a role in life, and the task of government is to provide a framework where each individual citizen can work out in his own way the calling which God has given him.

A FRAMEWORK OF PEACE

Some have a calling for activity, others are called to quiet and contemplation. There is a calling for wealth, and a calling for sacrifice. All the struggles and strivings and aspirations of a society, along with the need to earn a living, make up what we call a free market.

Government should only interfere with that market to keep certain individuals from harming others: keeping certain groups from acquiring so much wealth and power that they threaten the aspirations of others. Beyond that, government should provide a framework of peace and security where the streets are safe and the borders are secure from invasion.

Contrast that with the role of the government under communism, where the government became the enemy of the people, oppressing them in every single thing they did, forcing them to conform in their thoughts, words, and actions to the predetermined government policy and brutally repressing those who deviated from that policy. That system was so contrary to God's will and the basic yearning of people for freedom that it had to fall.

At least five years in advance I predicted that Soviet communism was going to fall. In his book about my campaign for the presidency, Dr.

Hubert Morken made note of my prediction along with the reactions of the national media who scoffed that anyone would suggest that communism might conceivably fail in Eastern Europe. But the record stands.

After the Russian debacle in Afghanistan I knew that the myth of Soviet invincibility had been shattered. I was not surprised by the fact that it happened, though I was surprised (as we all were) with the speed at which it happened. Certainly in the East Bloc countries—Poland, Czechoslovakia, East Germany, Romania, Hungary, Bulgaria, Albania—there is a clear move for freedom. And in the Soviet Union itself there seems to be a movement away from communism which is irreversible.

THE BREAKUP OF RED CHINA

Despite the evidences of the massacre at Tiananmen Square, I think the downfall of communism is certain in China. The repression of the popular will by the military and political leadership is merely a momentary setback for freedom in that country. **When the old men like Deng Xiaoping and Li Peng are moved out of the way, I think it is only a matter of time before full expression of freedom takes place there.**

China is a unique and paradoxical land, known in its own antiquity as the "Middle Kingdom," the center of the earth. By dint of its sheer magnitude and its long and exotic history, it has proven to be a land where the unexpected can happen. Given that history, I think there is another provocative scenario which could begin to play itself out within the next several years.

Specifically, I would not be surprised if that country did not break up and revert either to a system of warlords similar in many respects to the system that existed back before the Kuomintang and the presidency of General Chiang Kai Shek or to a series of provinces with different economic philosophies and governing units.

I don't know that there is enough strength in the nation to provide a system of free-market democracy to govern more than a billion people. The political and social pressures in such a vast land are simply too immense to contain. I suspect a breakup of some kind is a very real possibility, but if it holds together, a free united China could become an awesome power in the next century.

THE WOUNDED BEAR

The disintegration of a bankrupt system is a natural phase of political change. When empires fall, they crumble. Today many commentators feel that the formal union of fifteen Soviet states will inevitably break up as well. Mother Russia has voted for freedom from the Soviet Union. It seems apparent that the Baltic states and Eastern Europe are destined to go free. Georgia, the Ukraine, Moldavia, Azerbaijan, and the Tashkent-Kazakhstan regions might then form into some kind of autonomous or semi-autonomous states.

The danger of such an eventuality is not the difficult period of transition that would then come about, but the prospect that the Soviet leadership might try some desperate last-ditch effort to prevent the loss of their empire.

We already know that today the Soviets are still spending about as much on arms as they were before the talk of *glasnost*. They have an arsenal that may well be as great as the combined strength of the United States and Europe. The danger to all of us is that as their economy continues to collapse and the empire disintegrates, there might be some kind of military adventure as a means of holding the whole thing together.

Frankly, I think that for the next few years the Soviet Union will be a very dangerous player. The magnitude of their arsenal and their military power is formidable and rapidly growing.

Now, in terms of what has already happened, I think we have to acknowledge that all this is of God. I think the Spirit of the Lord is bringing liberty into these oppressed lands. If we continue the evangelistic work that has been going on in Eastern Europe and continually step up the intensity of our labors, these former communist countries may well be the launching pad for the evangelization, actually the re-evangelization, of Europe.

This is a place where there is great hope spiritually. Without that, Western Europe is lost to Christianity and could easily become the launching ground for a New Age dictator.

Western Europe as a whole is so lacking in any true spiritual roots that I would not be surprised to see the rise of some popular, charismatic leader who could win the hearts of the people by speaking of the noble goals and worldwide aspirations of a renewed Europe, much as Adolph Hitler did in Germany in the late 1930s.

THE PEACE DIVIDEND

Throughout its history, the world has experienced more than 4,000 wars. Therefore, statesmen who have predicted war have usually been correct because they have had the precedent of history on their side. Given the reality of a sinful world, those who really want peace usually attain it only by having a strong military establishment. In political language, "peace through strength."

Nevertheless, I think the United States no longer needs large forces in NATO, nor do we need large forces defending Japan. I think a great empire moves on the strength of its economy before it moves on the strength of its military. If the United States economy becomes bankrupt, then ultimately our military will become bankrupt as well.

The United States must first strengthen its own economy. Then it would not be a great burden to maintain forces adequate for our defense. Having maintained a huge force in Germany for 45 years, we must now turn that task over to the Germans and evacuate our troops.

The same holds true for Japan: the Japanese people can defend themselves. A July 1990 edition of *Business Week* reported that Japan is the world's third largest military spender, after the U.S. and the Soviet Union. The U.S. Defense Department has already announced an 11 percent cutback in military aid to Japan, but that number must increase.

As the Japanese fund more of their own military readiness, we can better balance the federal budget and begin paying off some of the debt, which is imperative. We should certainly do that before we undertake any new social programs. We cannot borrow any more to pay for well-meaning welfare plans.

REAGAN'S CAVEAT

We know only too well that freedom has a high price. Before we allow the media or the reformers to cause us to jump too quickly to the conclusion that we're in for an economic windfall, which they are calling the "peace dividend," we should know where we stand. Returning the defense of Germany and Japan to the people of those countries does not mean we should, at the same time, weaken America's military.

To speak with credibility, America must stand on its strength, and that means we not only speak with authority but that we are prepared to act with authority. A strong voice without a strong military is only a hollow threat.

In what may be his finest public address, Ronald Reagan spoke to the nation of England from the London Guildhall in June 1988. This was at a time when the prospects for reform in Eastern Europe were beginning to seem very real. We weren't sure what Gorbachev was up to, but it seemed as if there might be a realistic hope for peace.

The president reflected on the long and warm kinship between the English and the Americans, and he remembered stories from the Second World War when we struggled together against a common enemy. But, more important, the President warned the English and the world that we must not forget the lessons we have learned in our struggle for liberty. That entire address deserves to be quoted, again and again, but at least some of Mr. Reagan's conclusions are worth citing here. He said,

> We have learned the first objective of the adversaries of freedom is to make free nations question their own faith in freedom, to make us think that adhering to our principles and speaking out against human rights abuses or foreign aggression is somehow an act of belligerence. Over the long run, such inhibitions make free peoples silent and ultimately half-hearted about their cause. This is the first and most important defeat free nations can ever suffer. When free peoples cease telling the truth to their adversaries, they cease telling the truth to themselves. In matters of state, unless the truth be spoken, it ceases to exist.

The President told the nobles and statesmen assembled there, and the nations of the world who were listening, that in a sense our actions can be measured by our words. That is, if we really believe in freedom and dignity, and if we are truly prepared to defend our beliefs, then we will not hesitate to say so.

Too often in recent months we have seen our government cave in to foreign intimidation. Too often the diplomats have wanted to maintain their friendly smiles for Gorbachev and Deng Xiaoping and the other tyrants of the world instead of speaking the truth when human rights have been violated and when human dignity has been crushed. Candor and outright honesty, Reagan asserted, do not provoke war: they prevent war. For how else will our enemies know we mean business unless we speak without fear?

Finally in those remarks, Mr. Reagan also expressed the hope that we would one day recognize that our common journey has been a pilgrimage toward honor, love, human dignity, and freedom for all peoples and all nations. He closed by stating his own faith that, wherever the struggle for honor and freedom has prevailed, the hand of God has guided our way and brought the victory of good over evil. He said,

> Here is the strength of our civilization and our belief in the rights of humanity. Our faith is in a higher law. We hold that humanity was meant not to be dishonored by the all-powerful state, but to live in the image and likeness of Him who made us. Let us seek to do His will in all things, to stand for freedom, to speak for humanity.

The issues that confront us today are no less serious than they ever were. The threats to freedom and dignity are no less real. Smiles and diplomacy and friendly gestures are good for business, but they are also good for treason. Judas betrayed our Lord with a kiss.

The warnings of President Reagan should be a reminder to all of us that we cannot throw down our weapons in the hope the world will suddenly call us friend. Cut back on the defense of Europe? Yes. They are very strong now, and while we will remain a powerful ally, we don't have to pay their bills for them. Cut back our defense of Japan? Yes. But we must never let down our vigilance, our resolve, or our military preparedness. We can best deal with the villains of the world, however much they may smile, when they know we have a mighty saber at the ready.

GORBACHEV

Mikhail Gorbachev, who is he? What is he? Is he the great defender of freedom, the "Man of the Decade," or is he the next great villain? In order to understand this man, it is vital to remember that Gorbachev is a creature of the KGB. He was a protege of Yuri Andropov, who was formerly head of the KGB.

Gorbachev began his rise to power as head of the Communist Youth Movement in Stavrapol. He later succeeded his mentor, Feodor Kulakov, as Central Committee Secretary for Agriculture in Moscow, where he became the protege of Yuri Andropov. He was trained by Andropov, taught by him, and sanctioned by him. He rose to become head of the Communist Party and the nation itself. Clearly, he was the master's prize pupil. There is no other way his incredible rise to power can be explained.

In his book, *Gorbachev: The Path to Power*, C. S. Hauer notes that Gorbachev's direct and speedy rise is unprecedented in Soviet history. He succeeded Kulakov who died, Andropov who died, then Chernenko who died. He took power in the same spot where Lenin declared the Bolshevik victory in 1917, declaring his allegiance to the goals of world communism.

Since his rise to power, Gorbachev has said again and again that his aim is to strengthen and improve communism, not to weaken it. In December 1989, the *New York Times* quoted his speech to Communist Party officials in which he said, "There are attempts to make you believe that I am working on behalf of someone, that I want to tear apart the party, the state, to bury socialism. I reject that. I am a Communist, a convinced Communist. For some that may be a fantasy, but for me, it is my main goal."

From a political perspective, it is clear that there has to be strong backing of his actions by very powerful forces. Seemingly, Gorbachev has undercut the Communist Party, undercut the military, undercut the old guard, and has taken to himself more personal power than any other leader in the history of the Soviet Union, including Joseph Stalin.

He is already a virtual dictator if he wants to exercise his power, and with the expanded powers he lobbied for and won in early 1990 he can even declare war at his own personal discretion.

What does that mean? For one thing, it means that the Soviet President can put through dramatic economic reforms which are critically needed; or he could turn that society very repressive again in order to save his own power.

The Soviet economy is collapsing so fast that either Gorbachev is going to have to use the army to bring people into submission or else he's going to have to permit the Soviet empire to fall apart. But will he do that?

If he should permit the empire to fall apart, it is possible that Gorbachev himself could become the subject of a bloody coup, probably by the army and the radical hard-liners. We saw in the news reports from the 1990 National Party Congress that the old guard are saying they are ready to oust this paradoxical reformer. Only Gorbachev's strength abroad, and the ongoing popularity of dissident leaders such as Boris Yeltsin, seem to stand between the president and the ire of the communists.

The bad news of the Soviet economy is not really news any more. When he came to the West, Aleksandr Solzhenitsyn told us, "communism cannot improve, only die." And now in the aftermath of the economic collapse we are beginning to find out what was really going on behind the Iron Curtain.

We learned that 30 million Soviet citizens do not have pure drinking water, that six million are homeless, 13 million live in communal apartments where two or more couples are forced to share the same bathroom and kitchen, and less than 50 percent of Soviet families can afford a refrigerator.

Instead of the monolithic government touted as the rival of the world's greatest economies, suddenly we see Soviet Russia as a Third World nation. The people are desperately poor, and the idea of collective labor is a colossal failure.

Today we know that 20 percent of Russian crops rot in the field; and over 40 percent of all the machinery in their small businesses doesn't work. People say the sausage sold in the government stores is so bad even the cats won't eat it, and basic necessities such as soap and toilet paper are not even available much of the time.

The average Soviet citizen must work ten times longer than the average American to buy a pound of meat; the infant mortality rate is 250 percent higher than that of Western nations; and the average woman will undergo eight abortions in her lifetime. That's the communist idea of birth control.

All these facts, and many more like them which have surfaced over the past year, are clear evidence that the communist social order has failed on every front. Soviet economists are reporting that over 85 percent of the people live below the poverty line. But apparently none of that has deterred the communists from building their war machine. Nor has it dissuaded the liberals who bet their lives on that godless dream.

The jokes people tell often give a certain insight into national character. A story making the rounds in Eastern Europe these days is about an American, an Englishman and a Russian who ended up in hell. It seems they each got one last chance to call home. It cost the American 1,000 dollars; the Englishman had to pay 600 pounds; but it only cost the Russian one ruble. The first two didn't understand, so they asked the Russian why his call was so cheap. "Local call," he said.

To some, that apocryphal story may not even be a joke. Today it seems that the only people left in the world who still believe in the communist lie are United States college professors caught in a '60s time-warp.

PROPPING UP A DYING REGIME

According to the latest calculations of Secretary of Defense Dick Cheney, reported in *Janes' Defense Weekly*, at least 25 percent, and possibly as high as 40 percent, of the entire gross national product of the Soviet Union goes for arms and military spending.

Soviet support for communist satellite governments or communist insurgencies in Angola, Cuba, Nicaragua, El Salvador, Afghanistan, South Africa, Libya, North Korea, the Philippines, and other Third World nations has been an endless drain on the Soviet economy with no substantial gains in world communism. The Rand Corporation estimates that the USSR has been paying upwards of 15 billion dollars annually in military aid to their dependent regimes.

The Russian ruble is valueless as a currency outside the Soviet bloc. It is useless even in places like Finland, which is closely linked to the Soviet economy. One of the few leaders who seems to be willing to trade with the Soviets, to give approval to them, and to share the latest technological secrets with them is the President of the United States.

During his visit to Washington in June of 1990, President Gorbachev came with no chips and nothing to bargain, but he walked away with a treasure. At the moment when it was clear to the entire world that communism was at last defeated, Gorbachev came to America, and we gave him more than he could ever have dreamed possible.

The arms reduction agreements drafted by President Bush and Gorbachev do not give the West any means of monitoring actual reductions of Soviet nuclear or chemical weapons. We have not insisted that Soviet spy satellites, tracking stations, or antennae be dismantled, as all our defense analysts had demanded.

Despite the warnings of experts, we agreed to share our scientific secrets with Soviet engineers. In effect, George Bush put all the chips in the Soviet president's hands.

A preponderance of our most respected scientists and advisers have warned that we must not give the Soviets our technology, our computer systems, or our financial backing. Now we are shipping IBM PCs and Macintosh computers to Russia by the boatload.

All of the brave dissidents, exiles, KGB defectors, and escaped writers who have fled to the West have reminded us of the way our liberal leaders propped up Lenin's New Economic Policy in 1921; how Harry Truman propped up "Old Joe" Stalin, the most tyrannical of all the Soviet dictators, between 1946 and 1949. Do not be fooled again by Gorbachev, they warn. We have to wonder if anybody is listening.

A SINISTER NEW SCENARIO

I believe that the fall of communism is real. I believe that the democracy movement in Eastern Europe is real. However, to check our euphoria there have been raised serious voices of caution. Could the entire scenario be nothing but a KGB ruse conceived by the master, Yuri Andropov?

In his book, *New Lies for Old: The Communist Strategy of Deception and Disinformation*, published in 1984, former KGB agent Anatoliy Golitsyn predicted virtually every event that we have witnessed the past three years. The weakness and instability we perceive today, he said, is no more than a massive fraud, a deception being staged by the Kremlin while they attempt to extort aid from the West and implement certain economic changes, on the capitalist model.

Golitsyn cited the exact details of a Communist Party conspiracy to deceive the West into believing that the Soviet Union is falling apart; that its satellites are splintering; that its economy is threadbare. "All warfare is based on deception," they say, therefore "feign incapacity."

"Offer the enemy the bait to lure him; feign disorder and strike him." This military wisdom, from the pages of Sun Tzu's *Art of War*, was adapted by the Soviets in the late 1950s and was being played out for real in the late 1980s. Golitsyn wrote about it in 1984, but of course, the liberals in the academy were not listening. Instead, we have opened our hearts and our values to the Kremlin and brought the bear into our midst.

But even our misguided largess may not be enough to save the wounded beast. A new book, co-authored by Moscow correspondent Dusko Doder and Louise Branson, a *London Times* correspondent in

Beijing, says that Gorbachev is only a transitional figure in the Soviet government.

Entitled *Gorbachev: Heretic in the Kremlin*, this new book maintains that, like Czar Peter the Great, Gorbachev can see the Russian economy dissolving and the strength of the empire crumbling around him. He knows that his only help can come from the West, so he has made brash overtures to the United States and Europe. But, while he is a hero to many in the West, he is considered a failure and a heretic at home.

Doder and Branson foresee public unrest and riots in the Soviet Union, demanding the ouster of the radical leader. It is obvious that the election of Boris Yeltsin as President of the state of Russia was a rebuff to Gorbachev. Yet, because of his newly granted powers as Soviet President, it would be very hard to oust Gorbachev—it would take an act of the entire Soviet Parliament—and then a strong power would have to succeed him. These authors believe that these events are certain and will lead inevitably to a military dictatorship. Then what?

In another book, *Soviet Disunion*, by Bohdan Nahaylo and Victor Swoboda, two East European authors suggest that there are only four possible scenarios for the USSR at this point in time. Gradual breakup of the empire; creation of a new, looser confederation; federalization; or restoration of the empire through military oppression and a reimposition of control by the hard-liners. Three of those four options would keep the communists in strict control; and even the possibility of a breakup of the empire offers no guarantee that the emerging governments would necessarily reflect Western democratic principles.

So far, everything Gorbachev has done, with few exceptions, seems to be moving toward an open society, free markets, and peace. He has certainly convinced people in the State Department and the White House that he wears a white hat. But that could be an illusion and we would be foolish indeed to put everything we've got into the Soviet leader's basket. The situation is still unclear and, at best, two sided.

THE VIETNAM EFFECT

Vietnam very likely hastened the decline in the United States that was already under way. The Great Society spending of Lyndon Johnson was an enormous failure and no doubt helped push that decline along. It wasted huge amounts of money, but in terms of its impact on reducing poverty its effect has been negligible.

The axiom in war is very simple. There is no substitute for victory. There is no such thing as a limited, no-win war. We should never have gotten into Vietnam; we should never have tried to fight a land war in

Asia; we should not have overthrown the Diem regime by a coup and an assassination. We should not have escalated that war the way we did.

The whole thing was a tragic mistake. But if we were determined that a just war was necessary, then we should have moved in with all of our forces as fast as we could and ended it. There should have been no privileged sanctuaries, no targets that were off limits. Except for hospitals and orphanages and that sort of thing, we should have given no quarter.

If we had gone in with military resolve and mobilized our forces, I think that we could have concluded that war, probably in a couple of months. If we had used all of our strength, no nation could have withstood us. Certainly not the Viet Cong. As it is, though, we wasted our strength, demoralized our military, and still lost the war. That loss crippled the conscience of this nation and showed that we are lacking in resolve.

The Afghanistan experience showed the communists how weak they were in a very similar way. More than any other event, it proved that the Soviet machine was not invincible. Without question, Afghanistan started the spiral which made public the apparent decay within the Soviet Union. It was the trigger to the spiral that has been accelerating recently as their powers decline.

The long-term and lasting lesson from both these wars is that no amount of physical force can overrun a people who are determined to resist. It is impossible to kill everyone in a country. The Soviets tried to kill and subjugate, but they were unsuccessful. I think it's true anywhere in the world: brute force can never win over a determined ideology.

The yearning for freedom in the hearts of people, sooner or later, will win out over brute force. There may be suffering, starvation, death, disease, and vast numbers of refugees, and there may be people whose lives are destroyed, whose homes are gone, and whose bodies are maimed, but nevertheless, freedom will inevitably prevail over tyranny. The Soviets learned that lesson in Afghanistan in a dramatic and painful way. At least I hope so.

DEMOCRATIC REFORM

The truth is, except for Chile, no nation has ever voluntarily voted in communists, because the people instinctively understand that communism means tyranny, persecution, death, suffering, and poverty.

With an armed insurrection in Nicaragua and guerrilla insurrections in Guatemala and El Salvador, the communists tried to take over a region which would threaten Mexico and, in turn, imperil the United States. They were never able to get widespread popular support in either

Guatemala or El Salvador. And, of course, the resounding defeat of the Sandinistas in Nicaragua's free election showed that those people would prefer almost anything to the desolation that the years of communist misrule in that country has brought them.

The remarkable thing is that in Nicaragua, 17 percent of the people are evangelicals. In Guatemala and El Salvador the total is about 30 percent. Of that 30 percent, about 29 percent attend church on a regular basis. It is not just church affiliation, but very enthusiastic and vocal participation.

I was deeply touched by the contrasts when I visited there in 1989. There was such grinding poverty, the majority of the people had no hope of ever being free again. In Guatemala City the poverty was horrible. The mayor told me if they could just move from misery to poverty it would be an improvement!

You could actually sense the presence of the monstrous evil that was attempting to gain a foothold in those countries. If there was ever a place where God could send a unique spiritual revival, this was it.

On my visits there in 1989, I knew we had to do something to support the believers in that land. Consequently, I instructed our staff at CBN to mobilize all the mass communications skills and all the media that had been put at our disposal—high speed printing, motion pictures and film, television and radio spots, specials, newspaper advertising and bill-boards, plus church involvement and training of counselors.

Why should we sit around with our hands in our pockets moping about the pathetic conditions in those countries when we had access to the greatest technologies and the most sophisticated promotional con-cepts in the world? So we decided to blitz those countries with the gospel and see what God would do. We organized campaigns in all three countries to make it possible for a majority of people to hear the gospel and come to the Lord. And it is now clear that this is just what happened.

We had a massive campaign, with something like 73,000 radio spots; 3,300 television spots; 50 film teams equipped with portable generators, projectors and screens, showing a feature film on the life of Jesus 5,200 times. We had 20,000 trained counselors; 10 million pieces of literature; hundreds of billboards; 400 tons of food and medicine given to the poor; and then prime time television programs on what is called a "roadblock."

We essentially took all the air time on all the stations in the country during one evening. After the blitz, we commissioned six surveys to be done by secular agencies. They reported that these were the most-watched programs in the histories of those countries. In just Guatemala and El Salvador, some 2,090,000 people prayed with the television host to receive the Lord; in Nicaragua it was over one million.

That campaign was successful beyond all our expectations. It shows the tremendous receptivity of people to accept Jesus as Savior in these countries which have been under the intense assault of communism. They have now freely chosen to go another route.

THE FUTURE OF CAPITALISM

No system of government is ultimately perfect, and no government of men can truly solve all our problems or bring ultimate good. In our own country we can see that capitalism, without a foundation of moral and ethical principles, is capable of terrible greed and corruption. I talked about this in my book, *The Secret Kingdom*. Without moral enlightenment, any secular system will lead to exploitation.

The headlines of the *New York Times* and the *Washington Post* shout the news that capitalism without ethics is exploitational and unscrupulous and ultimately self-serving. The most dramatic expression of the new face of capitalism in Moscow these days, as it is throughout Europe, is McDonald's and Coca Cola and blue jeans and plastic cups and all the traditional symbols of commercialism and consumerism.

While it may be colorful and even funny to see these things against the rather grim backdrop of Soviet communism, there is also the suggestion that there is a potential for exploitation in any economic system.

But over the past 50 years we have observed the results of communism and socialism and the planned "Welfare State." We have been able to compare the results of free market capitalism with the best communism could offer, and the world has come to the conclusion that freedom works, not a centralized control economy.

There is only one system of economics in the history of mankind that truly makes sense and leads to the prosperity and well-being of the people, and that is the free-market profit-motivated economic system we know as Capitalism.

Jesus said, "Do unto others as you would have them do unto you." In that statement He recognized individual self-interest as being a very real part of the human makeup, and something not necessarily bad or sinful. The desire of an individual to improve his lot in life, to provide a dwelling place for himself and his family, to put food on his table, to save something for retirement, and to have some joy in life is very natural: it is the way we are made.

It is also reminiscent of the comment of Paul in his letter to Timothy in which he said, "To God who gives us all things richly to enjoy. . . ." The enjoyment of life was God's plan. Enlightened self-interest was also obviously His plan. So the profit motive, *per se,* the desire for economic betterment, is not at all contrary to Scripture.

There was some primitive communism in the early church, but it resulted in poverty. Everybody gave up what they had, but they did it voluntarily. It was a communal existence but it was based strictly on personal benevolence.

If you remember the story in the book of Acts, Ananias sold some land and, secretly holding back a little for himself, he told everyone he was giving all the money to the church. But Peter knew he was lying and told Ananias to look at the land. "When you had it, wasn't it yours? And when you sold it, couldn't you have done with the proceeds what you wanted to? So why did you come here and lie to us and pretend that you're more holy than you really are?"

Ananias dropped dead on the spot. That was his reward for lying. But there was never a demand from the apostles that all the early Christians give up their money and live communally. They did it voluntarily because they had such love for each other and such zeal for the Lord.

Later on the apostle Paul went around the Mediterranean world taking up money for the poor saints in Jerusalem. Possibly one of the reasons they were poor was that they had given up all their money in this first burst of love and zeal. Some scholars believe they sold everything in the belief that the Messiah would return very soon. Perhaps they truly wanted to live in a communal relationship with other believers; but in the long run, it made them lacking in the means of self-help.

The thing that must make capitalism humane is the corollary teaching of Jesus that said, "Unto whom much is given much will be required." It is the concept of *noblesse oblige,* that nobility (or privilege) obligates. If you have privilege you must use that privilege for others. The Bible has striking examples of those who had great material wealth but did nothing to help their brother in need.

How can the love of God reside in their hearts? Capitalism—the accumulation of capital, the placing of money to the exchangers, individual self-initiative, all this kind of thing—was taught and encouraged by the Lord. But at the same time He said, "A man's life does not consist in the abundance of the things that he possesses."

Jesus told the Roman governor of Judea, "My kindgom is not of this world," and He taught His disciples, "seek first the kingdom of God and his righteousness and these other things will be added unto you." He said, "Don't be anxious about what you should wear or what you should eat. Your heavenly Father knows you have need of these things."

Jesus said—and His apostles taught—to give to the poor and the needy, to give to the work of the Lord, and to lay aside generously. Christians were to be stewards. I am not master of 90 percent and steward of 10 percent. I am steward of 100 percent: all of my spending, all of my life should be lived in relation to what God wants me to do.

If I believe what He taught, I am to be considered a bond slave of Jesus, bought with a price, and therefore my money and possessions and capital are, in turn, His, not mine. I am merely a life tenant of the wealth placed at my disposal.

Only when given the nobility and responsibility of the Christian view of property can free market capitalism, however successful, rise above the dangers of greed and exploitation.

THE GOD OF THE GODLESS

The other forms of economic organization violate so many of the principles of God, they actually deny the rightful place of God in society and raise up idols in His place. They do not permit the individual to be blessed by God. They don't let the individual receive what God wants to give him. They don't let him express compassion for his fellow human beings by giving money as he would like to give.

Under the socialist forms of government, the individual is not a steward of God but a steward of the state. He works for the state, is paid by the state, his salary and wealth are regulated by the state. His emotions are regulated by the state, and therefore he is not a servant of God but of whomever happens to be the governing party, whether it is communist, socialist, Labour, or whatever.

This false religion substitutes the state of God, and the creed is that the state will care for my needs. The citizen cannot then say, "The Lord is my shepherd, I shall not want," but, "The Government is my shepherd, I shall not want." The government says, "In turn, we will take care of your needs, we will give you work and money and take care of you after you retire, but in exchange for that you must give up your freedom and liberty and make us your God."

That is the most horrible life I can imagine. Yet, it was an experiment in improving the lives of people who had been crushed by the ravages of the industrial revolution, and by the other damaging forms of exploitation which industrialization brought with it in its early stages.

But today we know that the people who have lived under communism have now rejected it and have risen up to expel all remaining vestiges of that abusive system. I believe in a very short time we will see the last of those systems.

The greatest irony now is the lingering presence of the all-encompassing welfare state in the United States Congress and the continued presence of tenured Marxists in America's schools and universities. We still have a coterie of misguided intellectuals in the church who are preaching a so-called "Liberation Theology," which is nothing short of communist repression dressed up as social reform. Perhaps now even the most progressive thinkers will begin to see these fellow travelers for what they are and either reform the reformers or cast them from the temple.

THE CHALLENGE OF EASTERN EUROPE

The greatest challenge for Christians standing at the threshold of Eastern Europe today is to fill a vacuum. Everyone knows that a vacuum sucks in air. It doesn't stay around in suspended animation for very long; it consumes whatever comes near. That's what we are facing in Eastern Europe right now. It is an enormous spiritual and cultural vacuum, and that vacuum is going to be filled very quickly.

Recently we heard that fully half of the money spent by the East Berliners who crossed into the West to shop during those first exciting months of 1989 and 1990 went for pornography. We also learned that within two weeks of the opening of the gates, when the Berlin Wall was flattened and the unification of the two Germanys was complete, *Playboy* magazines were being sold on newsstands in Leipzig and Dresden and East Berlin.

Now the fact that Christian worship and ethical values have been forbidden for so long means that entire generations have grown up without a system of applied moral values. The heady exhilaration of personal freedom suggests to these young men and women that now everything is possible, and the warfare of ideologies has clearly already begun. But will they merely trade the slavery of communist tyranny for the slavery of sin and carnality and materialism?

The need for Christian literature is very clear. Number one, the people of the East Bloc need Bibles in their own languages. There has been very little printing of Bibles. Number two, they need Bible helps. There has been very little of that. They need evangelistic literature, and they need the simple type of literature that explains to the new believer what he or she is supposed to do after a decision for Christ.

They also need books and teaching on the inner relationship of God to government, society, family life, and the events of their everyday lives. How does Christianity apply to my society?

The trouble is that in America we have been woefully lacking in that kind of teaching ourselves. There are very few Christians in America who have an intelligent concept of citizenship or of the way that God would have us interrelate to the body politic. So we have allowed alien ideologies to fill the vacuum in America, so much so that Christian values have virtually been crowded out.

Clearly, America is struggling with its own moral identity, but at least we have the benefit of an ethical tradition. If it were not for the incredible reservoir of Christian beliefs and customs which we have inherited from the precepts of our founding fathers and the framers of the Constitution, I have no doubt that we would have lost our own moral vision years ago.

Sadly, there is no such reservoir in Eastern Europe. Everything is being written on a blank slate, right now. The questions concerning the relationship of public policy and personal beliefs are incredibly urgent. As laws are being drafted, positions are being filled. As parties are being organized, leaders are being chosen. Who is going to be in those parties? What philosophy is going to be enshrined in the government?

In our founding documents here in America we enshrined Christian beliefs. The State of South Dakota, for example, has a wonderful motto, "Under God the People Rule." Our Declaration of Independence paid homage to a Creator and spoke of the fact that our freedoms came from a Creator.

The Constitution, rightly interpreted, was clearly a document based on Christian concepts of sin and justice. We believe that all men are born sinners and even the best of them cannot be trusted with absolute power. So in framing the nation, our founding fathers circumscribed the leaders with a great many checks and balances so no one group could dominate our government.

Unfortunately, some people want us to forget that Christian heritage. Even the World Council of Churches, who should be on the side of Christian faith and tradition, voted recently to censure Christopher Columbus for bringing racism, bigotry, and exploitation to the New World.

What a warped view of reality! Liberals of that ilk would have us believe that the Pilgrims who settled in this continent were secular dissidents, and not men and women who left Europe for religious freedom. But that is simply not the case, and those who say so are either woefully ignorant of their own history or patently dishonest.

More and more historians and scholars are coming forth with the proof of our Christian heritage. Dr. Gary Amos, a historian and lawyer who teaches at Regent University, has compiled conclusive historical evidence in his book, *Defending the Declaration*, which clearly refutes the anti-Christian hypothesis.

In a study on Federalism, Dr. Amos says that the secular historians have never understood the degree to which our founders were trained and schooled in biblical thinking. He shows that there is a direct, logical, and historical connection between the Protestant conception of scriptural truth and the American constitutional form of government.

The colonists had 150 years in this country to learn how to govern a society by a "written standard," preceded by 150 years among their Protestant ancestors in Britain, France, Holland, Germany, and Switzerland. They knew the Bible to be "the one infallible rule of faith and practice," and they built schools wherever they went so every man, woman and child could read and understand the Bible.

In his book, *Independence and Involvement,* another scholar, Rene de Visme Williamson, points out that the early settlers were steeped in biblical wisdom:

> They read and reread it, meditated upon it, memorized large portions of it, argued about it, listened to innumerable sermons expository of it. They were so filled with it that their vocabulary and their literary style bore an unmistakable biblical stamp. In colonial Connecticut the Bible was accepted as a basis for decisions by civil courts. In their churches they were accustomed to living under written confessions of faith and written church constitutions.

Their knowledge of covenant law and of the teachings of the New Testament gave the founding fathers an innate understanding of God's plan for mankind. The *Magna Carta,* published in 1215, embodied these same principles, making provisions for freedom of religion, protection of individual rights, free trade, unity for the common good, and protection of the people.

The first Americans obviously understood the nature of original sin as well as the means of structuring the documents of government with wisdom and compassion. Even if secular historians deny those facts, the truth remains. The genius of the American constitutional government is proof of that wisdom.

The doctrine of original sin doesn't exist in Eastern Europe these days. At least it is not very well defined. So when framing documents are set up, will they have the wisdom our forefathers did to write enduring constitutions and pieces of founding legislation?

Maybe. At least there seems to be a strong Christian faith in many parts. We know that Czechoslovakia became a Christian nation before the year 1000. Poland has a strong Catholic tradition, and even under persecution and adversity that nation produced the current Pope. Hungary, Czechoslovakia, and Romania were also strongly Christian at one time, but whether these nations hold any of the concepts our founding fathers brought with them to America, we cannot yet say.

There is a clear mandate now for concerned Christians in the West to support the growth and development of Christian principles in these emerging governments. We must get the Bible into the hands of the people. Christian principles have to be taught, and the people need to understand the kinds of institutions that should naturally come from a Bible-based faith.

THE WIND FROM THE EAST

It has been refreshing to see the influence of the Christian faith returning to us from lands which just decades ago were only mission fields. We have seen the gospel return from Korea, from China, and from Africa with wonderful vigor and enthusiasm, and now we are seeing the same things coming from the churches of Eastern Europe.

The American press, which is notoriously cold to Christianity and hardened against conservative Christian values, was forced to report on Romania, and those reports were highlighted by the comments of Christian leaders who told of prayer vigils, of the faith that sustained them through the dark years of communist repression, of believers meeting in ancient churches to pray for freedom.

But the other side of that story is that in many papers, and other media as well, the American press quickly began to edit out those declarations of faith and to report only the purely political statements.

A press corps that screams for freedom of speech when it comes to pornography, vulgarity, and blatant anti-religious forms of expression, and a national media that lambasts censorship of every kind, has done its best to censor out all references to Jesus Christ or to Christianity or to the profound faith that has kept Eastern Europe alive these many years.

When Vaclav Havel spoke to the American Congress he mentioned that Czechoslovakia was the crossroads of Christianity in Europe. He mentioned the first coming of Christianity; he talked about God. But according to a report in *USA Today*, those comments were expunged from his address in the reports in the *New York Times* and the *Washington Post*. That tells you that the American liberal media is predominantly anti-religion and is going to do everything it can to prevent the favored expression of faith in God from coming through to the people.

They will make fun of those who claim to stand for God if they can show them in some moral dilemma. But for a world leader who is becoming a hero, as Havel is doing, they don't want him to have Christian words coming from his mouth if they can help it. The first time many Americans could read for themselves the unexpurgated text of Havel's speech was when Philip Yancey quoted those parts in his column for the magazine *Christianity Today*.

But the truth will not be restrained. Those nations are going to show us something remarkable. But more than that, they may well be the future for the potential revitalization of the faith in Europe.

This is the great hope, and the great irony, that Europe, which has been so terribly secular, will rediscover the Word of God. The land where, at best, less than 10 percent of all the people attend church, may rediscover the vision and the spirit of Christianity through the awakening taking place in Poland, Hungary, Czechoslovakia, and Romania. **Those who survived a half century of persecution may awaken in us the force and the conviction that will lead us all back to faith in Christ.**

There is a revival taking place there even today, and there is the very real hope that those men and women who had endured decades of repression and humiliation will someday hear their fellow Europeans saying, "We believe in Jesus Christ, and He has given us new life!" That hope is one of the key reasons why it is vital that the church over there be strong and that revival continue.

It is so vital that on their blank slate we write large the words of our Lord. Especially in a country like Romania. They are so open it just touches the heart.

A HUNGER FOR THE WORD

I spoke in a church in the city of Timisoara, Romania, in the spring of 1990. The place was packed. It was meant to hold 2,100, and they had somewhere between five and six thousand people, standing up all the way down the front aisles, along the walls, in the balcony.

I gave what was for me a fairly long message, and when I sat down the pastor said, "Brother, you didn't talk enough. These people are hungry for the Bible. They want to hear more about the Word of God."

They had stood in this hot place for a couple of hours but they wanted more. There is an unbelievable spiritual hunger among these poor, suffering people, but I am convinced they can be the revival spark for all of Europe.

Wouldn't it be one of God's supreme ironies that just as America, once the stronghold of faith and religious freedom and a beacon of hope to the entire world, loses its faith and falls from power very much like the once-great Roman Empire, that the once-communist nations of Eastern Europe, where Christians have been persecuted, should be the ones to bring revival and renewal?

There's no question that American and Western Christians have a dynamic challenge. Despite being persecuted today in our own land, we also have the challenge to help make this vision of rebirth of faith in Eastern Europe a reality as well. There are hundreds of immediate and dramatic opportunities for Christian service in these emerging countries.

In Czechoslovakia and Hungary they are begging for teachers of English. American young people could go by the thousands. President Havel wants 12,000 English teachers in Czechoslovakia. There is a marvelous openness to any kind of belief, so there is a critical need for Bible teachers, for those who would work in Bible schools to train pastors.

There is also a vital need for talented professionals to teach Christians in those countries the principles of business administration. With everything so very primitive, the Christian church can rise very rapidly if the people are taught more advanced principles of management. They need to know about management procedures, business systems, accounting practices, computer applications, and all the other business skills that can contribute to financial independence.

I think it will be very important to go into these countries and support the church. Frequently the evangelicals have been the church of the poor. They have been regarded by the leaders as people who are not really relevant to what's going on since they are generally among the poor and downtrodden.

I would like to see those churches advance the roles they have had in feeding the poor, in helping with social problems, especially in educating the masses. But I would also like to see the coming generation of young Christian leaders trained for law and government, for economics, and for the media, so that the emerging elite in these countries will be evangelical Christians.

I think that is very possible right now. Now is the time to begin implementing a long-range strategic plan which will ensure the preservation of the Christian faith and of personal freedom in the emerging democracies of Central and Eastern Europe.

Unless there is immediate action to instill the principles of Bible-based constitutional government and individual self-restraint, the specter of chaos looms over the nations of Europe recently freed from communism.

3

The Rise and Fall of Secularism

Along with communism, secular humanism has failed. In this decade the believers will stand firmly astride the failed and crumbling ruin of the secular colossus.

As WE OBSERVE the failures of communism in Europe and Asia, it seems as if we may have finally come to the end of an era, to the conclusion of one of the long cycles of history. From the publication of the *Communist Manifesto* in 1848 to the collapse of the Berlin Wall in 1989, the world has witnessed a long and bitter warfare of ideologies that has engulfed entire continents and cost tens of millions of lives. Could the warfare suddenly be at an end?

It seems obvious that communism has failed as a practical system of economics. But there was always more to communism than the practical side; there was an emotional and intellectual side as well. While the practical seems to have failed, it is more certain today than ever that the ideology, the intellectual side of the nightmare, lives on. Not just in Cuba and Angola and North Korea, but in America, and especially in our universities.

First and foremost, communism sprang from a secular hypothesis. It was based on the belief that man can live without faith in God, that man is the master of his fate and the captain of his soul. Framed on the rudiments of G.F. Hegel's dialectical hypothesis, Marxist-style communism proposed that society is necessarily in a constant state of revolution and that the goal of society must be a classless state and a world without boundaries. In other words, the genuine aim of communism is one-world government.

A TALE OF TWO REVOLUTIONS

In recent years, secular historians have written about the affinities between the American Revolution of 1776 and the French Revolution of 1789, as if both were merely incarnations of the same dynamic force. But that is not true.

While there was a thriving commerce between the United States and France during the eighteenth century, both in goods and in ideas, the aims of the patriots in America and the ideologies of the revolutionaries in France were two very different forces.

The American Revolution produced a constitution and a government based on biblical principles of Christianity. The French Revolution was, at its core, anti-Christian. Motivated by rebellion against the Church, and influenced by the ideas of the deists and free-thinkers such as Rousseau and Descartes, the revolutionaries in France sought to remove God from His throne and to crown Reason in His place.

The French Revolution was a product of the Enlightenment. It was based on the glorification of man and the exaltation of wisdom and learning. While the colonial patriots in America humbled themselves before a wise and loving God, Rousseau proclaimed, "Man was born free, but everywhere he is in chains!"

One of the most touching stories of the American Revolution was that of a British officer who somehow got separated from his unit and was trying to make his way back to camp, silently, through the trees. As he approached a clearing, he was startled to see an American general on his knees, hands clasped before his face in deep and fervent prayer.

As the Englishman looked on, his heart sank and tears came to his eyes, for he saw that the praying officer was General George Washington, commander of the American forces. "When I saw that sight," he said later, "I knew we were defeated. For any army whose commander was so humble before Almighty God could never lose the war."

THE FRAMING DOCUMENTS

The authors of the American constitution did not lack for self-respect, but they also understood that without appropriate checks and balances any government of men would inevitably grow corrupt. They had seen it in England, and they had lived under it in colonial America. So they framed a document that limited the power and authority of government.

The Declaration of Independence proclaimed "it is self-evident" that all men are created equal and are "endowed by their Creator with certain unalienable rights. . . ." But those rights did not, by any means, suggest absolute license. James Madison, generally recognized as the father of the constitution, wrote, "If men were angels, no government would be necessary." So the American documents of government protected the rights of the individual while they also imposed certain responsibilities and limitations. That is the true genius of the Constitution.

The revolutionary government of France took a very different turn. It became the goal of the revolutionaries to dismantle the European heritage of civilization and the Christian heritage of faith. According to Ben Hart, author of *Faith & Freedom*, "Rousseau did not believe in original sin or private property. He hated European civilization precisely because he saw it as a product of Christianity."

Voltaire had once said that the only way to have good laws was to burn the existing ones and start all over again. In essence, that was what the revolutionaries sought to accomplish.

At one point the revolutionaries wanted to throw out the Christian calendar and start fresh, from year one of the revolution. Ultimately it was not moral outrage that stopped them but European nationalism. The nations on either side felt no such esteem for the French Revolution; if anything they feared and resented it, so they wouldn't support that arrogant notion. They simply refused to go along.

Another curious mark of the revolution's antagonism toward God was manifested in the way they labeled themselves as left-wingers. When the National Assembly split into factions, the conservatives sat on the right side of the hall and revolutionaries chose the left.

James Billington, historian and Librarian of Congress, writes, "The subsequent equation of the left with virtue dramatized revolutionary defiance of Christian tradition, which has always represented those on the right of God as saved and those on the left as damned."

Toward the end of his ministry on earth, Jesus told His disciples parables of the end times, and among those was the story of the Judgment. In Matthew 25:41, Jesus described how He would one day bring all the people together, separate the righteous from the unrighteous, and then pronounce judgment.

To those on the right He would say, "Come, ye blessed of my Father, inherit the kingdom prepared for you from the foundation of the world." But to those on the left He would say, "Depart from me, accursed ones, into the eternal fire which has been prepared for the devil and his angels."

So great was their hatred of Christ and His Church, the radical reformers chose to be identified with those on the left as evidence of their rage.

These revolutionaries sought to acknowledge man as God. They believed each individual had the power of the divine within himself and that he could do whatever he believed to be right, short of harming another. Today that precept is enshrined in the French Declaration of Rights, Article Four, which states "liberty consists in whatever does not harm another."

The aftermath of the Revolution of 1789 remains one of the bloodiest and most outrageous blots on history. The idealism of the early patriots quickly degenerated into terror and chaos. They executed their king, even after he had sworn allegiance to the new constitution. Then, under Robespierre, tens of thousands of merchants, tradesmen, landowners, and nobles were executed; and the rioting and bloodshed provided a pretext for slaughtering one's enemies, for whatever reasons, throughout France.

Eventually Robespierre, himself, was guillotined, and after a prolonged period of anarchy, Napoleon Bonaparte came forth from the rabble and crowned himself Emperor. It was a classic pattern; after the collapse of empire, a bloodthirsty dictator rises to power.

THE VIEW FROM THE SHAMBLES

The English statesman, Edmund Burke, had seen early what would come in France. After a trip to Paris in 1773 to see what was afoot, he warned the British Parliament that the political theories of the philosophers could only produce tyranny. Burke predicted it would be ". . . the most horrid and cruel blow that can be offered to civil society through atheism. . . ." After the fall of the Bastille in 1789, and the Reign of Terror that ensued, Burke placed the blame for France's miseries on the philosophy that denied God.

Ironically, that revolution actually proved the humanists' faith in man to be unfounded and unwise. James Hitchcock writes, "The Terror, an orgy of hate and revenge, was strong disproof of the Enlightenment belief that man, left to himself, would inevitably behave in a rational and just way. The dark side of human nature asserted itself with a literal vengeance in the mid-1790s." He continues,

> The Terror was the first example of a familiar modern phenomenon: a movement to remake the world in the name of humanity gives birth to a murderous and destructive fanaticism. Every modern revolution has borne the same witness. It is one of the strongest arguments against total reliance on man and his goodwill. It has also given rise, among thoughtful people, to

a strong distrust of all movements which proclaim that they have the welfare of "humanity" at heart. Time and again, this has meant the crushing of individual human beings in the name of a political abstraction.

The Terror and its outpouring in France was the true outpouring of what Rousseau had called "The General Will" as expressed through what John Locke had called "The Social Contract." That is, a moral consensus among men for the good of man. What it actually proved to be was one of the first and most poignant examples of humanism unchecked, and man given unlimited power apart from God.

Among the first items on the agenda of the revolutionaries was the debunking and the desecration of the Church. It was fashionable to scoff at religion. Hitchcock writes, "The intellectuals of the time portrayed the churches as reactionary enemies of progress." Sound familiar?

How often have we heard the charge in recent years that conservative Christians want to "turn back the clock" on progress to a "better time," before the great social advances of abortion on demand, homosexual liberation, no fault divorce, and the dissolution of the nuclear family?

Historians point out that all pretense of religious toleration among the French revolutionaries quickly turned into religious persecution. "Soon the government embarked on a systematic 'de-Christianizing' campaign." Hitchcock writes,

> Churches were closed and converted to profane uses, like stables for horses. Religious schools were destroyed. The religious press was outlawed. All religious services were forbidden. Priests and nuns were rounded up in large numbers and sent into exile, imprisoned, or executed. The aim of the government was to wipe out every remaining vestige of Christianity.

Our American forefathers had worked diligently to avoid these very things. They knew, as John Adams said, "The people, when they have been unchecked, have been as unjust, tyrannical, brutal, barbarous, and cruel as any king or senate possessed of uncontrolled power."

Another patriot said, "Whatever may be conceded to the influence of refined education on minds of peculiar structure, reason and experience both forbid us to expect that national morality can prevail in exclusion of religion." The speaker was George Washington, and you can be sure that he wasn't talking about just any religion. He wasn't speaking of cults, or Eastern religions, or humanist ideologies, for he also said, "It is impossible to govern rightly without God and the Bible."

TURNING THE CORNER

The motto of the French Revolution, as enshrined today on the national coat of arms, was "liberty, fraternity, equality." Author James Billington has suggested that the revolutionary egalitarianism of the French idea of liberty was the progenitor of modern communism. The "common happiness" idea in the French Revolution was "proto-communist."

And according to Hitchcock, "Although its full fury was found in France, similar ideas and practices spread to other parts of Europe where the Revolution itself spread. It became, in time, a permanent feature of European life."

In that sort of intellectual climate where man is supreme and God is irrelevant, society will ultimately sink to the level of expedience and self-centeredness. If there is no moral absolute; if I am the arbiter of right and wrong and the ultimate judge of worth; if I am all there is, then why shouldn't I have whatever I want? It is not hard to see where that line of thinking can lead. Courtesy is no longer a duty or a virtue but a way to "grease the wheels" so that I get what I want.

Jesus Christ taught that we should esteem our neighbor more highly than we do ourselves. In the section of Matthew quoted above, Christ told how He would say to the righteous, "I was hungry and you fed me; I was thirsty and you gave me drink." And it was not what they had given to Him directly, but what they had given to "the least of these." The righteous had given selflessly to the humble, the downcast, the frightened, the helpless. How contradictory that view is to the humanist ideology!

It was in just such a godless environment that Karl Marx formulated his ideas of communism. This man, a German Jew who had once been a pious Christian, had grown bitter and angry. He had been an activist in Germany during the 1840s and was eventually tried by the state for treason in the same year he published the Communist Manifesto. But he escaped to England and, from his cold, drafty dwelling in London, Marx systematically conceived his theories of dialectical materialism, which would ultimately threaten the entire world.

Communism succeeded in Moscow and, again, the king and his family were slaughtered. Tens of thousands who disagreed with the Bolsheviks were butchered in the streets and on the farms and in the villages. Today we know that Stalin murdered more than 20 million of his fellow countrymen and buried them, unceremoniously, in unmarked graves from one end of Russia to the other.

The humanism that lies within communism has not been a very noble theology. Tens of thousands of citizens who have committed the heinous crime of seeking travel permits, emigration papers, passports, or who have simply been in the wrong place at the wrong time have been sent for "retraining" to Siberia. Others have simply been murdered in cold blood, and who could question the executioners?

THE BOLSHEVIKS IN AMERICA

Relentlessly, communism spread throughout Europe and across to the United States where the firebrands of the Labor Movement eagerly championed the doctrines of Marx and Lenin in the 1920s and '30s. **While most of the ordinary Americans who had suffered greatest from the Depression years determined to get back on their feet the old-fashioned way, by hard work and sweat, the urban intellectuals in America gravitated to the Marxist ideologies with incredible fervor.**

Among them, Edmund Wilson, John Dos Passos, Malcolm Cowley, Theodore Dreiser and many others were singing the praises of communist ideology, and a new genre of "proletarian fiction" was born. John Steinbeck wrote it in *Grapes of Wrath*. Carl Sandburg wrote it in *The People, Yes*. Richard Wright wrote it in *Native Son*. There were poets, painters, musicians, and philosophers, and, as we shall see, more and more professors in major universities who have now passed their theories along to three generations of American scholars.

In his book, *Since Yesterday*, historian Frederick Lewis Allen wrote that in 1932, at the depth of the Depression, communism was notably gaining strength, not only among the unemployed but among the intellectual elite. "Ideas were in flux," he writes. "There was a sharp upsurge of interest in the Russian experiment. Lecturers of Russia were in demand; Maurice Hindu's *Humanity Uprooted* and *New Russia's Primer* were thumbed and puzzled over."

The editor of Hearst's "usually frivolous" *Cosmopolitan* magazine had gone to Moscow to sign up Soviet writers and, on his return, threw a lavish, capitalist dinner party. Allen writes, "Gentle liberals who prided themselves on their open-mindedness were assuring one another that 'after all we had something to learn from Russia,' especially about 'planning'; many of the more forthright liberals were tumbling head over heels into communism."

By 1932, 52 writers, critics, and college professors signed an endorsement of communist presidential candidate William Z. Foster. Marxism was in the air. However, as Paul McElvaine, author of *The Great Depression*, points out, Americans didn't buy the idea of collectivism so much as the belief that socialism would provide "the economic security necessary for people to be truly free to express their individuality." But wasn't that the dream behind the French Revolution as well?

In the 1940s, less than five million Americans actually completed four years of college; however, by the mid-1960s that number had swelled to twelve million. That increase is tied in to the social transitions taking place in America, the change from a rural to an urban society; but it also reflects a steady rise in the number of intellectuals and theoretical thinkers in the nation.

According to Stanley Rothman and Robert Lichter, in their book *The Roots of Radicalism*, the increasing numbers of intellectuals also reflects a greater spread of liberal and socialist influence. In the early years, that did not make as much of a difference as it would in the 1960s and '70s when the radical revolution truly hit home.

Rothman and Lichter report that "in 1944, college faculties voted only 3 percent more Democratic than the general public; in 1952 they voted 12 percent more Democratic; and in 1972 they gave George McGovern 18 percent more votes than did the general public."

But these authors also point out that if the universities were having an impact on the behavior of the American middle class, their influence was greatly magnified by the revolutions taking place in communications and transportation.

Now ideas could move freely. Theories learned in the colleges in the East were broadcast throughout the land, from coast to coast, and from the Northern steel mills of the Midwestern Bible belt. Now, more and more, the media was in the hands of college-educated liberals who were attracted to the whole range of liberal thinking, ranging from free speech to communist activism. And the gospel of socialism was blossoming in America and around the world.

AMERICA'S CLOSED MINDS

Today we are reaping the whirlwind of the academy's experimentation with communism and secularism. The educational collapse we are seeing in America's classrooms today is nothing more or less than the playing out of those flawed theories. The idea of a value-free culture is nothing but a humanist fantasy. Translate "open-mindedness" for "empty-headedness" and you have the real meaning of the socialist dream.

Today we are seeing that America's dalliance with experimental education has been a monumental failure, that people are beginning to wake up to the fact that it's not money, or buildings, or computers that we need but a new pedagogy.

For the first time, the intellectual establishment is saying that they are also fed up with the ignorance and anarchy of deconstructionist thinking in America's universities. Many were stung by Allan Bloom's monumental bestseller, *The Closing of the American Mind*, which pointed out the predominance and the folly of so-called "value neutral" thinking in our schools.

Bloom's book shows how generations of students have been so well trained to be so open minded, their minds are essentially empty. *Tabla rasa.* The subtitle of Bloom's book, *How Higher Education Has Failed Democracy and Impoverished the Souls of Today's Students*, really says it all. Secularism in the classroom, supported by socialist ideology, has raped the minds of America's young.

Millions of college graduates don't even have the mental tools to make basic decisions. It is no wonder they can't form lasting relationships, they have been brainwashed since kindergarten to be "open minded" and "non-judgmental." They may not have faith, and they may have no convictions, but they're open minded. And that is supposed to be a virtue?

Since Bloom's work first appeared in 1987, others have come along to add kindling to the fire. Most recently, Roger Kimball's book, *Tenured Radicals: How Politics Has Corrupted Our Higher Education*, depicts in detail the inglorious failures of university administrators and the systems of political manipulation within the academy; and Page Smith's *Killing the Spirit: Higher Education in America* adds another indictment to the charge that our students have been indoctrinated by Marxists, atheists, and skeptics who have robbed our children of values without offering anything of value in return.

Dr. Bruce Lockerbie's brilliant address to the Chautauqua Institution in New York in 1989 capsulized the contradictions of America's "moral neutrality" and the educational mediocrity of the last forty years. Throughout the history of education—at least since the time of Socrates—there has never been a serious quest of any kind for which Truth is not the objective.

Yet in absolute defiance of that fact, today's students have been taught that "truth is relative." Teachers and students in our universities hold the view that "truth" smells of "absolutism," and for them there is only one absolute: that is, "truth is relative."

Lockerbie told his audience that the kinds of absolute truth American college students know for certain are as follows:

1. "I think, therefore I am." (René Descartes)
2. "God is dead. God remains dead. And we have killed him." (Friedrich Nietzsche)
3. "There are truths but no truth." (Albert Camus)
4. "We have neither behind us, nor before us in a luminous realm of values, any means of justification or excuse. We are left alone, without excuse." (Jean-Paul Sartre)
5. "Life is hard, then you die." (bumper sticker)

For students, and their teachers, who have such a mind-set, the worst accusation you can make against anyone is to say that they believe strongly in anything other than everyone's right to his own opinions. Their greatest moral virtue is "openness," but in becoming so, they have become vacant-minded and empty-headed.

However, Lockerbie, who is Scholar-in-residence at the Stony Brook School, understands that there is no truth which does not recognize that the "the fear of the Lord" is the beginning, and even the end, of wisdom, and the criterion of all legitimate knowledge.

"Of course, we recognize that some human beings differ concerning our need to acknowledge a Supreme Being's existence and sovereignty over the affairs of the cosmos," said Lockerbie. The Psalms twice describe such persons. "The fool has said in his heart, 'There is no God.' To ignore or reject as fundamental truth the existence and sovereignty of God, in search of some alternative, isn't 'open-mindedness' but folly." In unison with Bloom, Lockerbie says that the university must stand for something: and that something must be Truth.

It should not be an altogether new revelation to most of us that the educational theorists have failed. In the early 1960s we first heard that "Johnny Can't Read"; then in 1981 Rudolph Flesch told us that "Johnny Still Can't Read," and not only that, he doesn't even know the basics that Americans have believed to be foundational for generations.

E. D. Hirsch's brilliant bestseller, *Cultural Literacy: What Every American Needs to Know,* outlined vast areas of ignorance of the average American and described the gulf America's educators must span in order to restore sound teaching and values to the classroom.

The official reports of former Secretary of Education William J. Bennett, and the recent public addresses of current Secretary of Education, Lauro F. Cavazos, have handed out stinging reproof of the policies of the National Education Association (NEA) and the methodologies of the education establishment. The scores of high school students on the Scholastic Aptitude Test (SAT) continue to drop year after year.

While liberals prefer to attack the surveys and to claim prejudicial language and bias, students are learning less and less and reports from university campuses all across this nation prove that entering freshmen are incredibly ignorant and apathetic. Many have lost faith in the system and in their ability to gain anything of value from education.

On the latest reports, American students have dropped to fourteenth place in educational achievement, ranking somewhere between Togo and Chad!

THE ONRUSHING TIDE

In 1983 the National Commission on Excellence in Education published its *Open Letter to the American People* with the subtitle, *A Nation at Risk: The*

Imperative for Educational Reform. It was that report which, more than any government study before or since, helped to portray the crisis that confronts us in the ominous phrase, "the educational foundations of our society are presently being eroded by *a rising tide of mediocrity* that threatens our very future as a nation and a people."

While it is demoralizing to see what the colleges have done to our youth, the legacy of failure in the elementary and secondary schools is even more heart-rending. In his excellent work, *Changing the Way America Thinks*, Regent University President and former *New York Times* editor Bob Slosser chronicles the collapse of the educational process with many pointed examples. Slosser writes that,

> Illiteracy is so pervasive in American schools today that it is no longer limited to crumbling cities, nor even to rural shacks. Illiteracy has become an equal-opportunity disgrace. The city of Boston, once the literacy capital of America, was described recently by a disgusted businessman as "not only second rate, but a disaster, a waste basket."

In *Illiterate America,* Jonathan Kozol pointed out that 25 million American adults are so illiterate they cannot read the warning label on a bottle of poison. Another 35 million read only at a survival level. This is the result of educational experimentation, and we have the principles of Dewey and the socialists to thank.

Marxists and socialists who have burrowed into the schools are going to have to be rooted out if we're going to change the way America thinks. They're going to be so discredited that nobody who's intellectually responsible is going to accept the Marxist view of life any more. Sadly, that has been the prevailing doctrine in America's schools for the better part of 40 years.

In 1989, Chester E. Finn, Jr., former Assistant Secretary of Education and now a professor at Vanderbilt University, reported in *Commentary* magazine that only 5 percent of 17-year-old high-school students can read well enough to understand technical documents, literary essays, or historical documents; barely 6 percent can solve multi-step math problems and use basic algebra; and only 7 percent are able to draw conclusions from scientific knowledge.

Finn said that 60 percent of eleventh graders do not know why the *Federalist* papers were written; three-fourths do not know when Lincoln was president; and just one in five knows what "Reconstruction" was about.

Furthermore, high school students are essentially ignorant of geography or international affairs. But lest we argue that the tests are prejudiced or unfair, Finn points out that in head-to-head comparison with teenagers in Europe and Asia, Americans are clearly out-classed in all categories. He writes,

> The most recent [study] reported by the Education Testing Service in January [1989] compares the performance of thirteen-year-olds in mathematics and science in six countries. In math, ours came in dead last. In science, American girls and boys were tied for last place (with Ireland and two Canadian provinces). Korea led in both subjects, and the United States was also bested in both by England, Spain, and three other Canadian provinces.

But, Finn reports, another part of the problem is denial. For example, even though the American students ranked at the bottom, the same study shows that the American kids had the highest self-regard. Fully 68 percent of the American 13-year-olds believed themselves to be "good at mathematics," while only 23 percent of the high-scoring Korean youngsters felt so. And while 91 percent of American mothers said their schools were doing an "excellent" or "good" job, only 42 percent of Chinese mothers and 39 percent of the Japanese surveyed rated their schools at those levels.

Complacency, denial, and divisiveness are rampant in all sectors, but the behaviorism and secularism of the '60s and '70s is still a prime ingredient of public education, and some of our educators are still actively engaged in the process of destroying schools.

We had a guest on the 700 Club television program who had been involved in some of the experiments where they literally made California schools into experiments for their so-called "social studies." They call it social science, but it is not science at all. It is pseudo-science, built upon very faulty statistics and untenable assumptions.

It is a game of educational experimentation and a mechanistic form of behaviorism straight out of Pavlov and B. F. Skinner. The social scientists hold a view of human beings which does not take into account the fact that our children are made in the image of God, or that God has anything to do with them.

BACK TO BASICS

Ironically, the government's destructive programs of the past decade are part of what was termed the "Back to Basics" movement. But whatever it was, it wasn't basic and it didn't work. The evidence is only too clear.

The results of a ten-year study of schooling in America and the various systems for financing public education concludes that the only way our schools can be made responsive to the legitimate educational needs of children is by eliminating bureaucratic control over education and returning the decision-making power to the parents.

The report, entitled *Politics, Markets and America's Schools,* is the work of John E. Chubb, a senior fellow at the Brookings Institution, and Terry M. Moe, a political scientist at Stanford University, who analyzed the experiences of more than 20,000 students, teachers, and principals in 500 public and private schools all across the country. It is important to see that these researchers, by taking a straightforward, objective look, discovered the inevitable truth that the natural way is the best way.

Bureaucracy is unnatural and ineffective. The institution created by God for development and nurturing is the family. Government's task should be to empower the family—whether through a system of vouchers for education or through substantial tax relief—and not to interfere in the natural order established by God.

The secularizing of education and the destruction of the natural order has served as the springboard for a vicious vendetta against religious values in the schools of America. The horror stories abound. Jay Sekulow, of CASE, a lawyer who defends cases of religious persecution, along with John Whitehead and attorneys at the Rutherford Institute, has told many of them; and we gathered others at the Freedom Council a few years ago.

One of the most shocking examples was the story of a student who was suspended from school in DeKalb County, Georgia, for "the possession of Christian literature." Not drugs, not alcohol, not firearms: but Christian literature! He handed a piece of paper to a friend inviting him to come to a Fellowship of Christian Athletes meeting, and it may have said something about Jesus.

The assistant principal was apparently in the hall and demanded to see the note. He read it, then suspended the boy for possession—possession of Christian literature! That is just one example of the kinds of antagonism toward Christian faith and values that has flourished in this country over the past two decades. And in some places that sort of prejudice and bias is still growing worse.

Somehow the secular establishment doesn't perceive the irony that the very same school that suspended this student for possession of Christian literature had Satanic literature on its bulletin board! When confronted with that fact, they said, we're not interested in talking about Satan; we're just interested in keeping Christianity out. At least that was their message. If this is worship of the true God, their actions implied, we won't tolerate it. Worship of a false god is okay.

You can't put the Ten Commandments on the classroom wall, but apparently there's nothing wrong with having gurus come in to lecture, or having seances and meditations. Those practices are going on right now in many schools. We know of schools where they are teaching astral projection in the classrooms. Students are taught that they are going out of their bodies into space, meeting with creatures in space, and bringing spirits back to earth with them.

We reported on television that in some schools in New Mexico, children are told to lie on the floor and meditate into a trance. At best this type of thing is absurd; at worst it is demonic, and opens up these innocent children to evil powers and spirits. But the school boards of America see nothing wrong!

Still, the handwriting is already on the wall, and I predict we will see dramatic changes in the coming decade. I believe we will see this nation moving away from rationalistic and atheistic thinking very quickly. There is going to be an openness of faith, and people all across this land will be taking a stand for their faith.

For many we trust it will be faith in Jesus Christ, but for others it will no doubt be faith in some other power. Whether it comes from the New Age or Hinduism or Buddhism or Islam or some other Eastern-type religion, there is going to be a sudden and overwhelming rise of religious belief in this country. We are going to witness a spiritual awakening of inconceivable proportions, and it will be a spiritual awakening ready-made for a post-Christian Europe as well.

THE ALLURE OF SECULARISM

From its inception, secularism has focused intently on the overt de-Christianizing of America. It starts with dialogue about "pluralism" and "tolerance" and "relative values," as it did in France 200 years ago, but it always ends with an outright assault on Christianity and the Church.

In the beginning, the intellectual allure of secularism is intriguing. Educated men and women are tantalized by the ideas and promises of the humanist dream, and it seems no great leap of faith to swallow the absurd logic of Darwinism, or Freudian psychology, or even of Marxist-Leninist social theory.

The mind becomes a playground of ideas. **It is the hunger for the apple all over again; the lust for the knowledge of good and evil; the desire to attain what Satan promised, "you shall be as gods."**

The idea of evolution has been taught as gospel truth in America's schools now for at least forty years. Except in Christian schools and a few small community schools where Christianity is still considered a virtue, the biblical account of creation is not even taught today.

The central idea of evolution is that there is no God; things occur by chance, which leads directly to the belief that values and mores are purely functional. "If it feel good, do it." Social scientists, from Carl Jung to B. F. Skinner, suddenly gained a new stature in the secularized society. Jung told us the collective conscience of the human race determines our values and our beliefs; Skinner taught that we practice norms of right and wrong by simply learning the natural behavioral patterns acceptable to the greatest number of people.

Human law, we then conclude, need not be based on eternal truth or the revealed Word of God, but on the basis of consensus, pluralism, relativism, and social determinism. And if we lose the promise of eternal life and a personal walk with the Lord God in the process, we at least gain the freedom to be fully human and masters of our own fate.

How ironic that in freeing himself from all moral restraint, mankind has become a slave to his own pride and immorality. By casting off his soul, he has put himself on the level of the animals. By disowning the family of God, he has alienated himself from God's most sacred institution on earth, the family of man.

It has become great public sport in the 1990s to scoff at Christians and Christianity. As film critic Michael Medved points out, "If someone turns up in a film today wearing a Roman collar or bearing the title Reverend, you can be fairly sure he will be crazy or corrupt—or both."

In the film, *Monsignor,* Christopher Reeve plays a priest who seduces a nun and invests Vatican money with the Mafia. In *Agnes of God,* Meg Tilly plays a nun who murders her own baby and stuffs it into a trash can. Others, from *True Confessions, Mass Appeal,* and *The Mission,* to the scurrilous and thoroughly artless *Last Temptation of Christ,* set out to prove the corruption and hypocrisy of Christianity and the Church.

In his lecture at Hillsdale College, quoted in *Reader's Digest,* Mr. Medved wondered why Hollywood is so intent in its hatred of religion that it produces one box office fiasco after another, like those named above, while the films which have portrayed the positive values of the faith have scored so well.

Chariots of Fire was a "worldwide box-office smash," he says. Robert Duvall won an oscar for his part in *Tender Mercies,* in which he played a washed-up country singer whose life is transformed by religious faith. "In one scene," says Medved, "he is baptized and most convincingly born again. The movie confounded the experts with its strong audience appeal."

There was a time when Hollywood seemed to understand and appreciate the deep religious faith of this nation. *The Ten Commandments, The Robe, Ben Hur,* and *The Greatest Story Ever Told* were sensational film successes. Actors such as Pat O'Brien, Bing Crosby, and Spencer Tracy made a tradition of playing "earthy, compassionate priests who gave hope to underprivileged kids or comforted GIs on the battlefield."

The film-makers have forgotten that tradition, however, and they are completely out of touch with what faith in God is all about. Medved said,

> A 1982 survey analyzing the attitudes of key figures in the movie business showed that only four percent regularly attend church or synagogue. In the country at large, by contrast, over 40 percent flock to services on a regular basis. If most big-screen images of religious leaders tend to resemble Jimmy Swaggart or Jim Bakker, it's because evangelists on TV are the only believers who are readily visible to members of the film colony.

Except for the cable networks and religious programming, television is essentially a desert. The implied morals of so-called family shows such as "My Two Dads," "Family Matters," "Empty Nest," "Roseanne," and all of the network soap operas suggest that American viewers have lost all sense of propriety or shame. Deviant sexual behavior is out in the open; sex outside of marriage is the norm; anger, bitterness, and exploitation are everywhere; and there is an outright glorification of carnality and brutality and godlessness. One can only wonder, where will it all end?

On network television and in the print media liberal, socialist, humanistic, and promiscuous values prevail. Those who stand for restraint, for religious values, or for moral codes are often branded extremists, fundamentalists, and reactionaries.

What outcry comes from the secular press when newsfilms document the images of riot squads breaking the arms of pro-life demonstrators? And even as the news readers recite the lurid evidence of drugs and violence in the streets of America, no one seems to make the connection between the loss of Christian values and the spiraling increase in crime.

For the time being, secular humanism is still held somewhat in check by America's long tradition of Christian values. Though it is a pale shadow of its former self, America's tradition of morality still ascribes some worth to the Ten Commandments and to the principles of compassion Jesus taught in the Sermon on the Mount. But for how long?

THE FRENCH WITNESS

About 40 years after the French Revolution—still troubled by the devils the Reign of Terror had unleashed at home—the French government commissioned Alexis de Tocqueville to journey through America to discover what it was about the American experiment that had made it such a conspicuous success. Like the French, the Americans had gone through a bloody revolution; yet, unlike the French, they had come out of it basically loyal, law-abiding citizens, charitable and respectful, and remarkably tranquil. Why?

In his book, *Democracy in America*, de Tocqueville told his countrymen it was their faith in God that made the American experiment unique. "I do not know whether all Americans have a sincere faith in their religion," he wrote, "for who can know the human heart?—but I am certain that they hold it to be indispensable for the maintenance of republican institutions. This opinion is not peculiar to a class of citizens or to a party, but it belongs to the whole rank of society."

America is, he wrote, "the place where the Christian religion has kept the greatest power over men's souls; and nothing better demonstrates how useful and natural it is to man, since the country where it now has the widest sway is both the most enlightened and the freest."

THE COMING COLLISION OF BELIEFS

Despite the apparent collapse of world communism, America is still wrestling with the specter of the humanists and socialists in our own midst. The advocates of the secular society, both inside and outside the established church, are preaching "separation of church and state."

By misconstruing the "no establishment" clause of the Constitution, which states that Congress must keep its hands out of matters concerning the church, the secularists have tried to throw out the last remnants of Christianity in America.

The spokesmen and gurus of popular society have been trying for 30 years to shove the church into a mold made in the shape of the Ku Klux Klan, Nazism, and racial bigotry. The perpetrators of that fraud say they simply want the church to restrict itself to ecclesiastical matters and to leave the running of society to the government, but their ambition is much larger than that. They want to destroy Christianity.

Under communism the church was not allowed a voice in secular affairs, in education, or in the policy issues that affected the welfare of the citizens. Bred from the same stock as the atheists, the rationalists, and the pragmatists, the communist leaders were in a war against God and His kingdom on earth. To silence God in society, they first had to silence the church and the men and women of faith who believed in Him. Today's secular humanists are their heirs.

The fact is, the church must always be able to speak out on anything of a moral nature. That includes the family, the bond of husband and wife, sexual relationships, the origin of life, the rearing of children, the education of the young, the welfare of the poor and needy, the faithful worship of Jesus Christ, and all the other issues which are the time-honored concerns of Christianity in Western society. **We simply will not let secularization crowd us out. After all, our forefathers founded this country, and we're not about to give it up!**

Today it is clear that secular humanism has failed. Like communism, to which it has been allied from the beginning, it is a bankrupt system without moral guidelines or reliable safeguards to protect the people from its own corruptions. It has degenerated into carnality, sensuality, lawlessness, and disease, and it has left millions of men and women all over the world adrift, without purpose, and emotionally crippled.

Nature abhors a vacuum, and secularism has left a spiritual vacuum in the hearts of all those who once turned to it for freedom and hope. To survive, the humanists will either have to decamp or change their ways, and this is the decade in which one of those two will most certainly come to pass.

Now after their half-century rampage through the pages of history, I am not holding out much hope that they will simply admit their folly and give up. I am not betting that they will suddenly see the moral and emotional carnage in their wake and reform, but I am betting they will change.

In *Megatrends 2000,* John Naisbitt and Patricia Aburdene forecast a mammoth boom in spirituality in this country in the years ahead: "a worldwide multidenominational religious revival" they call it. Reciting how American society has passed from genuine faith to a belief in science, passing through the "God is dead" movement at mid-century, these authors write that "Science and technology do not tell us what life means. We learn that through literature, the arts, and spirituality."

So the decade ahead will offer a supermarket of spirituality for the discriminating palate. Basic Christianity? Yes. New Age? You bet. Channeling, holistic healing, tarot, ancient lords, ascended masters, and alien visitors, all these will be readily available, packaged attractively and marketed tastefully for the perceptive consumer, and every one of them worthy of serious worship in the coming decade. These authors don't care which you choose.

Fundamentalists—that is, those who actually believe the Bible is the Word of God and that it contains truth which must be believed and followed—may now seem a nuisance to the humanistic power brokers. But in my judgment, after a period of intense struggle the believers will stand firmly astride the fallen and crumbling ruins of the secular colossus.

From the rise of secularism to the fall of communism, the world has now endured a 300-year assault on its very soul. Now the tide is turning.

The year 1990 will be remembered as the beginning of the end of secularism. For today we are standing at the threshold of a massive collision of beliefs.

From the French Revolution on, the secularists have tried to destroy the Christian religion. They are still entrenched in the schools, the courts, and many parts of government. The warfare between secularism and religious faith will conclude in this decade with the clear victory of faith.

4

The Rise of the Supernatural

During this decade we will witness a crumbling of the power of prevailing intellectual elites in the United States and Europe.

The 1990s will not be a decade dominated by rationalism or science, but a decade of religious faith. We are entering the age of the supernatural.

As THE DECADE of the 1980s was coming to a close, a keen observer could detect some clear trends. The traditional church in Western Europe lay prostrate before the centuries old attack of rationalism, humanism, and secularism.

Clearly the high ground of society in Western Europe and the United States—the universities, schools, media, think tanks, courts, and to a lesser extent the parliaments—had been captured by the forces of anti-Christian rationalism. The "Christendom" that had held sway since 500 A.D.—what Winston Churchill in 1940 had termed "Christian Civilisation"—was dead.

The Christian church behind the iron and bamboo curtains was alive but lacking influence. Persecuted, hunted, imprisoned, ridiculed, the church in these lands lacked trained priests, Bibles, basic literature, Bible schools and seminaries, and even places to meet. Most of all, they lacked freedom.

For over two billion of the earth's inhabitants, their gods were Marx, Lenin, Stalin, or Mao Tse Tung. The only heaven held out to them was the oppressive, stultifying "worker's paradise" of communism.

Then in a few electrifying months, the gods of East and West began to tumble. Marx, Lenin, Stalin, and Mao all came crashing down. Communism was revealed as the empty lie many of us have always known it to be.

The fall of the Berlin Wall, the execution of Nikolae and Elena Ceausescu, the election of Vaclav Havel, the political disintegration of the Soviet Union are all highly visible events. We can watch pictures of these events on television. We can see the leaders and hear the debates in their assemblies.

What we cannot see on television is the dismantling of the humanist philosophical superstructure that saw its hopes and dreams for a communist one-world utopia suddenly dashed by the emerging reality of faith in God, love for freedom, and the superiority of free-market economics.

During the next few years, particularly in the United States and to a lesser degree in Western Europe, a fierce, intense, and sometimes ugly battle is going to be waged to seize the control points of society away from the advocates of anti-Christian secularism.

When communism lost, the secularists lost. The problem is that they hold entrenched positions of power and, like the World War II Japanese defenders of Iwo Jima who holed up in caves and bunkers in the hills, they will have to be taken out of their strongholds one at a time.

In the United States, the skirmishes over abortion, government-funded obscenity, and parental rights are just part of the larger battle to take back education, the courts, governmental agencies and, indeed, our culture from the intellectual heirs of the French Revolution.

During this decade we will witness a crumbling of the power of prevailing intellectual elites in the United States and Western Europe. Atheistic communism is dying. Rationalism and atheistic humanism are also dying.

In my judgment, the 1990s will witness an intellectual and spiritual renaissance that can only be compared to that of the early days of the Christian Church or the emergence of the power of the Church after the fall of Rome.

The 1990s will not be a decade dominated by rationalism or science, but a decade of religious faith. We are entering the age of the supernatural.

What we don't yet know is what form the religious faith will take. Will the world embrace the claims of Jesus Christ and the truths of the Bible, or are we to expect the world to turn to an "Age of Aquarius" dominated by the Hindu religions and led by mystic holy men in touch with demonic spirits known as "ascended masters"?

AWAKENING IDEOLOGIES

Europe is a spawning ground for ideologies. They received the gospel from the apostle Paul and the early missionaries of the first century, and from then on through the Middle Ages until fairly recent times Europeans have been involved in evangelizing the world for Christ.

But now the direction may be changing, and I suspect we will see a new era of missionary activity in Europe as we move toward the new millennium. But in this case, the missionaries will be coming in to them from the Orient, bringing a new kind of religion.

The confrontation of Eastern and Western religions on the soil of Europe may well be the great struggle of the decade, and the new millennium is going to be shaped somehow by the spiritual forces that have been let loose in this age. Faced with the dismantling of the old ideologies of Marxism and atheism, the logical conclusion would be that the European people will begin to champion democratic ideals and the doctrines of love and brotherhood taught by Christianity.

They should say, "In the past we rejected Christianity, but now it is clear that Christianity is the answer. Therefore, we will turn to Christ." But I'm afraid that is not going to happen. Those people aren't going to do that. That would be too difficult, too self-effacing. It would mean loss of pride and prestige.

So what they will do, little by little, is to introduce another religion. They can't go with traditional Christianity which they rejected, so they will choose to embrace the secular religion of self-actualization, self-realization, and other New Age-type religious concepts born out of Hinduism.

Obviously, that sort of belief system is entirely compatible with the worship of Mother Earth, with the concept that we are all gods, we all come out of some universal consciousness. The philosophy of Carl Jung talks about a great universal sense of right and wrong, and the pre-existent consciousness of man. It is God-free and sanitary, and the whole concept of reincarnation fits so nicely with that.

Nobody is really responsible for his actions; after all, we each have a Karma attached to us that goes back to some grandparent, some debt that has to be paid because of some former life. What a convenient theology for a post-Christian world in a desperate search for values.

FALSE PROMISES OF THE NEW AGE

The promises of the New Age are so radical and subversive of everything Christ taught us, it seems to be tailor-made for a secular elite looking for a philosophy. Among the various cults and mysteries, there are those which promise unlimited wealth to anyone who wants it.

The Unity Church, for example, is a theology of prosperity which promises that the believer will accumulate wealth and prosperity as he or she accepts the divine nature—the Christ consciousness—within. "Be all that you can be," they say. "Achieve everything you've dreamed of"; but none of these cults has the slightest thought of repentance or the need for a Savior or a Cross. Even the concept, to these people, is foolishness.

When I look at the book of Revelation, I have to wonder if these kinds of cults might not be the origin of the Anti-Christ? It certainly seems that way. Things could already be in place for some kind of a world dictatorship based, not on communism or socialism or fascism or any of the man-made, mechanical, ideological systems we have known in the past which focus on government, but based on a one-world religion.

If you will recall, it was the religious vacuum caused by divisions in the Church that allowed the anti-Christian heresies and the secularization of the sixteenth century to begin. By the same token, the vacuum caused by the collapse of communism could create a very similar environment in this century in which a counterfeit religion could emerge, and it would be such a subtle counterfeit that people who are spiritually motivated would receive it. Especially those who have rejected Christianity.

I believe that is another major trend, and I believe that this is what we're going to be facing in the next decade. The manifestation of satanic power is going to come at us—that is, at Bible-believing Christians—in such a way we would not have believed it possible. But I also believe that during this decade there will be a counter-balancing Christian revival of the power of God's Holy Spirit.

In the coming decade there will be evangelism we could never have dreamed of at any other time. The power of mass communication will revolutionize the way we present the gospel, and millions all over the world will be exposed to the ministry of Jesus Christ who might never have heard the name before.

During April of 1990, our evangelistic teams saw 2,090,000 people accept the Lord in Central America in one week. That's more than we saw in 30 years of previous ministry. And I believe it's going to be that way in country after country after country. But, right now, the world is in the balance and it's going to be a spiritual struggle more than anything else.

If the communist political values have collapsed; if the atheistic, humanistic philosophy is in a state of collapse; and if the only other ready-made form of worship we have is materialism and there's a worldwide depression—which I believe there well may be because of the mounting debt crisis—that would mean the collapse of another materialistic god.

All of that would leave people desperately longing for something, somebody, some way, some philosophy to get them out of their mess. I suspect some will find it quite easy to put their faith in a bold New Age leader who offers them the world.

INSIDIOUS ALLEGIANCES

If you take a look at the full-page ads for the guru god, "Lord Meitreya," paid for by Benjamin Creme in the *New York Times* and other international papers, you can see what absurd ideologies people will accept and what lengths their false prophets will go to in promulgating them.

From his office at the Tara Center, a British cult organization, Creme told the world that the Lord Meitreya is the true Messiah. He said he is already here and is merely waiting the moment to arrive when he will lead the world into a glorious millennium.

Creme did not mention, however, that the name "Meitreya" is Sanskrit for the name Buddha, since the aim of the movement is to mislead those who would be more open to a Western concept of Messiah. Nevertheless, someone identified as Meitreya has reportedly made appearances in Europe and Africa and is only waiting for his followers around the world to help bring about his "Declaration Day," when he will declare himself the new Christ.

These people are clearly talking about a one-world government that will solve the problem of war, depression, famine, poverty, and bring an end to the cycles of suffering that are afflicting mankind. They are promising a new era of peace, and they describe it as the fulfillment of the Age of Aquarius.

In 1949 L. Ron Hubbard was a failed science fiction writer who authored a presumptuous book called *Dianetics, the Modern Science of Mental Health.* For whatever reasons, the book became an instant bestseller and virtually overnight a movement was born.

By 1952 Hubbard founded the Church of Scientology and, surrounded by drug addicts, teeny boppers, and movie stars, this "chain-smoking enigmatic bundle of contradictions" built a massive empire, including an entire ocean-going fleet, out of a desperate search for love and power.

Over the past forty years the Church of Scientology has become a multi-million dollar operation—some say a billion-dollar operation. In 1972 the *Encyclopedia Brittanica*, quoting Peter Rowley's work, *New Gods in America*, called it the largest new religion in America.

Werner Erhard, founder of EST, called Hubbard the "greatest philosopher of the twentieth century." For more than 25 years the rich and famous beat a path to his door, and celebrities such as John Travolta, Karen Black, Sonny Bono, Chick Corea, Stephen Boyd, Gloria Swanson, William Burroughs, Priscilla Presley and many more, worshipped at his shrine.

In the powerful expose written by Hubbard's oldest son and a collaborator, a man who had worked at Hubbard's side for many years, the father of Dianetics is shown to be a fraud, a pathological liar, and a deceitful manipulator who masterminded break-ins, theft, extortion, blackmail, revenge plots, murders, and many other felonies.

The book, *L. Ron Hubbard: Messiah or Madman?* shows how Hubbard identified himself with Meitreya, "he whose name is kindness," the god with the golden hair prophesied to appear in the West 2,500 years after the death of Buddha. And it cites Hubbard's lyric, "Address me and you address/Lord Buddha/Address Lord Buddha/And you then address/Meitreya."

Even though Hubbard died in 1986, the empire continues and the leaders of the militant cult claim the spirit of this "cosmic outlaw" still directs them from the astral plane. He leads them from his higher-level being. Accordingly, the bestsellers continue to pour off the presses, and each brings in multiplied millions of dollars to support the brain-washing, terrorism, and fraud which fuels the madman's empire.

Just knowing that hundreds of thousands of Americans, and hundreds of thousands more on all five major continents, are actually reading and believing—and more, joining and following—such outrageous ideologies should convince anyone that the dangers of the New Age are neither innocent nor benign.

Such cults are insidious and evil. Having styled himself on cultist Aleister Crowley, who calls himself "Beast 666," it is patently clear that one of Hubbard's chief aims was to eradicate Christianity from the face of the earth, to destroy the credibility of Jesus Christ, and to bring Christians into submission to the spirit of the Beast. Sooner or later, all false religions which deny the deity of Christ come back to the same satanic root.

INSIDE THE NEW AGE

The human potential movement may seem trendy and full of pop psychology, emotional therapy such as Silva Mind Control, the Forum (formerly known as EST), and high-priced bearded gurus chanting mantras over well-known rock and roll musicians. Actually, it is nothing new.

It was first found in the Garden of Eden when Satan whispered to innocent Eve, "you shall be as gods." At its core is a simple message: human beings who are able to develop their full potential of mystic and psychic powers can gain access to the hidden mysteries of occult knowledge and power and, thereby, be as God.

To the idealistic, the New Age offers a universal brotherhood of man, a one world government, no war, no heaven, no hell, only everlasting peace. The words of the song "Imagine," written by the late megastar, John Lennon, clearly set forth the New Age agenda for mankind. No church, no preachers, no need for repentance, and no salvation in Christ.

The message of the New Age is just as beguiling as the message of the serpent in the Garden, and it is every bit as insidious. It is not surprising that the New Age religion is spreading like wildfire into the spiritual vacuum that now exists in the world.

In his book, *Understanding the New Age*, Russell Chandler, a religion writer for the *Los Angeles Times*, says that the New Age movement is "a hybrid mix of spiritual, social, and political forces, and it encompasses sociology, theology, the physical sciences, medicine, anthropology, history, the human potential movement, sports, and science fiction."

It is not a single cult but an entire spectrum of beliefs, and although New Agers often disagree among themselves about what the essential precepts really are, the underlying proposition is a belief in the transcendence of mankind. It is prompted by a belief in an essential divinity.

Marketing savvy has a lot to do with the success of the movement as well. When George Gallup reported in 1978 that ten million Americans were involved in some form of Eastern mysticism and another nine million were into spiritual healing, that news seemed to trigger a feeding frenzy on Madison Avenue.

Suddenly television shows such as *Star Trek* and *Battlestar Galactica* were all the rage. Hollywood scored phenomenal hits with movies like *ET, Star Wars, Close Encounters of the Third Kind,* and the *Star Trek* series. In every case, revenues from the sale and licensing of products, toys, T-shirts, puppets and dolls, along with unlimited product endorsements, was many times greater than the box-office take alone.

Movies such as *The Exorcist, Poltergeist,* and *Rosemary's Baby*, and later *Alien,* along with the somewhat fluffier *Cocoon,* exposed specters and fantasies in the public imagination, but the new wave of space thrillers seemed to be an opening of the American soul to alien powers.

Most invoking was the paradoxical spirit George Lucas called "The Force," which has been variously described as a blending of biblical teachings and Eastern lore, along with a large dose of pop psychology and psycho-kinesis, which involves demonic forces.

THE MORONIC CONVERGENCE

In his book about the Hollywood film world, Lloyd Billingsley called the movement a *"gazpacho* of Eastern ideas and assorted nostrums, which the *New Republic* has called 'Moronic Convergence.'" It is true that many people have joked about the absurd claims of Shirley MacLaine and J. Z. Knight, who supposedly channels a 35,000-year-old warrior, Ramtha, from the lost continent of Atlantis. But it is much more than a joke. It is a multi-million dollar industry which boasts tens of thousands of converts and is having a tangible impact in virtually every city and town in North America.

In addition to all the show business celebrities associated with the New Age movement, from MacLaine to Sylvester Stallone, an increasing number of business and political leaders have identified themselves as New Agers.

At a conference in Denver, Atlanta broadcaster Ted Turner called for a New Age president to transport America into the new millennium. He said America needs a new moral code to give us a sense of order and dignity and he offered money to anyone who could come up with a document superior to the Ten Commandments which, in Turner's opinion, is hopelessly flawed and outdated.

In the United States Senate, Rhode Island Democrat Claiborne Pell, a dabbler in the occult and a New Age convert, introduced legislation in Congress in 1989 to fund a National Commission on Human Resource Development. Fortunately, Pell's efforts to legitimize the New Age movement and to funnel millions of taxpayer dollars into the hands of so-called "Mind-Body" experts failed, but just barely.

The national New Age policy lobbied by Pell would have set up a commission of 25 advisers and a full-fledged administration department. It was rebuffed largely through the protest of Senator Dan Coats, who reminded the Senate that they had already rejected a similar measure in 1988.

CHANNELING THE CORPORATION

In 1986 the *New York Times* reported on the increase of New Age mind control in the corporate world. The story showed how large corporations, under the misguided pretext of increasing efficiency and productivity, are pushing meditation, hypnosis, channeling, biofeedback, psychic manifestations, and other components of Eastern mysticism loosely built on Maslow's principles of "self actualization."

These "human potential" seminars and "mind control clinics" are still very much in vogue and are being required for employees in companies such as Ford, Chrysler, General Motors, Westinghouse, IBM, RCA, Boeing, TRW, Proctor & Gamble, Polaroid and other industry giants. In some cases, refusal to participate can mean loss of a job, harassment on the job, or denial of advancement opportunities.

Some of our largest airlines currently require all their flight personnel to undergo "psychic training" based on New Age concepts at least twice a year.

A survey of 500 California firms conducted by *California Business* magazine showed that fully half were already employing some kind of "consciousness-raising" techniques. And graduate schools of business, from Stanford to Yale, are experimenting with "creativity" training involving everything from witchcraft to primal therapy.

In her February 1990 newsletter, Phyllis Schlafly reported on many of these activities and described further the Department of Education hearing on "protection of pupil rights" which revealed that many of these same occult practices, along with many examples of outright Satanism, have been used in public schools to "retrain" our sons and daughters and to indoctrinate children into the New Age.

ROOTS OF THE OCCULT

New Age is another term for occult which became prominent as booksellers, in particular, discovered the growing appeal of metaphysical and occult books dealing with what the authors termed "a coming new age of spiritual enlightenment."

Simply reflecting the "Occult" label on the bookshelves with "New Age" escalated sales on everything in the section, from books on herbal cures to the Satanist Bible.

The idea of reincarnation, which is characteristic of many of the New Age religions, is a Hindu belief which has gained great popularity in this country because it offers a concept of eternal life. But it is very different from the doctrine of death and resurrection taught by the Bible.

Hindu beliefs offer a view of the world that is cyclical. The idea of *karma*, the Hindu wheel of fate, is a central concept. It is the belief that people continue to come around until their *karma*, or debt, is purged; but the *karma* never does get purged, unless they attain Nirvana, which is nothingness.

It is a chilling and joyless vision of life, but these beliefs are spreading like wildfire. We recently learned that a new Hindu temple goes up in the United States every 21 days. Swamis, Yogis, Gurus, and Zen Masters seem to be multiplying everywhere, particularly on the West Coast.

SALVATION FROM THE STARS

If that weren't enough, belief in UFOs is also growing rapidly. The movie *ET* was an immediate success in this country because it allowed a lot of people to hope that there might really be salvation for mankind from the stars. At the same time, the concept of Extra Sensory Perception (ESP) has become as commonplace as horoscopes. Author and sociologist Andrew Greeley reports that 70 million Americans have had ESP experiences, and a study done at Northern Illinois University suggests that nearly the same number follow their horoscopes on a regular basis.

Beyond that, there are a vast number of popular forms of spiritism, from Ouija boards to palm reading, and other things which are very much in vogue because people want to believe that the spirits guide them. I even heard recently that some psychics, including Jeanne Dixon, are advertising their services on television with a toll-free 800 number for call-in customers.

The sad irony is that spirits can and do guide them; but they are not the spirits the seekers are expecting. They are not innocent and benign spirits but evil ones who prey on the weak and ignorant. Those who dabble in the occult and who have rejected the atonement of Jesus Christ become the victims of demonic forces whose sole aim is to use up and destroy their victims.

It is pathetic to see mediums and gurus claiming to possess some magical combination lock to the unknown. There is no mystery to summoning up evil spirits. The Bible says, "Your adversary the devil walks about as a roaring lion seeking whom he may devour" (1 Peter 5:8). Satan roams the earth in search of victims, and his demons and minions of evil are constantly prowling in our very midst. Frank Peretti's book, *This Present Darkness*, portrays this reality so very forcefully, it is no wonder the novel has become a national bestseller.

The only thing easier than becoming a willing victim of Satan is renouncing sin and becoming a child of God. Yet, despite the promises of Jesus Christ and the essential simplicity of His message, the New Agers appear to be intent not only on leading millions astray but participating in their own self-destruction.

The leading mystics and seers of the movement have tried to incorporate some of the basic teachings of Christianity with the "all is one" ideology of the Eastern tradition to create a new image of god in man. Their theory is a hodgepodge, at best, but it is a heady mixture for those who have no roots and for those who have an openness to the occult.

The essential heresy of the entire movement is the denial of God's authority and the promotion of man into the role of God. Shirley MacLaine has written, "We already know everything. The knowingness of our divinity is the highest intelligence. And to *be* what we already know is the free will. Free will is simply the enactment of the realization you are God, a realization that you are the divine free will is making everything accessible to you."

Only the ignorant or the deceitful could ever accept such a twisted vision of God, but there are millions of ready converts among us. The Bible also says we should be strong in faith and resist evil. More and more, resisting that evil means we must endure the scorn and abuse of those who call us names, but it is not the laughter or even the violence of the scoffers that we should fear but God Himself, who will certainly judge the unfaithful witness.

SIGNS AND WONDERS

Already the false gods of the movement are gaining power, a power which comes straight from Satan. Accordingly, I believe we can expect to witness Satanic miracles, signs and wonders, and a host of demonic manifestations in the not-too-distant future. None of us should be surprised if during this decade we begin to see many more supernatural events taking place in our world.

Just as Christ foretold, demonic forces will be raging against the church of God, but the power of God will be alive in the church and we will also see incredible signs and wonders through the power of the Holy Spirit.

The clash we will experience, then, will not be between belief and unbelief, but between one form of belief and another. It will be faith in God versus faith in the Devil, and it will be very clear where the people of God will have to make their stand.

At the same time, cults which claim to be Christian will be blossoming among us. Jehovah's Witnesses, Unity, Christian Science, the Way, the Worldwide Church of God, and many others, are actively proselyting in this country and abroad. In every case, the fallacy of their claims is in the denial of the absolute deity of Jesus Christ and His lordship over mankind.

Either by watering down the gospel message or by adding false teachings and false writings to the Word of God, these false doctrines commit the sin of Revelation 22:18 by adding to this record and thereby bring down the wrath of God upon their own heads.

THE STAMP OF SATAN

Communism is also a religious belief, though it is more of a belief in the mechanical determinism of history than in any kind of supernatural force. But within the umbrella of the New Age there is room for a plethora of beliefs—not just the ones mentioned here, but all kinds, from Indian gurus to those who claim to be possessed by disembodied spirits who pass along messages.

There are those who claim to have had out-of-body experiences, some who claim to have been visited by beings from outer space, and others who believe in some kind of occult faith or luck. There is an enormous variety, but they all bear the unmistakable stamp of Satan.

Many of these phenomena can only be explained by reference to demons. So far the Devil and his demons have been hidden. Very few people in America believe in the Devil. They say they believe in God, but they don't believe in these things which are satanic manifestations.

It seems fairly clear that in the next ten years the manifestations will coalesce more and more into a unified whole and their satanic origins will become more and more visible. I think Satan is going to be showing himself.

Of course, there are satanic groups in this country who are nothing more than pornographers in disguise. They are using satanic rituals to make kiddie-porn and to engage in sadistic rituals that really have nothing to do with Satan except the name. Nevertheless, they are there and there is hardly a city in America where there have not been instances of ritual torture and repeated abuse of little children in the name of Satan. There is sexual abuse, physical torture and many instances of dismemberment and death—not only of animals, but of people. This is the work of Satan, and it is on the rise in America.

In some cases, Indian drugs such as peyote have been used in these rites. The Satanist group that murdered the American medical student in Matamoros, Mexico, is one such case. They were engaged in ritual sacrifice, but there was also drug involvement. Unfortunately, there are dozens of these kinds of cults, and they all come under the heading of Hindu thought and structures.

THE RISE OF ISLAM

We will also see a rise of militant Islam in this country during the coming decade. Islam is very active in America; its adherents are building mosques in hundreds of cities and towns. In a special report on the growth of Islam in the *Bible Baptist Tribune*, Dr. James Combs says that "In the 1990s there will be more Moslems in America than Jews! One out of every five persons on earth is a Moslem."

Money has a way of allowing people to propagate their religious beliefs, and since there is so much oil money flowing into the Arab world, it is being manifested in the spread of Islam into America, especially into the Black community.

The spread of Islam among African-Americans is such an incredible irony. It was the Arab and Muslim merchants in Africa who were the main proponents of the slave trade. They created it. Although English and American ships transported the slaves to the United States, it was the Arab Muslim traders who went into the heartland of Africa, captured the people, brought them to the coast, and sold them to the slavers.

Now to see Black Americans forsaking their Christian heritage, which has produced some of the most beautiful and godly people on earth, in order to turn to Islam—as if that were a way of bringing some sort of national deliverance to them—is utterly absurd and, frankly, heartbreaking.

But Louis Farrakhan and his ilk are pushing a militant and rabidly racist form of Islam which is growing dramatically on the pretext that somehow Islam offers Blacks in the inner-city a chance to express their heritage. That never was the case, and it is a fraud and a lie, but thousands of Blacks are buying it. Farrakhan's anti-Semitism is a matter of public record, yet he draws audiences of tens of thousands whenever he speaks.

There is a large Arab population in America, especially in Michigan and other industrial regions. In its militant, nationalistic form, Islam is a very powerful force. The Arab Brotherhood murdered Anwar Sadat, and fanatic Shiites were responsible for the kidnappings and murders that took place in Lebanon and Iran.

Whether Islam can break out beyond the boundaries of the Middle East into Europe is doubtful, but their continuing growth is still surprising. There is a huge population of people who believe in Islam. If Dr. Combs' estimates are correct, as many as a billion people on earth are Muslims.

The good news is that the Muslims share many common beliefs with Christians. It is a monotheistic religion, and the Allah of the Muslims is essentially the same as Jehovah. Only Christianity, Judaism, and Islam reject an evolutionary concept of man and therefore reject the doctrine of reincarnation. But from there the differences far outweigh the similarities.

It is my feeling that Islam is actually a Christian heresy. It was born at a time when the church was weak, when there was squabbling between Rome and Constantinople and when the theology of the church had degenerated into needless fantasy and speculation. The Christian church had lost both its fervor and its spiritual hold over the people of the Mediterranean world.

When Mohammed appeared on the scene in 622 A.D., he proclaimed himself a new prophet of the historic faith of the Bible. He wrote the books of the Koran very much as Jeremiah and Ezekiel had written the prophetic books of the Old Testament.

When his successors began to launch repeated Islamic Jihads, or holy wars, neither the Christian churches nor the Christian governments in the very cradle of Christianity could stand before them. What was taken has never been recovered. Only tiny Lebanon remained as a Christian enclave in the midst of a Muslim Middle East.

Followers of Mohammed believed in the idea of one God. They also believed in Abraham and Isaac and Ishmael and Jesus; the principal problem for Christians—and it is a very serious problem—is the role assigned to Mohammed as the last prophet and the fact that he did not recognize Jesus Christ as the Messiah, or the Mahdi.

Nevertheless, there is within Islam a tone that can respond somewhat to Christianity. Islam may be considered a Christian heresy, but at least it springs from the Bible. It is not a totally alien religion as is Hinduism.

OF ALIEN GODS

Although dangerous men like Saddam Hussein have called for unification of Muslim nations—what he calls the "Pan Arab World"—Islam is not the spiritual threat that Hinduism will be because Hinduism comes at us much more subtly and has, as its origin, demonic power.

There is really no common ground between the beliefs of Hinduism and the beliefs of Christianity. It is the product of a totally alien culture and an alien concept of religion which cannot be reconciled in any way with the Christian faith.

The Bible says that it is appointed once for man to die and after that the judgment. There is no possibility of coming back in different forms. Christians believe in the idea of original sin, in the possibility of redemption through faith in a sovereign God. We believe in the unique life of each human being. The Hindus really don't have any concept of a personal God or of sin or redemption by a God-sent personal Savior.

They believe that each human being lives this life then returns as a dog or a cow or a dung beetle, or even as the rain or another human being. Each stage in the transmigration of the soul is, to them, determined by karma. As for social justice, there is no necessity to improve the lot of the poor untouchables because their karma determined their status in life.

For a Westerner brought up according to the compassionate teachings of Jesus Christ, it is virtually inconceivable to behold the misery, the suffering, and the degradation that the Hindu beliefs bring about in a nation like India.

We should also be aware that the genius of the Buddha was to create some escape from the fiendish hell of Hinduism. The salvation he offered, unfortunately, was unattainable. Escape from karma to Nirvana, or paradise, was only possible to those who had ceased all human desire, and that any right-thinking person must realize will never happen short of death itself.

In the rigors of their worship and the attempts to change their karma, Hindus seek physical transcendence through out-of-body experiences, ecstatic trances, and the visitation of alien spirits. Hindu worship is aimed by and large at bribing the angry spirits and buying off the gods with gifts of appeasement, mortification, endless self-degradation, and humiliation. This totally alien system of beliefs can only lead people to poverty, anguish and, ultimately, to demon possession.

Nevertheless, as we have seen, many cults born out of Hinduism will emerge as rivals to the Christian faith during the coming decade. They will come with all the trappings of the New Age, with promises of sensuality and mystical transcendence to rush into the spiritual void existing in our world today. They will offer a host of bogus promises, and millions will believe.

FALSE MESSIAH

Lest anyone dismiss the New Age philosophy and its Hindu roots as too bizarre for serious consideration, we should recall the full-page advertisements announcing the appearance in the world of a new messiah, the Lord Meitreya.

In these advertisements we were told that this messiah figure would come to lead the peoples and governments of the world out of their problems because he would have at his disposal the spiritual wisdom of the ages.

From the time of people like Alice Bailey on, those at the heart of the New Age movement have promised solutions to the imponderable problems of the world through wisdom given to them from beings described as "ascended masters." Obviously these beings are calling for a one world government, the end of national sovereignty, and the elimination of those people who would resist their all-encompassing plans for the world.

I have twice interviewed Tal Brooke, the author of a fascinating book entitled *When the World Will Be One*. Brooke was in India as a disciple of the famed guru, Sai Baba. Sai Baba was in turn reputed to be a disciple of "ascended masters." Brooke told me that when he drew closer to Sai Baba it was evident the human being was no longer present. Sai Baba was completely inhabited by another being: a powerful demon which was giving him the concepts and plans that his disciples so eagerly followed, as well as the miracles which astonished his followers.

It is reasonable to believe that many of the present Western intellectuals and thought leaders who have fought Christianity so vehemently will not now turn to Christianity for their solutions. Instead, they will seek wisdom by becoming disciples of those who offer what appear to be eminently practical solutions served up by the emissaries of Satan himself.

The worldwide struggle in this decade will not be temporal but spiritual. As the apostle Paul put it, "We wrestle not against flesh and blood, but against principalities and powers, against spiritual wickedness in high places, against the rulers of the darkness of this age."

In this decade and beyond, how much more important will it be to weigh every public policy initiative and every church initiative to identify its true source and where it will eventually lead. When leaders speak of "one world" and "a new world order," what do they really mean? Where will their counsel take us?

THE COUNTERBALANCE

Before we succumb to the fear that these various cults, heresies, and New Age counterfeits will totally overtake us, we need to recognize that there has also been a groundswell of Christian renewal throughout the world during the past ten years, and the evidence suggests that trend will accelerate during the coming decade.

I believe that, irrespective of the apparent reason for glasnost, perestroika, and the collapse of communism, the momentum toward freedom was brought about by God as an occasion for evangelism.

As this book is being published, CBN will be in the process of distributing 13 million gospel booklets in Romania, eight broadcasts of Bible stories each week throughout the Soviet Union on Soviet television, the printing of 100,000 Bibles and 100,000 copies of a key Christian book in Poland, the licensing for printing four major Christian books in Hungary, the distribution of 15,000 Bibles in Bulgaria, and the donation of 100,000 dollars to evangelical churches in Czechoslovakia for the paper to print Bibles for that country.

Only two years ago, in Budapest, Hungary, Sandor Nemeth was conducting underground church services in fear of arrest. Now his Sunday services are so huge that his church is forced to meet in a sports arena. During the past year he has established 35 fast-growing satellite churches throughout Hungary.

Reports have reached me of powerful spiritual revival in the Ukraine. The move toward God is so strong in the Soviet Union that people are actually kneeling in Red Square to receive Jesus Christ as their Savior.

Everywhere that I went the message was clear. A spiritual revival of unprecedented magnitude is coming about in the former communist lands. Their reasoning is simple. Communist oppression is equated with atheism, freedom is equated with faith in God.

The needs are immense. There is a crucial need for pastors, for seminaries, and Bible training schools, for programs to train lay leaders, and to give them the tools to assist new converts just coming to the faith.

Even in communist China the religious revival is strong. In 1979, I spoke on the streets to friendly crowds in Guangdong (Canton Province) and Kweilin. Their voracious hunger to receive copies of the Bible and their warm-hearted willingness to receive salvation through Jesus Christ were as intense as anything I have witnessed anyplace in the world.

Although church statistics coming out of mainland China are unreliable, reports reaching me indicate that there are between 50 and 75 million professing Christians in China. Some sources estimate as high as 100 million. A powerful religious revival has been in progress in coastal Fukien Province with demonstrations of faith reminiscent of the New Testament church.

A particularly touching account of revival concerns the resisting students following the brutal suppression of their pro-democracy demonstrations in Tiananmen Square. Reports indicate that entire dormitories of students were renouncing communism and becoming Christians.

THE WORLD OF FAITH

My visits to Eastern Europe, to Central America, and to China have made one thing very clear to me. Communism and war have broken down the entrenched religious and social oligarchies which were opposed to Christianity. In mainland China, Buddhism was suppressed by the communists, and through them, one dialect, Mandarin, is now the only language suitable for conversation throughout the entire nation.

In the Soviet Union, Eastern Europe, and in Nicaragua, the communists repressed all religions and all classes of entrenched privilege. Once communism has been removed, there is now no impediment between the simple gospel of Jesus Christ and the hearts of deeply religious people.

Although North Africa is still hostile to Christianity, past colonial Black Africa is remarkably receptive to the Christian message. Some observers feel that a majority of Africa will be Christian by the end of the decade.

The ministry of German-born evangelist Reinhard Bonnke throughout Africa has been nothing short of phenomenal. In South Africa, Kenya, Burkina Faso, Mali, Malawi, and Nigeria, crowds numbering in the hundreds of thousands have come out to hear Bonnke preach. Sometimes the attendance at his meetings is equal to the entire population of the city in which he is speaking.

The population of the world has now exceeded five billion. Half of that number is made up of people under the age of 18. The total, we are told, exceeds the combined populations of the world from the time of Jesus Christ until now. Certainly this can be the church's finest hour as it experiences a spiritual harvest that could easily number during this decade between 500 million and a billion people.

GROWTH AND RENEWAL

One of the most exhaustive studies ever conducted of church growth in America was developed by Dr. John Vaughan, publisher and editor of the newsletter, "Church Growth Today," and his associates at Southwestern Baptist University in Bolivar, Missouri. The study completed in early 1990 shows that the churches which are growing the fastest are those which are preaching the gospel and sharing the love of Jesus Christ in their communities.

The denominational statistics are especially interesting. Vaughan reports that, of the 512 fastest growing churches in America, 117 are Southern Baptist, 79 are Assembly of God, 37 are independent charismatic, 36 are United Methodist, 29 are independent non-charismatic, 29 are Independent Baptist congregations, 19 are Lutheran Missouri-Synod, 18 are Evangelical Free Church, 14 are Church of Christ, 14 are Presbyterian Church USA, 14 are Presbyterian Church in America, and 10 are Foursquare Gospel.

Atlanta, Los Angeles, Houston and Dallas/Fort Worth topped the list of most spiritually dynamic cities while California, Texas, Florida and Georgia topped the most-dynamic states list.

What we are seeing are churches—such as Calvary Chapel in Costa Mesa, California, and Church on the Rock in Rockwall, Texas—which are not only dynamic congregations themselves, but are spinning off churches in their own cities and sometimes in far-flung communities.

The fastest growing church in America in 1989 was Calvary Chapel in Albuquerque, New Mexico, pastored by Skip Heitzig, a church planted by Chuck Smith's church in Costa Mesa. Congregations are emerging with ten to fifteen thousand people and a tremendous passion for service. They are growing, reproducing themselves, and they are changing the landscape of Christianity in this country.

A few years ago no one would have believed this kind of church growth was remotely possible, but the trend of the '80s is continuing into the '90s and appears to be growing stronger. Part of the reason it is happening now, I suspect, is the fact that Christian broadcasting has been accelerating all through the '80s.

Between 1980 and 1986, CBN recorded some 600,000 decisions for Christ during that time, hundreds of thousands of whom were referred to local churches. We found that the number of decisions were growing dramatically year by year. In 29 years of ministry, we have recorded 1.6 million decisions for Christ and our counselors have received over 35 million telephone calls for help.

Almost all of the new converts and many of those seeking counsel have been referred to local churches. How many thousands more have come from other similar ministries?

THE TURNING POINT

One of the critical points in America's spiritual life during the 1980s was the event called "Washington for Jesus," which Bill Bright of Campus Crusade for Christ has called "the turning point of our century." It was the largest inter-denominational gathering of Christians in the history of the country.

It was estimated that somewhere in the neighborhood of 500,000 people attended that conference, people from every corner of America. There were 45,000 people from the state of Massachusetts alone. There was a trainload from Florida. People flew in from Hawaii. They were from all over, from all races, and they represented every kind of organization, from Cops for Christ, to Catholic outreach ministries and Protestant bishops.

The event featured a tremendous time of prayer for revival in America. Clearly, that had a profound impact on the elections of 1980, on the presidency, and on the shift of influence in the United States Senate. Washington for Jesus was not in any way a political movement; it wasn't intended to influence politics. It was intended to fulfill 2 Chronicles 7:14 which says, "If my people, who are called by my name, shall humble themselves, and pray, and seek my face, and turn from their wicked ways; then will I hear from heaven, and will forgive their sin, and will heal their land."

It was a time of fasting and prayer and crying out to God for revival in our nation. The country was in a state of malaise, confusion, and drifting moral values. Washington for Jesus was a manifestation of Americans seeking the face of God.

Out of that conference, we believe, came a new sense of national purpose, a new strength of vision, and a new pride in this nation. Two years later there was a sense of national pride we hadn't seen in years. There is no question that God heard and answered prayer.

THE EVANGELICAL RIGHT

Time magazine's cover story, "The Year of the Evangelical," focused on the fact that evangelicals were on the move. Not only did we have a man in the presidency who called himself "born again," but evangelicals were instrumental in bringing in another man into the White House who professed most of the beliefs of the evangelical Christians.

Subsequent to the success of his book, *The Naked Public Square*—which told secular America we could not function as a society without religious and moral values—Richard John Neuhaus penned an article for *Commentary* in which he described "What the Fundamentalists Want," and informed liberal America that, like it or not, "the country cousins have shown up in force at the family picnic.

"They want a few rules changed right away," he said. "Other than that they promise to behave, provided we do not again try to exclude them from family deliberations." The book and the article merely voiced what was already becoming quite clear. Evangelicals had grown sick and tired of being sick and tired, and they were on the move.

Every time a great victory like that happens, it is natural to expect a counterattack. Every victory in battle, until the enemy is totally crushed, will bring forth a counterattack. Unfortunately, the counterattack in this case took place to coincide with my run for the nomination of the Republican Party for the presidency in 1988.

The secular press and those who are anti-Christian in our society were looking for any opportunity to discredit this enormous movement of renewal and revival in our country which was beginning to impact the secular order. They placarded the story of Jim and Tammy Bakker and Jimmy Swaggart on every television network and in the headlines, and they played it over and over again for the better part of two years. And with that they were successful in discouraging evangelicals from giving to all kinds of worthy causes.

Financial support for Christian work dropped dramatically, across the board, whether to the Wycliffe Bible Translators, to interdenominational mission work, or to the various Bible societies. It also had an enormous impact on the local churches and small ministries.

SHAKING THE CHURCH

But the truth is, this assault and regrouping was merely a lull to prepare for something greater. **The Bible makes it clear that judgment**

begins at the house of the Lord. Those of us who were looking at what God was doing realized two important things.

First, there could not be a continuation of revival as long as there was spiritual rot in the church: it had to be cleansed and cleansed publicly. But the second thing was that God as a righteous God could not judge the secular world for its evil if He permitted comparable evil within His church. So He first did a work of cleansing and purging.

Now we see that this wasn't bad, it was good. That period of purging laid the foundation for a decade of evangelism which is going to exceed anything we have known in the history of the world. **By shaking out the church, God actually prepared it for the greater challenge to come.**

Using the incredible tools that we have available to us through radio, TV, film, video, high speed printing, and all the various skills that we have accumulated over the past 30 years, it is literally possible to blitz an entire nation for Christ and to bring about a spiritual harvest of unprecedented magnitude. It can be done through the existing church structure so that our churches will be revitalized, trained and equipped, and given the opportunity to become leaders in the education, social welfare, and spiritual life of our communities.

RECLAIMING THE LAND

It is interesting that just as this decade dawned, the Lord enabled us at CBN to start a spiritual blitz into the three major countries of Central America: Guatemala, El Salvador, and Nicaragua. We called it *"Projecto Luz"* (Project Light). Our goal was to see two million decisions for Christ through a massive media blitz that would guarantee that every home throughout these three countries would hear the gospel. We were not disappointed. The response of the churches was overwhelming.

The church in Guatemala applauded our efforts. The ministerial head of the evangelicals in Guatemala told me that he wholeheartedly endorsed the campaign because it did not exalt any man; rather it exalted Jesus Christ. He said, this was the most unifying thing that had ever happened to those churches.

It was strictly an interdenominational activity to bring people to Christ and to enable the churches to take advantage of the opportunity in accordance with their own spiritual desires. If the local church chose to be active, they could see their church membership tripled or quadrupled in a year's time. And even those who were less diligent could still add a few more members.

In every church there was equal opportunity to reach out as far as they were able. We made available to them a climate in which people would listen to the claims of Christ, and actually receive those claims.

This kind of outreach can be repeated, and I assure you it will be repeated in the East Bloc countries, in the Soviet Union, all over Africa, in parts of the Middle East, in vast areas of Asia, and throughout Latin America. I have heard statistics which indicate that, in Latin America, if the gospel is clearly presented, one out of every two people who hear it will receive Christ on the spot. In Asia, that figure is more like one out of four; and the same figure holds for the United States!

To date, CBN has either initiated or taken part in outreach programs in 85 nations around the world. Our broadcasts have been carried throughout mainland China. In the Middle East, we are beaming the message to a potential audience of some 10 million people, both Arabs and Jews. In Argentina we are preparing a fresh media blitz. One month after this book reaches the bookstores of America, five million Argentinians are expected to have made decisions for Christ.

All that is necessary at the present time is to have a sense of spiritual awareness and revival within the church, and a sense of diligence, and then to take the resources we already have available into the traditional channels of the marketplace of these nations.

The object is not to broadcast on early Sunday morning when very few are watching, but to go into prime time with major spot announcements on the most popular programs on the most popular television and radio stations. We must go where the people are, to be where they're looking and listening. Having done it once in Central America, we now see that the potential harvest is beyond calculation.

THE MINISTRY EXPLOSION

I am convinced the coming decade will see an explosion of ministry, which means the number of people who will hear the gospel in the next few years will be greater than the total number of all those who have heard it, collectively, from the time of Jesus until now.

That means that our evangelistic activities can be more fruitful now, in terms of mass numbers, than at any time since the time of Christ. So the final harvest—and this may well be our final harvest—will be the most glorious in the history of the church.

Logistics became a major factor in the evangelical explosion of the 1980s. Some churches were having to go to three and even four services on Sundays to accommodate the crowds. In one church in Dallas, people literally ran to church to get a seat. You could see them hurrying into the church building to be assured of a place to sit.

Willow Creek Community Church, north of Chicago, has added a Saturday night service as well, and Bill Hybels is preaching to standing-room-only crowds. From a group of just 150 dedicated believers 15 years ago, Willow Creek grew to more than 14,000 members in 1990. That is a far cry from what we used to think of as typical church growth.

There is a real explosion of faith going on in the hearts of believers. But while we see the evangelical faith thriving as never before, we also see that the intellectual theology of doubters and equivocators is dying of self-inflicted wounds. Jesus told the Jews of His day, "The kingdom of God will be taken from you and given to those bearing the fruit thereof."

There is no question that the mainline churches—the Episcopal, Presbyterian, Methodist, Lutheran and other historic denominations—have been hemorrhaging members for the past 25 years. The reason is that, by and large, they have moved away from the clear proclamation of Jesus Christ, Who declared, "I am the way, the truth, and the life. No one comes to the Father but by Me."

In mid-1990, UPI reported on a study by the Lilly Endowment which indicates that doctrinal and political divisions in the mainline churches are eating away at these congregations. Episcopalians, Congregationalists, and Presbyterians were the dominant institutions in this nation for more than two centuries, since long before the Declaration of Independence.

Today, the UPI article suggests, it looks like the mainline has headed to the sidelines. After holding a near-monopoly on government in this country, the Presbyterians have lost fully a third of their membership in the past 25 years, along with much of their clout.

On January 29, 1990, Bishop Maurice M. Benitez, of the Episcopal Diocese of Texas, told the Church Club of New York, "Over the past twenty years the Episcopal Church dropped from 3.5 million baptized members to 2.5 million members." He then added,

> St. Paul and the other apostles did not barnstorm the Mediterranean world preaching social justice, preaching abolition of slavery, or calling the Roman Empire to provide housing for the homeless and a more equitable economic system. They preached Jesus Christ, crucified and raised from the dead for our salvation. They called all who would listen to repent, to turn their lives around . . .

The denominations that have permitted the secularization of their seminaries and the liberalizing of their theology have lost their grip on the core of the faith. They have forgotten the words of Christ when He said, "Except a man be born again, he shall in no wise see the kingdom of heaven." Instead, they have chosen to preach a "social Gospel," to dwell on the so-called "higher criticism" of scholars such as Bultmann, Heidegger, and others who cast doubt on the authenticity of the Bible, the miracles, and on Jesus Christ Himself.

THE LIBERAL AGENDA

As Jim Reapsome, editor of *Evangelical Missions Quarterly,* pointed out in a recent series, "Liberals claim that the world sets the agenda for the church. God's kingdom, they say, is not established by proclaiming the unique salvation message of Jesus Christ, but by restructuring the world's social, political, and economic order."

In the National Council of Churches, these people have further allied themselves with leftist movements in America, the most shocking of which was perhaps the contribution of 100,000 dollars by the Presbyterian Church to the Defense Fund of the Marxist radical, Angela Davis.

When I was in Columbia in the 1970s, a Presbyterian missionary told me of a 75,000 dollar gift that was going to support a rebel group seeking the overthrow of the democratically elected government of Columbia.

University of Oregon sociologist Benton Johnson, in his study of the Presbyterian Church U.S.A., reports that less than 55 percent of Presbyterians confirmed in the 1960s are still active in churches. Between 1970 and 1987, the denomination lost more than a million members.

Even though hard times have forced the social churches to rethink some of their policies, the Presbyterian General Assembly which met in Salt Lake City in June 1990 announced that the environment would be a major thrust of the denomination for the '90s and that the liturgy would now profess the female as well as male attributes of God.

It appears the people in the pews just don't want any part of that. They want their souls to be fed, and they want to have the faith proclaimed by men of God who know God and who are willing to teach that faith and to build them up in the faith once delivered to the saints. And when they don't get it, they leave.

God removes His hand from those churches which refuse to serve Him. The money dries up, and the churches inevitably fall into disrepair. And the pundits proclaim that God is dead, but God is not dead. He will not submit His Spirit to churches that *are* dead. God is very much alive and He is looking for men and women who believe it.

A DECADE OF OPPORTUNITY

The church is booming in America. Certain expressions of it are dying on the vine, but that can change. There are signs of revival in the Anglican and Episcopal churches. There are pockets of revival in the Methodist and the Presbyterian churches, but only in those congregations where Christ is being preached and the truth of Scripture is being proclaimed. God's Spirit will not remain in an atmosphere of compromise; but where Christ is preached, He lives.

In the inspired words of Bishop Benitez,

> I declare that people are looking for something, someone in whom they can believe, for a faith on which they can bet their lives . . . People in our world, people in our pews, are hungry for spiritual renewal, hungry not for more meetings, or more social issues, or more turmoil, they are hungry for God, and yearn to know His presence and power in their lives. People will go to a church that believes that Jesus Christ is the Way and the Truth and the Life and says it.

If there is to be revival in the land, it will not come through compromise and equivocation but through that kind of fervent faith in and passionate commitment to the gospel.

Today the world is poised for a spiritual revival. This is an incredible decade of opportunity for the Christian church.

Age old barriers to missionary activity have fallen and billions of people are open to receive the claims of Jesus Christ.

But if the Christian church fails, or if we fail to reach out with the genuine nourishment of God's Word, the world's present spiritual hunger will most certainly be filled with the Hindu-based spirituality of the New Age.

Part II

THE
TRI-LATERAL
WORLD

The United States borders two oceans, one facing Europe, the other facing Asia. . . . American people and American business can no longer comfort themselves by crowing over our superiority. All of us from now on are on a course of continuous gut-wrenching change and fierce competition from East and West. We will no longer be insulated from any development in our world whether it takes place in Brussels or Berlin, Moscow or the Persian Gulf, Tokyo or Beijing.

5

The Unification of Europe

Long weak and divided, Europe will soon unite as a powerful equal of the United States.

Unification should mean trade, investment potential, and jobs for Americans. Together we should share a rapidly growing world economy. But dangers exist.

Are powerful forces pulling strings to fold Western Europe, Eastern Europe, Japan, and the United States into a one world political system?

W HEN THE FINAL documents are signed and the official oaths are sworn, the world will experience an event reminiscent of that Christmas day in 800 A.D. when Charlemagne was crowned by Pope Leo III as emperor of a United Europe, then termed the Holy Roman Empire. For on December 31, 1992, in furtherance of what is called "The Single Europe Act," a European community will be formed as an economic and quasi-political federation of the twelve nations of France, Germany, Great Britain, Italy, Spain, Holland, Belgium, Ireland, Luxembourg, Denmark, Portugal, and Greece.

With its parliament in Strasbourg and its executive offices in Brussels, the single Europe will encompass a population of 323 million and a gross national product which at 4.274 trillion dollars will be about 19 percent smaller than the United States GNP and roughly equal to the combined output of Japan and the fast-growth economics of the Pacific Rim.

The current arrangement leaves more questions than answers. Will this be a loose customs union, or will there emerge a United States of Europe similar to the United States of America? Will the single Europe be a responsible trading partner for America, or will it erect barriers to shut out our products?

Why is the demise of communism in the Soviet Union occurring as if on cue to coincide with the 1992 European Union? Is this mere coincidence, or are powerful forces pulling strings in order to fold Western Europe, Central Europe, and Eastern Europe into some one world political system yet to be unveiled?

Of particular interest is the issue of a single European currency and a single European Central Bank. A European-style Federal Reserve Bank setting interest rates and regulating money supply would effectively negate national sovereignty among the twelve member nations. Why was Margaret Thatcher of Great Britain set upon so thoroughly by the establishment press when she chose to defend British sovereignty by opposing a Central European Bank?

What will happen to the freedom of every American if a European Central Bank were to combine with the seven-member American Federal Reserve Bank and they, in turn, were to combine its efforts with a seven-member Japanese or perhaps Japan-Asia Central Bank?

Such an arrangement might make the world's finances neat and tidy, but it would also mean that as few as twenty-one non-elected officials would control the money of the world! We can hark back to Lenin who declared that if he could control the world's money he would not care what else others controlled.

Regrettably, the time has already come when the interest rates paid by every American family or business are not being set just in Washington but by investors and bankers in Tokyo, Bonn, London, and Hong Kong. A group of powerful world leaders meeting under the auspices of what is known as the Tri-Lateral Commission—which is directly linked in turn to the New York-based Council on Foreign Relations—has repeatedly called for a "new world order based essentially on a one world government.

This means a diminished role for national sovereignty, especially for the United States of America. It means that the destiny of every American family would be taken from their hands, from the hands of their own elected officials, and given to some yet-to-be-determined supra-national governing body.

It hardly takes a genius to see that a closely coordinated world monetary policy between only three powerful central banks could bring about a de facto one world system long before the average man on the street knew what was going on. It could happen long before any elected official was even given the opportunity to vote on it.

The book of Revelation warns of a time in history when economic control will be so tight that no one could buy or sell without the identification number of the worldwide dictator.

Such gloomy thoughts aside, when most of us think of a United Europe we think of burgeoning markets to buy American goods. We think of prosperous Europeans visiting America and investing in our businesses, our securities, our real estate.

We see exciting opportunities to participate in an ever-growing world economy with those nations that produced our ancestors and many of our Western institutions, and with whom we as a nation have shared common ideals for centuries. We see in Europe those nations whose freedom we defended in two bitter world wars and whose economies we helped rebuild with the Marshall Plan.

We think of historic towns and cities that we have visited. Of universities where many of us have studied. Indeed, Western Europe's prosperity should be our prosperity, and a single Europe should mean jobs for Americans, a greater variety of goods for our consumers, and tremendous investment opportunities for our businesses.

Yet lingering in the back of the mind of every Christian should be one other question. A United Europe in 1992 will not be a "holy empire." Western Europe is probably the most cynical and irreligious part of the entire world. One stroll through the red light district of Amsterdam or Hamburg would shock even the most jaded.

Paul Henri Spaak, one of the primary post-World War II architects of a United Europe is reported to have blurted out the following: "Give us a man to solve our problems, and be he a god or a devil, we will follow him."

Could the bright hope we share for the future of a United Europe be dashed in the new millennium by the appearance of a charismatic leader who, like Adolf Hitler, resembles the Anti-Christ of the Bible?

Only time will tell.

HOW IT HAPPENED

For many years, political power in Western Europe has been controlled largely by its Christian Democratic parties. The tradition that began after World War II under the leadership of an Italian priest, Luigi Sturzo, has included such illustrious leaders as Konrad Adenauer of Germany, Robert Schuman of France, and Alcide de Gasperi of Italy. West German chancellor Helmut Kohl, of the Christian Democratic Union (CDU), is probably the best known of today's Christian Democratic leaders.

The founders of all those parties had deep Christian convictions which gave a focus and purpose to their political beliefs. The principles of their faith conformed their commitment to their culture. Furthermore, as reported by *The Economist* in March 1990, the founders of the movement were also the true founders of the European Community. As early as 1920 they were meeting to discuss the possibilities of a unified Europe based on principles of faith and service.

One of the unifying factors of these various national groups was French philosopher Jacques Maritain's concept of "personalism," which is the belief that mankind fulfills his innate purpose through service to others, particularly to his family and his community. Their idea of personalism was, therefore, strongly opposed to the competing beliefs of "liberal individualism" and "social collectivism" which have begun to dominate European political thought in recent years.

Even though many of these parties—in Italy, France, Germany, Holland, and Belgium—have continued to hold power, they have tended to do so over the past three decades by compromising with more liberal positions, by sacrificing principles for votes.

Fernan Herman, a member of the European Parliament and former Belgian minister of economy, claims "Christian Democracy has lost its soul and should go into opposition. The leaders now," he says, "accept anything to stay in power and they disregard our principles and traditions."

Herman scolded his colleagues, reminding them that they were the first federalists, "but now we focus too much on domestic politics and leave it to socialists like Delors and Mitterrand to push forward European integration."

LOOKING BEYOND THE WALL

The collapse of the Berlin Wall has done more than create new commerce in Europe, however, and conservative leaders among the Christian Democrats are pointing to the marriage of faith and political power that has brought new life to Poland, Hungary, Romania, Czechoslovakia, and all the rest of Eastern Europe. In those countries, they say, "50 years of persecution have made the new or revived Christian political groups unashamedly forthright."

Even the Soviet Union has a rapidly growing Christian Democratic Party whose chairman, Victor Aksyuchits, told *Forbes* magazine for its August 20, 1990, issue,

Social democracy, when it looks to the West, only sees material wealth. We, on the other hand, understand that the concept of Western liberalism (in its traditional sense) could only arise as the heir to Christian Civilization. Only the conviction that man is created in the image of God makes the individual inherently valuable.

To add evidence to their outcry, the Christian Democrats also cite the example of a group in Italy, called Communion and Liberation, which claims more than 100,000 active members and whose aim is "to put Christ at the centre of life and society." The party operates radio stations, businesses, publishing houses, and "solidarity centres" which offer training for the unemployed. *The Economist* reports that the group's most recent annual festival and political debate, in Rimini, Italy, drew more than 700,000 attendees, "most of them young."

The Christian leaders say there is no reason to cower in the shadows of the political arena when these others have proved that courage and dedication can give them authentic victory. The communists have failed, they say, and there is a window of opportunity today for Christian Democrats who will dare to hold fast to their convictions.

But the challenge is apparently not being taken up. Most spectators are predicting that the secular socialist position will continue to grow more rapidly than the conservative position in Europe and, consequently, the more secular parties, such as Kohl's CDU, will likely become the new model for European politics.

OF EMPIRE AND IDEOLOGY

The Unification of 1992 will be the final culmination of a plan signed into being in March 1957 at a conference of six European nations, which has come to be known as the Treaty of Rome. That document established the Common Market as the administrative headquarters of Europe for trade and trans-national dialog. Further, the treaty set forth the principles of an integrated market system based on "the four freedoms": free movement of goods, services, capital, and people.

Over the past thirty years, the European Community (EC) has grown to a league of twelve nations and has gone through periods of strife and compromise followed by periods of slow and painful consolidation some have called "Eurosclerosis."

During that time thousands of principles and policies have been enacted, most of which have required that delegates of the Community return to their homes and ensure that their respective nations make whatever changes may be required in their internal policies in order to bring all these disparate nations (and baroque bureaucratic systems) into accord before Unification Day in 1992.

Needless to say, it has not been an easy process. How do you get

Italians to agree with Frenchmen? And how do you get Belgians to accept a policy introduced by the Dutch? Politics has played an enormous role, but time and determination seem to have made a difference and, today, it does look as if the unification will take place as planned.

Part of the jockeying in the EC has been due to both perceived and real differences in character and worldview. For example, most of the member nations still admit to fear of the German state, since that nation was responsible for the two greatest conflagrations of this century. On the other hand, Germany's administrative and economic programs are as polished and efficient as their machinery, and the other European nations realize they very much need leaders with those traits.

ISSUES OF NATIONAL CHARACTER

Germany's role is already beginning to loom large in the unification game. The re-unification of the two Germanys in October 1990 will have economic consequences in the near future, but it is already having political and emotional consequences.

An accord in 1979 gave Germany's Bundesbank dominant influence over the European Monetary System (EMS) and its Exchange Rate Mechanism (ERM). That more than anything else has caused concern for Britian's Prime Minister, Margaret Thatcher, who has refused to submit the British pound or the English economic system to the EC or the Bundesbank.

Mrs. Thatcher disagrees with the protectionist-isolationist tendencies of the EC and its president, Jacques Delors, and favors a market-driven economy which would encourage the current open exchange with world nations, such as the United States. *Forbes* magazine quoted one American observer, Stanislav Yassukovich of Merrill Lynch, as saying that "The Continentals expect an institution-led approach. Her approach is more American; theirs reflects the influence of Catholic socialism. You have two fundamentally opposed political traditions."

Jacques Delors, in particular, has helped to foster the strongly socialist institutional policies of the EC. In fact, the blueprint for the Unification of 1992, frequently called the "Delors Report," calls for uniform economic policies imposed upon member nations by the EC. It calls for a *"transfer of decision-making power* from Member States to the Community," which means that the real power of the twelve independent nations of united Europe would actually rest in a single body, or worse, in a single man.

Along with that, Delors is big on social programs such as minimum wage and maximum work-week restraints. He would do away with the availability of "cheap labor" which (as in Asia, or the American Southwest) has given many smaller, poorer nations a distinct economic advantage in an increasingly competitive marketplace.

Having barely fought her own (and Britain's) way out of the depths of the socialist quagmire, Margaret Thatcher has no interest in going back into the pits. She inflamed her liberal opponents by saying so in a brilliant speech in Bruges, Belgium in September 1988. At that meeting she said, "We have not successfully rolled back the frontiers of the state in Britain only to see them reimposed at a European level with a European superstate exercising a new dominance from Brussels."

Her critics at home and abroad accuse Mrs. Thatcher of denying Britain a chance to compete fairly in the new Europe. They say she is obstinate and obstructionist. Ironically, *Forbes* also reports that Mrs. Thatcher's government has really been the most effective in actually implementing the various EC policies handed down by the administration in Brussels. Of the 88 directives, Britain has enacted 69. Italy, by comparison, has enacted 35. Only Denmark has enacted more.

Most observers of the ongoing debates and negotiations say it is also clear that the Delors economic model is exclusionist and protectionist, and that his trade plan specifically militates against free trade with the United States. That is another limitation Margaret Thatcher will not abide.

In concluding her remarks in Bruges, she made an appeal for a united Europe "which looks outward—not inward—and which preserves that Atlantic community—that Europe on both sides of the Atlantic—which is our noblest inheritance and our greatest strength." Clearly, she was referring to the United States.

THE TRI-LATERAL WORLD

Europe's unification finally brings into alignment a three-way division of world power that has been predicted for some time. The EC will quickly become the dominant force in the European sphere, surpassing NATO, the defunct Warsaw Pact, the communist economic organization, COMECON, and other agencies and organizations which once gave focus to the multinational interests of Western and Eastern Europe.

A world away, Japan, despite its troubles with a faltering stock market and sporadic economic readjustments, continues its plans to unite with China and its neighbors throughout Asia and the Pacific Rim. The combined economic impact of a trading block which includes the major nations of Asia will be staggering, and the Japan-Asia league will be a mighty player in the coming tri-lateral world.

Finally, the ongoing economic and diplomatic consolidations between Canada, Mexico, and the United States, part of a North American Free

Trade Zone, will form the third leg of the triangle which may set the tone for the world of the future.

According to the statistics of the International Monetary Fund, for the period 1981–1987, the three economies already stack up as generally equal competitors for global markets. Without the input of figures from China, Korea, or any of the other Asian partners, Japan's Gross National Product (GNP) is 2.9 trillion dollars. Comparatively, the combined GNP of the 12 EC nations is 4.3 trillion while the United States GNP just tops 5.2 trillion dollars.

On the same scale, Japan's population base is 123 million, while the EC reports 323 million and the USA 270 million. Perhaps the most interesting relationship of those numbers is the Per Capita GNP of the three. This time, Japan's tally is 23,600 dollars per person while the EC's is 13,300 dollars per person and the United States is 19,300. Suddenly the relationship comes more into balance.

Analysts project the EC's overall GNP to rise about 4.5 percent after unification, compared to a projected rise of about 2 percent in the United States. During the coming decade we will see those figures fleshed out with greater precision and, doubtless, we will see a greater parity between these three rivals.

INTERPRETING THE SIGNS

So what is the real consequence of all these matters for us in the decade ahead? For one thing, the way the European Community develops may have just as much historical and social impact on the world in the next ten years as the collapse of communism. The forms established now will determine the EC's role in world affairs well into the new millennium.

Europe's unification will give these 12 nations enormous clout in the increasingly competitive and complicated world economy. However, in a purely economic sense, the union of Europe has many complex implications for the United States, as it does for all the other players in the world economy. Many are good; some are bad.

While we once dealt with Germany or France or Italy as separate nations—with separate currencies and separate trade policies—unification will change all that. Now there will be a single currency, a uniform trade policy, very likely a single banking community, and twelve nations will deal effectively as one global superpower.

Unification has given these countries a feeling of "European" nationalism and an *esprit de corps* previously unknown to them, and it comes at a time when national pride was flagging badly. A 1989 Gallup Poll reported that only 41 percent of Italians, 33 percent of French, 21 percent of Germans, and 19 percent of Dutch express pride in their nationality. In citing this report, *Business Week* concluded that the idea of a powerful united Europe may appeal to citizens of these nations in search of some sort of "higher nationalism."

Germans in particular seem to find some relief in broadening their national identification. Haunted by the ghosts of their past, many would agree with Hartmut Ruge, managing editor of a German newspaper quoted recently in *Time* as saying, "We are part of the rubble generation, a generation of moral disorientation and guilt. Now there is normality."

The generation that lived through the last war has had to endure the recriminations and reprisals of a half century. Many, like Manfred Poeck, also quoted in *Time*, find remembering painful. "I have real problems with our past," he says, "a sense of deep shame." All agree that their new identity as "Europeans" mandated by unification helps to exorcise the demons of history.

WE ARE EUROPEANS

I recognized this attitude on my recent trip to Hungary. I thought it was striking that young political leaders I talked to said to me, "We are Europeans." They are not just Hungarians any more, but Europeans. And I think this attitude of European pride is going to be felt more and more, in Germany, but also in Austria, in the Benelux countries, as well as in France and Spain. More and more people are going to say, "We are part of Europe. We are a world superpower. Now you will have to take us more seriously."

Beyond a certain nationalistic arrogance, the promise of world power can create certain expectations in government and business leaders which are not altogether healthy.

As I suggested above, perhaps the greatest immediate concern to American interests abroad is the initiative for currency control being put forth by Jacques Delors in his attempts to create a European Central Bank. This central bank would level, effectively, the national interests of all the various countries.

While it might centralize and simplify many complex procedures, solve exchange rate problems, and provide certain other advantages for businesses involved in international trade, it would also be in control of all the currency of those twelve countries. It would, thereby, have enormous financial leverage and could manipulate markets and economies on a grand scale in order to improve its own financial position or perhaps to discriminate in favor of its own industries and holdings.

If we think the recent scandals on Wall Street are bad; if we're afraid of a few men who can drive the stock market up or down for personal gain; or if we recognize the legitimate dangers of the S&L collapse we are going through in this country, just think about the dangers of giving a handful of men the power to control the entire economic resources of a dozen nations.

If it chose, the European Central Bank could bring about inflation or deflation on demand. And if linked with the Federal Reserve Bank of Washington and the Central Bank of Japan—which has already been discussed—it would put absolute economic control of the world in the hands of 21 or 22 people.

AN ECONOMIC CARTEL

Frankly, that's a frightening prospect. These would be non-elected representatives who would effectively control the money supply of the entire world. They would be involved in hundreds of billions of dollars in transactions every single day, and could, thereby, affect the ultimate destiny of the entire world.

This is the thing that is most worrisome to me about the "New Europe." I am concerned that somehow the real power would fall into the hands of a few bankers. However honest or reliable they may be in the beginning, or at any point for that matter, the potential for corruption and misman-agement is just too great.

The thrust of the thinking in Europe now is that the banking commu-nity would not be autonomous as it is in the United States, but that it would be responsive to the European Parliament in Strasbourg. But that parliament, in turn, is unapologetically socialistic, generally militant against traditional Western-style capitalism, and some of the delegates are quite radical in their personal beliefs.

We know only too well from our own experience, and from the recent experience of Eastern Europe and the Soviet Union, that socialism will destroy a free market economy and lead to enslavement of the people. We have lived that nightmare, and we can't afford to fall into that trap again.

THE ATLANTIC ALLIANCE

Because of its enormous strength, the European Community has the potential of being a very valued ally to the United States. We have a deep, long-standing relationship with Great Britain, and we have great affection for our allies and trading partners throughout Europe. Even though they have often deserted us—even scorned us—in our efforts to defend

Western Democracy, we recognize our common heritage and destiny with them, and we want the best for them.

But at the same time, if Europe continues its flirtation with socialism and secularism, and particularly if it closes its doors to the influence of the United States, it could conceivably become the foundation for some type of dictatorial regime based 100 percent on a humanistic system, whose values are not only very different from our own, but threatening to them.

Despite the efforts of the Christian Democrats, and especially the Catholic Church in many countries, Europe is a post-Christian society and a thoroughly hedonistic culture. We can only pray that the flame of Christianity which has emerged from Eastern Europe—unextinguished and more powerful than anyone ever dared to imagine—may be the spark that ignites a great revival throughout Western Europe as well. But that is still just a hope and a prayer at this moment.

If the united Europe continues to develop as it has, there is always the possibility that those who have resented us in the past because of our economic or military power might discover the newfound power and unity of Europe as some means of redress.

There are many in Europe who resent the United States because of what they may have perceived as our meddling in their national affairs. There are some who resent us for our part in World War II.

The formation of a new, more powerful league of nations could give those voices a means of settling old scores. At the present moment they are our friends and our allies, and it is obviously a place where American business needs to be. But all these relationships are in some jeopardy until we can see better how it will develop. I believe this will be an area of great concern for Americans over the next decade.

FORTRESS EUROPE vs. FORTRESS USA

Charges have flown back and forth between business leaders in the United States and Europe over the last few years, Americans charging the EC of having a fortress mentality, excluding the U.S. and everybody else from their country club, and the Europeans saying they're just trying to get into position to deal with giants like America and Japan on an equal basis. There seems to be a lot of insecurity on both sides, but the formation of the European Community is going to bring about great advantages to its member countries.

It is clear that the EC will offer some type of associate memberships for countries outside the immediate European Community but still within the European land mass, but it is equally clear that there will be walls set up against the United States and Japan.

The creation of trade barriers and other restrictions of one kind or another will definitely change our current relationships, and in the beginning that will probably hurt us economically. But in time, I suspect that for its own self-interest the EC will have to make some accommodations for a more or less open market between the world's major trading nations.

To ensure their right to participate in the European market, many American companies are already rushing to get in on the action. They are buying European companies, opening plants and facilities in Europe, and creating various kinds of subsidiaries so they can get products produced and marketed inside the EC.

In the newest comprehensive study of the unification compiled by the Brookings Institution, Gary Hufbauer reports that the percentage of United States foreign investment stock placed in the EC rose from about 18 percent in 1960 to nearly 40 percent in 1988. Our trade balance with Europe fell substantially during that period of time, but some sources report that U.S. exports have climbed into surplus with Europe in the last two years.

Hufbauer reports in the book, *Europe 1992*, that U.S. firms already doing business in Europe see the coming unification as a bonanza, and they are not so much concerned about trans-Atlantic relations as they are about improved relations within Europe.

It is not surprising, he writes, that the principal organizations which speak for American business—the Business Roundtable, the U.S. Council for International Business, and the U.S. Chamber of Commerce—are enthusiastic about Europe 1992.

Although the community could be a great benefit as an ally to America in the years ahead, chances are it's going to wind up being a formidable rival. Combining the industrial and economic strength of the twelve European nations will change the face of the world as we know it.

These are ancient and proud countries with a deep sense of history and culture. They have been down—economically, militarily, and spiritually—for a long time, and now they are glowing with a sudden burst of entrepeneurial vigor. That chemistry cannot help but produce a gigantic impact.

RECONSTRUCTION IN THE EAST

In dramatic contrast to the growing prosperity in the West, Eastern Europe is extremely primitive in terms of economics. Their factories are hopelessly out of date. Their labor force is unskilled. They are choking in pollution. The Vistula River is essentially dead. Southern Poland, the Silesia area, is choked with filth.

In the cities of Romania, especially where there is heavy mining, the people are gasping with lung diseases and birth defects and other serious illnesses caused by pollution. This seems to be endemic in nations such as Poland which have been under the iron heel of communism for so many decades.

What happened at Chernobyl is merely one example of the communist system's callous disregard for the health and safety of its people. The explosions at the atomic energy plant at Chernobyl and the massive radiation exposure and resulting murders of untold thousands of people (as a direct result of the government's attempt to cover up the magnitude of that disaster) only prove what we already knew: that communism is not concerned with the life of the individual.

The big thing in any "socialistic" system is to produce, to get something out of the laborers, and to keep the wheels of industry rolling, regardless of what it does to the ecology or how much it may devastate the lives of individual men, women, and children.

It will cost multiplied billions of dollars to clean up the environment in that entire region of the Soviet Union. Recent evidence from studies in northern Europe indicate that Finland, Scandinavia and the Baltic countries may be contaminated by the nuclear fallout from that disaster and entire generations are doomed to suffer cancers, leukemia, and other radiation-related diseases.

Apparently the shocks to the ecology from the Soviet Union are still not over. Intelligence expert, Jack Wheeler, reports that in May of 1990 thousands of tons of rocket fuel leaked out of a storage tank at the nuclear submarine facility at Sverodvinsk. *Pravda* reported that one third of all marine life in that area of the White Sea, including five million fish and 100,000 seals, died as a result of the spill.

In the Siberian oil fields there have been 1,100 pipeline breaks and subsequent leaks causing the staggering loss of 700,000 tons of crude oil by August of 1990. Wheeler expressed his amazement that not one mention of these huge ecological disasters has ever appeared in the Western media.

It's going to cost the emerging communist nations billions more to overcome the infrastructure's deficiencies and to upgrade or replace their antiquated plants and equipment. But what the Eastern Europeans do have is a literate population and a tradition of high-quality workmanship that goes back centuries. At this point in time, though, they are still poor, underpaid in relation to the West, and they don't produce as much.

The Eastern European countries are like economic babes in the wilderness. Yet, from a spiritual standpoint they are much stronger than their counterparts in the West: they have been persecuted for their faith and have endured. They have been willing to fight and die for their freedom, and they have come to appreciate freedom so much more than anybody who has always taken it for granted ever can.

The men and women of Eastern Europe are willing to make sacrifices for the important things of life, and that depth of character and courage won't go away—at least not among the Christian people—any time soon.

On the one hand the West can infuse the East with the latest advances their technology can provide—computer skills, accounting and marketing expertise, manufacturing knowhow, and all the things needed to upgrade the standard of living—but the East has the potential to bring to the West a level of faith and dedication that has been unknown there for decades.

TECHNOLOGY'S GODS

It just could be one of God's wonderful ironies that the impulse to bring Europe back to Himself and to give them a chance at revival will come from these former strongholds of communism.

Even if that is to be the case, it will still be a struggle. Western Europe has been thoroughly secularized over the past forty years. In Germany as few as one percent of the people go to church. There is a type of thinking there that is totally anti-Christian and post-Christian, and the people have no understanding of even the most basic spiritual foundations of Christian life and behavior. That type of ignorance in Western Europe may well be harder to overcome than the mere technological ignorance of the East.

I was in Bavaria recently, in the Garmisch-Partenkirchen area of the Bavarian Alps, when a young man who had seen me on my television program came up to speak to me. He was a bright, handsome young man who had been with the Unifil forces on the border between Lebanon and Israel and had seen the 700 Club broadcast on Middle East Television.

When I asked him about his concept of God, he told me he didn't know much about God. "Actually, I don't believe in God," he said. "But if there is a God, He is certainly not the one you talk about on television. I don't know, maybe God is a computer."

Needless to say, I was saddened by his casual concept of the Creator, but even more, I was staggered by his apparent willingness to accept a computer as an object of worship if it simply possessed enough intelligence to take care of people's basic demands.

If there were a computer smart enough—and I have no doubt there will be some very sophisticated and intelligent machines in the not too distant future—this young man would worship it as his god. If the computer says, "I have the answers. I have unparalleled science and technology at my disposal. I will see that there are no more wars, and I will give you the means to have prosperity and a happy life," many would follow. This young man was willing, essentially, to deify intelligence, whatever kind of intelligence manifested itself. And I fear he is not unique.

That isn't too far away from what we read in the book of Revelation. John's prophecy indicates that there will be some incredible intelligence who will know where everybody is and will have great power for good as well as evil. And through the power of this super intelligence, there will be economic controls, so that the people can buy and sell only with the authority of the state, or with some kind of a mark or token of submission to the state.

But to think that this intelligent, college-trained Austrian would say, "Whoever God is, maybe he's a computer," just absolutely astounded me. And I'm afraid that he is much more typical of the emerging young generation in Europe today than we dare to think possible.

THE INSTITUTIONS OF COMMUNISM

It appears that the Warsaw Pact is finished as a military alliance, and what has been called COMECON, the economic alliance of Soviet satellites and communist-led countries, is essentially dead because the Soviet Union doesn't have anything of value with which to pay for its imports.

The United States and Europe will not take Soviet rubles, and all the Soviets have to export is gold and oil, and they don't have very much of them. So they desperately need Western support.

East Germany has already effectively joined West Germany as one nation. That big, powerful nation is going to set the tone in Western Europe. Before anything was signed, West German industrialists raced into the East to grab up everything of value while they still had an enormous capital advantage.

The big manufacturing plants, trading companies, and retailers have moved in to establish beachheads and to buy up East German companies as fast as they can. As the merger uniting East and West Germany as one nation takes final form, those frontrunners will be in a controlling position.

The same thing is happening—though perhaps to a lesser degree—in

Poland, Hungary, and Czechoslovakia. There is a tremendous movement of capital into those countries from Western Europe.

Once that happens, corporations in Germany, Austria, Italy, France, and other Western European nations will begin to put pressure on their governments to make concessions for goods coming out of the Eastern countries. In fact, in lieu of gigantic direct subsidies to East Bloc countries which will end up creating debt and dependency, the best way Western Europe can help the Eastern Europeans come back to economic health is through trade concessions and private investment. It looks as if that may be happening now.

It is not likely that East Bloc countries will be allowed to be members of the European Community, but they will most likely be accorded a favored trading relationship as associate members with full economic privileges for their goods, and a close relationship with the rest of Europe.

THE MORAL DILEMMA

Beyond political considerations, the moral collapse in Western Europe has reached epidemic proportions and, unfortunately, West Germany seems to be leading the way.

Even *Time* magazine seemed shocked by its own report in July 1990 that West German theater has sunk to the "vilest displays of the body onstage" along with the "vilest displays of the mind." In the article, *Time*'s reporter in Berlin offered a revolting inventory of crude and vulgar displays.

"Onstage vomiting, with visual effects, four times, including a mass upheaval by a dozen actors at once. Excretion, with sound effects, three times. Full frontal nudity, three times, plus two lavish displays of dildoes. Onstage copulation, involving every imaginable combination of genders, countless times in seven separate works. Plus incest, transvestism, self-mutilation, murder." And that is only a partial tally.

Now in Munich, Hamburg, Bremen, Bochum, Schwerin, and stages in East and West Berlin, such degradation is becoming common public fare. And to make matters worse, it is being supported at taxpayer expense. As much as 1.5 billion dollars a year is doled out to theater groups to bathe their audiences in obscenity.

But the public goes to these performances, and while a handful scoff or walk out of the theater, there is wild and exuberant applause from the majority. One can only wonder where it will lead. If this is public morality in West Germany, generally acknowledged by most Europeans as the most likely leaders of the forthcoming unification, what can be in store for the rest of the Continent?

For centuries men and women have considered such graphic display as immoral, degrading, and dehumanizing, for it sinks to the lowest and basest form of human experience. Since Plato, the aim of Art has been to present images of life and nature which are "elevating," not "degrading."

The masochistic absorption with filth and vulgarity displays a depraved state of the soul. The degradation of "art" to "pornography" proves that the soul of Europe may well be on its way to utter dehumanization.

When the first Westerners crossed the Berlin Wall in late 1989 and early 1990, they saw the stunned looks on the faces of the East Berliners coming out, as it were, to the light of a new day. One American pastor asked some of them how they felt about the possibility of reunification with the West, and he was shocked at their answer.

"We are happy," said one young woman, "but we are scared."

Pursuing that answer, the American asked why she felt both those emotions.

"We're happy for freedom," she responded. "We haven't much money, but we can buy in the stores now, and goods in the West are much better. We can also see our loved ones. But we are afraid for our country, afraid now we will be exposed to your Western materialism, to much greater crime, and to drugs and pornography."

What a sad, wise answer. For forty years the socialist government had denied the noble aspirations of its people; ironically, it had also shielded them from those aspects of Western culture of which we should be most ashamed. But how sad to see that, already, that woman's fears are being recognized. Consumerism, excessive self-indulgence, and the freedom to wallow in filth and pornography will certainly have an impact on these naive and oddly protected peoples from the East.

There is only one hope in such a situation, and that is the deep faith in Jesus Christ which has been growing strong under persecution. Again, we pray nourishment for that faith will come quickly.

THE POPULATION DILEMMA

While the Club of Rome, the environmentalists, the pro-death movement, and all those who support the Malthusian hypothesis that the world is being over-populated continue to hold forth, Europe has begun to realize that it is in a serious population dilemma. Not from over-population, but from under-population.

In his book, *The Birth Dearth*, Ben Wattenberg pointed out that during the first half of this century, the Western nations made up roughly 30 percent of the world's population. Today that percentage is in rapid decline and Europe in particular cannot keep up with the death rate.

By 1990 the percentage of people of European stock (including those

in America) has fallen to just 15 percent of the world's population. By the year 2035, if the present trends continue, these nations will constitute an insignificant 7.5 percent.

It is generally accepted that a modern nation must have a minimum of 2.1 births per woman to simply maintain its population at a constant level. Today, however, West Germany and Denmark have curbed the birth rate so sharply they are now at 1.3 births per woman and still declining.

The Netherlands and Italy are at 1.5, Britain 1.8, and the United States has fallen from 3.6 in 1955 to a low of 1.7 in 1976, and has recently leveled out at about 1.8.

Little has been reported in the American press, but the world's birth crisis—labeled by some now as the "Depopulation Bomb" (in response to Paul Ehrlich's book of the 1970s)—is beginning to raise eyebrows in Europe. Sorbonne professor Pierre Channu calls it the "European cancer" and correctly identifies the crisis as "a refusal of life itself." Others say, as reported by Allan C. Carlson in his book *Family Questions*, that the West is signing its own death warrant.

Oddly enough, French families are given substantial welfare assistance and tax incentives to have more children, but the plan has not worked. The Italian government is so concerned about their falling population they are trying to woo Italian emigrants back from Latin America.

One of the implications of the population crisis is the impact on the labor force. More and more companies are discovering they cannot find qualified natives to fill the jobs they have available. Most are being forced to hire immigrants, or in many cases, to actually import immigrants from Eastern Europe, Africa, and the Middle East.

Needless to say, these policies merely complicate the lives of the Europeans even further and lead to racial and social tensions most of these nations have, until now, never really experienced.

The decline of Europe's population is not just a function of abortion, but of a general unwillingness of Europeans to have children. Many believe the quality of life is unsuitable, and they offer many reasons for deferring or denying child-bearing.

In European Russia, where the average woman has eight abortions, the wretched condition of life under communism makes parenting an unwelcome option. In Western Europe, it may be the high cost of living combined with the post-World War II despair caused by lack of faith and lack of hope.

Between the United States Supreme Courts's Roe v. Wade decision legalizing abortion in 1973 and the year 2000, there will be 40,000,000 abortions in this country. The number in Europe is conceivably even higher. If so, the total number of abortions in Europe and America could reach an unbelievable 100,000,000 by the end of the decade. The nations of the West have literally committed genocide on themselves.

REGAINING THE STATUS QUO

In their address to members of the EC and the other major decision-making bodies in Europe, both President Bush and Secretary of State Baker have tried to encourage restraint and sound judgment, and a continuing role for the United States in Europe.

Speaking to the Berlin Press Club, Secretary Baker pressed for continuing support for NATO and its role in keeping the peace. He said the new "architecture" of Europe should help to preserve the link between Europe and North America, "politically, militarily, and economically." He also stressed the importance for cooperation in science, industry, environmental policy, and "a host of other fields."

Surely one of the key areas of cooperation and dialogue should be with regard to the social and moral issues that will confront the European Community and its growing sphere of influence in the coming decade.

Europe first became aware of itself as a unique entity and a force in a larger framework when Emperor Constantine united Europe in 320 A.D. under the Roman Empire and the cross of Jesus Christ. The dynamism of that union expanded and retracted over many centuries until today when, once again the Continent is being united under a powerful central authority.

But only one thing is missing: the hand of God.

Clearly the hand of God will not come from within, for the church has fallen on hard times throughout Western Europe. It will have to come from outside, and both Eastern Europe, with a new vision of faith and freedom, and the United States, with its legacy of Democratic freedom and a Christian Constitution, could possibly offer the vehicle of reform.

But will it be enough? Can it be done? Will there be time?

At the death of a star, it first implodes then bursts out in a fiery display. We call such stars "supernovae."

I believe that Western Europe is beginning one last bright burst of fire before it sinks into a major cycle of decline lasting for centuries.

Western Europe is now the most irreligious part of the world. Europe united under the control of a New Age dictator would menace the globe.

Will Christian Democratic ideals win out? Will there be a new influence of Christianity throughout Europe, flowing from the newly liberated communist countries?

6

The Rise of the East

The oil price shocks of 1973 and 1979 signaled the beginning of a 500-year cycle of Eastern ascendancy in the world.

Japan is the economic forerunner of the East Asian world powers.

The new millennium may see a post-communist, free-market, Christian China become the world's dominant power.

IN EARLY 1990 the land surrounding the Imperial Palace in Tokyo, Japan, was reported appraised at 70 billion dollars, a price equal to the total market value of all of the real estate in Florida.

Then we were told that the market value of the land in the tiny islands comprising the nation of Japan was five times that of the market value of all of the land in the United States from Maine to California.

Then a list of the world's largest banks was published. At the top was the Dai-Ichi Kangyo bank with assets approaching 400 billion dollars, twice those of Citibank, America's only entrant in the top ten of world banking. Of the top ten world banks, eight were Japanese.

When J.D. Power and Associates publishes various studies of consumer satisfaction with automobiles sold in the United States the Japanese built Acura tops the list year after year. In the latest study of reported automobile defects, a new Japanese luxury car, the Lexus, comes in with the fewest reported defects. Now the Lexus advertisements joke that owners of the highly regarded German made Mercedes Benz can actually step up in quality at half the price by buying a Japanese Lexus.

The only American car in the top ten is Buick, which is enthusiastically promoting its fifth place standing. We are no longer surprised to learn that by 1992 Japanese car makers will have a share of the United States automobile market equal to once mighty General Motors.

There are no broadcast television cameras manufactured today in the United States. The Japanese-built Sony Betacams have become the industry standard, as are Japanese home television sets, VCRs, camcorders, walkman audio recorders, and a host of other electronic products sold in America.

Japan has enjoyed an annual trade surplus of some 90 billion dollars, of which as much as 50 to 60 billion dollars comes from the United States. The money has been recycled to America by the Japanese, who have been purchasing up to 30 percent of all United States government debt securities, and in the process a sizable chunk of California banking assets and such choice parts of America as Rockefeller Center and Columbia Studios.

The Japanese are surpassing the United States in total share of world markets. In the semiconductor industry, which the U.S. pioneered and developed, the Japanese share of the world market rose from 33 percent in 1982 to 50 percent in 1990 while the U.S. share in the same period of time plummeted from 57 percent to 37 percent.

Now the Japanese are planning in the 1990s an industrial and financial thrust of such magnitude that we can only conclude its intent is to make Japan the dominant economy of the world. This thrust will be fueled by a hoard of cash unprecedented in world history and according to an American economist based in Tokyo, "It is literally frightening to contemplate the effects, within three or four years of the gigantic increase in exports" that the new Japanese capital is creating.

Consider the financial reserves available to them. We know that, even after the recent Nikkei nosedive and subsequent readjustments, at least eight of the world's 10 largest banks are Japanese. Beyond bank capital, Japanese industry is expected to have raised 200 billion dollars in equity capital during 1989, six or seven times what United States corporations raised that year.

By the first quarter of 1989, the war chests of Japanese firms were staggering. Hanwa steel had 17.2 billion dollars cash in reserve; Mitsubishi 15.2 billion; Toyota 11.8 billion; Sumitomo 11.3 billion; Hitachi 7.0 billion.

The 25 largest Japanese life insurance companies dwarf these figures. Their combined assets are 100 trillion yen, (700 billion dollars). And the money keeps pouring in. Nippon Life receives 12 billion yen, (75 million dollars) per day in premiums. Sumitomo Life, an estimated 8 billion yen (50 million U.S. dollars) each day.

Not content with home markets, Japanese companies have borrowed an additional 113 billion dollars on the international markets at shockingly low rates. In October of 1989, Nissan borrowed 1.5 billion at 3⅜ percent, a full 5 percent below what the most credit-worthy U.S. corporations have to pay.

Japanese interests bought 134 billion dollars in foreign manufacturing, real estate, and securities in 1988. In 1989 that figure is estimated to have grown to $170 billion. At home Japan is devoting a staggering 25 percent of its entire gross national product to capital spending in order to make more and better steel, automobiles, copiers, computers, electronics, and advanced technology aimed to overwhelm the United States.

In automobiles alone, Japanese companies are expected to spend 55 billion dollars during the decade to build 14 ultramodern factories able to produce another 2,800,000 new vehicles each year, most of which will be for export. Their plan is to be unbeatable in every technology before the United States during the 1990s can recover its fiscal senses and its lost marketing edge.

They don't plan to stop at manufacturing and technology. The Japanese now control one third of California's banking assets and within a year plan to expand into at least 45 of the 50 states. Japanese banks have access to virtually unlimited capital at 5.5 percent. They lend to their United States affiliates at 7.5 percent. From that point on, the United States affiliates of Japanese banks can most profitably undercut any bank in the United States in making commercial loans.

This would soon make the Japanese banks the principal lenders to much of American business. America got a taste of what that power meant when Japanese banks pulled out of the United Airlines leveraged buyout recently. Not only did United's stock crash, but the U.S. Stock market went for a dizzying fall along with it.

THE 500 YEAR CYCLE

The rise of Japan and of what are called the Asian Tigers comes as a shock to anyone who served in the pacific theatre in World War II or who served, as I did, in post war Japan and Korea during the Korean War in the early 1950s.

In 1945 the Japanese military had been crushed by American power. Her economy was bombed out and destitute; her emperor and god had been deposed; and an American Caesar, Douglas MacArthur, now ruled the nation from the Dai-Ichi Building in Central Tokyo. Japanese products were invariably shoddy. The label "Made in Japan" was synonymous with junk.

At war's end, China lay defeated not only by the brutal Japanese occupation but by the vicious struggle between the Nationalist forces of Chiang Kai-Shek and the communists under Mao Tse Tung. Taiwan did not exist as a nation. The Malay peninsula and Singapore had been devastated by war and occupation. Hong Kong was without economic significance.

Korea was a backward primarily agricultural nation which had been subjugated by the Japanese for decades and was soon to find itself ripped apart by another war which raged from the Yalu River in the North to the port of Pusan in the South.

This was a region of warlords, peasants, coolies, and rice paddies. These were the poverty-stricken Asian hordes. To any observer in 1950 it was clear that this region was destined to be an economic and cultural backwater well into the twenty-first century.

But at least one observer saw things differently. Dr. Raymond Wheeler, a professor and historian at the University of Kansas, after a monumental twenty years study of cyclical history, forecast that there would arise by the year 1980—a scant 28 years after the cessation of hostilities in Korea—a resurgence of Asia and an Asian leader.

Wheeler did not pick Japan but India. Perhaps he felt that India had suffered least during World War II and therefore was the most probable candidate. Wheeler's work did not consist, however, of forecasting the rise of individual nations but regions. He clearly saw a free and resurgent Orient before the end of the century.

Professor Wheeler's calculations encompass three one-thousand-year periods and six five-hundred-year periods during which the pendulum of world economic power, military power, and cultural influence swings from Europe to Asia and back again. During the beginning of the thousand years one society begins its upward growth for roughly 500 years then begins a slow decline for a similar period.

The chart on pp. 132–133 is a vastly oversimplified but relatively true to fact profile of Wheeler's cyclical view superimposed on what we know of history.

Dr. Wheeler called his work "human ecology," the study of environmental forces such as physical geography, climate, social interaction and economic change. His chief premise, however, was that "nations have risen or fallen on the tides of climatic change."

He determined that every five hundred years climatological factors in the biosphere produced a cold dry period which basically caused dislocation of nations all over the globe. With the cooler climate came political chaos, and a shift in power from East and West, but also increasing democratic freedom for the masses whenever these conditions occurred.

Looking ahead to the coming at the new millennium, and the arrival of

	EAST	WEST
	Rising	Declining
1000 B.C.	Kingdoms of David and Solomon; Assyrian Empire; Babylonian Empire; Persian Empire	Barbaric primitive tribes
	Declining	Rising
500 B.C.	Babylon falls; Persia defeated by Alexander; Alexander takes half of India and Egypt.	Beginning of Greek democracy; Empire of Alexander the Great; The growth and establishment of the Roman empire.
	Rising	Declining
1 A.D.	Birth of Christ; growth of Christianity; Christianity fills Middle East, Europe, and Africa, supplants Roman Empire.	Decline of Roman Empire, through spiritual and financial excess. Rome falls to successive waves of barbarians.
	Declining	Rising
500 A.D.	Islam rises and recedes. No significant Eastern empire on the world stage.	Beginning of European Christian civilization. Christianity spreads to France, Germany, England, Scandinavia, and Russia. Muslims defeated at Battle of Tours. Holy Roman Empire consolidates power.
	Rising	Declining
1000 A.D.	Mongol Empire under Genghis Khan, Kublai Khan, and later Tamerlane occupies greatest land mass in history. Threatens Western Europe.	Europe weakened by continual warfare among nations and within nations, disease, and famine. Church becomes divided and corrupt.

EAST	WEST
Rising	Declining
at Danube in Hungary. Flowering of Chinese culture. Ottoman Empire captures Middle East.	One quarter of total European population dies from plague known as "black death."
Declining	Rising
1500 A.D. China free from Mongol influence. Successive emperors grow weaker and inward looking. Ottoman Empire declining. India, Southeast Asia, backward, poor, superstitious.	Reformation and Renaissance, Voyages of discovery. Colonization of Western hemisphere. Industrial revolution. Rise of Portuguese, Spanish, French, British, Dutch, Italian, and German Colonial empires in Africa, Middle East, India, and Asia. Christian European nations totally dominate the globe. Rise of constitutional democracy, wealth, and military power of the United States as a Christian nation.
Rising	Declining
2000 A.D. Influx of wealth of OPEC nations and Japan. Dramatic rise of Japan and nations of Pacific rim. Rise of fundamentalist Islam and Hinduism. Technological superiority. Military power yet uncertain, but Saddam Hussein of Iraq a forerunner. Rapid spread of Christianity in Korea, China, the Philippines, and Taiwan.	Enormous debt. Budget instability. Family break-up, crime, drugs, declining educational standards. Losing technological advantage. Declining birthrate. Post-Christian era. Loss of religious faith. Threat of hyper inflation and economic collapse. Ability to maintain military power in grave doubt.

the twenty-first century, these massive studies drew Wheeler to the conclusion that European civilization was heading into decline while the Asian nations would come front and center on the world's stage. Events of the past 40 years have proved him remarkably prescient.

Wheeler is not the only thinker who has held a cyclical view of civilization. According to James Dale Davidson and Sir William Rees-Mogg in their book, *Blood in the Streets*, the authors of the American Constitution believed that "the destiny of nations was governed by long term cycles of growth and decay." Not the weather or the stars, but the physical, spiritual, and intellectual softness that comes from too much material prosperity.

Nations and empires do not usually fall by some sudden cataclysm but by a slowly accelerating departure from the individual initiative and moral self-control that laid the basis for their prosperity.

THE GREATEST EASTERN EMPIRE

If history indeed repeats itself, will the next millennium bring forth an oriental empire to rival the last one? In the late 1100s a Mongol Chieftain named Temujin took power. He was bloodthirsty and utterly ruthless. Under the name Genghis Khan he conquered North China in 1215 then turned to other conquests.

He subjugated China, Korea, Mongolia, Persia, Turkestan, and Armenia. His empire included parts of Burma, Vietnam, Thailand, and Russia. In 1241 his son, Ogotai, laid waste Hungary and Poland, and threatened the civilization of Western Europe.

When I was in Budapest, Hungary, this spring, my wife and I were taken at night to the Buda heights above the Danube and shown the statue of the king, St. Stephen, who brought Christianity to his people. From that vantage point we were then proudly told that in the plains beyond the Danube, Christian Hungary had stood fast to save Europe from the Mongol Hordes.

Ogotai's son, Kublai Khan, enlarged the empire, and then gave it the splendor recorded by Marco Polo. Kublai Khan sent a message to the Pope requesting missionaries to come and teach his people Christianity.

The British used to say, "Scratch a Russian and you find a Tartar." History shows us that a vast portion of the Soviet Union is more closely allied with the Middle East and Asia than with Europe. Only Russia, itself, the Ukraine, and Moldavia can truly be considered European.

The province of Georgia is East of Turkey, bordering Iran. For almost 3,000 miles the Soviet Union borders Manchuria, Mongolia, China, India, Afghanistan, and Iran.

In June 1990, leaders of Kazakhstan, Turkmenstan, Kirghizia, Usbekistan, and Tadzhikistan met to protect their interests from Russia. This was the first step toward establishing a large independent state of Turkestan, presumably independent of Moscow.

Will there be a resurgent empire coming from the East? We should expect that a possible break-up of the Soviet Union would bring forth a vast Oriental nation. Would it ally itself with China, Mongolia, and Manchuria to form a power like that of Genghis Khan and Kublai Khan? Would it then subjugate Southeast Asia and control the sea routes?

We may not live to see it happen, but eventually, absent God's intervention in history, such an Asian super power may emerge. If a modern nation of one and one half to two billion people were to come about, and such a thing is entirely possible, the description in the book of Revelation regarding the armies of the "Kings of the East" would be literally possible. Such a power could dominate the entire world.

On a less apocalyptic note, most likely the next several decades will bring about the fall of communism in mainland China and the break-up of the Soviet Union. In all probability, without a strong autocratic government, China will break-up into regions which differ from one another either by the military nature of their government or the economic theory under which they are organized.

When I visited China in 1979, I learned that a skilled artisan was then paid the equivalent of 26 dollars per month, and a foreman of a factory employing 2,000 workers 70 dollars per month.

The Chinese are probably the world's most astute business people. If mainland China moves to the same free market capitalism that has brought such a remarkable standard of living to Taiwan and Hong Kong, and if indeed the Chinese in vast numbers continue to embrace Christianity and the democratic freedoms which invariably accompany Christianity, within forty years the per capita income in China should reach 4,000 dollars and the Chinese economy would have grown to a level in excess of 4.5 trillion dollars per year.

The Central Asian landmass, with its vast population, would create the most extraordinary internal market in the world. Imagine what it would take to supply such a population with housing, transportation, clothing, furniture, electronic products, electricity, telecommunications, and services. **If the future of capitalism depends on markets, a free resurgent Central Asia could guarantee a booming internal market and a virtually limitless market for the surplus output of the world's farms and factories.**

As I see it, the key will be to teach the people now the truths of Christianity, the principles of democratic self-government, and free market economics. This is why Regent University, of which I am Founder and Chancellor, jumped at the invitation of the present government of China to establish a branch of our Graduate School of Business Administration at Yellow River University in Central China.

OIL POWER

In 1973, suddenly and without warning, the East reached from the sands of the Persian Gulf and began to choke the lifeblood of Europe and America. All modern industrial life was built upon petroleum—cheap petroleum. Our automobiles, our airplanes, our trucks, our farm tractors, our plastics, our fertilizers, our light, our heat, our machine lubricants and our defense establishment all required oil. Oil was so essential to our life that its price was a multiplying lever on the cost of every single product in our entire economy.

To our shock and amazement the Arabs and their OPEC partners raised the price of oil from $2.80 a barrel to $13.00 a barrel. Europe and America were totally unprepared for such a happening and watched in horror as some 80 billion dollars of their wealth poured into the coffers of the Arab sheiks each year.

The Western economies went into a serious recession. Bankruptcies by the thousands littered the economic landscape.

During the 1970s, Western economies alternated between virulent inflation and recession. When a religious fanatic, the Ayatollah Khomeini, took power in Iran, the price of oil tripled to $39 a barrel. The Western nations were gripped by inflation and no growth stagnation at the same time.

A new term, "stagflation," was introduced to describe what was happening. The American hostage crisis was merely a symbol that the Western nations were being held hostage and bled white by Eastern leaders around the Persian Gulf.

American inflation hit 13.3 percent and interest rates soared to an undreamed of 21.5 percent. Millions of Americans were put out of work. The powerful industrial heartland of America began to be known as the "Rust Belt." A crisis of major magnitude gripped America's farmbelt. The suffering and heartbreak of steelworkers, auto workers, and farmers was overwhelming.

The poorer, non-oil nations of the world, particularly those in South America and Africa, were forced to borrow tens of billions of dollars to pay for the increased price of oil in order to survive. These Third World debts now exceed one trillion dollars and still exist as a threat to the long-range future of major United States banks as well as the political and economic health of hundreds of millions of desperate people who live at or below a level of misery unthinkable in America.

In his book, *The Kingdom,* published in 1981, Robert Lacey tells of the rise of Saudi Arabia as a nation. In 1930 the founding monarch of Saudi Arabia, Abdul Aziz Ibn Saud, survived on a 200,000-dollar annual stipend from Great Britain. When King Ibn Saud in the 1920s began an expedition against Kuwait, he was stopped by British planes, British armed cars, and British ships. In Lacey's words, "It was his Majesty's Government who determined for Abdul Aziz the frontiers of the possible."

In 1990, the entire world shuddered when the Dictator of Iraq, Saddam Hussein, seized tiny Kuwait and thereby controlled an estimated twenty percent of the oil supply of the entire world. Hussein, with an army of 1,000,000 men, some 5,200 tanks, plus rockets and poison gas, suddenly became a world figure.

It is virtually impossible for Americans, accustomed to Middle East power, to realize that in March of 1921 Winston Churchill, as his Brittanic Majesty's Secretary of State for the Colonies, convened a conference in Cairo for the purpose of disposing of Hussein, the Sharif of Mecca, a rival to Abdul Aziz in Saudi Arabia.

Churchill's plan was simple. A map was drawn. Mesopotamia was called Iraq and given to Feisal, the son of Sharif Hussein, but under British tutelage. The Sharif's other son, Abdullah, Feisal's brother, (and grandfather of the present King of Jordan), was given a new territory adjoining Iraq called Transjordan.

Palestine was made a British mandate. The French kept Lebanon and Syria. Kuwait was a British protectorate. The Sharif was acknowledged as King of Hijaz in Saudi Arabia.

That is the way the Middle East worked just seventy years ago. Over a cup of tea the British divided territories, set up kings, and deposed kings. No one questioned their authority. They were a European power and the Middle East was their sphere of influence.

In 1973 the cycle of change from West to East began to work. By 1980 it was clearly set in place. By 1990 America is once again importing over fifty percent of her oil requirements. America's known reserves are steadily dwindling. The only known major pool of oil in the world exists in the Middle East.

Whatever the United States and Europe do to bolster their economies, the fact remains that from now on the economies of the once powerful Western nations are in some measure hostage to the nations of the Middle East who will continue to build up enormous wealth as it is being steadily drained from the rest of the world.

To be sure much of this oil wealth will be recycled back into Europe and America. The Japanese are doing the same thing with their wealth. But every dollar that is recycled makes the Arabs and the Japanese owners of that much more. Western real estate, banks, stock, bonds, and factories.

With loss of ownership goes loss of control. With loss of control goes the power to make the decisions which we deem good for our nation, our businesses, and our own lives. It is the long range loss of control over our own destinies which will be the price we pay when power flows from the West to the East.

THE ASIAN TIGERS

During the 1980s, the economic story did not focus on the Middle East or on the Asian landmass where the long range future lies, but on the extraordinary economic growth around what is called the Pacific Rim.

Japan is not the only booming economy in the East. China, Hong Kong, Taiwan, Singapore, Malaysia, and Korea, and others have been growing their business interests in the West and multiplying their export market exponentially over the past dozen years.

Robert Hormats, of Goldman Sachs in New York, believes that Japanese investment in the area has been the greatest single factor in the creation of a sort of Asian Common Market. What Hormats calls the "integrated production zone" actually involves more than a dozen separate nations, some who are suppliers and others who are primarily developers and entrepreneurs.

If we look at the dynamic growth among the six member nations of the Association of Southeast Asian Nations, which includes Thailand, Malaysia, Indonesia, Singapore, Brunei and the Philippines, we can see just how broadly that economic power has spread.

The *Wall Street Journal* reported that in the five years, from 1984 to 1989, Japanese companies tripled their investments in these Asian nations to 5.57 billion dollars. The Japanese investment in Thailand alone in 1988 topped 705 million dollars—ten times the United States investment that year in that country.

The network of trading and bartering between Southeast Asian nations has created a bonanza in the East. Japan's GNP, now topping 2.9 trillion dollars, has more than doubled since 1980 and has outstripped its 1965 level of 84.6 billion dollars by a factor of 35. Over the same period, the per capita income increased from an annual 8,638 dollars to over 23,600 dollars in 1988.

South Korea's GNP jumped from a mere 2.9 billion dollars in 1965 to 125 billion in 1988. Per capita income rose from a poverty level of 103 dollars per annum to almost 3,000 dollars. Singapore, now at 24.7 billion dollars, has experienced a 24-fold increase in GNP since 1965; and Hong

Kong jumped from just over 3 billion dollars to nearly 45 billion in the same 23-year period. In 1965 Hong Kong had a per capita income of barely 900 dollars. Today the figure is 10 times larger, topping 9,200 dollars per person.

When you total these various International Monetary Fund, World Bank, and United Nations figures, you begin to get the picture that something is indeed happening in the East. Suddenly, we see a major player in the world marketplace with a current combined GNP exceeding 4 trillion dollars, clearly on a par with Europe's 4.3 trillion and the United States' 5.2 trillion.

If the Japanese economy grows at 6 percent per year, then slows to 4 percent, by the year 2000 their economy would total 4.75 trillion dollars, roughly the size of the present U.S. economy. If Japan maintains its white hot 1980–88 growth rate, it will reach a staggering 7.98 trillion dollars by the year 2000.

Using the conservative growth calculation, in the 1990s South Korea's economy would grow in ten years to a 205 billion-dollar GNP; Hong Kong would be at 73 billion; and Singapore would likely top 40 billion.

THE ASIAN SECRET

At the end of World War II, a key group of Japanese business leaders invited a middle level manufacturing engineer from Westinghouse Electric to teach them techniques of manufacturing.

The principles set forth by their American teacher, W. Edwards Deming, were actually very simple. They were accepted by his Japanese pupils as holy writ and assiduously put into practice. Basically this extraordinarily humble man told the Japanese to insist on quality, to respect the dignity of their workers, and to organize their enterprises for maximum flexibility through the participation of workers in key manufacturing decisions.

In fact, Deming taught the Japanese two key tenets of Christianity. The first: "Let him who is great among you be the servant of all." Managers were to be servants of the workers, listening to them and providing them an environment in which they, in turn, could produce excellent products. The second principle was equally important: "A house divided against itself cannot stand." Management and labor should not be adversaries but co-workers in a shared enterprise.

As a people, the Japanese began saving money at a rate of almost 17 percent a year. At that pace money doubles every four years. By saving, they applied another key tenet of Jesus, related in what is called the parable of the talents: "Unto him who has more will more be given."

Their savings mounted, soon doubled, and then doubled again and again, to provide an enormous pool of capital to finance their industry expansions.

In Japan, as in the other fast growing Asian nations, the government has sponsored and promoted a pro-business environment. The Asians rejected European and American-style political liberalism and government-sponsored redistributive economics where a huge, wasteful bureaucracy set out to move vast sums of wealth from the producing segment of society to the non-producing segment.

It is also instructive to note that in Japan there are roughly 33,000 lawyers. In the United States there are 700,000 lawyers. Asian enterprise has been spared the internal warfare and economic drain which our litigious society has placed upon us.

In the Asian nations, a permissive attitude toward illegal narcotics and crime is just not tolerated. In Japan drug dealers are swiftly given life imprisonment. In Singapore they are summarily executed.

Finally the Asians have strong family ties and a strong, disciplined work ethic. Each family member is expected to work hard and support one another. When prosperity comes they have been known to spend very lavishly, but they are willing to sacrifice and defer spending until they succeed.

According to the conservative newspaper, *Human Events,* in 1985 the crude divorce rate in the United States was three and a half times as high as that found in Japan. Illegitimacy accounted for 21 percent of all American births in 1984, only 1 percent of all Japanese babies were born out of wedlock in the same year.

In the United States 50 to 65 percent of all 17-year-olds report sexual activity. Japanese officials express concern when just 10 percent of their high school students engaged in pre-marital sex.

Divorce and illegitimacy have helped drive up the cost of American welfare programs. American families are increasingly unwilling to care for their aging parents while Japanese families typically honor and care for their elderly.

Small wonder first generation Koreans, Chinese, and Vietnamese in the United States have been so successful. Despite language and cultural barriers these people have repeatedly risen within a few years of their arrival in this country to an income level equal to or exceeding our norms. And time after time their children take top honors in American schools and Universities.

The East is rising because the people there have embraced hard work, a disciplined life, individual initiative, family values, and in most cases strong religious faith.

Europe and America are declining because we have become self indulgent, dependent on large governments, and are permissive in our behavior. We have turned our backs on faith in God, individual self reliance, and strong family values.

The United States borders two oceans, one facing Europe, the other facing Asia. California, Oregon, Washington, Alaska, and Hawaii are all part of the Pacific Rim and even now are participating in the Asian boom. Our nation has a choice of following the sterile decline of post-Christian Europe or the long-range future of a booming Asia.

During the coming decades we should expect the Asian boom to act like a magnet to shift population and wealth from the East Coast toward the West and Southwest. The existing population growth trends in the Southern and Western portions of the United States will only increase in the years to come, and along with it the continued shift in economic and political power away from the Northeast and upper Midwest.

These trends will affect housing prices, jobs, and investment opportunities. Right now property prices are plunging in the Northeast and the infrastructure, crime and welfare problems of cities like New York are virtually insoluble. It is highly unlikely that the downward trend will reverse itself but will grow progressively worse in the Northeast over the next decades. The fall of Donald Trump's empire in 1990 may become a highly publicized symbol of the irreversible decline of the urban Northeast.

DANGER SIGNS IN JAPAN

After World War II, our brilliant commanding General Douglas MacArthur, flashed an urgent message to the churches of America, "Send me Bibles and 10,000 missionaries." The post-war American Christians had other things on their minds. There were families to be formed, jobs to begin, houses to build, children to educate, and churches to plant and build.

We had the opportunity to turn Japan from a nation of emperor worshipers to a nation of Christians. But the American Christians failed this unparalleled opportunity.

The Japanese are ready students, and they copied everything about America. They copied our law and government, our cars, our clothes, our communications, our motion pictures, our advertising, our music, our hamburger, our baseball, our golf. Many of the women even had plastic surgery done to copy actress Raquel Welch's belly button. They copied our Christmas celebration without reference to Jesus Christ. Most of all they copied our materialistic preoccupations and love of money.

Everything they copied they improved on. As one person told me, "The Japanese make everything smaller, cheaper, and better." The one thing that they did not copy was our soul: our faith in God, in Jesus Christ, and the Holy Bible.

The Japanese preoccupation and skill in making money has led to absurd anomalies. The United States Dow Jones stock average and the Japanese Nikkei average in the late sixties both stood at 1000. The so-called price earnings ratio of Dow stocks has traditionally been twelve or thirteen to one. The U.S. Stock market averages trended as high as 3000, but the Nikkei went to 39,000 and their stocks were selling at a wildly speculative price ratio of 60 to 1.

Their land values are reminiscent of the tulip bulb craze in Holland when one tulip bulb sold for 17,000 dollars. The *Wall Street Journal* quoted a foreign banker in Tokyo as saying, "The property market here reminds me of a boulder perched at the top of a pinnacle of ice. A little heat and it could all come crashing down."

The total property market in Japan is listed at 15 trillion dollars, and the most choice land in Tokyo is selling for 200,000 dollars a square meter which translates to 978 million dollars per acre.

If the Japanese land market crashes, the defaults could cripple some banks and dwarf America's savings and loan debacle. With cross ownership of stock among major Japanese corporations, and with the use of land for collateral to support stock purchases and stock for collateral to support land purchases, the possibility of a world-engulfing economic collapse taking place in Japan is very high.

Japan has a population of only 123 million on a relatively tiny landmass. They have incredible manufacturing capability at home and overseas, and astounding financial reserves, but more and more the Japanese people and their economy are beginning to show alarming signs of speculative hangover and premature aging.

If they could match their incredible material success with a deeply held religious faith, I would say that the Japanese economy will correct for its current excesses and sail ahead.

However, as things stand now, my money would be on Japan as the forerunner of the Asian renaissance, but on a spiritually renewed China after communism as the long-term Asian super power of the new millennium.

GROWING THE BUSINESS

The best management book that I have read, other than the Bible, is *Thriving On Chaos* by Tom Peters. Peters' basic theme is that rapid change and chaos will be the norm in business from now on. He proposes that decentralization, service, innovation, and creative problem solving will be the trademarks of business in the coming era.

American people and American business can no longer comfort themselves by crowing over our superiority. All of us from now on are on a course of continuous gut wrenching change and fierce competition from East and West. We will no longer be insulated from any development in our world whether it takes place in Brussels or Berlin, Moscow or the Persian Gulf, Tokyo or Beijing.

Seeing the role of business in such global terms offers a striking new vista. Imagine tracking the business news as it follows the rising sun. The stock market opens up in Japan, and as the day continues it opens in the Middle East and in Europe and across to the United States.

Satellites are beaming trading information as it happens to terminals connected by fiber-optic cables, and computers are standing by to assess and interpret trends in mere microseconds. Suddenly the world has become a gigantic trading bazaar.

People can no longer say, well that happened in Hong Kong, so it doesn't affect us. Everything is interconnected because the transfer of funds takes place so rapidly. The investments of United States capital in the Orient and in Europe, and the investment of Asian and European capital in the United States, is dynamic and absolutely volatile.

This kind of cross-cultural activity going on around the world will mean that national boundaries cannot stop the flow of information.

Of course, this trend started with the multinational corporations several years ago. At one point, Citibank was taking 74 percent of its profits from overseas loans. Once that happens, then a corporation isn't just concerned about its home country anymore.

In an international trading environment, the multinational corporation cares about its holding and investments in foreign capitals just as much as its operations at home. So if General Motors has a bigger operation in West Germany than it does in Detroit, then the health of West Germany will be just as important to General Motors management as the health of Detroit. They can no longer be concerned solely with the well-being of American workers.

This will also mean that the worker in America cannot be protected in the American environment. He or she is now in competition with workers in Taiwan, Japan, Singapore, and Hong Kong, as well workers in Europe and the Middle East. Consequently, those workers are in competition with America.

Because of the ease of the shipment of goods—although there might be a time when politicians do the wrong thing and raise tariff barriers—the trend now and from now on will be toward global markets or global trading blocks.

The developing American Free Trade Zone between Canada, America and Mexico—and very possibly including both North and South America—will have great importance in the emerging global marketplace.

For now, there will be three major players on the scene. The American contingent, the Japan-Asia contingent (along with the Pacific Rim), and of course the European Community contingent. So we are rapidly coming to the point where the three major trade blocks will be in direct competition with each other.

Some forecasts for the future are both mind-boggling and encouraging. Because they do not factor in recession or decline, I do not necessarily endorse these figures. Nevertheless, the Mitsui Research Institute has projected worldwide output to reach 39.2 trillion dollars by the year 2000.

Of that total, the United States is forecast to have a 10.4 trillion-dollar economy, Asia 10.2 trillion, and Western Europe 12.7 trillion.

Of course, these blocks may also complement each other. The rational way of encouraging fair trade on a global basis would be to lower barriers as fast as possible and encourage the free flow of goods. That seems to be the real mandate for the tri-lateral perspective.

INNOVATION AND EFFICIENCY

In certain industries that might mean that the standard of living would go down for American workers; but it could be a boon for American workers if the efficiency of American industry goes up as it should and if our historic level of innovation continues.

Despite the claims of people like Shintaro Ishihara—the Japanese author who claims Japan holds the definitive balance of power in world trade and is a formidable innovator—the Japanese do not originate technologies. They are shrewd marketers and superior in the lateral integration of ideas, but they have not invented things as a rule.

North American scientists invented the transistor, the television, super-conductors, robotics, mainframe computing, and most of the other modern technological innovations of our time. These things come from American research and development. What Americans have not been able to do is to exploit the commercial applications of the technology the way the Japanese have done.

Japanese engineers are very good at studying and analyzing these devices, learning how and why they work, and then through a process of incremental improvement on an ongoing basis, they manufacture and mass produce an even better product. They never stop improving.

They are constantly asking for information from their customers and their workers about ways to improve their products. Clearly, this is a better way, and today the Japanese are reaping the benefits of that system.

American business is going to be forced—in fact, is already being forced—to adopt some of these Japanese management techniques. Industries will die which cannot serve markets quickly with quality products. Industries will also die where autocratic bosses refuse to empower workers to make decisions.

THE QUALITY DIVIDED

The worker who only wants a nine-to-five job and who has no interest in or commitment to the business he or she is in will sink to the bottom of the system.

If the strength of the system is worker participation, then workers will have to care about their jobs; however, that is not a threat if the company fosters an environment where a worker's concern is rewarded and where workers and managers, together, take genuine pride in the jobs they do. There has to be an ongoing dedication on a daily, almost hourly, basis to upgrade products and services. There has to be an obsession with quality and innovation.

I don't think we can assume that a demand for quality and innovation on this level will necessarily bring instant peace and prosperity; in fact, in some ways this new system will make it much more difficult for managers and workers alike, since their creative and innovative skills will be taxed to the limit. There may ultimately be a high rate of burnout, increased stress, and even higher incidence of psychological damage. We have certainly seen that happen in Japan.

Nevertheless, I believe there is no way around the dilemma except through the power of faith and belief in God. There may be turmoil around us, but men and women who commit their lives and work to God will discover the real rewards of their labors.

They will have peace in their lives, and because they will have a clearer vision of who they are and what they believe, they will work better. I pray we will have the vision as a nation to have that kind of commitment.

INTERNATIONAL PERSPECTIVES

Even though America's role in world affairs has grown consistently larger over the past 300 years, it was not actually until the end of the Second World War that most Americans began to recognize the significance of the world beyond their own doorstep.

Tens of thousands of young men and women left the farms for the first time in the 1940s in order to help wage war in Europe, North Africa, and the Pacific. At the same time, the demands of war forced government and industry to pour millions of dollars into the development of new technologies, including new systems of communications and transportation. Those achievements not only helped win the war, but opened up new perspectives on the world.

Today, we have become a global community, or as Marshall McLuhan phrased it, a "global village." What happens in America affects the entire world; conversely, what happens in Europe or Africa or Asia now affects America. And one of the implications of seeing the world in those terms is the continual broadening of our horizons.

Once we establish links with the world around us, we can no longer see ourselves as a single group of people in a particular city or nation, but we must see ourselves as citizens of the world.

Looking beyond our shores today we observe that we are now over five billion people on this planet, some 220 nations, and 22,000 distinct groups of people. It has been estimated that 75 percent of the world's population speaks or understands one of the 25 major languages, but researchers believe there may actually be as many as 5,445 distinct language groups.

At the end of World War II, as mentioned earlier, Western nations comprised about 30 percent of the world's population; by 1990 that figure dropped to roughly 15 percent. By the year 2030, some say it will be down as low as seven and a half percent, which means that the influence of Western thought and culture on world affairs will be greatly reduced over the next 50 years, one day perhaps to irrelevance.

THE CHURCH WORLDWIDE

In China, we have now discovered, the church blossomed after the American and European missionaries were expelled in a way it had never done until that time. In Africa, where there is an exploding birth rate, we can see that there is also an incredible explosion of Christianity. Some researchers now estimate that by the year 2000, Africa will be predominantly Christian.

It is estimated that over half of Korea will be Christian by the end of the century. Dr. Paul Cho's church in Seoul is home church to nearly a million evangelical Christians.

According to some reports, there may be as many as 100 million Christians in Mainland China today, and their numbers will continue to grow dramatically over the next ten years. With the exception of India, which is still very much in the grasp of Hinduism and other idolatrous religions, there is a dramatic turning to Jesus Christ throughout the Far East, and around the world.

There is really no explanation for this surge of religious vitality,

except that it is the hand of God. The wind of God is stirring around the world, and hearts are desperately yearning for truth. That should give every Christian a personal mandate to get back into a close personal relationship with his God.

Even if traditional Western civilization based on Christianity should be diminished during the coming decade, we can take consolation in the knowledge that Christianity, itself, will not be diminished. There is a unique vitality and vibrancy in the world revival going on now, and God is reclaiming His kingdom.

Reportedly, over 1,800,000,000 people now profess faith in Christ. The Episcopal church, which is the American form of the Anglican church, has more members overseas by far than it does in its home country of England. Liberal teaching in that church has been pernicious until very recently. For every Bible-believing evangelical leader, like Bishop Michael Baughan in Chester, there are six liberals, in Durham and in Canterbury and around the world, fighting to secularize the Anglican creed.

While the problem is still far from over, there are signs of revival. Anglicans who would have been horrified to be labeled evangelical a decade ago are now proud of the term; and some of the most vibrant churches in America, in Africa, and in Asia are charismatic Episcopal churches.

The Anglican church has fallen on very hard times in England, and attendance there has dwindled down to less than three percent of the population. Great cathedrals designed for congregations of five hundred to a thousand people frequently minister to no more than five to ten worshipers on a typical Sunday; and in many cases those few are only there for the sake of form or lost traditions and not, by any means, in hopes of encountering the actual Word of God.

In Africa and Asia, on the other hand, the Anglican church is growing dramatically. Mainline Lutheran, Presbyterian, and Methodist churches, along with evangelical and family-centered Catholic congregations, are rising from the ashes of burned-out theology and misplaced allegiances.

These have become some of the most vibrant churches, with some of the most dynamic Christians, in the world. I have met men of God in Korea, Singapore, Hong Kong, and Mainland China whose faith and dedication and knowledge of the Word put all of us in the West to shame.

GROWING THE CHURCH

The Bible has now been translated in its entirety into more than 300 languages, and there are portions of it in another 1,900. As James Combs reports in the *Bible Baptist Tribune,* that means that 90 percent of the world now has some availability to the teachings of Christianity; but lest we feel the job of missions is done, a half-billion people (equivalent to the combined populations of the United States and the Soviet Union) have yet to hear the gospel message for the first time.

Charismatic congregations are helping to transform and reinvigorate tired old churches, and in some cases they are simply supplanting ministries that have been unable to do the job.

In Chile, for example, I understand that the Presbyterian mission gave over its evangelistic activity to the Pentecostals since more than 24 percent of the total population of that country is already Pentecostal and charismatic in their faith expression.

In terms of trends, as we look ahead to the year 2000, I believe that shifting of forms of expression is going to continue. **The gospel is going to have tremendous acceptance among all these other nations, but it isn't necessarily going to be in the context of Western Christendom or Western civilization as we know it. It is going to be in a totally different cultural environment.**

THE ONE-WORLD CULTURE

A trend we see growing rapidly around the world (which does have the Western stamp) is the homogenization of culture. English is now the accepted language of commerce everywhere in the world and, more and more, it is being sought after as *the* language to be taught in the schools.

In January 1990 Vaclav Havel asked for 12,000 teachers of English in the schools of Czechoslovakia. The same trend is evident in Hungary, Romania, Poland, and all of Eastern Europe. There is an earnest desire to move away from any other language.

English has even become the language of trade in Japan and the Far East, so in Tokyo you might well see a Japanese businessman speaking to a German or Russian businessman in English. They have no other common language, and the only way they can communicate with each other is through English.

English has become a *lingua franca* for the nations of the world as no other language has ever been. No other language has had such wide currency. I am told that in every commercial airport in the world there has to be at least one person who speaks English.

Another thing that tends to bring homogeneity to the world is the spread of American films and television.

Even though the things portrayed in Hollywood movies, and more and more on TV situation comedies, may not be true reflections of America nor the image of our culture by which we would want the world to judge us, the world is learning about us by watching TV.

Because we have such a long tradition of quality television production, and because of the sheer size of the market this country has created, we are a major supplier of programming to the world.

The quality of our motion pictures and television right now, from a purely technical standpoint, is so much better than any other nation's that we have a firm hold on the world market. The technology and the production quality of American film and video is so very high, no one, not even the Japanese, is likely to surpass that standard for years to come.

The consequences of this domination of the "entertainment" marketplace are many and varied. Some are good, some bad, and some are just funny. I remember Malcolm Muggeridge saying that on the fortieth anniversary of television the BBC wanted to determine which of all the shows they program around the world the people were actually watching. It turned out their favorite programs were "I Love Lucy" and "Wagon Train"! Not "elevating," perhaps, but at least the values were wholesome.

Another consequence of the almost universal exposure to American programming, even in nations we would consider very remote and very different, is a desire to emulate American styles, dress, language and customs. Unfortunately, what that means is that they are copying many of those things in our society that are very superficial. They are not at all what we would like to see emulated, but nevertheless the people of the world are doing it.

THE UNIVERSAL TONGUE

From the standpoint of television and radio missionary work, we are suddenly in a position very much like the early church, with a universal language. In the days of Rome, when there was the *Pax Romana,* and the one common language all over the Roman Empire presented a unique window of opportunity for the early missionaries.

Wherever they went, they could converse. Rome had prepared the way—first with Greek and then, from the third century on, with Latin. When the Empire began to disintegrate after the year 500, the usefulness of either Greek or Latin as a *lingua franca* was greatly diminished.

But when the saints traveled from Asia Minor to Malta and to Rome, and on to Spain and France and Germany and England, the gospel could spread very rapidly because everybody understood the words that were being spoken by the apostles. There was a ready basis of communication.

Today we have much the same situation. We have a language that is becoming increasingly universal, which will enable us to speak to people in a broad number of contexts in an idiom they generally understand. It is not as difficult now to go across cultural barriers because the cultural barriers have already been breached by television, film, radio, and by audio and video cassettes which have proliferated around the world.

I remember my shock in visiting ancient Ephesus where the early church had been born under the teaching of Paul. Standing there in a shop one morning, I was listening to a broadcast coming out of Izmir, Turkey, playing a record of Cat Stevens singing "Morning Has Broken."

It was an odd sensation and so out of context. But I experienced the same thing again later, on the Island of Rhodes, where American blue jeans and American-style portable radios were the rage. I remember how strange it seemed going into a shop there and seeing a Phillips tape recorder playing a song by a Dutch rock group singing in English, with a Southern accent! But this is the way it is. The blue jeans, the rock music, and the "modern" idiom have pretty much circled the globe.

When Elvis Presley did his international satellite telecast, it was reportedly viewed by a billion people. It may have been the most watched program in history up to that time, and all the people were tuned in to what Elvis was saying and how he was saying it. Although we might not like that type of acculturation, it is nevertheless there for us to use if we will just have sense enough to use it.

Given that platform, it is very foolish for the church to structure its appeal to the nations of the world in a methodology that is out of date, in the garb of the missionaries of fifty years ago, and in the typical idiom of the nineteenth century missionary mentality. All the important communications barriers have been broken down. All that is necessary is for Christians to use the channels and the idiom that have been opened up for us.

The transfer of vast wealth from the West to the East will mean the loss of decision-making power.

The United States is both a Pacific and an Atlantic nation.

Economic and political power will continue to flow out of the Northeast toward the South and West.

Christianity is not a Western religion. Christianity will flourish worldwide in the new millennium.

7

The Undermining of America

For 70 years America has experienced a relentless attack from its own elites.

If dramatic change does not occur in this decade the process of decay will be irreversible.

From its declaration of independence as a nation in 1776 until 1980, a period of 204 years, the United States of America accumulated a total unpaid national debt of one trillion dollars. During that time we fought the War of Independence, the War of 1812, the Civil War, the Spanish-American War, two World Wars, the Korean War, and the Vietnam War.

During the next six years, from 1980 to 1986, confronted only by a "Cold War" and a "War on Poverty," the United States Government spent so much more money than it received that the unpaid national debt escalated to two trillion dollars.

In six peacetime years we doubled the debt that had taken 204 years to accumulate. That is almost beyond imagination. And if that weren't enough, in the next four years, from 1986 to 1990, the Government did it again and loaded another trillion dollars onto the growing pyramid of unpaid debt.

President John F. Kennedy, who took office in 1961, said that he did not want to be the first president to preside over a 100-billion-dollar federal budget. In 1990 the interest alone on the federal debt, at some 176 billion dollars, was almost twice the total United States budget when Kennedy took office.

In 1980, the claims of the citizens and businesses of the United States against other nations were so large that this nation was considered the world's largest creditor. By 1987, the credit balances accumulated by our nation against the world since 1918 had been brought to zero. By 1990, the United States was the world's largest debtor nation, with net foreign claims against our assets standing at somewhere between 600 and 650 billion dollars.

Our foreign debt dwarfs that of the "debtor" nations of Mexico, Brazil, and Argentina. America is number one in the world in the category of debt owed.

We excel in other categories as well. We have the highest rate of illiteracy of any developed nation; the highest rate of violent crime and juvenile delinquency; the highest rate of teen pregnancy—six times that of Denmark and three times that of Sweden. We have the highest rate of illegal drug use in the world; and, next only to France and the Soviet Union, the highest rate of alcohol consumption and alcoholism.

The worldwide statistics on venereal disease are somewhat imprecise, but we may be edging up to first or second in these categories as well.

Americans have always considered their nation the world's greatest, and their people the best and brightest. We think of ourselves as winners, but do we really want to win in all these categories?

Isn't it time as a nation we ask how we got this way, and then how we can change?

THE POST WAR YEARS

America in 1945 was the greatest, most powerful nation the world had ever known. It had fought and won simultaneously in Europe and Asia the most terrible war the world has ever seen.

The strategic and tactical skills of our generals and admirals were remarkable by any standard. The bravery of our combat forces was legendary. But it was the ever-increasing output of American industry which enabled America and her allies to grind down the Axis powers. Tens of thousands of tanks, planes, trucks, artillery pieces, and vessels of all shapes and sizes poured out from the industrial might of America.

By the end of 1942, the outcome was no longer in doubt as what Winston Churchill called the "encircling ring" began to squeeze tighter and tighter around Nazi Germany, Fascist Italy, and militaristic Japan.

At war's end, Europe was war torn and prostrate. The Soviet Union had been left crippled and bleeding by the ruthless Nazi invasion. Japan and the rest of Asia were stunned and destitute. Only the United States of America remained—its industry intact, its farms brimming with surpluses, its cities untouched by war and ready to begin the post-war boom.

America was unselfish with its wealth. Through the Marshall Plan we helped rebuild Europe. Through direct aid we strengthened Soviet Russia. Through enlightened military occupation we introduced democratic government to Germany and Japan, then we gave generous aid to help them rebuild their ravaged economies.

The United States Navy ruled the seas, the United States nuclear shield controlled the skies. American automobiles, tractors, machine tools, computers, television sets, appliances, and hundreds of products dominated world commerce.

In 1944, the finance leaders of the major allied powers met at the Mount Washington Hotel in tiny Bretton Woods, New Hampshire, and agreed that the United States dollar would become the strong reserve currency of the world, backed by gold. As one participant gushed, "Gold is the sun, the dollar is the earth, and all other currencies are the moon."

Money was pouring into America, and the American dollar was "as good as gold." This was a different world than that of 1979 when presidential candidate Ronald Reagan quipped, "Yesterday my doctor checked my heart. He said it was sound as a dollar, and I almost passed out."

SEEDS OF DESTRUCTION

In the 1930s, while America endured a severe depression, we experienced 54 percent unemployment, bread lines, soup kitchens, a stock market collapse, and tragic business and bank failures.

Sensitive intellectuals saw the Great Depression as the failure of capitalism. They were easy prey to the hard core Marxists who had been organizing the United States since 1918.

In 1930, a powerful atheist and communist sympathizer, John Dewey, began his work in education at Columbia Teachers College. Undoubtedly the despair of the Depression era provided fertile soil for the rapid growth of Dewey's anti-Christian thinking.

During the height of the war effort, when Soviet Russia was our comrade in arms, it was easy enough for pro-Soviet Marxists to find a ready home in the State Department, the Treasury Department, and in those departments conducting crucial top secret research.

At war's end, a dying Franklin Roosevelt and his advisors held back our victorious forces from taking Berlin and East Germany. Then, in a misguided attempt to secure lasting world peace by what he called "*noblesse oblige*," Roosevelt gave over to the crazed butcher, Joseph Stalin, control of Poland, East Germany, Estonia, Latvia, Lithuania and, ultimately, Hungary, Czechoslovakia, Romania, Bulgaria, and Albania.

In the East, the Russians did not join the war effort against Japan until after the United States dropped atomic bombs on Hiroshima and Nagasaki. Then when it was obvious Japan was finished, Soviet Russia declared war. With United States acquiescence, the Russian troops looted Manchuria. It is reported that they stole everything—rail cars and locomotives, iron rails, whole factories, even metal doors.

Then under the constant barrage of left-wing press reports decrying the "stench of corruption" in China, the United States abandoned its wartime comrade in arms, Chiang Kai Shek, and turned the nation of China over to Mao Tse Tung and the communists.

In America, in the academic circles and the liberal press, they were described as "agrarian reformers" seeking a better life for their people by freeing them from the greed and corruption of their former leaders.

THE POLITICAL NATION

With a few notable exceptions, the foreign policy record of the United States from 1945 to 1980 is one of defeat, betrayal, and shame. Under the pounding of the liberal press and the powerful urging of what the London *Economist* termed the "Political Nation," America repeatedly undercut pro-Western and pro-Christian leaders of Third World countries in favor of Marxist or communist regimes.

The pattern was the same. Batista was corrupt, but Castro and Che Guevara were revolutionary heroes. Somoza was greedy and corrupt; the Sandinistas represented freedom. The Army of El Salvador is full of right wing bullies; the rebels represent justice. Haile Selassie in Ethiopia is old and corrupt; the communist Mengistu should take power. Ian Smith in Rhodesia is a racist oppressor; the Marxist Robert Mugabe represents his people and deserves our support. The communist Allende is the new savior of reactionary Chile.

The real stench was not the corruption of the pro-Western Third World governments but the incredible leftist, anti-Christian bias of leading American journalists covering the foreign desks of their respective news organizations.

I have been privileged to take my own cameras and news producers into some of the world's hot spots. I often have extensive briefing papers. I usually am able to interview key leaders in the places I visit.

My staff can talk to people in their own native languages. My only conclusion after years of experience is that with few exceptions the

American overseas press has been biased in favor of Marxism and communism and opposed to pro-Western governments. They in turn order the facts to fit their own biases and attempt to tilt American public opinion against our friends and in favor of our enemies.

If, as Marx once claimed, religion is the opiate of the people, then for the past 40 years Marxism has been the opiate of the media.

THE NEW WAR POLICY

In World War II, the United States and her allies were fighting a fascist country which had invaded the communist homeland. Therefore, the American left and the American right were joined together. We mobilized our entire industrial might with one objective—crush the Axis powers and bring about unconditional surrender.

We gave no quarter. There were no "privileged sanctuaries." There were no complex "rules of engagement" tying the hands of our military forces.

Four years after the war, the then Secretary of State, Dean Acheson, with the advice of suspected leftist, Owen Lattimore, sent a signal that the Korean peninsula was not a vital part of the American defense perimeter. In June of 1950, the communist government of North Korea took him at his word and invaded South Korea.

President Harry Truman, taking advantage of a time when the Soviet delegate was absent from the United Nations Security Council, was able to secure declarations from the United Nations which condemned North Korea's action and authorized a United Nations force to resist it.

American troops entered the fray but were quickly pushed back to a tiny defense perimeter around the southern port city of Pusan. Then General Douglas MacArthur in a brilliant but risky move, launched an amphibious strike near Seoul at the port of Inchon on the West Coast of South Korea.

Our forces outflanked the North Koreans, then cut their supply lines and began a race into North Korea. As they neared the border of China, at the Yalu River, large numbers of Chinese soldiers entered the conflict about the time that the bitter cold of winter swept in from Manchuria. Our troops were forced to withdraw but were able to regroup and begin a second advance further south.

MacArthur realized that if we could bomb the Yalu River bridges and then attack by air the troop emplacements on the Chinese side of the river, our forces could catch the North Koreans and Chinese troops in a relatively simple pincer movement and could utterly destroy them.

By these operations, our troops could have sealed Korea at the Yalu and instituted a free democratic government in a unified Korea. But this war had one very significant difference from World War II: now we were fighting a communist country, and the prevailing doctrine in Washington was that we could *fight* a communist country but we could not *defeat* a communist country.

KOREA AND VIETNAM

MacArthur, who knew that in war there is no substitute for victory, insisted on winning. Truman and his advisers insisted on giving the Chinese a privileged sanctuary even though they had been killing American troops with men and supplies from China.

So MacArthur was removed from command and we settled for a "peace line" on the 38th Parallel. North Korea stayed communist. South Korea stayed democratic. America had lost its first war.

I served in Korea with the First Marine Division. I felt we had made a mistake, a policy error to protect American lives. I thought it could never happen again.

But we repeated the same mistake in Vietnam. Only, this time I knew it was not a policy error but part of a deliberate calculated plan. The new policy put in place by those holding the ultimate power in our society, and supported unwittingly by a leftist press, was obvious.

For full employment, rising prices, and financial growth, the experts determined that the United States needed some mechanism by which roughly 10 percent of our output could be wasted each year.

A shooting war would accomplish full employment, but its results were unpredictable and messy. The ideal solution was a "cold war" during which the United States would maintain a semi-war footing against an enemy which we, in turn, propped up with loans and aid.

If communism were defeated, then there would be no more troops to pay, ships to build, airplanes to become obsolete, advanced weapons to develop, or government debt to finance. Either this is the underlying policy or our government had been seriously infiltrated by pro-Marxist liberals. No other explanation accounts for the continuous, ongoing foreign policy "blunders" of the United States for 30 years.

If a shooting war developed, as it did in Vietnam, it was acceptable for our servicemen to die and our treasure to be squandered, but no communist power was to be defeated by America.

The Vietnam War took the heart and resolve out of America. It drained our economy and debased our currency. It was the second war America lost. It was planned that way. American military power would never be the same again.

THE ACADEMIC FIFTH COLUMN

What we see in economics and foreign policy springs from attitudinal roots that are fashioned in the classroom, in academia, in the think tanks, and only then in the newsrooms.

Charles Sykes has caused a panic on the campus of Dartmouth College. Sykes, whose book, *ProfScam*, helped shake up faculties all over America in 1988, is now looking into the practices of the faculty, examining curricula, and exploring evidence of the continuing "politicization" of teaching philosophy at Dartmouth.

An article in the *Washington Times* reports that blood pressures are soaring on the New Hampshire campus. Sykes' research comes at a time when Americans are already beginning to question the things their sons and daughters are being taught. Faculty liberals are clearly nervous.

Like most American campuses, Dartmouth has been invaded by professors trained in the liberal, secular, socialist biases of the academy. Unfortunately, they have tried to inflict their beliefs upon students on a traditionally conservative campus, and at a time when the lie of Marxism is suddenly visible to the entire world.

With an Ivy League education costing upwards of $20,000 a year, parents are wondering why they should be paying that kind of money for college professors to train their children to be angry, rebellious, self-centered, and close-minded when the kids can stay home and be all those things for free. Sykes' forthcoming book on the Dartmouth affair should make interesting reading.

How long will it be until the radicals on America's campuses are finally exposed and deposed? Washington columnist and scholar Arnold Beichman recently wrote, "The Marxist academics are today's power elite in the universities, and by the magic of the tenure system they have become self-perpetuating." Instead of "a search for objective truth," he says, the academy has "successfully substituted Marxist social change as the goal of learning."

Columnist Georgie Anne Geyer has suggested that, despite the apparent collapse of East European and Soviet communism, Marxism continues to thrive in the universities because American academics are utopians, intellectual idealists who compare culture not to history or tradition but to some visionary dream.

CIVILIZATION'S DEATH WISH

Malcolm Muggeridge once said that Western civilization's flirtation with liberalism is evidence of its "death wish." The liberals in society seem to be hell bent on the ultimate destruction of Western culture.

In his Harvard lectures, Aleksandr Solzhenitsyn traced this flirtation back to the Enlightenment, but added that "liberalism" assumed its most somber and most sinister aspect in America. For in America, like nowhere else, a subculture of liberal intellectuals has attempted to undermine and to disassemble the entire fabric of Western society.

This plundering of traditional morality and Christian values was never accidental. It has been a deliberate and methodical assault on the tenets of society—what Muggeridge calls Christendom—and has proliferated from the classrooms to the courtrooms, and from the newsrooms to the living rooms of America. More and more, it even comes from the pulpits of America.

The end has not just been to supplant Christian values with humanism, but to weaken American sovereignty and supplant it with a one world socialist government.

In the book, *The End of Christendom*, which is a collection of classic lectures, Muggeridge offers a stunning insight. He says,

> Previous civilizations have been overthrown from without by the incursion of barbarian hordes. Christendom has dreamed up its own dissolution in the minds of its own intellectual elite. Our barbarians are home products, indoctrinated at the public expense, urged on by the media systematically, stage by stage, dismantling Christendom, depreciating and deprecating all its values. The whole social structure is now tumbling down, dethroning its God, undermining all its certainties. All this, woefully enough, is being done in the name of the health, wealth, and happiness of all mankind.

The great irony of this situation is that the very men and women we have entrusted to educate and challenge our children have been the corrupters. While few students have become communists or Marxists, per se, their trust has been shattered. Many no longer have faith in their nation; they no longer believe in God; they no longer believe justice and public service and patient labor within the framework of a Christian society will bring about progress and social change. They have been programmed either to drop out or to dissent. They no longer belong to the team.

Suddenly we are being challenged by new and powerful forces from many corners. At the international level we are feeling the pressure from the East which, as we have seen, will crescendo during the coming decade.

We are enduring the assault on faith and values in the courts as the ACLU and other liberal organizations wage their violent and relentless war. We are, of course, in a profound conflict with the false cults of the New Age.

Considering the death of our Western values, Muggeridge says,

Christendom has played a tremendous role in the art and literature, in the mores and jurisprudence, in the architecture, values, institutions, and whole way of life of Western man during the centuries of his dominance in the world. But now as Western man's power and influence recede, so Christendom itself comes to have an evermore ghostly air about it, to the point that it seems to belong to history already, rather than to present day actuality.

Over the past three decades we have seen a gradual chipping away of America's deepest and longest-held values. The family is under attack from feminists denying the legitimacy of motherhood and guardianship of the home; homosexuals and lesbians are waging a violent campaign against their natural gender; abortion activists are on the attack seeking the right to destroy the unborn; and secular humanists are bringing their overt God-hatred into the public forum and laying siege to the church.

FOUNDATIONS OF AMERICAN LIBERTY

When the founding fathers of America, who had been meeting at Independence Hall in Philadelphia completed on September 17, 1787, the drafting of a constitution for the newly formed United States of America, John Adams, who was to become our second president, remarked, "This constitution was made only for a moral and a religious people. It is wholly inadequate for the government of any other."

Washington, Adams, Jefferson, Madison, Franklin, and Patrick Henry—in fact all our founding fathers—recognized that constitutional government was only possible when the people being governed were ruled by inner moral restraint and self-control.

At the signing of the Constitution, the 13 colonies comprising the new nation contained an estimated 3,000,000 Protestants, 300,000 Roman Catholics, and 5,000 Jews. America was predominantly a Protestant Christian nation, united by a moral consensus based upon biblical values. When George Washington signed our constitution, he dated it "In the year of our Lord, 1787."

There was only one Lord whose birthday dated back 1787 years: Jesus Christ. The founding document of the United States of America acknowledges the Lordship of Jesus Christ, because we were a Christian nation.

Constitutions in effect at the time of the Declaration of Independence give the tenor of our national beliefs. The Delaware Constitution of 1776 proclaims, "Everyone appointed to public office must say, 'I do profess faith in God the Father, and in the Lord Jesus Christ His only Son, and in the Holy Ghost . . . and I do acknowledge the Holy Scriptures of the Old and New Testaments to be given by divine inspiration.[1]"

North Carolina's constitution of the same year states, "No person who should deny the being of a God, or the truth of the [Christian] religion or the divine authority . . . should be capable of holding any office or place of trust in the civil government of this state."

These laws and others like them were in effect in most of the states during the better part of the nineteenth century. In 1892 in the Supreme Court case titled, *Church of the Holy Trinity v. United States,* the court stated explicitly:

> Every constitution of every one of the forty-four states contains language which either directly or by clear implication recognizes a profound reverence for religion and an assumption that its influence in human affairs is essential to the well being of the community. . . . These and many other matters which might be noticed, add a volume of unofficial declarations to the mass of organic utterances that this is a Christian nation.

In 1931 in *United States v. Macintosh,* Justice Sutherland reiterated that part of the *Trinity Trustees* case when he wrote in the majority decision, "We are a Christian people."

A CHANGE OF VENUE

Only by destroying the Christian consensus could this nation be undermined and its power destroyed. The assault against America has taken the following avenues.

First, the liberal left realized that no elected body in the United States would adopt its radical agenda. Therefore, a deliberate plan was put in motion to claim for non-elected judges power that they had never been given under the United States Constitution. Lawyers and judges would then, under the guise of "constitutional rights," dismantle systematically the Judeo-Christian majority consensus that has guided this nation since its founding.

Second, and concurrently, the educational system would first be taken from its Christian roots and used as a psycho-political indoctrination ground to move the young toward the agenda of the left.

Third, the left would infiltrate wealthy and powerful tax-free foundations and government agencies where taxpayers' funds would begin to pour out to support the left at home and abroad.

Fourth, organizations such as Planned Parenthood, the National Education Association, and more recently the National Organization for Women, People for the American Way, the Gay-Lesbian Caucus, and their ilk would arise to champion unrestrained sex, homosexual rights, abortion on demand, while they attacked Christian beliefs, conservative organizations, and all the traditional family structures of America.

Fifth, the nation's once conservative Christian press would be virtually overwhelmed by those dedicated to undermining Christian America in favor of this brave new world of humanism and socialism.

In 1990 we see family disintegration, unrestrained sex, a holocaust of abortion, an epidemic of drugs and alcohol, deteriorating educational standards, growing poverty amidst unrestrained opulence, business greed and fraud, and a runaway federal budget.

We have these things because we have allowed Christian and biblical standards to be removed from our national life. It has taken the left some 70 years to reduce us to this level. As we enter the decade of the nineties and the coming new millennium, we must ask ourselves whether we have enough spiritual strength left to throw off the parasites that have been wasting our national strength, or whether there are now so many parasites leeching onto us that our nation has passed the point of no return.

REWRITING THE CONSTITUTION

Some years ago Supreme Court Justice Felix Frankfurter is said to have passed a note to Justice William O. Douglas which read, "If we can keep old bushy [Justice Charles Evans Hughes] on our side, there's no amount of rewriting the constitution that we can't do."

Here was a former Harvard law professor communicating with a former Yale law professor, candidly laying out his agenda, the judicial rewriting of the governing laws of America.

Equally cynical was the arrogant assertion of Justice Hughes, "The Constitution is whatever the court says it is." America no longer had a government elected by the people under a timeless constitution to be interpreted according to the clear intention of the framers. America no longer had judicial interpretation but legislative rule by five out of nine non-elected judges who had taken unto themselves the power to change the constitution of the United States to suit their own philosophical biases.

Thomas Jefferson had warned so forcefully that if on matters of constitutional interpretation the judges were the sole arbiters, "we will find ourselves under the tyranny of an oligarchy."

And tyrants they have become. They have virtually destroyed neighborhood schools; they have permitted a district judge to force Kansas City to levy 500 million dollars in taxes for social programs they support but the people do not; they have forced an irreligious value-neutral educational system down America's throat; they have dramatically hindered law enforcement; they have trampled on the prerogatives of the United States Congress and the legislatures of the fifty states; they have opened the doors for a bewildering array of high-damage plaintiff's tort rights; and most heinous of all, they have participated in legalizing the murder of 25 million unborn babies in America.

THE WRATH OF GOD

In 1958, in a case entitled *Cooper v. Aaron*, the Supreme Court announced that its decisions were the "supreme law of the land." Even though in my opinion this is an unconstitutional usurpation of power, since *Cooper v. Aaron* the Supreme Court itself, the lower court judges, and attorneys practicing before federal courts all act as if each decision of the Supreme Court is the supreme law. Therefore, under the evolutionary theory of the constitution, the court sits as a continuing constitutional convention making up new constitutions as it goes along. Therefore, since it controls the constitution, it has made itself the supreme branch of government. When it speaks, it speaks for all the people of America, and if it errs all the people must suffer.

On June 25, 1962, the Supreme Court ruled in a case titled *Engle v. Vitale* that state-sponsored prayer could not be said in public school rooms. On June 17, 1963, the court ruled in the case of *Abington v. Schempp* that the Holy Bible could not be read to students in classrooms.

On November 17, 1980, in *Stone v. Graham* the court ruled that the Ten Commandments could not be posted in the classrooms of America's schools. On June 4, 1984, in *Wallace v. Jaffrey* the court ruled that a moment of silence prior to a class was unconstitutional if that silence was called prayer. And more recently, they ruled that a state could not mandate the teaching of a course acknowledging that the origins of life began with a creator.

Acting on behalf of all the citizens of the United States, our government has officially insulted Almighty God and has effectively taken away from all public school children any opportunity for even the slightest acknowledgement of God's existence. By rejecting Him, we have made the Protector and Champion of the United States its enemy.

The events that followed are not coincidence. On November 22, 1963, less than six months after the Bible-reading decision, President John F. Kennedy was assassinated. Within two years after that decision, America was massively embroiled in its second most painful war, which decimated our treasury, our servicemen, and our national resolve.

By 1966 the real standard of living of the average American worker stopped growing. By 1969 the stock market took a dizzying plunge, and by 1971 because of inflation we took our currency off the gold standard.

By 1973 the OPEC nations quadrupled the price of oil, and the United States economy went into the worst recession since 1930.

In 1974, for the first time in American history, a president resigned in disgrace and a vice president pleaded *nolo contendre* (no contest) to a charge of extortion. All of this took place against a back-drop of violent student demonstrations which had set the nation's campuses aflame.

By 1978 our trade deficit was at an all-time high. Iranian students assaulted our embassy in Teheran, took our diplomatic officers and staff hostage, and we were seemingly impotent to help them.

By 1979 inflation was out of control and interest rates were pushed to an unbelievable 21 percent to stop it. Our president was the laughing stock of our allies and our country was termed "ungovernable."

LOSING CONTROL

Ten years later, when the 1980s ended, the United States had seen an assassination attempt against its very popular president who, in his second term, was discredited because of an arms for hostages transaction with Iran. And in a long list of media scandals, both the Speaker of the House of Representatives and the Majority Whip resigned in disgrace— one amid charges of profiteering, the other amid ethics charges.

By 1990, Michael Milken, the leader of the 200-billion-dollar junk bond industry, pled guilty to securities violations even as billions of dollars in junk bond values were collapsing along with the bankruptcies of over-leveraged major airlines and some of the nation's best-known department stores.

The savings and loan industry has collapsed and the price tag to clean it up may well top a trillion dollars. Real estate values have also collapsed, or are collapsing, and with them may go a sizable part of the banking and insurance industries.

Going into the 1990s, the United States Government has direct debt of three trillion dollars and contingent liabilities of some six and one-half trillion dollars. At some point government debt may become worthless; and we are faced with the very real prospect of a stock market collapse coupled with a collapse of the dollar and the government bond market. The prospect is for depression followed by run-away inflation.

Since 1962, intertwined with budget deficits, high interest rates, and business failures is the rapid breakup of the social fabric of America.

Since 1962 the number of divorces in America has increased 250 percent; the number of single family households headed by women increased 250 percent; the suicide rate in the 15 to 19 age group and the 20 to 24 age group has increased 253 percent.

From 1962 to 1981 the reported cases of sexually transmitted diseases climbed from 400,000 cases to 1,100,000 per year. By 1986, when diseases such as genital herpes and chlamydia were added, the annual number of new cases of sexually transmitted diseases soared to 12,000,000.

In 1962, 4 percent of high school seniors indicated they had tried marijuana. By 1982 that number was approaching 60 percent. Since 1962 the incidence of violent crime, alcohol and drug abuse, child abuse, teenage runaways, adultery, and "living together" outside of marriage has skyrocketed.

In short, over the last 28 years the moral and social fabric of the United States has been progressively torn apart. Has a watchful God given us up? These words from Benjamin Franklin spoken at the Constitutional Convention should be instructive.

> Have we forgotten this powerful Friend? Or do we imagine we no longer need His assistance? . . . without His concurring aid, we shall succeed in this potential building no better than the builders of Babel; we shall be divided by our little, partisan local interests; our projects will be confounded; and we ourselves shall become a reproach and a byword down to future ages.

THE DUMBING OF AMERICA

On March 17, 1984, New Jersey Senator Bill Bradley reported on the Senate floor the results of a survey taken two months earlier of 5,000 high school seniors.

Forty-five percent of those tested in Baltimore could not shade an area on a map where the United States was supposed to be. Nearly half the students in Hartford could not name even three countries in Africa. Thirty-nine percent of the students in Boston could not name the six states in the region where they lived, New England. Twenty-five percent of the students in Dallas could not name the country that bordered Texas on the south.

In two parallel tests of college students, 84 percent of students tested in 1950 identified Manila as the capital of the Philippines. By 1984, only 27 percent of the students tested gave the correct response. In 1984, 70 percent of the college students could not name one country in Africa between the Sahara and South Africa.

We sent our CBN news crews to the University of Maryland to ask a few college freshmen and sophomores there some random questions. None could name the three states bordering California. None that we spoke to could name the U.S. presidents between Truman and Reagan.

Only one could correctly identify the method of determining the area of a triangle.

I learned firsthand—and my wife confirmed the report on a subsequent visit—that 85 percent of the graduates of the high school in a city near Philadelphia had graduated as functional illiterates.

Is it any wonder that American business cannot find employees for high tech jobs? Is it any wonder the armed forces have had to "dumb down" their manuals to a minimal level for the new generation of recruits?

A program we started at CBN, called "Heads Up," has trained over 300,000 people to read and write during the past five years. I have personally brought literacy programs to Watts in Los Angeles, the South Side of Chicago, Bedford-Stuyvesant in Brooklyn, and the inner cities of Philadelphia, Detroit, Atlanta, Houston, Birmingham, and Memphis.

I have participated in literacy programs in the prisons and in communities in the Mississippi Delta. In all of these places, I have found learning of reading skills to be a breeze for people of all ages and social backgrounds. A breeze, that is, if reading is taught the way God made us to talk—by syllables, by what is called phonics, and not by the "look say" method forced on the schools by the behaviorist models.

But the tragedy of humanist education is that the educators do not believe that reading, math, history, and geography skills are important. The important thing is the sociological and behavioral indoctrination of the children.

THE BURDEN OF PROOF

So now, 60 years after John Dewey, we have 73 million Americans educated at less than a fifth grade level, 28 million functional illiterates, a school dropout rate of one million pupils per year, and an annual burden of 225 billion dollars on the American economy because of illiteracy.

The scores of American high school students on the Scholastic Aptitude Test (SAT) have dropped every single year from 1962 until 1980. There were 18 years of unbroken decline. In 1980 there was a slight increase in the average, but this was caused in whole or in part by the fact that some 32,000 Christian schools had come into being during this period and, together with private schools, accounted for 12.4 percent of the nation's student population: a total of some 5,580,000 pupils.

Depending on whose numbers you read, there are in addition between 300,000 and 600,000 students being educated at home, through home schooling programs, almost all of whom test superior to the products of the public schools.

When I served on President Ronald Reagan's Task Force on Victims of Crime, I learned that the public schools are the most dangerous places in America. More than 250,000 crimes are reported each month in the public schools. I am not referring to fist fights and scuffles, but to assault with a deadly weapon, rape, robbery, dealing narcotics, possession of narcotics, and other crimes of that nature.

I learned from our "Heads Up" sources that up to 70 percent of all students in the New York City public schools system read at or below the third grade level. This means that virtually all instruction from the third grade on is incomprehensible to them.

Boredom, coupled with crime and narcotics in the schools, has obviously created a hostile and dangerous environment. It should come as no great surprise that up to 45 percent of the students in that school system drop out before finishing high school.

THE WISDOM OF FOOLS

It has been stated that all that is necessary to succeed financially in this rich and free land is to graduate from high school, get married and stay married, and take an entry level job and keep it.

To see the hopelessness and despair of young people in our inner cities and to realize that the only future ahead for many (perhaps most) of them is a short and unhappy life of stealing, selling narcotics, prostitution, or welfare is to bring forth a cry of rage against an education establishment run by wise fools.

Despite spending hikes on education in America in excess of 600 percent from 1951 to 1988, and over 320 billion dollars annually, the 1989 SAT scores were described as "grim" and "especially disheartening" by Education Secretary, Lauro F. Cavazos.

America has heard appeals for more money for teachers, the need for lower teacher to pupil ratios, better staff to pupil ratios, on and on. The facts are plain. In 1949 there were 27 pupils per teacher, now there are about 17 pupils per teacher. Despite enormous increases in spending per pupil (from $900 per pupil in 1949 to over $4,800 per pupil today), the total portion of school expenditures devoted to teachers' salaries has fallen from 55 percent to 40.4 percent. In 1940–50, teachers represented 70 percent of the total adult employees in the school system. Now they represent only 53 percent.

According to *Forbes* magazine, only Switzerland spends more money on education per pupil than the United States, yet the United States ranks last among the industrialized nations in the relative performance of its students.

THE EDUCATION POWER

The National Education Association (NEA) is without question the most powerful labor union in America. Formed in 1857 as a follow-up to the anti-Christian revisionist education movement started by Horace Mann, it now has two million dues-paying members in all fifty states.

The NEA operates from a national headquarters through state chapters (known as the Michigan Education Association, the Virginia Education Association, the Texas Education Association, etc.). Because of the power of these state affiliates, the NEA has a virtual stranglehold on education in America.

The NEA is highly political and undeniably partisan. It was estimated that one third of all the delegates to the 1980 Presidential Convention of the Democratic Party were NEA members. Critics alleged at its creation by then President Jimmy Carter that the Department of Education was the only cabinet level department ever formed as a payoff to one labor union.

Since membership in the NEA is compulsory—or virtually compulsory for most teachers—it is obvious that there must be many fine teachers who are members of the NEA by force and who deplore the current state of American education. But that grass roots sentiment never influences the national leadership of the NEA.

At its top, the NEA is a radical, leftist organization which seems totally committed to the present course of education in America. One of its officials recently stated on my television program that the NEA was completely opposed to teaching any form of moral values in the schools of America.

He then gave the usual justification that the teaching of moral values would "be an unconstitutional establishment of religion."

The extremes that this NEA position can be taken to is illustrated by a television interview I conducted with a Christian teacher who had been using a "value neutral" teachers manual in a Mobile, Alabama, public high school. The teacher was told that if a discussion began about morality and a student should ask, "Is shoplifting right or wrong?" the answer from the teacher should be, "I can't tell you if it is right or wrong. You must find out for yourself."

If this was the answer about the potential commission of a crime punishable by prison, just consider the confusion of students in interpersonal relations, sexual relations, and marriage.

By its literature, seminars, and public utterances, it is clear that the number one goal of the NEA is to maintain power over schools to the clear exclusion of parents and taxpayers. Parents are the natural enemy of the NEA. Jim Mattox, former attorney general of the State of Texas, summed up the position of the NEA when he said, "The state owns your children."

It is equally clear that the NEA is committed to a radical socialist, one world agenda. The prime thrust of the NEA curricula is to wean children away from loyalty to "the outdated religious superstitions," loyalty to the family, loyalty to the United States, and belief in free market economics, and then to introduce them to socialism and world citizenship.

The actual education of the young is a totally secondary issue.

The NEA plays on the respect we accord education and educators in America, and it wraps itself in a mantle of the high and lofty goals of education. It tells us that it stands for the strength and independence of our public education. Since the press favors the NEA positions, and since most legislators don't dare come out against "public education" or the local teachers, it has been virtually impossible to dislodge the NEA from power.

In this decade I believe that the scandal of public education will have gotten so bad that the people will finally be willing to overthrow this radical power bloc in favor of a free market system that works.

EDUCATION IN THE FUTURE

Imagine a time in America when in late August the parents of school age children would be mailed a voucher worth $2,500 for each child in their family.

All summer long the parents and their children would have been poring over the brightly colored brochures advertising the available schools in their community. Some schools would be specializing in physics or computer science. Others would emphasize the study of Latin, romance languages, and the classics.

Some would stress religious teaching and Bible study. Some might advertise regulated dress codes and strict discipline. Some might stress a less structured environment and education based on field trips and laboratories. Some might claim a fast track for college entrance; others might emphasize vocational training. Each school would be accredited by a public or private agency and would be required to provide a basic core curriculum for each student.

Some schools would be in existing school buildings. Others might be located in newer facilities. All the schools would have transportation available to serve the citizens of their community.

There would be no more education monopoly where parents had one choice: the gray mediocrity of present-day public schools. If any of the schools in question did not deliver a product which satisfied their customers, these customers would take their vouchers and buy elsewhere.

Obviously if some schools wanted to offer a premium curriculum instead of the standard fare, they could charge more and apply the voucher toward the increased price. If parents could afford pricey extras, that would be their private decision.

All students would be guaranteed a basic quality education. Those who wanted more would not be forced to pay the full price of private education and the full tax burden of public education at the same time.

True parental choice is clearly an idea whose time has come, and it has been put in place in Milwaukee, Wisconsin, over the vehement protest of the education establishment and some civil rights groups. The plan was developed and implemented by an unlikely partnership between State Representative Polly Williams, the former Wisconsin chairman of liberal Jesse Jackson's presidential campaign, and conservative Republican Governor Tommy Thompson.

The plan, which has already cleared a court challenge, will allow parents of 1,000 low income public school students to receive a $2,500 voucher to pay for tuition at the private school of their choice. If the Milwaukee Plan (which does not currently include sectarian schools) is successful it will be expanded throughout Wisconsin.

Other programs like the Milwaukee Plan, and modifications of it, will be repeated over and over again all over America. By the year 2000 America will have firmly in place a free market educational system well on the way to returning quality to our classrooms. If 40 percent of our school systems move into the free market, I predict that the remainder will follow quickly.

The fight to establish the initial beachheads of quality education will be acrimonious and bloody. The old system cannot be reformed. Like communism, it must be replaced.

THE SUPREME COURT IN THE NINETIES

On July 20, 1990, 84-year-old Justice William Brennan resigned from the Supreme Court. This man was not just one more justice, but the intellectual leader of the Supreme Court liberal bloc which had pushed the judicial revision of the Constitution to its ultimate power.

Going into the 1990s, the court will be led by Chief Justice William Rehnquist, a strong conservative. It will also be influenced by two brilliant Roman Catholic conservatives, Justices Scalia and Kennedy. On most issues, Justice Sandra Day O'Connor can be counted in the conservative camp. If the strongly conservative Appeals Court Judge David Souter is confirmed by the Senate, there will exist a five vote conservative Supreme Court majority, to be frequently joined by Justice Byron White.

Both Justices Marshall and Blackmun are advanced in years and either could resign during the presidency of George Bush. If one or two younger conservatives were appointed to the court, there would be an overwhelming conservative presence on the court well into the twenty-first century.

With David Souter on board, in my opinion the court will, at its first opportunity, overturn the *Roe v. Wade* decision which in 1973 made abortion a constitutional right. Without a doubt, if the appropriate case is brought before them, the court may well reverse the tortured view of the establishment of religion clause of the First Amendment and lift the ban on prayer, Bible reading, and other expressions of religious belief in our public life.

This means that in the 1990s, the left will have lost its stronghold: the courts of America. And the power that has been accumulated for the left will more and more begin to serve conservative moral and social values.

However, courts customarily decide cases that have been brought to them by opposing parties. **During the 1990s, Christian pro-family, pro-life litigants have an increasingly positive opportunity to win lawsuits.** However, like the ACLU for the past 70 years, Christians must adopt a legal strategy which combines scholarly research with a strategic plan and powerful courtroom tactics.

The first major victory for the rights of students to observe their religious beliefs in the schools was decided by the Supreme Court on June 4, 1990, in a case titled *Mergens v. Westside Community School*. That case was funded by CBN through a legal foundation.

The case was argued and won at the Supreme Court by Jay Sekulow of CASE. Simply stated, in this landmark case the court ruled that the private expression of Bible study and prayer by a student club in an Omaha, Nebraska, high school did not constitute an impermissible establishment of religion under the First Amendment. The high court acknowledged the right of "equal access" for the religious interests of students by the same standards that sports or other extra-curricular activities are recognized.

This case will become a powerful weapon to stop the anti-Christian vendetta that has been waged incessantly in the schools of America. But a case or a law is no better than its enforcement; therefore, Christian people must be prepared to wage an ongoing and relentless battle against the educational establishment in every jurisdiction in America in support of the rights of Christian values in our schools.

Then there must be the preparation of the new cases to bring before the post-Brennan court to restore once again the legal foundation of the Judeo-Christian moral structure that this nation was built upon.

To this end, and in association with the Regent University Law School, CASE, and the Christian Coalition, CBN has established the American Center for Law and Justice to spearhead the exciting legal fight of the nineties.

TRIUMPH OF THE KINGDOM

The ten years from 1990 until the year 2000 will determine the destiny of America.

Despite our flaws, we are still the richest, most powerful nation on earth. We have more innovation, broader markets, a better standard of living, and greater opportunity than any place else on the globe. So far, the ships are still bringing the poor, huddled masses to our shores. They are not carrying them to other shores.

Beyond material things, America still has a vast tradition of faith, and the most vibrant and active church life of any developed country on earth. We may fail in literacy, but we rank number one among Western nations in spiritual faith and values.

It is ironic that these very Christians who are so despised by the secularists may be the only thing standing between them and the complete destruction of their way of life. Indeed, it can be said that the Christians and the Christian gospel are the early warning mechanism in any society, warning of the perils of rejecting God's standards, and urging moral self-control.

America can return to faith in God, individual initiative, and moral living. We can throw off the bondage of humanism, rid our institutions of the parasites which have been sapping our vitality, curb the excesses of big government, and turn the powerful engine of America's free enterprise system loose to pull us out of the current economic doldrums and into a new millennium filled with undreamed of technological and spiritual progress.

On the other hand, America can intensify its attacks on the Christian faith and spiritual values and, slowly and inexorably, watch its standard of living and its economic and political freedom be taken away and given to those who display the discipline and spiritual vision secular America so despises.

Christian people who have so loudly proclaimed that they are not interested in "politics" must realize that the decline in economic standards in America is not just going to affect the "heathen." The "dumbing of America" is not just going to affect the children of non-Christians. The rise in teen pregnancies and abortions in America is not merely for the unchurched. And the hand of some future conqueror of America will not rest only on those who have forsaken God.

Yet at the same time, we must be aware that the future of God's kingdom is not tied to Europe, America, the Middle East, Asia, or Africa. God's kingdom will triumph in the hearts of people. For Jesus said, "My kingdom is not of this world."

KNOWING THE DIFFERENCE

Although every one of the issues facing us—whether pornography, abortion, prayer in the schools, excessive government spending, or self-destructive foreign policy—may be very important for the moment, we must be careful that we do not identify the cause of Jesus Christ with passing, temporal concerns.

God's kingdom will stand whether or not people abort babies, read pornography, or desecrate the flag. God's kingdom will stand whether or not homosexuals proliferate in our society. We know that if abortion continues it will be hurtful to society and will ultimately bring God's wrath and judgment. We have a moral duty to speak out against evil, but we must make sure that our hope in Christ is at least as visible as our condemnation of sin.

Whatever we do as Christians in taking a stand against evil and abuse must reflect our faith in God and His right to judge evildoers. Even as we point out the evil, we must point out the kingdom of God. We must say the way of the world is death, but there is a better way!

The biblical way is against abortion. If children are unwanted, the solution is not abortion but adoption. Too often abortion has been a cheap, handy way of getting rid of the evidence of sin, or of killing off the child whose birth might force us to face up to adult responsibilities.

God's way is life. It is loving, caring families. It is a husband who loves his wife, and a wife who loves her husband; it is children brought up in the nurture and admonition of the Lord.

In the early Christian era, the Romans said of the Christians, look how they love one another! Coming from a pagan background and a violent and bloodthirsty culture, the Romans had never encountered such genuine love. They also said, they have such extraordinary women.

There was something about those Christians. The women weren't like the ordinary heathen women. They had a poise and a dignity, and a stability and radiance about them that was different.

That visible expression of Christianity from within was evidence of the light which would transform the world. It made Rome a Christian empire, and it allowed the Christian faith to span the globe. Christians today must live in that way. We have to proclaim the kingdom, and we have to point people to Jesus as the answer to the world's problems; then we must demonstrate our own faith in Him through exemplary living.

THE WAGES OF SIN

If the non-Christians, the ungodly, and the people who don't know Jesus continue in their sin, they will pay the price of that sin. If homosexuals continue in their homosexuality, they will commit genocide. Even without the implications of the AIDS epidemic, homosexuality is nothing short of self-extinction and suicide.

If the people who share that philosophy continue their self-destructive lifestyle, sooner or later their share of the population will die out. The same thing is true of abortion. Those who support the murder of the unborn will continue to kill off their own young, and sooner or later their share of the population will diminish and die out.

This is true of many other activities as well. Pornography is self-defeating. People who indulge in pornography desire more and more extremes of filth. Before long their perversion debases and destroys all their human relationships. It destroys their families, and it will destroy their lives.

Alcoholism, drug addiction, gambling, all these things will inevitably destroy the people who participate in them. In the depth of their self-destruction, such people will either realize that they must find a better way, or they will die. And, ultimately, they as a class of people will diminish because other people can see their self-destruction and will not want to participate in it.

There has to be a reaction sooner or later to homosexuality, adultery, abortion, alcoholism, drug addiction, the use of tobacco, and all the things the church has been saying are sin. It takes a few years sometimes; it may not happen overnight, but we are seeing signs of change.

Any time a society moves into blatant sexuality, especially into homosexuality and any type of sexuality in which the marriage vows are violated and there is widespread adultery, that nation can expect the judgment of God and the full weight of God's wrath against them.

From the beginning of time, any nation which has allowed itself to fall away from God and to fall into carnality and vice, and to continue willfully in that sin without national cleansing and repentance, that nation has suffered the scourge of degradation and disease and eventual destruction.

In the book of Leviticus, Chapter 18, there is a catalog of offenses so heinous they will not only cause a society to fall but will cause the land itself to "vomit out" its inhabitants. The list includes homosexuality, adultery, incest, bestiality, and the sacrifice of children. Every one of these offenses, with the exception of bestiality, is now rampant in America.

Either there will be a major national revival or there will be a national purging.

Have we gone so far that we cannot come back? No. Is there enough spiritual and moral strength in America to bring it back? Absolutely. Could there be a purging short of destruction and then a national restoration? It has happened before and can happen again.

Only God knows what the future holds for America, but this is certain. The decade of the 1990s will determine the future of America.

If God's people do not exert maximum effort in prayer, in evangelism, in education, in the courts, in the media, and in politics during this decade, America will have reached a point from which it cannot recover until after the massive judgment of God is visited upon it.

8

The Assault on the Family

Assaults on the traditional family by government and radical feminists have weakened the family.

In 1990 the traditional American family is neither in the majority or normative for others.

"MARRIAGE HAS EXISTED for the benefit of man; and has been a legally sanctioned method of control over women . . . we must work to destroy it. The end of the institution of marriage is a necessary condition for the liberation of women. Therefore, it is important for us to encourage women to leave their husbands. . . . All of history must be written in terms of the oppression of women. We must go back to ancient female religions like witchcraft."

So said the "Declaration of Feminism" drafted in Houston, Texas, in November 1971.

"In order to raise children with equality, we must take them away from families and communally raise them." So wrote D. Mary Jo Bane, assistant professor of education, Wellesley College and editor of *The Wellesley*.

"Overthrowing capitalism is too small for us. We must overthrow the whole f_____ patriarchy." So stated feminist activist Gloria Steinem, the editor of *Ms* magazine.

When asked what she thought of China's policy of compulsory abortion, Molly Yard, president of the National Organization of Women, was quoted in the October 10, 1989, issue of the *Washington Times* as saying, "I consider the Chinese government's policy among the most intelligent in the world."

Margaret Sanger, the founder of Planned Parenthood, which has received hundreds of millions of taxpayer dollars, wrote decades earlier, in her book, *Women and the New Race*, "The most merciful thing a large family can do to one of its infant members is to kill it."

To complete the anti-family, pro-feminist agenda, the appeal to women was not only to renounce marriage, murder children, overthrow capitalism, and seek spiritual insight from witchcraft. Sexual relations were to be transferred from heterosexual to homosexual.

In the January 1988 issue of the *National N.O.W. Times* were these words: "The simple fact is that every woman must be willing to be identified as a lesbian to be fully feminist."

THE MILITANTS

When I viewed films showing the uncontrollable rage of the National Organization of Women members against pro-life picketers at abortion clinics, I wondered what difference it should make to them whether women had babies or not. Frankly, I could not understand the pathological hatred of these militant feminists against unborn children.

Then one day I realized the answer: giving birth is the most feminine thing a woman can do. Motherhood is the most fulfilling activity a woman can ever enjoy. The radical feminists, especially the lesbians, realize instinctively that women who bear children have enormous emotional, psychological, and physical superiority over their radical counterparts. The real reason they oppose the birth of children is their agonizing desire to deny traditional women their clear advantage.

We have often heard that misery loves company. At our CBN phone centers we lovingly counsel some 2,000 gay and lesbian people every month. I can assure you that no homosexual is "gay." They and their lesbian sisters are among the most driven, confused, guilt-ridden, and miserable people on earth. To entertain their anti-family rhetoric and to give their lifestyle a legally protected place in our society is nothing short of lunacy.

NO MORE BEAVER CLEAVER

The typical American family of a wage-earner father, stay-at-home mother, and wholesome, mischievous, drug-free children was humorously portrayed in the very popular situation comedy, "Leave It to

Beaver." What we now know as the "Beaver Cleaver" family is no longer in the majority in America, nor is it any longer normative for all our families.

When President Jimmy Carter called for a "Conference on Families," many of us raised strenuous objections. To us there was only one family, that ordained by the Bible, with husband, wife, and children. But the White House was bowing to the realities of the day—homosexuals living together; couples living together outside of marriage; divorced men or women with children—all the non-traditional combinations now called families. So the government sponsored a conference on "families," not on "the family."

During the early part of this century, with one or two notable exceptions, every state had laws governing divorce that were based on biblical principles. The only biblical grounds for divorce and remarriage are adultery and desertion. It is obvious that physical cruelty is "constructive" desertion, and so were some types of mind destroying mental cruelty.

Each state recognized that stable families were the building blocks of society; therefore, state law protected marriages and made divorce difficult. To obtain a divorce it was necessary for the aggrieved spouse to prove legal "fault" on the part of the partner.

Beginning in 1970 in California, the first "no fault divorce" law was passed. A divorce could be granted on the petition of either party without proof of adultery, desertion, cruelty, or any fault. By the 1980s every state except South Dakota had some type of no-fault divorce laws.

According to the May 1990 issue of *The Family in America*, the divorce rate soared from 9.2 per thousand in 1960 to 20.3 per thousand in 1975.

With the *Roe v. Wade* decision in 1973, the number of legal abortions jumped from 100,000 in 1960 to 586,800 in 1972 and then to 1,409,650 in 1978. The number of illegitimate births climbed from 245,000 in 1962 to 400,000 in 1970, and to 448,000 in 1975. By 1988, one out of every four births in America was to an unwed mother, and 1,000,000 births were recorded to unmarried women.

THE FAMILY WAGE EARNER

In the traditional family, the father was the wage earner. Since he had the responsibility to support not only himself but a wife and several children, it was expected that his pay would exceed that of a single man or woman.

Of course, a man with a secure home and a wife caring for the children had a distinct advantage over a working woman, especially a working mother.

The feminists protested this supposed "discrimination" and in 1963 the Congress passed the Equal Pay Act and Title VII of the Civil Rights Act of 1964 which made payment of a "family wage" to male heads-of-household illegal.

Coupled with the anti-family rhetoric of the feminists and the release in 1969 of Paul Ehrlich's *The Population Bomb,* social planners in Washington, to quote Dr. Allan C. Carlson, ". . . opened a campaign against the fertility of the American people." As Dr. Carlson points out so cogently, "We get more of what we pay for and less of what we tax."

From the Vietnam War and President Lyndon Johnson's "Great Society" to the 1980s, the inflation burden on America's families rose rapidly, the tax burden on families with children went up about 225 percent, and male heads of families were placed at a competitive disadvantage.

Yet government welfare was now being generously extended to unmarried mothers with children. So the government got what it paid for—1,000,000 illegitimate children. It also succeeded in making motherhood so costly that couples began to have fewer children and many more women were forced to go to work.

The feminists also got what they asked for—a rapid breakup of families and along with it the pain and anguish of divorced women with children reduced to poverty, with no male family head or bread-winner.

As one woman put it, "A woman voting for divorce is like a turkey voting for Christmas."

THE DEATH OF A CULTURE

A report on the mounting dangers to the family in America prepared by the Washington, D.C.-based Family Research Council concludes that the negative trends which began in this country in the 1960s have not yet run their course. Citing the evidence of three decades of consistent decline, the report states that the outlook for the family for the rest of the 1990s is bleak.

The conclusions of the study show that the number of families headed by single women has increased 150 percent since 1960. Today, one in four families with children is headed by a single parent, and if the trend continues there will be 13 million single-parent households in this country by the end of the decade.

Perhaps even more disturbing, the number of illegitimate births has increased more than 300 percent since 1960. Yet that fact doesn't even reveal the true horror of the problem since unmarried women also have four out of five of the 1.6 million abortions in America each year.

The trend indicates that fully half of all births in America will be illegitimate by the end of this decade.

Today we are witnessing the disintegration of all the values we once considered "American virtues." The traditional family is in shambles; our culture is in a nosedive of moral decline; government is raping the American taxpayer through its own arrogant and self-absorbed greed; and the courts have legislated Judeo-Christian values out of American public life and, in effect, turned the nation over to the godless.

After a period of head-scratching and regrouping, conservative and religious Americans are beginning to realize that they are under assault. What is happening in America is not a debate, it is not a friendly disagreement between enlightened people. It is a vicious one-sided attack on our most cherished institutions.

Suddenly the confrontation is growing hotter and it just may become all out civil war. It is a war against the family and against conservative and Christian values.

Even as we are witnessing an ongoing crisis in the Middle East, we are engaged in a war in our midst of profound spiritual dimensions, and as stated so well by Gary Bauer, "To the victor goes the next generation of young Americans."

THE BREAKUP OF THE FAMILY

In his public addresses and writings, Gary Bauer, who is the president of the Family Research Council, has warned that the goal of the secular welfare state is to render the family obsolete and to usher in an age of "rule by experts." That is not surprising, but we have already seen that the consequences of secular rule without spiritual values can be disastrous.

Bauer says that modern history has shown us, over and over again, that "neither a free economy nor a strong national defense can be sustained without the Judeo-Christian bedrock. A nation of hedonists, incapable of postponing gratification, cannot resist the siren-song of big government; and a nation that smiles at the slaughter of its young, and leers at the degradation of the human person on the video screen, is probably doomed, in the long run, to go the way of Carthage."

It is truly shocking, by any standard, to see how the values of this nation have crumbled in such a short period of time. In 1950 the so-called nuclear family was based on the traditional model of one husband as the bread-winner, one wife at home, and a couple of children. At that time approximately 55 percent of all American families fit this model.

A couple of years ago, Bureau of Labor Statistics reports suggested that perhaps as few as 10 percent of all American families could be considered traditional. However, newer research from the Family Research Council suggests that about 39 percent of American families are traditional, in which the mother is the primary caregiver to her children; 18 percent are semi-traditional, where the children are continually cared for by at least one parent; 19 percent are careerist, meaning the children are regularly in day care; and 24 percent are single-parent families.

But regardless which standard you choose, the number of women working is continuously escalating. There is growing social pressure on mothers to work outside the home as well as a greater financial burden on the family which forces mothers into the workplace.

I fear that if this trend continues, it will take us to the point that as high as 90 percent of all married women will be working outside the home by the end of this century. What will that do to the family? What will it mean for the next generation of children?

The mere prospect offers a shocking vision of the future and has already had some far-reaching consequences. It does mean that the work force is expanded; it means that there are more skilled people in the work force, and that the pre-tax incomes of families will go up.

The median income of families in 1987 was just over 30,000 dollars. If the trend continues, the median family income could conceivably increase to as much as 50,000 dollars by the end of the decade. But there is another side to that promise. There will clearly be a direct impact on the structure of the family, and that will bring with it other far-reaching consequences.

THE UNCALCULATED COSTS

When you consider the relatively low pay most women receive, subtract taxes and the cost of transportation, extra clothing, cosmetics, meals at work, child care, and other related expenses, you discover that the actual take-home pay of the average working mother is insignificant.

Financial advisers Ron Blue and Russ Crosson have documented this fact in their research reports and books on the subject, suggesting that the actual net pay after expenses of the working mother is frequently no more than 1,900 to 2,000 dollars a year!

Even if most families haven't stopped to calculate such things, they know it's true when they discover that their two incomes have not actually improved the quality of their lives. Families who once thought the solution to their money problems would be for mom to work have discovered that suddenly they're deeper in debt than ever, they're no happier, and their kids are growing up with no mother, no father, and absolutely no sense of family.

Black Americans are at greatest risk. The Family Research Council report shows that 61 percent of all Black children are born out of wedlock, and 44 percent of all Black families are headed by a single woman. Those unfortunate trends suggest that by the end of the decade less than half of all Black families will be built on the traditional model of a married couple and children.

Since the first federally funded government welfare programs were introduced in the 1960s, teenage pregnancy, out-of-wedlock child birth, and abortions have skyrocketed. Value-free counseling and sex education has escalated the disintegration of the nuclear family at an astronomical rate.

It is as if the federal welfare system has set out to put government in the place of father and mother in the home. At the current frightening pace, Bauer states, "The family may soon be void of any significant role in society."

Even more compelling, we should be horrified that what we have created, instead of more security or greater affluence, is a day-care system which, without question, is harmful to children.

Every sociological test that has been taken for years has indicated that prolonged absence of either parent is damaging to children. Prolonged absence of the father or of the mother leads to dependency, lack of assertiveness, submission to peer pressure, susceptibility to drugs, inferior performance in school.

In addition, the increase of women in the work force has put ever greater strain on marriages. At this point, the financial and career ambitions of women equals that of men.

Just like the competitiveness and the stress and strain of the workplace, competition also develops in the home over which partner makes the greater contribution, which job takes precedence, and which roles various partners should take with regard to child care, housework, and all the various responsibilities of mothers and fathers in the home.

It is obvious that even greater strain is placed on women who feel a responsibility to be not only good employees but good mothers; the so-called "Super Mom" complex. In order for a woman to work, to maintain a home, and to look after her children, she has to have incredible endurance and resolve. All those demands can get to be nerve-wracking, and in many homes it leads to broken marriages and ruined lives.

If you look at the leading causes of divorce in this country you will discover that "lack of communication" is often listed as the number one reason. People just don't talk to each other. But it should be obvious that if they're not home at the same time, and especially if they're working shifts where they don't even get to see each other, then lack of communication is inevitable.

BECOMING STRANGERS

The nature of the work environment means that both husband and wife are now receiving most of their emotional and intellectual stimulation outside the home, in the workplace, and from different groups of people who never meet or interact with each other.

Given that situation, it's not hard at all to understand how a husband and wife can quickly become estranged from each other and from each other's friends, and how their conversations (which seem to grow fewer and fewer) reflect that differing input, different circle of friends, and different frames of reference.

When they do focus on the things they have in common, it is often only to solve problems with their children, the home, or their mounting debts. It's not the kind of loving interaction and kinship that brought them together in the first place.

The second leading cause of divorce is financial. Strains in relations due to bills and mounting debts and disputes over the allocation of funds are a genuine problem. And they become more and more problematical as the partners each have their own income, and as they squabble over who gets what.

Today the divorce rate has skyrocketed. For every two marriages formed in America, one marriage ends in divorce. There are more and more people these days who are chronic divorce victims, who may go through four or five marriages. The divorce rate is up 700 percent since the turn of the century.

The strain this puts on people's lives is unbelievable. Next to the death of a spouse, divorce is one of the most traumatic experiences anyone can have. The feelings of inadequacy, of failure, and of guilt can go on eating at both these individuals for years. But perhaps even worse, the damage to the children is beyond calculation.

I think everybody recognizes this fact, and we want the best for our children, but couples grow so embittered toward each other they willingly jeopardize the future welfare of their own children. In one survey I saw recently, even though the warring parents recognized, and freely admitted, that a divorce would damage their kids, 75 percent of them said they would go ahead and get the divorce, which shows again the selfishness and lack of commitment that can develop in a damaged marriage.

The awful trends these statistics are setting in motion are a shame and a scandal. The epidemic of shattered families and broken homes in this nation is producing a generation of emotionally and psychologically impaired young people who will, in turn, grow up to be adults who will be getting married with less and less commitment to marriage, which in turn will produce future generations even more impaired, and without a healthy sense of love or bonding. We can only wonder where it will end.

THE PATHOLOGY OF DAY CARE

I can't help but think of the seminal studies of Professor Harry Harlow and his team of behavioral researchers at the University of Wisconsin in the 1950s. Harlow discovered that little baby monkeys, when deprived of their birth mothers, would frantically cling for comfort and protection to stuffed mother substitutes. He learned that, even though the baby monkey could be fed from a wire mannikin, the infant would cling, when frightened, to the comforting, padded surrogate mother.

We know that infants deprived of the affection of a mother—and it is equally true for monkeys and humans alike—will become sick and die. The lesson is quite simple: we cannot live without love.

Any child who does not have a mother with it, especially in the early days, is deprived. In a research project at Regent University, we found that day care doesn't work, whether it's institutional day care, church-run day care, skilled franchised day care, or company-provided day care. It is absolutely certain that government-run day care will be devastating to little children.

It doesn't work because institutional day care does not provide the same support and psychological nurturing that a mother can give.

A few years ago we came up with an alternative child care program at CBN called Mother's Touch, in which a woman would take as many as six or seven children into her home during the day. The woman is very much like a loving aunt or grandmother to the children in an environment psychologists call *in loco parentis;* that is, "in the place of" parents.

We found that, unlike institutional day care, those situations worked very nicely. We believe it was successful because the element of nurturing and one-on-one affection and reinforcement was diligently provided for each child.

For years we have known that children need natural, one-on-one reinforcement. Each child must know that, to someone, and hopefully to his mother, he is the most special person in the world. The child needs warm, loving attention. When he says, "Mommy, look at me!" he is begging for that nod of approval, for that look that says, "Yes, my precious child, you are special to me." But group day care does not provide that.

After a remarkably short period of time, even little children grow cold and withdrawn. In some cases they grow shy, their personalities become stunted. Still others react in the opposite extreme by becoming loud and assertive and demanding.

As if they have given up on love and affection, many children confined in day care institutions for years become angry and antisocial. There're not enough bad things I can say about what day care does to children.

A new survey co-sponsored by the American Academy of Pediatrics and *Working Mother* magazine recently reported that medical professionals recognize that day care is especially harmful to children age three and under. Of the 1,100 pediatricians polled in the survey, more than two-thirds said they believe day care is harmful for children under six months; 61 percent said it may be harmful for children six months to one year old; and more than half, 52 percent, believe it is still harmful for children aged one to three.

That is strong evidence from a purely secular source. But sadly, the typical response of working mothers is to say they will simply demand better day care instead of saying they will give their children what the child wants—and needs—most in the world: its own mother.

Toward the end of its lengthy focus on the day care issue, *Newsweek* magazine actually confessed that infants in day care for 20 or more hours a week are at risk. The researchers said that the high turnover rate of paid caregivers and the high disease rate among institutionalized children make day care a very uncertain and unhappy place for children.

"Despite the compelling evidence about the dark side of day care," the magazine reported, "many experts say there's a great reluctance to discuss these problems publicly." Why? "Because they're afraid the right wing will use this to say that only mothers can care for babies, so women should stay home."

As so aptly expressed by Phyllis Schlafly in her April 1990 newsletter, "What the liberals and the feminists are really afraid of is not the right wing but the eternal truth that the traditional family is still the best way to live, and that babies still need mothers in the home."

The long range effects of the neglect and mistreatment of our young people is going to be the creation of a whole generation of people who will be lacking in commitment, shallow in their personalities, and unable to form lasting bonds and attachments. That may translate into an inability to form bonds with their business associates, their fellow employees, and with their community; or with their nation.

How will that affect our long-range ability to defend a country, to make sacrifices in terms of taxes, or to give the time and energy it takes to run a complex society? The prospect is frightening.

How sad to think that it comes down to the fact that we have become a consumer-oriented, greed-driven society whose motivations and morals are based on the acquisition of things, and the inevitable accumulation of enormous amounts of debt. And the commonly accepted belief, even among Christians, is that the way to accumulate the things that pay off the debts is for the wife to go to work.

THE HIGH PRICE OF FULFILLMENT

This is, in part, the legacy of the feminist movement which says, "Do your own thing, Baby. You are the New Woman. Fulfill yourself!" They are not willing to recognize that a commitment to the next generation is more important than fulfilling your own desires right now. For what does it profit a man or a woman if they gain the whole world but lose their own soul, and destroy the souls of their innocent children on the way down?

I readily acknowledge that some women do have to work. I also recognize that women without children and women whose children are grown may want to get involved in a career for many reasons.

However, let's be sure we understand that the problem we will have to face in the '90s is not that some women work, but that women who should be home nurturing and building the next generation are worshiping, instead, at the shrine of materialism: the lust for bigger and better and more, and lots more of it.

Indeed, as I illustrated above, many women have to work. They have no choice. But many do not have to work. These women must recognize that the nurture and training of the next generation is *the most important career any human being can have.*

Having so many mothers in the workplace now means that there is inadequate day care for the children of working mothers. So the government's new solution is to spend 23 billion dollars more of taxpayer money to provide for the children in day care. This in turn will bring on more inflation and force more women into the workplace.

Long range, children without commitment, latchkey children, children who are pregnant out of wedlock, children who begin sexual activity at age 12 or 13, children who are drinking alcohol at 11 or 12, teenage alcoholics and drug addicts, and other problems too outrageous to mention, can be traced directly to family breakup, poor home life, and the absence of both parents during the crucial formative years.

An article in the *Los Angeles Times* in September 1989—citing research in the journal, *Pediatrics*—reported that "latchkey" children, whether from rich or poor families, are twice as likely to use cigarettes, alcohol, and marijuana as youngsters cared for by adults after school. Yet 40 percent of children under 13—somewhere between 2 million and 6 million—go home to an empty house after school.

These reports may be low because parents are reluctant to admit that their young children have no adult supervision. Because of the growing problem of divorce, which has left an estimated 14.6 million children with single parents, there will be an ever increasing number of at risk, unsupervised young children.

GATEWAY TO DESPAIR

The impact of drugs and drug abuse on the American family does not seem to be going away. The casual attitude of many people toward so-called "recreational drugs" has had terrible consequences.

The 1988 Bureau of Justice Statistics Sourcebook reported that over 60 percent of people between the ages of 18 and 25 say they have used marijuana and 25 percent have used cocaine at least once.

Among Americans aged 26 to 34, 58.5 percent have used marijuana and 24.1 percent have used cocaine. This says that the younger you are, the more likely you are to experiment with marijuana or cocaine at some time. But it also says that getting drugs is easy, and a lot of people are doing it.

Even while many people say they do not consider such statistics a problem, there is a dramatic positive correlation between drugs and crime, and each year the evidence becomes more damning. Between 1974 and 1986 the proportion of state prisoners under the influence of an illegal drug at the time of the offense for which they were incarcerated increased from 25 to 35 percent. The number under the influence of cocaine alone increased from 1 percent to 10.7 percent.

The Bureau reports that typically the first use of drugs among prisoners surveyed was at age 15. The typical "user" first became a steady user at age 18. Even more distressing is the information gathered from users in juvenile facilities, where 19 percent said they first used drugs before age 10, and 40 percent said they were using before age 12.

The number of people convicted of drug possession in this country more than doubled from 1980 to 1988, while the number convicted for sale or manufacture of drugs went up 180 percent, from just under 103,000 in 1980 to 287,858 in 1988. This bad news affects every city and town in America, and involves every law enforcement agency.

The Federal Government seized 4,175 clandestine drug laboratories between 1975 and 1988. In 1988 alone, 810 labs were seized; 107 million marijuana plants were destroyed in 38,531 plots, leading to 6,062 arrests and the seizure of 2,034 weapons. In that same year, the Drug Enforcement Agency (DEA) confiscated 125,000 pounds of cocaine, 2,000 pounds of heroin, 73 pounds of opium, and 1.2 million pounds of marijuana.

Add to that the U.S. Customs Service seizure of 1.7 million pounds of marijuana, 87,900 pounds of cocaine and close to 4 million dosage units of LSD and other barbiturates; plus the Coast Guard's confiscation of 356,000 pounds of marijuana and 9,000 pounds of cocaine. The total number of suspects prosecuted for drug offenses escalated from 7,003 in 1980 to 17,729 in 1987, an increase of 153 percent.

What will it take for America to wake up to the danger of playing with drugs? A National Institute of Justice survey of 20 cities reports that from one fourth to one third of all males arrested in 1988 tested positive for marijuana.

In New York City, 75 percent of males and 74 percent of females arrested tested positive for cocaine. And of the juveniles incarcerated for violent crimes in 1986, 60 percent reported being regular drug users and 40 percent were under the influence of drugs at the time they committed the crime for which they were incarcerated.

THE WAY OUT

How many times have we heard bureaucrats scream, "We must educate the people to the dangers of drugs"? How many billions of dollars have we poured down the drains of federal bureaucracy? And why do we keep on thinking that education in the hands of federal bureaucrats will ever change the situation? Don't the statistics speak for themselves?

You don't have to be a genius to see that the billions we have thrown at "education" have failed to produce results. It is perfectly clear that drug use is worse now than ever, that alcoholism is on a crazy upward spiral, that drug- and alcohol-related crime show no signs of slowing down.

Every public and private agency in the world has been "educating" the American public to the dangers of tobacco for more than a decade. We have all seen every imaginable kind of media and advertising crusade telling Americans that smoking will cause cancer in long-term habitual users, yet nearly a third of all Americans continue to smoke.

Smokers interviewed about the obvious dangers of their habit say they know it is deadly, they know they are at risk, but they are willing to take the risk. In other words, they have the education, they know the facts, but it hasn't changed their lives.

Alcoholics know the dangers of alcohol abuse. Many of them, in similar interviews, say they know that driving under the influence of alcohol is dangerous and deadly, and they know they are at risk. They even know that alcoholism causes conflict in the home and broken marriages. But they continue to drink and to drive and to put lives in jeopardy because they cannot stop.

Either they believe they are in command when they are not, or they have accepted the fact that the habit owns them, or else they just don't care who they hurt.

Education has not changed them. So why is government telling us, "We need more education"? The answer to all these questions is the same. The federal bureaucracy doesn't have a clue. They have no idea what to do, because the answer does not lie in education or training or demonstration of the facts. Fundamental changes in the desires of the human heart are God's territory.

Changing lives is ultimately a profound philosophical and theological matter. It is an issue which can only be dealt with through submission of our own wills to the will of God.

PROTECTING OUR FUTURE

Unless there is a dramatic change in our habits and beliefs, there really is not a great deal of hope for the children of America in the next decade. The United States Department of Health and Human Services, which monitors the incidence and prevalence of abuse and neglect of children, has released figures which show that child abuse is increasing at an alarming rate in this country.

In their 1988 study, the figures showed that cases of maltreatment had increased 66 percent since 1980, with an increase of 74 percent in cases of physical and sexual abuse.

Some 63 percent of the cases reported in that study involved neglect, which means that out of every 1,000 children, 15.9 were reported as victims of neglect: 1,003,600 children. Another 43 percent suffered from abuse, which is 10.7 children in 1,000 and a total of 675,000 children reported.

The incidence of the sexual abuse of children has tripled since 1980. The sad fact is, this is only the tip of the iceberg. These are only the cases which are actually reported and which pass the government's screening verification processes. What must the actual numbers be?

When we look at the implication of such studies in the context of the overall cultural and spiritual climate of this nation, we have to recognize that it all comes back to the same foundation: selfish, egotistical self-interest.

Since the early 1970s the trend has been to ever greater levels of selfishness, materialism, addiction to sex, alcohol and drugs, the breakdown of the family, and the destruction of the natural bonding between parents and children.

Responsibility, restraint, concern for the welfare of others, and the kind of maturity that considers the future consequences of our actions seems to be missing in a huge segment of our society.

The type of self-indulgence we are seeing in this country today doesn't even stop at self-destruction; it even seeks to destroy others, and to eliminate the inconveniences created by its own excesses. That is the real sin at the heart of the abortion problem in this country.

MORAL ACTIVISM

The Bible makes it clear that we must lift the yoke of oppression. If we see a wrong being committed, we have a positive obligation to do something about it. In the Old Testament we read that anyone seeing his neighbor's ox in a ditch was supposed to go to the ox and pull it out. Certainly if we see an animal in trouble and have an obligation to help it, how much more do we have an obligation to help protect innocent children, to prevent them from being abused and, in the case of abortion, from being killed?

In the days of slavery, if a slave owner was seen whipping or abusing his slave, any Christian had an obligation to speak out about it. Slavery was a very old custom—as old as civilization—but there came a time when men and women of faith saw that they had to try to do something to change the laws to protect the people who had been enslaved.

Did Christians have an obligation to get involved in the legal processes? Yes. Were they responsible for doing their part to shut down slavery, which was a violation of human dignity? Absolutely.

It should be a symbol of just how far the values of this nation have fallen to see, as readers of the magazine *Christian Century* recently did, the comments of America's first suffragettes and feminists on the issue of abortion. A notice placed by a group called Feminists for Life of America quoted several of those early leaders and their opinions on the issue.

Susan B. Anthony, for example, said, "I deplore the horrible crime of child murder . . . No matter what the motive, love of ease, or a desire to save from suffering the unborn innocent, the woman is awfully guilty who commits the deed. . . ." And Elizabeth Cady Stanton, in a letter to her friend Julia Ward Howe, wrote, "it is degrading to women that we should treat our children as property to be disposed of as we see fit."

The essential morality of that earlier time was not due to the fact that men and women were better. Certainly children were conceived out-of-wedlock and at inconvenient times then as now. The women were not less militant; each of those women pointed out the complicity of the men in the conception and the abortion. But there was a foundation of morality, inherited from a Christian tradition, that set the natural frame of reference.

It is only now, in this modern and increasingly godless age, that women like Molly Yard and Jane Fonda dare claim that women have a "moral right" to murder their young.

THE LOST WILL AND TESTAMENT

As America has observed the birth and growing up of the enormous generation commonly called "The Baby-Boomers," we have witnessed the making of a generation of Americans who, to a large extent, have been unwilling to make the kinds of traditional family commitments society has always been based upon.

Instead of marriage, they have opted for "living together." Instead of child-rearing and the building of families, they have opted for promiscuous pre-marital and a-marital sex. Facing the prospect of conception, they have used birth control devices of every description and, failing that, they have resorted ultimately to abortion.

Many of the men and women of this generation have shunned the traditional male and female roles, refused traditional adult responsibilities, rejected the bearing of children in order to persist in a prolonged emotional adolescence and self-absorption. It is more than just a joke that they have surrounded themselves with every kind of creature comfort and every conceivable luxury that money and a Visa Gold Card can buy on time.

This huge demographic segment of the population, the pig in the python so to speak, is working its way through our system and is going to come to retirement age during the first and second decades of the new millennium; that is, from 2010 to 2020.

However, some rather mundane and practical issues have to be examined before that prospect can become reality. The only guarantee of a man or woman's retirement is the existence of a large, active work force: that is, their own children and grandchildren, who will be paying into the Social Security system (and various other retirement programs) in order to make their retirement possible.

Wouldn't it be one of those tragic ironies of life if those people who have opted for pleasure now, who have failed to make commitment or to invest in a family, to raise and nurture children, or to spend the time it takes to bring them up with love, will have no one to care for them in their old age?

Wouldn't it be ironic if those same people discovered their need of a family to help provide for their future, but there just wasn't anyone around to take care of them? They may well be the first generation to come to the point where the working young will say, "Enough! We refuse to support you." And those old hedonists who have sunk their life savings into their personal fulfillment and self-gratification may be reduced to abject poverty.

A May 1990 report in *Newsweek* indicated that the Social Security system is already under incredible strain as the numbers of contributing workers in America declines and the number of recipients continues to grow. In 1950 the ratio of workers to retirees was 120 to 1. At the current rate, the ratio will fall to only 2 workers per retiree by the year 2030.

And since they have been such vocal advocates of abortion and euthanasia, wouldn't it be ironic if some kind of government-sponsored euthanasia program is signed into law just in time to make sure they won't have to hang around too long in their lonely and miserable retirement years? We don't have to summon up the fable of the grasshopper and the ant to realize that this predicament is one of the results of hedonism.

The unwillingness to make commitments because they are afraid of what might happen, along with the desire to "fulfill" themselves, may well condemn an entire generation to a cold and lonely demise.

Their unwillingness to invest in the future is the very vehicle that will bring them into a pathetic and helpless old age. The joy and the light of men and women in their later years has always been their children and grandchildren: the family unit. These people will not have a family unit. I'm afraid there will be a great many elderly who will reap this whirlwind.

RETURNING HOME

But perhaps there is yet hope. Already I am seeing a definite trend among some of our young people to experience the rewards of a loving home, to give of themselves instead of always taking from others, and to discover the joys of traditional family life before it's too late.

Today we are seeing women in their thirties, young women reaching the other end of their child-bearing years, suddenly opting to take off from work to start a family. Motherhood is coming back "in." The maternity wards are beginning to get crowded; and fashions seem to be more feminine.

A recent study by the Population Reference Bureau in Washington reported that America has entered a new baby boom. Demographer Carl Haub was quoted in a syndicated news release as saying, "It does appear to be a real upswing in U.S. fertility."

The highest fertility rate in recent history was recorded in 1957, when the average was 3.77 births per woman of childbearing age. That rate dropped to its lowest point in 1976, at 1.76 births per woman. Unexpectedly, it moved up to 2 births per woman in 1989 and it looks as if it may well exceed that average for the next several years.

Gregory Spencer, of the United States Census Bureau, told reporters his department was caught off guard by the sudden increase in births in this country. "The last couple of years have surprised everybody," he said. Now, the demographers believe we are seeing a genuine trend. "People are really saying they don't want to be childless," said Spencer.

Women are having more children, and women in the Christian community are leading the way. As of this year, I am the grandfather of nine gorgeous children, and every one of them is beautiful and bright! If my sons and daughters are in any way representative of their peers and the other Christian moms and dads around the country, maybe some of our young couples are recognizing the importance of the family.

On the other hand, it is still a tragedy that so many women deferred child-bearing too long. In some cases, they may have had an abortion and since discovered that the abortion rendered them unable to bear children. There are many women who are incapable of having children because of abortions.

For years we have seen that it is more difficult to have children, and that the dangers of birth defects are increased substantially for women over 40. However, a new study by Dr. Henry Klapholtz of Boston's Beth Israel hospital suggests that women who keep fit, who are free of addictions, and who have good physical and emotional health may continue to conceive and bear healthy children even after 40.

Thanks to the fitness trend, more women in their 30s and 40s are staying trim and eating healthy food, but it is still a struggle to keep fit after 40. Having a first child after 30 can be difficult and, however you look at it, after 40 the risks are increased.

A CHRISTIAN MONOPOLY

Bill Gothard, who heads a number of excellent family-centered ministries in this country, has been teaching pastors the importance of communicating to their congregations the blessedness of having children. The whole concept of fruitfulness in the Bible context is that the family is a blessing from God.

The psalmist wrote, "Sons are a heritage from the Lord, children a reward from him. Like arrows in the hands of a warrior are sons born in one's youth." Everything about the Bible indicates that fruitfulness is God's blessing.

It seems abundantly clear to me that those who are political liberals—those who are left of center, and those who are atheists—are intent on destroying themselves. The pro-abortion crowd is essentially committing suicide.

The statistics show that it takes 2.1 live births per woman in a country such as the United States to maintain a population at a steady pace. We are now at about 1.9 per thousand in America, so the rate of growth is actually declining. We have already seen that it is equally low in industrialized Europe.

Allan Carlson told me that his studies for the Rockford Institute showed that the only people who want to have children are those who have a strong religious faith. Muslims, Christians, and certain other groups fit this description because they have confidence in the future. Because they believe in a Supreme Being, they are willing to take a chance on the future by bringing children into the world; they have the conviction that there really is a future and a hope. There is something better.

Those who have no religious faith say, this life is all there is. Why should I invest in the future if the future doesn't matter? I had better grab all the gusto I can get, because I only go around once. I might as well have fun and take care of number one. I deserve a break today.

Ever notice how the advertising is all focused on that very self-indulgent, self-gratifying hedonism? But the hedonism is a function of atheism, which says that I am the center of my universe. Looking out for myself and giving myself pleasure is, after all, the ultimate aim of life. So if I can find pleasure for myself and achieve self-actualization, then I will have achieved the goal of my life!

What a sad, disappointing way of life. What an unfortunate legacy to have given an entire generation on this planet. You only have to look at nature to realize that the goal of any biological species is to reproduce itself. Any plant or flower that is sterile is a biological failure.

It's an irony that the greatest sex symbol of the '50s and '60s, Marilyn Monroe, couldn't even bear children. She was a "sex goddess," but she couldn't do what sex was about: namely, reproduce.

But among all these ironies, there is one other which should not escape our notice. If Christians continue having large families and do not have abortions, our percentage of the population is going to rise dramatically, just on the basis of birth-rate alone.

Those who are our philosophical adversaries are deliberately committing genocide. They are doing away with their young, they are not reproducing themselves, and it is only a matter of time until their kind dies out completely. Certainly homosexuality should die out since the homosexuals are unable to reproduce themselves.

Christians and all those who believe in God, in the blessings of life and in the wonder of God's creation, along with all those who love children and want to share their lives with their families, will continue to prosper and their philosophies will grow stronger as their numbers increase. The future is on our side.

I am not in favor of self-inflicted genocide even for the adversaries of Christianity. But nevertheless, as their numbers decrease, our numbers will increase, and our influence will continue to grow.

SOME PRACTICAL SOLUTIONS

Several years ago two young teenagers in a suburb of Los Angeles brutally murdered a young man and his girlfriend who were attending a public sports event at an outdoor stadium. The murderers then sauntered nonchalantly to a MacDonald's restaurant where they ate a "cheeseburger, french fries, and a coke."

There was no guilt. No remorse. Two promising young lives were extinguished in a pool of blood, and these young killers calmly ate cheeseburgers.

Such unfeeling brutality is not unusual in our land any more. I once ministered to a professional killer on death row at the maximum security prison in Raeford, Florida. This young man, under age thirty, had murdered twenty people and not once had he ever cried. Not once, that is, until he experienced the love and forgiveness of Jesus Christ and was born again.

These young people have grown up without hugs, without kisses, without attention, without care. Often the only contact they receive with adults is through physical or mental abuse. They are emotional zombies, lacking human feelings. What they can do to other human beings is horrible to contemplate.

The children of divorce and those who grow up in day care institutions are not that bad, but they are clearly stunted, short of their full potential. **Something has to be done to restore the traditional families in America. Unless drastic changes are made now, by the year 2000 a generation will be lost.**

Here are a few proposals that merit consideration:

First, we should do away with no-fault divorce and, again, make it difficult for couples to sever the bonds of marriage.

Second, we must reward stable families with financial incentives. I believe that tax deductions of up to $5,000 per child and tax sheltered educational Individual Retirement Accounts (IRA) will be an enormous incentive for families with children.

Third, there should be tax credits to reward women who wish to be homemakers. If we can give tax deductions for child care expense for working mothers, we can certainly afford tax benefits for women who want to stay home and care for their children.

Fourth, welfare laws that deny benefits when there is a "man in the house" should be revoked. We cannot allow welfare to become a disincentive for family formation.

Fifth, there should be no welfare benefits for unwed mothers. Those teenage girls who receive welfare should not be able to use welfare to leave their parents' home and establish their own residence. Welfare checks should no longer be viewed as a benefit for illegitimacy.

There should be reward, not punishment, if a girl who has a baby out of wedlock decides to marry the child's father.

Sixth, men who father children should be forced to support their own children. The burden should be theirs, not society's.

Finally, this society must be taught that sex before marriage, adultery, and abortion are sinful and wrong. People must be taught that God hates divorce. They must learn that only through stable, loving marriages where children are raised in the "nurture and admonition of the Lord" can this nation rise to its potential and be spared anarchy and heartbreak.

An entire generation of children are now clearly at risk in America.

Part III

2000
AND BEYOND

We have in our power the ability to conquer disease, to extend life, to remove genetic abnormalities, to supply a reasonably abundant standard of living to every human being on this planet, to bring forth an ever increasing cornucopia of technological products to make each of our lives more pleasant, to have at our disposal increased learning, culture, and leisure.

Today we are citizens of a new and different world. As we cast our eyes from East to West we see new allies and new adversaries on every horizon. Furthermore, we are no longer an island, for the world has come to our shores to buy and sell, to proselyte, and to live.

9

Technology and the Environment

Major technological advances await us in the next millennium. At the forefront will be discoveries to unlock the potential of the human mind and spirit.

The primacy of environmental concerns may hinder technology and prove a front for massive new governmental spending and intrusion into our lives.

WHEN CANADIAN SCHOLAR Marshall McLuhan coined the phrase "the global village" in 1964, he had no idea just how soon or how relentlessly the new media technology would circle the globe.

Along with the newest rage for fax machines, cellular phones, answering machines, compact disc players, VCRs, Nintendo and Atari games, and wide-screen TV, we now have sophisticated cable systems, and backyard satellite dishes bringing entertainment into family rooms all over the world.

In more and more American homes you now see personal computers connected to modems connected to libraries, consumer bulletin boards, information services, shopping services, stock brokers, and news retrieval sources nationwide. People are banking with automatic teller machines, by telephone and computer, and suddenly McLuhan's prophecy has come true in the most unbelievable way.

In March 1990, *Scientific American* reported on the broad range of information technologies already in our grasp. From "minitel" computerized telephone systems, like those being used in France, to the high-tech online funds transfer networks—such as the SWIFT system, which is engaged in the exchange of hundreds of billions of dollars every single day—the range of technology we're already using is mind-boggling.

Not only does the presence of all this sophisticated technology change the way we communicate with each other, but it changes the way we work. Today thousands of people are working from their homes, using technology to link up with their employers, customers, and suppliers.

The new technology has also allowed American business to focus heavily on information and service-based activities. Today nearly 75 percent of the entire labor force in America is employed in the service sector, compared to only 55 percent in the years right after the Second World War.

Communications and related systems for information delivery are the biggest things on the industrial horizon; and the biggest thing on the communications horizon is fiber optics. Those tiny filaments of dense fiber are incredibly efficient conductors of light, and therefore, they can also transmit all kinds of data in a highly efficient way.

Over a period of time, as it is mechanically and economically feasible, telephone companies will replace traditional cable with fiber optic cable as their primary delivery system for information, and at that point I believe we are going to see a whole new era of communications technology.

In combination with the power of fiber optic transmission of information, satellite links will become more and more sophisticated. Soon we will be leap-frogging voice, data, and image transmission from huge satellites around the world. We're just on the threshold of having access to the types of satellites that can do this.

There will soon be antennae no larger than a couple of panes of glass, which means that every home will have access to satellite. Satellite transmission will leap across national boundaries and physical barriers so that there will be increasingly broader global communication.

We can do it now of course—three satellites can cover the world—but the new satellite-to-home transmitters are going to be much more powerful than anything we have seen before.

FASTER, MORE AFFORDABLE

The information-bearing capacity of optical fibers is skyrocketing with each new stratum of research. We have read that the newest cable can transmit one trillion bits of information per second; at the same time, the cost of manufacturing and installing the cable continues to fall.

One of the marvelous curiosities of the technology boom is that as the technology becomes more powerful it also becomes more affordable.

Successful innovations attract a consumer base almost instantaneously in today's economic climate, which allows industry, in turn, to continue development and to reduce costs.

From a broadcaster's perspective, the programming opportunities are really exciting. Very soon it will be possible to send out several thousand programs simultaneously, which will give viewers a tremendous diversity of programming to choose from. People will be able to access motion pictures, educational programs, or whatever they want, around the clock.

This means, in turn, that the three major networks in America will continue to lose audience and power. Combined, they're already down to maybe 60 percent of the audience, and I predict that figure will drop very soon below 50 percent.

Not only will cable take more of the audience, but the satellite in the sky and the Baby Bells, the telephone companies with their fiber optic delivery systems, will all be major players.

At present we have the capacity to put one picture in the sky and sideband a number of audio tracks so that one message—one motion picture or one program—can be seen by multitudes and heard in their own language.

This also means that there will be a huge demand for software. I think there will be a broad proliferation of film companies in the years just ahead. The public demand for programming on these high quality delivery systems will be an absolute monster, devouring everything we can produce.

GLOBALIZING THE MEDIA

From a Christian standpoint, the opportunities are just enormous to produce movie and video programming. In the coming decade we will see the formation of new production companies creating very sophisticated motion picture materials. This is why we have such a strong film department at Regent University. We are training people to do films. Many of our graduates are already producing films, and we are in the process of establishing a fairly large motion picture company to do this kind of work.

Through our International Family Entertainment group, we are in partnership now with producers in France, Canada, and Australia. We have produced a major series in Japan. In the coming years there will be a globalization of this kind of activity.

We have seen the Japanese coming into America to buy up companies like Columbia so they can have access to their libraries of motion pictures. But I also see creative talent coming out of the East Bloc nations as well, and out of Europe and other parts of the world, beginning to challenge U.S. filmmakers on costs and quality.

Again, from a Christian standpoint, there is a hunger now for high quality programs that have family values. The emerging nations do not want the sex, crime, and violence that is so typical of American television. They want high quality shows, but they don't have them available.

So much of today's European fare is extraordinarily dull. They haven't had the production budgets necessary to move into the type of massive motion pictures that the United States is familiar with. The new Europe will become a huge market for quality films in the coming decade.

RETIRING THE GATEKEEPERS

Until now, about 200 writers, producers, and directors in Hollywood have determined what people around the world get to see and believe. They have been the gatekeepers and, by and large, not very good ones. That will have to change.

Global competition will diminish the role of the old gatekeepers and bring in new ones with fresh ideas and better character. In the future there will be much more diversity.

With the emergence of the new technologies there will also be many more gatekeepers to help ensure quality programming. The new writers, producers, and directors, must have a clearer vision of their message. Ultimately they will provide many more opportunities for the kinds of productions the world wants to see.

If the Christian church will take advantage of the technology, it can have at its disposal delivery systems for high-quality programming that have been virtually undreamed of in the past.

IMPROVING THE VISION

It is clear that we will be moving into high definition television that will be crystal clear, much more beautiful than anything we have imagined, and much more realistic. Consumers will have not only compact disc audio, but compact disc video, which means that soon people will be able to record on disc at home. That means program producers can, in turn, dramatically simplify the distribution of programs to the world.

Compact disc technology provides incredible quality. In recorded music, in digital imagery, in compact data storage, and in speed of access, the compact disc has opened up entirely new horizons. That trend will continue in the decade ahead.

Right now the proliferation of video recorders is very high. In the Middle

East, in Africa, in Eastern Europe, everywhere you go, people have video recorders because the state television has been so bad that the people have come up with their own alternative sources.

PIRATING THE GOSPEL

There is already a fabulous market in the Third World for any kind of videos. We produce a series of programs for the Japanese market called *SuperBook* and *Flying House*. These are animated Bible stories for children that were produced in Japan for CBN. We have heard that today they are the best-selling videos in Turkey, a Muslim country.

Basically, local entrepreneurs have pirated our programs! They are reproducing them without any kind of copyright license fees and they are selling them in video stores and kiosks all over the country. Consequently, hundreds of thousands of people are watching Bible stories and hearing the gospel in their homes because we have entered into the channels of commerce in that country.

It would be impossible to get a Christian program on the air in Turkey on their government television, but the people are hearing the gospel because people want to make money, and they can do that by fulfilling the voracious demand of the audiences for high-quality, Western-style television.

In terms of evangelism, this is the opportunity of a lifetime. It will break down any type of control. It will mean that speech, thought, and religious values can be disseminated much more rapidly. This will be a great opportunity for missionaries and other Christian workers if they will take advantage of it, but the benefits of the technology flow to everybody else as well.

It means that anybody with a thought he wants to disseminate can have some channels available to him—many, many of them. Whether it is Shirley MacLaine with her occult fantasies, or some sort of self-help motivational program, there will be channels for every conceivable interest. These will range from aerobics to geriatrics, and from aviation to zoology. All of these things will now have worldwide distribution potential.

The importance of this kind of information explosion is that now we can get the ideas to the people. The bad news is that it will also be possible for some dangerous charlatan to have global distribution capability which is literally awesome in its scope. Because of that threat, we must always be on the alert that the technology is used for good and not for evil.

WORLDWIDE NEWS

Already, the Cable News Network (CNN) is global. It is all over Europe, in parts of Asia. It is certainly in the hotels wherever you go. This network provides worldwide, up-to-the-minute news. The markets of the world are integrated. This is now a very small globe we live on.

News-gathering services such as Reuters, Worldwide, CNN and others are now doing something that has never been done before: bringing instant news and pictures of everything that happens, as it happens. The sophistication of information that is being beamed out to the world is extraordinary. There is nothing any longer that is done in a corner.

We have access to a global information system, which allows us to focus in on places like Washington and Moscow, and soon possibly Brussels or Strasbourg with the European Community coming into being. As these things happen we will all be much more involved in the global community, and the names and faces of public figures in these countries will be as well known to us as the leaders in our own country.

Because of datalinks and satellite transmission of information, we will have instant access to business and financial information and commercial transactions with unprecedented quality and speed. I understand that the SWIFT system—the Society of Worldwide Interfund Transfers which runs out of a great big computer in Brussels—handles over one hundred billion dollars a day in bank transfers. The amounts involved with currency transactions—the actual buying and selling of currencies—are reportedly vastly larger than that.

TECHNOLOGY IN REVOLUTION

Absent some war or other catastrophe, the consumer able to afford the product is going to be getting much better quality, in almost everything. Appliances, automobiles, consumer electronics, all these products will be much better. Also, they will become more affordable as the markets expand.

I expect to see explosive new developments in these and many other areas during the coming decade. This will happen not so much through dynamic breakthroughs in technology, not just through new products and discoveries, but incremental increases and improvements in the products we already rely on. During the coming decade we will see product *improvements* that will amount to dramatic breakthroughs.

This will be "the age of the supers." Superconductor technology is racing ahead at breakneck speed. Powerful new super-fast chips being produced both in the United States and Japan are capable of out-performing today's standards by factors as high as 10,000 to 1.

Some of the newest silicon products coming from the laboratories into the marketplace are nothing short of revolutionary. In mid-1990 the Japanese announced that they are developing neural networks on silicon wafers that duplicate the functions of the human brain. They say one five-inch microchip can contain the equivalent of 19 million transistors and operates 100,000 times faster than existing supercomputers.

One of the most fascinating insights I have seen concerning the proliferation of computers in our society comes from George Gilder, author of many important works including *The Spirit of Enterprise*. In an essay for the volume, *An American Vision*, published by the Cato Institute in Washington, Gilder suggests that micro-computers have also helped to prove the futility of socialism.

In the beginning, IBM thought the small "personal computer" (PC) would be a simple tool to help them sell more mainframe computers; however, what they actually discovered was that PC networks were out-performing their mainframes and, in millions of instructions per second per dollar, were 90 times more cost efficient than supercomputers.

Gilder's conclusion is that "computers make socialism totally futile and obsolete. By their very nature, computers distribute power rather than centralize it. . . . The evolution of the industry therefore constantly increases the power of the individual workstation. . . ." The very architecture of the technology decentralizes and gives immense value to the distribution of power.

The "economies of microscale," as Gilder calls it, dictates that "power continually devolves into the hands and onto the laps of individuals." Having demonstrated some of the fallacies of Marshall McLuhan's predictions of the 1970s, I have to agree with Gilder that "What is important is not the medium but the message."

HARD REALITIES

We will have to face many problematical issues in the decade ahead concerning biotechnology, gene splicing, and the like. The use of fetal tissue for medical experimentation, the modification of the fetus in the womb to alter the genetic code or the physical and mental traits of the unborn child, along with experiments in cloning human beings—these and other very questionable issues are being debated even now.

We will have to address the practice of euthanasia, issues such as Dr. Jack Kervorkian's suicide device, as well as use of the RU-486 abortion pill from France which not only strangles the fetus in the womb but threatens the life of the rejecting mother.

We will also see revolutions in the application of computer technology to certain types of medical experiments—fusing biology and cybernetics. Dr. Louis Sullivan, Secretary of Health and Human Services, recently announced that the government is launching a massive program to study the power of the human brain.

In one experiment cited by Sullivan, researchers implanted a microchip into the brain of a laboratory rat. Not only did the chip transmit signals successfully, but the rat's brain actually accepted and fused with the chip. Will human beings be the next to carry digital programming in their brains?

The new gallium-arsenide (GaAs) microchip technology—or perhaps some hybrid derivative of it—may soon allow scientists to store as much information in a single bank of chips as is contained in all the books in the Library of Congress. They say that's not even a very far-fetched dream; it's practically a reality now.

Super-computers like those being developed by Seymour Cray—along with new discoveries from Alan Huang, engineers at IBM, and others now in the hunt—will continue to blossom. *U.S. News* and *Time* both reported that Huang recently previewed a new optical computer, powered by light, that can run up to 1,000 times faster than today's most powerful supercomputers. There seems to be no limits to this type of technology.

In physics, the super-collider will also be very much in the news as the scientists in Texas begin to explore the processes and applications of advanced nuclear dynamics.

In transportation, we will see even more revolutionary advances. We are certainly going to see super high speed bullet trains that ride on air cushions with a potential speed of anywhere from 500 to a thousand miles per hour. We are going to see supersonic airplanes that can go from Washington to Tokyo in two and a half to three hours in a sort of sub-orbital flight.

In the foreseeable future, we will have smart highways where people can lock their cars onto an underground computer system and essentially punch up their destination and sit back and enjoy the ride while the highway conducts them to their point of exit, then lets them off.

Recently General Motors announced it has already designed the prototype of a whole new generation of automobiles that will be powered by high-energy batteries. Subsequently, *Time* reported on research for a new highway system featuring an electrified underground cable that would allow electrically powered cars to recharge their batteries while driving.

COMBINED TECHNOLOGIES

There will also be a continuing trend to merge all these technologies. For example, there will be increasing uses of computers in the automobile industry, not only the computer consoles we now have to monitor operating systems, but also to avoid accidents, cars that can avoid impending collisions and apply the necessary safety precautions to prevent accidents.

Along with the advances in computer technology, improved fiber optic communications, improved transportation, and advances in engineering procedures, there will be changes in the physical workplace. Perhaps most notable, the demand for improved quality of life will accelerate the tendency for many more people to work at home, or in smaller offices close to home.

Airports all over the world are so congested today, there will have to be some new breakthroughs in air transportation. The vertical takeoff and landing method, generally called VTOL, may well be the answer, especially for commuter flights.

The aircraft of the very near future will likely be something that can hover, land in a small area, take off and then fly very rapidly to its destination. On a commercial level, this could be something like the Harrier Jump Jet.

Instead of the long landing patterns we have in our airports today, we will see landing pads no larger than a small parking lot. Instead of being located very far outside the cities, they can be much closer, more convenient, and less noisy.

Ever-increasing congestion in our major cities will add additional impetus to the public's desire to move to smaller towns where the quality of life will be much higher. This will be a major issue for cities like New York, Boston, Chicago, Detroit, and others which will be losing huge numbers of people over a fairly short period of time.

When the trend toward home business was first predicted a decade ago, nobody really believed it would happen; but it is happening, and it's changing the way America does business.

Just look at the way the fax machine has changed business in the last three years. And for many people, especially for those who work outside the office, the cellular phone has become indispensable. We have access to instant communications from anywhere in the world at any time. This is not only the trend for tomorrow, it is the reality of today.

It is a reality in churches as well. A nationwide poll of Protestant churches conducted by the Barna Research Group found that fully half of the churches they contacted currently own or use computers in their ministry. That is a dramatic increase from the 21 percent who reported using computers in their work in a 1985 study.

UNLOCKING RAIN MAN'S SECRET

In what may well have been the finest motion picture of the past decade, *Rain Man,* actor Dustin Hoffman delivered an award-winning performance as the autistic older brother opposite fast talking Tom Cruise. Hoffman's character, Raymond, was what psychologists term an "idiot-savant," someone with the IQ of a moron yet who has a mental ability which seems superhuman. Raymond was unable to care for himself in society, yet had the ability to do complex mathematical calculations in his head almost instantly with absolute accuracy down to three or four decimal points.

Such people are rare, but they do indeed exist. Last year my co-hostess, Sheila Walsh, had the privilege of interviewing such a remarkable individual on the 700 Club television program. He was a young black man named Alonzo Clemons from Denver, Colorado.

We were told that Alonzo's IQ was a sub-moronic 55. Yet he had two extraordinary gifts—artistic expression and total detailed recall. If, for instance, he could look once at an animal, he could then return to his studio and craft a clay statue of the animal, perfect in dimension and accurate in every detail.

Alonzo was shown a large color photograph of my big stallion, Aristocrat. Then without further reference to the photograph, within 15 minutes he had crafted a perfect scale model of the horse—head, ears, neck, shoulder, legs, feet, barrel, flanks—all beautifully symmetrical and true to life. I was frankly overwhelmed.

Some savants are gifted musically. They can play from memory complex musical scores. Others, like the movie character, Raymond, are gifted in math. It is possible, for example, to ask such a person what day of the week Christmas fell on in 1776. Within seconds they can give an absolutely correct answer. Others can perform calculations that would strain the ability of our finest computers.

I learned that savants are windows God has given us into the true ability of the human brain. As best I can determine, the normal human brain functions at about 10 percent of capacity. The truly gifted among us may reach 20 percent. In their compensating specialties, the savants have been allowed to move up to 80 percent or 90 percent of capacity.

Think what would happen if God would somehow enable all people to operate at the level of wisdom and discernment of which we are capable.

The discoveries and breakthroughs in science and technology would beggar belief.

More recently some not too scientific experiments have been made in pre-natal teaching with startling results. Pregnant women are playing gospel music or recorded scripture readings to their unborn children along with clear, distinct prayer. I have been told, but I hasten to add without scientific verification, that children so taught before birth later evidence IQs which are off the top of the genius range.

The Bible says, "Your sins have separated you from God." Can it be possible that innocent little children—like the completely innocent idiot-savants—could receive extensions of their abilities that are nothing short of remarkable? I think this is possible and may prove, along with the understanding of the human spirit, one of the great breakthroughs in the decades ahead.

In my opinion the experiments of J. B. Rhine at Duke University and other researchers into ESP and paranormal phenomena are merely conducting kindergarten classes in spiritism. We must understand that there exist in the world God's intelligence revealed by His Holy Spirit, man's intelligence, angelic intelligence, and demonic intelligence. God's intelligence comes to man through man's spirit. Demonic intelligence comes to man through his soul. The Greek word for soul is *psyche* from which we get our English word psychic.

Those who begin to enter the realm of intelligence beyond ourselves—without the spiritual rebirth that comes from Jesus Christ and a clear understanding of the Holy Bible—will invariably find that they have neither tapped into an extension of man's intelligence or God's intelligence, but demonic intelligence.

I hasten to add—as I have already outlined in detail in chapter 4—that we are entering the age of the supernatural. To quote the apostle Paul, there will be "lying signs and wonders to deceive as it were the very elect." We can expect extraordinary breakthroughs accompanied by extensive media publicity in the field of paranormal activity. Invariably these signs and wonders will beckon us to a brave new world and salvation—*apart from Jesus Christ.*

As the old fades away and new perceptions of reality come quickly into focus, it will be absolutely crucial that Christian people have a thorough understanding of the Bible and that they are trained in spiritual discernment and perception to identify clearly what is true and what is false in the coming new millennium.

COUNTING THE COST

As always, there will be economic and cultural repercussions from the advances in science and technology. As individuals move away from the mega-cities, rental and ownership patterns will begin to change. Real estate values in small and medium-sized cities will go up, and some of the core cities that are so terribly congested now are going to begin breaking down.

Both economy and quality-of-life changes will impact these cities, and we will see some rather substantial out-migration from cities where congestion and pollution and the breakdown of the infrastructure have already become intolerable.

After a long period of intense debate over the importance and the uses of nuclear energy, I think we have finally come to the time when we have to admit that controlled and responsible use of atomic power is essential to our future.

We have learned—not only from Chernobyl but from a long list of films, movies, and books on the potential dangers of mishandling nuclear power—that there are legitimate concerns. But we are also discovering that there are substantial advantages as well, and we simply have to begin to discover how we can use these advantages realistically.

I believe that we will harness the power and the technology for efficient applications of nuclear energy in the very near future. One of the developers of the Chicago Project—an engineer who worked with Enrico Fermi on atomic fission—was a guest on our television program. In the course of our interview, he said that with 20 billion dollars and a dedicated program, America could achieve nuclear fusion. I believe he is right, and I believe we must do it.

We cannot continue to rely on fossil fuel indefinitely. We are consuming our resources at a staggering rate. It is absolutely essential that we have alternate sources of energy, and solar power has proven to be too expensive and too unreliable. So I maintain that the long range hope is nuclear fusion, and it seems to me that America should take the lead in producing and using it.

That is an attainable goal. We can get controlled fusion, but we need to focus our research efforts on it now to maintain our lead. The Japanese are already at work in this area because they also recognize that it is the power for the future. We know the Germans, the Russians, and several Middle Eastern countries have constructed very advanced systems. In 1990, France was receiving fully half of its power from safe nuclear reactors. The French goal is 100 percent nuclear power by 1995.

Nuclear power—especially that from the development of hydrogen fusion—could be created from water. It boggles the mind to conceive of the world we could have if both poorer and richer nations had unlimited cheap power at their disposal with no more dependence on sky-high fossil fuels.

Think what could happen when one day we are able to enter the world of what we now call science fiction and ride on bullet trains powered by nuclear energy and floating on electromagnetic cushions, hurtling across continents at two or three times the speed of sound.

Think of vehicles powered by tiny nuclear reactors, and houses where the power bill was less than $100 each year.

Even more utopian, consider the world that we could have if the nearly one trillion dollar arms budget of the world were turned to innovation, to improving our cities, making the deserts green, lifting the masses from poverty, and sharing the goodness of this earth.

MAINTAINING AN EDGE

If Americans learn from the Japanese and are willing to be humble and listen, we can exceed any other nation in terms of the quality of our products. That has been a dream and goal of mine, that the term "Made in America" can be synonymous with "the Best in the World."

There's no question that we can do it, it's just a question of whether or not we have the will to do it and take the necessary action. If we insist in our factories that nothing goes out unless it is the best, and if we demand the intelligent participation of our workers to the extent the Japanese do, we cannot help but achieve this goal.

Becoming that kind of nation is really an emotional commitment. It is having the attitude and belief that we cannot permit errors. Milliken, a South Carolina textile manufacturer, has shown us that it can happen here. That plant is a leader in involving workers in improving the quality of their products, and as a result there has been a dramatic improvement in quality in their mills, in their techniques, in the worker involvement, and in upgrading their manufacturing systems.

Creative worker involvement sets them in the top rank of textile manufacturers in the whole world. There is no question that this kind of company can compete on a global basis with anybody.

In the marketplace of the next decade, it will be government's responsibility—and consequently our responsibility as citizens—to see that there is a fair and open market for American products. There cannot be discrimination against American products if we are to survive.

From the long view, I believe government will begin to take the initiative in these matters and use America's diplomatic clout to pry open world markets. In the short range, however, I suspect we could see some punitive tariffs that come out as we approach the end of the current business cycle and begin to work out our existing debt.

If American business interests suffer, there will be a cry for protection-

ism and, in my opinion, that would be the wrong thing to do. Protectionism will not help America. Instead, I fear it would bring on a replay of
1930 all over again, and we could see a devastating depression which
could hurt the world very badly. What we need are free and open markets
with fair trade among equal partners.

ECONOMIC PRECAUTIONS

This is the thing I fear most when looking at the prospects for the
decade ahead. There could be such a major economic dislocation that it
would plunge the world into economic chaos which would lead, in turn,
to political chaos and possibly even war. That's the dark side of the
scenario.

In a sense, we are at a crossroads in our history where we have in our
power the ability to move either toward Christian values in our spiritual
life and enlightened capitalism in our material life, or toward a much
more somber alternative.

We can choose to move toward less government regulation and more
openness among nations, which would lead to international prosperity, or
we could move toward the tightening of barriers, of tariffs, trying to
protect inefficient industries in order to preserve domestic jobs a little bit
longer.

One way will help bring us an era of prosperity and peace, the other
would very likely plunge the world into a depression which could lead to
war and collapse.

The image which then comes to mind is too much like the prophecies
of Revelation for comfort; for within the collapse of the peace and order
of the world there is the threat of a global dictatorship and the end of
democracy as we know it. That's a scenario no one looks forward to.

We have in our power the ability to conquer disease, to extend life, to
remove genetic abnormalities, to supply a reasonably abundant standard
of living to every human being on this planet, to bring forth an ever
increasing cornucopia of technological products to make each of our lives
more pleasant, to have at our disposal increased learning, culture, and
leisure.

We could have all of that but for one thing. We lack the spiritual and
ethical standards to stop killing, cheating, and oppressing our fellow
human beings. And we lack the wisdom and self-restraint to stop
pillaging, raping, and polluting the land, and the sea, and the air, and the
other creatures that share this planet with us. In short, we realize that the
Millennium cannot come unless God brings it by changing all our hearts.

WHO OWNS THE ENVIRONMENT?

Along with the mushrooming of technology, the environment is suddenly on everybody's mind. As if someone had turned on the faucet, suddenly we are being flooded with articles and ads and campaigns of every description urging us to save the environment.

Obviously, this will be one of the issues of the '90s, but where does it come from and what does it mean? When we look at any subject that receives as much exposure as this one has had over the past couple of years, it's generally a good idea to see who's involved. Who are the out-front, outspoken leaders of the environmental movement? What is their past record of accomplishment? What have they done to make the quality of life better in America?

When a detective starts to investigate a murder, the first question he asks is, who stands to benefit? When you find out who stands to gain the most you generally find the fatal motive. By the same token, when I see the passion of this new movement, I'm impelled to ask that question. Who stands to benefit?

Those who are interested in getting their hands into the government purse are usually close by when such movements begin. Liberal interests in this country have always pushed for greater government involvement in the lives of people.

For one thing, the government habitually tries to solve problems by throwing money at them. Also, when government takes over, it begins to take control of the lives of everyone involved. It does not take a genius to see that federal programs have failed miserably in this country. So who's pushing for a new one?

It's astonishing how often you see the same people who have always tried to socialize business and run the lives of the American people. They seem to come out of the woodwork for movements like this. Now, as if frustrated by the failure of communism, the activists have all shifted en masse to a new cause. Again, their purpose is to get government involved in controlling our lives.

Their real agenda is not the environment: the movements they cluster around are never more than a cover for their hidden agenda. Their agenda is control, and it is almost always anti-business and anti-growth. In fact, this is the very same bunch of radicals who have been wrong so many times before.

EMBRACING THE MOVEMENT

I believe we have a genuine right and responsibility to be good stewards of our environment. The Bible is very clear that we are to plant and harvest wisely, to use the animals and the other resources wisely. So I agree with many of the scientists and professionals who are pointing out the genuine dangers to the environment. But I think we have to be very cautious before we embrace the agenda of "the Movement." We certainly have to be wary of embracing it as some have done, as a religion.

Former Secretary of the Interior Donald Hodel told me that I would never understand the wilderness movement until I recognized that to these people, the activists, the wilderness is an object of worship. It is something they worship as an ideal.

It is not practical to suggest that we can promote tree growth through forest management, or that we build better roads so people can enjoy the wilderness. The wilderness activists believe they are defending Mother Earth and we cannot touch her, that whatever happens in the wilderness is sacred and holy.

Just prior to Earth Day 1990, a *Wall Street Journal* editorial lampooned the event as one of the rites of a new world religion. The writer pointed out that the environmentalists appear to be seeking "contact with the transcendental" in the universe beyond themselves. "We are coming to see the environment as a religion, rather, in a quest for understanding." The author of that piece writes that the movement defies mere logic,

> As the second millennium approaches, the apocalypse must be upon us. The devout search frantically to learn which of the seven ends ensues: The fire of nuclear winter. The ice of nuclear winter. The unseen peril of radiation, or a new plague as a judgment for genetic tampering. The roast of global warming, or the judgment of a new ice age, the climatological fear of only a decade ago. Or merely perhaps terminal boredom in the end of history?

An amusing observation, but perhaps not all that far from the truth. Actually, it should not be surprising to see the passion with which activists have leaped into the battle for the environment.

In an age in which religious faith has been slandered and discredited by secular institutions, many of these people are desperately searching for something to fill the void in their own souls. Like the New Agers, these people have lost touch with God Almighty and they are reaching out to Nature as their God.

What happens in the wilderness may be important to nature and the natural processes of the earth, but it certainly is not holy. It is simply "natural," and as such it is subject to all the laws and processes of nature. We must realize that sometimes those changes are dramatic and destructive.

Trees decay and die; there are forest fires, wind storms, lightning damage, insect infestations, and many other types of destruction that come from natural causes. Animals prey upon one another; deserts and woodlands and wetlands expand and contract with the climatic changes that vary from year to year. Man is also a part of nature, and even when he is irresponsible and destroys some part of the environment, he is still a part of nature and does not necessarily change the laws of nature by his presence or his actions.

CYCLES OF GROWTH

Intelligent management of the forests and woodlands is a very wise and important thing. Trees actually grow better when they are not in too close proximity to each other. Trees have a certain life cycle and when they reach the end of that cycle—whether it's 70 years, 80 years, or longer—they begin to die, so it is wise at that point to harvest them, to enable smaller trees to come up, or to replant with nursery-grown seedlings.

Even such things as forest fires may be good for certain species, because only after the earth has been singed by the heat of a forest fire and certain areas have been cleared of timber can new seedlings germinate and bring life to whole new forests. The redwoods of California and some of the other trees considered sacred to the environmentalists are actually in that category.

The natural thing is to permit a certain amount of clearing of growth. Wildlife management is much the same. Unless the populations of North American deer that run wild in many parts of this country are thinned out by manmade methods, predators or disease will take them.

When their herds grow larger than one deer per acre, deer cannot forage or breed freely, and many times the ravages of nature are more costly than the alternative, which is to permit hunters to thin the herds.

If the reverence we have for the wilderness becomes a kind of religion, and if what we feel for the environment is not just respect but worship, then the environment actually becomes our god and it cannot be touched by anyone. That sort of idolatry is a frontal assault on our concept of stewardship.

The biblical mandate is for man to have dominion over the earth, over all living things, over the animals, over the creeping things and flying things, over the forests and rivers and seas. As intelligent stewards, under the authority of God, we are to tend the garden and cultivate it and look after it.

CYCLES OF DESTRUCTION

We are to care for the environment, but never did God give us a mandate to desecrate it. What has happened in some places is that lumber companies have gone in and clear cut virgin forests for pure greed and with no concept of stewardship. That kind of wanton deforestation is alarming.

In Brazil in 1989 unlicensed lumbermen and poachers were chopping down as high as 18,000 acres of virgin timber a day; that is not only a crime, it is immoral. We know that the rain forests of Brazil, Central Africa, and Southeast Asia are unique biological laboratories. These forests are primary resources for reproducing the world's supply of nitrogen and oxygen, and for maintaining the balance of humidity in the atmosphere.

Many of the forests that are being ravaged, especially in the Third World, are irreplaceable. But the cycle of devastation only begins with the trees. Once the forests are cut down, seasonal rains come and wash away the topsoil.

The arable soil in which crops are grown has a unique composition which, with very little variance, is the same all over the world. It is approximately half mineral, 3 to 5 percent vegetable, and the remainder about equal proportions of air and water; but the average depth of that soil is only about 8 to 10 inches. When we lose that topsoil, we endanger our ability to survive on this planet.

We must have harmony between man and the environment. The tragedy of North Africa, for example, is the clearing of forests, all the way from the Mediterranean Coast south to Mali, Chad, and Nigeria. As a consequence of indiscriminate clearing, nearly half the continent has been consumed by desert, and the toll on human life has been devastating.

We only need to think of the photographs from Ethiopia and the Sudan to recognize the toll in human life. At one time that whole area was forested, but over the years, through war and through periods of prosperity and famine, men have cleared the forests farther and farther south, and as the trees are cut the wind and rain wash away the topsoil until nothing is left but sand and desert.

Satellite photos reveal the consequences, with the desert creeping southward across Africa at a relentless pace of seven to eight miles every year. The nomadic tribes are always running just ahead of the desert, but they cannot outrun the famine. Millions of people have starved to death because there isn't enough food for them and the productive capacity of the land has been utterly destroyed for years, possibly ages, to come.

BRINGING NEW LIFE

I saw that damage when I flew from Khartoum in the Sudan across Egypt and over the Mediterranean. Over Egypt, I noticed little puffs of clouds over the few scattered areas where trees were growing.

I realized then—since I had seen it proven in Israel—that planting trees helps bring about cooling, which brings moisture and rain, which can also help accelerate other climatic changes. And as the trees drop their leaves in the fall, over a period of time there is a gradual building of solus and humus, which form the topsoil.

So I asked a friend, Bob Macauley, who is head of a company with timber interests, why don't we plant a million trees as a demonstration project and let others join with us? Bob jumped at the idea, so CBN formed a partnership to add trees to a project begun by a Danish agronomist active in Kenya. With Bob's help we have now planted close to 3 million trees, and some of them are 12 to 20 feet high!

An area that was once hard, unyielding, near desert, has suddenly begun to flourish. Our agronomist and his team dug a lake, and the weather cycles in the region began to change, it began to rain more and more, and now the lake is full of water. He has now reintroduced the various species of wildlife that disappeared during the drought and famine, and there are even hippopotami in the water. There are birds and literally hundreds of the natural creatures which had virtually disappeared from this natural habitat.

Now, from those first plantings we did, the scientists and the local managers have established a very prolific seedling nursery so they can give plants to other villages who want trees. At this point I am proposing we take what we have learned from that operation and plant a hundred million trees to begin to reclaim Africa from the desert.

President Bush said he would like to see America plant one billion trees a year. That is not an unattainable goal for Africa. It should have been done a long time ago, but it also needs to be done in Southeast Asia, and South America, and in all the areas of the world where the forests are being cut down.

The governments must cooperate not only in reforestation but in conservation. For some reason, in Brazil and other Third World nations, there has not been a responsible effort to preserve the forests. The forests are not only important to recycle the air, to filter out poisons, and to replenish moisture, chlorophyll, oxygen and nitrogen, and other important properties of the air. But the vegetation holds the soil in place and regulates the run-off of water, which in turn helps to prevent devastating floods.

THE BALANCE OF NATURE

The balance of nature is crucial, but we violate it almost casually. We have also violated it in the water. We have dumped toxic wastes into the oceans, lakes, rivers, and streams. We have used increasingly toxic chemicals, and the chemicals run off into the water and kill the wildlife and the aquatic life, and that imperils, in turn, those who live by and from the sea.

Instead of responsibility, we find people whose main concern is with bottom-line profits. They don't stop to think about the air we breathe, so they build factories and mills that belch out fumes, saturating the air with colloidal compounds, such as acid and coal smoke.

Irresponsible managers dump poisonous wastes in areas where it can leach into the water supply. There is no telling how many people die of cancer or how many babies are born with birth defects every year through the irresponsible behavior of managers and supervisors who think that because nobody will see what they have done, nobody will be hurt.

Virginia experienced one of the worst ecological disasters in American history a few years ago because of just such carelessness. It seems that a small, fly-by-night chemical supplier for giant Allied Chemical Company stored some barrels of the deadly chemical, Kepone, in a little storage building the size of a residential two-car garage.

This building was near the banks of the James River at a city called Hopewell, some 40 or 50 miles upstream from the Chesapeake Bay. Some of the barrels containing the Kepone began to leak and the Kepone oozed out of the building and into the James River. As a result, the entire lower Chesapeake Bay was contaminated and the fishing and oyster business in the region was shut down completely.

That single leak destroyed the fishing for several years. It did untold damage to living fish, not to mention the potential danger to humans and animals who ate the fish. It was just a small amount of a deadly chemical, but it was caused by the carelessness of people who didn't understand the incredible potential for harm in today's chemical products.

THE OTHER SIDE OF SCIENCE

When we saw the Bhopal disaster in India and the Chernobyl disaster in Russia, we got just a small glimpse of the horrific consequences of modern technology when the toxic by-products it produces fall into the hands of thoughtless and careless people.

I am for atomic energy, and I think that ultimately the principal energy source of the new millennium will be nuclear power. Hydrogen power is an idea whose time has come. I am convinced that someday we will have a cheap form of energy, as cheap as all the oceans of the world. It will give the world a limitless energy supply, and it won't be priced on the basis of scarcity.

This new energy resource will be available to everybody, but it will involve certain risks and it will demand certain precautions. If we cannot accept the risks and take the proper steps to safeguard ourselves from the risks, then we will have to forego the benefits of the technology. We cannot have nuclear reactors if we have no regard for safety.

The accident at Chernobyl has caused incalculable damage over an immeasurable area. As we know now, people all over northern Europe are still being exposed to dangerous levels of radiation from that accident.

The London *Economist* reported recently that Britain's sheep, contaminated by fallout and poisoned rain from Chernobyl, have to be color-coded according to their level of radioactivity. Those marked with green paint are considered safe, while the sheep with apricot markings are still off limits. The comedy of such a system is hardly offset by the real-life horror.

There is not a lot we can physically do to reverse the damage that has been done there, but we must learn from Chernobyl. We must at least gain an immense respect for the power of technology and for the potential it possesses both for good and for evil.

Incidentally, an ominous biblical prophecy says that in the end times a bright star will fall to earth, and this bitter star will poison the waters of the earth. The name of the star is wormwood. The passage, in the eighth chapter of Revelation, predicts that a third of the earth will be destroyed because the waters will be made bitter. Curiously, the word for wormwood in Russian is *chernobyl*.

We must be cautious that we do not endanger our populations. Under communism, all that mattered was the ongoing economic welfare of the state, to the exclusion of any outside concerns about the health of the population. A government trying to squeeze every last ounce of productivity from the people, particularly when the people are already impoverished and the economy is collapsing, will not spend much time worrying about pollution.

But pollution is a legitimate concern. Whether it is from trash and garbage, from radioactive contamination, or from lead or aluminum contamination, we have to care.

Many scientists now believe that Alzheimer's disease may be caused by aluminum poisoning, from cooking with aluminum utensils. We already know that excessive exposure to or ingestion of lead causes mental retardation and birth defects of various kinds, so it is not unreasonable to suspect that aluminum—an alloy—may have a similar effect.

As a matter of fact, historians and scientists have applied some of the new findings to earlier cultures with some startling results. Many believe that the short lifespans of people in the Middle Ages may have been due to the fact that their utensils and tableware were commonly made from pewter: pewter is an alloy of lead and tin.

The same evidence suggests that one reason the Roman Empire began to die out was because they used so much lead, not only in their eating utensils, but in the water pipes and sewage systems. They were dying of lead poisoning and didn't know it.

Carcinogenic materials, poisons, and contaminants which damage the central nervous system or which cause birth defects and other serious impairments are matters of great urgency and we have the right as citizens of a free democratic nation to see that the risks are eliminated.

PREVALENT DANGERS

I think we have to take the dangers of pollution caused by automobile emissions very seriously. We have been told that every car and truck on the highways in this country spews its own weight in carbons back into the atmosphere every year. Multiply that times the number of vehicles you see around you every day and the thought is mind boggling.

There isn't a single country anywhere in the world that doesn't have a serious pollution problem. Poorly developed Third World countries; highly developed industrial nations; they all have serious problems. Mexico City is choking on pollution. Tokyo, Rio, and Sao Paulo are all choking on pollution. Every major city in Europe has a serious problem.

Many of us have seen the grim photos from West Germany showing the almost total destruction of the historic Black Forest. It is heartbreaking to see that stately and historic forest being devastated by acid rain caused by the poisonous coal smoke belching from factories in Poland, Czechoslovakia, and East Germany.

In Italy the trees and ancient statuary along the Appian Way, along with many of the great cathedrals and landmarks of Europe, are being eaten away by the ravages of pollution, coal smoke, and acid rain. Unfortunately, we don't yet know what the acid rain is doing to the lakes of New England or the Great Lakes.

In Athens, the air quality is so bad it is nearly impossible to breathe on a hot day. Shirley Temple Black, our ambassador to Czechoslovakia, has said that living in Prague is like smoking two packs of cigarettes a day.

One thing after another indicates that massive pollution is having disastrous consequences all over the world, degrading the environment, causing lung disease, causing emphysema, birth defects, senile dementia, and a whole host of other ills.

GETTING IT RIGHT

The comprehensive reports of the United States Environmental Protection Agency offer grim evidence of the dangers within our communities and public lands. A quick review of the summary documents of the EPA activities published in early 1990 reveals the massive scope of the problem the agency has begun to attack.

Under the single category of clean air, they are involved in programs for control of acid rain, smog, and toxic pollutants. They deal with the problems caused by benzene emissions and radioactivity from mining operations, along with controlling airborne pollutants from the incineration of municipal waste.

Other programs address oil spills, municipal waste disposal, and domestic pollution, plus asbestos contamination, chlorofluorocarbons, global warming, hazardous waste, radon contamination, medical waste, ocean dumping, dangerous pesticides, and the banning of agricultural products such as Alar.

The EPA is also involved with the FDA, USDA, and the Department of Justice in policing poisons, hazardous waste, and cleanup activities, and in the prosecution of offenders.

Obviously, righting the wrongs already done to the world about us is going to be a major task. It is going to cost hundreds of billions of dollars. First of all we have to clean up the smokestacks and come up with alternate sources of fuel. We not only have to come up with some sort of scrubbers and air filters on the smokestacks, but we have to clean coal at the mine that is being burned in the smokestacks, and ultimately we have to go to some kind of non-fossil fuels.

We have to do something about the fact that automobiles are filling the air with petrocarbons. Right now automobiles are the principal means of transportation in every industrialized nation in the world and, in such massive quantities, automobile fumes are deadly.

But what about the proven dangers of cigarette smoke surrounding us everywhere we go? They tell us that Americans are cutting back on cigarette smoking. In 1964, approximately 60 percent of Americans smoked; today that figure is reported at just over 29 percent. Apparently some people are beginning to get the message, but cigarette smoking still has a stranglehold on millions and it is killing thousands every day.

The vice of cigarette smoking seems to prey on the weak. Teenagers and young adults trying so hard to be cool, to prove their independence, are ready victims of smoking. Inner-city families, low-income Blacks, Hispanics, and now women are the greatest at-risk categories among smokers.

The women's liberation movement, by making women believe they have to be macho, has induced tens of thousands to smoke as a sign of freedom and rebellion, and it is killing women today at a staggering rate.

To their eternal shame, American tobacco companies are luring children and teens and young singles through pernicious advertising playing on sex and glamour. They are luring them to their deaths. These same companies are stepping up exports at an alarming rate, and because of the greed and exploitation of the American tobacco companies, people in Third World countries are, literally, smoking themselves to death.

I invite anyone who believes it's okay to smoke to go down to the nearest nursing home and talk to the old men with emphysema and lung disease. Visit the rooms of the young men and women with bronchial diseases; or go to any major hospital in any city in the world and speak to the doctors in the cancer wards.

Look in on the patients dying of lung and bronchial and esophageal cancers. These people will not hesitate to tell you what smoking is all about. They will not hesitate to condemn the evil of smoking. Cigarettes and all other forms of tobacco are a man-made source of pollution that is self-induced and is more common, more deadly and, because it is so insidious, is more perceptibly evil than any of the others.

As Christians, we have a duty to be worthy custodians of the environment, but we are also commanded to take care of our bodies, which are the temple of the Lord.

We are to be the stewards and live in harmony with the plants, the animals, the birds, the fish. Yes, we can harvest them for food, but we must protect and cultivate and harvest wisely. Any form of wanton destruction is evil, whether it is destruction of our world or our own bodies.

STANDARDS AND DOUBLE STANDARDS

We must be realistic, and we don't need to be faddish. So many at the forefront of the environmental movement have such a double standard, it's clear that the idea of a movement—any movement—means more to them than the issues themselves.

I find it pathetically ironic that the same environmentalists you see at the protest rallies against air pollution and nuclear contamination can't go more than a few minutes without a cigarette break. It's also telling to see that the people who are such staunch opponents of hunting and the use of furs are all wearing leather shoes. Odd they're not saying anything about that. After all, steers have to die for us to have leather.

We have harvested animals since time immemorial; we have always used animals for our food and clothing. Since the earliest days of Genesis, we have used the meat and skins of animals. Meat is a necessary part of the human diet, and fur coats are no more wrong, in themselves, than leather shoes or handbags.

What is wrong, however, is the wanton slaughter of wildlife for the sake of fashion, or greed, or simple exploitation of nature for personal gain. Think what the early trappers and traders did in their appalling slaughter of the domestic buffalo.

A century ago there was wanton slaughter of the egrets in the Everglades of Florida just so the elegant ladies of New York and Boston could have plumes for their finery. Today there is an ongoing slaughter of the elephants in Africa. Poachers kill the elephants but only take the tusks, which are sold for jewelry, and leave the carcasses to rot.

The African rhino is being threatened with extinction because some people believe the tusks make good aphrodisiacs. The tusk of a single rhino can bring up to 20,000 dollars; consequently, poachers are killing them by the thousands. These are horrible losses and an outrage against nature.

The large-scale netting of fish has also been appalling. It is tragic to see dolphins, which are such beautiful, intelligent creatures, being trapped in tuna nets and thrown away, lifeless, because the commercial fisheries are in such a hurry to catch a few tuna.

When it gets to the point that we are no longer catching food for the good of mankind or harvesting crops according to responsible management practices, we are guilty of wanton slaughter and greed. The kind of exploitation which threatens the extinction of entire species is sinful and wrong.

UNNATURAL ACTS

We cannot condone that kind of exploitation, and it has to be controlled by law. But what we don't need, in the process, are wild-eyed fanatics voting legislation to prohibit hunting, fishing, or the killing of beef cattle, hogs, sheep, and chickens. Unrealistic and unnatural protectionism brings about an imbalance in the opposite direction.

For example, once they became legally protected the alligators in Florida began to multiply at such a high rate they have imperiled the population. Today there are alligators everywhere, and they are growing so fast they have become a threat. There has to be an intelligent harvesting of these creatures or mankind cannot live in relationship to them. Even in a wild state, man was able to protect himself against animals and to use them for his own good, and this should continue.

It is amazing to me that the same people who fulminate against the killing of baby seals and who stand in horror of wearing fur coats and who talk about protecting the bald eagle are at the same time at the forefront of the movement to slaughter human beings in the womb. There is an obvious inconsistency in their thinking. They worship the wild beasts and destroy human life made in the image of God! It is paradoxical, confusing, and hard for a rational person to reconcile.

THE GOD OF NATURE

If Christians will bring the biblical worldview to these issues, we can take the lead in this area, because we have insight as to how these environmental concerns need to be managed.

The liberals and radicals who are getting involved for various personal, political, or social reasons are often fanatics, and they are using the environment for their own hidden agenda. While we support the ideas of responsibility and restraint, we must also be cautious who we support and what we sanction.

There are volumes being written about the environment today, and the political movements to protect and maintain the balance of nature just continue to grow, but there is no question that in the next ten years the issue of the environment is going to take on massive proportions. It is probably going to be the number one public concern.

Environmental clean up, especially in the Soviet Union and Eastern Europe, is a top priority. Preserving our world from ecological harm is a clear priority for us all. But let us all be on our guard against that which is excessive, faddish, fanatical, and is being manipulated by people who want to use this issue as a means of introducing government control back into the lives of people on a massive scale.

The Christian view of ecological stewardship can provide the only satisfactory answer to pollution and desertification.

10

The New Economics

The specter of massive debt overhangs the world economy. American debt ratios are dramatically more threatening in 1990 than in 1929.

THE FRENCH HAVE a saying, *"Plus ça change, plus la même chose."* The writer of the book of Ecclesiastes said the same thing differently, "What has been will be again, what has been done will be done again; there is nothing new under the sun." Jesus put it differently, "As long as the earth remains there will be summer and winter, seed time and harvest."

As we seek somewhat frantically in the days ahead amidst what seems violent economic changes to discern the economic course for our families, our businesses, our nation, and our world, we should know that although the pace of change may intensify and the people on this planet are drawn closer together than ever before, the economic cycles and rhythms of history will continue over and over again.

In other words, nothing is going to happen in the 1990s and beyond, absent the return of Jesus Christ to establish His kingdom on earth, that has not happened sometime, somewhere before.

Empires have risen and empires have fallen. There has been good weather and bad weather. Abundant crops and food shortages. Economic prosperity and depression. Stable currencies and inflated currencies.

Peace and happiness, war and misery. The earth always remains. The economic laws always remain. There is nothing new under the sun.

INEXORABLE EXPONENTIAL COMPOUNDING

Baron Rothschild called it the "eighth wonder of the world." The first head of the Bank of England, Sir John Houblon, undoubtedly rubbed his hands in joy at the secret he had learned from William Paterson, the wily Scot who had founded the bank in 1694, "We will charge interest on money which we create out of nothing."

These two secrets, the exponential compounding of interest and what is called "fractional reserve" banking can go a long way toward explaining what is going to happen to the economies of the world in the days ahead.

These two principles can bring untold wealth to those who use them and untold misery to the people and nations trapped in their web. It was no accident that God Almighty forbade His people in Israel to charge usury from one another, nor was it accidental that He then instructed them to proclaim a time of debt release every 50 years.

The mystery of exponential compounding works as follows. Money placed at compound interest begins to multiply slowly then at an accelerating pace which over the course of 20 to 50 years becomes absolutely astounding. To determine how fast money will grow with compound interest or how fast compound inflation will make money worthless, simply divide the number 72 by the rate of interest, or the rate of inflation.

At 10 percent simple interest compounded annually money doubles in 7.2 years. At just 10 percent compounded, 100,000 dollars, invested with no additional investment, no work, or no effort, silently, almost mysteriously would grow in 50 years to 12,800,000 dollars.

At 10 percent inflation, a dormant nest egg of 12,800,000 dollars would virtually disappear over 50 years to a real "inflation adjusted" value of only 100,000 dollars. And even as wealth compounds exponentially, even so debt when allowed to compound will grow inexorably until it overwhelms the debtor's ability ever to repay at which time he either repudiates his debts or becomes a slave of the lender.

In making investment decisions, it is crucial to remember that money invested must earn more than inflation or it is being lost. It is tragic to see someone who has put money aside for retirement fail to realize that the money must be sufficient to pay today's retirement needs plus future retirement needs after compounding inflation.

For example, if inflation is 5 percent, then bank accounts which yield only 5 percent are not growing at all. At 5 percent inflation, the price of everything will be double in fifteen years. Consequently if a retired person will need 25,000 dollars for living expenses at age 65, he or she will require 50,000 dollars to continue the same standard of living after age 80.

The potential tragedy that inflation can bring on retirees with fixed incomes is evident. What is not evident is that today's young workers who are planning to retire in 2020 would need four times the 1990 level of benefits just to exist if inflation continues to compound at 5 percent per year for the next 30 years. And for everyone this could mean low priced automobiles selling for 40,000 dollars, average houses selling for 400,000 dollars, and meat at 10 dollars per pound.

This illustration should make it clear that interest or dividends which merely keep up with the rate of inflation are no gain at all. Yet current income taxes fall on interest and dividends with no regard for inflation. Clearly the amount of inflation should be deducted not only from capital gains but from all income derived from interest or dividends.

Bad as the exponential compounding of debt is, consider how much worse it can be when multiplied with so-called fractional reserve banking. Here is how that works. Assume that you are paid $100 and deposit that money in your bank. The bank sets aside a fraction, about 5 percent, and loans out the remaining $95.

Assume that the borrower deposits the $95 in the same bank, which again reserves 5 percent, and loans out $90.25. That money is redeposited and can be reserved, and the balance loaned out again. The first $100 has through fractional reserve banking been transformed into many times again as much in loans, all of which are supported by only 5 percent in reserves.

It becomes obvious that almost all bank assets are actually borrowed into existence. If people stop borrowing and begin to pay off their loans, the total supply of credit and banking assets can shrink in the same dramatic way they were created.

It is equally obvious that bank assets are not "money." They are computer print-outs representing the pledged credit of the businesses and individual people that banks are charging interest on loaned "money" which the banks "created out of nothing." When banks deal with one another, they don't pass cash money or gold back and forth. They trade entry balances on computer print-outs.

Since bank "assets" are based primarily on the credit of people who have borrowed from them, or the real assets which stand behind the paper, it is easy to see how a sizable number of bad credits could act like a loose thread in a knit sweater and unravel the entire fabric of world banking. If a "run" were to develop in which all the depositors wanted their money back from the world's banks, it is clear that no real money exists to pay them.

In case of a run, banks absent government help are out of business. Worldwide banking in the final analysis is a finely tuned, completely legal Ponzi scheme that depends 100 percent on the restraint of depositors, the credit of borrowers, and a generous appeal to the law of averages.

The danger of a rupture of the entire financial system is so perilously great in our over-leveraged world that when one sector of the banking industry, the Savings and Loan (S&L) Banks, began to fall apart, President Bush and Secretary of the Treasury Brady were forced to risk a second term in office for the president and the credit standing of the United States government in order to pay off S&L depositors and keep the game going a little longer.

This rescue effort may cost the United States government a total of one trillion dollars. But worse things may be ahead. The commercial banking industry is much larger than the Savings and Loan industry. There exists at best only 70 cents of federal insurance money for every 100 dollars of bank deposits. In recent years commercial banks have been failing at a higher rate than at any time since the Great Depression, and that rate shows no sign of diminishing.

If the government were forced to step up again with a one trillion dollar banking bailout, I believe that the credit standing of the United States would be severely damaged. The government already has guaranteed farm loans, several types of housing loans, education loans, small business loans, veterans loans, amounting to 2.8 trillion dollars plus a host of other off budget obligations which together total some 6.5 trillion dollars. All this is on top of the direct national debt which now exceeds 3 trillion dollars.

If the credit rating of this nation falls, several things begin to happen. (Some are already happening.) The prices of existing government bonds begin to decline. As they drop in price their interest yield begins to rise. This in turn forces up business rates, home mortgage rates, consumer loan rates, and newly issued government bond rates. Secondly, the value of the dollar declines on world markets which has the further effect of lowering bond prices, raising interest rates, and fueling inflation.

The higher interest rates set off a recession which means less tax revenues for the government and greater federal deficits. Greater deficits mean more federal borrowing, a further lowering of the credit rating, and higher interest rates, which trigger another round of the vicious cycle.

If the central bank tries to lower interest rates, investors will seek some other place for their money and in the process bonds are punished and interest rates do not drop but rise farther.

This story scenario has been played out for the past ten years or more in Brazil, Argentina, Mexico, Israel, the Sudan, Nicaragua and a host of other countries. Ultimately inflation gets out of hand, fixed securities become useless, and interest rates rise so high that they are meaningless.

There can then be a repudiation of debt, a new political initiative, and usually a new currency backed by some tangible exterior standard of value such as gold or representative commodities.

We are not there yet, but any thinking person must realize that the excess debt creation in America and the rest of the world must someday come to an end. Many observers feel that this decade may see a fiscal blow-out and a new beginning based on sound money and sound economic practices.

THE DEBT TIME BOMB

John Naisbitt, the author of the much quoted books, *Megatrends* and *Megatrends 2000* was both a charming and fascinating guest on my television program. However, I have to take issue with at least one of his very optimistic assertions in *Megatrends 2000,* that the federal deficit is a false mirror, a false reflection giving an unrealistic and hypothetical image of America's debt crises.

Certainly bureaucrats and political pundits have been cheered by Naisbitt's observations and his unreserved optimism, but, sadly, Naisbitt is wrong. The key indicator to look at is the federal debt in relation to our national output, what is called the debt/GNP ratio.

In the late days of the Carter administration inflation was rising rapidly at over 13 percent a year, and the GNP and federal revenues were rising with inflation. In those days the total federal debt was 34.5 percent of the entire gross national product of the country—a very manageable amount.

Under Ronald Reagan two things happened. Inflation shuddered to a halt, federal revenues slowed, and the federal deficit leaped to some 200 billion dollars a year. Along with it the national debt soared to undreamed of heights. The present 1990 debt to GNP ratio has doubled in the past ten years to 60 percent.

This is a very sobering statistic to any economic analyst. Equally sobering is the fact that total on and off budget debt of the federal government is almost twice the total annual output of this nation. If we add debt of business corporations, private citizens, plus the actual federal debt and its contingent liabilities we find that the total stands at 18 trillion dollars which is 367 percent of the annual output of the nation and only slightly less than the value of all of the public and private assets of the entire country.

These figures are imprecise because of possible double counting of private debt and overlapping contingent debt of the government. However one counts the numbers, it is clear that America is in hock up to its eyeballs, with a public and private debt load standing at a markedly higher level than what we had just prior to the Great Depression of the 1930s.

Overall corporate debt figures are not known precisely but I have seen estimates that the debt of American corporations in 1989 stood at 70 percent of their total assets. In 1929 that number was estimated at 25 percent. In 1929 the federal debt was only 16.9 billion dollars, the GNP was 103.4 billion dollars and the debt to GNP ratio was only 16 percent, not the 60 percent it is in 1990.

The total national debt of this country exceeds the combined external debts of the other nations of the world. Our balance of payments deficit reflects an inability to live within our means.

We have been consuming foreign products—automobiles, computers, electronic devices, clothing, and household goods, along with jewels, perfumes, and all the luxuries that come to us from other nations—and we have been borrowing to pay for our enormous consumption.

The closest analogy to the impending debt crisis in America is the unfortunate example of Argentina just before World War I. Argentina had one of the top ten standards of living at that time. They were incredibly rich, as anyone could see.

The principal river in Buenos Aires is the Rio Plata, the River of Silver, the very name reflecting the atmosphere and attitude of opulence which existed there. The land is nearly as rich as ours, the climate is very similar to ours, there is an abundance of mineral wealth.

But with a great deal of political and material idealism, and with a seemingly monumental capacity for self-indulgence, the country went on an orgy of spending and borrowing to pay for the wild excesses of their lifestyle.

Today Argentina is not even in the top 50 nations of the world. It is subject to continuous political and economic upheavals, and the people are thoroughly demoralized. Unless there is an intervention of God in that nation, Argentina seems destined for some kind of oblivion.

Their sad example should be only too clear to us at a time like this. Yet, despite all we know about the dangers of debt and reckless spending, the same thing seems to be happening in America at this very moment.

CAN GOVERNMENT MAKE IT BETTER?

As I write this chapter the United States economy is either in a recession or approaching one. The stock market was beginning to decline when Saddam Hussein launched a war against Kuwait. Now the market has lost 15 percent of its total value since it reached a high point of 3000 on the Dow Jones Index, a loss in dollar value of approximately one half a trillion dollars.

The Federal Reserve has been tightening the money supply for six months and the broad level of money known as M-3 when adjusted for inflation has been experiencing a 2.5 percent negative growth for almost three years.

Congress desperately needed to balance the budget and was set to raise taxes and cut spending. Oil price hikes following the Middle East crisis may take 60 billion dollars out of the economy and tax hikes are out of the question. The federal deficit may go above 200 billion dollars in the new fiscal year, and if the recession deepens the total could reach a record 300 billion or more.

Congress cannot raise taxes in a recession. It cannot lower taxes with huge deficits. The Federal Reserve Board cannot lower interest rates because the markets will react to fears of inflation, nor can it raise interest rates for fear of making the recession worse.

People and businesses are afraid so they are not borrowing or buying as they once did. Banks are not loaning because of federal regulators and the fear of loan defaults. The growth of credit is dropping.

The huge overhang of property left over from the Savings and Loan collapse has not been sold, so prices for both private and commercial real estate have continuously edged lower.

Undoubtedly we can work our way out of it, but I believe the scene is set for a major global recession, more likely a depression. Frankly, there is nothing much the government can do now to make things better. They helped put us in this mess, but there is very little they can do now to get us out of it.

THE DEBT COLLAPSE

History does repeat itself, and one of the primary lessons of history from Bible days until now is that a society can only accumulate so much debt before something gives. Historically it is possible for national debt to grow somewhere around 50 or 60 years. That was the conclusion of the Russian economist Nikolai Kondratieff, for whom the Kondratieff long wave debt cycle is named.

Simply put, a capitalistic society will begin a period of growth and debt accumulation until a future time when there is excess unused capacity, obsolescence of technology and products, and insupportable debt. After a period of debt cancellation and closing excess obsolete capacity, new products and fresh capital come forward to begin the next cycle of growth.

Some of this has already happened in America. Our steel plants were obsolete and inefficient. Most of them have been closed. So also obsolete automobile plants have been closed down all over the country.

There has been a vast excess of inner city rental office space, some of which in cities like Dallas, is slowly beginning to be occupied. Other rental office buildings stand lonely and empty in cities across the land. There are hundreds of thousands of excess hotel rooms as a result of speculative over-building, and a shake out in that industry is yet to be dealt with.

The market has been swamped by the excess of debt in high interest leveraged buyouts featuring reset bonds, high interest zero bonds, mezzanine debt, and the better known junk bonds. Sellers of junk bonds like Canadian developer, Robert Campeau, have experienced spectacular and highly publicized bankruptcies. Many lesser known companies have defaulted on their debts and have gone into bankruptcy.

I would estimate that no less than 50 billion dollars has been lost by junk bond investors, and that figure may move much higher.

The major banks have been forced to write off billions of dollars in debt owed them by third world countries, and the present and future defaults among United States real estate investors may dwarf that amount. At present the capital structure of most of the big city money center banks is quite strained and vulnerable to any further debt shocks.

So far our economy has weathered progressively devastating economic events with remarkable resilience. I, like many, fervently hope that we can work our way out of it. But as things stand now, if there is a serious recession which takes under a number of over-leveraged businesses, the strain may be too much for an already weakened financial system and we may see a debt collapse of worldwide proportions followed by a painful and protracted depression.

With these prospects before us people would be well advised to avoid the stock market until the smoke clears, to stay clear of all but the most advantageous and necessary real estate purchases, to get out of debt, and to have available investments of the safest and most liquid sort, such as U.S. Treasury bills.

The government will never default on its current short term paper, and it must market treasury bills, as it always has, to yield interest at a rate at least 3 percent higher than the then current rate of inflation. For this reason funds placed in treasury bills are safe from default and reasonably safe from all but the most virulent inflation.

FOOLISH GOVERNMENT ACTION

In 1929 when the long wave debt cycle was winding down with a stock market crash, the government tried to help the economy out. As is always the case, our government took action to try to change the past not help the future. Incredibly they raised taxes and raised tariff barriers.

It is still a matter of debate as to who took the third false step, the Federal Reserve Board or the credit creating borrowing public, but we now know that between 1930 and 1932, in a time of desperate need of capital, the United States money supply shrank by an unbelievable 25 percent.

People today say that a 1929 style depression cannot happen because the government has too many mechanisms in place to prevent it. The record clearly shows that it was unwise government action before and after the great depression which helped bring it on and then made it much worse after it had happened.

In our day it was government action which allowed the Savings and Loan debacle to occur. The Congress raised the insurance limit on S&L accounts to 100,000 dollars and then authorized the S&Ls to make whatever loans they wished with the government insured money.

The Congressionally mandated lure to fraud was virtually irresistible. Now, true to form, the government by overreacting to the past abuses is bringing on a credit crunch which is helping push the economy into recession. Congressional action, by dramatically raising reserve requirements, has forced even solvent S&Ls into receivership.

Government auditors are poring over bank records, questioning existing loans and in some cases forcing banks to call fully performing loans. As a result bank officials are fearful of taking even modest risks, and a full blown credit crunch has developed which is giving the economy a major shove into recession.

Government does not produce anything. Government never creates wealth. It is one of the illusions of socialism that government somehow makes wealth. All government does is redistribute wealth, and it does so by extracting an enormous administrative penalty.

Some estimates of government programs indicate that something on the order of 70 percent of the total spending goes for administrative costs and only about 30 percent gets out to the recipients. The idea that higher taxes will improve economic conditions is a false promise of those who support the idea of a welfare state and ever-greater expenditures by government.

Thomas Jefferson's opinion of government was very clear in his oft-quoted statement, "That government governs best that governs least." He warned us at the founding of this nation about intrusive government programs and the resulting tax burden. Americans in the highest tax bracket are already paying close to 40 percent now for state, federal, and Social Security taxes, and the average taxpayer is paying upwards of 25 percent of family income for more bureaucracy.

In addition, the burden of Social Security continues to mount. In 1990, the cost of Social Security and Medicaid will top 345 billion dollars, equal to half of all Federal spending if you discount military spending and interest on the national debt. Where most of us feel the crunch, though, is in our paychecks.

In 1958 the maximum withholding was about 189 dollars for Social Security; by 1977 it was up to about 1,900 dollars. But thanks to seven rate hikes during the 1980s, by 1989 it was up to 7,850 dollars. David Boaz, vice president of the Cato Institute in Washington, D.C., wrote in a commentary in the *New York Times* that today the typical American worker actually gives up more of his income for Social Security than for income taxes.

That cost is not going down. To make Social Security solvent, by the year 2020 the combined Social Security tax will be 22,000 dollars (in 1989 dollars), or 88,000 dollars at 5 percent compounded inflation.

For many years, Congress has used the resources of the Social Security Administration like a checking account. No capital has ever been accumulated, and no interest or other benefits have ever been allowed to accrue to these vital accounts.

It is clear now that government has lost its vision and its ability to manage these programs, and it should come as no surprise that Boaz and other Cato Institute experts, such as Peter J. Ferrara, have been calling for the privatization of the government retirement and Social Security systems.

TAKING THE HIT

The double whammy of high income taxes and high Social Security withholding has created an incredible burden on the average wage-earner. In March 1989 the United States Census Bureau announced that the median annual family income in 1987 was approximately 30,850 dollars. That was the first real inflation-adjusted gain since the previous high of 1973. But again, the average family in America had to work from January 1st to May 5th to pay their tax debt.

Despite the higher incomes and the so-called "tax reductions" of the past five years, that's the longest period of time Americans have ever had to work for the IRS before earning the first nickel for themselves. Shouldn't it be clear to everybody that we don't need more taxes?

Liberal commentators were applauding the 1990 Tax Summit in Washington, saying it was about time Americans realized that somebody has to pay for government. In fact, John Chancellor said that on an NBC News commentary. But Americans haven't missed the point at all; John Chancellor has missed the point, and the liberal Democrats have missed the point.

Americans don't want more government, or even the same amount of government. We want less, not more. We want a lower tax debt, fewer bureaucrats, less meddling in the lives of Americans, fewer socialist giveaway schemes, and less scalping of American wage-earners.

In his remarkable book, *Losing Ground: American Social Policy, 1950–1980*, Charles Murray described a program which would accomplish many if not all of the goals of the socialist agenda. He said it could turn the hard-core unemployed into steady workers, reduce the birthrate among single girls, reduce the breakup of poor families, and improve morale among the underclass.

Quite simply, his suggestion was to scrap the entire federal welfare system, "including AFDC, Medicaid, Food Stamps, Unemployment Insurance, Worker's Compensation, subsidized housing, disability insurance, and the rest." Murray's logic was that "it would leave the working-aged person with no recourse whatsoever except the job market, family members, friends, and public or private locally funded services."

Now if they could be assured of achieving all these goals, government would gladly spend billions, Murray reasoned, and this program would be absolutely free! But naturally the liberal majority, who feel the solution to every problem is to raise taxes and to increase federal control, scoffed at Murray's proposal. To them it was simply too outrageous.

What we must remember is that government is not ultimately interested in helping the under-privileged; government is interested in building programs that extend the power and control of government.

GROWING THE UNDERCLASS

Boaz cites Murray's research in his essay on "Saving the Inner City," in which he shows how the so-called "underclass" was, in fact, a creation of the welfare system.

While there have always been, and will always be, poor in the land, the hard-core unemployable, and those people who have become entirely dependent on government programs, never existed in this nation until Lyndon Johnson's "Great Society" gave them a place to hang out.

The things the Eastern Europeans are learning fast is that central planning, socialistic economies, and government-owned enterprises are wasteful and inefficient. Everywhere I've gone in Poland, in Hungary, and in Czechoslovakia, there has been talk of privatizing state-owned enterprises because people know they are wasting resources, and they're not contributing to the economy.

As a matter of fact, when I was in Hungary an American appraiser of state enterprises told me that a typical beauty shop operator in the United States or Canada with three women working for her would know more about business accounting and economics after three years than the general manager of a state-owned enterprise with 10,000 employees in Hungary.

The accounting—and the level of business accountability—is horrible because the goals are not set by the markets. The key to successful enterprise is a free market. The market tells business what it wants and what it does not want. The state, on the other hand, tells business what it should make, whether the people want it or not.

Accountants in Hungary, for example, are not concerned by what actually sells but what makes it into the warehouse to fulfill the government-mandated quota. If 3,000 pairs of shoes were made but nobody wanted them, the books still show that they sold 3,000 pairs of shoes because they made them and put them into the warehouse.

When state quotas are met in many of these enterprises, they stop counting because they have met their quota and anything else is not relevant. They have satisfied the demands of the state.

CURBING GOVERNMENT'S CONTROL

The aim of free people everywhere is to limit the power and the scope of the government in any way they can, and the best way to do that is through lower taxes. Unfortunately, the bureaucratic lobby is large and powerful.

Those who seek to wield power and control the people have great skill in manipulating the system, while the average taxpayer isn't organized at all. There are very sophisticated pressure groups to represent those who expect to get money out of the system.

The people who profit from the poor have a vested interest in maintaining poverty programs, so they have an effective lobby because they want to keep the things they are receiving from the government.

There can be a taxpayer's revolt, as there was in California. There is certainly a tendency toward (perhaps even a mandate for) lower taxes in this country—and ultimately that trend will have to continue—but the liberal power block is always on the side of higher taxes, increased government involvement in people's lives, and more of the product of our working people going into the hands of bureaucrats.

In a conference sponsored by the Family Research Council in Washington, D.C., Dr. Allan Carlson, president of the Rockford Institute, said that the financial pressure on the two-parent family has become unbearable. He told the conferees that between 1960 and 1984, the tax burden on a two-parent family with four children increased by 224 percent. During the same period of time, there was a 600 percent increase in the family's Social Security tax.

What these figures show is that there is a deliberate discriminatory bias toward the traditional family in this country. The government's welfare programs reward the disadvantaged family, encourage single-parent homes, and provide substantial benefits to dysfunctional families, while the traditional two-parent home is expected to pay the freight for the government's giveaways.

Under such pressure, is it any wonder that Americans have resorted to credit and compounding debt as a solution to their dilemma? Is there any doubt that over the last two decades Americans have learned to believe that debt is desirable, that credit is always available, and that the desires of their hearts are as near as their handy bank card?

WANTING IT NOW

The moral breakdown we have experienced in this nation and the world over the past 40 years indicates a growing lack of self-control. Someone defined lust as "wanting it now." Wanting *anything* now. We have been trained as consumers over the years in America to "buy now and pay later."

We are taught to desire material goods as the means of gaining satisfaction, and then we have placed in our hands an extremely permissive credit system which makes it possible for us to fulfill our desires for material things with little regard for the consequences.

It all starts with the fact that people cannot live within their means. In most cases they are unwilling to trust God for their material needs, so they bow to the false gods of credit and materialism.

The first commandment says, "Thou shalt have no other gods before me," but people begin to set up materialism as a god and they begin to think if only I could have that car, or this house, that boat, or this set of furniture, or this vacation, or that suit of clothes or some other status symbol, then I would be happy.

So there is an unending cycle of materialism. First there is violation of

the first commandment. Then coveting, a violation of the tenth commandment. Finally people begin to steal to satisfy their wants. They either go
into credit bondage, where the borrower is the servant of the lender, or
they will default on their debts which in essence is a form of theft. The
honest man pays back his debt, but the thief borrows and he doesn't pay.

By this credit creation, we have introduced a type of corruption into
our whole national life. When you add to that the fact that 51 percent of
the people take something from government, we have introduced another
factor, getting something for free because it comes out of government.

On top of that, we now have lotteries in state after state to help pay for
added government expenses. The states are deliberately training people
to gamble instead of to save their money.

We no longer train them that wealth comes from hard work, savings,
and compound interest. Instead, we have trained people to be wasteful in
their economic affairs then to wait for that great windfall profit that
comes about when they hit the lottery.

We are corrupting ourselves by our credit and spending policies. Then
our government comes in with a further corrupting influence with legalized
gambling. We get a false sense of satisfaction, a false sense of wealth. These
false values and the resulting dissatisfaction and high debt are major
contributing factors to the tremendous anxiety among so many people.

Our people are very anxious. Look at the number of librium and valium
tablets Americans consume: some figures indicate it is as high as ten billion
a year. When we consider the increased number of visits to psychiatrists, the
breakups of marriages, increased family violence and abuse, we have to
recognize that at least a big part of the emotional problems in this country
must be attributed to financial mismanagement and the financial bondage
which is attributable to our national worship of false gods.

We read in the book of Deuteronomy in the Old Testament that God
told Moses that if His people would shun false idols and continue to seek
His face, the people would prosper and flourish in the land, through all
time and wherever they went. But He also warned them that if they
turned away their hearts and were lured by their own pleasures and their
wealth and the idols of foreign lands, they would be cut off and their land
would be laid waste.

Whether we apply God's covenant to the children of Israel or to the
Christian nations of the world which inherited God's promises, it is easy
to see that we have failed God's commandments.

We go back to the fact that for most Americans their satisfaction is not
in God, is not in spiritual relations, or the inter-personal relations which
should give us happiness—the love of our wife, our husband, our
children and parents—but it is centered in things and the acquisition of
more things.

YUPPIES BEGIN TO SAVE

In the 1980s America and the industrialized world went on a spending spree the apex of which is chronicled by a weekly television show hosted by Robin Leach called, "The Lifestyles of the Rich and Famous."

The young urban professionals, or yuppies, led the way. These were the swinging singles or two income couples where annual family incomes of 90,000 to 100,000 dollars were the norm, and salaries of 250,000 to 1,000,000 dollars and beyond were not uncommon.

They went skiing at Aspen or Vail, dined on nouvelle cuisine on the Riviera, shopped on Rodeo Drive, drove BMWs or Mercedes cars, paid big money for memberships in luncheon and golf clubs, and fitted their homes and apartments with jacuzzis, giant screen televisions, surround stereo sound, and the latest and best video recorders, compact disc players, and symphony quality hi-fidelity music systems.

They spent money faster than they earned it and undoubtedly helped push America's saving rate to what may have been its lowest rate in history, a skimpy 2.8 percent.

In the 1990s, the yuppies are older, their children are growing up, and they have either bought everything they need or else they have grown tired of wasting money. So we are told consumption is out, frugality is in. BMWs and Mercedes are out, Jeeps and Ford Broncos are in. Designer clothes are out, discount specials are in. The wine and brie set may be turning into the lemonade and ritz cracker bunch.

The biggest news though is that consumption is out and savings are in. In the September, 1990 issue of *Money* magazine the lead feature was entitled, "9 Great Savings Moves." One of those featured savers was a certified member of yuppidom. He was a 45-year-old newspaper editor of a metropolitan newspaper whose wife is a writer.

This couple with one 17-year-old daughter have been saving 51 percent of the husband's salary, and in five years of frugal living (driving a 1984 Volkswagen Rabbit without a radio) have been able to pay off the mortgage on their 126,000-dollar-home in Southern Florida and accumulate savings and investments of 200,000 dollars.

Economist Dr. Gary Shilling of the New-York-City-based A. Gary Shilling and Company tells me that the trend in America from consumption to saving will be adequate to fund even larger federal deficits than we have now plus the investment needs of the growing United States industry. Shilling, who by the way feels we are heading into a really nasty worldwide recession, is quite optimistic for the long term prospects later in the decade.

The real secret of the economic rise of Japan since World War II has been the extraordinary 17 percent Japanese saving rate. If the American people would move their personal savings rate from its present level to anywhere near the Japanese level, American industry would have more than enough capital to challenge the world. And along with industrial renaissance we could see a zero rate of inflation, a prime interest rate of 3 percent, and home mortgage rates of 4.5 to 5 percent.

If there is any policy that the government should adopt during the next decade it should be a policy that reduces government spending, lowers taxes, and rewards saving. At present, government policy rewards borrowing and penalizes saving.

Corporations are permitted to deduct interest on bonds held by investors, but not the dividends paid on stock held by investors. People who finance their homes on credit are rewarded. People who pay cash for property are not. Interest and dividends received by savers are taxed without taking into consideration the inflation rate.

Savings placed into various types of pensions are highly restricted and limited in scope. No provision is made to allow the tax free build up of funds so that young couples can purchase a first home or pay for the college education for their children.

When an alcoholic or drug addict stops using drugs and goes "cold turkey" the immediate effect is horrible. He experiences chills, cramps, fever, sweating, delirium, and agonizing craving for a drink or a "fix." After a while the body of the addict or the alcoholic cleanses itself of the poison, and the normal processes begin to work again as wholesome food, rest, and exercise do their work.

The physical addiction is gone. All that remains is a possible physical tendency toward addiction and a steadily declining mental addiction.

The debt binge of the past 25 years is over. The punch bowl and the needle are being taken away. We would like to taper off gradually. A depression might demand that we go "cold turkey." If so, the temporary pain will be intense, but if the problems discussed in chapter 7 are solved we can come through it and return to vibrant health. The issue is not whether there will be debt withdrawal—only how and when.

THE ROLE OF THE CHURCH

The church stands to today's society very much as the church stood to Rome at the collapse of the Roman Empire. It does seem that what has been called Christendom, to use Muggeridge's phrase, is in decline. When the Roman Empire collapsed, it took with it the greatest system of political, economic and military power the world had ever known. And in the very dark days of the Roman Empire, after the collapse, the Church of Rome was the only stable force available to rebuild society.

Out of the collapse of one came the flowering of the other, and that flowering and rebirth were based on Christian tenets and Christian morality.

As the most dominant empire since Roman times, America has helped to bring great wealth and prosperity to the world, but its moral strength and vitality have begun to wane. The strong dose of renewal and vitality so greatly needed by American government and business can best be delivered by an injection of democratic morality.

Richard John Neuhaus recently said, "I believe that democratic morality will be both a means toward its achievement and a product of its achievement." In other words, when we commit ourselves to the aims of moral structures and moral government in a pluralist society, our faith in the process of democracy helps to bring about its existence and continuation.

Our faith in the worth of morality and the fruits of democracy offers America and the world its greatest weapon against defeat and decline.

But many argue today that we are already living in a post-Christian era, as far as the culture, traditions and mores of the people are concerned. And it seems that Western civilization—at least in America—is in a period of decline. It is only too clear that much of the vitality and economic power we once prized so highly is moving to the East.

Today we are seeing an even more striking paradox in Eastern Europe. In an area of the world where Christendom has not been a dominant influence for at least 50 years, suddenly there is moral renewal.

In communist countries where the Christian church has been oppressed, and where the political and economic system has been organized around militant atheism and the trampling of individual values under the iron heel of the collective, there now appears to be a new birth of Christian democracy.

The only unifying force in those countries with any moral authority is the Church, and throughout Eastern Europe—in Hungary and Czechoslovakia and in Poland—the Roman Catholic church and the Evangelical Protestant churches have become the rallying point of moral and democratic renewal.

I believe that the role of the church is to call people back to New Testament faith and New Testament beliefs that put transcendent values ahead of present day materialism. Even if the political and economic system that we currently enjoy goes into decline, Jesus Christ will not decline and His kingdom will endure forever.

This can be the church's finest hour, but I believe that we must rise to the challenge by working for spiritual renewal, giving a whole new ethos to Western culture. The church must be prepared to pick up the pieces of shattered materialism.

What a great tragedy it would be for those emerging Eastern European countries if they were to survive the ravages of communist-style materialism and to overcome the tyranny of atheist philosophies only to fall victim to a capitalist-style materialism devoid of the underlying spiritual values that make capitalism human and bearable.

When I met with Billy Graham at the Brandenburg Gate in 1990, he told me that the East Germans he met were shocked when they came across the wall and saw West Berlin. They thought they would be met by fellow believers who would be singing hymns and praising the Lord and rejoicing at their freedom. But there were no believers to welcome them; instead, all they saw was shops and cars and X-rated movies and all of the decadence that now exists in Western Europe. Plentiful goods to be sure, but a heart-breaking lack of moral and spiritual values.

I remember my own shock in making the journey from Hong Kong to Mainland China and seeing the contrast between those two cultures. There was a simplicity, an honestly and openness, even a kind of purity in the people I met in China that was absolutely appealing and beautiful.

When I came back out to Hong Kong and the unbelievable opulence that exists in that colony, I was jolted by the excesses. It was such an incredible irony to see the greed and decadence of Hong Kong juxtaposed against the austerity of Mainland China. There is no question that spiritual values languish when we have material excess.

As we look about us, we see everywhere the signs of collapse. The rationalistic ideologies have failed, the reign of communist tyranny has failed, and the materialistic systems of American-style wealth-building have failed.

But the source of our renewal remains, and there is hope. For the kingdom of God has not failed, and Jesus Christ has not failed. In that truth alone we have reason to hope that the coming decade can be a promising era for freedom and truth, and for building the future world God has prophetically ordained.

That world will not come through greed or materialism or any of the worn-out values of consumerism, but through a new commitment to biblical morality. The very hand of God is stirring in the land, and those who survive and prosper will be those who humbly seek His face and seek His guidance. I am convinced that only a national renewal can save us. Only a global renewal can save the world.

The 1990s will see a debt blow-out which could trigger a serious worldwide depression.

11

The Rise of Anti-Semitism

Anti-semitism will continue to rise in this decade.

The nations of the earth have united against the nation which occupies the site of the Tower of Babel to form a New World Order.

EARLY ON THE morning of August 2, 1990, the forces of Iraq at the command of Iraqi dictator, Saddam Hussein, invaded their tiny neighbor, Kuwait, looted the Kuwaiti banks, seized their gold and currency, raped their women, and then annexed their country.

Suddenly a wily megalomaniac at the helm of a nation with only 17 million people, yet possessing a large army, over 5000 tanks, chemical weapons, and the rudiments of atomic bombs, had taken control of 20 percent of the world's oil and was threatening 30 percent more.

The rest of the world, led by the United States, assembled a vast force of planes, ships, and fighting men to blockade Iraq and then neutralize its leader.

A comment in the August 27, 1990, issue of *U.S. News and World Report* gives a true perspective of what was happening, ". . . the looming conflict in the Persian Gulf is not simply a battle for Kuwait, or even for mastery of the Middle East's oil. It is the latest chapter in a 14-century-old battle between East and West, between Islam and its monotheistic rivals, Christianity and Judaism."

THE TRUE MEANING OF SADDAM HUSSEIN

The world's present civilization began in the Tigris-Euphrates valley first with Summer, where Ur of Chaldees, the ancestral home of Abraham was located. Slightly north the civilizations of Nineveh and Akkad emerged, then successively in the same territory arose the Assyrian and Babylonian civilizations.

The modern nation of Iraq is located precisely where the civilizations of both the East and the West began, in the land of Nineveh, Assyria, and Babylon.

This region has been known as the center of mystical and occult religions—Nimrod, Astarte, the tower of Babel, the false god, Baal, Baalzebub, the court magicians and Chaldean soothsayers of Nebuchadnezzar, and the Babylonian Mysteries of the Roman era—all originated here. In the book of Revelation the Roman Empire and type of a future anti-Christ is identified as "Mystery Babylon, the mother of harlots."

I would not want to make more out of the current trouble than the facts warrant, but it seems to me that the world should take notice that a major conflict at the end of this millennium is pitting all the nations of the earth against the nation which occupies the place where all of our cultures began in ancient history.

Iraq also happens to be in a place identified by the Bible as the land where successive revolts against God have taken place since the beginning of time.

The Sumerian civilization dates back at least to 3500 B.C., possibly earlier. In a Sumerian city called Ur a boy was born about 2000 B.C. whose name was Abram. After Abram was married, his father took him, his wife Sarai, and his nephew Lot to a place in Canaan north of present Israel called Haran.

Abram, who later became known as Abraham, left Haran at the age of 75 because God had promised him the land we now know as Palestine. Abraham had two sons, one was Isaac, the forefather of the Jewish people. The other was Ishmael, the child of a servant girl, Hagar, and was the forefather of the Arab people.

Abraham was 100 years of age when his wife Sarai conceived Isaac, fulfilling God's promise to make Abraham's seed a blessing to all of the nations of the earth. When God told Abraham to sacrifice the young Isaac at a place called Mount Moriah, Abraham's obedience was being tested. But Abraham proved worthy, and the boy was spared by the intervention of God.

This place of holy dedication and unquestioning obedience to God is thought to be the site of the Temple Mount in the city of Jerusalem. By his act of sacrifice and obedience at Mount Moriah, Abraham made Jerusalem the spiritual center for those who, like Abraham and later Jesus Christ, were willing by faith to give everything to serve God.

Jerusalem is therefore the center of the true worship of God. Babylon, on the other hand, is the spiritual symbol of those who refuse God's grace but insist on building systems and institutions which, like the tower of Babel, were to challenge God's rule and authority.

The Bible tells us that at one time all the people of the earth were united with one purpose and one language. At Babel, however, God confused their languages and separated them to prevent a unified, one-world revolt against Him.

Until very recently, I had always felt that Babylon was merely a symbol. Until the Saddam Hussein affair, I never felt that anything would actually bring the power of the entire world to physical Babylon. But this is the era when we should expect the unexpected!

THE NEW WORLD ORDER

On Saturday, August 25, 1990, the United Nations Security Council voted unanimously, with the participation of both China and the Soviet Union, to permit the joint force gathering in the Middle East to use appropriate power to back up the United Nations blockade against Iraq. That afternoon, Lieutenant General Brent Scowcroft, the protege of Henry Kissinger, and National Security Advisor to President George Bush, was interviewed by Charles Bierbauer for Cable News Network.

General Scowcroft was obviously pleased and in his pleasure let slip a phrase that he had learned over and over as a member of the Council on Foreign Relations, "A New World Order." The action of the United Nations to permit military action against an aggressor nation such as Iraq was, in the words of the highest ranking strategist in the Bush administration, the start of "a new world order."

Obviously to those of us who are weary and disgusted by a world divided into rival squabbling camps, the prospect of unanimous joint action by a world body sounds good. But is it really good? Has the crisis in Babylon actually been used to usher onto the world scene something that is not good at all?

Since its founding in the late 1920s, the Council on Foreign Relations has played a dominant role in the foreign and economic policy of the United States. If there is a true establishment, this is it.

Funded and directed in large measure by the Rockefeller family, the CFR has long held what must seem to them a noble goal, the establishment of a one-world government. To that end the repeated thrust of CFR related literature has been the diminishing of the power and sovereignty of the United States of America and the establishment of a global government with courts and military and currency—and yes, of course, banks—which take precedence over the institutions of the United States.

In a benign world where all men are angels such an arrangement might actually be desirable. But given a world in which dictators, fanatics, revolutionaries, and assassins are as often as not in control of nations, the prospect of being governed by such people is not very appealing.

For Christians, the idea of surrendering sovereignty to Muslims and Hindus who are dedicated to the destruction of what we consider holy is anathema. The nation of Israel most certainly has a very similar attitude.

I am writing now somewhat ahead of events developing in the Middle East but, to my thinking, some of the portents seem very clear. If Saddam Hussein is really smart, he will meet with key Arab leaders, and then permit himself to be talked into withdrawing from Kuwait in exchange for an agreement by his Arab brethren to maintain the price of oil at a level of $22 per barrel or more.

At that point, President Bush will have no choice but to bring U.S. troops, planes, tanks, and ships back home, leaving Saddam free to use his oil wealth to build atomic bombs and a more deadly arsenal.

Saddam can then rail at America, and call for a revolt in Saudi Arabia against the family of Ibn Saud, who will be presented as the lackeys of the imperialist anti-Arab American aggressors. If there is then an internal overthrow of ruling monarchs, there is no way the public opinion of the world can be mobilized to resist it.

Saddam may lack that wisdom, but I doubt it. If he withdraws, President George Bush will be revived in popularity as a cool leader who backed down a 1990s version of Adolf Hitler. In reality, a more sinister scenario may actually be unfolding.

The real long term meaning of the Saddam Hussein affair would be this: at the site of the Tower of Babel where the nations of the world were once dispersed, all the nations of the earth came together and entered into a military alliance which began, according to a high ranking American official, "a new world order."

It would be a new world order with military power to force upon individual nations a standard of conduct that the nations of the world believe is proper. It is this power that may one day be used against Christians. It certainly will be used one day against the nation of Israel.

The real future story of biblical world history is not about all the nations on earth coming against Babylon, the center of false religion, but about all the nations on earth coming against Israel, the site and origin of

God's true religion. Jerusalem, not Baghdad, is the capital of the land described by the Bible as the navel of the earth.

WASHINGTON CHANGES COURSE

If what President George Bush said in his February 1990 address represents any sort of shift in American policy toward Israel, we can expect to see a much harder line in this country in the months ahead. And if the level of pressure against Israel from within and from without continues to mount as it has in the past 12 months, by the year 2000 we may well see the nation of Israel standing virtually alone.

In his public and private remarks, President Bush has told Yitzhak Shamir that East Jerusalem and the West Bank are still considered off limits to Jewish settlers. He further warned the Israeli Prime Minister that he could not continue to take three billion dollars a year in aid from the United States on the pretext he would work for peace and bring about an end to the strife with the Palestinians, then do nothing about peace.

Bush's words were understood as a threat to withdraw aid and support to Israel, and in some ways a statement that our long diplomatic relationship with Israel was being reexamined. As a result, the Likud lost the support of the Parliament. Shamir's government fell in March 1990 and it took two attempts and nearly four months, until June 1990, to rebuild a stable coalition.

The problem for the Likud, the conservative wing of government, is that the hard-liners want to ignore the Arab problem and make it go away. The Labour Party, on the other hand, wants to settle with the Arabs and, like Ben-Gurion and Menachem Begin before them, trade land for peace.

The two major parties cannot even agree to disagree, but to complicate matters dramatically there are 35 dissident and splinter parties in the Parliament, circling like gnats, constantly agitating and rendering the prospects of a peaceful resolution virtually impossible.

President Bush and Secretary of State James Baker have repeatedly told Shamir to get serious. They are saying that America and the world will not be patient with the internal bickering within the Parliament forever. If, in addition to all the external pressure from Saddam Hussein and the militant Arab nations and their own internal squabbles, there is also a concerted effort to pressure the Jews, then I believe matters can only worsen.

However, from all indications, the action of Saddam Hussein has shocked many of the Israeli "doves" to the danger the nation would face from a Palestinian state on the West Bank, connected to Jordan, and then

connected to Iraq. Prime Minister Shamir's hardline stance has been
clearly vindicated and strengthened.

SHIFTING WORLD OPINION

Whether America's new get-tough policy is motivated by sincere
diplomatic concern or by more pragmatic financial reasons—because of
Middle East oil, the threats of Arab boycotts, or the expense of a
three-billion-dollar aid program—there has been a definite shifting in
American foreign policy toward Israel.

In addition to the shift in public policy, there seems also to be a shift of
the sympathies of the American people toward Israel. Recent public
opinion polls show that most Americans feel that other nations are now
better friends of America than Israel.

In the press, and in the public opinion, there is a growing consensus
that Israel is not as important to us as it once was, and the support for
Israel which has come predominantly out of the evangelical, biblical
worldview, has diminished even as that Christian worldview has been
diminished in American life.

THE HISTORICAL RECORD

**The Holy Land is called the navel of the earth in the Bible. It is the
spiritual hub of the world. The ancient city of Jerusalem is considered
to be the most holy place for both Jews and Christians and, to a lesser
degree, for Muslims as well.**

If we believe the Bible, the Messiah will come back to Jerusalem, His
feet resting on the Mount of Olives, followed by earthquakes and celestial
events of catastrophic proportions. The mountains will split from north to
south and a great waterway will form in the valley which runs from
Jerusalem down to the Dead Sea. The city of Jerusalem will be leveled by
the earthquake and become a large plateau.

The book of Revelation offers many such dramatic images, but whether
they are all to be taken literally or whether they should be understood to
imply some spiritual truth, I can't say categorically. Bible scholars have
excellent reasons in support of each point of view.

However you choose to interpret these passages, the Bible clearly
speaks of a literal conflict with the nations surrounding Jerusalem and the
deliverance of the Jews coming from the Lord Himself. The Old Testament used the phrase, "The Time of Jacob's Trouble." The New Testament
called it, "The Tribulation."

I believe there will come a time when the nations of the earth will turn against Israel and isolate her, and that she will only be saved by the direct intervention of God.

THE DREAM OF ZION

As we know, Zionism is a political force. It is not a spiritual force. While its underlying beliefs and goals are as ancient as the nation of Judah itself, Zionism has been the unifying dream of the Jewish people since Theodore Herzl and others came together in the last years of the nineteenth century to formulate plans for the establishment of a homeland for the Jews in Palestine.

If we look back to the history of this region, we discover that King David first took the Citadel of Zion by conquest in about 1000 B.C. As I pointed out, it is believed that what is called "The Temple Mount" is Mount Moriah where Abraham went to sacrifice his son, Isaac. It is part of the land given by God to Abraham, and it was given later by God to Moses and Joshua and the people who came up from captivity in Egypt by conquest around 1400 B.C.

As recorded in Genesis 15, God granted all the land between the River of Egypt (The *Wadi El Arish* near Gaza) north to the Euphrates (which flows through Syria) to the children of Israel. And we know that this grant was not only by divine mandate, but it was also by military conquest, and the Bible tells us that 400 years elapsed from the promise of Abraham until the people returned to the land because what was termed "the iniquity of the Amorites" was not yet complete.

We know, further, that when the northern kingdom of Israel was conquered by the Assyrians in 722 B.C., thousands of Jews were massacred by the invading armies of King Sargon II and as many as 30,000 were carried off into captivity.

In the midst of the slaughter, many of the people of Israel fled north and east and west and eventually covered the earth. Those people who are known romantically as the "ten lost tribes of Israel," found homes in many nations and have seemingly vanished from history.

THE REMNANT OF JUDAH

Those who remained in the southern kingdom were the tribes of Benjamin and Judah. It was from Judah that the modern word, Jew, is taken. It was these people who preserved the Israelite traditions and culture through the dark years between the Assyrian invasion and the next great tragedy in 586 B.C. when they were conquered, carried off, and enslaved to Nebuchadnezzar, King of Babylon, in the region we now know as Iraq.

In those turbulent years between 734 and 580 B.C., there were six separate depredations against the Israelites, and each attack scattered the people and drove them out of the land. Only a small band escaped the Babylonian invasion and remained in Palestine until the captives returned from Babylon, about 70 years later.

But, the people of Judah, the Jews, occupied Jerusalem under foreign rule through the time of Christ, and they remained there until the Romans finally burned and flattened the city in 70 A.D., "leaving not one stone on top of another."

Rome's final desecration of Jerusalem came in 135 A.D. On the pretext of quashing the civil war between the Greeks and the Jews, the Romans attacked the Jewish Zealots in the hills around Jerusalem, and then Hadrian's legions sacked and destroyed all that remained of that once-great capital, thereby ending the Jewish presence in Israel for the next 1,800 years.

REBUILDING A NATION

By the nature of history and the nature of war, it is humanly impossible that the Jews could ever have returned to Israel after 1,800 years to build a nation. While a small number of Jews managed to remain in the land through each of the successive devastations, the surrounding nations moved in quickly and populated the camps and villages, took over the fields and vineyards, and claimed the land.

Every other people on earth lose their national identity after years of living in another country. Only the Jews refused to assimilate, to give up their separate identity, their faith in God, and their hope of returning to their own land. At the annual Passover they would say, "Next year in Jerusalem."

Only God could have worked such an incredible miracle. He had told the Jews that they were His chosen people. They were to keep alive the true faith in the true God. Despite thousands who fell away, the Jewish remnant kept the faith.

The story is told of a conversation between the mighty monarch, Queen Victoria of England, and her Prime Minister, Benjamin Disraeli. "Mr. Prime Minister," she asked, "what is the greatest evidence of God's existence?" After brief reflection, Disraeli replied, "The Jew, your majesty."

By the late 1880s, Jews started buying land in Israel, particularly in the Galilee and the valleys north of Jerusalem, with a new dream and vision of Zion. Encouraged by zealous young leaders from the wealthy Jewish families of Germany, Poland, France, and Great Britain, they began reclaiming arid, empty land and swamps, wherever they could get a foothold.

In some of those settlements they brought swampy, mosquito-ridden, malaria-infested lands which had to be reclaimed from the sea. They went out into the marshes and planted eucalyptus trees to soak up the water so they could use the land.

The inhabitants of the land prior to the coming of the Jewish settlers were nomadic, by and large. There were few cities of note. Tel Aviv was a relatively small town. The old city of Jerusalem was still small. There were other isolated Arab villages and settlements in some parts of Palestine, but there was not a lot of activity among either the Arabs or Jews in those days.

RECLAIMING THE PROMISE

The movement to reclaim Palestine as a Jewish homeland grew into a major diplomatic issue during the first two decades of this century. By the early 1920s, both sides, Arabs and Jews, were participating in skirmishes and terrorist activities to try and swing the tide of world opinion in their own favor.

It was soon to be a turbulent period of struggle and bloodshed. Men like Chaim Wiezmann, a highly educated German Jew with capitalist perspectives, and David Ben-Gurion, who came to Israel in the early 1920s from Poland with strong socialist sympathies, rose as leaders of the Zionists.

Ironically, it was Winston Churchill who, as Colonial Secretary of the British government in March of 1921, took it upon himself to settle the situation by giving a territory called Transjordan to Abdullah, the son of the Sharif of Mecca in Saudi Arabia.

Churchill never quite sorted out his feelings about Palestine, the third territory under his authority, but he acknowledged the Jewish right of return and seemed to believe that Arabs and Jews would somehow co-exist there quite peaceably.

Nevertheless, from the end of World War I until the end of World War II, the land of Palestine remained in nearly constant turmoil. Even though Jews all over the world claimed the dream of Zion, it wasn't until the Holocaust and the slaughter of more than six million European Jews that the immigrations to Palestine became a reality.

Suddenly Jews who a decade earlier had thought of Germany or France or Poland as their native home were forced to face the fact that there could only be one home for the Jews.

In 1917 Lord Balfour wrote a letter to Lord Rothschild—who was the most distinguished Jewish financier, philanthropist, and statesman in the world at that time. Balfour declared his support for the establishment of a "Jewish homeland." The Balfour Declaration didn't make the Jewish state a reality, but it gave focus to the hopes of young men like Weizmann and Ben-Gurion.

It was not until after World War II, in 1948, that the United Nations (at the insistence of Harry Truman and the American people) acknowledged the national statehood of Israel. By a vote of 33 in favor, 13 against, and 10 abstentions, the UN gave the Jews a narrow strip of land which included the area around Tel Aviv and north into the Galilee area, but excluding what is now the West Bank. East Jerusalem and the West Bank were then still a part of Transjordan. The Gaza Strip belonged to Egypt.

But Churchill's surmise had been wrong. There could be no peace. Arabs in Palestine and throughout the Middle East were incensed that this essentially Western, European-style, and seemingly democratic nation was being inserted, like a virus, into their midst.

Suddenly the land of Palestine had become inhospitable to the Arabs living there and many fled to Transjordan, Lebanon, Iraq, Syria, Egypt, Gaza and the West Bank. Altogether, more than 600,000 Arabs took refuge outside Palestine.

PROVOCATIONS TO HOSTILITY

But these refugees were also ready warriors, and bolstered by the promise of support by their Arab brothers, the Palestinians declared war on the new State of Israel with the aim of driving the Jews into the sea.

At the same time, a wave of repression of Jews in the Arab countries— from Morocco in the West to Syria in the East—brought more than a half million Jews into Israel at a time when the Israelis were marshaling their own forces. By late 1948, the Israelis had put together an army of 100,000 men with weapons they had purchased from Czechoslovakia, or which had been provided by supporters of Zion in America and other places.

The difference in the re-settlement practices of the Jews with their refugees versus the refusal of the Arab nations to provide a long term solution for their refugees was to become a major factor in the ongoing struggle.

When the Jews arrived from the Arab countries, or from Europe, North Africa, Scandinavia, or any of the other places they had lived, they were immediately given land and shelter in Israel and made citizens of the nation.

The Arabs, on the other hand, were put into temporary dwellings, tents, and refugee camps. They were not settled permanently since they believed it was only a matter of time until the Jews would be evicted and Arabs would regain their homes in Palestine.

The Arabs were confident they would come back victorious and resume their lives. But the Israelis won that war, as they have won every war since that time, and the territories which had been held by the Arabs in 1947 were now possessed by the Jews.

A sort of troubled peace existed in the region for the next 20 years. While there were clashes and skirmishes between Jewish settlers and the half million Arabs who remained in Palestine throughout those years, the first full-scale war came in 1967 when Gamal Abdel Nasser of Egypt provoked what is now known as the "Six Day War." The *causus belli* was the closing of the Gulf of Aqaba to Israeli shipping, which was interpreted by the Jews, understandably, as an act of war.

Israel responded to the provocation with a lightning strike into the Sinai region, and in six days, with the might of the tank battalions commanded by Moshe Dayan, defeated the forces of Egypt, while another Israeli force captured the West Bank, including East Jerusalem, from Jordan.

For the first time in about 2,500 years, the Jews occupied the eastern sector of Jerusalem, including the Temple Mount and the Wailing Wall. They made Jerusalem the capital of Israel, and within weeks they began settling the captured regions of what they began to call, by their biblical names, Judea and Samaria.

After a restive peace, the Egyptians along with the Syrians struck again in 1973 and launched what is now known as the "Yom Kippur War," on Israel's most holy day. Again they were roundly defeated. Israel had trapped a major Egyptian army corps and could have marched on Cairo but was held back by the United States for the sake of world opinion.

At that time they took back from Syria, and later annexed, the high plateau north of the Sea of Galilee up to the Syrian border called the Golan Heights. For years Syrian gunners had used these heights to rain down mortar and artillery fire on the hapless Jewish settlers in the Galilee valley. The battle for the Golan filled the headlines at that time, and television news reports showing the fire power and the devastation in that area were terrifying.

Christians around the world wondered if this wasn't the start of Armageddon—after all, the plain of Megiddo was barely ten miles to the south. As it became clear that the Israelis had won the battle for the Golan, tensions subsided somewhat. The battle goes down as one of the biggest tank battles in the history of warfare. As many tanks massed in that one small area as had ever been marshaled in any battle in history, giving Israel an enormous victory.

THE DISPOSSESSED

The amazing thing about the Palestinians' apparent loss of their land is the reluctance of other Arab nations to take the Palestinians into their midst. The Palestinians are the most highly educated people in the entire region. They are highly skilled artisans, craftsmen, and engineers. They have a tradition of learning that goes back thousands of years, to the first universities and libraries in the world.

But the Arab emirates and surrounding nations were almost afraid of them—apparently afraid their learning and skill might allow them to become the dominant nationality in the lands where they were working.

Consequently, while the Arab nations have allowed the Palestinians to remain as workers, executives, and administrators, they have not really taken them in. With the single exception of King Hussein, who formerly exercised civil government over Jordanian Palestinians on the West Bank, no Arab nation has tried seriously to re-settle them.

Gaza could have been re-settled at any time, yet it has been kept as a United Nations refugee camp for nearly 25 years, which is virtually unheard of. Today the Gaza Strip is the most densely populated area on earth, with more than 3,800 persons per square mile.

When you think that the average population density of the United States is about 66 persons per square mile and England, which has always been considered one of the most congested nations on earth, is only about 600 per square mile, you realize just what a pressure cooker that area has become.

But one wonders if one reason for the continued homelessness of the Palestinians isn't because their leaders—along with their advisers and friends from Syria, Iraq, and the other Arab nations—believe that it will be of greater political advantage to keep them homeless, congested, and belligerent so they can be used as political pawns in the struggle against Israel.

A MANDATE FOR PEACE

Out of that background came the Camp David Accords in September 1978, at the behest of President Jimmy Carter who paid for, and reportedly stage-managed, the event. I am convinced that all the parties to those accords were sincere and believed they had a mandate for peace.

Representing the Arab interests was Anwar Sadat of Egypt, who was a highly religious man. He felt he had a mission from God and was willing to take the risks. On the other side was Menachem Begin, a long-time activist and militant, a warrior, a leader and twice prime minister, and the son of a distinguished rabbi.

Begin agreed at Camp David to surrender the Sinai to the Arabs— along with its oil fields, settlements, and military installations—in order to gain peace. Not since the administration of Ben-Gurion had an Israeli leader been willing to make such a bold compromise.

That compromise was costly to Begin at home and he lost the friendship of many long-time political confidants. The greater cost, though, fell upon Sadat.

For a while after Camp David, it began to look as if peace was, in fact, a possibility. Cabinet meetings were being held and negotiations were going on around the clock, seemingly with great success. But within a matter of weeks it was clear that the Egyptians were being excluded from the councils of the Arab leaders, even though Egypt had always been at the center of Islamic culture and theology, and was the biggest of the Arab nations.

Sadat's sincere effort to find a reconciliation with Israel had made Egypt a pariah in the Arab world. The old animosity between the Arabs and the Jews was just too deep, the tragic evidence of that fact being the bloody assassination of Sadat by Muslim fundamentalists at a parade ceremony in 1981.

Many of the West Bank Arabs work in Israel. They go into Jewish areas to work. The bridge over the Jordan is open for the transport of Palestinian citrus and other produce. They go across Jordan to Iraq, Kuwait, or down to Saudi Arabia and the Gulf. There has been very active trade. Without question, the status of Palestinian Arabs improved under Israeli occupation.

A CLOSER LOOK

During my visits to Israel in the late 1970s, there seemed to be a genuine movement toward peace and reconciliation in the area. The leader of the Labour Party, Shimon Peres, told me he wanted to establish a confederation where Israel could have secure borders around the whole territory. He hoped for an agreement in which the Palestinians could have self-government and autonomy within the boundaries of greater Israel.

The West Bank Arabs could form a state within a state. He thought that for its own security Israel would have to maintain a defense perimeter around the area. After all, the neck of land between Tel Aviv and the West

Bank is no more than nine miles at its widest, so it would be virtually defenseless in the event of a military strike. Peres has been willing all along to make concessions at that point.

However, Menachem Begin and his successor, Yitzhak Shamir, feel that Judea and Samaria are not Arab lands at all, and that in fact they are an integral and vital part of Israel's historic patrimony. To them trading the heartland of Israel for peace will never work and will only serve to weaken the nation by establishing a militantly hostile entity within Israel's natural defenses—which would be like a dagger aimed at their heart.

There were many who felt Israel should have annexed the West Bank territories after the Six Day War. They annexed the Golan Heights after 1973 with virtually no complaint. Golan is now part of Israel and that's the end of it. But the West Bank was allowed to become a seething cauldron, and the repercussions of that fact are not likely to be settled in the foreseeable future.

IRRECONCILABLE DIFFERENCES

The Palestinians have in their leadership some moderates with a desire to make some kind of accommodation with the Jews in Israel and to live at peace with them. People like Elias Freij, the Mayor of Bethlehem, and leaders of village councils, were beginning to take steps toward reconciliation. The process continued in that direction until more and more hard-liners in both camps began to emerge in the late 1980s.

The conservative wing of the Israeli parliament, the Likud, has become very unyielding in its attitude. Since 1987 the pace of building Israeli high rise towers and pre-fab towns called "settlements" has escalated in the West Bank.

One of the extreme groups made headlines in early 1990 by taking over an apartment building in Arab East Jerusalem, owned by the Greek Orthodox Church. They chose Holy Week to do it. These orthodox Jews declared their right to settle anywhere they pleased. The chosen people of Israel, they refused to concern themselves with Arab rights. And so they achieved worldwide press because of their timing, their militancy, and their seeming insensitivity to the rights of others.

While this is going on, the Arab world recognized the Palestinian Liberation Organization, the PLO, as the natural representative of the Palestinian people. Tawfik Abu Ghazala, a lawyer and counselor at the Gaza Center for Rights and Law, said, "The Palestinian people are the leaders, and Yasser Arafat is their representative." Before the beginning of the

Intifada, such an observation might have seemed like just so much rhetoric, but now we see the truth of that comment.

The Intifada has inflamed to white hot intensity the passions of Palestinians in Gaza, the West Bank, and Jordan. Unfortunately, the PLO has in its midst some very radical people. Men like George Habash continue to prey on innocent victims. Whether or not he is still a member of the PLO, Habash is a Marxist and an extremely violent man.

Extremist Mohammed Abbas led the attempted invasion of Tel Aviv from the sea in May 1990. He is not only a cohort of terrorist Abu Nidal and head of the extremely dangerous Al Fatah phalange group— formerly a wing of the PLO—but he is also a member of the PLO executive committee.

Arafat, himself, is also a dangerous man. Though he wants to be perceived as a peacemaker, he has repeatedly advocated terrorism and violence to achieve the goals of the Palestinians. Is it any wonder the world is leery of his overtures?

Others outside the Palestinian camp also counsel violence against Israel and participate in overt terrorism. Their targets are not only Jews, but the United States and other nations who actively support Israel. Western interests in the Middle East are constantly in jeopardy of terrorism because of our support for the Jews.

FIGURES OF SPEECH

Whether or not our perception of Yasser Arafat is correct, he has been the leader of the PLO since its inception, and he has repeatedly stated his conviction that Israel must not exist as a state.

He has made public declaration that his aim and goal is to drive this foreign influence out of the Middle East. He has said he does not want Israel as a sovereign nation within recognized and defensible borders; he wants Israel eliminated, out of the Middle East, and he has said so repeatedly.

In early 1990 Arafat was pressured by the United States State Department to read a line or two in Geneva which indicated that he has renounced those goals, but that isn't what he says in private, from what we can gather.

One gets the impression that Arafat's meetings with Jimmy Carter and the Pope have been staged for political advantage and do not truly reflect any change in his political stance.

To gain attention for their cause, the Palestinian people started a resistance movement inside Israel, Gaza, and the West Bank, called the uprising, or the "Intifada." While it has disrupted the normal pace of the economy, making day-to-day life harder on Jews and Arabs alike, it has really been a highly successful media campaign to gain sympathy for the Arab cause.

Three years ago I was told that on a slow day the Western media could call up and ask for a demonstration before noon and still have time to get something on the evening news in New York. If a demonstration is already planned for noon, the cameras will be in place at 11:45 to film it.

But the uprising has been very successful. The Israelis presumed that the Intifada would go away, but it hasn't gone away; it has only grown more and more determined, and in the process Israeli troops have grown more and more battle weary. In many instances, the soldiers have resorted to tactics that are nothing short of brutal.

OBJECTIONABLE FORCE

In its efforts to silence the disruptive Palestinians, the Israeli military has not used restraint as it should have. They have repeatedly used excessive force which has gone far beyond any recognized or acceptable norms of crowd control.

There are many cases of the deliberate breaking of bones. People's arms and legs have been stomped or twisted with truncheons so they will break. Soldiers have beaten civilians with gun butts, and many shoot to kill. Even rubber bullets, which are actually heavy metal balls covered with a thin rubber hide, are deadly at moderate range.

I have seen the medical reports analyzing the types of injuries found on demonstrators and detainees. These reports show that they are not accidental, but are deliberate attempts to maim and to punish the Palestinians in the most painful way. The violence has been indiscriminate: women and children have been brutalized as well as boys and men.

However you look at it, this kind of behavior shows a serious breakdown of discipline among the Jewish forces. There are similarities to what happened at the 1968 Democratic National Convention in Chicago when hippies went wild and the police, who couldn't take the abuse any more, began using brutality far beyond anything that could be considered acceptable in civilian restraint or crowd control.

We are seeing the same things being done to pro-life protesters all over America today. Under the pretext of enforcing an unjust law, police are viciously brutalizing decent, God-fearing people who simply want to point out the injustices of the system that permits, and encourages, the murder of the unborn.

SERIOUS CHARGES

The violence which erupted in Israel, in Jordan, and in Egypt in the spring of 1990 after a deranged soldier murdered a half dozen Palestinians and wounded scores more, caused a dreadful blood bath. The event spawned military reprisals with death and injuries to another hundred people. As long as that kind of mayhem continues, there can be no peace.

Among the factors that continue to bring censure upon Israel from the United Nations and other world peace organizations is the seeming contempt of the Jewish bureaucratic system for the Palestinian Arabs. It shows up in many forms, from foot-dragging in judicial and administrative matters to the overt destruction of Arab property.

The Israeli Foreign Ministry labels these the Three-Ds: demolition, detention, and deportation. The fact that some 400 Arab villages inside Israel have been demolished since 1948 has been a historic source of antagonism, but sometimes the covert antagonism and reprisals are an even greater irritation.

Arab homes are routinely bull-dozed for undisclosed reasons, and permits to rebuild are either denied or delayed for years. Palestinians can be held in "administrative detention" for undisclosed reasons and imprisoned for up to a year in virtual concentration camps in the Negev Desert. No charges need be brought; and if a detainee can afford an attorney, neither the prisoner nor his attorney may have access to the actual charges. Arabs can be held on the grounds of "secret evidence."

Arabs may be deported from Israel at the discretion of the government or, as has happened with many Palestinians studying abroad, their passport and right of return can be canceled while they are out of the country, leaving them stranded and effectively deported.

Automobiles and trucks belonging to most West Bank citizens must display blue license plates to distinguish them from people living in the Jewish areas, who use yellow plates. Vehicles with blue tags are routinely stopped, searched, and the drivers are physically and emotionally harassed. This is degrading, but worse in the long run, these kinds of harassment incite the Palestinians to seek revenge. Unfortunately, they already have enough reasons.

Statistics compiled by the United Nations Works and Relief Agency and other sources are equally distressing. They show that more than 75,000 Palestinians have suffered serious injuries in Gaza, the West Bank, and Eretz Israel since the beginning of the Intifada in December 1987.

Reports of the Israeli Information Center for Human Rights in the Occupied Territories, a Jewish organization, show that 637 Palestinians have been killed by Israeli military actions, 604 by shooting (including rubber bullets), and 33 by beatings, burns, and other causes. Of those, 41 were children under age 12; 101 were youths 13 to 16.

Tear gas exposure killed another 77, of whom 30 were infants. The figures also report 29 Palestinians killed by Jewish civilians and 5 apparently killed by Arab collaborators.

According to United Nations figures, there have been 8,000 cases of broken bones since the Intifada began, and more than 60,000 Palestinians have been held in administrative detention.

But lest we think the pressure is all one-sided, during the same period, 10 Israeli soldiers and 9 Jewish civilians were reported as killed by Palestinians, and 46 Israeli soldiers have committed suicide. Clearly there is a level of hostility and violence here that is intolerable to the human spirit.

Eventually, it all comes back to the ancient and bitter strife between these two peoples and the reluctance of either side to accept a peace which does not give them final control. It is hard for us in the West to understand the emotions at work here. In America and Europe we are negotiators and compromisers by nature. The idea of each side giving up some of its rights in order to settle a dispute is an old and trusted concept with us. Not so in the Middle East; not so to the Arabs and the Jews.

ASSESSING ALTERNATIVES

So what are the alternatives? Bible scholars feel that the West Bank belongs to Israel. Certainly the City of Jerusalem is—must be—a Jewish city.

Jesus predicted that Jerusalem would be trodden under foot until the time of the Gentiles was fulfilled. Bible scholars decided that when the Israelis took possession of Jerusalem in 1967, this was the completion of a prophecy that had waited some 2,500 years for fulfillment.

Many felt the return of the Jews to Jerusalem was very possibly the most important event of biblical history to take place in our lifetime. Jerusalem was once again in Jewish hands, for the first time since the Babylonian captivity.

Evangelicals do not want the Jews to lose control of that city any more, and the Jews have sworn to maintain possession with their lives. In 66 to 73 A.D., during the terrible revolt of the Jews against Rome, a small band of survivors gathered at a mountain fortress called Masada in the Judean desert near the Dead Sea. There they fought and died, to the last man. The name of Masada has become a symbol of the will of modern Israel to fight to the last man, woman, or child rather than accept slavery again.

A highly respected Defense Department analyst in Washington, D.C. told me that before they will surrender the Old City of Jerusalem and divide Jerusalem into two cities again, the Jews will use any weapon in their arsenal, including atomic weapons if they have to.

If any nation were to attempt to divide Jerusalem, that nation would run the risk of plunging the world into nuclear holocaust. The issue of East and West Jerusalem under Jewish control is the central issue, and it will not go away because of official pronouncements or press releases from Washington, D.C.

The Palestinians talk about Jerusalem being the capital of their state. But, given the realities of this world, it is not practical to have a landlocked state within a state, or for any other nation to accept in its midst a hostile, independent nation.

An autonomous division within military borders would be one thing, but an autonomous state using Jerusalem as its capital just isn't going to happen, so that is an unrealistic expectation for the Palestinians.

If their leaders continue to hold to that goal, the only possible result will be a devastating war. And however large the numbers weighed against Israel in this particular event, Israel will be prepared to fight. They will fight the Russians, the Western Europeans, or the United States if they have to. And they would be willing to fight to the last man, as their forefathers did at Masada.

The conflict in Israel today has the potential of being a tinder-box for the whole world. If somehow the Arab nations push for control of Jerusalem; if Saddam Hussein pursues his threat to use poisonous gas; or if he were to form some league with the Libyan madman, Mohamar Qadaffi, or the Syrians, I believe we would see a cataclysmic war in the Middle East.

The long range goal of the surrounding Arab nations is to eradicate Israel, not just accommodate her. The Israelis know this, and they know they will be fighting for their very lives. Given that provocation, it is not inconceivable that they could be tempted to launch a pre-emptive strike if they ever felt unduly threatened.

If all attempts at peace fail, and if pushed into a corner beyond which they cannot concede any more, the Jews might just say, what else do we have to lose? Let's use the armed might we have at our disposal to eliminate our enemies before they eliminate us. Not a desirable option for anyone, but still conceivable.

MOUNTING PRESSURES FROM ABROAD

Such an event could then be the flashpoint for a much greater war. I don't really foresee a World War III developing between the superpowers or between any of the European forces, but I could see a collection of nations—yes, including the United States—coming against Israel.

The rising tide of anti-Semitism in the Soviet Union and the East Bloc nations may also have far-reaching biblical significance.

No one could have dreamed that the horrors of the holocaust would not have buried the European hatred of Jews forever. Outside the Soviet Union, Jews do not form significant populations in Eastern Europe. There are now estimated to be only 4,000 Jews in Poland, 8,000 in Czechoslovakia, 500 in East Germany, and 60,000 in Hungary. The largest population of Jews in Europe lives in the Soviet Union. Population estimates vary between 1.5 and 2.5 million Soviet Jews, but these figures represent only a meager 1 percent or less of the Soviet population.

Yet my sources tell me that in the Soviet Union a fanatical anti-Jewish group, called Pamyat, is actually searching 400 years back in Russian genealogical tables in an attempt to harass anyone with Jewish blood.

On my recent visits to Eastern Europe I was astounded to encounter virulent anti-Semitic sentiment in Romania, where there are only 22,000 Jews, but where the current Prime Minister, Petre Roman, is of Jewish descent.

Regrettably, after World War II, some Jews, grateful to be liberated from Adolf Hitler, allied themselves with Stalin and were reported to be members of the KGB and some communist politburos which suppressed the captive peoples of Eastern Europe. However, the actions of a few can hardly be used to justify making scapegoats of an entire race.

In Nazi Germany it was easy for an eloquent demagogue such as Adolf Hitler to blame the economic collapse of post-World War I Germany on a conspiracy led by "International Zionist Bankers." This was a lie, but desperate people need someone to blame for their problems. They willingly believe lies, especially when those lies originate from the government leaders they are expected to trust.

Now in the Soviet Union and the East Bloc nations a new lie is emerging, that communism and the collapse of communism was engineered by a "Zionist conspiracy."

At present the anti-Semitism in the Soviet Union and Eastern Europe has no government sanction. But a highly placed source within the Jewish community tells me that Soviet Jews are terrified that the wave of hatred there could be at any time result in a full scale pogrom.

Up to 280,000 Soviet Jews are seeking to emigrate to Israel this year. This is a flood compared to 8,000, 12,000, and 28,000 in previous years. The government of Israel is estimating 4 billion dollars in resettlement costs. Jews in America have an emergency "Operation Exodus" fundraising effort under way and are seeking 600 million dollars in supplemental aid from the United States government.

In recent months the United States Government has become more and more demanding in its pressure on Israel to reach an accord with the Palestinians. Clearly the Israelis are nervous about that, since the deeper implication is that the United States could withdraw both its financial and diplomatic support. There is also a fear that the bond between America and Israel may be weakening.

Articles have recently appeared in a number of magazines and journals asking if America has deserted Israel. Someone even raised the question on public radio a few months ago, what would George Bush say if you woke him at 3:00 A.M. and whispered the word, "Israel"? Would he respond "friend" or "foe"?

I don't know the answer to that, but I do know this. So long as this nation has any concern for God's favor, we cannot turn our backs on Israel. Throughout Scripture, the prophets warned that God will judge the nations that stand against Israel.

Intolerance in any quarter is wrong, but inasmuch as we are able, we must ensure that the trend throughout the 1990s remains in favor of a Jewish homeland in Israel and not for the elimination of the Jews.

THE FUTURE OF THE JEWS

Some sources have estimated that the total number of Jews coming to Israel from Russia could be well over a million people. If that is in fact the case, the burden on social and medical programs, not to mention the resettlement costs, are going to be enormous for the Israelis, as much as 16 to 25 billion dollars.

A massive influx of Jews will also exacerbate the tensions between the Jews and the Arabs because the Palestinians see the arrival of more and more Jews as a threat to their livelihood, to their national welfare, and to their prospects for an independent homeland of their own.

Population is key to the success of Israel, yet the demographics are clearly working against the Israelis, who have adopted the European and American custom of limited or childless marriages. The Arabs in Israel on the other hand have been exploding in population. The birthrate among Arabs in Israel is 31 per 1,000, the Israeli birthrate is 13 per 1,000.

According to the London *Economist* there are 3.5 million Jews in Israel and 822,000 Arabs. Palestinians living in the West Bank and Gaza number 1.7 million. At present birthrates, and with no major immigration, there will be 4.2 million Jews and 3.1 million Arabs in the area under Jewish control by the year 2000.

By the year 2020, at present birthrates, Arabs will be in the majority in the entire country.

It is obvious that the Israelis face a major problem. If they accept Palestinians as citizens of Israel, in a short while they will be a minority race in an Arab country. If they establish an Arab state of Palestine, they may be inviting a threat to their future security.

If they deport all the Palestinians, they will take the place of South Africa as the pariah nation of the earth. What they have now is a type of Apartheid, and it is only a question of time before the nations of "the new world order" begin to force Israel to abandon her settlements and give up the West Bank. When the demand by force extends to East Jerusalem there will be a nuclear war.

Perhaps the clearest answer to the Israeli problem, and one that would at least temporarily relieve world pressure, would be the arrival of one million or more Jews from the Soviet Union, despite the enormous costs involved.

Shimon Peres once told me a story about former Israeli Prime Minister David Ben-Gurion and the former President of France, Charles DeGaulle, walking along together, talking confidentially about the problems of Israel.

DeGaulle said, "Mr. Prime Minister, tell me frankly. What do you want? Do you want a larger army? Do you want more territory? Do you want a harbor? What do you want?" Ben-Gurion just looked at him and said, "I want more Jews!"

DeGaulle couldn't believe his ears, but Ben-Gurion realized that the success of Israel was going to depend not on military or technical achievements but on a vibrant population, and despite the potential cost of settlement, he wanted more Jews.

POPULATING ZION

Even though he died in 1973, Ben-Gurion is getting his wish. New settlers are coming in huge numbers. If the numbers they are projecting actually come, this will be the largest migration of Jews into Israel since the holocaust. They are mainly coming from Russia, from Eastern and Western Europe, and also from parts of Asia, though in much smaller numbers.

The greatest concentration of Jews in the world is still in the United States. It is not likely that many of America's Jewish families will volunteer to give up their secure lives here in order to go into that hotbed of racial tension and unrest, but I suppose it could happen.

I have been told that over the last 25 years more than 400,000 American Jews who immigrated to Israel have returned home. The problems there were just too great for them. In my estimation, nothing short of a holocaust or a global conflict will ever bring about a mass exodus of American Jews to Israel.

Jews have come to Israel from Iran, Iraq, and the rest of the Middle East; they have come out of North Africa, Europe, and to a lesser degree, South America, even though there never was a large Jewish population there.

Because of America's long-term commitment to and support of Israel, and because of our allegiance to the six million Jews in this country, the United States will in all likelihood continue to be Israel's strongest ally. That will likely keep America in the position of being the prime defender of Jewish interests in the Middle East.

Even though it seems inconceivable that anything will happen in the United States to cause an out-migration of the Jewish population here, it would be foolish to assume such a thing could not or will never happen. We trust it will not; but if it ever does, we will certainly know that the last days are upon us.

The fact that there are only two major populations of Jews in the world today is extraordinarily significant. In Isaiah 43, the Bible says, "I will bring your children from the east and gather you from the west. I will say to the north, 'Give them up!' and to the south, 'Do not hold them back.' Bring my sons from afar and my daughters from the ends of the earth." That seems to be what's happening now. This is a strong prophetic word which, in my view, is already being fulfilled.

Given the rise of anti-Semitism in the East bloc and the Soviet Union, and the pre-existence of strong anti-Semitic feelings in Western Europe (the bitterness in Germany has not gone away), there is a very real possibility that the United Nations may turn against Israel. The Arab-African non-aligned bloc has been anti-Israeli all along. The only defender of Israel besides the United States has been South Africa, and they have been made a pariah nation by these same people.

THE CHRISTIAN ALLIANCE

Even with some six million American-born Jews living in this country, we should not think that it is only the Jews in America who have supported Israel. Since the Reformation, Western Christians of all races and denominations have accepted the biblical teaching concerning the Jews as the "chosen people."

Yes, Christians believe that the Jews rejected their own Messiah, just as the Jewish prophets foretold they would. That rejection then brought about a **New Covenant** with God—succeeding the **Old Covenant** which God had given to Abraham—by which both Jews and Gentiles who renounced their sin and accepted Christ as the Messiah could inherit the promise of Salvation.

The obstinate denial of the Messiah by the vast majority of Jews has always concerned Christians. To anyone whose eyes are not closed, it seems so obvious that Christ fulfilled every single prophecy of the Scriptures! But the frustration and sorrow for these Jews does not, in any way, mean that Christians do not recognize the Jews as chosen of God and a special people. By and large Protestants and Catholics alike have upheld the Jewish nation throughout history.

A sad irony of the last 40 years, though, is the fact that the liberal Jewish population in America has been intent on diminishing Christian influence in the public life of America. They believe that Christianity is a threat to Judaism, and many recite the terrors of the Holocaust as evidence of the Christian "blood libel" against the Jews.

The crimes perpetrated against the Jews by the Nazis are an unspeakable horror. Christians are not guilty of that charge. The Nazis were guilty. Some of them may have claimed to be Christians, but everything in the New Testament condemns hatred, murder and revenge, especially against Jews. Anyone who believes Christianity is against Jews does not know the Bible.

Bible history tells us that because of their hardness of heart, God scattered the Jews time and time again. The Egyptians and the Babylonians and the Assyrians were allowed to make slaves of them. However, God eventually brought down His wrath upon those nations and eradicated their empires.

THE IMAGINARY ADVERSARY

Regrettably, the efforts of liberal Jews to destroy the Christian position in the world has, in fact, weakened the moral consensus that has supported Israel from the start.

About 30 years ago, futurist Herman Kahn, of the Hudson Institute in New York, warned Jewish leaders that Christians in America would not stand for the loss of their traditions. In forestalling the desires of certain Jewish leaders to denigrate and vilify Christian expressions and symbolism, Kahn said such behavior would bring inevitable reprisals against Jews.

Kahn was a brilliant man. His book, *Thinking the Unthinkable,* forced a generation to take a realistic look at some very serious issues concerning nuclear war and the welfare of the global community. Thinking people listened to him. But he is gone now. Those who advise restraint seem to be gone, and the assault against Christianity is on, and it is very strong.

Since the Christian Broadcasting Network and all our affiliates here and around the world are vitally concerned with issues concerning Christianity and the gospel of Jesus Christ, we get a lot of attention, not only from other Christians but from those who want to destroy our heritage and take away our freedom.

In recent months we have been involved in disputes with Hollywood executives over the defamatory film, *The Last Temptation of Christ*, with the anti-religious People for the American Way headed by Norman Lear, and with the agenda of the National Endowment for the Arts which has used taxpayers' money to support pornography, sacrilege, and blatant homosexuality. More and more we are in debates with writers and journalists who seem to be activists in the destruction of Christianity.

It has become perfectly clear over the past 20 years that any type of discrimination on the basis of race or gender or sexual preference will be condemned in this country. Blacks, Asians, Hispanics, and all other minorities are guaranteed equal rights under the law. Women are guaranteed rights in the workplace. Even homosexuals and Satanists are guaranteed certain rights.

But Christians are becoming fair game for the media, for authors and columnists, for filmmakers, for artists, for strident feminists, for abortionists, for drug pushers and their fellow travelers, for Marxists, for pornographers, for liberal politicians, for atheists, and even some who call themselves Christians.

A CONFLICT OF IDEOLOGY

The American Jewish community is not monolithic. Some are most sympathetic to the social concern of Evangelical Christians. Some are indifferent. But the Liberal Jews have actually forsaken Biblical faith in God, and make a religion of political liberalism.

For example, they think government welfare somehow is Judaism. They think a pro-abortion stand and the absence of religious activity in the schools are Judaism.

If someone attacks abortion-on-demand or asks for prayer in the schools, the liberal Jewish community reacts as if this stand were somehow anti-Semitic. They have anti-Christian liberalism intermingled with Judaism to such a degree they can't distinguish anymore.

Liberal Jews are passionately in favor of the pro-choice, pro-abortion position—which doesn't make any sense, since the abortion position uses the same language and techniques that the Nazis used in exterminating Jews. Of all people, the Jews, who toast *LeChaim* ("to life") should be for life not death. They are dead set against prayer in the schools and public expressions of religion. Yet, anyone who has ever been to Israel knows that prayer is open and public in that nation. And why shouldn't it be?

The Jews in Israel are trying to build and populate a nation! There is no debate over prayer in the schools. People pray in the schools and read the Bible; so if anybody wants to pray in the schools, the Israelis don't care. They welcome religious expression.

So many of the political issues that the conservative evangelicals embrace in the United States are not even a debate in Israel—in fact they are very much in keeping with the feelings and beliefs of the Israelis.

The sabras—that is, those who were born and raised in Israel—don't have the same suspicions and animosities of their fathers and grandfathers. They were born free, born in their own nation, and they never knew the discrimination and the persecution of places like Germany.

So many of the Israelis I have met have been quite willing to talk about Jesus, to listen to the gospel, and to receive Christ as Messiah. I have talked to people in the army, I have been to meetings, I've met with people at all levels of society, and in every instance I have found a great openness and cordiality.

It is distressing that the situation is so different in the United States. While there is a great sense of unity between conservative Jews and the evangelical political position, liberal Jews feel threatened by Christians.

CRITICAL CONCERNS

Absolute liberty and unrestrained license have always been the slogans of the liberal; but even if that stance may work for the cosmopolitan, liberal, secular Jews, it does not work so well for the religious Jews. Religious Jews have always believed in ethical responsibility and moral restraint.

Perhaps the greatest irony of the liberal position is their split personality. They are outraged by anyone who would try to limit their own freedom of speech; but, on the other hand, they are absolutely insensitive to the rights of those they oppose.

Norman Lear wants unrestricted freedom for smut and pornography and the murder of the unborn, but anyone who speaks against kiddie porn or vulgarity on television is branded a reactionary and silenced without a hearing.

The part that Jewish intellectuals and media activists have played in the assault on Christianity may very possibly prove to be a grave mistake. It is beginning to appear that support for Israel in America may already have been weakened in the political arena, and soon the Christians may be in no condition to help.

For centuries, Christians have supported the dream of Zion, and they have supported Jews in their dream of a national homeland. But American Jews invested great energy in attacking these very allies. That investment may pay a terrible dividend. If a shift should come in America's public opinion toward Israel, the Christians who have stood for them throughout the ages may not be able to reverse the trend.

This situation can also have dire consequences for our nation. Based on my understanding of the Scriptures, it is my conviction that if our nation turns against Israel, it will incur the wrath of God. This has happened in modern times to nations like Spain, England, and Germany when they have persecuted the Jews. And we as a nation will reap the same judgment if, in our public posture, we turn against Israel.

ISOLATION AND ATTACK

In this decade the isolation of the Jews will intensify. A world alliance is forming which is to become a new world order. The United Nations, without such an order, branded "Zionism as racism." The vast majority of the nations which make up the United Nations General Assembly have an almost pathological hatred of Israel.

If the Arabs are at the forefront of the movement against Israel, they will use their oil weapon to the maximum. The current president of the United States and his Secretary of State are both from the Texas oil industry. Israel is a secondary concern for people whose focus in private life has been petroleum and petro-dollars and whose personal friendships have for years been made with the rulers of the pro-Western Arab states.

We have mentioned the ongoing attempt of liberal Jews in America to undermine the public strength of Christianity. It should be equally clear that the liberal, wealthy Jews voted for Democratic candidates Carter, Mondale, and Dukakis, not Reagan and Bush. They have been on the losing side of the political battle for years and the present administration owes them no favors.

One day a vote against Israel will come in the United Nations when the United States neither abstains or uses its veto in the Security Council to protect Israel.

When that happens that tiny little nation will find itself all alone in the world. Then, according to the Bible, the Jews will cry out to the one they have so long rejected, and He will come in heavenly power to give them deliverance from the earthly power of all the nations of the earth.

Then we will have a reign of peace on earth known as "The Millennium." But more on that in the following chapter.

Saddam Hussein has set the machinery in motion which one day will bring the military force of world government against Israel.

12

Looking Ahead

The Bible promises a heaven-sent one world government to supersede the Gentile powers.

Attempts by the nations to establish by human effort a counterfeit millennium based on one world government will bring on an unspeakable nightmare.

TO BORROW A biblical phrase, America has long been in the world but not of the world. Since at least the mid-eighteenth century, the United States has maintained a position of isolationism and insularity, standing aloof from the global marketplace.

Even as we have sent armies, embassies, and missions abroad, we have stood back emotionally like stoic observers, protected to a large extent by our geography and our democratic individualism. But that era has now come to an end.

Suddenly the world has come to America and America must go to the world. Military and economic incursions abroad can no longer be construed as value-free operations. The world has grown too small, the interchange of ideas and ideologies has become the rule of the day, and every expression of American economy or foreign policy will henceforth be interpreted by the world as expressions of America's will and ideology.

In a recent column, Patrick Buchanan pointed out that America has participated in three great crusades in this century. First was Woodrow Wilson's attempt to make the world safe for democracy. The failure of Wilson's "Fourteen Points" was demonstrated in the failure of the Treaty of Versailles. There was no enduring peace after the First World War. The subsequent war, World War II, was our second crusade. The third was the Cold War, the longest and costliest of the lot.

Today we are citizens of a new and different world. As we cast our eyes from East to West we see new allies and new adversaries on every horizon. Furthermore, we are no longer an island, for the world has come to our shores to buy and sell, to proselyte, and to live.

Tens of thousands of men, women, and children from the Third World have become citizens of our land, and they have helped to accelerate America's commerce with the world. Europe and Asia are no longer external and extraneous ideas. They have become as real to us as the cars we drive and the foods we eat. We are among them and they are among us.

The crusades of the past described in Buchanan's column were military and diplomatic incursions brought about by invasion, by conquest and surrender. The new crusades are invasions of population, not only here but around the world. Armies of immigrants from North Africa and the Middle East are swarming north and west into the homelands of the old colonial nations.

Hordes of Latins are moving north into the United States and Canada. The columnist suggests the question is not whether we will be invaded by warriors but whether our cultural identities will survive the immigrations from the Third World. Will the new invasions bring decline, or will they, perhaps, bring renewal?

Buchanan made one other observation which I believe to be not only true but very much a concern of this book. He quotes Albert Jay Nock who once wrote that, "We are in no danger whatever from any government except our own, and the danger from that is very great; therefore our own government is the one to be watched and kept on a short leash." How sad that Nock's observation remains so true.

At the conclusion of *Religion in American Public Life*, James Reichley writes that religion and the practice of democracy have been closely intertwined since the foundation of this country. Reichley believes that relationship will continue in the years ahead. George Washington certainly believed the two were inseparable and said so in his farewell address.

Washington said, "Of all the dispositions and habits which lead to political prosperity, religion and morality are indispensable supports. In vain would that man claim the tribute of patriotism, who should labor to subvert these great pillars of human happiness, these firmest props of the duties of men and citizens."

When we see the handiwork of the ACLU everywhere dismantling the traditions of a moral culture, can we believe that this nation remains committed to morality? When we see the work of the behaviorists who control the education establishment continuing to pollute the minds of our youth with deconstructionist rhetoric and anarchist ideologies, can we believe political prosperity is even a remote hope?

When we see the false religions of the New Age rising from the ruins of the rationalistic and humanistic culture, can we ever again hope that America will know itself to be "one nation under God"? If a moral democracy is the key to prosperity, what is our realistic hope for the future?

THE LAY OF THE LAND

As we move inexorably toward the dawn of the new millennium we ought to look back once again and review where we have come from as a civilization. To set the stage and to help us draw some conclusions about the broad range of issues we have considered in this book, I would also like to take a brief survey of some of the traditions of the modern age which have come down to us from the legacy of Rome and the Christian foundations laid down in Roman times.

Rome was the last major organizing unit of the old world. It was not only the greatest empire of its time, but the greatest of all the empires up until its time. The empire of the Caesars extended beyond any previous empire, to the ends of the known world. It brought about peace and a system of law and justice, and through the use of Greek, it gave the world a universal language.

This was a powerful empire. It extended from Turkey in the East to Great Britain in the West, and from the northern shores of Germany to the southern deserts of Ethiopia. The Roman Empire literally controlled the entire Mediterranean world.

When the empire finally collapsed around 476 A.D., there was a period of decline throughout Europe. By the year 600 A.D., the Muslim world began to flourish. The religion of Mohammed spread rapidly into the gap left by Rome, and up until the Battle of Tours in 732, when the Franks under Charles Martel defeated the Saracens, the Islamic religion virtually engulfed Europe.

Later on we find the Mongol empires on the rise, Genghis Khan and others, who swept across the Steppes of Russia and came into what is now Hungary. Europe and the last vestiges of the Roman Empire were under assault by Islamic forces from the Middle East and the ravaging hordes coming out of Mongolia and China. The Europeans were frankly no match for these mighty armies.

But by 800 A.D., Charlemagne was beginning to unify the forces of

Europe in what was called the Holy Roman Empire. Charles was made the Frankish king. By the time of the Renaissance, around 1500, Europe moved into the ascendancy in the world. In terms of economics and culture, and due in part to the spread of ideas brought about by the invention of the printing press in Germany, Europe entered the "Age of Exploration."

For the next 300 years, the European culture, which was now solidly Christian, was united first by the Church of Rome and subsequently by the Protestant churches. Colonists from Europe moved into India, Africa, and North and South America. They took possession of the Middle East and subjugated China. Although they didn't make China a possession, they nevertheless conquered it.

While Christendom was in the ascendancy, the Asiatic and Middle Eastern countries were in decline. That was the flowering of Western power and influence in the world.

The United States of America today is the last great expression of the triumph of Christendom. America has been the strongest of all the nations that came out of the Christian tradition extending from Charlemagne to the present.

But as we look back upon the vast sweep of history, it now appears that the end of this millennium will signal the end of a long and colorful cycle of history in which the Christian tradition had been the dominant moral and social force.

After World War II, America had more military might than any nation in history. It had more wealth and more global reach than any nation of this or any other time. The trouble was that America had never been prepared by its culture to assume the role of Empire.

Americans did not want overseas colonial possessions or empire, they merely wanted to help others to be free. Since the time of George Washington, the United States had been developing its tradition of isolation, so that it would not get involved in "entangling alliances" in Europe or other countries.

The role of global defender was alien to America, and yet after World War II—with all the nations of the world in chaos both in Asia and in Europe—the American dollar became the universal currency, and the American system of business (especially the mass production of goods) was the dominant system. American goods went everywhere, and America's share of the world's markets and the world's wealth was enormous.

So from its sleepy isolationism and 9 billion dollar annual budget, America set out to rebuild the world. We funded the Marshall Plan, sent industrial economists and engineers into Japan, built military bases around the globe, and began paying multiplied billions of dollars in aid to dozens of foreign nations on five continents.

THE MISSING MOTIVATION

But suddenly there was another problem. In the post-war era, America lost the things that had made us great: namely, our faith in God and our individual self-reliance. Although we continued to make enormous profits, we were consuming the spoils without any contingencies for the prospect of change in the future.

In essence, business leaders were doing what the British had done in the era just prior to World War II. They were milking their businesses and depreciating their plants and equipment without replacing them. They were consuming the future.

They were profit oriented, and in that era of monumental growth there was little or no competition in the world. American industries such as steel and automobiles had protected markets, and within a monopolistic, protective context, they could grant raises to workers and give financial concessions to the labor unions without any concern for the global consequences. We believed American products were just considered the best and everyone was copying us.

In this era Americans became "consumers." We had survived a period of decline during the Depression, we had won a war, and now we were exploiting this period of expansion to the limit. Homes were being formed; young people were getting married and starting families.

They were buying houses and automobiles and appliances, and there was enormous expansion of our economy and our society. But no one gave any thought to the possibility that someday we would have to be concerned about such things as inflation and domestic budgets.

During the Eisenhower years, things were kept pretty much in balance. But subsequently, the government began a process of rapid inflation, and during the tragedy of the Vietnam War, our society inflated rapidly without realizing that America's currency was the reserve currency, like gold, for the rest of the world.

By 1971 we had discarded the gold standard, and the dollar, at first, floated, then dropped in relation to other major currencies. So we exported American-style inflation overseas. Instead of being the stable, bellwether leader for the rest of the world, we became the irresponsible partner who inevitably earned the condemnation of our allies and trading partners.

We were still the strongest and had the nuclear umbrella. We still took the lead, but more and more our allies were reluctant to acknowledge our lead because of our irresponsible behavior. During this period we were still waging the false war—the so-called Cold War—and we wasted our resources on it in prodigal fashion.

It was as if somebody was intent on bringing America down from its pinnacle of world leadership. We were wasting our resources on an enormous arms build-up against an adversary that has later proven to be more illusory than real.

The Soviet threat perhaps was never as bad as we thought it was because their underlying economy was so terribly weak. In the last two years the Soviet Union has proven to be, in every meaningful respect, a Third World nation.

America has been drained of its resources and, to a degree, its resourcefulness. First in Korea, then in Vietnam, then in a cold war, we have been hamstrung and prevented from exercising our military strength. We have not been allowed to win a war or to defeat an enemy, but we've spent enormous amounts of money on an arms build-up, for a war we were never allowed to fight.

During the Vietnam war someone came up with the term "guns and butter." This was the idea that we would run a war and spend enormous amounts of money on the military while, at the same time, launch a costly war on poverty and social programs.

Thus we began a seemingly endless period of enormous domestic spending which sent us into a cycle of debt creation and inflation which has not ended to this day. It has, in turn, destabilized the entire world.

By 1966, the dramatic increase in the per capita income of the American worker in real, inflation-adjusted dollars simply stopped growing. By 1978 we had a trade deficit of 33 billion dollars, which climbed to 152.7 billion in the following decade; and by 1989 the federal debt surpassed the unbelievable 3 trillion dollar mark. The interest alone on the national debt is now 18 times the total national debt at the beginning of the Second World War.

A CRISIS OF CREDIT

The debt spiral and the mushrooming of consumer credit meant the creation of wealth through borrowing; but that wealth has not brought prosperity to the poorer nations. In fact, wealth creation through debt has impoverished countries like Nigeria and Brazil and the Congo and Mexico and the Argentine and Peru and many other countries that believed this American ideology would solve their domestic worries.

Yes, the game of debt creation has enriched those engaged in the money transfers to a degree beyond the wildest dreams of Croesus. But in the process, it has virtually crippled the economy of the entire world.

We are now at the end of a cycle of wealth creation through debt that has got to be worked out. In the process there may well be a massive economic collapse, and if not a collapse, at least a major slowdown.

Today the nations of Europe have forsaken Christianity, thus denying their spiritual heritage. They have moved into state socialism which, even in the most enlightened countries, consumes as much as 58 percent of the gross national product. The United States, too, is taking an increasingly large share of the people's income, but America has begun losing its competitive edge, just like Europe.

Today Japan is the largest creditor nation in the world while the United States has become the largest debtor. There was a time when American citizens had the highest standard of living in the world; today the Japanese and Germans surpass us in virtually every category, and the French, Danes, Swiss, and Italians are moving ahead as well.

It only takes a trip to Europe to see how weak the dollar has become. While Americans are shocked at the prices of food and hotels and incidental expenses, Japanese and European tourists are everywhere, buying up everything in sight. In the past 20 years the dollar has fallen from 350 yen to roughly 140, and from 4 German marks to roughly 1.5. In effect, that means Americans pay double for everything in Europe and Japan while the Germans and Japanese pay half price for American goods.

So, it seems as if we have come to the end of a major cycle, and as we look to the future, we see a revival coming out of the East. After some 500 years of decline, the East is coming back. Today the nations of the Orient are beginning to rise again, just as they did in the days after the Roman Empire, before the spread of Christendom.

They are flexing their economic muscles, taking a commanding position in world commerce, controlling the flow of capital in world markets. But it is not merely an economic revival, it is a spiritual revival as well.

In parts of Asia there is a spirituality custom designed for a new age, but it is clearly not compatible with the beliefs of Christianity. The beliefs—and the movement this revival entails—will most likely lead to the kind of poverty and misery associated with Bombay and Calcutta, and the desperation of the rigid caste system supported by adherents of Hinduism.

There is another system which features the kind of fanaticism that has been associated with the Shiite Muslims, the Ayatollah Khomeini, and those of his ilk who launch holy wars against infidels in order to bring about their own ends.

If the world's oil problems continue, we can expect more crises like

those in the mid-1970s when the energy supply was curtailed and manipulated for profit, for political advantage, or for harassment of the West.

The major supply of oil in the world is in the Saudi Peninsula, and in those nations that are predominantly Islamic. Many people have not stopped to realize that even the oil from Indonesia, Nigeria, and practically all the other sources is under Islamic control. Non-Islamic countries have a greatly reduced share of the petroleum that is vital to their existence, and that could easily become a major source of conflict in the immediate future.

In terms of trade imbalance, we know today that the United States has been running up a substantial deficit in trade equity with the Japanese, the Koreans, the Taiwanese, and the so-called "newly industrialized countries," called the NICs or the "Asian Tigers."

The growth rates of those nations, in terms of corporate earnings and individual savings alike, are dramatically ahead of the United States. One reason is that they have emphasized individual initiative, hard work, family values, and strong religious faith: all the things we used to have in America; the things that helped make us great.

THE NEED FOR RADICAL CHANGE

No one believes in some sort of blind determinism in history. No one is going to say that at the stroke of the year 2000 the focus changes and the world suddenly faces from West to East. Nevertheless, from a cyclical standpoint, it does seem that there is a definite shifting from West to East and a flow of wealth and technology and spiritual ideology to the East.

This does not mean that America is finished, but it does mean that unless we regain our roots, we in the West are doomed to fail. We need a radical change, in the original sense of the word "radical," meaning roots. Without a sense of our heritage, our democratic roots, we do not have a guiding ideology.

We cannot guide and motivate a society purely on the basis of politics or economics; and unless there is a spiritual revival of massive proportions, it seems to me that Western civilization, long range, will decline.

What could happen at the outset of such a time of decline? First of all, a political convulsion to bring forth a powerful charismatic leader, a dictator. In these cycles, as we have noticed, first the economics weaken, then comes a period of disarmament, then a dangerous autocratic leader.

We saw that in the 1920s. The economics of the major countries began to weaken so they decided it was in their best interest to cut back on arms, which they did, which in turn weakened the defenders of liberty and permitted one renegade in their midst to begin to arm dramatically.

By that time, the will of the people in Britain and France to use their might had been completely sapped by the post-World War I recovery. They had disarmed and did not have the military, financial, or spiritual will to rally against Adolph Hitler. As a result the world was plunged into war.

The early 1990s will certainly witness a period of dramatic disarmament. We have to stop spending so much on arms until we can get our budget balanced and begin to cut our national debt. That is a fact. But if it means that, in the wake of Vietnam we have lost our will to defend ourselves, then the chance that a person or nation might rise up as a result of an economic convulsion is a very real possibility.

If we have any kind of major economic crash in the 1990s, it could mean that the United States of Europe could fall into the hands of a demagogue, as I suggested earlier, who might well mobilize military power to go on a series of military adventures overseas in order to preserve his own dominion. In fact, it is not unrealistic to suppose that the Soviet Union might be the one: one last gasp as they are dying economically and being dismembered.

It is entirely possible that military rulers within that country might call a halt to *glasnost* and the dissolution of their empire and say since we do have this enormous arsenal, let's use it to re-establish once again Soviet hegemony, especially in the Middle East.

They could easily make a play for the oilfields in Iran, Iraq, and the Persian Gulf, and that in turn could trigger a war with a weakened United States—unless by that point the United States has already lost its will and would wait too late to intervene.

THE EASTWARD SHIFT

If the Lord doesn't return soon, and if there is not a major spiritual revival, we can expect the next hundred years to see a dramatic shift in wealth, in culture, and in military power from Western Europe and America into the nations of the Orient.

The Orient will have more active young people while the populations of Europe are growing older. By the year 2050, Western nations will likely have just over seven percent of the world's population. Their corresponding share of the world's wealth, power, and influence will be diminished accordingly. Trends are in progress which are irreversible without dramatic change.

These trends may or may not affect anyone alive today, but they will mean that the days of American ascendancy have come to an end. The Pax Romana, Pax Britannia, or the Pax Americana may well be a thing of the past. If we look at long-range trends based on demographics, economic flow, savings, competitive edge, education and other concurrent indicators, the prognosis for America in not terribly good.

That does not mean there cannot be a spiritual revival, or a renewal of education and the national will, or a curing of the moral rot in this country. It does not mean we cannot attack and eliminate the drug plague, the abortion plague, the divorce plague, and other forms of corruption in the land.

It does not mean that these social ills cannot be cured by an intervention of the hand of God. But absent that intervention, America is already in a state of decline which is going to accelerate. There is not a whole lot we can do to stop it *without* a revival.

I am not sure the trend is reversible even if there is a spiritual revival. If we lose our collective will to get our budgets balanced, to live within our means, and to return to a sense of individual self-reliance and faith in God, then the long shadows over this land are indeed dark and deep.

When I ran for the presidency in 1988, I campaigned on the premise that we have to restore the greatness of America through moral strength. If that moral strength is gone, then all the other things will disappear along with it. We are still the greatest nation on the face of the earth. We still have not lost the number one position.

We are much bigger and stronger than Japan. We may not be bigger and stronger than the collective United States of Europe, but we have a better long-term understanding of world economies, so we will continue to have economic advantages for a time.

And while we will not be nearly as big as a revived China—or especially a revived China combined with Japan, Southeast Asia, and the Pacific Rim—nevertheless, for at least this moment in history we are on the high ground. Where we go from here will make the difference in whether or not we can survive as a force in the world.

But America seems to be determined to destroy itself. While the Japanese have done everything they can to strengthen business, the liberal lobby in this country has done everything in its power to weaken business, to handicap government, business, and labor organizations, and to cripple the middle class with punitive taxation.

The major public institutions in Japan have worked in partnership to create a constructive economic environment. They see themselves as Japan Incorporated: they're all in it together. How can two such contrary systems truly compete?

In the United States, government has worked against business, business against labor, and all three have desperately worked to diminish the influence of the others. They say they can't trust each other. Yet we know that a divided nation cannot compete successfully in world competition.

The threat of a united Asia and a united Europe has opened our eyes, however, and perhaps we're beginning to get a little bit smarter, but we have a lot of learning yet to do.

The next ten years are going to be crucial in deciding the fate of this nation. If we don't surmount the moral problem, and if we don't meet the economic problems that Japan and the European Community are posing to us, we are going to find ourselves in an increasingly weak and defenseless posture.

GOD'S LOVE FOR THE FAMILY

There is a saying that a rising tide lifts all boats. When the tide rises there is more prosperity for everybody, and when the tide goes out, there is less. But whether or not we can anticipate an economic high tide in this nation in the near future, we know that God will care for those who honor Him. However desperate we may become, or however prosperous, God remains close by if we but seek Him.

During the Depression of the 1930s, 25 percent of the people in America were unemployed. That was a bitter and difficult time, but we often forget that 75 percent of the people were working. The vast majority of the people had jobs. Prices dropped dramatically, so a family with an income of just 10,000 dollars during the Depression could live very well, and could even afford domestic help.

God is able to take care of His people during a depression, just as He is during times of plenty. The average family does not feel the distress to any great degree, unless there is a military takeover, which is unlikely in this country. But that is not to say that there might not be a bondage of our national pride.

If our will remains weak and the Japanese boom continues, instead of working for American companies, we may well be working for Japanese companies before long. Instead of owing money to American banks, we will be owing money to Japanese banks. That means that ultimately the destiny of our nation is no longer in the hands of Americans but in the hands of foreign businessmen and bankers. That is not a very pleasant prospect, but, again, it isn't the end of the world.

The security for our nation does not depend on how many weapons we have stockpiled or how much wealth we have in reserve, but how strong is the family.

Jesus taught that love and self-sacrifice were among the greatest achievements in the kingdom of heaven. Instead of always looking out for number one, we must care for others, particularly those who look to us for affirmation and support.

I think it worthwhile to hear what the first lady, Barbara Bush, had to say at the Wellesley College graduation ceremonies in May 1990. After being slandered for her pro-family statements and threatened with boycott by militant feminists on campus, Mrs. Bush came and gave an eloquent address. Toward the end of that talk, she said,

> For several years you have had impressed upon you the importance to your career of dedication and hard work, and of course that's true. But as important as your obligations as a doctor, a lawyer, a business leader will be, you are a human being first and those human connections with spouses, with children, with friends are the most important investment you will ever make.
>
> At the end of your life, you will never regret not having passed one more test, winning one more verdict, or not closing one more deal. You will regret time not spent with a husband, a child, a friend, or a parent . . . .
>
> Whatever the era, whatever the times, one thing will never change: Fathers and mothers, if you have children, they must come first. You must read to your children and you must hug your children, and you must love your children. Your success as a family, our success as a society, depends not on what happens in the White House but on what happens inside your house.

What a moving and important statement! Through whatever times of struggle may lie ahead, the ability to believe in the future of such families, and on homes built upon the premise of mutual support and love, takes the apprehension out of the future and the potential changes ahead.

Beyond any doubt, we are in for a period of turmoil for the individual family. We must acknowledge that. The decade ahead will be a period of economic turmoil, which means that caution should be the rule of the day, not wild optimism. We should be cautious in terms of investment policies and in terms of debt accumulation, whether for housing, automobiles, school tuition, or any other activity. But there is long-term hope, and there are ways to ensure our peace of mind and survival through these times.

First of all, every worker should be sure that he or she has marketable skills. The best investment anybody can make is in education, to ensure that they and their children have skills and abilities others will pay for. Women need to have that assurance, just as men do.

Nobody should feel that because today there's the promise of a pension guarantee from some corporation, or that they have put away a sizable economic nest egg, that it will be there forever. In uncertain times, we need to have available reserves that we can get our hands on, the short-term obligations of the United States Government. Yet, in the final analysis, only our investment in the kingdom of God will survive the ravages of inflation or depression.

THE TRENDS

As we look back at the trends we have discussed, we can see that the future promises many revolutionary changes, but it also offers the hope of a profound revival and renewal in the world, from West to East. We know that Christians will play a much larger role during the coming decade but that our beliefs and our perspectives will be challenged on many fronts.

Nevertheless, we will prevail, for we have the assurance of God's love, and we have confidence in His plans for us. As written in Jeremiah, "I know the plans I have for you," says the Lord, "that they are plans for good and not for evil, that you may have a future and a hope."

So here, then, are the issues we have explored:

1. The collapse of world communism
2. The rise and fall of secularization in the West
3. The surge of interest in the supernatural
4. The shift of influence from the West to the East
5. The deliberate undermining of America
6. The continuing assault on the traditional family
7. The boom in technology and environmental issues
8. The growing importance of global economics
9. Anti-Semitism and the meaning of Saddam Hussein
10. The challenge of the new millennium

These issues will loom large in the next ten years, and how successful we are in dealing with them—both individually and as a nation—will depend not only on our intellectual and professional skills, but on our spiritual depth.

We have come to a time and place in history when human intellect alone is no match for the problems we must confront. If we are to win the race for survival, we will need super-human powers. We will need the help of a loving and powerful God.

Collectively as Christians in America, each family, working together, can do two very important things. They can continue in prayer, asking that God will heal this land, and they can contribute their time and talents to the work of revival.

As we continue in steadfast prayer and contribute to the cause of Christ through our own efforts, we can bring about a spiritual revival in this nation. Now is the greatest opportunity in the history of the world to get the gospel out. We should be willing to spend and be spent in the service of the Lord.

The Bible talks about a time when the night comes when no man can work. What is down the road none of us can say with absolute certainty, but we can say that now while we are in the daylight, and now while there is receptivity to the gospel all over the world, we can help to shape the future that we and our children are going to live in by bringing the gospel to those nations who don't know our Lord.

If Japan is a Christian country which shares our values, then it is really of no great consequence whether they succeed economically or not. If Germany, England, France, Spain, and Italy share our values, then the fact that they invest huge sums in our country and employ American workers is not something to be feared: it can be something good rather than bad. It is only a thing to be feared if we are going to be dominated by those who worship the devil, who are malicious, or who only desire to hurt people.

Each individual family—in our neighborhoods and across this land—must use our wealth and our energy wherever we can to help spread the gospel around the world. Personally, I believe we have a two-year window in the East bloc countries and the Soviet Union when the opportunities will be beyond anything we ever dared to believe possible. But now is the time to work. A night will come when those opportunities are no longer there.

MAKING A DIFFERENCE

We cannot sit by and wring our hands and say, well it would be nice if those people in the Congress and the Legislature would vote laws that we like. Waiting around won't make it happen. We must be prepared to vote and to join with our neighbors, especially with our Christian neighbors, in influencing the laws under which we live. We must become involved.

The way we do that is by writing to our legislators, by calling our congressmen and senators, by visiting with them and talking to them, by explaining our issues, and by supporting candidates who have pledged themselves to issues we support.

The oft-quoted statement of Edmund Burke is certainly true, "All that is necessary for evil to prevail is for good men to do nothing." For too long the Christian people of America have done nothing, so it is absolutely imperative that we learn about the structure of our local precincts, about political organizations, and the formation of our parties.

We should attend party caucuses, and if we have the leadership skills, stand for election as precinct chairmen. We need to get out and knock on doors and ring telephones and send letters on behalf of candidates, and give money to them, and let our voices be heard.

With the apathy that exists in our nation, a small, well-organized minority can influence the selection of candidates of both major parties to an astonishing degree.

In the past, hippies, radicals, feminists, and deconstructionist liberals have had a field day with that fact. Now it is our turn to monopolize the system, to demand a place of political involvement, and to have a say in what happens in this country. In essence, the destiny of this nation is in the hands of the Christians.

I love the old story about the two young men who came up to the ancient Chinese sage to try to stump him. One had a bird clasped in his hand and he said, "Old man, tell me about this bird. Is it alive or dead?"

Now, if the old man said the bird was alive, the young man planned to close his fist and kill the bird; but if the sage said it was dead, the youth would open his hand and let the bird fly away. But the old man, perceiving the plan, said, "As thou wilt, young man. As thou wilt."

In the United States right now, it is very much as we will. The opportunity is ours to fashion a just society based on biblical principles which can endure strong and proud and free well into the twenty-first century.

BIBLICAL CERTAINTIES

As we look ahead to the fulfillment of the decade of the nineties and the beginning of the next millennium I would like to lay out in very concise form some of the biblical certainties which may impact your life and mine in the days ahead.

I would like also to engage in some speculation about future events which these biblical certainties may have foretold. If you happen to be one who dislikes a bit of intrigue and speculation, this section of this chapter is not for you. For others I hope you enjoy this section but please feel free to judge carefully and critically.

To me the most powerful word in the scripture concerning the present course of the nations of the world is found in chapter 21 of the Gospel of Luke, where the Lord Jesus Christ says, "And Jerusalem shall be trodden under foot of the Gentiles until the times of the Gentiles are fulfilled."

The "times of the gentiles" refers to the ascendancy of the great world powers from Assyria to Babylon to Alexander to Rome and to the offshoots of Rome. According to Jesus, Jerusalem would not be under the control of the Jews until the ascendancy of the Gentile powers was at an end.

This prophecy was literally fulfilled in June of 1967 at the end of the Six Day War, when a Jewish nation, for the first time since 586 B.C., had gained military control over all of Jerusalem. When that event took place a clock began to tick that signaled the downfall of the great Gentile powers, the last and greatest of which is the United States of America. It also began the rise of Israel. What we would like to learn now is, very simply, how long will the clock be ticking?

We do not know for sure, but here is one speculation. A biblical generation is 40 years. If June 1967 began the "generation" of the end of the times of the Gentiles, then 40 years takes us to the year 2007.

In Biblical numbers 10 is the number of completion. Usually the completion of provocation, sins, and judgment. Forty, a generation, times 10 is 400, the number of years that God, for instance, permitted the Amorites living in Canaan to sin against Him before He gave their land to the nation of Israel. The Bible tells us that God told Abraham that his descendants would sojourn for 400 years in Egypt and then would inherit the holy land, because "the iniquity of the Amorites is not yet full."

In the city of Virginia Beach, where I live, is a point of the Atlantic shore called Cape Henry. The United States Interior Department erected a sign at this place reading, "Act 1, Scene 1 of the unfolding drama which became the United States of America."

History tells us that the first official act of the first permanent English settlers at the beginning of America took place on April 29, 1607 when the settlers planted a seven-foot oak cross in the sand, then knelt in prayer and claimed this new nation for the glory of God and His Son Jesus Christ. In God's eyes the United States of America did not begin on July 4, 1776, but on April 29, 1607.

Four hundred years from the beginning of America—ten full biblical generations—takes place on April 29, 2007. By some amazing coincidence—or might we not say foresight of God—the 400th anniversary of the greatest Gentile power that the world has ever known coincides precisely with the 40th year conclusion of the generation of the "end of the Gentile power."

More remarkably the anniversary dates of the two events—Cape Henry and the taking of Jerusalem by the Israelis—(if my calculations are correct) are 40 days apart within the calendar year. (The spring of that year, I might add, this observer of events will have turned exactly 77 years old.)

Could this be a time of collapse of the Gentile powers? None of us knows the times and seasons which God has reserved for Himself, but this scenario is fascinating to contemplate. If correct, it reinforces some of the other conclusions of this book that indicate the long cycle of Western European ascendancy has come to an end.

The year 2007 is only 17 years away. But we should remember that an incredible number of convulsing events can take place in 17 years. In 1933 when Germany was prostrate economically Adolf Hitler came from nowhere and seized power.

In just seven years from that time he had plunged Europe into a devastating war. In only twelve years his evil had brought devastation to the entire globe and he lay dead as a suicide. Seventeen years can be a very long time if a demonic dictator is let loose on the earth.

An economic collapse in Germany set the stage for Hitler. An economic collapse of worldwide proportions could set the stage for some leader equally bad.

The second scriptural event which impinges on our understanding of the future course of nations is found in the book of the prophet Daniel in the Old Testament. On successive raids against Judah which finally culminated in the sack of Jerusalem in 586 B.C., Nebuchadnezzar, King of Babylon took Jewish hostages in Babylon so that he could indoctrinate them in the culture of his country.

One named Daniel showed such wisdom that he was given a prominent place among Nebuchadnezzar's spiritual advisors. The Bible tells us that Nebuchadnezzar had an alarming dream, promptly forgot it, then demanded upon pain of death that the Chaldeans, astrologers, and soothsayers who were advising him should tell him what the dream was and what it meant.

God revealed to Daniel both the dream and its meaning. Nebuchadnezzar had seen a large statue of a man. The head was gold, the torso and arms were of silver, the thighs and belly were bronze, the legs were iron, and the toes were iron mixed with clay. Then a stone, not cut by human hands, fell upon the toes, crushed them and the rest of the statue, and then became a mountain filling the whole earth.

The interpretation given to David is clear to us who live today. The head of gold was Nebuchadnezzar who had absolute authority. The silver torso represented the Persian Empire, where the King was bound by laws which he himself had made. The bronze thighs represented the Macedonian empire of Alexander where even the powerful world ruler could not stop a near mutiny of his army.

The next empire of Rome had a fighting machine of steel, but was governed, at least early on, by a senate and a clear rule of law. Finally, the ten toes represent the successors to Rome where the central authority has been mixed more and more with and derived from popular democracy and representative parliamentary government.

If we understand Daniel on this point, a government instituted by God will arise to supersede all of the previous world empires. But the specific group of nations then in existence which are to be superseded by God's kingdoms are those ten or more successors of the Roman Empire which are governed by a combination of strength, possibly socialism, and democracy.

The kingdom of God which crushes the preceding empires will "fill the earth," so it is not merely a European or a Middle East phenomenon but a worldwide kingdom.

King Nebuchadnezzar took Jerusalem away from the Jews in 586 B.C. They got it back in 1967. Jesus' prophecy concerning the end of the times of the Gentiles was made around 30 A.D. It seems to me that Nebuchadnezzar's dream and Jesus' prophecy are two sides of the same thing. It also seems that since Nebuchadnezzar was the one who conquered Jerusalem, his dream would span the period of empires and nations that existed during the time of conquest until Jerusalem was restored.

What then is the rock cut without hands that crushes the nations and fills the earth? Jesus told His disciples that "this gospel of the kingdom shall be preached in all the world for a witness, and then the end shall come."

Clearly, Jesus who said, "My kingdom is not of this world," intended that there would be a spiritual expansion of His kingdom into all the earth. In fact most Bible scholars agree that the one clear sign of the end of this age will be a vast worldwide proclamation of the good news of Christ's kingdom, not unlike the events described in chapter four.

But Nebuchadnezzar's dream was about earthly kingdoms, not spiritual kingdoms. Certainly the rise of the Roman Catholic church in 453, the Holy Roman Empire in 800, and the worldwide victory of Christendom during the post Reformation period could clearly satisfy what Nebuchadnezzar saw. But it does not satisfy Jesus's prophecy for two reasons.

First, from 453 A.D. on, though the Roman Empire was in decline, Gentile powers were in ascendancy somewhere in the world until the present day. Although Christian in name, it is hard to believe that nations who fought successively bloody wars against one another up through World War I and World War II were Christian in spirit.

Never in its history was this mass of ignorance, treachery, intrigue, greed, and oppression to be considered the "Kingdom of God." Many representatives of Christ's invisible kingdom lived in Christendom, and Christian principles were clearly the basis of its legal and social organization, but Christendom was not God's ultimate plan for earth.

Secondly, it is equally clear that during the entire period from 453 A.D. until 1967, Gentile powers—Romans, Turks, Arabs, British—controlled Jerusalem. Only at the end of Christendom did the Jews take back Jerusalem.

What then is the worldwide kingdom of God to be like—this mountain not cut with hands—that will supplant the Gentile Kingdoms? Certainly the tiny nation of Israel does not have the population, the wealth, or the military power to become a world power. Here again the Bible gives us a clue. The prophet Micah has this to say:

> And it will come about in the last days
> That the mountain of the house of the Lord
> Will be established as the chief of the mountains
> It will be raised above the hills, And the peoples will stream
>   to it.
> And many nations will come and say,
> "Come and let us go up to the mountain of the Lord
> And to the house of the God of Jacob
> That He may teach us about His ways
> And that we may walk in his paths."
> For from Zion will go forth the law,
> Even the word of the Lord from Jerusalem.
> And he will judge between many peoples
> And render decisions for mighty, distant nations.
> Then they will hammer their swords into plowshares
> And their spears into pruning hooks;
> Nation will not lift up sword against nation,
> And never again will they train for war.
> And each of them will sit under his vine
> And under his fig tree,
> With no one to make them afraid . . . and the LORD will
>   reign over them in Mount Zion.
>   Micah 4:1–4

This is the government that God Himself will institute from the city that Jesus Christ and Abraham before Him, hallowed by supreme acts of faith and obedience to God.

There will then be a one world government, headed by Jesus Christ, and there will be one system of laws for all of the inhabitants of the earth based on righteousness, justice, and fairness. The hard cases will be settled by the Lord Himself with absolute wisdom.

There will be no more war anywhere because all residents of the earth will agree to abide by the total wisdom and justice of the Lord. The military academies will all be closed, and the enormous worldwide expenditure for arms will be diverted to peacetime use.

The right of private property will be respected, and no man need feel threatened in the enjoyment of his possessions by his fellow citizens or by his government. There will be no oppression of the rights of any group by any other.

The power and cost of individual governments will dramatically decrease and under the new system of law people will be citizens of the world with the greatest individual freedom that people have ever enjoyed since the Garden of Eden.

The reason is simple. All people will be directed by an inner code of conduct whose basis is the golden rule, "Do unto others as you will have them do unto you." External restraints on the citizens will be unnecessary for all people will have the benevolent law of God written in their hearts.

The standard of living, the technological advances, the freedom from stress and disease, and the happiness of the people will be beyond calculation. Not only will men live at peace with one another, but the Bible says that even the animals will live at peace with man and with one another to such an extent that a little child can play safely at the den of a venomous cobra. The *Lex Talionis,* the law of the jungle, will be a thing of the past.

Wouldn't it be wonderful to be alive to see such a day? Some, in fact, want this day so badly that they have decided that they will help God out and bring it in for Him. Marx wrote of a classless society of such equality and bounty that soon struggle would be over and governments would become unnecessary and fade away. The Marxist Utopia brought on a hell on earth for two billion people. Millions died as central planners tried to force "heaven" upon them.

Hitler wrote of a 1000 year (a millennium) kingdom, the Third Reich, which would bring splendor, majesty, and happiness to the German people. His Utopia ended in the bombed out destruction of his nation and the death from war of 50 million people.

Now the Utopian vision of the people of wealth and power is for a "New World Order" in which there is such a strong central authority that individual nations will not dare to engage in war or to violate international norms.

On their part, the New Age believers yearn for a brotherhood of man and a one world government under a counterfeit Christ whose wisdom comes from demons they call "ascended masters."

With all of the strength at my command I warn the readers of this book that a one world government which tries to be a counterfeit of the millennial government that Christ will establish will become the most hellish nightmare this world has ever known.

Fortunately for us all the Utopian schemes of men, despite the damage they can do, must fall. The glorious kingdom of Jesus Christ is certain. It may appear in our lifetime with the return of Jesus Christ to earth. When it comes, the earth will know a thousand years of peace and joy.

May the new millennium be the Millennium of the rule and reign of Jesus Christ.

Bibliography

Allen, Frederick Lewis, *Only Yesterday: An Informal History of the 1920s* (New York: Harper & Brothers, 1931, rev. 1962).

Amos, Gray, *Defending the Declaration* (Brentwood, TN: Wolgemuth & Hyatt, 1989).

Barna, George, *The Frog in the Kettle: What Christians Need to Know about Life in the Year 2000* (Ventura, CA: Regal, 1990).

Billingsley, K. L., *The Seductive Image: A Christian Critique of the World of Film* (Westchester, IL: Crossway, 1989).

Billington, James, *Fire in the Minds of Men: Origins of the Revolutionary Faith* (New York: Basic Books, 1980).

Bloom, Allan, *The Closing of the American Mind* (New York: Simon & Schuster, 1987).

Blue, Ron, *The Debt Squeeze: How Your Family Can Become Financially Free* (Pomona, CA: Focus on the Family, 1989).

Blumenfeld, Samuel, *NEA: Trojan Horse in American Education* (Boise, ID: Paradigm, 1984).

Bosworth, Barry P., et al., *Critical Choices: What the President Should Know about the Economy and Foreign Policy* (Washington, D. C.: Brookings Institution, 1989).

Bozell, L. Brent and Brent Baker, eds., *And That's the Way It Isn't* (Alexandria, VA: Media Research Center, 1990).

Brooke, Tal, *When the World Will Be One: The Coming New World Order in the New Age* (Eugene, OR: Harvest House, 1989).

B'Tselem, the Israeli Information Center for Human Rights in the Occupied Territories, *Annual Report 1989* (Jerusalem: B'Tselem, 1989). Includes April 1990 Update.

Bureau of Justice Statistics, *Drug Use and Crime* (Washington, D. C.: U. S. Department of Justice, 1989). Plus reports of the National Institute of Justice.

Carlson, Allan C., *Family Questions: Reflections on the American Social Crisis* (New Brunswick, NJ: Transaction, 1988).

Chandler, Russell, *Understanding the New Age* (Dallas: Word, 1988).

Chubb, John E. and Terry M. Moe, *Politics, Markets, and the Organization of Schools* (Washington, D. C.: Brookings, 1989).

Crane, Edward H. and David Boaz, *An American Vision: Policies for the '90s* (Washington, D. C.: Cato Institute, 1989).

Cromartie, Michael, ed., *Evangelicals and Foreign Policy: Four Perspectives* (Washington, D. C.: Ethics and Public Policy Center, 1989).

Crosson, Russ, *Money and Your Marriage* (Dallas: Word, 1989).

Davidson, James Dale and Sir William Rees-Mogg, *Blood in the Streets: Investment Profits in a World Gone Mad* (New York: Summit, 1987).

FRC Publications, *Cultural Trends and the American Family* (Washington, D. C.: Family Research Council, 1987).

Golitsyn, Anatoliy, *New Lies for Old: The Communist Strategy of Deception and Disinformation* (New York: Dodd, Mead, 1984).

Groothius, Douglas R., *Unmasking the New Age* (Downers Grove, IL: InterVarsity, 1986).

Hart, Benjamin, *Faith & Freedom: The Christian Roots of American Liberty* (San Bernardino, CA: Here's Life, 1988).

Henry, Carl F. H., *Twilight of a Great Civilization: The Drift Toward Neo-Paganism* (Westchester, IL: Crossway, 1988).

Herman, Victor, *Coming Out of the Ice: An Unexpected Life* (New York: Harcourt Brace Jovanovich, 1979).

Hirsch, E. D., *Cultural Literacy: What Every American Needs to Know* (New York: Houghton Mifflin, 1987).

Hitchcock, James, *What Is Secular Humanism?* (Ann Arbor, MI: Servant, 1982).

Hufbauer, Gary Clyde, *Europe 1992: An American Perspective* (Washington, D. C.: Brookings Institution, 1990).

Johnson, Paul, *A History of the Jews* (New York: Harper & Row, 1987).

Johnson, Paul, *Intellectuals* (New York: Harper & Row, 1988).

Johnson, Paul, *Modern Times: The World from the Twenties to the Eighties* (New York: Harper & Row, 1983).

Kimball, Roger, *Tenured Radicals: How Politics Has Corrupted Our Higher Education* (New York: Harper & Row, 1990).

Kurtz, Paul, ed., *A Secular Humanist Declaration* (New York: Prometheus Books, 1980).

Kurtz, Paul and Edwin H. Wilson, *Humanist Manifesto* (1933), and *Humanist Manifesto II* (1973), published jointly (New York: Prometheus Books, 1984).

Lacey, Robert, *The Kingdom* (New York: Harcourt Brace Jovanovich, 1981).

Lockerbie, Bruce, *Who Educates Your Child?* Garden City, NY: Doubleday, 1980).

McElvaine, Robert, *The Great Depression* (New York: Times Books, 1984).

Medved, Diane, *The Case Against Divorce* (New York: Donald I. Fine, 1989).

Morken, Hubert, *Pat Robertson: Where He Stands* (Old Tappan, NJ: Revell, 1988).

Muggeridge, Malcolm, *The End of Christendom* (Grand Rapids: Wm. B. Eerdmans, 1983).

Neuhaus, Richard John and Michael Cromartie, eds., *Piety & Politics: Evangelicals and Fundamentalists Confront the World* (Washington, D. C.: Ethics & Public Policy Center, 1987).

Office of National Drug Control Policy, *National Drug Control Strategy, 1990 and 1989 Reports* (Washington, D. C.: Executive Office of the President, 1989, 1990).

Peters, Tom, *Thriving on Chaos: Handbook for a Management Revolution* (New York: Alfred A. Knopf, 1987).

Reichley, A. James, *Religion in American Public Life* (Washington, D. C.: Brookings Institution, 1985).

Robertson, Pat, *The Secret Kingdom* (Nashville: Thomas Nelson, 1982).

Rothman, Stanley and S. Robert Lichter, *Roots of Radicalism: Jews, Christians, and the New Left* (New York: Oxford, 1982).

Slosser, Bob and Cynthia Ellenwood, *Changing the Way America Thinks* (Dallas: Word, 1989).

Smith, Page, *Killing the Spirit: Higher Education in America* (New York: Viking, 1990).

Sykes, Charles J., *Profscam: Professors and the Demise of Higher Education* (Washington, D. C.: Regnery-Gateway, 1988).

Tocqueville, Alexis de, *Democracy in America,* trans. Henry Reeve, rev. Francis Bowen and Phillips Bradley (New York: Alfred A. Knopf, 1956).

U. S. Department of Health and Human Services, *Annual Data from the Drug Abuse Warning Network* (Rockville, MD: National Institute on Drug Policy, 1989).

U. S. Department of Health and Human Services, *Drug Use, Drinking, and Smoking: National Survey Results from High School, College, and Young Adult Populations 1975–1988* (Rockville, MD: National Institute on Drug Policy, 1989).

U. S. Department of Health and Human Services, *National Household Survey on Drug Abuse* (Rockville, MD: National Institute on Drug Policy, 1989).

Vaughan, John N., *Church Growth Today* (Bolivar, MO: Southwestern Baptist University, series vol. 4 no. 4 1989—vol. 5 no. 1 1990).

Vertefeuille, John N., *Sexual Chaos: The Personal and Social Consequences of the Sexual Revolution* (Westchester, IL: Crossway, 1988).

Walters, Philip, ed., *World Christianity: Eastern Europe* (Eastbourne, Sussex, U. K.: MARC, 1988).

Wattenberg, Ben, *The Birth Dearth* (New York: Pharos, 1987).

Volume Two

The
New World
Order

Then the devil, taking Him up on a high mountain,
showed Him all the kingdoms of the world
in a moment of time.

And the devil said to Him, "All this authority
I will give You, and their glory; for this has been
delivered to me, and I give it to whomever I wish.

"Therefore, if You will worship before me,
all will be Yours."

And Jesus answered and said to him,
"Get behind Me, Satan! For it is written, 'You shall
worship the Lord your God, and Him only
you shall serve.'"

Luke 4:5–8

Contents

Foreword   287

Part I
Perspectives on World Order

1 The World Order Agenda   295
2 The Cry for Change   305
3 The Old World Order   321
4 The Old Order Crumbles   343

Part II
Threats to Freedom

5 The Establishment   369
6 Follow the Money   386
7 School for Scandal   409
8 New Order for the New Age   426

Part III
A Glimpse of the Coming World

9 A Promise of Hope   445
10 A Cruel Hoax   456
11 The Words of the Prophets   473
12 The Great Divide   492

Bibliography   508

Foreword

M̲y work on the manuscript of *The New World Order* was completed, the final proofs had been checked, and the book was essentially on the presses when the first satellite reports flashed on the monitors in our CBN broadcast center with the news that Soviet President Mikhail Gorbachev had been overthrown in a coup led by the KGB, the Soviet Army, and the secret police. His hand-picked vice-president, Gennady Yanayev, had been named by the hard-liners to head their revolutionary government.

But as suddenly as it all happened, this action was not entirely unexpected. Despite his popularity abroad, Gorbachev had been becoming increasingly unpopular at home. Some said he had walked too long on the razor's edge of compromise, but there were other possibilities.

The "coup" began on Monday, August 19, 1991. By Wednesday, August 21, it had collapsed. Boris Yeltsin, the charismatic president of the Russian Federation, emerged as the leader who had defeated the gang of eight. At his side was none other than Gorbachev's longtime ally, Eduard Shevardnadze, the former Soviet foreign minister and a former head of the interior ministry, the body which controls the secret police. Shortly thereafter, word came that Gorbachev was returning to Moscow as the "constitutionally elected" head of a "Democratic Soviet Union." Only time will tell what sort of structure will actually emerge.

From President George Bush's vacation home in Kennebunkport, Maine, on Wednesday, August 21, the day it became clear that the coup had failed, came the startling observation of CNN reporter Mary Tillotson that the president's *"new world order* is back on track, now stronger than ever." And suddenly the perspective becomes clearer.

On pages 359 through 363 of this book, I quote from Anatoliy Golitsyn's book, *New Lies for Old*, written in 1984, which gives a startling and detailed account of the KGB plan that was actually played out in 1989 to lull the West with false "liberalization." On page 357–58 I quote headlines from the *New York Times* which reveal a virtually identical program carried out by Nikolai Lenin in 1921, a program he called *glasnost.* Such precedents for deception should jolt the public conscience, but memories are short.

As I kept track of events—actually the remarkable lack of them— during the August "coup," it became all too clear that many facts just did not add up, except as an attempt to make the Soviet Union more palatable as a partner for the United States in the coming new world order. Consider the following.

The eight "coup" leaders were all part of the group that had engineered the rise of Mikhail Gorbachev to power. KGB Chief Vladimir Kryuchkov, Defense Minister Dmitri Yazov, Deputy Defense Chairman Oleg Baklanov, Prime Minister Valentin Pavlov, Farmer's Union Chairman Vasily Starodubtsev, Interior Minister Boris Pugo, Industrial Chairman A.I. Tizyakov, and Vice-President Gennady Yanayev were all placed in power relatively recently by Gorbachev himself. The first question to ask is why these members of Gorbachev's hand-picked team would turn against the man who not only placed them in power but was effectively keeping them there?

Another very odd fact, duly noted by several network analysts, was the failure to cut outside communications. That is the first thing any revolution would do. I was in Greece right after the so-called Colonel's Coup of 1974. When that revolution occurred, both domestic and overseas phone lines were cut; all radio, television, and press were silenced immediately; and all potential opponents were jailed. Neither the Greek citizens nor the world press knew what had happened until the revolutionary council was firmly in control and unassailable.

In the Soviet Union, the leaders of the August "coup" controlled the army, the secret police, and the KGB. They were all highly trained and experienced in espionage, military tactics, and propaganda. Furthermore, they were cautious older men, not impetuous youths given to reckless adventurism. Yet their "coup" seemed reckless, ill-conceived, half-hearted, and incredibly inept.

All the Soviet airports remained open. Domestic and long-distance telephone service was uninterrupted. Opposition newspapers were allowed to publish. Boris Yeltsin was permitted access to national television and even had the opportunity to address the world from the podium of the Russian Parliament. No arrests were made of any leaders or potential leaders of any group that would naturally rise to oppose the "coup."

Even more striking, the entire spectacle was allowed to play itself out before the television cameras and the press of the free world. Instead of the obligatory press shut down, it was as if those planning the "coup" actually wanted the entire world to see what was taking place—a move that by itself would virtually guarantee the failing of their undertaking.

In short, this "coup" was programmed from the beginning to fail. So, if that is the case, why did it take place at all?

The reason is obvious. Any careful observer of recent Soviet history must realize that Gorbachev was the hand-picked protégé of Yuri Andropov, the late Soviet premier and the head of the KGB. People were suspicious that Gorbachev's reforms were merely cosmetic, not genuine, and that lurking around him were hard-line Stalinists and Marxists eager to revive the military confrontation with the United States.

I noticed that a number of Soviet commentators used an American phrase to describe the source of the "coup" as the Soviet "military-industrial complex." Boris Yeltsin said that, if allowed to succeed, the "coup" would mean an end of freedom in the Soviet Union and a return to the military confrontation of the Cold War.

Now Gorbachev, Yeltsin, and Shevardnadze can proclaim that democracy has triumphed in the Soviet Union, that the reforms of the past are permanent, and that the hard-line, reactionary communist elements of the "military-industrial complex" have been banished from the land forever. Therefore, it must follow that the Western democracies can make massive reductions in their military arsenals without risk while they, in turn, pump billions of dollars into the Soviet economy to " keep democracy alive."

Are we so gullible as to believe that all this could be accomplished by a silly little three-day adventure during which four people were killed and one armored vehicle was set on fire? If the Stock Market is any barometer of public opinion, the answer is yes. We are that gullible. We want so desperately to live in a peaceful world that we will accept virtually any fraud which offers that hope.

Whatever happens in the days and months following the "coup," I do not believe that the global design for a new world order will be hampered by this kind of acceleration. Those who favor the globalist vision of world order will quickly find the necessary rhetoric to glorify the implications of the August "coup" and then to whitewash the rest.

For me, the "August Surprise" of 1991 is not unlike the similar surprise we received in the early morning hours of August 2, 1990, when we saw the first reports of the impending Persian Gulf crisis. At that time, I had just completed work on my book, *The New Millennium*, when the satellites began beaming the news of Saddam Hussein's incursion into Kuwait.

As the day unfolded, the CBN newsroom was on constant alert to see what, if anything, would transpire and how this latest flareup in the Middle East would affect world events. At the same time, I was anxious to know how the crisis would affect my work of the past several months on the book.

When it became clear what was happening, and that a military showdown of some kind was indeed very likely, I quickly updated the manuscript, and the book was released shortly thereafter. Now the manuscript of this book, *The New World Order*, has been updated in much the same way, to take into account this latest development in world history.

The ramifications of that historic week in 1990 have not yet been fully absorbed. Operation Desert Storm, the One-Hundred-Hour War, the March 1st "cease-fire," and the proclamations of a "new world order" that came out of the crisis in the Persian Gulf have added a new dimension to our lives. If there is greater hope in the world, there is also greater anxiety, and as we move ever closer to the coming *new millennium*, we can hardly doubt that other and more auspicious dramas lie just ahead.

It is clear now that this book, *The New World Order*, is actually a continuation of the last one. Today we can see more clearly than ever that the coming decade will be a time of turmoil, of controversy, and of even greater political and spiritual unrest. I believe that the issues I have addressed in these pages are proof of the depth and complexity of the problem.

While I have tried to challenge each reader to take them seriously—as life-and-death issues—I have an undeniable sense that we are witnessing the unfolding of a historic age, "a time of troubles," if you will, of biblical proportions, and the end of the age will truly bring the revelation of a new world order to justify the hopes and dreams of all mankind and the divine will of God. That, in essence, is the perspective I have tried to bring to this narrative.

For their assistance in preparing this work, I would like to express my gratitude to all the people who have helped with the research, analysis, and information gathering. Thanks to Dr. Jim Black for his able assistance in the organization and preparation of the work; to CBN News Director Drew Parkhill, whose professional research and fact checking have been invaluable. And special thanks to Beverly Milner from my staff for her long hours deciphering my handwritten notes and preparing the manuscript.

I would also like to thank Word Publishing executives Kip Jordon and Joey Paul for their ongoing stimulation and support and for their commitment to publishing the truth in these troubled times. And I would especially like to thank my wife, Dede, for her faithful support and encouragement, for reading and critiquing the work in progress, and for her patience throughout the months of reading, writing, and seemingly endless revision.

And finally, I would like to thank you, the readers, for your participation in this adventure, for you are the ones who, in the long run, will make the real difference. It is you who must exercise the rights and responsibilities of your citizenship, to make appropriate demands on your elected representatives, and ultimately to hold accountable all those who offer a vision of a new world order.

Pat Robertson
Virginia Beach, Virginia

Part I

PERSPECTIVES ON WORLD ORDER

1

The World Order Agenda

IN THE FALL and winter of 1989, communism collapsed in Eastern Europe. By mid-1990, the once-mighty Soviet Union was in economic and political ruin. In the late summer of 1990, war erupted between Iraq and Kuwait, and the following spring America and her allies—on the strength of superior technology and dynamic leadership—crushed Iraq's military force in a lightning-fast, one-hundred-hour war that was witnessed, via satellite, by virtually the entire world.

In 1992 the European community will emerge as the possible forerunner of the United States of Europe. And just eight years from the first publication of this book, the world will conclude the second millennium of its existence since the birth of Jesus Christ, and will begin the third millennium, A.D.

Against this backdrop of history, from the podium of the legislative chamber of the United States House of Representatives, the elected president of the United States of America has announced the beginning of a *New World Order.*

It was a deliberate and significant announcement, but what does this promise of a new regime mean to you, to me, and to our families? What kind of world will this new world order bring us? For the first time in their lives, many people have the undeniable sensation that they are living in a time when history is being made—when events are taking place in the world that will have a profound effect on their future lives.

In preparation for a television special entitled, "Don't Ask Me, Ask God," which was to become, we believe, the top-rated religious television special in American history, the Christian Broadcasting Network commissioned the Gallup Poll to survey a representative cross section of the American people to discover the answer to this proposition, "If you could ask God one question, what would it be?"

We tabulated the top ten concerns of the American people and then enlisted the aid of such well-known personalities as Steve Allen, Ned Beatty, Ruth Buzzi, Tony Danza, Norman Fell, Michael J. Fox, Anita Gillette, Dean Jones, Marvin Kaplan, Doug McClure, Jayne Meadows, Vincent Price, Ben Vereen, and many others to dramatize the top five questions that were on the hearts and minds of the American people.

Those who advocate a new world order are trying to answer these crucial questions by political means:

1. Why is there suffering in the world?
2. Why is there evil in the world?
3. Will there ever be lasting world peace?
4. Will man ever love his fellow man?
5. What does the future hold for me and my family?

AN IMPOSSIBLE DREAM

To some the new world order will usher in an era of unprecedented peace, harmony, justice, and prosperity. In one chapter of this book I will address the utopian dreamers and their plans through the ages. Typical of their thinking is the musing of the late megastar John Lennon, whose song "Imagine" has been sung without true comprehension by hundreds of millions of misty-eyed teenagers and young adults worldwide.

Lennon asked those listening to his song to imagine a time when there were "no countries," "no religion," "no heaven," "no hell," "no possessions," everyone "living for today," and the world "as one."

The former Beatle's dream world would be a world of hedonism—without religious faith, without national pride or sovereignty, without "anything to fight for," without any private property—but with a one-world government and communal property. Of course, if a one-world government had taken away all our property, our values, our faith, and our freedom, there indeed would be nothing left worth fighting for—unless we decided, like the people under the slavery of communism, that our precious freedom was worth fighting and dying to get back.

Some of his most ardent fans apparently have failed to recognize one glaring and essentially hypocritical inconsistency between the words and the life of this much-acclaimed troubador. Lennon, who sang about a new world with no private property, left to his Japanese widow an estate valued at a staggering $250 million. In fact, in almost every world utopian scheme, from Karl Marx on, there is a chasm between the lyrical rhetoric meant to ensnare the masses and the personal lifestyles of the expositors and leaders of the planned utopia.

George Bush and John Lennon are not alone in championing a new world order. Consider the following words that have spanned decades, even centuries of history:

> The Colonel's [Colonel Edward Mandell House, aide to Woodrow Wilson] sole justification for preparing such a bath of blood for his countrymen was his hope of establishing a new world order of peace and security as a result.
> Walter Millis, *Road to War: America, 1914–1917*

> In an address to the International Platform Association at the Sheraton-Park Hotel, [New York Governor Nelson] Rockefeller called for the creation of a "new world order."
> *New York Times*, July 26, 1968

> National socialism will use its own revolution for the establishing of 'a new world order.'
> Adolf Hitler, cited in
> *The Occult and the Third Reich*

> In short, the 'house of world order' will have to be built from the bottom up rather than from the top down. . . .
> An end run around national sovereignty, eroding it piece by piece, will accomplish much more than the old fashioned assault.
> Richard N. Gardner, former deputy assistant
> secretary of state for international organizations
> under Presidents John F. Kennedy and Lyndon
> B. Johnson, in *Foreign Affairs*, April 1974

> We must replace balance of power politics with world order politics.
> Jimmy Carter
> Democratic presidential candidate, 1976

> It is necessary to establish a universal regime and empire over the whole world.
> Writings of the Illuminati, ca. 1780

We deplore the division of humankind on nationalistic grounds. We have reached a turning point in human history where the best option is to transcend the limits of national sovereignty and to move toward the building of a world community . . . a system of world law and world order based upon transnational federal government.

The Humanist Manifesto II (1973)

What is the Plan? It includes the installation of a new world government and a new world religion under Maitreia.

Benjamin Creme, New Age leader
April 25, 1982

IMPLACABLE REALITIES

A single thread runs from the White House to the State Department to the Council on Foreign Relations to the Trilateral Commission to secret societies to extreme New Agers. There must be a new world order. It must eliminate national sovereignty. There must be world government, a world police force, world courts, world banking and currency, and a world elite in charge of it all. To some there must be a complete redistribution of wealth; to others there must be an elimination of Christianity; to some extreme New Agers there must be the deaths of two or three billion people in the Third World by the end of this decade.

In an article on the new world order in the Summer 1991 edition of *SCP Journal*, Tal Brooke quotes Brock Chisolm, director of the United Nations World Health Organization, as making the following appalling conclusions:

> To achieve world government, it is necessary to remove from the minds of men their individualism, loyalty to family traditions, national patriotism, and religious dogmas.

Whatever fringe groups might say or believe, the core premise of a new world order is aptly summarized in the Rothschild publication, *The Economist*, in its cover story of June 28, 1991, entitled, "The World Order Changeth," which says:

> There should, however, be no illusion that a global police force run by a global democracy is feasible. Those who have carried the winning ideas to the top of the mountain, and now wish to spread them, will not allow this process to be vetoed by the semi-converted or by plain toughs. . . .
>
> And if that sounds painless, it is not. The mountaintop is thick with those who would rather not see trade that is liberal, aid that is too principled, or arms control that is too self denying. And America needs to remember that a willingness to involve others is not enough to make a collective world order work. *There must also be readiness to submit to it. If America really wants*

such an order, it will have to be ready to take its complaints to the GATT, finance the
multilateral aid agencies, submit itself to the International Court, bow to some
system to monitor arms exports, and make a habit of consulting the U.N. (Emphasis
added.)

But do Americans want the government of the United States to defer to
the United Nations General Assembly before initiating an action it
considers in this nation's best interest? Do they want to be taxed to
support an international assistance agency? Do they want cases involving
themselves or their families to be tried by world courts? Do they want to
be citizens of the world instead of citizens of the United States?

Conversely, are Americans willing to be bound by the actions of the
United Nations to condemn a nation, such as Israel, that might not be
following the dictates of the new world order? For that matter, would
they be willing to be drafted into an army by United Nations mandate to
fight a war of its choosing?

Will the new world order usher in a glorious era of peace, or is it
the beginning of a dictatorial world nightmare? This book will raise the
troubling questions and, where possible, give some answers to those
questions.

THE INVISIBLE CORD

As a broadcaster, an author, and a longtime follower of and participant
in the political process, I have been an observer of world events for
several decades and have known personally a considerable number of
this nation's political and industrial leaders. It is clear to me, beyond a
shadow of a doubt, that for decades there has been a continuity of policy
and leadership in the United States that operates the same regardless of
which nominee of the major political parties gains access to the White
House.

It is relatively easy to trace the continuity of thought and purpose of
our policy elites from Cecil Rhodes, whose fortune rested on African gold
and diamonds; to the Federal Reserve Board; to Colonel E. M. House, the
éminence grise of the Woodrow Wilson presidency; to the English Round
Table; to the J. P. Morgan bank; to the Rockefellers and the Council on
Foreign Relations in New York; to the powerful Carnegie, Rockefeller,
and Ford Foundations; to the United Nations; to Henry Kissinger; to the
Trilateral Commission; to Jimmy Carter; and finally to George Bush.

What is not easy to explain is why the concept of a new world order,
taking as it does so many overtones from secret societies and the occult,
could have been handed down and then carried forward in a purely
natural progression for such an extended period of time.

Wealth does not explain it, for the people behind the concept have gained wealth beyond the dreams of avarice. Political power does not explain it, for all these players have reached the very pinnacles of power. Monopolistic capitalism does not explain it, because although one man or group of men may be seized with megalomania, the heirs and successors to the business soon forget the dreams of empire held by their ancestors and predecessors in order to enjoy the possessions at hand.

No, there has to be something more. There has to be some other power at work which has succeeded in molding and shaping United States public policy toward one clear goal—world government—from generation to successive generation. Some authors and researchers have pointed to the influence of the eighteenth-century elite group, the Illuminati. Others have pointed to the demonic "ascended masters" of the New Age religion—and still others have pointed to the world designs of a well-known but secret fraternal order. Some point to the greed of international banks, multinational corporations, and the vested aristocracy of the old and new world.

There are many suspects, but little consensus. Whichever is correct, it is my firm belief that the events of public policy are not the accidents and coincidences we are generally led to believe. They are planned. Further, I do not believe that normal men and women, if left to themselves, would spend a lifetime to form the world into a unified whole in order to control it after it had been so unified. No, impulses of that sort do not spring from the human heart, or for that matter from God's heart. They spring, instead, from the depth of something that is evil, neither well intentioned nor benevolent.

THE GULF CONNECTION

As it happens, the recent war in the Persian Gulf served as the convenient backdrop for the most recent announcement of the arrival of a new world order. Despite the brilliant victory, there are troubling facts that raise very serious questions about the integrity of the origins of that war and its ultimate conclusions. Is it possible that the Gulf War was, in fact, a setup? Consider carefully the following irrefutable facts.

On August 2, 1990, Iraqi tanks and armored personnel carriers poured across the border into tiny Kuwait. The Iraqis then proceeded to kill, rape, burn, loot, and pillage the people and property of that hapless land.

The game begun in Kuwait by the ruthless dictator, Saddam Hussein, had been played out for centuries in the Middle East. The strong have always preyed on the weak. Had not the forces of Syria's Hafez Al Assad ruthlessly butchered twenty thousand members of the Muslim Brotherhood in the Syrian city of Hama? Didn't Assad launch a murderous tank and artillery battle against the predominantly Christian Lebanese city of two hundred thousand inhabitants called Zahle?

Didn't the streets of Beirut, once known as the "Paris of the Middle East," flow red with blood when shells launched by invading Syrian forces ripped into buildings, maiming and killing innocent women and children? Wasn't it true in Lebanon that Palestinians killed Christians and Christians killed Palestinians? Druses shelled both Christians and Palestinians, and Christians and Palestinians shelled Druses, and Syrian gunners indiscriminately shelled them all.

Indeed modern Saudi Arabia was formed as a nation only after the brutal military conquest of smaller sheikdoms by King Abdul Assiz Ibn Saud. Ibn Saud was feted by the world's leaders, not condemned by them. Was it not true that the great powers had all but ignored Iraq's territorial grab against Iran that set off the carnage that lasted for eight years and cost more than one million lives?

So why would Iraqi aggression against neighboring Kuwait be treated any differently by the world powers? In fact was it not true that April Glaspie, the United States ambassador to Iraq, had assured Saddam Hussein that Kuwait enjoyed no special defense treaty with the United States? Hussein must have taken note that on July 31, 1990, in testimony before a House Foreign Affairs Subcommittee on the Near East, Assistant Secretary of State John Kelly made it clear that there was no mutual defense treaty between the United States and Kuwait. His words were echoed in precise detail by Margaret Tutwiler, an official spokeswoman of the United States State Department, who assured a press conference that the United States had no special obligation to come to the defense of Kuwait. Washington sources told CBN News that in April 1990, John Kelly and another individual spoke with Secretary of State James Baker to warn him that America needed to send Saddam a strong warning, even accompanied by economic sanctions. Baker apparently agreed, but somehow the concept died.

Saddam Hussein knew that United States satellite reconnaissance had charted precisely the formations of Iraqi troops and armor on the Kuwaiti border, obviously in preparation for war. He calculated that if the United States objected to what he was planning, it had plenty of ways to communicate its displeasure. It used none of them! By words and by silence, the United States flashed Saddam Hussein a green light.

SOVIET INVOLVEMENT

But what of the other superpower, the Soviet Union? At least thirty-five hundred key Soviet military advisers were stationed in Iraq under the command of a high-ranking Soviet general officer, training Saddam's troops. Saddam was armed with Soviet weapons, from Scud missiles to MiG fighters. Iraq was a Soviet client state.

By invading Kuwait, Saddam was putting billions of dollars into the Soviet economy. The Soviet Union is the second-largest oil producer in the world, with an annual output of 10.5 million barrels per day. Kuwait in 1990 was producing 4 percent of the world's oil and had been fudging on the OPEC cartel's production and pricing guidelines. Saddam and the Soviets wanted a price of $22 per barrel, not the $16 to $18 price per barrel that had resulted from a worldwide glut of crude oil.

This uptick in the price of oil would be worth as much as $20 billion annually to the cash-starved Soviets. The invasion of Kuwait by Iraq would have given the Soviets fabulous gains at no risk. Can any thinking person believe that Saddam's Soviet advisers did not encourage him to invade Kuwait and raise oil prices?

By invading Kuwait, Saddam could wipe out $10 billion of Iraq's debt incurred during his war with Iran, steal Kuwait's gold reserves, control the vast Kuwaiti oil fields, and raise the price of each barrel of Iraq's oil production at the same time.

He would also dominate almost one-quarter of the world's oil production with which he could have held hostage the economy of the entire world. Given this dictator's overwhelming military superiority in the Gulf, he then could either invade Saudi Arabia and the other oil-producing nations in the Gulf, or he could bend them to do his bidding.

Saddam Hussein, therefore, was clearly not just one more in a long line of Arab bullies trying to pick up some fast booty. Any junior analyst at the CIA, the Defense Department, or the State Department could have seen the threat that an invasion of Kuwait by Iraq posed to the economic security of the Free World.

The prospect of a single madman controlling commodity prices, energy prices, manufacturing costs, inflation, deflation, unemployment, in fact, the economic and political well-being of every human being on this planet is, frankly, too horrible to contemplate. On the face of it, that was the certain outcome of an undisputed, successful military takeover of Kuwait by Iraq.

Why then did the United States government not warn Saddam away from his course of folly? Why on three occasions did we encourage him? Why did we not send a clear message to the Soviets that any attempt to manipulate world oil prices through Iraqi military force in the Persian Gulf would be viewed as an act of hostility against the United States? Why did the admirals, the generals, the scientists, the economists, the politicians and the spies working for the entire United States government not take any action to head off a military adventure that could have destablized the world?

Why, in essence, did our government treat the entire incident as if it involved just one more desert bandit attacking a wealthy merchant's camel caravan?

HIDDEN MOTIVES

Could it have been that the wrong signals were sent to Saddam because powerful people wanted a situation that was so obviously dangerous to the entire world that all nations would join together to deal with it? A situation, indeed, that would cause the nations of the world to forget for a time their own claims of sovereignty in order to submerge their interests into that of a worldwide authority such as the United Nations? A situation which seemed on its face very ominous, yet which was certain of military victory by the massed armed forces of the world?

However formidable Iraq could have become with nuclear weapons and the world's oil wealth, it certainly was not that formidable on August 2, 1990, when the invasion of Kuwait began. There was a limited Iraqi navy, no Iraqi submarines, few modern aircraft in the Iraqi air force, no Iraqi spy satellites, no Iraqi AWACS spy planes, no Iraqi nuclear weapons, few Iraqi high-tech communications, and few truly motivated fighting men in Iraq's battalions. The United Nations forces had a leisurely six months to assemble a vast array of the most sophisticated battle gear on earth without any real threat of naval or air bombardment. Without in any way denigrating the brilliant leadership of our forces or their discipline and courage, the "One-Hundred-Hour War" in the desert was a clearly predictable turkey shoot.

Why then was Saddam Hussein given a green light by the United States to begin a war during which his forces would be demolished? Why permit a war to begin which cost over $50 billion and risked the lives of our fighting men and women, when a clear warning and a show of force probably would have kept the entire thing from starting?

Perhaps the leaders of America were preoccupied with other, more pressing matters. Perhaps they truly did not understand the geopolitical significance of Middle Eastern oil. Perhaps key data were kept from them. Or perhaps some very powerful being or some very powerful group, somewhere, wanted it all to happen just the way it did to set the stage for something that indeed transcended Saddam Hussein, or Iraq, or Kuwait, or even Middle East oil.

For out of the War in the Gulf emerged, full blown, what President George Bush and General Brent Scowcroft, his national security adviser, have proudly proclaimed as the new world order. In fact, our president has said publicly that the fate of Kuwait was not the main issue. Launching the new world order *was* the main thing.

He told the Congress and the nation on January 29, 1991:

> What is at stake is more than one small country, it is a big idea—a new world order, where diverse nations are drawn together in common cause to achieve the universal aspirations of mankind: peace and security, freedom, and the rule of law. Such is a world worthy of our struggle, and worthy of our children's future!

THE COMING JOURNEY

This book is written in an attempt to explain to each reader what this new world order is all about, how it came to be, who its advocates are, and, most important of all, what the meaning of the new world order will be to you and your family. Especially, I will show how the new world order, if allowed to proceed as planned, will radically alter the life you lead and the freedoms you now enjoy.

Finally, this book will place the origin, meaning, and ultimate destiny of the new world order within the clear purview of Bible prophecy, so that you can understand what God has to say about the one-world government that from 1990 onward may trace its public and official debut back to the Tigris-Euphrates Valley, where the first known civilization was born and from whence mankind was scattered because it had rebelled against God, and into which was born Abraham—the man whose seed was appointed by God to redeem the world.

That is the journey we are now set upon.

2

The Cry for Change

IN 1984 AND 1985, our television screens were filled with images of emaciated Ethiopian men, women, and children, near comatose from starvation, flies crawling over their faces, and their eyes staring blankly from skeleton-like sockets. The world was shocked into action to send relief. Hollywood megastars donated their time for the record "We Are the World," and a huge world satellite rock music festival called "LiveAid" raised tens of millions of dollars for emergency relief to Ethiopia.

Six years later, almost 6 million people in Ethiopia face imminent starvation, and most of the world no longer cares.

But the starvation has spread to Sudan and into Somalia, where a vicious civil war—as was the case in Ethiopia—has prevented the shipment of food to the people. A recent report in Congress declared that a disaster of "biblical proportions" was taking place in the Horn of Africa. Yet the rival factions fight on, the people are suffering unimagined agony, and the world looks away—uncomfortable at being reminded of the tragedy.

Simultaneously with the famine in Africa, a killer typhoon struck

Bangladesh, that poverty-stricken country carved out of India and Pakistan, in the spring of 1991. Flooding was so bad that a hundred thousand people lost their lives, a million were rendered homeless, and the entire population, where the per capita income is barely $179 per year, was pushed deeper into grinding poverty.

Surely the hearts of those who suffer in what is known as the "Third World" and the hearts of those affluent countries who care must cry for change. Something—anything—to make life more bearable. In fact, some urgent change is needed just to let them live.

As we look at the world around us, we see such an enormous disparity between the quality of life in the northern and southern nations. On the one hand, we see nations like the United States, Europe, and certain Asian nations in the Northern Hemisphere enjoying a high standard of wealth and prosperity; on the other hand, we see grinding poverty in Africa, Central and South America, India, and other nations in the Southern Hemisphere and the tropical regions.

While one segment of the world's population enjoys an incredible abundance, and the very rich among us enjoy extravagant excess, an equal or greater segment is living in absolute squalor with famine, political chaos, civil unrest, personal cruelty, and environmental disaster.

THE SPECTER OF DEATH

From the Sudan and Ethiopia in the Southern Sahara, and from Northern Mexico to Argentina, we see the darkest images of human suffering. With the exception of South Africa and nations such as Tunisia on the Mediterranean Coast, there isn't a single politically stable and fiscally solvent nation on the entire continent of Africa. In fact, the entire economic output of all 450 million people in sub-Saharan Africa barely equals that of tiny Belgium.

In Latin America and the Caribbean, we find nations such as Nicaragua and Haiti where the per capita income is at a misery level of $330 a year. In Guatemala, which has had its share of revolution and trouble, I saw people living on garbage dumps, competing with the vultures to get to the refuse.

In Guatemala City, I was personally giving out relief supplies to some of the eight thousand people who stood in line for hours in the broiling hot sun at the city dump just to get a bag of rice and beans which CBN's Operation Blessing was giving to each of them. This is life well below the subsistence level. The mayor of Guatemala City told me later that if his citizens could just move from "misery to poverty" it would be a great improvement.

Most of us cannot even imagine this kind of degradation. It is impossible for even the poorest American to conceive of the near-subsistence poverty that exists in nations like this all around the globe. Tens of millions of people of every race and culture are living in stark, dehumanizing poverty. They are not on strike; they will do anything for work. They're not screaming political slogans and ideological rhetoric; their lives are much too hard for theories and dreams. Ideologies are the luxuries of the privileged classes.

All the extreme political ideologies in the world—whether they come from the extreme right or the extreme left—have come from the privileged classes. Those who want to determine how the poor should live have never endured or even seen real poverty. Socialism in Britain was a creature of the aristocracy. Communism was the brainchild of German-Jewish intellectuals. Grand ideas don't come from the slums, they come from Idealists and dreamers.

The poor in Africa, Asia, and Latin America are so beaten down they don't have time for idealistic theories. When the poor rise up it's because there's an upper-class reformer somewhere stirring them up.

THE POOR OF THIS WORLD

Peru and other South American nations are being savaged by cholera at this very moment. Cholera is called the disease of the poor. The people contract it by eating fish from polluted waters and by washing their clothes and drawing their drinking water from garbage-laden rivers and streams.

In most of these places, people are pouring raw, untreated sewage into the streams and into the oceans, and disease breeds there. That is precisely how the Black Death started in Europe in the fourteenth century. There is hardly a single place in all of South America where the water is safe to drink.

In Egypt, halfway around the globe, the water is absolutely filthy, full of liver flukes and amoebas. People are wasted by intestinal disease and dysentery. This and the other diseases that breed in the rivers and streams and dumpsites spread contagion throughout the land and just sap the life out of the people. Ironically, natives who have developed some tolerance to the conditions may live for years with these diseases, while infected foreigners often die within days.

Nevertheless, the mortality rate is very high, especially among the children in these countries. The children succumb quickly to dysentery, and they are totally dehydrated by it. I have been told that just a little sugar water from a pure source can keep a child alive, but the natives have been told to give the children formula mixed with the local drinking water, and the water is so bad it is killing the little children in the hundreds.

Hopeless poverty combines with crushing monetary debt in these Third World nations, and this is compounded by ongoing environmental rape. The most critical environmental problem in tropical countries today is desertification, which comes from cutting down the forests. The rain forests are being decimated in Brazil; the beautiful hardwood forests of Southeast Asia are being systematically plundered. The ominous growth of the Sahel region in Africa is gradually turning the entire northern half of that continent into desert at the rate of eight or nine miles a year.

It is a vicious cycle. The poor need fuel to cook and to provide warmth. They cut down the trees because trees don't cost them anything. Some years ago I visited an Afghan refugee camp in an area of Pakistan called Baluchistan. The entire landscape was so pockmarked that it resembled the surface of the moon. My guide informed me that the refugees cut down all the trees and shrubs for fire and shelter, then they dug up all the roots and burned them as well.

THE UNENDING CYCLE

Of course the poor neither know nor care about ecology. When the trees go, the topsoil also goes. When the topsoil goes, not only does the food supply drop sharply, but mud slides wipe out houses, silt up rivers, and damage the water. Then, without trees, the ambient temperature rises, and natural wildlife and plant life disappear. So the people, now facing starvation, move on to start the cycle again.

I lunched several years ago in Jerusalem with the assistant minister of commerce of Israel. He was an ardent scuba diver. After Israel took over the Sinai Peninsula, he used to go down to the Red Sea where he took great pleasure in exploring the exotic plant and animal life in those waters. He told me how the Israeli Ministry of the Interior had done everything it could during the occupation of the Sinai to preserve the natural habitat of the coral and the various tropical fish in the Red Sea.

But when the Israeli government gave back the Sinai, he said, the unlettered Egyptian fishermen in the Red Sea would position their boats over schools of fish and toss sticks of dynamite into the water. The edible fish that floated to the top after the resulting explosions would be sold. Everything else was wasted. As anyone knows, that is the most destructive thing they could have done. The explosions destroyed the coral, decimated entire species of tropical fish, and demolished the food chain and the environment of all the closely interdependent aquatic life in that area for generations. And all the delicate and precarious natural environment of that ancient body of water has been changed forever.

Gorgeous, priceless species of fish—which, incidentally, are totally inedible—and the beautiful natural paradise that existed there were devastated by these thoughtless marauders. Why? Because they were ignorant of the repercussions of what they were doing. They had no natural heritage. They had no idea what the effects of pollution and man-made destruction of these natural treasures would be.

But like the ignorant woodcutters, these "fishermen" were pushing their nation further into poverty. Not only were they ruining the food chain and destroying the breeding grounds of edible species of fish, they were destroying a major source of hard currency for their economy.

The Red Sea waters were a mecca for European and American tourists because they offered probably the finest scuba diving environment in the world. As is the case of the Red Sea fishermen, the poachers of Africa injured long-range tourism by their slaughter of elephants and rhinos for ivory. Such short-term thinking, ignorance, and selfish greed have effectively sealed the economic fate of millions of innocent people in the Third World.

But are such men who poach and pillage the only ones guilty of wanton destruction? Certainly not. Things just as ignorant and destructive are taking place in this country right now. And this concerns not just the destruction of wildlife, but also human life.

For example, it is absolutely incredible to me that United States tobacco companies are exporting cigarettes to these same Third World countries by the ton. In this country we're learning about the dangers of tobacco, about lung cancer and emphysema. Every day thousands of people are quitting this deadly habit. But we export millions of tons of tobacco products to poverty-stricken nations, guaranteeing more death, disease, and suffering. The trade in tobacco is every bit as bad as the opium trade in China at the turn of the century, and, ultimately, I suspect, no less costly in terms of human life.

WHO'S TO BLAME?

Beyond the threat of environmental rape, we have also had nuclear terror hanging over our heads ever since World War II. When will some superpower confrontation take place? And if not a superpower, when will some madman like Mohamar Qaddafi steal a potable device; or when will a dictator like Saddam Hussein succeed building his own nuclear arsenal with which he can hold the rest of the world hostage?

Already we have had wars and revolutions on every continent. There have been communist-inspired revolutions in Asia, Africa, and Latin America virtually continuously since 1945. There have been military coups and countercoups in the Sudan, Uganda, Ghana, Liberia, Zimbabwe (Rhodesia), Mozambique, and Angola, along with socialist-type takeovers in places like Tanzania. We have a silent war going on now in North Africa, carried out by Qaddafi against the nation of Chad on his southern border. Obviously the racial strife of white versus black and Zulu verses ANC is not over in South Africa. And you can project a rising level of violence all around the world.

Consider Southeast Asia and the terrible struggles that have been going on there during the last thirty years. First in Vietnam, then in Laos and Cambodia, and then along the Cambodian border with Thailand. There have been revolutions and counter-revolutions in Burma, and continuous political instability throughout the region.

There have been problems of equal or greater magnitude in Central and South America with communist-led revolutions in Cuba, Chile, and Peru. Most recently we have witnessed the bloodbaths in Nicaragua and El Salvador. Sometimes it seems our world is bleeding to death, and everywhere people are crying out for solutions to the problem of war.

WHO'LL STOP THE RAIN?

How do we stop terrorism? How do we stop the killing of innocent civilians? How do we stop the Arab-Israeli conflict that has been so bloody in the Middle East, or the factional killing in Lebanon? The Iraqis have been fighting the Iranians. The Soviets have been fighting the Afghans. Armed conflict is breaking out in Yugoslavia between Croats, Slovenes, and Serbs. Tension is building between Czechs and Slovaks, and between Rumanians and their Hungarian minority.

More ominous for us all are the heightened tensions and conflicts in the Soviet Union between the central government and the republics of Latvia, Estonia, and Lithuania. There is a growing protest for secession in Russia, the Ukraine, and the Muslim republics. Will the Soviet Union disintegrate in the next couple of years, or will the forces of reaction and repression begin a crackdown that will bring back memories of the terror last known under Joseph Stalin?

Consider the age-old tensions between India and Pakistan, the internal warfare between the traditional Hindu ruling caste in India and the Sikhs, Tamils, and Sinhalese, all fighting on separate fronts for autonomy and independence. In the last decade the world has witnessed the deaths of three key political leaders in that country, including the plane crash that killed Rajid Gandhi, being groomed at that time for political office, the assassination of Mrs. Indira Gandhi, and the recent assassination of Rajiv Gandhi, Mrs. Gandhi's youngest son, in May 1991.

Further north, we have seen the rape of Nepal and Tibet by Communist China. The world is being torn apart by war and confusion and repression. Some 2 billion people have been under the heel of communism. We have seen the unstoppable ravages of poverty, war, and pestilence.

We have seen typhoons, cyclones, tornadoes, hurricanes, floods, and earthquakes in every corner of the globe. Of course there were terrible civil wars in Bangladesh, Biafra, and Nigeria. For forty years there has been carnage and destruction, both man-made and natural.

The cry rings out from every nation in a single voice, "Isn't there a better way?" Isn't there some way we can ensure justice, peace, law and order, an orderly approach to the environment, and greater equity between the wealth of rich and poor nations?

When we see such agony, is there any wonder that people applaud the concept of world order? It seems there has to be some forum for universal justice. There must be something we can do. The world tried after World War I with the League of Nations, which was shunned by the United States. Then we finally established the United Nations in 1945, in the wake of World War II, but that organization has been notoriously ineffective.

Now in the 1990s our leaders are telling us that the better way has already begun. But has it really?

FEEDING ON THE POOR

Unfortunately, in these Third World countries there are not only unavoidable problems, but overt oppression of the people by their own leaders. A close look reveals people like Lopez Portillo, the former president of Mexico, who reportedly enriched himself by as much as $3 billion. Ferdinand Marcos of the Philippines may have looted as much as $2 billion from the treasury of his country. The leaders of African nations have reputedly looted billions, and we have recently read that Saddam Hussein and his family may already have helped themselves to as much as $10 billion from the beleaguered people of Iraq.

Despite incredible poverty, Third World leaders continue to enrich themselves at the expense of the poor. In Mexico, upwards of 60 percent of the nation's foreign debt under previous administrations went back out of the country in so-called expatriate remittances. The same is true of Argentina and Brazil. Money that has been given in aid to the poor has been put into the hands of the wealthy few and passed right back out to the international banks in Switzerland, the United States, the Cayman Islands, or pumped into real estate in South Florida.

The amounts of these "expatriate remittances" are huge. The United States ambassador to Argentina told me when I met with him in Buenos Aires that the figure of "flight capital" in Argentina was $27 billion. In Guatemala I learned that under the administration of President Lopez Garcia, 30 percent of the price of every public works project went directly to the president and his cronies. In the Philippines, I was told by a Chinese property developer in Manila that a surcharge of 10 percent of the cost of every major private building project had to be paid as a bribe to a relative of Imelda Marcos, the wife of then President Ferdinand Marcos.

Third World debt stands at some $1 trillion, and it is a dagger pointing at the financial heart of the Western banking system. Most of these loans are a joke. The attitude of the newly enriched leaders is simple, "If you were stupid enough to loan us the money, why do you think we are stupid enough to pay it back?"

In Indonesia there was a terrible scandal involving the Pertamina Oil Company concerning bribery, looting, graft, and the loss of billions of dollars. In state-run companies in the Third World, the damage from gross mismanagement and overstaffing probably exceeds the damage from venality and looting. These problems are reaching epidemic proportions all over the world; so the poor stay poor and the rich grow even richer. And when you add to that the fallout of the 1973 oil crisis, it means that the people of the poor nations have had the blood sucked out of them for the better part of the past two decades, and most of the time by their own selfish and incompetent leaders.

These poor nations cannot pay these escalating debt charges, so they go deeper and deeper into debt to the international banks. At times debt service on their loans may equal their entire revenue from external trade. Now because of their misuse of previous credit, no new credit is available to them. There seems to be no way out of it for most of them. At least to human eyes they appear to be hopeless. They are caught in a constant cycle of runaway inflation, degradation, despair, and rapidly compounding debt. Something needs to come along to clean the slate.

THE SITUATION IN ZAIRE

I visited the nation of Zaire in July 1991 at the invitation of its president, Mobutu Sese Seko. Zaire, formerly known as the Belgian Congo, occupies a strategic area of Central Africa three times the size of Texas. With 35 million inhabitants barely existing on a per capita annual income of $150, Zaire is a microcosm of the troubles facing the entire Third World.

The Congo, once the private possession of King Leopold of Belgium, was granted independence from Belgium on June 30, 1960. Parliamentary elections were held in April 1960, and a pro-communist, Patrice Lumumba, was named prime minister.

Peace lasted just one week. On July 5, 1960, the army mutinied, and political authority broke down. Belgium intervened on July 10, and on July 11, Moise Tshombe set up a separate government in the mineral-rich Shaba district, then called Katanga.

When Patrice Lumumba turned to the Soviets for help, the United States CIA chose an army colonel, Joseph Mobutu, to take over the government, expel all Soviet diplomats, and imprison Lumumba. Lumumba later died under mysterious circumstances and was proclaimed an honored martyr by the Soviets.

Mobutu then returned the government to civilian hands, but from February 1961 until 1965 the nation was racked by a violent civil war that seriously damaged its economic infrastructure. The former colonel (now lieutenant general), Joseph Mobutu once again took control of the government and declared himself Mobutu Sese Seko, the "Guide."

Since that time Zaire has had one party in power, one national leader, and except for a murderous rebellion in Katanga in 1977, relative peace and security. Mobutu, for all practical purposes, is the supreme leader of the nation—enjoying a parliament from his own party, choosing the cabinet, choosing judges, ruling by decree if parliament is not in session, and leading the army.

Mobutu Sese Seko rules as an African chief, regarding the people somewhat like his family and the wealth of the nation as his own, to keep or disperse to friends at his pleasure. Published reports place his accumulated personal wealth at $5 billion—equal to the annual gross national product of the nation of Zaire. He admits to a more modest $50 million, but his lifestyle is much grander than a mere $50 million would permit.

During the past twenty-five years, almost all European or other white technicians and managers have been expelled or have left the country voluntarily. Since only a handful of college-trained specialists remain, the infrastructure, services, agriculture, and goods-producing sectors are in shambles.

The nation owes $8 billion and has defaulted once again on its latest attempt at debt restructuring organized by the International Monetary Fund (IMF). Inflation is running at 1,000 percent. There is not enough food. Telephone communication with the outside world is almost impossible. There are only a hundred thousand automobiles for 35 million inhabitants. Health care and education are in a state of crisis.

The city streets are pockmarked and filthy. In the countryside the eighty-three thousand miles of roads left by the Belgian colonial government have deteriorated to a sparse twelve thousand miles. Farmers in the interior have no way to transport their crops to the cities, which are experiencing critical food shortages.

A COLLAPSING SYSTEM

Before independence, Zaire was an agricultural powerhouse—a net exporter of rice, corn, sugar, cocoa, palm oil, cotton, and coffee. Now it must import large quantities of rice, corn, soybeans, and other food to feed its people.

I visited one agricultural complex that had originally been managed by some Israelis. Well-built and well-equipped chicken houses were standing in neat rows, completely empty, without evidence of a single chicken. Eighteen years before they had housed at a single time 270,000 chickens and had sent up to a million chickens each year for domestic consumption into the capital city. Then, for political reasons, the Israeli managers were deported. There was no one to take their place. Now Zaire imports most of its edible chickens from faraway Belgium, and domestic poultry production is virtually non-existent.

I visited an inefficient canning factory turning out tiny cans of tomato paste. We were told that the tomatoes used by this small operation had to be imported from Italy. We visited an egg production operation where the chickens were falling ill because of guano disease. The reason? No one could fix or replace a one-half horsepower motor that was there to drain the chicken droppings into septic tanks outside the building where the chickens were located. The manager of the complex told me he had to haul water for the chickens in a small trailer. Since the facility was located adjoining a river, I asked the obvious question, "Why don't you drill a well for your water?" His answer reveals the essence of Zaire's problems, "No one has come to dig a well for us."

Prior to 1960, this nation had one of the most highly developed and diversified economies in sub-Saharan Africa. It was, and is, unbelievably rich in national resources. It has fertile soil and multiple growing seasons. Sixty-seven types of tropical fruit grow in the country. Delicious mangoes and papayas grow wild throughout the land. Virtually every known edible variety of vegetable can be grown somewhere between Zaire's lowlands and the inland mountain ranges.

The nation has abundant deposits of iron, copper, nickel, tin, cobalt, gold, diamonds, rare earths, and oil. It has between 40 and 50 percent of all the hardwoods in Africa. It has 13 percent of all the hydroelectric capacity in the entire world. Yet with all that wealth, there is a budget out of balance, a $400 million balance-of-payments deficit, and a defaulted debt of $8 billion.

KEEPING UP STANDARDS

When someone discovers the answer to how Zaire got to where it is today, they will also find the answer to the riddle of poverty in the Third World.

First, we must remember that during colonialism the wealth of the colonies was used for the benefit of the mother country, the white plantation owners, and the white traders and business men. To be sure, there were roads and communication and clinics and law and order. But the native populations were often not given opportunities for the university educations and practical apprenticeships needed to develop business managers, civil servants, health professionals, agricultural specialists, mining engineers, finance specialists, marketing experts, and the host of other skills that a complex society demands.

In the United States there are in excess of 14 million students in colleges and universities, and at least 70 million Americans have some college training. Out of Zaire's population of 35 million, only a relative handful have university training. (There are now eight thousand Zairians who have graduated from American colleges and universities.) The technical base below the top levels is woefully inadequate.

Emerging nations, like Zaire, have been racked by bitter warfare between rival tribes, or communists insurgences, or liberation movements against communists, or army-led coups, or uprisings against colonial structures, or strife between religious groups. Each civil war or insurgency is devastating to the material well-being of the nation involved and often those nations that adjoin it as well.

But war and the lack of education are not the only problems. There is a fierce desire for racial independence that seeks to rid the nation of every vestige of those perceived as oppressors. Too soon they learn the truth of Shakespeare's words, "The fault, dear Brutus, is not in the stars but in ourselves." Or in the words of Pogo, the sage of the swamps. "We have met the enemy and he is us."

In 1973, President Mobutu announced measures to place all firms in the hands of Zairians. Bigger firms were nationalized. Following the decree, commerce was devastated. Although the decree was rescinded in 1976 to restore ownership as before, the damage had been done. Many businesses were either in poor condition or had closed. But there were other assaults inflicted by the government of Zaire on its own economy.

Following the course of many Third World nations, the government of Zaire tried to appease its rapidly growing urban population by placing price controls on agricultural products. Price controls on food had an opposite effect from that intended. Farmers stopped growing crops and moved to the cities, which meant more demand, less food, and higher market prices than before.

The devastation that nationalization, socialism, and economic misman-agement has brought about in Africa was summed up in this candid admission by the former socialist leader of Tanzania, Julius Nyerere, "We have ruined the plantations so badly that their former owners would not want them if we gave them back to them at no charge."

The unlettered and untrained leaders of Zaire, like those of other Third World countries, appeared to the salesmen from more developed nations like pigeons waiting to be plucked. They came with a bagful of monu-mental development projects, ill-conceived public works, and sophisti-cated weapons. By the salesmen's sides were government banks, private banks, regional banks, and world banks willing to shovel billions of dollars into projects of questionable value and lacking in fiscal controls.

FINANCIAL RUIN

The magnitude of the projects and the lax fiscal controls of the leaders were a breeding ground for fraud. Who could blame an official with a wretched salary and little business sophistication for occasionally dip-ping into the torrent of money passing before him?

But once the deals were done, the commissions and bribes paid, the buildings built, and the machinery in place, no one stayed around to show the people how to make everything operate well or profitably.

From then on they were to depend on the vagaries of the world commodities markets to service huge debts and operate their govern-ments. From that point there quickly followed disappointing earnings and frequently defaulted loans. Then there was no credit for repairs, replacement parts, and other necessary services.

With its back to the wall because of a deteriorating situation that was primarily of its own making, the government of Zaire decided to print the money it needed. They did this to such an extent that during my visit I learned that the local currency on the black market had depreciated about eight thousand times against the dollar. A modest lunch for two that used to cost about Z29 now cost Z235,000. It goes without saying that the soaring price of food and the other necessities of life brought the population to riots, demonstrations, and possible revolt.

A new program of participatory democracy and privatization is being put into place in Zaire. Religious expression is encouraged by the government. Foreign investors are being offered undreamed of concessions. It is much too early to tell whether gradual reform will succeed, or whether the country will disintegrate into warring factions. It seemed to me that only a spiritual revival and leadership by a strong economic Czar working under a powerful transitional head of state (like General August Pinochet of Chile) would restore the economy sufficiently for democracy to take root and flourish. If not, with no strong, reliable center, the entire nation will fall apart. Only time will tell what the ultimate outcome will be in Zaire. Anyone who visits that potentially wonderful land comes away with a clear conviction—something must be done to give these people hope.

ONE WORLD CURRENCY

Two things relating to the main subject of this book surfaced while our group was visiting Zaire. Although there were no phone lines or telefax links between Zaire and the rest of the world, when the group vice-president of CBN's international division, Michael Little, presented an American Express card to guarantee our hotel bill, an amazing thing happened.

The hotel clerk in Kinshasa, Zaire, inserted Michael's credit card into a standard verification machine that requested a search of a databank in Brussels, which in turn searched data records in New York. Within two minutes from the initiation of the process, the credit verification and credit limits had been received back in Kinshasa from New York.

If plastic money can be accepted or rejected within two minutes from New York to a broken-down city in Central Africa, can any of us doubt the truth expressed in the Book of Revelation that all credit could one day be controlled by a central one-world financial authority and that no one could buy or sell without its approval. As we will discuss in later chapters, it is abundantly clear that a one-world credit system, a one-world currency and a one-world central bank has been the center-piece of all significant planning for the new world order.

Of lesser significance was the seeming unwillingness of United States AID officials to address solutions to Zaire's most obvious and pressing economic problem, agricultural self-sufficiency. The United States government, on the other hand, is more than willing to loan money at interest to Zaire to purchase, under what is called Public Law 480, the surplus corn, rice, and soybeans grown by American farmers.

Belgium not only does not help Zaire become self-sufficient in poultry production, it actually dumps chickens on the market in Zaire at prices cheaper than what it costs the farmers of Zaire to raise chickens inside their own country.

It is obviously dangerous to generalize from fragmentary information, but I believe that neither Europe nor the United States is anxious to have Zaire become a net exporter of agricultural products in competition with their own farmers. Even widespread sales of American grain on credit at low prices, while appearing to be a humanitarian gesture, actually tend to depress agricultural productivity in a Third World country.

Maybe the troubles of Africa, the Soviet Union, and other Third World countries happened because of ignorance, corruption, and socialism. But it is also fair, I believe, for us to ask ourselves whether, in order to prepare for the new world order, powerful international economic interests have pushed the nations of Africa prematurely into freedom so that their faltering steps into socialism would in turn ruin the agriculture to such a degree that they would not be able to challenge the agriculture of the world's leaders, and in turn their vast mineral riches could one day be had for a song.

And we also must ask why, with all of sub-Saharan Africa in economic shambles, has the political left mounted such an unremitting campaign to bring about the same chaos in the only vibrantly healthy economy on the African continent—South Africa? In fact, is there not a possibility that the Wall Street bankers, who have so enthusiastically financed Bolshevism in the Soviet Union since 1917, did so not for the purpose of promoting world communism but for the purpose of saddling the potentially rich Soviet Union with a totally wasteful and inefficient system that in turn would force the Soviet government to be dependent on Western bankers for its survival?

Will indeed the new world order be a mechanism to enslave, control, and loot vast portions of the world's populations, rather than a mechanism to give them economic self-sufficiency and freedom?

WHO'S PAYING THE BILLS?

From a different perspective, there are also some who wonder how the biggest banks in the United States, in concert with our government, could have poured out billions upon billions of dollars to failing communist governments and crooked Third World dictators who had no intention of paying us back. Surely we knew that hundreds of billions of that loan money was leaving those nations and that the loan proceeds would never be used for their intended purpose.

Now that it has been done, will the American taxpayers be asked to make the banks financially whole? Only a few Americans are aware that under the Monetary Control Act of 1980, the Federal Reserve Board of the United States has the authority to issue United States dollars in exchange for the debt securities of any nation for any purpose, including, of course, repaying United States banks.

Was the debt problem of Third World countries something that happened accidentally as part of the long wave economic cycle? Was it an attempt by the lenders to dominate and control these people? Or has there been a deliberate attempt to weaken America's financial strength by improvident lending so that it would enter meekly into the one-world government of the new world order?

Whatever the economic causes, we see a world that is bleeding, crying out for relief, for justice, for a chance for normal human existence. We all want a better world.

But like the line in the popular song of a few years ago, "Looking for Love in All the Wrong Places," are we looking for something that is too good to be true, or for that matter, something that could turn out to be false and dangerous? Are we looking in all the wrong places for the answers to the world's dilemmas?

Particularly, we must ask ourselves if the internationalists, the banking and industrial complex, the European socialists, and their allies are truly desirous of establishing a world order to help the poor, to end wars, to balance budgets, and to give the little guy a better world for himself and his children. Or are these advocates of the new world order really seeking global control of the world's money, natural resources, and military power so that they can establish themselves, whether the people like it or not, as the dominant elite to determine the type of world in which we all will live?

The moving spirit of the Trilateral Commission, the mentor of former President Jimmy Carter (later his national security adviser) and the leading advocate of a new world order, Zbigniew Brezinski, had this to say in his book *Between Two Ages,* written in 1970, about his vision of the new society:

> [T]he gradual shaping of a community of the developed nations would be a realistic expression of our emerging global consciousness; concentration on disseminating scientific and technological information would reflect a more functional approach to man's problems; both the foregoing would help to encourage the spread of a more personalized rational humanist outlook that would gradually replace the institutionalized religious, ideological, and intensely national perspectives that have dominated modern history.

This does not sound to me like a concept for democratic freedom to meet the needs of the poor and downtrodden. It sounds much more like the command society of socialism or communism. Since the Council on Foreign Relations and the Trilateral Commission are the dominant force espousing a new world order, and since President George Bush has not only been a member of both organizations, but has surrounded himself with many of their members, it will be appropriate in a later chapter to focus on what the Council on Foreign Relations is, what its vision of the world order is, and what it means to you.

In the following chapters I would like to put some perspective on these issues by briefly reviewing the historical record. In order to judge the events of the past half century with any clarity of vision, it will be important to see how the map of the world was laid out and how it has changed over time. In that light, then, we will be prepared to examine the political and economic challenges of our own time in the context of the old world order, the age of transition, and the utopian dreams that have led us to this moment.

3

The Old World Order

PRINTED ON THE reverse side of every United States one-dollar bill is what is called the Great Seal of the United States. This seal was adopted by Congress in 1782.

Both faces of the seal are printed on the currency. One shows the American eagle with an olive branch of peace in one claw and thirteen arrows of war in the other. The second face of the seal depicts an unfinished pyramid, above which is an eye set in a blaze of glory. At the base of the pyramid are inscribed the Roman numerals MDCCLXXVI, or 1776. Overarching the pyramid are the Latin words "Annuit Coeptis," loosely translated as "He looks favorably on our endeavor," and below the pyramid is the Latin phrase, "Novus Ordo Seclorum," a line by the poet Virgil, meaning a "new order of the ages," or *a new world order.*

The designer of the great seal was Charles Thompson, a member of the Masonic order who served as secretary to the Continental Congress. This pyramid has special meaning for Masons, even as crystals and "pyramid power" today hold occultic significance for followers of the so-called New Age movement.

To some, the "all-seeing eye" represents divine providence. To others it does not represent the God of the Bible, as some think, but the eye of an ancient Egyptian deity, Osiris, who is revered in the secret high ceremonies and sacred rites of the Masonic Order. I will review some of these beliefs and practices of high-degree Masons and how their "mystery cult" figures into the new world order in a later chapter.

However, the pyramid shown on the seal is not complete, thus indicating that the task of nation building had not been accomplished. Thus, the implication for Thompson and others was that under the watchful eye of Osiris, the endeavor begun in 1776 would, according to their secret Masonic rituals, bring forth a new world order.

But a "new order of the ages" in relation to which old world order? Was it to be *new* in relation to the old monarchies of the time, or in regard to the old aristocratic ideas of nobility? Was it new in regard to human rights and freedom? Was it new in relation to the old idea of private ownership of property? Or did the "new order of the ages" have a double meaning?

Is it possible that a select few had a plan, revealed in the great seal adopted at the founding of the United States, to bring forth, not the nation that our founders and champions of liberty desired, but a totally different world order under a mystery religion designed to replace the old Christian world order of Europe and America?

THE MORE THINGS CHANGE

From 1782 to the present day, the call for a new world order continued against a backdrop of radically different times and places. The agricultural society of 1782 was obviously different from that of 1848, when the Industrial Revolution blossomed, yet Karl Marx published his *Communist Manifesto* and called for his own version of a new world order in that year.

The world of 1917 differed from both 1782 and 1848, yet Colonel Edward House and Woodrow Wilson called for a new world order in 1917. The world in 1938 differed from that of 1917, yet Adolf Hitler called for his new world order in 1938. And the world in 1968 differed from the world of 1938, yet Nelson Rockefeller called for his new world order in 1968.

Indeed the world has changed many times during two hundred years. The forms of government are different. The quantity and distribution of wealth and privilege are different. The power of individual nations and alliances of nations is different. Communications are vastly different among people, and, if in scientific achievement our world is light-years ahead of the world of just fifty years ago, how much more scientifically advanced is it than the world of two hundred years ago?

Every generation represents a new world order. The life and customs and mores of the world are constantly undergoing change. Old things die;

new things are born. This common-sense observation may explain in part why the noninitiated among us are somewhat baffled when certain elites tell us that they are bringing us a new world order.

But given the clearly observable reality of change and renewal, how can we account for the fact that for over two hundred years a small group, their spiritual successors, and their converts have labored ceaselessly to bring us what we thought we already had—a renewed world order?

Can it be that the phrase *the new world order* means something entirely different to the inner circle of a secret society than it does to the ordinary person? In fact my research leads me to believe that within the very organizations promoting the new world order, the term has one meaning to the general membership and an entirely different meaning to the small inner circle of leadership.

Indeed, it may well be that men of goodwill like Woodrow Wilson, Jimmy Carter, and George Bush, who sincerely want a larger community of nations living at peace in our world, are in reality unknowingly and unwittingly carrying out the mission and mouthing the phrases of a tightly knit cabal whose goal is nothing less than a new order for the human race under the domination of Lucifer and his followers.

THE KINDER, GENTLER WORLD

Laying aside until a later chapter the thoughts of such a possibility, just what does President George Bush have in mind when he and his aides speak of the new world order?

When the president declared in early 1991 that the end of the Cold War had helped to usher in a new world order, it seemed to be his contention that the law of the jungle was on the way out, along with all the old rules of strife and discord. The "kinder, gentler world" the president first promised in his 1988 campaign would be a place where tyranny could not (or at least should not) prevail.

The very words, *new world order*, have a utopian flavor to them. Nations within this new system are to be governed by the democratic principles of consent and agreement—the paving stones of the president's "kinder, gentler world."

But to most of us the term *new world order* is uncertain and imprecise—apparently more fantasy than fact, more rhetoric than reality. It is a vision of global peace submerged in a sea of political theory dating in modern times back at least to the time of Woodrow Wilson and the League of Nations. It seems to be little more than an elegant image for a somewhat ambiguous agenda for order that has made its way from the think tanks of Washington, D.C., to the nightly news in millions of American homes.

Fred Barnes wrote in *The New Republic* that the idea of a new world order has been tossed around in private conversations at the White House for a long time, although the exact meaning of the term was always uncertain and imprecise. "Whatever cropped up post-cold war, that was the new world order."

In an interview on CNN at the height of the Persian Gulf Crisis, General Brent Scowcroft, the current national security adviser, former aide to Henry Kissinger, and a one-time director of the Council on Foreign Relations, said he had doubts about the significance of Middle Eastern objectives concerning global policy. When asked, "Does that mean you don't believe in the new world order?" Scowcroft snapped back, "Oh, I believe in it. But our definition, not theirs!"

President Bush used the phrase in a speech at a San Francisco fund-raiser in February 1990, saying, "Time and again in this century, the political map of the world was transformed. And in each instance, a new world order came about through the advent of a new tyrant or the outbreak of a bloody global war, or its end."

Soon the president was speaking of "collective security," describing it as virtually synonymous with the new world order. Later his speeches were sprinkled with terms such as "collective resistance" and "collective defense," and the escalation of the Persian Gulf crisis as "a test" of the theory.

In any event, Bush was determined to test the idea on the American people, and it soon became a feature of every public address. In his September 11, 1990, televised address to Congress, he said, in part:

A new partnership of nations has begun. We stand today at a unique and extraordinary moment. The crisis in the Persian Gulf, as grave as it is, also offers a rare opportunity to move toward an historic period of cooperation. Out of these troubled times, our fifth objective—a new world order—can emerge: a new era, freer from the threat of terror, stronger in the pursuit of justice, and more secure in the quest for peace. An era in which the nations of the world, east and west, north and south, can prosper in harmony.

A hundred generations have searched for this elusive path to peace, while a thousand wars raged across the span of human endeavor. Today that new world is struggling to be born. A world quite different from the one we've known. A world in which the rule of law supplants the rule of the jungle.

Later, the president added:

When we are successful, and we will be, we have a real chance at this new world order, an order in which a credible United Nations can use its peacekeeping role to fulfill the promise and vision of the United Nations' founders.

On October 30, 1990, Bush commended the role of the United Nations Security Council and suggested that the United Nations could help create "a new world order and a long era of peace." In his address to the people of Prague on November 17, 1990, the president said the situation in the Persian Gulf provided "an opportunity to draw upon the great and growing strength of the commonwealth of freedom and forge for all nations a new world order far more stable and secure than any we have known."

On January 29, 1991, during his State of the Union address, President Bush said that the military response to Iraq's invasion of Kuwait was meant to be a bold statement of international purpose. "What is at stake is more than one small country," he said, "it is a big idea—a new world order, where diverse nations are drawn together in common cause to achieve the universal aspirations of mankind: peace and security, freedom, and the rule of law. Such is a world worthy of our struggle, and worthy of our children's future."

A FRAMEWORK FOR PEACE

The central issue, President Bush said, was the "long-held promise of a new world order," a promise which maintains that "brutality will go unrewarded and aggression will meet collective resistance."

During his whirlwind tour of military bases, the president spoke to families of servicemen at Fort Gordon, Georgia, on February 1, 1991, saying, "When we win, and we will, we will have taught a dangerous dictator, and any tyrant tempted to follow in his footsteps, that the United States has a new credibility and that what we say goes, and that there is no place for lawless aggression in the Persian Gulf and in this new world order that we seek to create." Bush used the phrase *new world order* three times that day alone.

Fred Barnes observed that the term has found a new currency since the conclusion of the Gulf War. "At the White House the phrase 'new world order' has all but become holy writ," he says. "Speech-writers now routinely include it in every military or foreign policy speech by the president."

Reportedly National Security Adviser Scowcroft was the first White House executive to use the phrase, but he has now grown tired of it. The president's press secretary, Marlin Fitzwater, thinks some new expression will come along to replace it, while others find the phrase uncomfortably close to Hitler's phrase, "the new order." Barnes suggests, "They fear it sounds too fuzzy-minded and one-worldish."

Nevertheless, in his March 6, 1991, address to Congress, commemorating the successful conclusion of the Gulf War—the speech subtitled "A Framework for Peace"—Bush said,

> Until now, the world we've known has been a world divided—a world of barbed wire and concrete block, conflict and cold war. Now, we can see a new world coming into view. A world in which there is the very real prospect of a new world order. In the words of Winston Churchill, a "world order" in which "the principles of justice and fair play . . . protect the weak against the strong." A world where the United Nations, freed from cold war stalemate, is poised to fulfill the historic vision of its founders. A world in which freedom and respect for human rights find a home among all nations.

He added, "Our success in the gulf will shape not only the new world order we seek but our mission here at home."

In reality it is clear that the United States foreign policy establishment used the United Nations mandate as a pretext for the Gulf War. Even as the administration said, "This action was mandated by the United Nations," the president called it "a test" of the new world order apparatus.

We were told that our involvement was at the urgent request of the United Nations Security Council, but in days gone by anyone in his right mind would have said, "Who cares?!" We would never have considered following the dictates of the United Nations unless it was something America already wanted.

Then when the dictator of Iraq lashed out against people in his own country who supported the allies, suddenly America refused to intervene. We cannot support the Kurds, we were told, because it was not part of the United Nations "mandate." In the past it was, "What's best for America? What's the right thing to do?"

At the end of all this, will we find that we have handed over our long-range foreign policy to an international body that is not concerned with our internal problems—such as genocide? Many fear that has already been done—*fait accompli*. So, the next time an American president says, "I think we should send troops into Lebanon, or some other hot spot," his advisers will say, "Sorry, Mr. President. The precedent was set in the Gulf War. If you don't get a United Nations resolution you can't send troops anywhere!"

A *Washington Times* editorial recently expressed the attitude of a lot of people: "Are we hearing this right? For twenty-five years the United Nations has been little more than a joke, and now you're telling us they're going to run the world? Is that what you're saying?"

Whatever he means by it, one thing is certain. The president of the United States has become the key player to prepare the world for the introduction of a new world order which may one day resemble an order defined by someone else, not him.

Since its inception the United Nations has been an example of bureaucracy run amok. It is rife with fraud, pointless debates, internal mismanagement, and ludicrous behavior. Nikita Kruschev's shoe-pounding tirades were only one early example. Jeanne Kirkpatrick, who was our ambassador to the United Nations from 1981 to 1985, blasted the organization over and over again. But how can such an organization ever hope to be effective? Tiny, unsophisticated nations which hold 80 percent of the voting power pay less than 1 percent of the budget, and the people paying 99 percent have only a minority vote.

The attitude of the United Nations member nations hardly suggests a realistic forum for world order. They wholeheartedly applauded the tyrant of Uganda, Idi Amin; 80 percent of them vote with the Soviet Union and against the United States on virtually every issue. Are we to believe that somehow this organization has suddenly been transformed by the action in the Persian Gulf? These distinguished people will lead us to world peace?

THE NEW PARADIGM

The rhetoric of President Bush's public statements is strikingly similar to statements being made by other officials throughout the administration. The same words and phrases appear again and again. In his address entitled "Building a Framework for the Rule of Law," presented at a judicial conference in July 1990, CIA Director William Webster commented that,

> A new European order of stable, prosperous and just democracies is still a long way off. It will require a new framework of political and economic systems. It will demand transitions—from rule by individuals to the rule of law. And finally, a new order will be meaningful only if there is trust—trust in the leaders and in the institutions of government.

The ideas and the expressions have become commonplace. Earlier, in an April 1990 address to the Reason Foundation in Los Angeles, another White House official, James Pinkerton, deputy assistant for policy planning, said, "If the last decade will be remembered as the time when the New Deal model broke down, I believe this decade will be remembered as the time when a new order for the age was established, not only in the U.S., but around the world."

Pinkerton also remarked—prematurely as it turned out—that, "In defiance of received opinion, the president has kept his campaign promises of a Kinder, Gentler Nation, and No New Taxes. Because of his policies, America stands at the horizon, ready for the dawning of the New Paradigm around the world." Bush had originally used the term "new paradigm" in his inaugural address, but he now apparently prefers the phrase *new world order*. At any rate, less than nine months after Pinkerton's comments in Los Angeles, the president had broken his tax pledge and immediately ordered American troops into combat in Kuwait.

Pinkerton credited his use of the term *new paradigm* to Thomas Kuhn's *The Structure of Scientific Revolutions*—which chronicles historical read-justments of scientific thinking about the world. He then listed five principles of the new paradigm which the Bush administration is following. Perhaps these principles will offer some insight into the objectives of the new world order.

First, Pinkerton said, the new paradigm recognizes a greater influence of market forces upon government than ever before; second, there will be increasing individual choice (especially in education); third, there is empowerment of the people to choose for themselves; fourth, there is greater decentralization of authority; and fifth, there is great emphasis on results rather than on theories.

The emphasis on business is not surprising, and the focus on the individual is consoling, but it is hard for most of us to see the reality in such statements. And even if the administration's vision of world order still seems to be more wishful thinking than practical reality, it is nevertheless an idea that has touched the public imagination and raised many new questions. Even the most passive observer must wonder what the president has in mind. Certainly the world took notice when, in announcing the siege of Iraq on January 17, 1991, Bush took such pains to promise this new vision of unity to the world.

BIRTHING A GLOBAL VISION

For all its vagaries, the phrase *new world order* was anything but concrete earlier this century when it first began to appear in the conversations of scholars and policy gurus meeting at Pratt House, at Sixty-Eighth and Park in New York City. It was only an idea, a catch phrase, but it offered an apt expression for Woodrow Wilson's premature vision of world unity which sparked his Fourteen-Point Plan and his ill-fated hopes for a League of Nations.

To members of the Council on Foreign Relations (CFR)—the nongov-ernmental body that has advised presidents and politicians since Wilson's time—the concept of a *new world order* became a useful paradigm for expressing the image of a managed global economy where reason and order supplanted the shifty and uncertain machinations of public policy debates. It was an idea that offered a grander vision of the art of statecraft and the rightful business of nations.

Harvard Professor Stanley Hoffman, writing in *Foreign Affairs*, the journal of the CFR, claims we are in "a new phase of history." This scholar certainly speaks for the consensus of CFR analysts when he says, "The world after the Cold War will not resemble any world of the past." This belief has been a central tenet of CFR policy for so long, Hoffman could hardly come to any other conclusion.

Then he adds another observation that is central to the idea of the new world order. He says:

> The fate of this new world will depend on the ability of the [sources of military, economic, and demographic power] to cooperate enough in order to prevent or moderate conflicts, including regional ones, and to correct those imbalances of the world economy that would otherwise induce some states, or their publics, to pull away from or to disrupt the momentum of interdependence.

Interdependence is a key concept of the globalist vision. Whether it would be called the League of Nations, the United Nations, or the new world order, the idea of a world organization to monitor world peace and foster interdependence has had many vocal supporters, both friend and foe. In 1937 Winston Churchill urged the English Parliament to proclaim its allegiance to the League of Nations, saying, "What is there ridiculous about collective security? The only thing that is ridiculous about it is that we haven't got it." The idea of collective security depends entirely upon the interdependence of nations.

Recently, conservative author George Weigel, director of the Ethics and Public Policy Center in Washington, D.C., said, "If the United States does not unashamedly lay down the rules of world order and enforce them—in both instances, the allies if possible, but unilaterally if necessary—then there is little reason to think that peace, security, freedom or prosperity will be served."

In an article for *World* magazine's special issue on the new world order, Mark Amstutz pointed out that the foundational principles of the new world order are outlined in the mandate of the United Nations peacekeeping apparatus. These principles are:

> (1) the integrity of territorial boundaries and the political independence of nation-states; (2) the legitimacy of force in repelling aggression; and (3) the legitimacy of collective defense and punishment of aggression.

The real teeth of this concept of interdependence were exposed in United Nations Resolution 678, which authorized the deployment of combined allied forces in the Persian Gulf area if Iraq did not voluntarily withdraw from Kuwait by the January 15, 1991, deadline set by the Security Council. It also provided the justification for war.

A TIME FOR CHANGE

Today the idea of a new world order is a part of the currency of contemporary foreign affairs ideology. The editors of the journal *New Perspectives Quarterly*, published by the Center for the Study of Democratic Institutions, a liberal think tank, commented in their special issue on the new world order that "The opening months of 1990 will be remembered as the time when the founding assumptions of postwar power alignments crumbled, bringing into view the outlines of a new world order."

Political events that began unfolding in the closing months of the last decade have indeed shaken everyone's image of the global political structure. The end of the Cold War has changed not only the hypotheses of the old world order but the creative tensions upon which our understanding of the world once depended.

In less than eighteen months, literally hundreds of scholarly texts were invalidated, along with innumerable social theories. And the shock waves of political and economic change—particularly within the Soviet Empire and the Eastern Bloc—continue to rumble and reverberate through the halls of power.

Mikhail Gorbachev has been a spectral figure throughout these events, and much of the current debate focuses on him. But there are many dimensions to the emerging vision of the coming new world order. There are political, demographic, geographic, and economic dimensions, but there are also philosophical and spiritual ones.

Jacques Attali, French President François Mitterand's top aide, made a particularly striking observation in a *New Perspectives* article when he wrote:

> Like Luther and Muhammed before him, Gorbachev is bending history. And he is doing it at such a speed that it is impossible to know the results. The world, it seems, will change more in the next ten years than in any other period of history. What was beyond the grasp of imagination yesterday is already happening today.

As the world approaches the beginning of a new millennium, Attali believes the superpowers of the old millennium, the United States and the

Soviet Union, are "slouching toward relative, if not absolute, decline." Military might is no longer the token of power in the world. The new order, he says, will be the "Order of Money," and in that light the big money players—the Pacific Rim nations and the European Community—will lead the way to a new age of "hyper-individualism" and unprecedented materialism.

Nobel laureate and political leader Willy Brandt of Germany wrote, "The logic of reform has already taken Gorbachev far beyond where he originally intended to go." And today, Brandt believes, "the trend is irreversible." At first glance, Brandt's vision seems prophetic. But we have to wonder how much Gorbachev may have known about the August 1991 "coup" beforehand, since his agenda for a new world order has suddenly gained such incredible momentum.

THE VIEW FROM THE TOP

Henry Kissinger, a member and the former director of the Council on Foreign Relations and foreign policy adviser to two presidents, wrote in the January 28, 1991, issue of *Newsweek* magazine that America's biggest challenge in the coming decade will be to preserve "the new balance of power" that is emerging from the Persian Gulf conflict. He says:

> Today, it translates into the notion of "a new world order," which would emerge from a set of legal arrangements and be safeguarded by collective security. The problem with such an approach is that it assumes that every nation perceives every challenge to the international order in the same way, and is prepared to run the same risks to preserve it. In fact, the new international order will see many centers of power, both within regions and between them. These power centers reflect different histories and perceptions. In such a world, peace can be maintained in only one of two ways: by domination or by equilibrium. The United States neither wants to dominate, nor is it any longer able to do so. Therefore, we need to rely on a balance of power, globally as well as regionally.

This is a peculiar statement, since the balance-of-power strategy was one of the things rendered useless by the end of the Cold War and the birth of the new world order. But most notably, Kissinger observes that the clash of arms in the Middle East is part of an ancient historical problem at the epicenter and birthplace of three world religions.

He says, "In several thousand years of recorded history, the Middle East has produced more conflicts than any other region. As the source of three great religions, it has always inspired great passions." The stalemate between Arabs and Jews, Arabs and the West, and the Jews and "world opinion," he says, has kept tensions at fever pitch in the region for the last half century. But in his summation, the elder statesman writes, "Victory in the gulf will create a historic opportunity to alter that particular equation—and it should be seized."

But it is not just the Middle East that has inspired the passion of war. General William Westmoreland, the former commander of all U.S. forces in Vietnam, once told me that in the history of the world there had been over forty-one hundred wars. The old world order has never known lasting peace.

Listen to the sounds of twenty centuries of war. Hear the ominous thunder of armed legions marching on foot, the relentless clatter of chariots over ancient cobblestones. Listen to the clash of steel on steel, the roar of fires ravaging entire cities, and the sound of buildings crashing to earth in ruins. Hear the panic of animals trapped in the midst of battle, the screams of women and children, the moans of the dying. Year after year, century after century, the legacy of man's rage, jealousy, and greed has spilled blood across the pages of history.

Time and progress march hand in hand through the centuries, and as mankind has learned to harness the power of steam, coal, electricity, oil, and nuclear fuels, his capacity for carnage has continually multiplied. Is it any wonder that as war grows ever more terrible, more and more men of goodwill should seek the ways of peace?

As we scan the pages of history, can we be surprised to discover that people would gladly accept the rule of tyrants when their only recourse was anarchy? As Rome conquered the Mediterranean world, the people gladly accepted the laws of the Roman dictators, for the legions also brought the Pax Romana—a measured peace under the hegemony of Rome.

In the ninth century, European nations submitted themselves to the Holy Roman Empire, which historians assert was neither holy, nor Roman, nor even an empire. But peace remained elusive for the next thousand years as an unending succession of warrior-kings and would-be emperors continued to rise to challenge the world order.

Out of the anarchy of revolution in France arose a twenty-six-year-old general named Bonaparte who brought an illusion of stability for a season. But this vainglorious conqueror wasted the flower of French youth on his own personal dreams of empire and ultimately turned Europe into a charnel house.

THE BALANCE OF POWER

After Napoleon's final defeat in 1815, the Congress of Vienna met to lay out the new map of Europe. Prince Klemens von Metternich of Austria dominated the conference, and he was certainly no idealist. Recognizing the cupidity of the various European powers and the ever-present threat of war, he proposed a balance of power—not that dissimilar from the concept of *détente*—by which no group of nations would have the strength to force its will upon another.

Further, preserving the balance in Europe required that no European nation would be permitted to gain added strength in the New World of North and South America. To ensure the European balance of power, England's Lord George Canning persuaded President James Monroe to issue what became known as the Monroe Doctrine, which declared North and South America off-limits to the Europeans. The Monroe Doctrine was honored because it was backed first by British power, then, until the Cuban Missile Crisis of 1962, by the power of the United States.

With balance-of-power politics in place in Europe, and with the incredible ascendancy of British economic power—along with Britain's worldwide naval presence—the nineteenth century became a time of relative peace under what we now recognize as the Pax Britannia.

The most devastating conflict of the period was not between nations but within our own nation. This was, of course, what historians now call the Civil War and what we in Virginia call the War of Northern Aggression!

Indeed, the nineteenth century was a time of great optimism and pride. Mankind was soaring. It was inventing, producing, discovering, transforming, and proving everywhere the eminence of its science and its mind. And in an orgy of self-congratulation, the intellectual, spiritual, and social leaders began moving away from their roots and their heritage of ethical values.

But hadn't twentieth-century man proved himself superior to his ancestors? Shouldn't he naturally discard those ancient traditions and beliefs—and especially those based on the idea that man was an instrument of divine authority—and embrace a newer, grander vision of humanity in charge of its own destiny?

At the very moment we began to see ourselves as too wise for war, our intellectual dreams were shattered by an assassin's bullet at Sarajevo, Yugoslavia. The assassination of Archduke Ferdinand of Austria immediately ignited World War I and led to four years of terror and carnage beyond anything the human mind could have imagined. Never in history had war been so terrible. Never had weapons of destruction levied such a ghastly toll.

And never has a war spawned such a bloody aftermath. An ailing president of the United States virtually ignored the Treaty of Versailles, which ended the war, while he gave what little strength he had left to the formation of a League of Nations to help ensure a world safe from war.

By 1920, after years of angry debate, the plan collapsed. Wilson's health failed, and the peace in Europe began to fray.

WILSON'S TRAGIC FLAW

It is one of the tragic ironies of history that the punitive terms of the Versailles treaty—which emasculated Germany's military power and forced it to pay $5 billion in war reparations—actually paved the way for the rise of Adolf Hitler and foreshadowed a second world war. Meanwhile, Wilson's cherished League of Nations was dying of impotence. His Fourteen Points, which offered a framework for a world without war, failed to keep the peace.

Could people living in 1900 have dreamed of the horrors of Joseph Stalin's starvation of the Soviet Kulaks, of Hitler's concentration camps and the gas ovens of the Final Solution, or of the war in the Pacific? Could anyone have imagined that even worse disasters would grip the entire world only fourteen years after the ratification of the Treaty of Versailles?

Would they have believed the panic and hysteria that ensued only a decade after the end of the first-ever world war, the collapse of the stock market, the Great Depression, and the outbreak of another world war more horrifying and more dehumanizing than the first?

In less than fifty years the world was transformed from the exuberance and whimsy of the Gay Nineties to one seized by the trauma of two terrible wars and a half century of mind-boggling change. Following the carnage of World War II, nations suddenly numbed by their own capacity for violence yearned for a genuine and lasting peace.

Only such an attitude can explain Franklin Roosevelt's idealistic but incredibly naive explanation of his concessions to Stalin. In his account of Roosevelt's words, Winston Churchill wrote:

> "I think," he said of Stalin, "that if I give him everything I possibly can and ask nothing from him in return, *noblesse oblige*, he won't try to annex anything and will work with me for a world of Democracy and peace."

Although Roosevelt's "Four Freedoms Speech" and the subsequent "Declaration of the Twenty-Six United Nations" on January 1, 1942, gave the impetus for the establishment of the United Nations, Roosevelt did not live to see the founding of the organization itself. Yet he would no doubt have shared the idealistic fervor of those who hailed its creation.

When the United Nations Charter was signed on June 16, 1945, in San Francisco, fifty nations were signatories to the agreement. The official documents were then transported to the White House by none other than

Alger Hiss, the presidential adviser who was later charged with giving state secrets to the Soviets and was convicted of perjury in 1949. Five years after the United Nations was founded, the organization participated in its first major action, agreeing to intervene in the civil dispute in Korea.

The United Nations was presented to the American people in glowing terms. In Dean Acheson's words, "As almost holy writ, with the evangelical enthusiasm of a major advertising campaign. It seemed to me," Acheson said, "to raise popular hopes that could only lead to bitter disappointment. . . . The General Assembly appeared to be the town meeting of the world."

THE UNCERTAIN PEACE

Brief highlights stand out along the road to the "bitter disappointment" of which Acheson spoke. In June 1950, Harry S. Truman persuaded the General Assembly to mobilize its police action against North Korea. In 1958, President Dwight Eisenhower broke up the Anglo-French effort to maintain access through the Suez Canal. When he turned the matter over to the United Nations, Dag Hammarskjold used the occasion to blast European imperialism and to extol the virtues of the so-called Afro-Asian nonaligned nations.

It is instructive to note that neither the rhetoric nor the actions of the general secretary were ever directed against the Soviet Union, which had brutally repressed the freedom fighters in Hungary under cover of the Suez Canal Crisis. Hammarskjold's anger was carefully reserved for Western democratic nations.

In 1960, when Belgium began to withdraw from the Congo, civil war broke out. The Belgian government waited for United Nations action. When none was forthcoming, the Belgian army moved in to restore order. Immediately Hammarskjold condemned the Belgians and raised a United Nations force from the nonaligned nations.

Mineral-rich Katanga Province had seceded from the chaos to form a separate state under its nationalist leader, Moise Tshombe. In the melee that followed, the United Nations forces turned on the European settlers and attacked Katanga. Can any of us forget the *Life* magazine photo of a bullet-riddled Volkswagen with a dead woman and child inside and a dazed and blood-spattered Belgian settler raising his head to implore his attackers, or heaven above, to understand why the United Nations "peacekeeping" forces had just done this terrible thing to him and his family?

Since that time, a new philosophy emerged at the United Nations. Right was on the side of the emerging nonaligned nations. Tribal warfare, revolution, dictatorship, terrorism, torture, murder, graft, and corruption within these nations were glossed over. The former Western allies and the United States became, in the words of a later nonaligned leader, "the Great Satan."

The most grotesque example of the United Nations' morality took place on October 1, 1975, when the dictator of Uganda, Idi Amin, who was then chairman of the Organization for African Unity, addressed the General Assembly. This bloodthirsty tyrant denounced an imaginary Zionist-U.S. conspiracy and called not merely for the expulsion of Israel from the United Nations but for its "extinction."

The combined assembly gave him a standing ovation when he arrived, applauded him throughout his address, and rose again to their feet when he left. The following day the secretary-general and the president of the General Assembly hosted a public dinner in Amin's honor.

DUBIOUS HONOR

This was the honor given a man who had murdered no fewer than two hundred thousand of his fellow citizens, including Anglican Archbishop Luwum. Julius Nyerere of Tanzania said, "Since Amin usurped power he has murdered more people than Smith in Rhodesia, more than Vorster in South Africa." Yet not once would the United Nations move either to censure the bloody dictator or to prevent his further rape of what was once the loveliest land in all of Africa.

Since the early 1970s, perhaps in a desire to give legitimacy to its bizarre perspectives, the United Nations has brought forth resolutions on the New International Economic Order and the Charter on the Economic Rights and Duties of States.

The thrust of these and related studies was for a world devoid of ideological differences, a built-in poor-versus-rich bias, a new information order severely restricting press freedom, and a new international legal order mandating by fiat world peace as an "inalienable right of humanity." It was a mandate, in effect, for peace at any price, a proposal that could ultimately result in the loss of all other human rights under a one-world dictatorship.

The United Nations' real concern for human rights snaps into clear focus when we realize that from 1980 to 1984 the United Nations' Third Committee concentrated its entire attention on the question of human rights violations in El Salvador, Guatemala, and Chile. Until public outcry finally demanded consideration of human rights violations by the Soviets in Afghanistan in 1986, no communist country had ever been placed on the agenda of the General Assembly or any of its committees.

But why should this be surprising? The nonaligned nations which make up the majority of United Nations delegations, vote with the communist line fully 85 percent of the time in the General Assembly. In 1987, member nations voted with the United States only 18.7 percent of the time.

From a business standpoint, the fiscal mismanagement and inequity within the United Nations is colossal. The poorest countries contribute less than one-hundredth of 1 percent of the United Nations budget. Together, eighty of these countries, with a numerical voting majority in the General Assembly, contribute less than 1 percent of the United Nations budget.

On the other hand, the United States pays 25 percent of the total United Nations annual budget—in excess of $1 billion each year—and an even larger percentage of the actual costs of some agencies. The United States has contributed $17 billion of the estimated $87 billion spent by the United Nations since its founding in 1945 through 1987. Yet our share amounts to only one-sixth of United Nations Secretariat personnel, and to only 12.6 percent of the agency professional posts.

Where does our money go? In the 1984–85 fiscal year the United Nations funded 2.2 billion pages of documents. The secretariat employs fifty-two thousand civil servants, who were paid 32 percent higher than their American counterparts. After fifteen years of service, employees on the lower levels are guaranteed pensions 80 percent higher than their American counterparts, and those with the rank of under secretary or higher will depart after thirty years service with a $310,000 tax-free farewell bonus—in addition to their generous pensions.

Dean Acheson's warnings were proved correct. The United Nations has led to "bitter disappointment." It has not preserved peace, and it assuredly has not served as a dispassionate forum for the benefit of all mankind.

A COMMUNITY OF NATIONS

In my 1987 address to the Council on Foreign Relations in New York, I proposed a new organization of nations to supersede and replace the United Nations. Such an organization would be, I suggested, an organization based not on failed utopian idealism but on realism, not on the shifting sands of ideological expediency but on a foundation of time-honored principles.

What I proposed then, and what I still believe would be a much more reasonable forum for international understanding and cooperation, is a community of sovereign nations based on democratic institutions, representative government, and respect for the rule of law. Such an organization would offer respect for the individual freedoms, private property, and the basic rights of free speech, assembly, religion, and the press. And nations that neither use terrorism against other nations nor employ torture and terror against their own citizens would be eligible to join such a body.

The organization, which I called the Community of Democratic Nations, would be open to all nations whose governments have achieved legitimacy by embracing democratic processes. When any nation can show that it has moved from totalitarianism to true democracy for a specified period of time, it would then be eligible for membership in the Community of Democratic Nations.

In such a body, the artificial distinctions of First, Second, and Third World status would disappear. There would be no Eastern or Western power cliques, no nonaligned nations. The international institutional dynamics flowing from the anticolonial period would be superseded by the new realities of the twenty-first century.

Since member nations would represent the lion's share of the world's economic powers, the Community of Democratic Nations would be able to use its power constructively and efficiently. There would be construction without Soviet obstruction. Furthermore, in matters of trade, loans, credit, economic development, and military assistance, the Community of Democratic Nations could use its power to give international support to those governments that do respect democratic principles and promote constructive change.

An organization that would include such diverse nations as Sweden, Costa Rica, and Japan could scarcely be called an American propaganda machine. In my proposal to the CFR, I suggested that the United States reduce its funding to the United Nations by at least $250 million and use that sum for a number of years as seed money for this new organization.

Over the years, the present United Nations could concentrate more on the things it does best in the technological arena, while it continues to serve as a place of discussions between delegates of various opposing camps. Such a move would mean the end of the era of failed idealism and political disappointment and the beginning of a new era of realism and the struggle of freedom against totalitarian tyranny.

A SOURCE OF DIVISION

George Bush served as the United States ambassador to the United Nations. He knows what an impractical, unwieldy vehicle it is. The present United Nations was created as a post-World War II mechanism and excluded both Japan and Germany from the Security Council. It also is a vehicle that gave the Soviet Union one seat in the General Assembly for each of its fifteen republics, a veto in the Security Council, and key positions in both the personnel and security offices.

More disturbing, in 1991 the bureaucracy of the United Nations still opposes free enterprise capitalism in favor of government planning and socialism, supporting statist regimes everywhere and withholding assistance from nations that seek to move away from central planning. Christopher Whalen, a Washington, D.C., consultant writing in the July 22, 1991 issue of *Barron's*, reports that the United Nations Development Programme (UNDP), headed by a close friend of President Bush, William Draper III, spends $1.5 billion a year "helping authoritarian governments preserve the status quo." A few of the shocking misuses of UNDP money include $10.9 million to prop up Fidel Castro in Cuba, $42 million to the Marxist government of Yemen, $99 million to the socialist government of Tanzania, $93 million to communist Vietnam, and $108 million to communist China. Yet those countries that are bravely attempting to move into free market capitalism are being strangled. Poland's UNDP aid was cut from $7.5 million when it was communist to $3.5 million now that it is free. Hungary received $7.5 million when it was under communist control. Now Hungary, which is rapidly moving toward freedom, will receive a tiny $1.7 million.

One veteran United Nations official, according to the *Barron's* report, said, "The underlying theme [at the United Nations] is that the present economic crisis throughout the Soviet Bloc countries is due to the pursuit of ill-conceived free market solutions."

A new world order under the United Nations as it is presently constituted is guaranteed to be a socialist, not a free-market capitalist, world system. The former United Nations ambassador, former CIA director, former ambassador to China, former Republican party chairman must have a pretty good idea of the socialistic and antidemocratic bias of all but a very few members of that assembly. But is he ignoring such facts, as did Franklin Roosevelt in 1944, in order to follow a utopian dream?

Is George Bush merely an idealist or are there plans now under way to merge the interest of the United States and the Soviet Union in the United Nations—to substitute "world order" power for "balance of power," and install a socialist "world order" in place of a free market system?

IN THE FACE OF REALITY

Rest assured, utopian fantasy does not work in the real world. The old balance-of-power strategy is still better. At least the balance-of-power concept is based on opposing cycles of greed! If you recognize that people in power tend to be venal, then a balance of power that counterpoises strong forces with differing views for mutual security is a real-live world system.

When Prince Metternich proposed the idea of a balance of power, he was acknowledging a basic fact of life, namely, the sinful nature of man. He balanced Europe the way we have balanced our government, with checks and balances and the separation of powers.

As scholar and author Michael Novak has observed, the United States Constitution was made for sinners. It was presumed that man was sinful, and sinful man could not be trusted. So the framers of the Constitution locked them up and made things deliberately cumbersome. That was their method of arranging the government so that government could not hurt the people, and so no one group could gain control to the detriment of others. It was an ingenious plan.

Thomas Jefferson warned of an unrestrained Supreme Court. In a letter to an opponent he said, "In matters of Constitutional interpretation you seem to feel that the Supreme Court is the ultimate arbiter." He called such sentiments "a very dangerous doctrine, indeed, and one that could lead us to the despotism of an oligarchy."

Unfortunately, this is precisely what has happened during the past three decades. We have turned the power of the people over to a nonelected body of eight men and one woman, five of whom can effectively control the moral and social destiny of the nation. And along with the Supreme Court, we have empowered another non-elected oligarchy in the form of the Federal Reserve Board. This was not the system the framers of our Constitution intended for this country.

The system of checks and balances they devised included a powerful judiciary, a powerful legislative branch, and a strong executive branch, all balanced in turn by the powerful rights of free citizens. For better or worse, Prince Metternich expressed essentially the same principles in his proposal that strength be limited by strength. His aim was not to take power away from nations, but to balance opposing powers in order to strengthen the resolve growing out of their national self-interest.

That was the old order, and for a time it worked very well. But the world order was bound to change; the seeds of change had been planted around the world during the age of empire. By the mid-nineteenth century those seeds were already bearing fruit.

SPHERES OF INFLUENCE

In an earlier age, when the Spanish and the Portuguese were vying for territory around the globe, powerful nations controlled their "spheres of influence" in the world. These spheres determined the characteristic cultures in parts of Africa, South America, the Southwestern United States, and many island groups from the Azores to the Philippines.

During the nineteenth century colonialism was still a major factor. The spheres of influence carved out by colonial powers in the Third World (to use the modern term) gave today's characteristic shape to the world, but they also laid the foundations for much of the racial strife that continues to this day.

The old world order gave us the adventurism of the eighteenth and nineteenth centuries and the awakening of the Industrial Age. It gave us the Pax Britannia, along with the colonial empires of the Spanish, Portuguese, Dutch, French, Germans, and British. It was essentially a time of peace based on a Christian code of ethics. However, the instinctive bias of the colonists—that the Third World was inherently inferior to the civilized society of Western Europe—would inevitably lead to the collapse of colonialism and the end of the Age of Empire.

Nevertheless, a fair analysis of the colonial policy of England, for example, must show that it was a relatively enlightened time. In terms of bringing to the colonies education, sanitation, the rule of constitutional law, and some kind of economic order, the colonists were genuinely humanitarian.

Before the beginning of the Pax Britannia, America was already a force in the world. The desire of various European nations to manipulate the destiny of the New World had to be dealt with again and again after the British defeat at Yorktown, Virginia, in 1781. Although the French Revolution was still eight years away, the old order of the world was altered there for all time. The old methods of war, the old ambitions of empire, and the old moral code were irrevocably changed.

When America began to flex its muscles, it quickly became the desire of the Europeans to preserve their own balance of power in Europe by keeping America out of "foreign entanglements." When President James Monroe issued his proclamation, he depended on the promise of British support to help keep the others at bay. In fact, if it hadn't been for the support of the European powers, the Monroe Doctrine would never have worked.

Later, the European economic powers began to see the wealth of North America as a great treasure, and some of them still wanted to get their tentacles into America's economy. They eventually did so not by force but by investing their money here, by sending people, and by buying land. Europe could not defeat the United States by military force, but the European financiers knew that they could control the United States economy if they could saddle us with an American equivalent of the German Bundesbank or the Bank of England. Their efforts failed until

1913, when a German banker, Paul Warburg, succeeded in establishing the Federal Reserve Board, America's privately owned central bank.

The old world order was crumbling bit by bit. Monarchies were going out of style. A wave of democratic reform was sweeping across the map. In America, Canada, Great Britain, Switzerland, and France, democracy was working and the atmosphere of change was pervasive. But there were ominous clouds on the horizon.

The twentieth century had hardly begun when the tensions of this changing world brought about a spontaneous eruption, and the assassination of Archduke Franz Ferdinand of Austria at Sarajevo became the pretext for the First World War. With the war, more terrible than any in the history of mankind, the post-Napoleonic world order of kings, nobles, serfs, and small aristocratically led armies came to an end, and a radically different world order began.

4

The Old Order Crumbles

Two ATTEMPTS TO create a new world order arose out of the turmoil surrounding World War I. One was the League of Nations put forward by President Woodrow Wilson; the other was the Communist International put forward by Nikolai Lenin. On the face of it, these two concepts were light-years apart. In this chapter, however, we will see that both plans actually flowed from the same wellspring.

At the beginning of the second decade of the twentieth century Europe was balanced precariously between the French, the British, the Prussian monarchy in Germany, the Hapsburg Austro-Hungarian Empire, and the Tsarist Empire of Russia. Touching Europe at what later became the nation of Yugoslavia was the Ottoman Empire of the Turks, which remained the dominant power in the Middle East until the end of the First World War.

The point of tension that existed in 1917 was back in the news in 1991, when rival factions in Croatia and Slovenia began warring again. These former provinces of the Hapsburg Empire that bordered on the Serbian portion of the Ottoman Empire were joined together to create the nation of Yugoslavia, but it has never been a happy marriage. In fact it was there that the incident which instigated World War I took place in Sarejevo, Yugoslavia, on June 28, 1914.

After the war, the Prussian Kaiser was gone, the Ottoman Empire was gone, the Hapsburg Empire was gone, and the Tsarist Empire was gone. The result was so profound and the excuse for war so flimsy, that casual observers would have reason to suspect that someone had planned the whole thing.

Before the war, monarchies held sway. After the war, socialism and high finance held sway. Was it planned that way or was it merely an "accident" of history?

What was clearly not an accident of history was the entry of the United States into the war. Woodrow Wilson, a Democrat, was elected president of the United States in 1912, primarily because a split developed between the Republican president, William Howard Taft, and the former Republican president, Theodore Roosevelt, who had since formed the Bull Moose party.

Wilson was a devout Presbyterian born in Staunton, Virginia, just thirty-three miles from my hometown of Lexington. Wilson became the president of Princeton University, a Presbyterian school that claims as one of its past presidents the Reverend John Witherspoon. Witherspoon was a member of the Continental Congress and the man who trained James Madison, the author of the U.S. Constitution, in law and theology.

HIGH-LEVEL MANEUVERS

According to Georgetown University Professor Carroll Quigley in his provocative tome, *Tragedy and Hope: A History of the World in Our Time,* Wilson was chosen by what was then known as the Money Trust to become governor of New Jersey. From that position, his backers successfully ran him for president. This auspicious group of supporters included the Rockefellers, Jacob Schiff, Bernard Baruch, Thomas Fortune Ryan, and Adolf Ochs.

Since some members of the Money Trust supported Teddy Roosevelt, it is apparent that they deliberately split the Republican party in order to guarantee Wilson's victory. Two agents of J. P. Morgan, Frank Munsey and George Perkins, were pouring in money to support Roosevelt, while at the same time giving large sums to Wilson.

Wilson was dignified, beyond reproach, and a dedicated Christian. However, he was completely naive about the intricacies of international finance and the complex workings of the federal government. He would have been the perfect front man for the financiers of his day, especially when paired with a man of their choosing, Colonel Edward Mandell

House, the British-educated son of a Texas financier who represented British financial interests. Scribner's *Concise Dictionary of Biography* says of Colonel House: "No other American of his time was on such close terms with so many men of international fame."

Colonel House handpicked the majority of Wilson's cabinet. But together, Wilson and House quickly paid off their backers when, in 1913, President Wilson helped facilitate the two pillars of the international financial assault on the freedom and integrity of America. The first was the act that created America's privately owned central bank, the Federal Reserve Board; the second was the passage of the federal income tax under the authority of the Internal Revenue Service.

Created by the German banker Paul Warburg, the Morgans, and the Rockefellers, the Federal Reserve Board was custom designed as an instrument of immense power. Colonel House was the key figure in the passage of this legislation, and he was in constant contact with Warburg about it. The companion piece to that play was to change the United States Constitution to force the American citizens to pay for the loans these bankers would make through the Federal Reserve Board to the treasury. The federal income tax would become the most powerful fund-raising mechanism ever devised.

ENTANGLING ALLIANCES

But Colonel House, the "intimate friend of international men of fame," dreamed of much more. He wanted a new world order dominated by American finance—with himself as its head. It was House who talked the president into breaking his campaign pledge to keep the nation out of war and to support a war resolution, which, for the first time in history, broke George Washington's solemn pledge to stay clear of "entangling alliances" in the internecine intrigues of Europe.

Colonel House and his American and European friends undoubtedly hoped for two outcomes from the war. One was the dissolution of the monarchies of the old order—to clear the decks for a new world government. Second, they wanted to be sure that they had a powerful enough seat at the postwar bargaining table to influence the destiny of postwar Europe.

Just prior to the war, House penned a novel entitled *Phillip Dru, Administrator: A Story of Tomorrow.* In this remarkable book, published in 1912, the colonel bared his real soul. Imagine, if you can, the foreign affairs adviser to President Wilson planning a Marxist or socialist economic system as a replacement for monarchy.

Beyond state socialism, House wanted a one-world government, a one-world army, a one-world economy under an Anglo-Saxon financial oligarchy, and a world dictator served by a council of twelve faithful men. The vision of a new world order depicted in this novel included a radically revised United States Constitution and, of course, the United States leading the way, but ultimately submerged into a world government. Clearly, the League of Nations was just one small part of House's grand design.

In a spring 1991 article entitled, "A Much-Deserved Hearing for Wilson's 'New Order,'" *Washington Post* columnist Edwin M. Yoder, Jr., said that it was about time the world gave appropriate credit to President Wilson and Colonel House as the true authors of the new world order. One wonders if Yoder intended to applaud the new world order of *Phillip Dru, Administrator?*

House was a founding member of the Council on Foreign Relations which was conceived in 1919 and established in 1921. This august body of "wise men" has effectively dominated the making of foreign policy by the United States government since before World War II. The CFR has included virtually every key national security and foreign policy adviser of this nation for the past seventy years. Its impressive roster also includes the former congressman, former ambassador to China and the United Nations, former head of the CIA, and now president, George Bush, who was a CFR director between 1977 and 1979.

Is it not proper, therefore, to ask whether or not the new world order envisaged in 1991 by the Council on Foreign Relations and its former members, Bush and Scowcroft, is indeed the same new world order set forth in detail by the founder of the Council of Foreign Relations in 1921?

In my own opinion, it is highly doubtful that George Bush shares any of the notions of Colonel Edward House. But what about the behind-the-scenes leaders within the CFR who have been promoting and engineering the new world order these past seventy years? Dare we say?

THE ILLUMINATI

The end of World War I brought another world vision more terrible than a mere League of Nations. It brought the triumph of the Bolsheviks in Russia and the rapid growth of international communism. But where did Russian communism get its vision of a new world order?

On May 1, 1776 (May Day is still considered to be the key annual holiday for communists), a Bavarian professor named Adam Weishaupt launched a small secret society called the Order of the Illuminati. Weishaupt's aims were to establish a new world order based on the overthrow of civil governments, the church, and private property and the elevation to world leadership of a group of hand-picked "adepts" or "illumined" ones.

Weishaupt chose as his vehicle for infiltration and takeover the established Continental Order of Freemasons, of which Frederick the Great of Prussia had become sovereign grand commander and the wealthy Philippe of France, Duc d'Orleans, had been elevated to grand master of the grand orient, as his lieutenant. In 1782, Weishaupt succeeded at the international convention of Freemasons held in Wilhelmsbad, Germany, with his planned infiltration of the Continental Masonic Order and the creation of what he termed "Illuminated Freemasonry."

His conspiracy was sufficiently successful from that point on to use French Freemasonry as a vehicle for placing members of the French Illuminati into key governmental positions. Once installed, these members set about to undermine the Bourbon dynasty of France and to prepare the way for the French Revolution. It is believed that several of the key leaders of the French Revolution were members of the Illuminati.

The slaughter that followed was not merely an assault on the king and the aristocracy—what was called the ancient regime—it was an assault against everyone, even the leaders of the Reign of Terror that followed on the heels of the revolution. The satanic carnage that the Illuminati brought to France was the clear predecessor of the bloodbaths and successive party purges visited on the Soviet Union by the communists under both Lenin and Stalin.

When the French Revolution had run its course, more than a million Frenchmen were dead; the government, commerce, and agriculture were destroyed; the currency was debased; and the savings of the people were worthless. France was ready for dictatorship, not by the Illuminati, but by Napoleon. Thus ended the first modern new world order. Lenin later said that the French Revolution did not go far enough. Russian communism showed how much farther it could go.

THE LEAGUE OF JUST MEN

Although Illuminism had been banned in Germany and was discredited in France, it surfaced again in the 1800s through secret revolutionary societies holding to the basic tenets of Illuminism. Operating in France and Germany, these societies commissioned the writing of a militant manifesto.

In the preface to the 1872 German edition of the *Communist Manifesto,* the authors said,

The Communist League (formerly called the "League of Just Men") . . . which could only be a secret one . . . commissioned the undersigned [Karl Marx and Fredrich Engels], at the Congress held in London in November 1847, to draw up for publication a detailed theoretical and practical program of the party. Such was the origin of the following Manifesto, the manuscript of which traveled to London to be printed a few weeks before the February revolution.

So wrote Marx and Engels themselves!

In 1885, Cardinal Henry Manning wrote that the Communist International was not the work of Karl Marx but that "of secret political societies, which from 1789 to this day have been perfecting their formation, and . . . have drawn closer together in mutual alliance and cooperation. In 1848 they were sufficiently powerful to threaten almost every capital in Europe by a simultaneous rising."

The precise connecting link between the German Illuminati and the beginning of world communism was furnished by a German radical named Moses Hess. According to Eugene H. Methvin, in his book, *Rise of Radicalism: The Social Psychology of Messianic Extremism*,

[I]n October of 1842 Frederick Engels stopped in Cologne and spent an afternoon with Moses Hess, then 30, who was known as the "communist rabbi" for his missionary zeal in proselyting for *French utopian ideas*.

Hess later wrote a friend: "Engels, an embryonic revolutionary, *parted from me the most enthusiastic communist*." Engels himself credited his conversion to Dr. Hess, and a year later expressly declared that the latter was "the first to make communism plausible to me and my circle."

He goes on to say, "Marx and Engels planned to publish a German edition of Buonarroti's *Conspiration pour l'egalité* [Conspiracy for Equality], translated by Moses Hess. . . . Marx's extensive collection of books on the French Revolution contained a copy of Buonarroti's *Conspiration*."

Further attestation to the link between the communists, the French Revolution, and the Illuminati comes from Saul Padover, in his work, *Karl Marx: An Intimate Biography*, in which he tells of Marx, then aged twenty-three, meeting with the thirty-year-old Moses Hess in Cologne. Hess later wrote, "Dr. Marx is still a very young man, who will give the coup de grace to the medieval religion and politics."

WORK OF THE MASTERS

In his authoritative book on revolutionary movements, *Fire in the Minds of Men*, James Billington says that the organizational plan that Filipo Michele Buonarroti distilled from two generations of revolutionary experience in Geneva was simply lifted from the teachings of the

Bavarian Order of Illuminists. Buonarroti codified the legend of a French Illuminist, François Babeuf, who spoke of "the knights of the order of the equals" and called himself l'HSD (*l'homme sans Dieu*)—by which he meant to imply that he was a man made perfect as a god, without the help of God.

Buonarroti's first revolutionary organization was called the Sublime Perfect Masters. The revolutionary Buonarroti touched the thinking of a group of young Italians who had been influenced by Illuminism while studying in Bavaria. They drew up plans to establish a journal capable of promoting the total transformation of humanity set forth in the Illuminist ideal. The occultic impulses of Illuminism, despite claims to the contrary, were very much alive in European secret societies in the nineteenth century.

The Illuminist streams clearly flowed in Marxist communism in the 1840s. Whether there was a meaningful confluence of these streams in Europe and elsewhere, then and now, remains to be seen.

The atheism, destruction of property, hatred of civil government, ruthless reign of terror, lies and deception, and gross mismanagement of resources of world communism are all mirror images of the French Revolution. Communism draws its spiritual soul from the same impulses that were present in 1789.

In 1988, in a major address to the national convention of the Republican party in New Orleans, I mentioned the atheistic excesses of the French Revolution—a recognized fact of history. Imagine my surprise when the political reporter for *Time* magazine blasted me and called my well-received remarks "a loser" because I had criticized the French Revolution. Apparently those in the United States who want a socialistic new world order are not enthusiastic about hearing criticism of the origins of their concepts.

In 1848, when the *Communist Manifesto* was published, Marx and Engels and their backers looked forward to a new world order that would emerge when the world's urban working classes would lead a revolution against property owners that would one day create a stateless, classless society.

As I have pointed out, the common strain that permeates much of the thinking about a new world order involves four basic premises: (1) the elimination of private property, (2) the elimination of national governments and national sovereignty, (3) the elimination of traditional Judeo-Christian theism, and (4) a world government controlled by an elite made up of those who are considered to be superior, or in the occultic sense, "adepts" or "illuminated."

THE POWER BEHIND THE BOLSHEVIKS

Americans are appropriately shocked when they find that the one-worlders of the early twentieth-century American Money Trust have financed the one-worlders of the Kremlin, not realizing that both groups hold larger goals and aims for the world that apparently complement one another. Until we understand this commonality of interest between left-wing Bolsheviks and right-wing monopolistic capitalists, we cannot fully comprehend the last seventy years of world history nor the ongoing movement toward world government.

British author Nesta Webster researched and wrote extensively on subversive movements. She described a group in Switzerland claiming direct descent from the founder of the Illuminati, Adam Weishaupt. She says,

> [T]he same secret ring of Illuminati is believed to have been intimately connected with the organization of the Bolshevist revolution. . . . None of the leading Bolsheviks are said to have been members of the innermost circle, which is understood to consist of men belonging to the highest intellectual and financial classes, whose names remain absolutely unknown. Outside this absolutely secret ring there existed, however, a semi-secret circle of high initiates of subversive societies drawn from all over the world and belonging to various nationalities.

Authors who expose subversive secret organizations are usually ridiculed because, when asked for proof of the identity of participants in secret societies, they have to answer, "That is impossible, since the names are secret." But, invariably, there is a tiny secret core ring, a larger and slightly less secret middle ring, then a much broader and more public group.

The Illuminati symbol, the dot within the circle, suggests this often-repeated pattern. Nevertheless there is enough evidence and enough unexplained phenomena in the past two hundred years that clearly points to a hidden plan intended to establish the new world order. Looking back, it is possible to discover certain clear links. I believe we can then trust reason and intuition to bridge the gaps.

The Roman pontiff, with his access to worldwide intelligence, made a statement that buttresses this view. Pope Pius XI declared in 1937 that communism has behind it "occult forces which for a long time have been working to overthrow the Christian Social Order." I believe that a statement from a person of such esteem must be given great credence.

The theories of Marx and his backers expressed in 1848 in the

Communist Manifesto, and later in 1867 in *Das Kapital*, began to take root in the oppressive society of Tsarist Russia. Between 1898 and 1903 the doctrine of Russian communism emerged under the leadership of a young radical named Vladimir Ilyich Ulyanov—later known as Lenin.

Between 1903 and 1917 the Communist party was shaped as an instrument of revolution, with the clear goal of overthrowing the established order in Russia and creating an atheistic command economy ruled by what the communists called the "dictatorship of the proletariat." True to Marx, the new order swept away property, the government, and the outward worship of God. The communists taught a ruthless suppression of their enemies, a radical elimination of the old ways, and the nationalization of not only the means of production but ultimately all private property as well.

The communists, in theory at least, expected that with the end of the class struggle, government would gradually wither away. Instead, their view of utopia led to a totalitarianism in which no sphere of human life was outside the grip of the state. This view of a new world order led almost 2 billion people to enslavement under the most hellish nightmare that the world has ever known, and at least 100 million of those have been ruthlessly killed. Lenin and his disciples indeed went "farther than the French Revolution" by a margin of a hundred to one.

What the average man and woman find so difficult to understand, however, is how a Wall Street banker such as Jacob Schiff of Kuhn, Loeb and Company could personally transport $20 million in gold to help salvage the near-bankrupt, fledgling communist government of the new Soviet Russia—or how a man like Lord Milner of the British Round Table could provide funds in 1917 to get them started again—or how United States industrialists and bankers could repeatedly assist them in receiving massive private and governmental aid over the decades that followed.

THE WAIL OF OPPRESSION

The postwar 1920s brought America prosperity, despite three colorless presidents, Prohibition, and the carefree gaiety of the "flappers." Postwar Germany was a seething cauldron of hyperinflation, desperate poverty, and rising radicalism. Russia, now the Soviet Union, largely isolated from the rest of the world, groaned under the suffering imposed by communism.

The Great Depression of the early thirties crippled the economies of the world and led to a massive disruption of finance and industry. The tragedy of the unemployed and the long bread lines were heartrending. The plaintive voice of crooner Bing Crosby singing, "Once I built the railroads, made 'em run on time; now the work is ended; Buddy, can you spare a dime?" must have convinced millions that free enterprise capitalism could not work.

In the days of the Depression, disillusioned intellectuals like the brilliant, Harvard-educated Alger Hiss apparently turned to an idealistic version of the Marxist-Leninist Communist International, and in the process, decided to betray the United States. Hiss and men like Harry Dexter White and Owen Lattimore began pushing United States foreign policy toward a pro-Soviet tilt, while a succession of New Deal domestic programs began the process of moving Washington, D.C., from a sleepy Southern town on the Potomac housing an $11 billion government to the home of the enormous $1.3 trillion colossus whose tentacles now clutch for control of the life and destiny of every man, woman, and child in the land.

In 1932, an Austrian-born madman determined that he indeed had been chosen by spiritual powers as the anointed savior, not only of Germany but of the world. Adolf Hitler, a man trained in the occult and surrounded by occultists ("demonized" in the words of William L. Shirer, author of the epic *Rise and Fall of the Third Reich*), felt a powerful calling to bring about "a new order" for the world—a thousand-year empire of supremacy that he termed the "Third Reich"—the third kingdom.

It is simply inconceivable to realize that in only thirteen years this poorly educated nobody took control of one of the great nations of the earth, armed it to the teeth, bluffed England and France into letting him dismantle two neighboring democracies, and began a systematic genocide against God's chosen people, the Jews. He subjugated almost all of Continental Europe, while launching a world war of ferocity and barbarity never known in the history of mankind.

After thirteen years of Hitler's madness, Germany was reduced to a heap of rubble, and the world was reminded once again to beware the siren song of utopian dreamers.

THE GREAT COMPROMISE

What remained of the old world order after World War I was indeed demolished after World War II. At Yalta, an ailing President Franklin Roosevelt, with the spy Alger Hiss at his side, surrendered control of the sovereign nations of Lithuania, Latvia, and Estonia to the Soviets. And with these tiny Baltic states came East Germany, Poland, Czechoslovakia, Hungary, Bulgaria, Rumania, Albania, and Manchuria.

But that was not all. Communists threatened the governments of Italy and France. Greece was barely spared a communist takeover. The Labour party socialized major industry in Great Britain. Sweden elected a socialist government. And burdensome government taxes were levied on the rest of Europe to support massive welfare programs.

After Roosevelt's death, his successor, Harry S. Truman, barraged by leftist stories about "the corruption of the nationalist government of China," turned his back on Chiang Kai-shek, our staunch friend and World War II ally. America then allowed the Chinese communists under Mao Tse Tung to subjugate, communize, and brutally purge the Chinese people.

The world order after World War II was different from any other, because for the first time in the history of mankind, two great nations had developed weapons capable of destroying all life on the planet.

Since 1945, the American people were told that this nation and the Soviet Union were engaged in a Cold War. The official policy of the government was the "containment of communism," enunciated by what came to be known as the Truman Doctrine. In Fulton, Missouri, the great world strategist Winston Churchill uttered the famous line, "From Stetin in the Baltic to Trieste in the Adriatic, an iron curtain has fallen across Europe."

We were told that behind the Iron Curtain—and later the Bamboo Curtain—lived the enemy. The Cold War required constant massive expenditures for arms, maintaining large numbers of United States ground forces in Europe and Asia, and stockpiling an ever-growing arsenal of thermonuclear weapons.

The post-World War II world order was characterized by the global nuclear standoff between the two superpowers, the United States and the Soviet Union. Each side developed increasingly powerful bombs whose destructiveness was measured in million of tons (megatons). Our leaders talked of the "throw weight" of missiles, then missiles that could carry up to ten nuclear warheads to separate targets, the so-called MIRV missiles.

Along the way we developed extraordinary accuracy in submarine-launched nuclear devices. We improved on that with a D-2 missile. We developed and deployed the most accurate intermediate-range (twelve hundred miles) missile in the world, the Pershing II. Missiles were placed in silos, on trucks, and on railroad cars. Our latest generation of "smart" bombs, cruise missiles, stealth aircraft, night vision equipment, and satellite surveillance is nothing short of awesome—and, I must add, awesomely expensive.

After we had spent the money developing these weapons, our leaders then negotiated with the Soviets to limit or destroy them. The buzzword that characterized the Strategic Arms Limitation Treaties (SALT I and SALT II) was "strategic parity." In other words, the United States that came out of World War II as the undisputed military and industrial power of the world had agreed to permit the Soviet Union, which came out of World War II as a ravaged, backward, Third World power, to build a nuclear arsenal that would be essentially equal to our own.

BUILD AND DESTROY

After months of debate in the early 1970s, Richard Nixon signed the so-called Anti-Ballistic Missile (ABM) Treaty in 1972, which limited the right of the United States to defend itself against nuclear attack. The operative buzzword here was an acronym, MAD, or Mutual Assured Destruction. In other words, neither the Soviets nor the United States were permitted to defend their civilian populations against the nuclear attack of the other.

The theory was that if the civilian populations of both parties were vulnerable, neither nation would launch an attack on the other. That was a nice theory, except we learned that not only did the Soviets prepare massive installations to protect against nuclear war, they also cheated on the ABM treaty by building the famed Krasnoyarsk phased-radar array.

In 1987, Ronald Reagan signed the Intermediate Nuclear Forces (INF) Treaty, which required that the United States destroy its deadly accurate Pershing II missiles and that the Soviet Union destroy its SS-20, SS-4, and SS-5 missiles. On the face of it, this treaty seemed equitable, but underneath, it was another trap for the United States.

Under the INF Treaty, the United States removed forever the nuclear shield protecting Europe from potential aggression by Soviet conventional forces and, in the process, the only meaningful U.S. linkage to European security. The Soviets, on the other hand, removed the obsolete SS-20 missile launchers but were permitted by the treaty to keep their SS-20 nuclear warheads—the bombs—which they have since been installing in their own territory on ultramodern SS-25 hidden, rail-mounted launchers.

The events surrounding the INF treaty are particularly poignant to me, because during the presidential debates I personally challenged then Vice President Bush on a key provision of the treaty which he was vigorously advocating. I discovered, to my shock, that he was completely ignorant of the fact that this treaty permitted the Soviets to keep their SS-20 nuclear warheads.

I also asserted that the treaty should include on-site verification of the presence of intermediate nuclear missiles in Cuba. At the mere suggestion of missiles in Cuba, I was castigated by Fidel Castro and the liberal press in this country for making what they considered an outrageous suggestion. I was interested to read, three years later, a column by Robert Evans and Michael Novak carried in the *Washington Post* which stated that SS-20 missiles were sighted in Cuba in the spring of 1991—missiles, I might add, that are entirely capable of hitting Washington, D.C.

By the summer of 1991, our president had signed a treaty that promised to destroy even more of our nuclear arsenal. Instead of SALT, or strategic arms *limitation*, the new acronym is START for Strategic Arms *Reduction* Treaty. Time will tell what American strategic advantages will be destroyed by a treaty whose verification procedures are perceived by experts to be seriously flawed. I suspect, as has happened all too often before, the United States will carefully abide by the spirit and letter of the START Treaty, and the Soviets will be free to break both the spirit and letter when it serves their interests to do so.

UNWINNABLE WARS

During the unfolding of the post-World War II world order, our leaders sent United States ground forces into battle to fight Soviet and Chinese communist surrogates in Korea in 1950 and in Vietnam in 1965. For the first time in the history of the United States, our armed forces were not allowed to win a war.

I served with the First Marine Division in Korea under the overall command of General Douglas MacArthur, and later General Matthew Ridgeway. Korea is a small peninsula, joined to China at its extreme northern border on the Yalu River. There is absolutely no question that if General MacArthur had been permitted to bomb Chinese troops and supplies north of the Yalu River, our armed forces in Korea could easily have sealed off the Korean Peninsula and then systematically, by air and ground action, destroyed the North Korean army.

But MacArthur, who insisted on the only intelligent military option, was instead fired by President Truman. His offense was that of failing to acknowledge civilian authority. In truth he was fired for the unpardonable sin of wanting to win the war.

At the time, I felt that the end of the Korean War, which followed so closely World War II, could be explained in part by war weariness. To me this was a mistake that would not be repeated. After Korea, it was clear that the United States should never allow itself to be drawn into another land war in Asia. Yet when the Vietnam War broke out, I could not believe that was happening! It was Korea all over again, only many times worse.

Civilian authorities were actually prohibiting our troops from winning. They conceived incredible rules of engagement, which meant that we could jeopardize *our* troops, *our* aircraft, and *our* ally, South Vietnam, but we gave privileged sanctuary to the North Vietnamese nation and communist troops in Cambodia. I strongly believe that had the United

States mined Haiphong Harbor, bombed Hanoi extensively, cut the North Vietnamese dikes, and then launched an amphibious operation against North Vietnam itself, that country would have collapsed and the Vietcong would have been without support in no time at all.

MacArthur had warned, "In war, there is no substitute for victory." Instead of victory, in Vietnam we played at war, and we bled our young men and women to death. We bled our treasury. And worst of all, we bled our national resolve. In Vietnam, the United States was forced by its leaders to suffer the first military loss in its history.

Above all else, we showed the world daily in the world press that the foreign policy establishment of the United States and its allies would not permit this nation ever to "defeat" communism. We could struggle against communism; we could arm against communism; but we could not win against communism.

Their plan for this country was not victory over communism but ultimate union with the Soviet Union in a one-world government. Roman Gaither, former head of the Ford Foundation, was quoted as saying that the resources of his foundation were to be used to "comfortably merge the United States with the Soviet Union."

IMPENETRABLE LOGIC

During the postwar years the obvious plan was to drain the resources of the United States in preparation for a war that was never to be. This accomplished, the time would be ripe for—in the words of Bruce Russett (the Dean Acheson Professor of International Relations and Political Science at Yale) and James Sutterlin (former director of the executive office of the United Nations secretary-general), writing in the Spring 1991 issue of Foreign Affairs, the official organ of the Council on Foreign Relations—"a new world order envisioned by Presidents Bush and Gorbachev."

Military preparation for the Cold War during the last forty-five years kept our economy approaching $4 trillion in direct debt at the end of the fiscal year. This same economy is sufficiently weakened to accept joyfully the promised end of the Cold War. Now that our former communist "enemy" has been converted to *perestroika* and *glasnost*, we are being prepared for the beginning of a new world order under the aegis of the United Nations. This is the "Bush-Grobachev world order" into which America and the Soviet Union are being "comfortably merged."

During the Cold War and *détente*, we were told that the Soviet Union was an economic powerhouse between one-quarter and one-half the size of the United States. The ruble was convertible into dollars at the rate of

$1.60 per ruble. We were told that the Soviet Army was formidable, Soviet weapons virtually invincible, and that the threat of those colossus justified a $300 billion defense budget, on the one hand, and military parity and shared global leadership on the other.

Then in 1989, just as the United States of Europe prepared for its 1992 debut, as if some silent director gave the signal, all of our preconceptions were dashed. Suddenly we learned that the awesome Soviet colossus is, in reality, a broken-down Third World economy.

Six million Soviets are homeless and another 13 million live in communal apartments of two or more families and must share a bathroom and kitchen. Less than a third of Soviet households have telephones; only half have refrigerators. The number of blacks in South Africa who own automobiles is greater than the total of all the automobiles in the Soviet Union. There are chronic food shortages. Health care and sanitation are appalling. The rate of alcoholism is eleven times that of the West. And the people are totally dispirited.

From $1.60 a few years ago, the ruble is now worth less than five cents. The gross national product of the Soviet Union has been shriveling for decades, and the country is in absolute economic, political, humanitarian, and moral chaos.

So where were the CIA, the State Department, and all those government agencies charged with keeping tabs on the economic and military status of other nations while all this was happening? Why weren't we receiving year-by-year assessments of the Soviet decline? The first such official report I ever saw was in 1989. If there has been such a dramatic Soviet decline, it did not happen overnight.

One of two things is certain: Either the CIA and the foreign policy establishment deliberately misled the American people about the strength of the Soviet Union so that the United States would continue its Cold War levels of wasteful spending, or the communists (like the Gideonites of biblical times) have deliberately sabotaged the consumer economy for the purpose of lulling the West into letting down its military, intellectual, and spiritual guard so that aid would flow, treaties would be signed, and (more particularly) alliances would form. In light of the abortive "coup" of 1991, the latter alternative seems much more likely.

THE LESSONS OF HISTORY

Consider these news headlines from the *New York Times:* AMERICANS TRADE WITH RUSSIA DESPITE BANS, SOVIET OIL OFFER TO AMERICAN FIRM, AMERICANS TO WORK RUSSIAN OIL TRACT, SOVIET GRANT TO BRITISH-PRELIMINARY AGREEMENT FOR

DEVELOPMENT OF OIL FIELDS IS REACHED. These are legitimate headlines, not from the 1990s but from the 1920s!

One in particular stands out above all the rest. On May 31, 1921, the *New York Times* reported, SOVIETS BANKRUPT, LENIN ADMITS, with the subtitle, MOSCOW DISPATCH QUOTES HIM SAYING THAT CAPITALISM MUST BE UNFETTERED. The process of candor and capitalism was called, of all things, *glasnost*. Does any of this sound familiar?

In 1937, the butcher Joseph Stalin stopped his bloodthirsty purges long enough to begin a program of liberalization of the communist apparatus in the Soviet Union. To those today who feel the term is unique to Mikhail Gorbachev, Stalin called his new program *perestroika*. Can any thinking person honestly believe that the Soviets under Lenin changed their course because Lenin started *glasnost?* And in the light of history, can anyone believe that the Soviet menace was any less intense under Stalin because of *perestroika?* But we may yet see the unfolding of a more repressive regime within the Soviet Union. When that happens, the dreamer's who believed the communist reformers' cries of "Peace, peace!" will have to find some new explanations for their gullibility.

The apparent dismantling of communism in Poland, East Germany, Hungary, Rumania, Bulgaria, Albania, and Czechoslovakia seems genuine enough. Changes there have been monumental, and the failure of the August 1991 "coup" in the Soviet Union has put their hopes for reform into high gear. But lest we become too giddy, let us remember that Gorbachev, the architect of "reform," is the protégé of Yuri Andropov, former head of the KGB and the man who is believed to be responsible for masterminding the assassination attempt against Pope John Paul II.

Despite the rhetoric of *glasnost* and *perestroika*, we should also remember that Gorbachev handpicked all eight of the August 1991 "coup" plotters. He named the hardened KGB operative, Boris Pugo, as minister of the interior, and Gennady Gromov as his deputy. Their front man, Gennady Yanayev, was Gorbachev's own second in command. He placed Vladimir Kryuchkov in charge of the KGB. Wasn't it a bit much to believe that those hard-liners would suddenly become champions of democracy and capitalism, or that their police organization, the KGB, would support a system to take away their own power?

Forbes magazine published an interview with Gorbachev's principal economic adviser, Leonid Abalkin, in its October 19, 1987 issue. Abalkin candidly admitted, as did Lenin before him, "The Soviet economy is in a grave state." However, after discussing *perestroika* and *glasnost*, he made one very telling admission: "We must always bear in mind that we are dealing with two completely different systems. We are a *socialist* country with a *planned economy*. Our *perestroika* will not change this."

Indeed only idealistic dreamers believe it will!

Despite recent events in the Soviet Union, I fervently hope that the move toward democracy in the Eastern Bloc is real. I recognize that within this arena in the present time there exists the greatest opportunity for Christian evangelism that has ever existed since the birth of Jesus Christ. However, our associates who are responsible for placing our animated Bible cartoon series and other programs on Soviet television have been told to work quickly. They may have only months before this window of opportunity is closed by the possibility of new policy changes and restrictions inside the Soviet Union.

THE MASTER PLAN

There are some who say that the events since 1989 in Eastern Europe and the Soviet Union were all carefully orchestrated by the KGB. In his gripping book, *New Lies for Old,* published in 1984, Anatoliy Golitsyn, a high-level KGB defector, laid out in meticulous detail—five years in advance of the liberalization movement in Eastern Europe—the precise blueprint for what has occurred over the past two years. Golitsyn's book is taken from knowledge of Soviet intentions gained much earlier.

The American CIA division chief who believed Golitsyn's story was dismissed. Now his words serve as a warning of impending deception. Because what he says is so significant, I would like to quote generously without comment from his chapter entitled, "The Final Phase." Please note again, Golitsyn reported these things to the CIA in the 1970s and published them in 1984, well before any of us had heard of *glasnost* and *perestroika*. He writes:

> [T]he communist strategists are now poised to enter into the final, offensive phase of the long-range policy, entailing a joint struggle for the complete triumph of communism. Given the multiplicity of parties in power, the close links between them, and the opportunities they have had to broaden their bases and build up experienced cadres, the communist strategists are equipped, in pursuing their policy, to engage in maneuvers and stratagems beyond the imagination of Marx or the practical reach of Lenin and unthinkable to Stalin. Among such previously unthinkable stratagems are the introduction of false liberalization in Eastern Europe and, probably, in the Soviet Union and the exhibition of spurious independence on the part of the regimes in Romania, Czechoslovakia, and Poland. . . .
>
> Because the West has failed either to understand communist strategy and disinformation or to appreciate the commitment to it of the resources of the bloc security and intelligence services and their high-level agents of political influence, the appearance of Solidarity in Poland has been accepted as a spontaneous occurrence comparable with the Hungarian revolt of 1956 and as portending the demise of communism in Poland. The fact that the Italian,

French, and Spanish Communist parties all took up pro-Solidarity positions gives grounds for suspecting the validity of this interpretation.

Western misreading of events led to predictions of Soviet intervention in Poland in 1981, which turned out to be unjustified. It may lead to more serious errors in the future.

There are strong indications that the Polish version of "democratization," based in part on the Czechoslovak model, was prepared and controlled from the outset within the framework of bloc policy and strategy. . . .

As with the "Prague spring" of 1968, the motives for the Polish "renewal" were a combination of the internal and external. Internally it was designed to broaden the political base of the communist party in the trade unions and to convert the narrow, elitist dictatorship of the party into a Leninist dictatorship of the whole working class that would revitalize the Polish political and economic system. The "renewal" followed the lines of Lenin's speech to the Comintern congress in July 1921. "Our only strategy at present," said Lenin, "is to become stronger and therefore wiser, more reasonable, more opportunistic. The more opportunistic, the sooner will you assemble again the masses around you. When we have won over the masses by our reasonable approach, we shall then apply offensive tactics in the strictest sense of the word."

A coalition government in Poland would in fact be totalitarianism under a new, deceptive, and more dangerous guise. Accepted as the spontaneous emergence of a new form of multiparty, semidemocratic regime, it would serve to undermine resistance to communism inside and outside the communist bloc. The need for massive defense expenditure would increasingly be questioned in the West. New possibilities would arise for splitting Western Europe away from the United States, of neutralizing Germany, and destroying NATO. With North American influence in Latin America also undermined, the stage would be set for achieving actual revolutionary changes in the Western world through spurious changes in the communist system. . . .

Externally, the role of dissidents will be to persuade the West that the "liberalization" is spontaneous and not controlled. "Liberalization" will create conditions for establishing solidarity between trade unions and intellectuals in the communist and noncommunist worlds. In time such alliances will generate new forms of pressure against Western "militarism," "racism," and "military-industrial complexes" and in favor of disarmament and the kind of structural changes in the West predicted in [Andrei] Sakharov's writings.

If "liberalization" is successful and accepted by the West as genuine, it may well be followed by the apparent withdrawal of one or more communist countries from the Warsaw Pact to serve as the model of a "neutral" socialist state for the whole of Europe to follow. Some "dissidents" are already speaking in these terms. . . .

The Iraqi attack on Iran looks like a concerted effort by radical Arab states, each of which is in a united front relationship with the Soviet Union against "imperialism," to use dual tactics (hostilities by Iraq, assistance by Syria and Libya) with the single overall objective of bringing Iran into an anti-Western alliance with them. The object of the alliance would be to gain control over a strategically vital area of the Middle East. Its success could but serve the strategic interests of the communist bloc. Despite Saddam Hussein's alleged purges of communists in Iraq and the moderation in his attitude toward the United States, he is continuing to receive arms supplies from communist sources, as are his Iranian opponents.

The overall aim will be to bring about a major and irreversible shift in the balance of world power in favor of the bloc as a preliminary to the final ideological objective of establishing a worldwide federation of communist states.

The suggested European option would be promoted by a revival of controlled "democratization" on the Czechoslovak pattern in Eastern Europe, including probably Czechoslovakia and the Soviet Union. The intensification of hard-line policies and methods in the Soviet Union, exemplified by Sakharov's arrest and the occupation of Afghanistan, presages a switch to "democratization" following, perhaps, [Leonid] Brezhnev's departure from the political scene.

The following observations were made prior to Brezhnev's death. They are followed by comments on developments subsequent to that event.

Brezhnev's successor may well appear to be a kind of Soviet Dubcek. The succession will be important only in a presentational sense. The reality of collective leadership and the leaders' common commitment to the long-range policy will continue unaffected. Conceivably an announcement will be made to the effect that the economic and political foundations of communism in the Soviet Union have been laid and that democratization is therefore possible. This would provide the framework for the introduction of a new set of "reforms."

In the economic field reforms might be expected to bring Soviet practice more into line with Yugoslav, or even, seemingly, with Western socialist models. Some economic ministries might be dissolved; control would be more decentralized; individual self-managing firms might be created from existing plants and factories; material incentives would be increased; the independent role of technocrats, workers' councils, and trade unions would be enhanced; the party's control over the economy would be apparently diminished. Such reforms would be based on Soviet experience in the 1920s and 1960s, as well as on Yugoslav experience. The party would be less conspicuous, but would continue to control the economy from behind the scenes as before. The picture being deliberately painted now of stagnation and deficiencies in the Soviet economy should be seen as part of the preparation for deceptive innovations; it is intended to give the innovations greater impact on the West when they are introduced.

Political "liberalization" and "democratization" would follow the general lines of the Czechoslovak rehearsal in 1968. This rehearsal might well have been the kind of political experiment Mironov had in mind as early as 1960. The "liberalization" would be spectacular and impressive. Formal pronouncements might be made about a reduction in the communist party's role; its monopoly would be apparently curtailed. An ostensible separation of powers between the legislative, the executive, and the judiciary might be introduced. The Supreme Soviet would be given greater apparent power and the president and deputies greater apparent independence. The posts of president of the Soviet Union and first secretary of the party might well be separated. The KGB would be "reformed." Dissidents at home would be amnestied; those in exile abroad would be allowed to return, and some would take up positions of leadership in government. Sakharov might be included in some capacity in the government or allowed to teach abroad. The creative arts and cultural and scientific organizations, such as the writers' unions and Academy of Sciences, would become apparently more independent, as would the trade unions. Political clubs would be opened to nonmembers of the communist party. Leading dissidents might form one or more alternative political parties. Censorship would be relaxed; controversial books, plays, films, and art would be published, performed, and exhibited. Many prominent Soviet performing artists now abroad would return to the Soviet Union and resume their professional careers. Constitutional amendments would be adopted to guarantee fulfillment of the provisions of the Helsinki agreements and a semblance of compliance would be maintained. There would be greater freedom for Soviet citizens to travel. Western and United Nations observers would be invited to the Soviet Union to witness the reforms in action.

But, as in the Czechoslovak case, the "liberalization" would be calculated and deceptive in that it would be introduced from above.

Dissolution of the Warsaw Pact would have little effect on the coordination of the communist bloc, but the dissolution of NATO could well mean the departure of American forces from the European continent and a closer European alignment with a "liberalized" Soviet bloc. Perhaps in the longer run, a similar process might affect the relationship between the United States and Japan leading to abrogation of the security pact between them.

"Liberalization" in Eastern Europe on the scale suggested could have a social and political impact on the United States itself, especially if it coincided with a severe economic depression. The communist strategists are on the lookout for such an opportunity. Soviet and other communist economists keep a careful watch on the American economic situation. Since the adoption of the long-range policy, an Institute of World Economy and International Relations, originally under Arzumanyan and now under Inozemtsev, has been analyzing and forecasting for the Central Committee the performance of the noncommunist, and especially the American, economic system. Inozemtsev is a frequent visitor to the United States and was a member of a Soviet delegation received by the U.S. Congress in January 1978. The communist bloc will not repeat its error in failing to exploit a slump as it did in 1929–32. At that time the Soviet Union was weak politically and economically; next time the situation would be different. Politically the bloc would be better poised to exploit economic depression as proof of the failure of the capitalist system.

Information from communist sources that the bloc is short of oil and grain should be treated with particular reserve, since it could well be intended to conceal preparation for the final phase of the policy and to induce the West to underestimate the potency of the bloc's economic weapons.

A Soviet-socialist European coalition, acting in concert with the nonaligned movement in the United Nations, would create favorable conditions for communist strategy on disarmament. The American military-industrial complex would come under heavy fire. "Liberalization" in the Soviet Union and Eastern Europe would provide additional stimulus to disarmament. A massive U.S. defense budget might be found no longer justified. The argument for accommodation would be strengthened. Even China might throw in its weight in favor of a Soviet-socialist line on arms control and disarmament.

These predictions and analyses were made during Brezhnev's tenure in office in anticipation of his departure. Brezhnev's succession and other developments confirm, in essence, the validity of the author's views. For example, the expeditiousness of the appointment of Andropov as Brezhnev's successor confirmed one of the main theses of this book; namely, that the succession problem in the Soviet leadership has been resolved. The practical consideration of the long-term strategies has become the major stabilizing factor in this solution. The promotion of the former KGB chief, who was responsible for the preparation of the false liberalization strategy in the USSR, indicates that this factor was decisive in his selection and further points to the imminent advent of such "liberalization" in the near future.

It is more than likely that these cosmetic steps will be taken as genuine by the West and will trigger a reunification and neutralization of West Germany and further the collapse of NATO. The pressure on the United States for concessions on disarmament and accommodation with the Soviets will increase. During this period there might be an extensive display of the fictional struggle for power in the Soviet leadership. One cannot exclude that at the next party congress or earlier, Andropov will be replaced by a younger leader with a more liberal image who will continue the so-called "liberalization" more intensively.

THE SHOCKING TRUTH

Are these the ravings of a madman? Is his narrative of detailed, dated political events wild-eyed and radical, or is it calm and precise?

Please note that Golitsyn accurately predicted, detail by detail, the very events that made news in the communist world in 1989, 1990, and 1991. Yet the establishment power block in this country chose to suppress his words so that the American people could not be warned by them. The Soviet Union has 4 million men in arms. It has been feverishly building modern submarines and ultramodern missiles. Despite the squalor and desperation in Russia, the Soviet government is still spending as much as 25 percent of its entire national output on arms. Somewhere a voice must be raised in warning!

There is one last interesting footnote to what the *Foreign Affairs* journal is now calling the "new world order as conceived by Presidents Bush and Gorbachev." Mikhail Gorbachev was Communist party first secretary in a province known as Stavropol. The party first secretary of the adjoining province of Georgia was Eduard Shevardnadze. Andropov brought Gorbachev to Moscow as minister of agriculture. Gorbachev brought Shevardnadze to Moscow in July of 1985 as minister of the interior, a police function, and then made him minister of foreign affairs.

In his native Georgia, Shevardnadze was minister of internal affairs and a major general in the secret police, reportedly involved in suppression and torture. Shevardnadze has now become a close friend of Secretary of State James Baker and, according to a report given to me personally by an eminent evangelical leader, a born-again Christian. So suddenly Shevardnadze becomes a great champion of democracy and blasts his old friend and mentor Gorbachev publicly for the "specter of dictatorship" arising in the Soviet Union. Such a statement has to be trumped-up nonsense! The Soviet people have known nothing but ruthless dictatorship since 1917. How could a major general in the secret police be surprised by dictatorship? He was a key part of it!

But today the move is on in the establishment press in key places to break tradition and place Eduard Shevardnadze in the post of secretary-general of the United Nations. Just imagine the implications of this *new world order* under the aegis of a fully armed United Nations whose leader is none other than a former major general of the Soviet secret police. The scenario is too much like a chess game! Each move seems logical. Each move seems plausible. Each move has immense consequences and wide-ranging public support because those in charge of foreign policy are also in charge of key segments of the world's press.

What's worse, the American people are buying the concept. An August 1991 *Newsweek* poll shows that over half of the American public, largely in response to the role of the United Nations/United States joint effort in the Persian Gulf, supports the renewed empowerment of the United Nations and the submission of U.S. national interests to a world governing body.

THE DEVIL'S ADVOCATE

The old adage is that when things seem too good to be true they usually are. Just think of the good news as seen through the eyes of the average citizen. America has had a fabulous, almost unbelievable victory in the Gulf. The defeatism of what is called the Vietnam Syndrome has been purged from our consciousness by a national festival of patriotic parades and welcome-home celebrations for the troops.

America is now the undisputed leader of the Free World. Our economy has faltered a bit, but our military might is unrivaled. Our industry, which has been mauled by the Japanese, has modernized, reorganized, and is ready to compete with the best in the world.

More than anything, the long Cold War seemed over, and the terrible threat of nuclear annihilation has receded from our national imagination. We seem to be entering an era of peace—the Pax Americana—during which our massive spending on the military establishment could be reduced.

We are living in a time of an unbelievable acceptance of spiritual values in the Soviet Union, Eastern Europe, Latin America, Africa, and Asia. In 1990 alone, the organization I head, the Christian Broadcasting Network, sponsored a gospel media blitz in Nicaragua, El Salvador, Guatemala, and Argentina that resulted in 6 million decisions for Christ. In the Soviet Union our offices have received over 2 million handwritten letters from across the nation. We are planning a television blitz this year, similar to that in Central and South America, which we believe will result in 20 million people receiving Jesus Christ as their Savior in the Soviet Union. A similar effort in Zaire in 1991 is expected to bring comparable results.

With good news like this to bolster our nation, it would be most unwise to embark on a program to surrender the sovereignty of the United States to any world body, and particularly one that is as poorly constituted and inept as the present United Nations.

I know George Bush. I have met with him in the White House, and I personally believe that President Bush is an honorable man and a man of integrity. Nevertheless, I believe that he has become convinced, as Woodrow Wilson was before him, of the idealistic possibilities of a world at peace under the benign leadership of a forum for all nations.

But I am equally convinced that for the past two hundred years the term *new world order* has been the code phrase of those who desired to destroy the Christian faith and what Pope Pius XI termed the "Christian social order." They wish to replace it with an occult-inspired world socialist dictatorship.

The task of good men now will be to fight with all their strength to preserve the gains in liberty and freedom that have recently come to the people of the world, while resisting with equal strength all attempts—however idealistic and well-meaning—to subvert the sovereignty of this great nation and place it into a one-world socialistic order.

To begin this struggle, we must learn more about the idealists, the dreamers, the manipulators, and the money men who through the decades have grasped for such control of the world.

And, more than that, we must learn a better way.

Part II

THREATS TO FREEDOM

5

The Establishment

T HE DISTINGUISHED PRIME minister of England, Benjamin Disraeli, once wrote, "The world is governed by very different personages than what is imagined by those who are not behind the scenes."

Woodrow Wilson, whose principal adviser was a behind-the-scenes operator, said, "There is a power somewhere so organized, so subtle, so watchful, so interlocked, so complete, so pervasive that they better not speak above their breath when they speak in condemnation of it."

Historians normally recount the deeds and exploits of kings, presidents, prime ministers, secretaries, and cabinet ministers. In truth, the real power to choose presidents and prime ministers is not in public view—it is behind the scenes. Such men generally prefer to operate in great secrecy, although some have a certain public face. Invariably, however, they control such enormous wealth that their collective voices can cause rulers to tremble and governments—along with their national economics—to fall.

If indeed there is in the United States a powerful group attempting to control our world, who is it and how did it get its start?

Rest assured, there is a behind-the-scenes Establishment in this nation, as in every other. It has enormous power. It has controlled the economic and foreign policy objectives of the United States for the past seventy years, whether the man sitting in the White House is a Democrat or a Republican, a liberal or a conservative, a moderate or an extremist. This power is above elections, but it has been able to control the results of elections. Beyond the control of wealth, its principal goal is the establishment of a one-world government where the control of money is in the hands of one or more privately owned but government-chartered central banks.

The visible home of the Establishment is Pratt House, on the corner of Park Avenue and Sixty-Eighth Street in New York City, right across the street from the Soviet embassy to the United Nations. This is the headquarters of the Council on Foreign Relations, and from here the Establishment reaches out to the many power centers. Here are just a few: the U.S. State Department, the U.S. Treasury Department, the Federal Reserve Board, the Export-Import Bank, the Rockefeller Foundation, the Rockefeller family, the Rockefeller Brothers Fund, the Ford Foundation, the Carnegie Foundation, the Chase Manhattan Bank, First National City Bank, J. P. Morgan and Company, Harvard University, Columbia University, Yale University, the University of Chicago, the *Washington Post*, the *New York Times*, the *Los Angeles Times*, and scores of international corporations, investment banking houses, private foundations, and media outlets in this country, in England, and on the continent of Europe.

MAKING FOREIGN POLICY

In government policy, the most visible expression of the Establishment is the Council on Foreign Relations and its publication, *Foreign Affairs*. Out of some twenty-nine hundred members, at least five hundred are very powerful, another five hundred are from centers of influence, and the rest are influential in academia, the media, business and finance, the military, or government. A few are token conservatives.

According to a man who had been a member for fifteen years, Rear Admiral Chester Ward, former judge advocate general of the navy from 1956 to 1960,

[T]his purpose of promoting disarmament and submergence of U.S. sovereignty and national independence into an all-powerful one-world government is the only objective revealed to about 95 percent of 1,551 members [in 1975]. There are two other ulterior purposes that CFR influence is being used to promote; but it is improbable that they are known to more than 75 members, or that these purposes ever have even been identified in writing.

The goals of the Establishment are somewhat strange, and we will discuss them in detail. At the central core is a belief in the superiority of their own skill to form a world system in which enlightened monopolistic capitalism can bring all of the diverse currencies, banking systems, credit, manufacturing, and raw materials into one government-supervised whole, policed of course by their own world army.

To accomplish what they perceive as this enlightened goal, they have set out in dozens of ways to weaken the national sovereignty of the United States so that it will be too weak to withstand the coercive pressure of a world government. At the same time, they have perceived that radical Marxism is an important intermediate step toward their goal of a managed world economy, so they have used their influence to promote the communist takeover of Russia, China, Eastern Europe, and parts of Central America and Africa. Some members are genuinely idealistic and feel this is the only way to world peace. Others are simply greedy and power hungry. And some, I fear, are motivated by other powers.

There have been communists or Soviet centers of influence such as Alger Hiss, Owen Lattimore, and Corliss Lamont among them, but on the whole these people are not communists. They are well-bred, highly refined, quite wealthy world leaders. Somewhere along the way they fell victim to the philosophic fallacy that the end justifies the means. And for many of them, the means (communist revolution and world government) became the end itself.

Some political leaders—including Jimmy Carter, Woodrow Wilson, and hopefully George Bush—have spouted the slogans of the Establishment theoreticians without fully understanding what they were saying and doing. Others have used positions of power in the government of the United States for programs that are nothing short of treason.

SPECIAL PRIVILEGE

Keep in mind, when speaking of the CFR, the *Washington Post*, the *New York Times*, or Harvard University, that these are not left-wing, pinko organizations. They are instead Establishment organizations that desire a one-world government. Many among them feel that supporting world socialism in one of its forms will facilitate their own long-range goals.

The views of these people toward world government are frankly so impractical and bizarre as to earn them a place of shame. Instead, they run huge banks, multinational corporations, the nation's financial system, the State Department, the Treasury Department, and the better part of the entire world.

The power of the Establishment is beyond question. Since 1940 every United States secretary of state except one (former Governor James Byrnes of South Carolina) has been a CFR member. And since 1940, all secretaries of war/defense, from Henry L. Stimson through Richard Cheney, have been CFR members. Here is the list:

SECRETARY OF STATE	SECRETARY OF WAR/DEFENSE
Robert Lansing†	Newton N. Baker†
Charles Evans Hughes	Dwight F. Davis
Frank B. Kellogg	Henry L. Stimson
Henry L. Stimson	Robert Patterson
Cordell Hull	James Forrestal
Edward R. Stettinius	George Marshall
George Marshall	Robert Lovett
Dean Acheson	Charles Wilson
John Foster Dulles	Neal H. McElroy
Christian Herter	Thomas S. Gates, Jr.
Dean Rusk	Robert McNamara
William F. Rogers	Elliott Richardson
Henry Kissinger	James Schlesinger
Cyrus Vance	Donald Rumsfield
Edmund Muskie	Harold Brown
Alexander Haig	Casper Weinberger
George Schultz	Frank Carlucci
James Baker	Richard Cheney

†CFR Founders

The CIA during most of the years since its creation has been under CFR control, starting with Allen Dulles, founding member of the CFR and brother of another founding CFR member and later secretary of state under President Eisenhower, John Foster Dulles.

Many of these men have held other influential posts. Dean Rusk and Cyrus Vance had been presidents of the Rockefeller Foundation. Charles Evans Hughes, in addition to serving on the board of the Rockefeller Foundation, was appointed chief justice of the U.S. Supreme Court. Admiral James Forrestal became secretary of defense and died some years later under very unusual circumstances.

During the Kennedy and Johnson administrations, more than sixty CFR members held top policy-making positions. McGeorge Bundy was employed on the staff of the Council on Foreign Relations, went from there to be the dean of the faculty of Arts and Sciences at Harvard, then became a key aide and national security adviser to John F. Kennedy. Bundy left that post to head the Ford Foundation. His brother, William Bundy, served as editor of *Foreign Affairs*, the CFR publication deemed so influential that it was even read by Lenin.

Under Richard Nixon the number of CFR members in major policy positions leapt to a hundred, and the story of their selection is mind-boggling. Former Secretary of the Navy William Mittendorf told me that he served as finance chairman of the 1968 Nixon campaign. On the night of the election he occupied a hotel room across the hall from the candidate. At 5:30 A.M. on the morning after Nixon's election victory,

Mittendorf saw Nelson Rockefeller and William Rogers come down the hotel corridor and enter Nixon's room. Later Rogers told Mittendorf that they were there to help select the cabinet.

INSIDE INFORMATION

What is not known is that Richard Nixon joined the CFR in 1961 and then resigned in 1965. He worked as a partner in the law firm of Nelson Rockefeller's bond counsel, John Mitchell, and occupied an apartment at 810 Fifth Avenue that was owned by Nelson Rockefeller, which adjoined the place where Rockefeller lived. During the mid-1960s, for the first time in his life, Nixon was making substantial sums of money. To quote another commentator on that subject, "Nelson Rockefeller was Nixon's employer, benefactor, landlord, and neighbor" during this period.

Insiders, like Mittendorf, were not surprised when Nixon chose Henry Kissinger, a man whom he had reportedly never met, to become his national security adviser and later secretary of state. Kissinger, as it turned out, was a protégé of Nelson Rockefeller and entered the White House straight from the staff of the Council on Foreign Relations—with, I might add, a $50,000 Rockefeller check to help with the expenses of the transition.

Nixon appointed Charles Yost, another paid CFR staff member, to be United Nations Ambassador. He chose CFR members Arthur Burns to head the Federal Reserve Board, Gerald Smith to be director of the Arms Control and Disarmament Agency, Dr. Paul McCracken to head the Council of Economic Advisers, Joseph J. Sisco to be assistant secretary of state for the Middle East and South Asia, and, of course, Bill Rogers became secretary of state. Nixon actually detached, on September 7, 1970, Brigadier General Robert L. Gard, Jr., from the office of the assistant chief of staff for force development for assignment to the headquarters of the Council on Foreign Relations in New York.

We must not forget that it was Nixon who also selected a young former Texas congressman, who had lost a Senate race against Democrat Lloyd Bentsen, to be chairman of the Republican party, ambassador to the United Nations, ambassador to China, and director of the CIA. That former congressman was a longtime CFR member and a CFR director in the late 1970s. He was none other than George Bush.

Perhaps knowing who his foreign policy advisers were may help explain why Nixon, the strong anticommunist, faithfully carried out major CFR goals—recognition of Communist China, signing the Anti-Ballistic Missile Treaty and the Strategic Arms Limitation Treaty with the

Soviets, continuing a Keynesian economic policy, and decoupling the U.S. dollar from gold.

Nixon, as you may remember, rose to power as the vice president under the Eastern Establishment candidate Dwight Eisenhower, who ran for the presidency as a Republican against another CFR member, Adlai Stevenson, who later became John Kennedy's ambassador to (you guessed it) the United Nations.

LONG-RANGE CONTROL

Of course, the present United Nations organization is actually the creation of the CFR and is housed on land in Manhattan donated to it by the family of current CFR chairman David Rockefeller. According to State Department Publication 2349, entitled "Report to the President on the Results of the San Francisco Conference" submitted by CFR member and then Secretary of State Edward R. Stettinius, "a committee on post-war problems was set up before the end of 1939 at the suggestion of the CFR."

Imagine! *Two years before the United States entered World War II, the CFR was already planning how to order the world when the war was over.* We may assume from this initiative that the entry of the United States into World War II was certain to these people two years before the "dastardly attack" at Pearl Harbor on December 7, 1941. How reminiscent this was of the entry of the United States into World War I at the urging of a founder of the CFR, President Wilson's key aide, Colonel Edward House.

The American delegation to the San Francisco meeting that drafted the charter of the United Nations included CFR members Nelson Rockefeller, John Foster Dulles, John McCloy, and CFR members who were communist agents—Alger Hiss, Harry Dexter White, and Owen Lattimore. In all, the Council sent forty-seven of its members in the United States delegation, effectively controlling the outcome.

For better or worse, the United Nations as we now have it, the International Monetary Fund, the World Bank, and the Bretton Woods monetary agreement were not the work of the United States government, per se, but that of the members of the Council on Foreign Relations carrying out the stated (and perhaps unstated) goals of that organization.

Perhaps the most blatant exercise of the power of the Establishment occurred in the selection of their 1976 presidential candidate.

In 1970 a young Polish intellectual named Zbigniew Brezinski foresaw the rising economic power of Japan and postwar Europe. Brezinski idealized the theories of Karl Marx. In his book, *Between Two Ages*, as in subsequent writings, he argued that balance-of-power politics was out and world-order politics was in. The initial world order was to be a trilateral economic linkage between Japan, Europe, and the United States. David Rockefeller funded Brezinski and called together an organization, named the Trilateral Commission, with Brezinski as its first executive secretary and director.

The stated goals of the Trilateral Commission are: "Close Trilateral cooperation in keeping the peace, *in managing the world economy*, in fostering economic re-development and alleviating world poverty will improve the chances of a *smooth and peaceful evolution of the global system.*" (Emphasis added.)

In other words, a three-cornered world system to "manage the world economy" will pave the way to world government. Senator Barry Goldwater's critique was scathing.

What the Trilaterals truly intend is the creation of a *worldwide economic power superior to the political government of the nation states involved. As managers and creators of the system, they will rule the future.* (Emphasis added.)

Brezinski took under his wing a born-again Baptist peanut farmer from South Georgia named Jimmy Carter, who had served one term as governor of that state. Brezinski took Carter as his pupil, filled him full of the philosophy of global government, and then brought him on as a member of the Trilateral Commission. Carter was an eager pupil who later wrote in his book, *Why Not the Best?* "Membership on this Commission has provided me with a splendid learning opportunity, and many of the other members have helped me in my study of foreign affairs."

CHANGING HORSES

It was obvious that after the Watergate scandal the Republican nominee, Gerald Ford, was in trouble going into the 1976 election. The population of the country had been moving south and west. After Vietnam and Watergate, there was a search for honesty and integrity. What better candidate for president than an unknown Southerner, an outsider, and a born-again Christian whose principal campaign pledge was, "You can trust me!"

Sometime in 1973, David Rockefeller picked Carter, and soon after the Establishment machinery went to work on his behalf. I learned in 1989, a long time after the fact, that a private security agency had been hired to meet a private plane at the Des Moines, Iowa, airport one night and to bring the passenger, Jimmy Carter, to a private meeting at the offices of the *Des Moines Register*, presumably for a briefing on the crucial 1976 Iowa presidential caucuses. The *Register* was formerly part of the Cowles

Publishing empire, the owner of which was an ardent CFR member. My source in Des Moines said that in those days the *Des Moines Register* considered itself the Midwest outpost of the CFR.

Given a favorable press umbrella by the state's most powerful newspaper and by dint of incredible personal exertion, the man who had been called "Jimmy who?" won the Iowa caucuses and was whisked by jet that night to New York City for appearances on all three of the morning national network television programs. The next crucial test was the New Hampshire primary where Carter won in a crowded field with only about twenty-eight thousand votes for a 33 percent plurality. From then on "front runner" Carter was covered with favorable press by the CFR media.

I personally was thrilled to think that a born-again Christian might gain the White House, and I gave Carter a boost with some friends of mine who were active in organized labor in Pennsylvania. After Carter won the Pennsylvania primary (believed, incorrectly I might add, to be a Northern, liberal, industrial state), the Southern peanut farmer had effectively won the Democratic nomination.

After the general election in November, I spoke to President-Elect Carter during a three-way telephone conversation along with pro-family activist Lou Sheldon of California. I suggested to Governor Carter that he, as a strong evangelical, might want to include some evangelical Christians among his appointments. He greeted the idea with enthusiasm and agreed to receive a list if we could get it to him within two weeks.

Lou Sheldon and I worked night and day to put together a short roster of names and résumés. The finished product was outstanding. All of the candidates were Democrats. All were highly distinguished in government, business, or education. The composition of the group looked like what Jesse Jackson sometime later called the Rainbow Coalition.

We had included male and female blacks, whites, Hispanics, native Hawaiians, and, I believe, a Chinese-American. A friend of a friend even obtained a preliminary thumbs up/thumbs down FBI screening to keep us from wasting the president-elect's time. (We had to omit one born-again Democratic governor from the South because of alleged campaign contributions by reputed Mafia figures.)

When the document was ready, I chartered a small aircraft to take Lou Sheldon to the grassy strip in Georgia we laughingly called "Plains International." Sheldon arrived at the Carter residence to find the next president barefoot and in blue jeans. They greeted each other warmly, and Sheldon proudly presented the booklet. Carter took it, read it, and began to cry.

When he got back to Virginia Beach, Sheldon said, "Jimmy was so touched by all the work that we did that tears came to his eyes." I said, "Lou, you are wrong. The reason he cried is because the appointment process is out of his hands, and he is not going to appoint any of those people." And indeed my words were true. Not one of our recommendations—men and women who on the surface shared every principle that Jimmy Carter espoused—was appointed to public office, or even seriously considered.

RASH PROMISES

Hamilton Jordan, Carter's brilliant but socially obnoxious campaign manager, was also surprised. Jordan reportedly said, "If, after the inauguration you find Cy Vance as secretary of state and Zbigniew Brezinski as head of national security, then I would say that we failed, and I'd quit."

But, in fact, that is precisely what happened. Carter's teacher, Brezinski, took the national security council post. Cyrus Vance who, like John Kennedy's secretary of state, Dean Rusk, had previously served as president of the Rockefeller Foundation, was made secretary of state.

Trilateral Commission member Walter Mondale, whose brother had signed the first *Humanist Manifesto*, was selected as vice president. CFR member Stansfield Turner was placed in charge of the CIA. Trilateral member Mike Blumenthal, whose family connections went back to internationalist banker Lazard Freres, was put in charge of the treasury. But more significant to the average American, Paul Volcker, a former employee of Rockefeller's Chase Manhattan Bank, was given the powerful role of chairman of the Federal Reserve Board. Out of only sixty-five American members on the Trilateral Commission, thirteen, including the president and vice president, were given top posts in the Carter administration.

Lest we forget, the Trilateral Commission, tagged by Senator Barry Goldwater as a scheme to place control of the world in the hands of "a worldwide economic power superior to the political government of the nation states involved," included in its membership (until he resigned about the time of the 1980 election) George Bush.

Jimmy Carter, who seems to be a decent enough person, was by aptitude and training totally unsuited for the presidency of the most powerful nation on earth. But in his four short years, he served his backers well.

Carter chose CFR member Sol Linowitz, a board member of a bank that had made loans to Panama, to be his emissary to negotiate away the United States ownership of the vital Panama Canal to Panamanian

Dictator Omar Torrijos. Torrijos was succeeded in office by that paragon of virtue, accused drug smuggler Manuel Noriega.

In 1977, Panama owed $1.7 billion, much of it to U.S. banks, which included Chase Manhattan, First National City Bank (now Citicorp), Bank of America, Banker's Trust, First National Bank of Chicago, and Marine Midland Bank (where Sol Linowitz was a director). Revenues from canal fees would be used to pay down the bank loans. Later Panama created a tax-free banking haven to reward its friends for their help.

The Panama Canal is a vital link for shipping from the West Coast of the United States to the East Coast and vice versa. It is one of the strategic choke points of the world. A look at the map quickly reveals that no other waterway exists for that purpose. The other sea route is to go all the way around Tierra del Fuego, at the extreme tip of South America, which is a totally unrealistic option for regular shipping.

The only other likely site for an alternate canal is in Nicaragua, which has two large inland lakes that could easily be connected by an inland waterway from the Pacific to the Caribbean. But under the Carter administration, the second canal option was violently taken away when Carter's people engineered the ouster of the pro-American leader of Nicaragua, West Point-trained Anastasio Somoza, and then brought in the Soviet- and Cuban-backed communist Sandinistas.

THE DEADLY TRUTH

Jack Cox's book, *Nicaragua Betrayed*, features a bombshell—an extended interview with Somoza. I interviewed Cox on my television program and learned the shocking truth about the betrayal of a United States ally by the Carter administration's State Department. In Somoza's own words:

> [Carter's] single-minded and overwhelming purpose has been to put Nicaragua in the hands of the communists. . . . Mr. Carter had effectively cut off Nicaragua from any possible source of supply.

At the conclusion of the book General Somoza makes this incredible charge:

> [T]he betrayal of steadfast anti-communist allies places Mr. Carter in the company of worldwide conspiratorial forces. I repeat, the treacherous course charted by Mr. Carter was not through ignorance, but by design.

Then Somoza continued:

[W]hile I'm privileged to tread this planet called earth, I shall do all within my power to see that other free nations do not suffer the agonizing death which struck Nicaragua. In my own way I am sounding the alarm. It is my wish, it is my impassioned hope that the freedom loving people of the United States will hear the alarm and they will respond without delay. There is no time for dalliance.

Shortly after *Nicaragua Betrayed* was published, however, General Somoza's time to "tread this earth" was cut short when a rocket fired by an unknown assassin blew up his vehicle on a street in Paraguay, where he had gone seeking asylum. He apparently knew too much to be allowed to live.

I visited Nicaragua just before the recent election. I talked with Violeta Chamorro before she was elected president. I met with various church leaders and a key member of the ruling Sandinista junta. Previously I had visited a Contra camp in Honduras located on the border of Nicaragua. I also have met and interviewed the current president and the past two presidents of El Salvador. I have a first-hand view of the truth in Central America that goes back many years.

BETRAYAL AND INSULT

The legacy of the Carter presidency in Central America is horrible. Nicaragua under the Sandinistas is one of the most wretched places I have ever visited. Around the capital of Managua there are miles of wretched hovels that resemble children's tree houses. Annual inflation at the time of my visit was 30,000 percent. The economy has been virtually destroyed. Unemployment is epidemic. The per capita income of the people is, along with Haiti, the lowest in the Western Hemisphere.

But Nicaragua under communism gave Fidel Castro a base for subversion against El Salvador, Guatemala, and Mexico. The flyleaf of *Nicaragua Betrayed* quotes the *Valeurs Actuelles*, a French political and economic weekly that carried on July 23, 1979, a conversation between Henry Kissinger and Lopez Portillo, then president of Mexico. Portillo said that he had told President Carter:

"I do not particularly like Somoza or his regime, as you know. But if the Sandinistas unseat him and replace him with a Castro-picked government it will touch off a slide to the left in my country."

"What did President Carter reply?"

"It was as though he did not hear a word I said," Portillo confided "He told me: 'Oh, Mr. President, you must do something to help me get rid of this Somoza.'"

A communist government in Nicaragua gave the Soviets two extraordinarily important military assets. First, air bases to receive long-range bombers and surveillance planes after they had flown from the Soviet Union along the West Coast of the United States. Second, Nicaragua has a superb harbor called El Bluff, which is perfect for submarines that could threaten vital U.S. shipping through the Panama Canal and in and out of the Gulf ports of Houston, Galveston, and New Orleans. As photographs revealed on national television by President Ronald Reagan showed, Nicaragua also became a key safe haven and staging area for drug trafficking from Colombia into the United States.

Postcommunist Nicaragua is a perfect laboratory for us in 1991 to examine the CFR dreams of a new world order. This single exercise of new order foreign policy brought a ruthless dictatorship, violation of human rights, confiscation of property, state socialism, a wrecked economy, subversion of neighboring democratic nations, and the undermining of the economic health and strategic security of the United States.

When the facts are known it is clear to me that anyone who takes an oath of office to uphold and defend the Constitution of the United States and then deliberately attempts to subvert the sovereignty and the strategic interest of this nation in favor of those of another government— world order or not—is guilty of, in a word, treason. Think again of the words of Richard Gardner, former deputy assistant secretary of state, that appeared in the CFR journal: "We are likely to do better by building our 'house of world order' from bottom up rather than from the top down . . . *an end run around national sovereignty, eroding it piece by piece,* is likely to get us to world order faster than the old fashioned assault." (Emphasis added.)

How dare an official (or even a former official) of the United States government set out to erode the sovereignty of the United States piece by piece! How dare a cabal of elected and unelected officials set out to subvert our constitution, our national sovereignty, and our democratic way of life!

Have any of us been told that the secretaries of state, the secretaries of the treasury, the heads of the CIA, the heads of the National Security Council, the heads of the Federal Reserve Board, and countless others are in agreement that American sovereignty is to be "eroded piece by piece"? When has there ever been a referendum for all of the people to decide whether they want to discard our Constitution in favor of a one-world government? The clear answer is, "Never!" Yet that is what the Establishment was preparing for us well before 1917.

THE WORK OF A DREAMER

Obviously the Establishment was not lowered down from heaven, nor did it rise full blown from hell. The best available records show that it sprang from the minds of an amazing man named John Ruskin and of his most apt pupil, Cecil Rhodes.

It was while he was attending Oxford University that Rhodes came under the influence of Ruskin. Ruskin believed in a platonic ideal society in which the state would control the means of production and distribution and which, in turn, is itself controlled for the benefit of all by those best suited by aptitude for the task. He believed, in other words, in the rule of the elite.

Ruskin taught Rhodes that the British upper classes possessed a "magnificent tradition of education, beauty, rule of law, decency, and self-discipline" that could not be saved unless it were extended to "the lower classes in England and to the non-English masses throughout the world."

The price of failure would be that the minority of upper-class Englishmen would ultimately be submerged by these majorities and their tradition lost. We learn that Ruskin read Plato every day. Plato wanted a ruling class with a powerful army and society subservient to it. Old social classes should be wiped away to give a clean slate for the new world to follow.

What seemingly evolved was an Anglo-Saxon platonic utopianism under which the old order of the world would be stripped away to prepare the world for the benign rule of the Anglo-Saxon aristocratic and monied classes. Most thinking people would say, as I do, that such notions are unadulterated hogwash, but sometimes the aberrant ravings of a so-called scholar, tucked away in a cloistered ivory tower, bear seed in a man of action.

Rhodes was such a man. In his maturity Rhodes exploited the diamond mines and gold fields of South Africa and founded the nation that came to be known as Rhodesia. With financial help from the powerful Rothschild banking interests he founded the DeBeers Consolidated Mines and the Consolidated Gold Fields. He conceived of a telegraph and rail link from the Cape of Good Hope to Cairo. And by the mid-1890s, Rhodes had a personal annual income of 1 million pounds sterling (the probable inflation adjusted equivalent of $100 million today).

Georgetown Professor Carroll Quigley, in his book *Tragedy and Hope,* which has been excerpted so skillfully by my friend Cleon Skousen in his excellent work *The Naked Capitalist,* says that despite this enormous income, Rhodes was spending so much on fulfilling the dreams of Ruskin that he was usually overdrawn on his account. Skousen writes:

> These purposes centered on his desire to federate the English-speaking peoples and to bring *all the habitable portions of the world under their control.* For this purpose Rhodes left part of his great fortune to found the Rhodes

Scholarships at Oxford in order to spread the English ruling class tradition. (Emphasis added.)

Again, Quigley tells us that Rhodes and other of Ruskin's pupils formed a secret society. Rhodes was the leader; Lord Esher, Lord Milner, and a man named Stead were the executive committee. Lord Balfour, Sir Henry Johnson, Lord Rothschild, Lord Gray, and others were listed as a circle of initiates. Then an outer circle of initiates was later organized by Lord Milner and called the Round Table.

THE BRITISH ROUND TABLE

The Round Table gained access to Rhodes's money after his death in 1902, and Lord Milner became the trustee of the Rhodes trust. Lord Milner was also governor-general and high commissioner of South Africa from 1897–1905. He gathered young men around him then and placed them in key positions in government and finance.

From 1909–13, Lord Milner organized semi-secret groups, known as Round Table Groups, in the British dependencies and America. In 1919, they founded the Royal Institute of International Affairs (Chatham House), financed by Sir Abe Bailey and the Astor family. The Council on Foreign Relations was conceived of at the same time in Paris by Colonel Edward M. House as the United States affiliate of the Royal Institute of International Affairs and, of course, the various Round Table groups.

According to Quigley:

> From 1884 to about 1915 the members of the group worked valiantly to extend the British empire and to organize it into a federal system. . . . Stead was able to get Rhodes to accept, in principle, a solution which might have made Washington the capital of the whole organization or allow parts of the empire to become states of the American Union.

Quigley continues:

> [T]he American branch of this organization (sometimes called the "Eastern Establishment") has played a very significant role in the United States in the last generation.

> The chief backbone of this organization grew up along the already existing financial cooperation running from the Morgan Bank in New York to a group of international financiers in London led by Lazard Brothers. Lord Milner became a director of the precursor to the giant Midland Bank. He became one of the greatest political and financial powers in England with his disciples placed throughout England in significant places, such as the editorship of the *Times*, the editorship of the *Observer*, the managing

directorship of Lazard Brothers, various administrative posts, and even Cabinet positions. Ramifications were established in politics, high finance, Oxford and London Universities, periodicals, the civil service, and tax-exempt foundations.

In other words, the pattern of operation was set in England, but the American Establishment has played it out to the letter. Quigley also claimed that, in New York, the Council on Foreign Relations was a front for J. P. Morgan and Company.

The New York branch was dominated by associates of the Morgan Bank. For example, in 1928 the Council on Foreign Relations had John W. Davis as president, Paul Cravath as vice president, and a council of thirteen others, which included Owen D. Young, Russell Leffingwell, Norman Davis, Allen Dulles, George Wickersham, Frank L. Polk, Whitney Sheperdson, Isaiah Bowman, Stephen P. Duggan, and Otto Kahn.

The group was "cosmopolitan, Anglophile, internationalist, Ivy League, Eastern seaboard, high Episcopalian, and European-culture conscious."

THE POWER OF INFLUENCE

By virtue of large grants and control of endowments, these men came to dominate the Ivy League universities and the selection of their presidents. Closely allied with Morgan, and later the Rockefellers, were the powerful Wall Street lawyers from John W. Davis and Paul Cravath to the Dulles brothers and John J. McCloy. Through direct ownership, use of trust and pension money, or by influence over powerful editors, their thoughts came to dominate the Establishment newspapers, then major broadcast chains, and then major magazines and scholarly periodicals.

First with the Morgan Bank, then with the Rockefellers and their Chase Manhattan and First National City Banks, then with foundations established by Carnegie, Ford, and the Rockefellers, the money power of the CFR has come to be enormous. But why would the big money interests veer away from the goal of Anglo-Saxon world domination to flirt with radical Marxism?

The reason is simple. It is easier to deal with a single autocratic authority than with the divided political forces of a democracy. A few years ago when I began the negotiations for a broadcast outlet in Israel—which ultimately led to CBN's television station on the Lebanese border—a kindly Israeli official suggested, "Why don't you try Jordan? Jordan has a king." In other words, a single powerful ruler can make decrees and enforce them. In the case of Israel, a government can fall because of the disaffection of one or more splinter parties; therefore, some things were not politically feasible even if the government wanted them.

Professor Quigley, who professed admiration for the goals of the Establishment and claimed to have been given access to the papers from their secret inner councils, confessed that the men of power and finance who had set out to remake the world were perfectly confident that they could use their money to acquire the cooperation and eventual control of the communist-socialist groups. Ruskin had taught (and Colonel House had written) that the new world federation was to have all property, industry, agriculture, communications, transportation, education, and political affairs in the hands of a small cadre of financially controlled political leaders.

As Cleon Skousen, commenting on Quigley's exposé, points out:

> The master planners have attempted to control the global conspiratorial groups by feeding them vast quantities of money for their revolutionary work and then financing their opposition if they seemed to be getting out of control. This policy has required the leaders of London and Wall Street to deliberately align themselves with dictatorial forces which have committed crimes against humanity in volume and severity unprecedented in history.

Quigley, the historian, makes this final observation:

> It was this group of people, whose wealth and influence so exceeded their experience and understanding, who provided much of the framework of influence which the communist sympathizers and fellow travelers took over in the United States in the 1930s. It must be recognized that the power that these energetic left-wingers exercised was never their own power or communist power but was ultimately the power of the international financial coterie.

Thus, we have the unbelievable result of the marriage of money and utopian theory. Earlier I mentioned the hypocrisy of utopian John Lennon calling for the abolition of private property for the human race, then leaving an estate of $250 million to his Japanese-born widow. But consider also David Rockefeller, enjoying a personal fortune in excess of $1 billion, living in a gracious estate and his elegant residences in the capitals of the world, driving in chauffeured limousines, flying private jets, dining on the finest food, yet giving massive financial assistance for decades to demonic tyrants to enable them to crush and grind the poor into the earth.

What possible self-delusion can come upon those with multi-million-dollar incomes, enjoying personally the fruits of a free society, who place their money and influence at the service of utopian fantasies which will doubtlessly create a world of slavery and undermine the nation that brought forth their own wealth? Will it not be one of the supreme ironies of history that the madness they have unleashed on the world will one day consume them, too?

THE DRIVING FORCE

The stream of world order flowing from the Illuminati is clearly occultic and satanic. The carnage that they have brought about is also understandable, given its ultimate source.

What is not clear is how monied, privileged, ostensibly Christian people could willingly and knowingly support the cruel, the barbaric, and the satanic. Quigley's hypothesis, on the surface, seems to provide the explanation. The power of money, by itself, also explains a great deal.

We have explored the link between Marxist communism and the occult Illuminati. What we have not touched upon is a link between these centers of privilege (which have been paying the bills for the communists in order to bring about a new world order) and the occultic, New Age agenda which, in turn, promises a mystical new world order.

Both groups are moving toward one goal, but at the highest, most secret levels. Is there a tie? But more on that in a later chapter.

6

Follow the Money

THE ORIGIN OF money is mysterious to most people. It is something they receive as wages and in turn spend for food, clothing, recreation, transportation, and shelter. A sizable portion of their money goes for taxes, but under pay-as-you-go taxation, taxes are not "paid," only deducted.

The international bankers have tried to tell us that money is a commodity, like flour or cement, which rises and falls in price depending on demand. But to most people money consists of pieces of paper printed in numerous denominations with pictures of various presidents and famous men. To some, money is the balance a computer tells them is deposited in their name at a bank or in some money market fund. When asked what the source of money is, they usually reply, "The government."

When the founders of the United States drew up our governing document, the Constitution, they were very specific about the creation of money. The key constitutional provision is Article 1, Section 8, which clearly charges the people's representatives, the Congress, with the "power to coin money and regulate the value thereof." To ensure a national currency, the states of the new union were forbidden to make anything but gold or silver payment for debts.

The power to create money and to regulate its quantity and value is the power to control the life of a nation. If there is too much money, prices rise. Inflation then causes interest rates to rise, and the value of the savings of the people is destroyed. If there is not enough money, the economy will collapse. Debts cannot be paid. Workers will be laid off. Construction and retail activity will slow down or dry up. And poorly funded owners of business or property will lost their businesses and property.

Obviously, if any private group could guarantee easy money to the economy, they would be in a position to loan money, build factories, buy stocks, and participate in growth opportunities. Conversely, if they could guarantee tight money, they could reduce loan exposure, short stocks, sell businesses, and then buy them back later at distressed prices at the bottom of what is called a recession or a depression. All things being equal, the control of money is the ability to bring prosperity or disaster on a nation.

Any nation that gives control of its money creation and regulation to any authority outside itself has effectively turned over control of its own future to that body. Ultimately, this was the battle that cost former British Prime Minister Margaret Thatcher her job.

Thatcher knew that linking the British pound to the European Currency Unit (ECU) and then agreeing to merge the British pound into a European currency would effectively put Great Britain in the hands of the president of the European Community, Jacques DeLors (a socialist), the other European socialist countries, and a European central bank controlled by the German Bundesbank. This would mean the loss of British sovereignty over its economic destiny, and Thatcher wanted no part of it. But powerful forces within her own party, moving toward monetary union, made quick work of her seemingly impregnable political position, and she was forced to resign.

SOURCES OF WEALTH

Because most average voters do not understand money, they will blame their economic woes on their political leaders and will, by the same token, credit their leaders for prosperity. Therefore, if any group has control of a nation's money, it has the power to create economic conditions that will bring success or ruin to elected officials.

As a former candidate for the presidential nomination of the Republican party, and later as a surrogate speaker for the successful candidate of the party, George Bush, I made my share of speeches extolling the low inflation rates of the Reagan administration which created 17 million new jobs. I also took my share of digs at the previous Democratic administration that "gave this country inflation at 13.5 percent, a 21.5 percent prime rate, and a major recession." The next line would usually be, "Do you want Michael Dukakis to bring you once again the failed economic policy of Jimmy Carter?" Crowds would cheer Bush and Reagan and boo Carter, then vote for four more years of prosperity.

What a stump speech of this sort would not say, however, is the very simple fact that the United States monetary policy of 1979 and 1980 was out of Jimmy Carter's control. Carter got the blame, but it was Paul Volcker, the man who really controlled America's money, who gave us the 21.5 percent prime interest rate and the recession that beat Carter. It was Paul Volcker who produced the low rate of inflation that allowed Ronald Reagan to begin massive deficit spending, create jobs, spur a powerful stock market rally, and enjoy his own reelection in 1984 and the successful succession of his vice president to the Oval Office in 1988.

If the power to create money is taken away from those whom the nation has elected to guide its destiny—the president and the Congress—then the people will have lost their democratic control. Obviously a nonelected body, serving terms that do not coincide with the terms of the presidents who appoint them and whose actions are not controlled or audited by Congress, does great violence to the carefully crafted system of checks and balances that our founding fathers established in the Constitution.

In fact, Thomas Jefferson said that a private central bank issuing the public currency was "a greater menace to the liberties of the people than a standing army." Except for Alexander Hamilton, all of the founders of this nation and their successors fought any attempt to take the power of money creation away from the people in order to place it in a privately owned or foreign-dominated central bank.

THE CENTRAL BANK

But what is a central bank? The idea first occurred to a canny Scot named William Paterson, who in 1694 agreed to establish a joint stock company to loan £1.2 million at 8 percent interest to William of Orange to help the king pay the cost of his war with Louis XIV of France. In return, the bank received a royal charter granting a number of privileges, including the right to issue notes payable on demand up to the amount of and against the security of the bank's loan to the crown.

The great secret that Paterson discovered was later blurted out by a London merchant, John Houblon, who became the first governor of the

Bank of England. He said, "We will charge interest on money which we create out of nothing." In other words, under the government's authority, the Bank of England would issue paper money created out of thin air, which would in turn be loaned at interest to various borrowers. These notes were not backed by gold or silver, but by a fraction of the note representing its loan to the crown.

American money is also made up of "notes" of the central bank. Take a dollar bill out of your wallet and read what it says. It is not a silver or gold certificate. It is a "note" issued by America's central bank. If you for any reason don't like it, all you will get in exchange is another Federal Reserve note. It is money created out of nothing, printed paper backed only by a private central bank. Yet it says, contrary to the Constitution, it is "legal tender for all debts, public and private."

All banks today use what is called *fractional reserve banking*. This means that if their starting capital is $1 million, they keep $50,000 in reserve and loan out $950,000. Assuming their borrowers redeposit the amount they borrow, the bank can then reserve 5 percent of the $950,000 in deposits and loan out the rest.

As depositors place money with the bank, the bank in turn reserves 5 percent, and loans out the rest, continuing the process as long as deposits or fresh capital is available. Therefore, by using fractional reserves a bank can ultimately pyramid modest capital into an enormous sum of money. Depending on various banking laws, theoretically at least, with capital of $5 million and reserves of $45 million, a bank can support a loan portfolio of $1 billion that would normally net, after interest payments to depositors and all other expenses, about 1 percent, or $10 million annually. This means that the bank has been receiving about $90 million in gross interest on money which it has created out of nothing.

WEALTH BY THE NUMBERS

It is easy to see the enormous leverage that is created by the banking system. The multiplication of money through fractional reserve banking is simply incredible, but at the same time the dangers of a debt pyramid are equally incredible. A debt pyramid where $50 million supports $1 billion of loans can be collapsed by five defaulted loans of $10 million each. These two facts explain the opportunity for fraud in the savings-and-loan industry, and the ever-expanding liability of the United States government when it is urged to pay for the improvident mistakes of greedy bankers who try to charge interest on money that they created from nothing.

It also shows what incredible damage can be done to the banking system and the economy in general if a central bank has the power to shrink the money supply, force the default of loans, and collapse weak banks. It also shows clearly the power and leverage that a central bank has when it lowers interest rates and increases the supply of money available for lending by the banks of a nation.

The companion secret to wealth building is compound interest, called by Baron Rothschild "the eighth wonder of the world." If it is possible to create money out of nothing, then loan it at interest, think how much more wealth can be created if the money is not repaid but allowed to compound year after year.

Money at compound interest doubles according to what is called the Rule of Seventy-Two. The number of years required for doubling is calculated by dividing seventy-two by the rate of interest charged. At 10 percent interest compounded annually, a $1 million loan will become $2 million in 7.2 years, $4 million in 14.4 years, $8 million in 21.6 years, $16 million in 28.8 years, and $32 million in 36 years. Put another way, wealth grows 3,200 percent in 36 years at 10 percent interest. In time, those who can make such loans grow rich beyond imagination, but those who borrow become impoverished.

In fact, no individual has the resources to sustain long-term compounding of interest. Only a sovereign government, armed with the enforcement mechanism of an income tax, can sustain the long-term compounding of debt.

The money barons of Europe, who had established privately owned central banks like the Bank of England, found in war the excuse to make large loans to sovereign nations from money that they created out of nothing to be repaid by taxes from the people of the borrowing nations. The object of the lenders was to stimulate government deficit spending and subsequent borrowing. War served that purpose nicely, but from 1945 to 1990 the full mobilization for the Cold War and the resulting massive national borrowings accomplished the result just as well without a full-scale shooting war.

So the monopoly bankers had two major goals. First, they sought to control the creation of money and the underlying political power of a nation. Second, they needed to encourage actions that would result in large-scale government deficit spending and debt creation at compound interest rates, paid for by taxes and tax increases when they become necessary.

PROPORTIONAL BLINDNESS

I read many periodicals and frankly I am amazed to read newspaper headlines about the "scandal" of a government official who took a $350 ride from Washington, D.C., to New York City in his government-allocated limousine, or the "scandal" of a patriotic U.S. Marine lieutenant colonel who tried to get some money to help freedom fighters in Central America.

But I never read about the scandal of those who have systematically and legally looted hundreds of billions of dollars from the taxpayers of America over the past seventy-eight years. I am reminded of the writing of Oliver Goldsmith, whose satire impaled those in England who put a man in jail for stealing a goose from off the common, but did nothing to the man who steals the common from under the goose.

History records that shortly after the establishment of the United States, the Rothschild interests attempted to saddle the country with a private central bank. The so-called Bank of the United States (1816–36) was abolished by President Andrew Jackson with these words,

> The bold effort the present bank has made to control the government, the distress it had wantonly produced . . . are but premonitions of the fate that awaits the American people should they be deluded into a perpetuation of this institution or the establishment of another like it.

But the centers of European finance could not rest until they had brought the powerhouse of the New World into their orbit. In 1902, Paul Warburg, an associate of the Rothschilds and an expert on European central banking, came to this country as a partner in the powerful Kuhn, Loeb and Company. He married the daughter of Solomon Loeb, one of the founders of the firm. The head of Kuhn, Loeb was Jacob Schiff, whose gift of $20 million in gold to the struggling Russian communists in 1917 no doubt saved their revolution.

A CAPITALIST CARTEL

Warburg was to become the catalyst, when joined with the Rockefeller and Morgan banking interests, to bring about the creation of a central bank for the United States. Here is how it happened.

In 1907, the Morgan interests were believed to have provoked a national money panic to such a degree that Congress established in 1908 a National Monetary Authority under Senator Nelson Aldrich of Rhode Island (whose daughter married John D. Rockefeller II, and one of whose sons was named Nelson Aldrich Rockefeller). Aldrich was considered a close ally of the Rockefeller interests.

From all indications, the National Monetary Commission wasted two fruitless years, including some aimless travel in Europe. On November 22, 1910, another group was formed, consisting of Senator Nelson

Aldrich; A. Piatt Andrews, assistant secretary of the treasury; Frank Vanderlip, president of the Rockefeller National City Bank of New York; Henry P. Davison, senior partner of J. P. Morgan Company; Charles D. Norton, president of the Morgan-dominated First National Bank of New York; Benjamin Strong, another Morgan lieutenant; and Paul Warburg. The group left secretly by rail from Hoboken, New Jersey, and traveled anonymously to a private hunting lodge on Jekyll Island, Georgia.

The meeting was so secret that none referred to the other by his last name. In 1935 Frank Vanderlip wrote in *The Saturday Evening Post*,

> [T]here was an occasion near the close of 1910, when I was secretive, indeed as furtive as any conspirator. . . . since it would have been fatal to Senator Aldrich's plan to have it known that he was calling on anybody from Wall Street to help him in preparing his bill. . . . I do not feel it is any exaggeration to speak of our secret expedition to Jekyll Island as the occasion of the actual conception of what eventually became the Federal Reserve System.

At Jekyll Island, the true draftsman for the Federal Reserve was Warburg. The plan was simple. The new central bank could not be called a central bank because America did not want one, so it had to be given a deceptive name. Ostensibly, the bank was to be controlled by Congress, but a majority of its members were to be selected by the private banks that would own its stock.

To keep the public from thinking that the Federal Reserve would be controlled from New York, there was a system of twelve regional banks. Given the enormous concentration of money and credit in New York, the Federal Reserve Bank of New York controlled the system, making the regional concept initially nothing but a ruse.

The board and chairman were to be selected by the president, but in the words of Colonel Edward House, the board would serve such a term as to "put them out of the power of the president." The power over the creation of money was to be taken from the people and placed in the hands of private bankers who could expand or contract credit as they felt best suited their needs.

DISSENTING VOICES

Congressman Charles A. Lindbergh, Sr., the father of the famed aviator, was the most vocal critic of the plan. He and others bitterly criticized a private stock company that could use the credit of the government for its own profit, take control of the nation's money and credit resources, and exercise a monopoly on the issue of "bank notes." One witness who testified against the plan said, "Both measures rob the government and the people of all effective control over the public's money, and vest in the banks the power to make money scarce or plenty."

The banking interests felt that President Taft could not manage the passage of the Aldrich Bill, so they engineered the three-party race in 1912 which ensured the election of Woodrow Wilson. Wilson's adviser, Colonel House, wrote in his personal memoranda:

—December 19, 1912.
I talked with Paul Warburg over the phone concerning currency reform. I told of my trip to Washington and what I had done there to get it in working order. I told him that the Senate and the Congressmen seemed anxious to do what he desired, and that President-elect Wilson thought straight concerning the issue.

Intimate Papers of Colonel House

George Sylvester Viereck wrote in *The Strangest Friendship in History: Woodrow Wilson and Colonel House*, "The Schiffs, the Warburgs, the Kahns, the Rockefellers, the Morgans put their faith in House. When the Federal Reserve legislation at last assumed definite shape, House was the intermediary between the White House and the financiers."

The Republican or Aldrich Bill of the Taft Administration was replaced with a virtually identical Democratic bill, signed by Woodrow Wilson, known as the Federal Reserve Act, which had been sponsored by the chairman of the House Banking Committee, Virginia Congressman and later Senator Carter Glass.

As a brief personal note, my father, A. Willis Robertson, succeeded his fellow Virginian, Carter Glass, in the United States Senate in 1946. Glass had chaired the House Banking and Currency Committee, and my father went on to chair its counterpart in the Senate, where he had the hearty support of the banking community. As I write this I am looking at a lovely sterling silver tray given him by the American Bankers Association at their annual meeting in San Francisco, October 25, 1966. My father was also a colleague in the Senate of Prescott Bush, the father of George Bush.

In 1968, I received on my father's behalf the award of the Woodrow Wilson Society in appreciation for his thirty-four years of distinguished service in the United States Congress.

As I am digging through all of the research and analysis in these chapters, some readers might wish to say to me: Pat, you are an Anglo-Saxon and an Ivy League law graduate. Your father was a senior United States Senator, and you have a distinguished heritage that goes from colonial days back to the nobility of England. You qualify to play a leadership role in the Establishment and its plan for a new world order.

So why don't you just keep your mouth shut, go along, and take the wealth and privilege that is there to enjoy?

My answer to such a question is very simple. I believe in freedom. I believe in equal opportunity for all people. I believe in free enterprise capitalism. I believe in the wisdom of the market.

Furthermore, I believe in the sovereignty of the United States of America. More than anything I believe in Jesus Christ, and I do not think that a man-made new world order is His will for mankind. I believe that God has never given anyone other than Jesus Christ enough wisdom to run this world, and it is my frank belief that some of these Ivy League characters trying to do so, have up to now made a colossal mess of it.

LOOMING DISASTERS

On December 21, 1913, American finance was captured by European finance and their powerful American allies in the Money Trust. How much of a financial benefit this central bank has given us can be judged from the fact that between 1913 (when the debt of the United States government was virtually zero) and October 1991, the nation's debt will have compounded exponentially to a staggering sum approaching $4 trillion, with annual interest charges that will exceed $200 billion per year. The federal debt load upon each family of four now totals roughly $64,000, and the annual tax burden upon every citizen is now calculated to be higher than the percentage exaction demanded of the serfs during the Middle Ages.

As for financial stability, we have only to look at the record of the Federal Reserve Board during the 1920s and early 1930s to realize that its policies were disastrous.

In 1928, Montague Norman, governor of the Bank of England, made the preposterous assertion about his banking power, "I have the hegemony of the world." In 1928 and 1929, the money powers of Britain and the United States coordinated their efforts in behalf of England because Montague Norman's hegemony was fast coming unglued.

The Federal Reserve Board embarked on a rescue effort to save the British gold supplies and the British pound sterling by forcing United States interest rates to an artificially low level. Cheap and plentiful money had the effect it always had: It drove the price of stocks and bonds through the roof. In 1929, because of 10 percent margin requirements for the purchase of stocks, stock buying turned into a speculative orgy.

The prices of securities became overvalued and vulnerable to bad news. Thus, when news of the collapse of the Credit-Anstalt Bank in Austria hit the market, there was a wave of selling, margin calls, more selling, and more margin calls. Instead of stepping in to ease the situation, history records that the Federal Reserve Board, faced with the collapse of many banks in the nation, did little to alleviate the crisis of a 25 percent decline in the money supply .

This shortage of money left the economy prostrate and a full quarter of the labor force out of work. Certainly from 1968 until 1991 the erratic expansion and contraction of the money supply by the Federal Reserve Board has caused serious recessions in 1969, 1973, 1979, 1982, and 1990.

Now in the United States the savings-and-loan industry has collapsed. A thousand banks are in trouble. The insurance industry is falling apart. It seems that by 1993 there may well be a massive stock market sell-off and, very probably, a worldwide credit collapse.

Since 1988 the Federal Reserve Board has restricted the money supply to such an extent that the economy has been placed in a painful recession. The so-called board (or M-3) money supply—which includes all currency, all demand deposits at banks, plus money market funds, along with overnight repurchase agreements, savings accounts, large time deposits, term repurchase agreements, and bank-held Eurodollars—has actually been shrinking in real inflation-adjusted terms from 1988 until the time of publication of this book.

The Federal Reserve Board's mechanism to deal with a healthy growing economy is to cause its collapse in order to reduce inflation. What I fear is that in order to prepare for the reelection of the president in 1992, the Federal Reserve Board will allow the money supply to grow more vigorously to create the appearance of prosperity and then slam on the money brakes around election time, an action that may well cause a debt collapse, a stock market collapse, and a global depression of unprecedented ferocity.

For that reason I am strongly urging readers of my newsletter, *Pat Robertson's Perspective,* to pay off debts now, take stock market profits by summer 1992, and place the bulk of their holdings in short-term treasury bills until the dust settles.

CALCULATED RISKS

If there is a crash, the Republican party will be blamed for it, and their candidate in 1996 will be defeated. Democrats will then take the White House. The Establishment had originally picked former Virginia Governor and now Senator Chuck Robb as their candidate (Robb was one of two senators invited to Trilateral Commission meetings). Unfortunately for Robb, the revelation of his presence in a sex-and-cocaine scandal in my hometown of Virginia Beach while he was governor, coupled with a criminal investigation into recorded taps of Virginia's current black Democratic governor's cellular telephone conversations, have blown Robb, like Gary Hart before him, completely out of contention for any higher political office.

Now the insiders have determined that a surrogate is not necessary when they can have the real thing. They have begun to move centi-millionaire Senator John D. Rockefeller III of West Virginia into the limelight!

Their first move was to name Rockefeller as chairman of a commission to protect the family, where he put forward proposals that won the support of defenders of the poor on the left and pro-family conservatives on the right. His relatively innocuous criticism of George Bush's Euro-pean forays and his seeming inattention to domestic policy in mid-1991 was spotlighted on the evening news of all three television networks. Absent a miracle, President Rockefeller has been tapped by the elite to bring us that much closer to world government in 1996.

So much for the benefits of a privately owned, and to my mind unconstitutional, central bank. But since most people are not aware that the Federal Reserve System is owned by member banks, which are in turn owned by private investors, it might be instructive to show who had stock in the Federal Reserve Board at its inception. Since the Federal Reserve Bank of New York was to set interest rates and direct open market operations, this bank was far more powerful than any other. Its first governor was Benjamin Strong, president of the Morgan Bank, and one of the participants at Jekyll Island. He brought the Reserve System into interlocking relations with the Bank of England and the Bank of France.

Of the reportedly 203,053 shares of the Federal Reserve Bank of New York, Rockefeller's National City Bank took 30,000 shares; Morgan's First National Bank took 15,000 shares; Chase National took 6,000 shares; and the National Bank of Commerce, now known as Morgan Guaranty Trust, took 21,000 shares. Any of the banks holding the shares could, in turn, be purchased in whole or in part by foreign interests. As I understand it, such a move would mean that control of the public money supply of the United States was not only in private hands but could be, at least in theory, in foreign hands as well.

THE IMPACT OF A UNITED EUROPE

In 1992, the world will see for the first time since Charlemagne a united Europe. The linchpin of that union will be a European central bank with powers similar to the Federal Reserve Board of the United States and some type of common currency, now called the European Currency Unit or ECU.

Presently the German Bundesbank is calling the shots for the flow of interest rates and currency alignment for all of Europe. But think what would happen if the emerging United States of Europe opts for one central bank with seven members. Then realize that Japan also has a central bank controlling its interest rates, money supply, and banking practices. Perhaps this bank might expand to become an Asian central bank.

Consider what would then happen if, in a Trilateral world, the central bank of Europe, the central bank of Japan, and the central bank of the United States began to coordinate their efforts, or even to merge. If that happened, some twenty-one people, possibly as few as three people, could control they money and credit of essentially the entire world. They would not only be able to affect the fortunes of every human being on earth, but they could create an economic climate to keep in power or take from office any government or public figure.

This is precisely the situation that former Senator Barry Goldwater warned about when he spoke of economic power capable of bypassing or controlling the political power of any nation. If national sovereignty collapses on the money front, then the media and public opinion's power will be available to collapse political and military sovereignty, thus bringing the dreams of the one-worlders to reality.

This day is coming much closer than anyone believes. Only one thing will stop it, and that is the concerted effort of concerned Americans who will vote into office a Congress who will repeal the Federal Reserve Act and restore the constitutional power given to the people's elected officials. The price of apathy on this score means the loss of liberty for every American.

IMPROVIDENT LOANS

The money barons are getting much closer to control of the world's economy than even they may have believed was possible. But like the dog who chased after the bus and didn't know what to do when he had caught it, these men don't really know what to do next.

David Rockefeller's Chase Manhattan Bank is swimming in nonperforming foreign loans and foreclosed domestic real estate. The credit rating of the Chase has been downgraded, and its stock value has collapsed. Although Rockefeller has tremendous political power, his financial acumen has been seriously questioned. A former vice president of the Federal Reserve Board once commented that David Rockefeller spends all morning giving away the assets of the bank, and George Champion (its president at that time) spends all afternoon getting it back again.

Citicorp, which grew out of the Rockefeller-dominated First National City Bank, was so heavily involved with loans to countries like Brazil, Argentina, and Mexico that its continued existence is threatened. Not only was its paper downgraded and its stock value dropped by two-thirds, it was saved, at least temporarily, by a humiliating rescue effort made by a rich Saudi Arabian prince who bought some $750 million in Citicorp convertible preferred stock carrying a usurious guaranteed dividend yield.

The great Bank of America was barely saved from collapse when its longtime chairman, A. W. Clausen, returned from retirement and a stint at the World Bank to assume active management.

Manufacturer's Hanover Bank had shaky Third World loans that exceeded twice its stated capital. If these loans had been marked to market value, the bank would have collapsed. Now Manufacturers Hanover and Chemical Bank are merging in the hope of finding operating savings to continue profitably in the future.

I remember a meeting in the late 1970s at the Morgan Bank on Wall Street where I had gone to acquire some distressed real estate. I found three very troubled middle executives who had shoveled $100 million of the bank's money into three hotel projects that were all in default and were costing the bank millions to carry. There were no guarantees of repayment on any of the projects and the loans were, in a word, improvident. These projects were not unusual but typical of the go-go lending of the early 1970s and certainly of the 1980s.

The giant Continental-Illinois Bank was stuck with a $1 billion bad loan to Penn Square Bank in Oklahoma and would have collapsed but for a government bailout.

Recently the Bank of New England collapsed and was taken over by regulators and sold. The giant Bank of Boston almost went under, but it is trying to struggle back.

The hottest banking news in 1991 concerned the largest bank collapse in history, the Pakistan- and Luxembourg-based Bank of Credit and Commerce International (BCCI), a $20 billion institution. This bank not only made unsecured loans to its friends concerning hundreds of millions of dollars, it had a "black" department that laundered drug money, financed arms shipments, held deposits for the CIA, drug dealers, the PLO, and the terrorist Abu Nidal. It financed secret Israeli arms shipments, engaged in terrorism against its enemies, and reportedly distributed $5 million in bribes to United States congressmen and government officials.

The collapse of BCCI leaves depositors with no way of recovering their deposits. Instead, these deposits in fact may have already been dissipated because of this incredible corrupt Ponzi scheme.

Ironically, the BCCI collapse is accelerating the move toward world banking. An urgent call is being made for global bank regulation to prevent a bank that has been chartered under the lax banking laws of such nations as Luxembourg or the Cayman Islands from committing such massive worldwide fraud again. The vehicle being put forward is the Geneva-based Bank of International Settlements, which is controlled by the major central banks of the world. Again, it is as if an unseen director keeps putting the pieces in place.

In 1991, the world owed and an unbelievable $25 trillion dollars in private and public debt. The exponential compounding of debt based on fractional reserve banking has created a monster that no central bank, no combination of banks, no single government, and no world government— especially the inefficient and corrupt United Nations—can solve. When the debt bubble finally bursts, the financial wreckage will be the worst in the history of the world.

WHO CAN YOU TRUST?

In my view the last people in the world to be entrusted with picking up the pieces will be those who caused the problem in the first place. Think about it. They helped destroy Russia, Poland, Czechoslovakia, Hungary, Rumania, China, Southeast Asia, Ethiopia, Angola, Mozambique, Tanzania, Rhodesia, Cuba, and Nicaragua. They brought us the Great Depression and many subsequent recessions. They have almost destroyed their own banks and financial institutions, and in 1991 they came perilously close to destroying the financial system of the entire world.

For years, to further their utopian one-world plans, they have been trying to undermine American education, moral values, sense of patriotism, and national pride. They will destroy everything else they get their hands on.

In the turbulent pre-Christmas days of 1989, an uprising of Christian people had broken out in the city of Timisoara, Rumania, protesting government abuses. The cry of the tens of thousands of people who filled the city square was, "God is alive!" Their peaceful protest was met with gunfire from members of the state security forces that had stationed themselves on the rooftops of buildings surrounding the public square. Some two thousand of those innocent civilians fell dead and wounded.

The news horrified the nation and the world, and on the next day the dictator, Nicolae Ceausescu, called for a large rally in the main square of the capital city of Bucharest. As the dictator began to speak to what he thought was a friendly crowd, one woman shouted out, "You are a liar!" Those around her began shouting "you are a liar!" Then the whole crowd began to shout it, and Ceausescu fled the platform. On Christmas Day 1989, he and his wife were executed, and the nation was freed from his abuses.

It is time that a new shout go up against the money barons who use such slick phrases to sell their next plans to ruin the world. Americans need to cry at the top of their lungs, "You are liars! We have had enough! Your time is up!"

THE POWER OF PERSUASION

The task of bringing forth a cry of rage that will be clearly heard will not be easy. The power of the Money Trust does not end at the banks. It goes deep into our largest media corporations, private and federal institutions, and educational establishment. Here is how it works.

All major banks develop relationships with large corporate clients. They make lines of credit available to finance inventories and receivables. They provide construction financing and real estate financing. They make bridge loans and term loans for corporate expansion or acquisitions. They help with cash management, currency transactions, letters of credit, and, of course, depository and check-writing services. Most banks maintain a private banking service for the executives of their large corporate clients in case these executives need ready cash for their own personal use.

For the really big loan requirements of their clients, a large bank may become the lead bank to syndicate a loan among several other national, regional, or foreign banks.

To cement relationships, the chief executives of the major corporate customers of a bank are invited to sit on the bank's board of directors, and often key bank officials sit on the boards of the corporations with which they do business. It goes without saying that a lead bank has firsthand, intimate knowledge of the inner workings of its corporate clients.

But the interconnection goes even deeper. All banks have trust departments, but some, like J. P. Morgan, manage trusts and pension funds in the billions of dollars. Several years ago such funds were in excess of $25 billion at Morgan alone. If that trust money is invested in the common stock of major corporations, especially those companies in media, it would in turn buy a great deal of influence. Because of the dispersal of public ownership of stock, a 5 percent stake in some corporations is tantamount to outright control.

It is my understanding that the major New York banks, and the trust funds that they manage, have substantial stock holdings in the *New York Times* Corporation, CBS, ABC, General Electric (which owns NBC), the *Washington Post* Company, the Times Mirror Corporation, and the Dow Jones Company (which publishes the *Wall Street Journal*).

These corporations, and hundreds more industrial corporations, cannot afford to have demand loans called, credit lines canceled, essential expansion loans denied, their credit standing impugned, or a bear raid on their stock. Huge holdings depend on credit. Those who get it have prospered greatly in the past decades; those without access to credit suffer.

This awesome power—tantamount to the power of financial life and death—accounts for the fact that there never is a critical article about David Rockefeller or the CFR in the major national media. The power is subtle but incredibly intense. In high finance, all it takes is a quiet word from the right person to destroy the future of any public company that is carrying substantial debt. Every owner of every major public media company is fully aware of how the game is played, and it is hardball.

TAKING THE BRUNT

The coup de grace is always administered in a paneled, deeply carpeted environment in the most genteel of tones. "I am sorry, but our loan committee does not believe that this is a bankable proposition." "Our loan committee has voted not to renew your company's annual line." "Your company's demand note signed last December is now due and payable. Our loan committee has voted not to renew it."

This is not a court. There is no judge, no jury, and no appeal. There are, of course, other banks, but a discreet leak for publication, as follows, will cool their interest.

This publication has learned from reliable sources that the Chase bank has called $50 million in demand loans made by it to the XYZ Publishing Corporation. The stock of XYZ plunged five points in active trading on the news. Speculation is rife concerning the source of the problems at the troubled media concern.

If XYZ Publishing recovers, you can rest assured that the managing editor knows that he will be fired and blackballed throughout the industry if ever a critical word against the Rockefellers or their CFR associates appears in the XYZ newspapers or on its television stations. If anyone else criticizes these people in public, XYZ Publications will polish its Establishment image by branding the critics as ill-informed, right-wing, fundamentalist reactionaries.

FOUNDATION RESOURCES

By the judicious use of credit, the Establishment has built a network of interlocking corporate and bank boards in every phase of American life, including the media, which control close to 60 percent of the total financial assets of the United States. Each of the leaders of these powerful companies are introduced, in turn, to the travel settings, the overseas business opportunities, the governmental aid sources, and the academic resources that would lead inescapably toward the philosophy of managed globalism.

When Cecil Rhodes died, he left a huge fortune in a tax-free foundation, the Rhodes Trust, which Lord Milner used to fund multiple causes in furtherance of Rhodes's global schemes. The importance of such tax-free foundations should not be underestimated.

First, they permit enormously wealthy individuals to leave huge fortunes free of inheritance taxes in the hands of family members or trusted allies. The wealth within foundations can compound in perpetuity, free of income or capital gains taxes. Foundations can own stock in banks or business corporations, and through foundation tax-planning techniques, families can retain voting control of large corporations while placing much of the beneficial interest into a tax-free foundation which they also control.

Relatively recent tax laws forced private foundations to pay out in grants up to 5 percent of their assets each year. Serious restrictions and penalties have been imposed on the most blatant forms of self-dealing between foundations and those who control them. But absent these modest restrictions, allowable foundation functions and grant-making power is broad and varied.

Andrew Carnegie, a personal friend of Rhodes, sold his Carnegie Steel Works to J. P. Morgan for $400 million. Most of that money, the equivalent of at least $4 billion today, went into the Carnegie Corporation and the Carnegie Endowment for Peace.

John D. Rockefeller gave away about $530 million in his day, worth billions in today's money, much of it to the Rockefeller Foundation. His son added to the sums, and his grandchildren endowed the Rockefeller Brothers Fund.

The largest foundation on record is the Ford Foundation, funded when Henry Ford, Sr., died in 1947, to allow the Ford family to retain voting control of the Ford Motor Company, and I might add, control of the foundation. The Ford Foundation had starting assets of $3 billion, a huge sum at the time.

Despite the express wishes of Henry Ford, Sr., leadership of the Ford Foundation wound up in the hands of Paul Hoffman, a principal player in the CFR and a trustee of the far-left Institute of Pacific Relations. Although Hoffman was removed from the Ford Foundation, its policies strayed continuously so far to the left that Henry Ford II, grandson of the founder, recently resigned in disgust.

THE ENEMY WITHIN

It goes without saying that leftists gravitated to the big foundations like flies to a honey pot. But who better to control and manage this money than the finance men and lawyers of the Establishment, like the CFR stalwarts, John McCloy or McGeorge Bundy, who at different times ran the Ford Foundation? Of no small note, for that matter, convicted perjurer Alger Hiss later ran the Carnegie Endowment for International Peace.

In 1989, the Ford Foundation listed assets of $5,832,426,000 and gave grants the previous year of $211,769,514. The foundation listed as one of its major purposes:

> [I]nternational affairs—analysis, research, dialogue, and public education on such issues as policies affecting immigrants and refugees, arms control and international security, and the changing world economy and U.S. foreign policy; and governance and public policy—including governmental and public policy issues.

That is their real power. The foundation has the ability to give away up to $164 million however it chooses to study and propagandize the nation on such foreign policy and world economy issues as the CFR and its one-world allies dictate.

For reference, it may be helpful to look at specifics on how some of the Ford Foundation's money is spent:

> $1 million to the Council on Foreign Relations. $300,000 to study the influence of communism in contemporary America, with Earl Browder, national secretary of the Communist party as a key stuff member

> $1,134,000 to the American Friends Service Committee to support a study of the communist takeover of China

> $630,000 to the Southwest Council of La Raza, allegedly headed by a known communist

Not only has the Ford Foundation poured out hundreds of millions of tax-free grants to fund leftist and global initiatives, but by 1970 it had given a billion dollars to educational projects in support of the same goals. Of interest is the fact that the Ford Foundation makes no grants at all for any religious purpose.

The Rockefeller Foundation in 1989 listed its assets at $2,140,244,924 with grants of $59,996,580. The goal of this fund is "to promote the well-being of mankind throughout the world."

This fund has been a major contributing source to the Council on Foreign Relations and its affiliate organizations, including the far-left Institute for Pacific Affairs. It also has been a training ground for future public servants. The secretary of state under Jimmy Carter, Cyrus Vance, and the secretary of state under John F. Kennedy, Dean Rusk, were both, prior to their appointments, presidents of the Rockefeller Foundation.

FUNDING THE ONE WORLD AGENDA

In 1946, immediately after World War II, the report of the Rockefeller Foundation stated clearly, "The challenge of the future is to make this one world." In forty-five years they have not deviated from that course.

It is the Rockefeller Brothers Fund, which was valued in 1989 at $242,120,725 with $7,999,659 in grants where the true purposes of the globalist establishment is seen. The mask is off in this incredible published statement of purpose:

> Support of efforts in the U.S. and abroad that contribute ideas, develop leaders, and encourage institutions in the transition to global interdependence.

In other words the resources of the Rockefeller Brothers Fund are to be used to develop propaganda, educate future leaders, and move institutions (including the United States government) toward a one-world government.

These three foundations have over $8.2 billion in tax-free wealth placed at the service of propaganda, education, leadership training, and "institutional encouragement" to move toward a one-world government and its companion piece, world socialism.

The Carnegie Corporation of New York in 1989 listed assets of $905,106,313 and annual grants of $47,587,022. Carnegie money was used earlier for extremely beneficial activities like the construction of public libraries and technical colleges. For the past few decades, through a propaganda machine called the Carnegie Endowment for Peace, with

1989 assets of $93,184,721, the Carnegie money has often been used in the service of pro-Soviet initiatives. Three of the stated purposes of the Carnegie Corporation are the diffusion of knowledge and understanding among the people of the United States and nations (in the manner of Carnegie's friend, Cecil Rhodes) that have been members of the British Commonwealth, the avoidance of nuclear war, and the improvement of U.S.-Soviet relations.

A listing of such foundation grants is available at any public library. The list is exhaustive and gives many examples of contributions to worthwhile causes. But here are some uses of foundation money that underscore the Establishment goals of influencing the press, Congress, and public policy:

Arms Control Association, $200,000. Toward program on arms control and national security for the Washington, D.C., press corps

Aspen Institute for Humanistic Studies, $550,800. Toward meetings on U.S.-Soviet relations with American lawmakers

Aspen Institute for Humanistic Studies, $300,000. Toward meetings on U.S. relations with South Africa for American lawmakers

Council on Foreign Relations, $208,000. For study of U.S.-Soviet relations

Institute for East-West Security Studies, $50,000. Toward international volume of essays on conventional arms control

United Nations Association of the United States, $300,000. Toward project on U.S.-Soviet policy dialogue on the United Nations

American Civil Liberties Union Foundation, $200,000. For national security studies on government secrecy

Council on Foreign Relation, $208,000. To study U.S.-Soviet relations in next decade

Council on Foreign Relations, $445,000. To enable ten U.S. scholars and government officials to serve apprenticeships in U.S. foreign policy agencies

Council on Foreign Relations, $45,000. Organizing symposia in five U.S. cities to bring African issues into mainstream of U.S. foreign policy concerns (multiple foundation grants toward this project)

There are hundreds of grants toward projects like these aimed at disarmament, linkage of the United States and the Soviet Union, and propaganda in support of Establishment global concerns aimed at press, lawmakers, and community groups. All these causes subtly move public opinion toward the preconceived goal of world government.

THE TILT TO THE LEFT

The "interlocking nexus of tax-exempt foundations" was so tilted toward left-wing associations that in July 1953 Congress set up a special committee under Representative B. Carroll Reece of Tennessee to investigate them. The pressure and vituperation that came upon this committee from very powerful sources ultimately ended with its unpublicized demise.

In 1958, a book by its counsel, Rene A. Wormser, called *Foundations: Their Power and Influence,* tells the story of what this committee accomplished and releases the evidence it uncovered to the public. The summary finding of the Reece Committee was shockingly simple: tax-exempt foundations were deliberately using their wealth and privilege to attack the basic structure of the U.S. Constitution and the Judeo-Christian American culture.

Wormser said quite eloquently that no society should grant tax exemption to any organizations seeking to destroy it. In his chapter entitled "Foundation Impact on Foreign Policy," Wormser cites the Carnegie Endowment for Peace as one of those attempting to mold public opinion and to decide "what should be read in our schools and colleges." He went on to say:

> Foundation activity has nowhere had a greater impact than in the field of foreign affairs. It has conquered public opinion and has largely established the international political goals of our country. . . . This was comparatively easy to accomplish because there was no organized or foundation supported opposition.

Wormser continued his shocking analysis of the evidence presented to the Reece Committee. He wrote:

> The influence of the foundation complex in internationalism has reached far into government, into the policy-making circles of Congress and into the State Department. This has been effected through the pressure of public opinion, mobilized by the instruments of foundations; through the promotion of foundation favorites as teachers and experts in foreign affairs; through a domination of the learned journals in international affairs; through the frequent appointment of State Department officials to foundation jobs; and through the frequent appointment of foundation officials to State Department jobs.

He then showed how the Carnegie Corporation, the Carnegie Endowment for Peace, the Rockefeller Foundation, and the Ford Foundation jointly sponsored conferences and forums filled with one-sided rhetoric advocating United Nations control of U.S. foreign aid, unilateral disarmament, recognition of Red China, and admission of China to the United Nations.

The Reece Committee came to this conclusion:

> The weight of evidence before this committee . . . indicates that the form of globalism which the foundation have so actively promoted and from which our foreign policy has suffered seriously, relates definitely to a collectivist point of view.

As to the aid given to communist causes by major foundations, Wormser points out that the predecessor of the Reece Commission, the Cox Commission, discovered one hundred grants that had been made to individuals and organizations with extreme leftist records from the Rockefeller Foundation, the Carnegie Corporation, the Carnegie Endowment for International Peace, the John Simon Guggenheim Foundation, the Russell Sage Foundation, the William C. Whitney Foundation, and the Marshall Field Foundation.

Wormser's conclusion from the lengthy investigations of the Reece Committee probably doesn't ring clearly on American ears of the 1990s, but they are nonetheless true.

> If one accepts the concepts and principles of the Declaration of Independence and the Constitution as *the existing order,* then any attempt to replace them with the concepts and principles of socialism must be considered "subversive" and "un-American."

The blending of the pro-Soviet, monopoly capital, globalism of the Establishment, the Establishment foundations, and the Establishment media—particularly when coupled with secular humanism, radical communism, the human sexuality movement, and New Age religion—makes a strange and potent cocktail in America's universities, high schools, and elementary schools.

Can this nation survive such a concerted and powerful effort to dismantle our sovereignty, our national spirit, and the legacy of self-reliance and independence won for us at such great cost? This is an urgent and troubling question, and the answer is not at all certain.

But before I even attempt to answer or to offer a point of conjecture, we will need to explore a few of these critical issues—the educational, religious, and political objectives of the globalist agenda—and with these insights we will gain a more stable footing for some of the assessments that follow.

I turn now to a discussion of the educational programs designed to prepare our youth for the new world order.

7

School for Scandal

IN THE BOOK *The Price of Power*, written shortly after the Second World War for the Council on Foreign Relations, a group of ranking CFR analysts led by Hanson Baldwin made the contention that "our ultimate objective, even though it may be decades or centuries away, must be one world, and we must constantly try to heal and patch and bind to avoid the final hardening of Europe into two camps."

The fear of atomic war seemed a real enough threat in 1948, and fear of imminent mass destruction was a genuine and powerful enigma, a vision that, unfortunately, elicited sinister responses. Expressing grave misgivings, Baldwin wrote, "The face of tomorrow is a bleak visage; we are embarked on a 'time of troubles.'" The images of mass destruction created by World War II brought a sense of overpowering dread to intellectuals which seemed to overpower their reason with irrational fears of the Apocalypse.

Baldwin went on to say, "We have opened for all time the lid of Pandora's box of evils. We cannot now push the genii back into the box. We may not like it, but we must face it. Atomic bombs, biological agents and other weapons of mass destruction are now a permanent part of man's society; and no perfect physical system of control is possible for all these weapons."

Then he added: "But today war—international war—can mean chaos. And so the face of tomorrow is the face of danger; we must anticipate a 'time of troubles' while man learns to make peace with himself."

In fact, this vision of a troubled world has hardly diminished during the past forty years. Former Attorney General Robert Kennedy, brother of President John Kennedy, wrote a passionate, almost evangelical appeal for world peace and a new world order in his 1967 book *To Seek a Newer World*. The postscript to this book is a virtual paean to the unity of mankind, the homogeneity of all races and cultures, and the necessity of "building a new world society."

It was in this book that the younger Kennedy announced his candidacy for the presidency of the United States, and in it he called on the power and idealism of youth (the most visible power block of the 1960s and early 1970s) to fight against any sense of futility, expediency, timidity, or love of comfort in order to bring about a revolution that would help to reshape the destiny of the world. But that destiny would be a challenge the author would not live to fulfill.

FROM THE WHITE HOUSE

A few years later, on February 14, 1977, in his address to representatives from many nations—symbolizing the global community—President-Elect Jimmy Carter said:

> I want to assure you that the relations of the United States with the other countries and peoples of the world will be guided during my own Administration by our desire to shape a world order that is more responsive to human aspirations. The United States will meet its obligation to help create a stable, just, and peaceful world order.

Most Americans hardly noticed the new president's peculiar statement or realized that, as a protégé of David Rockefeller and a member of the Trilateral Commission and the Council on Foreign Relations, this born-again Southern Democrat was communicating a deliberate and articulate statement of a specific vision of world government.

But most Americans are equally surprised to learn that the idea of a new world and the use of the term is not at all new or novel to hundreds of intellectuals, university professors, and public policy professionals in this country. Entire departments and degree programs in dozens of colleges and universities have been built around the premise of planning "alternate futures" for the world and agitating for elimination of the current system of autonomous statehood in favor of one-world government.

Allied with futurists, ecologists, economists, and specialists in many other academic disciplines, these world-order professionals have created an entire industry and a mythology around themselves. Dozens of textbooks, guides, and reference sources have been published over the past dozen years to support this study and to help facilitate the creation of a system of terminology and rhetoric for peace, justice, and ecology.

FROM THE IVORY TOWER

In recent years such idealistic dreams have come in a steady stream from the ivory tower. In their 1983 book, *Perspectives on American Foreign Policy,* Professors Charles W. Kegley, Jr., and Eugene R. Wittkopf assembled a series of essays by a number of intellectuals and commentators on the idea of a world superstate. Prompted by the same apocalyptic visions—world crisis and a troubled future—these scholars argued boldly and without pretense for a one-world government that would supersede national identity.

In one article, Henry Steele Commager wrote:

> The inescapable fact, dramatized by the energy crisis, the population crisis, the armaments race, and so forth, is that nationalism as we have known it in the nineteenth and much of the twentieth century is as much of an anachronism today as was States Rights when Calhoun preached it and Jefferson Davis fought for it. Just as we know, or should know, that none of our domestic problems can be solved within the artificial boundaries of the states, so none of our global problems can be solved within the largely artificial boundaries of nations—artificial not so much in the eyes of history as in the eyes of Nature.

This writer then goes on to say:

> Of all the assumptions I have discussed, that which takes nationalism for granted is perhaps the most deeply rooted and the most tenacious. Yet when we reflect that assumptions, even certainties, no less tenacious in the past—about the very nature of the cosmic system, about the superiority of one race to all others, about the naturalness of women's subordination to men, about the providential order of a class society, about the absolute necessity of a state church or religion—have all given way to the implacable pressure of science and reality, we may conclude that what Tocqueville wrote well over a century ago is still valid:
>
>> The world that is rising into existence is still half encumbered by the remains of the world that is waning into decay; and amid the vast perplexity of human affairs none can say how much of ancient institutions and former customs will remain or how much will completely disappear.

If some of our ancient institutions do not disappear [the writer observes darkly], there is little likelihood that we shall remain.

For all the horrifying implications of such statements, by far the most alarming evidence of the widespread influence and the future peril of this kind of idealistic rhetoric in the halls of academia can be found in the guidebooks published by the World Policy Institute (located at the United Nations Plaza in New York) entitled *Peace and World Order Studies: A Curriculum Guide*.

These guidebooks offer a comprehensive view of well over a hundred world-order majors and study programs at American colleges and universities, along with their course synopses, syllabi, and statements of purpose. More than any other single source I have seen, these guides indicate the incredible degree to which new-world-order thinking has infiltrated the academy.

THE REVOLUTIONARY GOSPEL

For most of these programs, the language of the new world order is no longer theory or mere rhetoric—it is gospel. The only hesitation in any of the literature presented in these books is in expressing openly their clear consensus that nationalism (or pride in one's nation, state, or region) is an ideological travesty and a political dinosaur.

In the introduction to the fourth edition, Peter Dale Scott, a Berkeley professor and former Canadian delegate to the United Nations, states, "Peace studies, while not necessarily committed to more radical proposals for amendment of global problems, still is committed to an enlarged intellectual viewpoint in which such radical critiques of the status quo can be contemplated and discussed."

The excitement of such programs, the author contends, is that they encourage both "global awareness" and a "self-critical attitude" which foments change. Terms such as *hierarchical order* and *authoritarian rule* are profane concepts in such programs, while ideas such as *global unity* and *anarchy* are ideals to be held in reverence.

The third edition of the series of course guides presented comprehensive course outlines on a wide range of courses in globalist issues currently being taught on campuses, in the editor's words, "from Santa Clara to Harvard." The sixty synopses published in that edition were merely the most comprehensive of more than four hundred course and program outlines submitted by colleges and universities all across America.

At UCLA the aim for the Global Issues Program described in the fourth edition of the guide is to examine issues "which have transformed the globe into an interdependent planet" and to prepare students with "international competence, citizen action and personal values for living in the twenty-first-century 'global village.'"

The aim of the curriculum developers at UCLA and many other campuses is to indoctrinate a new generation of Americans into the globalist and nonstatist mode of thinking. That means creating educational structures for thought modification (read that, "thought control") and accepting idealistic theories that will lead inevitably to revolutionary activism.

One such program directive states that the principal requirement for admission is "an open mind." You will recall that such open-mindedness was precisely the goal of the educators Allan Bloom described in his eye-opening bestseller *The Closing of the American Mind*. Open-minded students are those who believe that everything is relative, that there are no absolutes, and that a socialist vision is the only realistic approach to life and society.

According to Professor Walker Bush, the long-term goal of the World Order Program at UCLA is to provide an introductory course in globalist thinking to every entering student. Their aim is, in short, to refocus the entire ethos of higher education. In addition, the university will offer upper-level degrees in various global issues in order to turn out a cadre of new-world-order scholars and strategists.

Along with required reading from the works of Richard Falk and Buckminster Fuller, students study the writings of Norman Cousins, Margaret Mead, Daniel Ellsberg, and other contributors to the literature and mythology of this revolutionary discipline. These are the voices of those who understand the globalist view. For counterpoint, students read the works of the forerunners from the old world order, such as Henry Kissinger, Zbigniew Brezinski, and Cyrus Vance.

RADICAL MYTHS

Christine Sylvester teaches a class entitled Alternative World Futures at Gettysburg College in Pennsylvania. She writes:

We are endangered by structures which encourage a global war system, gross development disequilia, ecological abuse, the violation of human rights, and a "we-they" view of the species. We are also endangered by our seeming inability or disinclination to think seriously and creatively about our options. We are impaled in a world of structural injustice and intellectual paralysis.

The purpose of her course is (1) to foster a politics of species identity; (2) to highlight our collective sources of endangerment; (3) to gain an appreciation of alternative approaches to global management; and (4) to encourage creative, systematic thought on the future.

Required reading includes *The Third Wave* by Alvin Toffler; the novel *The Dispossessed* by Ursula LeGuin; *Toward a Just World Order* by Richard Falk, Samuel Kim, and Saul Mendlovitz; *Mankind at the Turning Point* by Mihajlo Mesarovic and Edward Pestel; and *The Communist Manifesto* by Karl Marx and Friedrich Engels.

Additional reading includes "Religion, Futurism, and Models of Social Change" by Elise Boulding, and "Constructing Models of Presents, Futures, and Transitions: An Approach to Alternative World Futures" by Harry R. Targ.

Among the solutions explored by students in Sylvester's course are a review of utopian ideologies, such as those in LeGuin's science fiction, a review of behaviorist and social engineering models, and in-depth review and writing on the principles of humanistic transformation.

At Amherst, SUNY, Chapel Hill, and Princeton, world order courses focus specifically on women's issues. At the Universities of Florida, Connecticut, Vermont, Northern Illinois, and Columbia, courses focus directly on the methodology of educating both teachers and students into the vocabulary and doctrines of the new world order. To instill the globalist perspective, the system's promoters believe they must train their future leaders from the ground up.

Florida International University's Global Awareness Program (GAP), housed in the School of Education, attempts to act as "a shaper of global futures" by making students more globally minded. Their explicit goal is to train a generation of teachers to see things globally rather than from the traditional perspective of the community, nation, or region.

Professor Arthur Newman at the University of Florida says,

> It is unquestionably wrong to assume naively that the world's schools are able to wave a magic wand and usher in the new millennium. On the other hand, it is just as inexcusable to suggest the converse, i.e., that the schools are impotent as regards engendering an awareness of, identification with, and commitment to universal humankind.

In application, Newman's thesis is intended to discredit the emotions, habits, and historical beliefs associated with nationalism, national sovereignty, and patriotism in order to form a new generation of globalists.

At Syracuse, Virginia Polytechnic, Duke, Tufts, and Denver, courses focus on human rights issues and on reforming the nation's social policies. At Stanford, Colgate, Boston College, Brown, SUNY, Princeton, and others, the prospective student can focus on militarism and the arms race.

SCHOLASTIC GLOBALISTS

Other programs focus on ecological concerns, on hunger and the politics of food distribution, or on the theories associated with the new global economics. But consistently, the view is futurist, applying alternative visions, imaging, and other fanciful means of exploring the promised globalist world-view which they believe is just ahead of us.

Supporting the research and development of all these programs are some 150 foundations, funding agencies, and research councils, ranging from Amnesty International to the World Future Society. Dozens of films and media resources are already available, from PBS documentaries to Time-Life films. The services of an immense range of scholars, statisticians, and scientists are also combined with those of medical, legal, economics, publishing, and theology professionals, to help make the entire globalist community one of the most auspicious and formidable emerging industries in the world today.

Professor Richard Falk of Princeton University has been one of the principal contributors to the new lexicon of world order studies. In his writings—such as his book *The End of World Order*—Falk has helped to clarify the aims and goals of world-order politics, calling for a realignment of national and federal policy in favor of a globalist one-world government. The statements of such works are so logical and dispassionate, one hardly notices their flagrant revolutionary implications.

In describing the context of world-order studies, Falk writes:

> Founded on dissatisfaction with the professional judgment that a statist framework of world politics is here to stay, the world order approach critically examines the durability and adequacy of statism, proposes alternative political frameworks, and considers strategies and scenarios that might facilitate the transition to a post-statist type of world order. Furthermore, it takes the realization of values (peacefulness, economic well-being, social and political justice, ecological balance, and humane governance), rather than materialistic and technological gains, as the decisive criterion of progress in human affairs.

In other words, this professor is helping to promote and define an academic discipline that proposes a general worldwide revolution against nationhood as we now know it in favor of a one-world socialist government. While discrediting technological progress and private property as tokens of the old, militaristic, nationalistic world order, he is calling for the empowerment of ecology, human rights, and socialist activism.

Throughout this movement, as in some throwback to the hippie culture of the 1960s, three predominant concerns stand out in virtually every discussion:

1. Antiwar and antinuclear activism
2. Ecology and environmental protection
3. Emergence of a global New Age religion

Falk writes:

This movement pits the "oppressed" against the entrenched elites, in and out of government, who continue to affirm, however reluctantly, a nuclear future. It is a matter of prediction, not prophecy, to contend that this struggle will intensify in the future and link antinuclear concerns with these wider antimilitary and ecological quality issues.

THE CLASS STRUGGLE, AGAIN?

What Falk describes is a warfare—not unlike a Marxist class struggle—between the oppressed peoples, prodded by their ideological leaders, and what he perceives as the "imperalists" and "militarists" of the world. It is curious how such spokesmen, (hiding behind a facade of antiwar rhetoric) have absolutely no hesitation to threaten violence to accomplish their purposes. But it is also eye-opening to observe that these idealists foresee the potential of a new religious movement within their cause.
Falk writes:

Finally, there is the question of whether, beneath the negotiations, a new, globally oriented religiosity will emerge to generate new myths, creeds, and symbols. This remains a major, perhaps decisive, uncertainty.

For his model of leadership, the author has gone back to the seventeenth century, to Hugo Grotius, a Dutch Calvinist reformer who was imprisoned for his ideas. For the scholar, Grotius represents the radical antiwar activist who was willing to speak out and to suffer for his unpopular beliefs. But more significantly, he is also the model for the future spiritual leader whom Falk believes will come forth to lead the nations. He says:

Perhaps we await a Grotius who can teach us to "see" the shadowland [of political transformation] and, without losing persuasiveness, to accord sufficient status to international developments that depart from the premises of the state system. Grotius came from an independent state in the Protestant north of Europe. . . . One would similarly expect that our Grotius, if he or she emerges, will come from the Third World rather than from the advanced industrial countries. The shadowland is more accessible to those who are victims of the old order and apostles of the new order. . . . Without indulging illusions, I believe that the Grotian quest remains our best hope.

Since its founding in 1968, another group, the Institute for World Order, has been investigating an area called "alternative futures" to determine how national frontiers and interests can be dissolved. At the heart of its World Order Models Projects (WOMP and WOMP II) are a host of related political interests concerning nuclear nonproliferation, human rights activism, social welfare, and the implementation of a new international economic order.

Again, the terms and ideologies of the think tanks are synonymous throughout all the various institutional programs. But over and over, the models and heroes being evaluated by these groups are such forward thinkers as Lenin, Marx, and Trotsky, along with Mao Tse Tung, Mahatma Gandhi, and even Adolf Hitler.

Inspiration for the models and the turn of mind required by these disciplines comes most often from Zen and Hinduism, from New Age clones such as est and Unity, or from science fiction—in works such as Ursula LeGuin's *The Dispossessed*. Is this really the new order that awaits us?

THE GLOBALIST'S CREED

Norman Cousins, the former editor of *Saturday Review* magazine, a bestselling author, and a longtime member of the Council on Foreign Relations, is another prominent contributor to the vocabulary of the new world order. His last work, revised and rereleased in early 1991 some months after his death, is entitled *The Celebration of Life*, and it offers a sort of Socratic dialogue on life and faith and mystical essences.

In this book, first published in 1974, Cousins holds forth an almost poetic image of the "oneness of all life," which is clearly from Hindu thought and mysticism. "Human unity," he says, "is the fulfillment of diversity. It is the harmony of opposites. It is a many-stranded texture, with color and depth."

Together, he reasons, all men and women make up "the oneness of man," and while our lives and memory are "personal and finite," we are part of a universal substance which is "boundless and infinite."

With such a view, it is not difficult to imagine that Cousins could easily espouse a one-world government that scorns individuality, personality, nationhood, and even private property. He notes that Eastern thought, especially in the teachings of Baha Allah, the founder of the Bahai cult, holds that, "The test of spiritual doctrine was in its application to every aspect of life and government." He says, "Baha Allah anticipated the implications of modern destructive science when he advocated world political unity." A thought apparently attractive to the author.

Cousins concludes this final book of his life, in fact, with his own statement of faith, which is his belief that we are all on a shared journey through some sort of mystical unity of body and spirit. He says:

> Together, we share the quest for a society of the whole equal to our needs, a society in which we neither have to kill nor be killed, a society congenial to the full exercise of the creative intelligence, a society in which we need not live under our moral capacity, and in which justice has a life of its own.
> Singly and together, we can live without dread and without helplessness.
> We are single cells in a body of five billion cells. The body is humankind.

Is this really immortality? Is this really the life that God has designed for humankind? Absolutely not. But this is the sort of mystical idealism which pervades so much of modern philosophy and science. With such a dehumanized and impersonal belief, it is no wonder supporters of the one-world ideology find it so easy to assault the ideas of national pride and the sovereignty of independent nations.

THE SCIENTIST AS MYSTIC

Fritjof Capra, another outspoken proponent of one-worldism, was educated as a physicist in Vienna, Paris, and California before becoming a leader of the New Age movement. His book, *The Tao of Physics,* launched his star among West Coast radicals and New Agers with its attempt to demonstrate the mystical elements of natural science. His most recent book, *Uncommon Wisdom,* includes a rambling account of the author's conversations with various scholars, mystics, and sages.

Through his journeys on several continents, dabbling in everything from quantum physics to economics, this spiritual dilettante superimposes his own wistful imagery upon a desperate search for a mystical reality that he hopes will reveal the cosmic unity of all energy and matter.

Like so many voices from the New Age—seekers lost in time and space—Capra is a victim of his own godlessness, a refugee from the hippie culture of the 1960s straining for some hidden reality beyond the perception of his natural senses. He, too, preaches a "challenge to the existing social order" and a mission to seek out "a new vision of reality."

It is sometimes difficult for Christians to understand the implications of such attitudes, since we believe our faith is strong and vital and very much alive. But it is important to realize that these intellectuals have already acknowledged the death of God and the demise of the church as a force in modern culture. Some claim that the publication of *The Communist Manifesto* in 1848 hailed the symbolic death knell of Christendom. Yet few today fail to recognize the need for moral underpinnings in society and even the need for mystical and spiritual values.

In his classic work, *Introduction to International Relations*, Charles P. Schleicher wrote that traditional religion is a dividing force in modern society that pits one group against another over emotional issues and which encourages bloody rivalries. He suggests that only the "decline in religious faith" in this century has helped to reduce social conflict. But more pointedly, he writes:

> There are those who believe that only a universal religion to which men are fervently devoted, one which unites men in devotion to a single god and in a common brotherhood, will serve to overcome divisions among men and the worship of the secular nation-state.

Obviously, Christians agree that faith builds brotherhood and understanding, but the scholar's pragmatic view of religion as a sort of social solvent is not particularly comfortable. Nevertheless, in light of the utopian heritage of today's vision of a new world order, the idea that the state or some other political institutions would aspire to divine authority is not at all surprising.

THE COUNTERCULTURE

In a 1968 work edited by Harvard scholar Stanley Hoffman and entitled *Conditions of World Order*, the European scholar Helio Jaguaribe takes the perspective that the spiritual context of life in the coming world order will be the moral responsibility, not of the church, but of the intellectuals. It is the intellectuals, he says, who have the vision and the objectivity to represent "the spiritual unity of men, beyond any conflict of interests, ideologies, and religions."

More sinister though, Jaguaribe also says that the scholars' task includes "the destruction of all romantic illusions regarding the good old days and the smug security provided by a Christian cosmos." In order to build a religion of the state, the scholar must first work to dismantle the religion of the church.

For an idea of what sort of doctrines a religion of the state would enshrine, it may be helpful to look at the work of one powerful organization, the Club of Rome. Citing the forward-thinking plans of the Club of Rome—the notorious pro-death group that preaches the doctrine of Zero Population Growth—many new order advocates support abortion as a practical means of birth control, and they support euthanasia as a way of ridding the new order of the old, the feeble, the tired, and the unproductive. This is their humanistic spiritual reality.

The Club of Rome in its 1976 report entitled *Reshaping the International Order* said that we live in a divided world: on one side is the rich world of the developed nations, on the other, the poor world of the underdeveloped. In saying that a "poverty curtain" divides these worlds, both materially and philosophically, they write:

> One world is literate, the other largely illiterate; one industrial and urban, the other predominantly agrarian and rural; one consumption oriented, the other striving for survival. In the rich world, there is concern about the quality of life, in the poor world about life itself which is threatened by disease, hunger and malnutrition.

The writers and researchers wrote that today there is a new search for order in the world, a new philosophy in which the rich nations are required to contribute materially to the welfare of the poor. "In a fast shrinking planet," they said, "it was inevitable that this 'new' philosophy would not stop at national borders; and, since there is no world government, the poor nations are bringing this concern to its closest substitute, the United Nations."

They observe, ominously, that "the rich cannot conceal their wealth in a 'global village.' The glaring differences are perceived by the poor thanks, perhaps paradoxically, to the rich world's technological dexterity. And their perception of these differences will, in a shrinking world, exert growing stress on already frail international institutions." Then they add that "the adjustment needed in the long terms is undoubtedly to be found in an increased flow of funds from the rich to the poor nations."

One has to wonder how this differs from outright communism! Their proposal is, in fact, an ideology known as state socialism. They want a world where those who work and produce and enjoy a high standard of living pay, not only taxes to support their own federal bureaucracy and welfare institutions through constantly rising taxes, but additional taxes to support the poor nations of the world who do not work or produce effectively.

But be certain, they do not expect government to take money from existing revenues to support this Third World. They know, without a doubt, that government will simply levy new taxes. What they are saying, then, is that you and I must pay more taxes to the government to support the Third World, and we must trust that our money will be used for good purposes and not simply more guns, more revolution, more graft and corruption, and more of the same folly that has kept the Third World largely unprofitable and unproductive throughout history.

The Club of Rome researchers propose a new international Treaty of Rome that would lay down the "rules of the international game," and which calls for, in its final provisions, a one-world government. This is spelled out in detail, with specific provisions and codes, in the documents of the report.

THE LIMITS OF REASON

Predictably, scholars such as Richard Falk have nothing but praise for the Club of Rome's initiative and insight in their search for a world-order hypothesis. He says, "The Club of Rome represents perhaps the most significant effort to date to gain a hearing for an interpretation of the future presented in quantitative forms and offered as new knowledge."

In their Project on the Predicament of Mankind, executed in 1970, the Club hired a group of MIT scholars, headed by Jay Forrester, to conduct a sophisticated research project based on global factors. Falk writes that "their purpose was to design a world model for computer analysis organized around the interactions of dynamic processes such as resource use, food production, population growth, capital investment, and industrial output." Their study was eventually published in the 1972 book *The Limits to Growth*.

Many critical reviewers and analysts said that Forrester's computer was reacting to insufficient data and crying "wolf." Even though Falk commended the research, he admitted that "Futurology is intrinsically flawed by the tension between the methodology and its policy recommendations. The method is not presently capable of producing a convincing argument unless it is supplemented by subjective factors—judgments, values, preferences."

But then the Princeton professor goes on to commend another writer, William Irwin Thompson, who in the process of taking issue with some of the technological failures of the Rome report, calls for a new spiritual dynamic to give vitality to such projections.

Falk writes:

Thompson believes that a new consciousness, based on a new spiritual awareness and appreciation of the realities of planetary culture, is a necessary precondition for any kind of successful response to the world order crises now being acknowledged even by statesmen. As Thompson put it, "If you are going to humanize technology, you're not going to be able to do it without the limited terms of books and civilization and other older containers. You've got to go very far out."

So what does he mean by "far out"? Specifically he proposes "a reunion of scientific and mystical thinking in small-scale institutions that embody a vision of the future." Suddenly Falk's own imagery is alive with models, and he proposes that Hermann Hesse's mystical novel *Magister Ludi* is the very model of such a spiritual linkage of power which merits closer study.

He goes on to say,

> For America, at least, it is morally and hence intellectually impossible to propose a new Jerusalem and yet at the same time remain agnostic or indifferent about genocide and ecocide in Indochina. . . . These comments about a new consciousness are designed to set the stage for an inquiry into the future of world order. . . . With these considerations in mind, it seems possible and desirable, indeed necessary, to propose new ways of envisioning—really revisioning—the future so as to break the bonds of present constraints on moral and political imagination. My primary purpose is therefore educational, to awaken man's reason to the idea of wholeness as the basis for individual or collective sanity.

Isn't it interesting that Falk, like the European scholars mentioned earlier, links the terms *intellectual* and *moral*. He is in fact contending that the scholar, not the priest, is the arbiter of morality.

THE PRICE OF FREEDOM

In another essay entitled "The Trend Toward World Community," included in the Festschrift *The Search for World Order*, Professor Falk writes, "[T]here are many signs of reaction against traditions of blind patriotism, at least in the liberal democracies of the West—in countries, that is, that are both modern and generally indulgent of political dissent."

The author says further that "traditional political symbols have lost much of their meaning. Partly it arises from the positive appeal of transnational moral and legal norms which embody both a generalized revulsion against unjust war, and a kind of cosmopolitan humanism that extends compassion to any victim [of] society. And partly it reflects the renewed appeal of anarchistic politics, with its opposition to all claims over life asserted on behalf of the sovereign state." Are we to understand such observations as fact, or merely as the scholar's wishful thinking?

But he goes on to say,

> There is also now occasion and need for a reorientation of ideas of national citizenship and national interest. In the socializing process that goes on in principal societies of the world, the essential need is to associate "security" more closely with the attainment of world unity than with national or even

regional separatism, and to this, education of the young could make a very large contribution. One may hope that the elites throughout the world will begin to be constituted and served by individuals who have been socialized in such a way that they see global norms as automatically relevant to the choice of means to implement societal goals.

It is interesting to note that this author also glows with the observations that the Teheran Conference of the United Nations on Human Rights passed a resolution declaring that developed countries are under a moral obligation to donate 1 percent of their entire GNP to the poor countries. He also notes that the newly revised charter of the Organization of American States argues for much the same principle. Both of these documents argue for the principle of *community* over those of *sovereignty*.

Falk also says that already, "in all major countries there are developing counter-elite groups with a futuristic and cosmopolitan conception of the proper organization of social and political life." Even if they fail to gain power, such groups will continue to foment revolt, resistance, and dissatisfaction within existing governments, whatever their stripe.

THE WISDOM OF THE ACADEMY

This is the wisdom of the academy. This is the rhetoric professors are drilling into our children at this very moment. Even if only a handful of students buy the rhetoric or respond in some fashion with their lives, what will the long-range implications of such radical ideology be? Remember that Falk is the same man who says that a new religiosity (presumably a New Age-type religion) is needed to shape the "myths, creeds, and symbols" of the new world order.

How will these educators change the world? Can they make a radical change in the way our young men and women behave? Harvard Professor Stanley Hoffman, in his book *Primacy or World Order*, writes, "What will have to take place is a gradual adaptation of the social, economic, and political system of the United States to the imperatives of world order." Clearly, educators are prepared to follow John Dewey's model of a slow, persistent, and relentless re-education of America's values and mores. Having seen the fruit of Dewey's labor, can anyone doubt what havoc the prophets of the new order will wreak?

The American system has lived to see the total collapse of the Soviet economy. Gorbachev, who came to our doorstep begging for aid, survived the apparent threats to his life during the August 1991 "coup," then emerged with the support of the enigmatic Boris Yeltsin. But now, with what appears to be fresh evidence of the Russian democratic spirit, the scholars are racing once again to cede the moral advantage to the Soviets.

Hoffman writes, "[T]he demands of world order entail a painful process of discovery for many Americans. They will have to realize that others do not share all our values and practices and that the world is not a field in which we can go and apply our preferred policies and techniques with impunity."

Education of the young to a new way of thinking must begin in the academy: teaching teachers who teach students who, in turn, grow into predictable products of the system. It is the conviction of these world-order advocates that subtle, patient, and gradual changes in education, shaping the minds of the youth of our democratic nations, will bring the real victory of the new world order.

Hoffman writes, "[A] world order policy is a pattern of education. By trial and error, American leaders must show the people whom they represent why traditional policies must change and obtain enough support to turn these changes into new laws, institutions, and habits. And American intellectuals must keep trying, not to behave as if the world of power were the kingdom of heaven, but to enlighten the public and the leaders about the problems of the present world, about the demands of world order, about the pitfalls of any attempt to meet them, and about the greater peril of politics-as-usual."

FALSE MESSIAHS

Since Dewey began his notorious career at Columbia, twisting and shaping the values and behaviors of American scholars and teachers, the secular establishment has been patiently and persistently dismantling America's inherited value system and its ethical foundations.

In times past their cause was most clearly identified in the language of communism, socialism, humanism, and anarchy. Today the language of the new world order offers a whole new vocabulary and an even more sinister agenda for reshaping our world for its ends. It is universalist, globalist, and spiritual in nature. And since it brings with it, in its very language, the specter of Apocalypse, it may well be the most threatening vision of reality ever conceived.

The false prophets of humanism are committed to their agenda of radical change, and they will not spare any means of bringing about their ends. Whether it is slow, like the work of the wind and rain, or fast, like a military revolution, they are committed to this struggle.

In *The Gold of the Gods*, Erich Von Daniken, a scholar and a dreamer, said,

I suspect that with the step into the interstellar third millennium the end of terrestrial polytheism will inevitably come.

With the assumption that we are all parts of the mighty IT, God no longer has to be simultaneously good and bad in some inconceivable way; He is no longer responsible for sorrow and happiness, for ordeals and acts of providence. We ourselves have the positive and negative powers within us, because we come from the IT that always was.

Such sentiments are hardly different from those of New Age celebrity Shirley MacLaine who, in *Dancing in the Light*, appropriated the language of God Almighty in her statement at the end of the book, "I AM that I AM." The new mystical order and the new secular order are hardly different in their ultimate ambitions.

In his 1979 book, *Tides Among Nations*, Karl W. Deutsch appropriated the language of the Messiah in his declaration that, through the patient and dedicated effort of reformers, "Humanity will be able to take its own fate into its own hands, and see to it that our children, and our children's children, shall have life and have it more abundantly." Clearly, such visionaries have no need of the kingdom of God or of His Christ, since they are driven by the compelling vision that they "shall be as gods."

What are the implications of such beliefs? In the following chapter I would like to examine these and other promises of the new secular agenda in greater detail and review the long-range implications of the ongoing manipulation of America's hopes, dreams, and its place in the world.

8

New Order for the New Age

A SIGNIFICANT SEGMENT of the forces birthing the new world order is not motivated merely by economic, sociological, or ecological concerns. To be sure, the most highly placed players are clearly centered around the banking-corporate-foundation nexus of big money, and their principal goal appears to be control of the banking power of a world government, along with the power such authority would give them over elected politicians and their policies.

However, when the spiritual dimensions of the new world order are discussed, they invariably take on the appearance of what we have come to know as the New Age. Author Tal Brooke, whose book *When the World Will Be As One* details the satanic background of the New Age, was at one time a disciple of a Hindu holy man, Sai Baba. Sai Baba was possessed by one of a group of powerful demons known to New Agers as "ascended masters."

Brooke wrote in July 1991, in his *SCP Journal,*

One of the dangers of the New Age Movement is that it is the perfect creed for globalism. It can syncretize with any faith except Christianity. It does not use the language of judgment or sin, but speaks in sweeping terms—about the sacredness of nature and the spark of divinity in the human race. It uses positive language and idealized human potential. It is utterly post modern and outwardly far more attractive to post-Christian baby boomers than the "outmoded" church. It is up to date, vogue, and politically correct. It could also undergird a planetary faith or spawn something else that will—such as Gaia. In brief, the New Age movement, and its progeny, Gaia, are spiritually correct for a new world order. Christianity is not.

A generic spirituality is necessary to fuse diverse, even hostile, cultures and faiths into a unity. To fit the world together, religious boundaries must be eliminated.

To those of us who realize the invisible spiritual dimension of the struggle to overthrow the existing world order and its Christian roots, the emergence of a New Age world religion is of paramount importance, because the human potential movement, as if part of a continuum, invariably leads to psychic power; and occult power leads straight to demonic power; and these lead, in turn, to a single source of evil identified by the Bible as Satan (the adversary), the Devil (the accuser), Lucifer (the light one), or Abaddon (the one who rules over hell and destruction).

To understand this concern, I recommend a careful reading of a 1977 book by Dusty Sklar, called *The Nazis and the Occult,* which details what happens to a government and its people when occultic forces begin to influence its leaders. Occultism was pervasive among the leaders of Nazi Germany, and it clearly influenced their ghastly programs for world domination.

THE SPIRITUAL NATION

Regardless of what anyone may say, America is still a religious nation. The court system and various liberal action groups in this country have tried for more than forty years to dismantle America's religious heritage, but they have not entirely succeeded, and by the grace of God they may not if the revival of Christian values continues to surge forth in the coming years as it has in the past decade.

Washington scholar James Reichley, a senior fellow at the Brookings Institute, reported in his book *Religion in American Public Life* that more than 90 percent of all Americans identify with some religious faith, and on any given Sunday more than 40 percent attend church. The common theology of America is not strict Christianity but what Reichley calls "theist-humanism," that is, a general religious view of the world with the specific duality of Christ's admonition to love the Lord thy God and to love they neighbor as thyself.

Despite the statistical evidence, the dominant value system in American society during this century, Reichley says, has become a sort of *secular egoism* combined with a flexible *economic individualism*. This radical consumerist view has taken such a commanding lead in the world's value system that it has led, irrevocably, to a glorification of the self and to conspicuous self-gratification, so easily seen in advertising, popular psychological therapy, and entertainment.

According to the numbers, mainline Protestant denominations make up roughly 30 percent of the U.S. population; Roman Catholics make up 25 percent; white evangelical Protestants make up about 20 percent; Black Protestant churches add about 8 percent; Jews are about 3 percent; and others, ranging from Mormons to Hare Krishnas, contribute an additional 5 percent. The remainder are presumably unaffiliated with any particular faith.

It was Joseph Schumpeter who pointed out that the doctrine of Marxism was essentially theological in nature, identifying the proletariat as the chosen people and the state as the ultimate ecclesiastical authority. But if Reichley's observations are correct, the doctrine of capitalism is no less theological, only in this case the god of this new secular religion is the self.

We see the teachings of this theology of self in books, magazines, and activities of every description: self-awareness materials; tapes, videos, and seminars for self-actualization; the national fascination with muscles, fitness, health, and beauty; a growing demand for luxury and creature comforts, even in the face of a difficult recession; and magazines such as *Us* and *Self* and many others that glorify the individual man or woman.

Despite the various religious affiliations Americans claim in the polls and surveys, secular civil humanism (what is generally known as secular humanism) has become the prevailing ideology of most of America's intellectuals and cultural elite. This is a doctrine of the self that traces its roots to the ancient Greeks and was perhaps best expressed by Protagoras (who gave the humanists their essential credo) in his statement that "Man is the measure of all things."

DARK SECRETS

The theosophist author and founder of the Arcane School, Alice Bailey, was reportedly the first to use the term *New Age* and also the first to expropriate the image of "the Christ" for New Age purposes. As a prototype of the priestly ascended masters—whom Bailey and other occultists claimed to be involved in working out mankind's spiritual destiny from some remote Himalayan retreat—the New Age Christ was transformed from the true Son of God to a convenient symbol. Bailey claimed her own words were transmitted to her telepathically by the Tibetan Djuhal Khul, who predicted the appearance of a new world government and a world religion. She followed a New Age Christ.

Members of Adolf Hitler's occultic organization within the National Socialist party, the Thule-Gesellschaft, had referred to themselves as the founders of *die neue Zeit*, the New Age, and they promised a thousand-year reign and a mystical godlike transcendence. Like the Rosicrucians and the higher orders of Masons, the Nazis practiced secret ceremonies that invoked mystical powers and included the worship of Lucifer, their god of light.

During the 1930s and 1940s, it was clear that Hitler saw himself as the father of a new world order. He preached a doctrine of Aryan supremacy, and he apparently believed himself to be the Messiah, the promised one, who would lead the world out of darkness into the light. That was just *one* false Messiah.

Years later the British New Ager Benjamin Creme proclaimed that the true Messiah—a combination of Jesus Christ, the Buddhist Lord Meitreya, and the Muslim Mahdi, all rolled into one—was already here and living in east London. Then, with the immense resources of the Tara Center, a New Age headquarters, he paid for full-page ads in many of the leading newspapers of the world in which he declared this millenarian vision.

New Agers of all stripes continued to long for "transcendence" and "transformation," which makes them natural prophets of and contributors to society's insatiable longing for a new world order. In light of the growing spiritual awareness of all fronts in the past two decades, mystics and sages are declaring the imminent arrival of a new spiritual order which coincides with the political vision. According to New Age author Peter Lemesurier of Scotland's Findhorn Institute,

> Extraordinary things are happening. Great and far-reaching changes are afoot. A strange, autonomous transformation is spreading like some irresistible virus through society. . . . Whether founded on factual evidence or merely on a desperate rejection of the idea that things can possibly go on as they are, the word is out that a new age is upon us, a new dispensation ready to begin, a revolutionary World Order about to supervene.

In an effort to correct the drift, so to speak, of the New Age movement and refocus some of its dualistic thinking, Lemesurier has prepared an astonishingly comprehensive overview of the various heresies, treacheries, cults, plots, and counterfeits (although he would not describe them in those terms) that have paraded as theological wisdom over the past thirty-five hundred years. In his book *This New Age Business*, the latest of his half-dozen offerings, he says that the New Age and the new world order are essentially synonymous concepts that have co-existed since man's emergence from Eden. Of this unified order he writes:

> At one time or another, indeed, it has been regarded as only common sense by large parts of the Earth's population. "New Ageism"—or millenarianism in its broadest sense—is in fact one of the oldest and most widespread ideas known to humanity. And to this day it remains (as the writings of Mikhail Gorbachev explicitly make clear) every bit as basic to the official outlook of the Marxist East as it does to that of the capitalist and science-oriented West.

KINGDOMS OF GOD AND MAN

The idea of a marriage of secular and spiritual images in the new world order is disturbingly real and potentially very dangerous. Certainly Alice Bailey, believed in it, and in her 1947 book *Problems of Humanity*, she wrote:

> The Kingdom of God will inaugurate a world which will be one in which it will be realized that—politically speaking—humanity, as a whole, is of far greater importance than any one nation; it will be a new world order, built upon different principles to those in the past, and one in which men will carry the spiritual vision into their national governments, into their economic planning and into all measures taken to bring about security and right human relations.

Bailey's spiritual vision was both sacred and profane, secular and occult, and she held out a metaphysical image of world order in which the individual was to be swallowed up in the state and individual nations were to be subsumed within a global community. This view was the political equivalent of the Hindu oversoul, or, as Norman Cousins described it, the image of a single human cell surrounded by 5 billion identical and anonymous cells of equal shape and value. Bailey said that:

> What we need above all to see—as a result of spiritual maturity—is the abolition of those two principles which have wrought so much evil in the world and which are summed up in the two words: Sovereignty and Nationalism.

That is such a shocking statement for our traditional sensibilities, but isn't it really the same ideology being touted by today's new world order advocates: a globalist world without national sovereignty or independence and a zeal for global political unity of spiritual dimensions?

In the late eighteenth century, the English philosopher Edmund Burke said that man is by nature a religious animal. Burke understood that man has a deep, heartfelt need for spiritual significance and purpose and that these emotions could only be satisfied by religious experience. The French thinker Blaise Pascal had expressed much the same thought a hundred years earlier in his maxim that there exists a God-shaped vacuum in the human heart that only God can fill. But for the passionate seekers in the New Age, the political agenda leaves little room for traditional moral values, and the religious agenda leaves little room for the rights of freedom-loving men.

If you consider the aims and the pervasiveness of such rich and powerful movements as Silva Mind Control, Eckankar, est (or the forum), Scientology, Unity, the Course in Miracles, various forms of ancestor and spirit worship, channeling, ufology, and crystalology—not to mention the renewed interest in more classical Eastern religions, from Zen Buddhism to Taoism—it is easy to see how spiritual visionaries such as Alice Bailey and L. Ron Hubbard could so easily exploit and despoil the historic values of this nation.

As early as 1978, a Gallup Poll reported that more than 10 million Americans were involved in some form of Eastern mysticism or activities associated with the New Age movement, and another 9 million are involved in some form of holistic and spiritual healing. With the continued growth of the human potential movement and sensitivity seminars in hundreds of America's largest corporations, this disturbing trend continues to grow and gain new converts year after year.

A SUBVERSIVE AGENDA

Willis Harman, formerly a social scientist at SRI International and now a consultant to U.S. corporations, government agencies, and various other institutions, is a highly sought-after New Age author and lecturer. His book, *Global Mind Change,* describes the ways that globalist, occultic, and one-world thinking are infiltrating the elite establishments of both Europe and the United States.

Harman is just one of the thousands of "counselors" being invited by training directors into U.S. companies to teach employee seminars on principles of creativity, imagination, and intuition—concepts derived exclusively from occultic practices that promise to enhance both the practical and the spiritual powers of its practitioners.

As with Fritjof Capra, whom I mentioned in the last chapter, such self-styled corporate gurus are trying to bring about a mystical fusion of science and spirituality—to heal the fragmentation of the human soul, in their own terms—which is very much in keeping with the growing belief that the new world order will bring about both a spiritual and a political unity.

In *The Crime of World Power*, Richard A. Aliano writes, "Ideology may be considered merely as the rationalization of self interest." It has been used as such in times past in order to motivate, inspire, and threaten, but he says that an ideology—whether it is that of a capitalist, socialist, or spiritual regime—is always presented by its proponents as truth and as the ultimate expression of reality.

Seemingly, that is the situation we are confronted with today. Presented as truth and reality, the ideology of a new world order being offered is, in fact, a rationalization for some form of political or spiritual self-interest and a means of achieving a particular end.

As I review the literature of the New Age and examine the self-evident trends within it, I am continually aware of three particular ends that surface again and again:

1. The subversion and denial of divine revelation
2. The deification of the self
3. The submersion of the individual personality within a larger whole

THE DARING HYPOTHESIS

If you are a religious skeptic, I invite you to suspend your judgment for a moment and explore a challenging concept with me. If you are a Christian or a Jew, I invite you to think about this scenario. Suppose that a powerful spiritual being, a supernatural force such as Satan, a being who is contrary to God and opposed to whatever He does, wanted to overthrow the kingdom of God and to install himself in the seat of power. What would be his agenda? How would he go about implementing such as plan?

First, he would have to cast doubts on God's authority and righteousness. He would have to subvert and undermine God's work among men and His guiding principles whenever and wherever possible. In some cases he could do this himself, but to be fully effective in a world such as ours he would need surrogates, agents, and representatives to carry out this mission among his potential subjects—the nearly 5 billion inhabitants of this planet.

Very likely he would use spiritual beings for this duty, and they could be very effective since they would be both unseen and sinister. But to reach effectively into human society he would have to recruit tens of thousands of willing servants among the sons of men to represent him to other men, not as an evil or sinister force, but as an enticing, wise, loving, and powerful force.

Instead of a source of hate and deception, he would want to persuade men and women that his motives were just, that he had been deprived of his rightful place of authority. He would need to show how mankind is, even now, struggling from darkness toward the light that only he can offer. That would, seemingly, be his natural first objective.

Second, he would no doubt feel that he could easily attract followers with the promise that they could share his kingdom. They, too, would be as gods, have power and dominion, rule the air, the sea, the sky, and hold eternity within their grasp. Poetic metaphors could barely grasp the grandness of such a vision, and the human ego could hardly bear the images of joy such a promise would hold out.

But if his first motive were truly subversion—to overthrow the God of the universe and supplant His authority—not all his methods would necessarily be clean and pure. He would have to do some dark and underhanded things from time to time—which is just common sense; after all, all is fair in love and war, isn't it?—so in some cases he would have to make people understand that dark is light and light is dark. In other words, he would need to create an environment in which any subversive and destructive act would be appropriate and irreproachable.

Third, if his ambition were to rise to godship and to wield divine authority in the world, he could not really share his power. To divide his kingdom would be to take away a part of his glory and dominion, so he would quickly need to submerge this divinity he had promised his subjects in some sort of oversoul or some other cosmic disguise which, in reality, is powerless and noncompetitive with him.

As in the objective stated above, he would also have to convince his would-be followers that the loss of their authority and identity would be the beginning of their godlike powers. Jesus Christ once said (under quite different circumstances) that he who would find his life must lose it. Surely the aspiring sovereign could apply Christ's words for his own purposes.

It is not hard to see that this very simple plan, if applied patiently and consistently over time, could be very effective. Were it not for the power of the authentic God and His followers among men, the job would be much easier. The institutions of the church, evangelical Christians (who actually believe what they profess), and any other recognition of God would be obstructions to his plan. But knowing the weak character of man and mankind's tendency to bend to persistent pressure, this supernatural interloper could surely have his way with the world over time.

THE GRAND DESIGN

It is as if a giant plan is unfolding, everything perfectly on cue. Europe sets the date for its union. Communism collapses. A hugely popular war is fought in the Middle East. The United Nations is rescued from scorn by an easily swayed public. A new world order is announced. Christianity has been battered in the public arena, and New Age religions are in place in the schools and corporations, and among the elite. Then a financial collapse accelerates the move toward a world money system.

The United States cannot afford defense, so it turns its defense requirements over to the United Nations, along with its sovereignty. The United Nations severely limits property rights and clumps down on all Christian evangelism and Christian distinctives under the Declaration of the Elimination of All Forms of Intolerance and Discrimination Based on Religious Belief already adopted by the General Assembly on November 25, 1981.

Then the New Age religion of humanity becomes official, and the new world order leaders embrace it. Then they elect a world president with plenary powers who is totally given to the religion of humanity.

Forty-five years ago such a scenario would have been unthinkable— but the unthinkable is happening. On July 26, 1991, Haynes Johnson wrote a piece in the *Washington Post* reporting a poll which stated "59 percent of the public believes that United Nations resolutions 'should rule over the actions and laws of individual countries, including the United States.'"

He also stated, "They want the United Nations, not the United States, to take the lead in solving international conflicts . . . as head of an international combat force that wages war." This poll may have been rigged to further condition the public toward globalism. But assuming it is accurate, we may presume that the Persian Gulf War has proved to be an enormous success for the globalists in creating a groundswell reversal of public opinion against the interests of this country.

In earlier chapters, we have traced the infiltration of Continental Freemasonry by the new world philosophy of the Order of the Illuminati, and its subsequent role in the French Revolution. We then were able to find clear documentation that the occultic-oriented secret societies claiming descent from Illuminism and the French Revolution played a seminal role in the thinking of Marx and Lenin.

In fact, one historian has asserted that wealthy and influential Europeans with direct roots to Illuminism operated a very secret society out of Geneva, which in fact controlled the Bolshevik movement. We also know that Lord Milner of the British Round Table and Jacob Schiff, of Federal Reserve Board creator Paul Warburg's banking firm, gave the essential seed money to finance the Russian Revolution.

But where is the link between the Continental Illuminati occultic influences on communism and British and American financial support of the same cause? Let's continue.

THE MASONIC CONNECTION

We do not know whether such a tie does exist; there is not presently any known direct evidence to support it. However, one magazine source, whose data have not been verified, indicated that all of the French membership on the Trilateral Commission were members of French Freemasonry. This may just be a coincidence, or it may mean that prominent Frenchmen are also Masons, or it may actually be the missing link tying these sordid elements together.

In any event, this book would be incomplete without a look at the impact of Freemasonry on the current thought processes moving toward a new world. To quote from the *Encyclopedia Britannica*:

> Having begun in medieval times as an association of craftsmen, hence its name—Freemasonry has been since the eighteenth century a speculative system. It admits adherents of all faiths, claiming to be based upon those fundamentals of religion held in common by all men . . . it is secret in so far as it has rituals and other matters which those admitted take an oath never to divulge.

But then the encyclopedist goes on to say:

> Since 1738 the Roman Catholic Church repeatedly has declared those of its faithful who join the fraternity to be guilty of grave sin and therefore excommunicated; the chief reason for this is that the church holds that the beliefs of Freemasonry constitute a deistic or pagan religion.

It is obvious from the teachings of Freemasonry that its doctrines are not Christian but indeed track identically with the syncretism of the so-called New Age religions of today. I think it is especially interesting that one of the official publications of American Masons was called until 1990 *The New Age*.

The power of the Masonic Order was extraordinary, and in England it quickly spread among the highest classes. Lord Alexander, General Alexander Hamilton, Quartermaster General Robert Moray, the Earl of Erroll, Lord Pitsligo, and the Duke of Richmond were members in the

1600s. The aristocracy completely took over the leadership. According to the *Britannica*:

> From 1737 to 1907 about sixteen English princes of royal blood joined the order. The list of past grand masters included eight princes who later become monarchs: George IV, Edward VII, Edward VIII and George VI of England; Oscar II and Gustav V of Sweden; and Frederick VIII and Christian X of Denmark.

With this incredibly array of royal power associated with Freemasonry, can we believe it possible that the powerful Cecil Rhodes and his secret society did not have some involvement with the Freemasons of England or those on the Continent?

CONTRASTING VIEWS

In the United States we know the various Masonic lodges as being composed of people who are engaged in a number of projects for community betterment. In my community, the Shriners sponsor the Oyster Bowl, which pits collegiate football teams in a contest to raise money for crippled children. Their slogan, "Strong legs will run, that weak legs may walk," his enormous appeal. Their benevolent traditions are commendable.

Both George Washington and Benjamin Franklin were Masons. If there is a dark side to Freemasonry, and there is, it should be carefully pointed out that the average American Mason—especially those in the lower orders—is not in any way aware of it. If he were a student of the Bible, he would realize that the Masonic rituals are neither biblical nor Christian, but most Americans know very little about the Bible. To them Freemasonry is a family-centered, fraternal, benevolent organization.

Earlier we pointed out that Adam Weishaupt (the founder of the Order of the Illuminati) had determined to infiltrate the Continental branch of Freemasonry. Weishaupt had been indoctrinated into Egyptian occultism in 1771 by a merchant of unknown origin named Kolmer, who had been seeking European converts. It was said that for five years Weishaupt formulated a plan by which all occultic systems could be reduced to a single powerful organization. He launched the Order of the Illuminati just two months prior to the drafting of the American colonies' Declaration of Independence.

Apparently Weishaupt tried assiduously to promote the concept that the Illuminati, whose offices in Bavaria had been raided and closed down, were therefore merely a transitory phenomenon. But Illuminism was not transitory, and Weishaupt's principles, his disciples, and his influence continue to resurface to this day.

Virtually every single proponent of a complete new world order repeats Weishaupt's concepts, virtually word for word. Here are his revolutionary, destructive goals:

1. Abolition of monarchies and all ordered governments
2. Abolition of private property and inheritances
3. Abolition of patriotism and nationalism
4. Abolition of family life and the institution of marriage, and the establishment of communal education for children
5. Abolition of all religion

In 1921, English historian Nesta Webster, author of *World Revolution*, wrote,

> This is the precise language of internationalists today, and it is, of course, easy to point out the evils of exaggerated patriotism. But it will not be found that the man who loves his country is less able to respect foreign patriots any more than the man who loves his family is a worse neighbor than one who cares little for wife and children.

Weishaupt's goal was not just the destruction of monarchy, but the destruction of society. In July 1782, Continental Freemasonry was infiltrated and captured by what Weishaupt called Illuminated Freemasonry. I have read a report by a former Mason, Comte de Virieu, who related his shock at the infiltration of Freemasonry in these words:

> Tragic secrets. I will not confide them to you. I can only tell you that all this is very much more serious than you think. The conspiracy which is being woven is so well thought out that it will be impossible for the Monarchy and the Church to escape it.

THE MISSING LINK?

That same year, 1782, the headquarters of Illuminated Freemasonry moved to Frankfurt, a center controlled by the Rothschild family. It is reported that in Frankfurt, Jews for the first time were admitted to the order of Freemasons. If indeed members of the Rothschild family or their close associates were polluted by the occultism of Weishaupt's Illuminated Freemasonry, we may have discovered the link between the occult and the world of high finance. Remember, the Rothschilds financed Cecil Rhodes in Africa; Lord Rothschild was a member of the inner circle of

Rhodes's English Round Tables; and Paul Warburg, architect of the Federal Reserve System, was a Rothschild agent.

New money suddenly poured into the Frankfurt lodge, and from there a well-funded plan for world revolution was carried forth. During a Masonic congress in 1786, the deaths of both Louis XVI of France and Gustavus III of Sweden were decreed.

William Still, in his book on the new world order, indicates that the Illuminati, with their Masonic front organization, were actually a secret society within a secret society. In 1798, Professor John Robison, a highly respected British historian and longtime Mason, wrote in his *Proofs of a Conspiracy*.

> I have found that the covert secrecy of a Mason Lodge has been employed in every country for venting and propagating sentiments in religion and politics, that could not have been circulated in public without exposing the author to grave danger. I have observed these doctrines gradually diffusing and mixing with all the different systems of Free Masonry till, at last, AN ASSOCIATION HAS BEEN FORMED FOR THE EXPRESS PURPOSE OF ROOTING OUT ALL OF THE RELIGIOUS ESTABLISHMENTS, AND OVERTURNING ALL THE EXISTING GOVERNMENTS OF EUROPE.

The publishers of Robison's book commented, "A conspiracy conceived not by Masons as Masons, but by evil men using Freemasonry as a vehicle for their own purposes."

Weishaupt enticed people into Illuminated Freemasonry with promises of influence, power, and worldly success. But he also ensured that the members were so compromised by personal revelations about themselves or even the commission of crimes, that denying the order could bring disgrace or even prison. He, and the Masons, had lower orders of rank where the initiates were either lied to or kept in the dark about further secrets. But his biggest appeal was to raw, naked power. He wrote,

> The pupils are convinced that the Order will rule the world. Every member therefore becomes a ruler. We all think of ourselves as qualified to rule. It is therefore an alluring thought both to good and bad men. Therefore the Order will spread.

Perhaps more than anything, the following candid admission by Weishaupt can explain the secret of the Illuminati and all those who are seeking world power:

> Do you realize sufficiently what it means to rule—to rule in a secret society? Not only over the lesser or more important of the populace, but over the best men, over men of all ranks, nations, and religions, to rule without external force, to unite them indissolubly, to breathe one spirit and soul into them, men distributed over all parts of the world.

Perhaps this statement answers the question I raised in the first section of this book: how could a concept like world order be kept alive and vital for two hundred years? If successive generations of men indeed bought into Weishaupt's occultic dream of power, they could indeed be willing (or obligated) to perpetuate it.

TO GAIN THE WHOLE WORLD

Members of the Illuminati at the highest levels of the order were atheists and Satanists. To the public they professed a desire to make mankind "one good and happy family." They made every effort to conceal their true purposes by use of the name of Freemasonry. By every ruse imaginable, the Illuminists were able to attract to their numbers the rich and powerful of Europe, very possibly including Europe's most powerful bankers.

Illuminism reportedly had large wealth at its disposal. Its influence is clearly alive and powerful today in the doctrines of both the one-world communists and the one-world captains of wealth.

Before we leave the influence of Freemasonry on the quest for a New Age and new world order, we should examine the writings of Albert Pike, whose *Morals and Dogma of the Ancient and Accepted Scottish Rite of Freemasonry* was first published in 1871 and subsequently republished in 1966. It was intended for use by the Thirty-Third Degree Masonic Councils. Pike probably was the most prominent expositor of the creed and doctrines of the Masons.

It should be understood that the Scottish Rite is not from Scotland. It was an American adaptation of the Rite of Perfection of the French Freemasons, which were in turn heavily influenced by Illuminated Freemasonry. Keep in mind that Weishaupt learned the Egyptian rites of the occult, so Egyptian symbolism plays a strong role in the Scottish (or French Perfection) Rite of Freemasonry.

Without comment, I will quote directly from the 1966 edition of the principles of the Scottish Rite by its leading expositor in America.

"Every Masonic temple is a temple of religion." (p. 213)

"The first Masonic legislator . . . was Buddha." (p. 277)

"Masonry, around whose altars the Christian, the Hebrew, the Muslim, the Brahmin, the followers of Confucius and Zoroaster, can assemble as brethren and unite in prayer to the one God who is above all the Baalim." (p. 226)

"Everything good in nature comes from Osiris." [the Egyptian sun God; the all-seeing eye is a Masonic representation of Osiris] (p. 476)

"Masonry . . . conceals its mysteries from all except Adepts and Sages, and uses false symbols to mislead those who deserve to be misled." (pp. 104–5)

"Everything scientific and grand in the religious dreams of the Illuminati . . . is borrowed from the Kabalah; all Masonic associations owe to it their secrets and their symbols." (p. 744)

"When the Mason learns that the key to the warrior on the block is the proper application of the dynamo of living power, he has learned the Mystery of his Craft. The seething energies of Lucifer are in his hands."

Manly Hall, *Lost Keys of Freemasonry*, p. 48

"To you, Sovereign Grand Inspectors General, we say this, that you may repeat it to the Brethren of the 32nd, 31st, and 30th degrees—The Masonic Religion should be, by all of us initiates to the high degrees, maintained in the purity of the Luciferian Doctrine.

"Yes, Lucifer is God, and unfortunately Adonay is also God. . . . Lucifer, God of Light and God of good is struggling for humanity against Adonay, the God of Darkness and Evil."

Albert Pike, Sovereign Pontiff of Universal
Freemasonry, Instructions to the twenty-three
Supreme Councils of the World, July 14, 1889

To my mind, there is no more monstrous evil than to bring public-spirited, often churchgoing, men into an organization that looks like a fraternal lodge, then deliberately mislead them until they are solid members. Then move them up thirty degrees to the place where they are ready to learn that Satan is the good god waiting to liberate mankind, and the Creator of the Universe (Yahweh, Elohim, Adonai) is, in their theology, the malicious prince of darkness.

It is my understanding that as part of the initiation for the Thirty-Second Degree, the candidate is told that Hiram, the builder of Solomon's temple, was killed by three assassins. The candidate therefore must strike back at those assassins which are, courtesy of the Illuminati, the government, organized religion, and private property.

This particular ritual is not Egyptian but from the Hung society of China, based on the cult of Amitabha Buddha. The ceremony, which clearly resembles those of the Egyptian *Book of the Dead*, was apparently copied as well by the Freemasons. It involves not a builder named Hiram, but a group of Buddhist monks, all but five of whom were slain by three villains, one of whom was the Manchu Emperor Khang Hsi.

It is self-evident that Masonic beliefs and rituals flow from the occult. Beliefs from Egyptian mysticism, Chinese Buddhism, and the ancient mysteries of the Hebrew Kabalah have been resuscitated to infuse their doctrines. What a splendid training ground for a new world/New Age citizen!

The New Age religions, the beliefs of the Illuminati, and Illuminated Freemasonry all seem to move along parallel tracks with world communism and world finance. Their appeals vary somewhat, but essentially they are striving for the same very frightening vision.

Now that we have taken a closer look at these spiritual and mystical threads which intertwine to form the historic ideology of a new world order, it is time to take a more precise and in-depth look at what this new world will actually be like.

Part III

A GLIMPSE
OF THE
COMING WORLD

9

A Promise of Hope

IT IS TIME now for us to consider the real possibilities that would exist for every human being if we all could indeed craft a world society where there was a wise administration of law, an end to war and oppression, and a guarantee of the basic necessities of life for every human being.

Indeed people have dreamed of such an age for at least three thousand years. Because the philosophers and dreamers leave out the two ingredients that are guaranteed to sabotage their beautiful dreams—the corruptible nature of man and the presence of spiritual evil—these dreams usually are impractical.

Such societies have been given a name—Utopia—from the island with a perfect government and perfect social system envisaged in 1516 by Sir Thomas More of England. The word *utopia* is from one of two almost identical Greek words that mean "good place" or "no place." It has come to mean in our language not only "perfectionism," but "unrealistic" and "impractical."

The earliest concept of a utopian society that we know of was conceived by Hesiod who lived 750 years before Christ. In his *Works and Days,* Hesiod described his dream of a time when "the fruitful earth spontaneously bore abundant fruit without stint. And they lived in ease and peace upon their land with many good things, rich in flocks and beloved of the blessed gods."

Is there any thinking person whose heart doesn't jump in anticipation when he or she reads such words? Is there any sane person who wants war, disease, famine, or injustice? We all want a life of peace and abundant blessing. If utopia were possible, most people would want it.

Plato was more of a realist in his utopian vision, and it is the platonic vision of a new world that our leaders are urging on us. Plato knew that people were too indifferent or lazy or venal to want his version of utopia, so he crafted an ideal society in which the wise men would rule. In turn, they would control every aspect of social existence in the name of justice, order, freedom, peace, strength, stability, and goodness.

The wise philosopher-kings would not work, but would organize the masses in their proper training and for their designated places in society. The contemporary upper-class term of derision for the laboring masses, hoi polloi, comes directly from the Greek words meaning "the people." According to Plato, the elite classes would not only assign the people their places, but would regulate optimal production and would keep the population at an optimal level as well.

As an aside, the late John D. Rockefeller II was obsessed with burgeoning world population growth and the necessity for birth control in the undeveloped nations. His foundation gave at least $50 million to Margaret Sanger. William Draper II, a key internationalist, came from government service in Europe to establish the Draper World Population Fund and to help form the Population Crisis Committee.

It was a Rockefeller Foundation treatise on abortion that served as the only philosophical support for Supreme Court Justice Harry Balckmun's incredible discovery of a "Constitutional right to abortion" in the case of *Roe v. Wade*.

As we watch our world hurtling toward the elite-controlled utopianism of Plato, another Greek utopianism may well come upon us shortly thereafter—that of Sparta. In Sparta, Lycurgus was the charismatic leader who seized dictatorial power and then created social institutions to make the people of Sparta austere, morally upright, simple, self-sacrificing, brave, and hardy. Lycurgus equalized property in Sparta, all but abolished money, and regulated and ordered the lives of the citizens for what he considered their good and the state's good. Plutarch, in his *Life of Lycurgus*, tells us that the Spartans honored Lycurgus as a god and consecrated a temple in his memory.

If the world embraces the platonic utopianism of Cecil Rhodes, the Rockefellers, and their followers, it is absolutely certain (according to the

Bible) that the world patterned after the Spartan utopianism of Lycurgus will follow soon after.

THE GRAND VISION OF WORLD ORDER

The general in the Union Army during the Civil War who was responsible for the scorched-earth policy in Georgia, William Tecumseh Sherman, said it best: "War is hell." When I met with the then prime minister of Israel, Yitzak Rabin, in 1974, he told me that Israel did not want war but a peace treaty. The most prestigious award in our world today is the Nobel Peace Prize—ironically underwritten from the proceeds of the fortune of the inventor of modern explosives. From generals to statesmen, people yearn for peace.

A new world order promises what we all want—world peace. In the Cato Institute volume *Collective Defense or Strategic Independence,* Georgetown Professor Earl C. Ravenal projects that by the year 1998 the U.S. Defense budget will top $451 billion, with cumulative defense spending in excess of $3.6 trillion. At the present time the expenditures on arms for the rest of the world equal or exceed that of the United States. The economies of Europe and Japan may equal or exceed the economy of the United States during this decade, so given a Cold War balance-of-power world, it is not at all unrealistic to project worldwide arms expenditures of $1 trillion per year—$10 trillion over ten years.

If the nations were disarmed, there would be a sum more vast than the mind can readily accommodate available for peacetime development. What would $10 trillion buy? An inexhaustible source of power from the fusion of hydrogen atoms and cheap electricity for every city and village on earth. Forests of billions of trees to reclaim the desert and restore the ecological balance so badly damaged by man. Plenty of clean, pure water for all the people, along with a bountiful food supply and the necessary infrastructure of roads and harbors to transport food from rural areas to the urban dwellers. Medical breakthroughs as well as the distribution of existing medical technology to the poor, who are so ravaged by easily preventable disease. The drastic reduction of infant mortality as levels of prenatal and postnatal care are raised in the so-called Third World.

Yes, the elimination of the spending for war and the preparation for war could free up enough of the world's resources to create what today's poor might consider nothing short of paradise on earth.

PRECEPTS OF WORLD LAW

The advocates of the new world order hold out a promise of peace, but a true world community promises many other benefits. We all can imagine supposed benefits. Here are my thoughts about some that will undoubtedly be advanced:

The Law of the Sea. A worldwide government could make and enforce a law regulating maritime commerce, shipping, navigation, harbor rights, and fishing rights. By a worldwide regulation of allowable catches and fishing techniques, the world could halt the depletion of various species of fish in the world's waters as well as the needless killing of dolphins in large commercial nets. Not only would shipping be forbidden to dump pollutants in the waters, nations would be forbidden to dump untreated sewage, chemical pollutants, insecticides, and disease-causing bacteria into the oceans. No tanker would be permitted on the world's waterways without a double hull or similar safety mechanism.

The Law of the Skies. Not only would the safety and dimensions of world aviation be protected and regulated, there would be laws preventing air pollution from auto emissions, power plants, chemical factories, steel mills, paper mills, and the like. No nation would be allowed to use ozone-depleting chemicals or any other emissions beyond a specified level. No one would be allowed to pollute the air that the people of the world, its plants, and its animal life must breathe.

The Law of Land and Forest. Trees would be considered the heritage of the human race and no trees could be cut for lumber or fuel unless it was according to the global forestry plan. Rain forests with their valuable exotic and medicinal plants would be preserved inviolate as "the lungs of the world." A global plan would be developed to protect land from erosion, mud slides, and the silting of rivers and harbors.

Of course, there would be a global law to protect fish and marine life, wild animals, and birds. The ecological balance of the earth would be preserved irrespective of national boundaries. There would be an allocation of land for use in agriculture, urban dwelling, and industry. There would be restrictions not only on the use of land, but on the quantity of land that any individuals or company could use. All land would be considered the patrimony of all people and would be allocated for term use according to the global plan.

There would be detailed regulations forbidding the use of dioxin or DDT or other harmful pesticides on the land, plus worldwide laws regulating the transportation and storage of chemical and industrial waste and the safety of industrial factories, nuclear power plants, oil drilling, oil wells, etc.

The Law of Energy Conservation. Fossil fuels would be regarded as a diminishing world resource, so worldwide laws would be enacted to prohibit wasteful energy practices in industry, transportation, and private residences. Stringent mileage requirements would be levied on automobiles along with subsidies to develop electric automobiles, alternate power sources, and safe, cheap nuclear power.

The Law of Industry and Agriculture. Worldwide output would be regulated to prevent overproduction and dumping. Agriculture would be strictly controlled so that only needed supplies of food were available to avoid the buildup of massive agricultural surpluses.

There would be strict standards of industrial safety for workers along with a guaranteed minimum wage for workers, everywhere, guaranteed health benefits, and guaranteed retirement.

World standards would be set to warrant product quality and safety. No food, drug, industrial, or consumer product would be sold that did not meet world standards.

Price controls would be in effect for most of the necessities of life. Costs of health care would be limited under a World Medical Board that would certify physicians, who in turn would be employed with regulated wages under a government-operated health care system.

The growing, manufacturing, sale, and use of marijuana, heroin, cocaine, chemical hallucinogens, and tobacco would be prohibited.

Payments for damages arising out of industrial accidents, product defects, traffic accidents, and malpractice would be limited to specific amounts only. Severe penalties would be imposed on lawyers and clients making frivolous claims.

All customs duties would be eliminated, as well as all immigration laws. All people would be registered as citizens of the world and would be free to live and work wherever they wished—until the time comes when the World Peoples Bureau requires permission to work and travel.

The Law of Credit and Finance. There would be one world currency, backed by a central world bank. This bank would have the authority to expand or contract the money supply of the world to permit industrial growth or to prohibit inflation.

There would be no currency imbalances and all prices would be quoted in the world currency. The central bank would, in turn, charter various world banks and would make currency and credit available at a "discount window" to its affiliate branches, which would in turn regulate smaller member banks. This banking arrangement would be intended to eliminate currency imbalances, misallocations of credit, and disparities of wealth. All peoples everywhere would be guaranteed abundant world credit, a guaranteed world currency, and an inflation-free environment.

Most industrial corporations would be organized on a world-wide basis. Therefore there would be a world stock exchange regulated by the world bank with international shares trading in world currency units. The world stock market would be in session twenty-four hours a day as trading would begin in Tokyo, continue in India, the Middle East, Europe, the East Coast of America, the West Coast of America, and finally end the twenty-four-hour Greenwich cycle in Honolulu.

The Law of Arms and Aggression. No nation would be allowed to take aggressive action against another, under penalty of severe sanctions. All chemical, biological, and nuclear weapons would be banned. Only such arms as would be necessary for local police functions would be permitted.

The World Human Rights Organization would prohibit human rights abuses against any citizen of the world. Torture, terrorism, and state oppression would be prohibited. Human rights abuses would be rectified under the aegis of the world court. Obviously, genocide such as happened in recent history against the Jews of Germany, the Ibos of Nigeria, and the Kurds of Iraq would be prohibited and prevented.

SAVORING THE DREAM

Hum quietly to yourself the words of John Lennon's "Imagine," and dozens of laws, rights, and benefits of one world may pop into your head. Rest assured that the finest dream merchants of the world will be employed in the sales job to come. Of course, it would be wonderful if it were all true. So would the vision behind the dream of Marxism, as it has been put out for public consumption: "A stateless classless society. From each according to his ability, to each according to his need."

But we see on our television screens almost daily how the reality of Marxist utopianism actually played out in real life. How will the dream merchants get across their vision of new world utopianism? Frankly, the task is easy, because the hope of the new world order answers the most pressing questions on the minds of people everywhere—world peace, relief of suffering, relief of cruelty, the mystery of the future.

The concept *will* move inexorably through world legislatures. Those who oppose it *will* be labeled obstructionist, reactionary, and out of step with the times. Just think about the color brochures, motion pictures, and television documentaries about this new world order and the promise of hope it offers. We will contemplate the wonders to come about when we enter into this beautiful relationship with each other as the United Nations administers all these laws with compassion, justice, and mercy.

As the world begins to deteriorate into warring trade factions and the inequities of the Third World loom larger and more grotesque, you can see that the promise of the new world order is truly within our grasp. And, following the Gulf War, it will be salable as being attainable. Didn't we go in and rescue this poor beleaguered nation? Didn't we use the force of the United Nations to accomplish it? It was little more than a close order drill, carried off with scientific precision.

Unlike the utopian dreams of the seventeenth, eighteenth, and nineteenth centuries, and unlike the utopias at the roots of the two world wars of this century, this will be a bolder, more practical vision. The other utopias did not have the same level of thought and experience behind them, and they did not come at a time when the human race was ready to hear this kind of news. Now it is.

If during this decade there is a worldwide banking collapse and a worldwide crash of the proportions of the Great Depression of the 1930s, people will be ready for a new order. When there are starving people standing in bread lines, when their physical needs are not being met, they will be ready for change.

The world may see a repeat of these words from 1932:

> The streets of our country are in turmoil. The universities are filled with students rebelling and rioting. Communists are seeking to destroy our country. Russia is threatening us with her might. And the Republic is in danger. Yes, danger from within and without. We need law and order. Without law and order our nation cannot survive.

The author of this most reasonable proposal calculated to touch the heart of every German was none other than Adolf Hitler.

Precisely what happened when Franklin Roosevelt offered his New Deal will happen again. Never before in history had both houses of the Congress of the United States agreed to grant a president such wide-ranging and potentially dictatorial powers in the first hundred days of his administration. But our Congress did that in 1932 with Roosevelt. They gave him virtually everything he asked for because he promised a way out of the Great Depression. The sweeping laws rushed through Congress to begin the New Deal radically changed the face of American federal policy. And they passed with virtually no opposition.

A CLIMATE OF FEAR

Think of the various New Deal agencies Roosevelt created by fiat. His use of executive power was so unprecedented that the Supreme Court initially struck down key parts of the New Deal program. But when Roosevelt threatened to pack the court and change its character, the justices changed their minds. Roosevelt could do whatever he wanted, because the economic crisis created a compliant majority in the Congress who would blindly follow his lead. Any reasonable offer of hope was acceptable.

A worldwide crisis today would create the same environment we saw during the Depression. This would be the first time in history that the entire globe could be made aware of these issues, simultaneously, via satellite communications. The model was set in place with the incredible coverage of the multinational force assembled in the Persian Gulf, ostensibly to curb the expansionist aggression of Iraq—and it demonstrates the ability to mold the world into one.

CNN was seen virtually around the world. Our world speaks English— the leadership of virtually every nation speaks English. United States films, television programs, records, tapes, and books have spread to every nation on the globe. With satellite technology, the ability to mold a world together is here. The international flow of funds is in place—we have never had anything like it before.

The ease of traveling from one nation to another is unprecedented. You can fly from London to New York City in three hours, seventeen minutes and basically outrun the sun. Facsimile machines, high-speed computers, datalinks, twenty-four-hour rolling markets: all these things make immediate communication and response a reality. The entire world can be instantly involved in every decision.

The United States has had a leadership role, not only as a permanent member of the United Nations and its Security Council, but in conceiving and implementing the ideology of the new world order. The fathers of the new world order are virtually all Americans, and they desire to have continuing, profitable international power out of America.

Their power is not limited by American laws or borders. They can exercise it wherever their money is. Frankly, it is easier to exercise arbitrary power overseas than it is in the United States. There are things you cannot possibly do in America that you can do very easily overseas. There are many restrictions on the freedom of commercial activity here that do not exist in other nations. How convenient it would be for them if world laws could override the regulations of the United States.

The rapid and unexpected changes of the past two years have taken the world by surprise. The Soviet Union is a basket case. They have had to send envoys to America, Europe, and Japan to beg for financial assistance. Eastern Europe is in nearly the same predicament. If the debt burden that exists in the world were to suddenly collapse, you can be assured the wheels of change would begin to spin.

In 1990, we saw the virtual collapse of the Japanese Stock Market, the Nikkei Dow. It has leveled out over the past year but is still in a volatile position, not unlike what the United States is going through at this moment. The underlying problems are about as bad as they always were. Loans are made on the strength of stocks; stocks are run up on the basis of appreciation of real estate; and real estate is escalating on the strength of bank loans and stock market prices.

The result is overpriced real estate, overpriced stocks, interconnected stocks, and weak if not insolvent banks, holding loans based on inflated real estate prices and a synthetic stock market, which, combined, have created a pyramiding of wealth that is completely artificial. That is a dangerous and potentially disastrous situation, which has not changed since the 1991 shakeup. The disaster has only been postponed.

Citizens groups were protesting in early 1991, pushing for a gradual readjustment of Japan's inflated markets before conditions worsen, but the balloon only seems to get larger and larger. When the air suddenly goes out of a balloon, it shrinks to nothing with shocking suddenness. That may be what's in store for the Japanese market if their economists don't wise up soon.

GROWING UNCERTAINTIES

Fear is a compelling force, but the human mind instinctively seeks relief from fear and dread. Christians naturally seek consolation from Scripture and through prayer and faith in God in times of crisis. But sometimes our hopes may be met by a hope, a dream, or an ideology that may be totally unrealistic and irrational. This can produce some curious reactions.

Robert Nisbet, in his provocative little book, *The Present Age: Progress and Anarchy in Modern America*, makes a very interesting observation about the collapse of socialism. He points out, "The death of socialism in the West opened the field of ideology, of 'isms,' to a number of entries which had not been especially noticeable before the Second World War."

These include such things as egalitarianism—meaning equality for women, races, religions, sex, and the like—and a host of other liberal concerns. Nisbet suggests that the void in the minds of intellectuals left by the death of their beloved socialist theories led to the rise of a host of strange cults, radical causes, and utopias. He writes:

> Socialism, held these vagaries—to the extent that they even existed as ideals in the minds of most intellectuals—together or kept them down as mere latencies—for exfoliation perhaps in the very distant future. But when socialism ceased to be the energizing faith of the Left in the West—primarily because of the repulsiveness of the Soviet Union, Fascist Italy, and Nazi Germany, one and all founded by lifelong socialists, but also because of the indisputable fact that the Third World nations that took up capitalism—as in

the Pacific Rim countries to the west—were faring immeasurably better than were those that took up socialism—when the socialist dream passed, the result was a mess of new idols in the marketplace.

Is the current fascination with politically correct thinking we read about in the news magazines a passion brought about in the universities by the death of the socialist dream? Possibly. Could it also be true that the defrocking of a political ideology such as socialism could add intensity and urgency to the Establishment hope for a new world order and a one-world government? Probably.

THE COMING REVOLUTION

In the conclusion to his book, Nisbet suggests that the climate in America today appears to be as ripe for a revolution in the world of ideas as it was in the eighteenth century, when our Founding Fathers first established a constitutional democracy in the New World. That seems to be precisely where the advocates of a new world order would like us to be. Poised on the threshold of a new era, a new world, and a new political theory.

Another author, Thomas J. McCormick, in his book, *America's Half Century*, argues that the era of American hegemony in the world is long dead and that new international forces will most certainly carry us into, first, a trilateral world and, next, a one-world internationalist system. Writing from a historical, almost prophetic, frame of reference, he says:

> As the 1990s loomed on the horizon, the world that Americans had made after World War II had come to an end. As yet, no new one had taken its place. The outline of world-system decentering had long been clear, but the contours of its recentering were so far murky and problematical. . . .
>
> American hegemony was dead and Russia in crisis and decline. Japan was the new economic giant and Europe was poised on the brink of true community, and China was ready to leapfrog everyone. This composed the new core of a world in which change was dynamic, uneven, multidirectional, and unpredictable.

The image drawn by McCormick, a Wisconsin history professor, is to some degree disconcerting. But not nearly so much as the author's proposals for a replacement for the now-defunct old world system. The two models he finds most interesting are those of Lenin and the German Marxist, Karl Kautsky. Of the two, he prefers Kautsky's, which argued that "world capitalism would transcend its nationalistic competitions and produce a new order of ultra-imperialism. Core countries, tied together by increasing economic interdependence, would integrate and dominate the Third World collectively."

Then the author rhapsodizes, "The gradual replacement of national industry with multinational industry had carried the world a long way toward a degree of oneness and interdependence." The author makes no effort to disguise the identity of this option as the one-world utopian government of the new world order.

10

A Cruel Hoax

THE ONE THING the Utopian dreamers always omit is actually the centerpiece of the Constitution of the United States—the sinful nature of man. Twenty-six hundred years ago—about the time of the Greek utopians—the Hebrew prophet, Jeremiah, spoke of that missing element when he wrote, "The heart of man is deceitful above all things, and desperately wicked; who can know it?"

Every utopia presumes that it can build a perfect world order with imperfect people. So, like the Marxist dream, it attempts by indoctrination, coercion, torture, and execution to change the hearts of its citizens. Or, in the case of Plato, it puts the citizens in perpetual bondage to a class of rulers whose natural aptitude and understanding of philosophy place them above the people. Or, in the case of the Illuminati and the New Agers, leadership is to be entrusted to those who have had psychic "illumination" and are, in fact, being instructed by demonic beings referred to as "ascended masters."

But despite utopian claims, Lord Acton's dictum still holds true, "Power corrupts; absolute power corrupts absolutely." Unfortunately, the proof of the idiom is not hard to find.

Revelations have recently come out that the "enlightened" Marxist Sandinista leaders of Nicaragua, the Ortega brothers, Thomas Borge, and their allies have stolen $1 billion worth of property, including luxurious homes and estates. Their grab for free wealth is being called "the Piñata," after the name for the children's toy full of goodies.

Erich Honecker of Germany took for himself luxurious accommodations. Some three hundred criminal investigations are under way involving currency manipulation, theft of state property, and embezzlement totaling $2.7 billion by East German communists. While his people were dying of starvation, disease, and squalor, the "enlightened" Rumanian dictator, Nicolae Ceausescu, had thirty-two private residences plus a still unfinished palace carrying at least a $1 billion price tag.

The founders of America created a constitutional republic where power was divided among the people, the state governments, and the federal government. At the federal level, power was again divided across executive, legislative, and judicial lines. Power was then limited again, not only by a written constitution, but by brief terms for officeholders who were forced to face regular elections and potential impeachment for misconduct.

To be sure, in order to form a "more perfect union," the thirteen sovereign states of America merged their sovereignty at that time into that of the United States of America. But we cannot forget this about America: they and their ancestors had lived in this country in harmony for 169 years, all as subjects of another country, Great Britain. They all shared the same language, traditions, and political concepts about the nature of man and the will of God.

All but about five thousand of the total population were recorded as either Protestant or Roman Catholic Christians, and almost all were committed to the biblical world-view. All the early American leaders had been trained in some fashion or other in statecraft. Furthermore, there was a restricted franchise when this country started, so that only property owners could vote in popular elections. People had to have a stake in society before they were allowed to determine its laws.

There was no inherent danger in merging South Carolina with Virginia or Connecticut with Massachusetts, because they were all basically from one common stock and one common philosophy. Benjamin Franklin in Pennsylvania, John Adams in Massachusetts, and Thomas Jefferson in Virginia were all highly educated men who had a tremendous respect, honed over decades of study, for the God-given rights and freedoms of each individual.

They had read broadly and studied the civilizations of the last thirty centuries, all the way back to the Greeks and Romans. The experience of the founding of America is in no way a precedent for forming a world government of totally diverse peoples. To have people of colonial America coming together in federation is one thing, but moving the United States of America into a world government on an equal footing with Muslim dictators like Mohamar Qaddafi of Libya and Hashemi Rafsanjani of Iran, or Marxist dictators like Deng Xiaoping of Communist China and Robert Mugabe of Zimbabwe, and then meekly saying, "We are all one, and we, therefore, surrender our sovereignty to you," is sheer, unmitigated nonsense. But that is precisely what a world government will one day insist upon!

TROUBLESOME FACTS

Bureaucrats feel that people have a rather annoying tendency of wanting to live their own lives the way they want, where they want, with whom they want. In the United States this drives the social engineers of government into apoplexy, and they cannot rest until they force the citizens to bus their children away from their friends, hire by quota instead of aptitude, make loans to people who won't pay them back, go to doctors who secretly have deadly diseases, and rent their property to undesirables with aberrant sexual habits.

Utopian ideas can only become reality through a change in the human heart or the force of law. Human government can never change people's hearts, so that leaves the fulfillment of the wonderful dreams of the new world order in the hands of a massive military force and an equally massive police power. Of course, world armies, world police, and world bureaucrats don't come cheaply.

Several years ago a close aide of the late Congressman Claude Pepper appeared as a guest on my television program to advocate a federal program to mandate compulsory catastrophic health coverage for the elderly. I felt that the elderly did not favor this program, and I knew that its cost was projected to be $30 billion. I asked Pepper's associate how much his program would cost. His answer was astounding, "I have no idea." The bill passed overwhelmingly, and no one knew for sure what it would cost. But once the tax bill to pay for it hit the elderly, their outrage forced Congress to beat a hasty retreat.

A similar lapse of knowledge was revealed in 1986 when I appeared before the Senate Labor Committee at the request of the chairman, Senator Orin Hatch, to oppose the sweeping government intrusion proposed by Edward Kennedy, under the euphemistic title, The Civil Rights Restoration Act.

Senator Howard Metzenbaum of Ohio was questioning me in a hostile fashion about the bill, when I asked him point-blank, "Senator, has there been any staff study of any nature to determine the cost to the government of this bill?" He stuttered and blustered and said there had not been. The bill passed ultimately by a wide margin, and no one, Democrat or Republican, had the slightest idea of the potential cost to the government or the people affected by it.

Rest assured that the new world order is going to cost plenty. If you like the Internal Revenue Service, you will love the tax police of the new world order.

Imagine that you, a citizen of the United States, are assessed a tax on your income to pay for a project in Africa that you totally disagree with. Since you are "rich," the representatives of the United Nations from the poor countries will now have a claim on your assets. The levy initially would be on the United States government, which would pass it on to you in the form of higher taxes. One day it may be a United Nations levy on you directly.

You want to complain to your representatives at the United Nations, because the entire nation has voted on the selection of our few U.S. representatives to that body. Unfortunately, the United States now has only 5 percent of the world's total population, and therefore would be entitled to 5 percent of the vote. If the United Nations wanted to drain the wealth of America, it would be free to do so by popular vote. By then we would have no choice but to acquiesce, because America would have been disarmed and the United Nations would control all the weapons.

PRESENT REALITIES

This type of wealth-transfer legislation is not futuristic, however, but already on the books of the present United Nations, which our leaders want to lead the world. In 1974, the Declaration on the Establishment of a New International Economic Order was adopted by the United Nations General Assembly, advocating that "the prevailing disparities in the world be abolished."

According to author Tal Brooke, "This world welfare system would insist on (1) The transfer of wealth from the first to Third World nations; (2) Nationalization by Third World governments, and (3) Economic special protection for poorer countries." In simple language, the Third World in the United Nations has already voted to take away by decree the wealth of Europe and America and give it to themselves. Only the impotence of the current United Nations General Assembly and the veto power of the Security Council has prevented this resolution from being implemented.

The IRS under successive United States laws has been given sweeping powers over the citizens of this nation in order to collect enough money to pay the bill for the federal deficits borrowed from the Establishment bankers. A worldwide IRS under a banking oligarchy would become the American citizen's worst nightmare.

But remember, before the financial bloodsucking begins in earnest on the newly minted American citizens of the world, the monopoly bankers will have placed themselves and their central banks above the law and out of reach of the taxing power. They did it in 1913 in America, and, rest assured, they plan to do it again in the new world order.

Punitive taxes would just be the beginning. The world government would also need a standing army. The spring 1991 issue of *Foreign Affairs* calls for a United Nations standing army, not under the command of United States officers as was the case of the United Nations-mandated Gulf War, but directly under the control of the United Nations Security Council.

Personnel for such an army would have to come from somewhere. If America wanted a voice in the action, it would either have to provide volunteers or draftees. But what would happen if young Americans did not want to participate in a United Nations war against one of our allies, such as Israel? The answer is simple, they would be forced to serve under penalty of prison.

What would happen if United Nations sanctions were levied against America? Would young Americans serving in a United Nations Army be forced to fire on their own countrymen? If not, who would do the job? As I mentioned earlier, I cannot forget the bloody picture in *Life* magazine of the young Belgian settler in Katanga whose wife and children lay dead behind him in a little Volkswagen, brutally killed by black African soldiers serving in a United Nations contingent. If it happened there, it can happen here.

THE TRUE RISKS

What are the downside risks of world citizenship? First of all, it would mean that the protection of the U.S. Bill of Rights would no longer apply. The principle of extra-territoriality applies, which means that the American citizens in the new world order could be arrested in this country or out of it and tried for violation of United Nations laws before a world court, which could just as likely operate under the Muslim Sharia as the Judeo-Christian Ten Commandments.

Whatever laws might be passed by Congress or interpreted by the U.S. Supreme Court could be superseded by world government laws and world court decision. This is, of course, what happens now in the United

States. I live in Virginia and am governed by Virginia's code of laws, Virginia's police, Virginia's courts, and Virginia's taxation. But the federal Congress, the federal marshals, the federal courts, and the federal taxing authorities all have jurisdiction over me, which either supplements or supersedes Virginia's claims.

I accept that gladly, for I like being a citizen of the United States. But world citizenship, however wonderful it may sound, clearly means that our unique privileges as American citizens will be ended whenever this nation buys wholly into the concept of a world government with military enforcement power and the disarmament of individual nations.

Just think of this. Suppose you are an American citizen, your name is Salman Rushdie, and you decide to write a book of poems mildly critical of the Shi'ite branch of the Muslim religion. In America, as it is now constituted, you are perfectly free to do so. But suppose the existing world law of genocide is modified slightly to include the politically correct speech in vogue on American college campuses. Under a world government you could be taken from America and tried before a world court for a world crime without necessarily being afforded confrontation by your accusers, a jury of your peers, counsel of your choosing, freedom from cruel punishment, freedom from excessive bail, freedom from unreasonable searches and seizures, or any of the other legal rights you now take for granted.

Just what does it mean not to be tried by a jury of your peers? In America we know that in our local community a jury will have some appreciation of our shared view of right and wrong, freedom, fairness, and longstanding constitutional liberty. People make up our juries whose material possessions and education is not greatly different from those of the one accused of a crime.

How would you feel as one accused of a crime if you appeared before a people's court composed if illiterate peasants, with annual incomes of $300 to $500, to whom your income of $25,000 a year made you out to be a greedy capitalist exploiter? What appeal would you have to justice, reason, or shared values? None!

But there is more. All the wonderful laws that give freedom from air pollution, water pollution, improper land use, respect for the animals, workers' rights, minimum wages, universal health care, and so on must be enforced by administrative oversight and ultimate punitive sanctions. Bureaucracy means forms, paperwork, inspections, appeals, delay, uncertainty, and unbelievable expense. It also means the possibility of shame, disgrace, fines, or prison if a person or company runs afoul of the regulations as interpreted by a low-level bureaucrat and some politically ambitious prosecutor.

TESTING THE APPARATUS

I read to my horror of a landowner who possessed an unsightly piece of land littered with debris. He hauled some dirt onto his land, smoothed it out, and planted grass on it. For this "crime" against the law, he was given three years in a federal prison. Another upstanding businessman, charged and found guilty of a technical violation of recent laws, was given ten years in a federal prison because of the rigid application of federal sentencing guidelines. The judge in that case broke down and cried because he had no discretion over the severity of the sentence.

It is estimated that the *Federal Register* this year will include sixty thousand pages of new federal administrative regulations. The regulations and enforcement proceedings under these regulations have made rich some of America's thousands of lawyers who practice administrative or tax law, but they only do damage to the citizens harassed by them.

The American and European welfare states are bad, but just consider what it will be like when pollution or energy inspectors from Burma and Sri Lanka visit your facility on orders from the World Energy and Pollution Control Authority in New Delhi, whose deputy administrator in charge of Europe and America speaks French and is headquartered in Brussels.

Given the almost unbelievable propensity of Third World officials to look for bribes, will the new set of world laws turn into nothing more or less than a worldwide protection racket? Those who can pay are cleared of "violations." Those who cannot pay are closed down or sent to prison.

Finally, it goes without saying, the world government would of necessity demand a law against sedition and treason. Most of the world knows nothing about the First Amendment freedoms that have been won for those of us who live in America by those who were Christians, who believed the Bible, and who were steeped in the Anglo-Saxon concepts of jurisprudence. In many countries those who criticize the government in the press or in assembly are executed, imprisoned, or muzzled. How can we possibly believe that these people, sharing other concepts of human rights all their lives, will suddenly switch to American concepts of freedom and free enterprise at the stroke of a pen? It is unrealistic to expect it. It just will not happen.

The downside of the promise for a new world order is that for laws to work, they have to be backed up by sanctions, and the sanctions can be disastrous.

Modern technology has performed wonders in this century. In just the last ten years we have seen an exponential increase in the sophistication of global communications. Think of how satellites, microwaves, fiber optics, computers, fax machines, and magnetic recording devices have changed the way we communicate. Think of how this same technology has given a powerful central government the ability to inform, indoctrinate, monitor, and control the will of the people.

THE LEVELING PROCESS

Some of the popular motion pictures of the last few years have international and intergalactic forces all interacting. Not only do you have different nations and races all flying together, but animals, reptile creatures, and other alien forms, as if they were all equal. The implication of these scenes is that man is no different or better than any other form of life, and certainly Americans are no different or better than any other nation.

Even if it is not popular to say so, the Europeans and the Americans have had a positive influence on world culture because of their religious beliefs, their work habits, their creative ingenuity, and their desire for a peaceful and productive life.

In my book, *The New Millennium,* I suggested that the pendulum of civilization may now be swinging back toward the East, and the Asian cultures may be once again on the rise. The Chinese and Japanese have had high cultures, far beyond those of most Third World nations today. To blur those distinctions and to act as if every culture and every system is of equal quality is absurd.

Of course, we are all sons and daughters of Adam, but nevertheless we have centuries of cultural differences, and those cannot be ignored. But there is every likelihood that the coming world government would make a declaration of equality of all people.

They would also have to have a law of arms control. They could not have a system that allowed people to keep arms, because that would allow dissenters to foment revolution. So our constitutional right to keep and bear arms would be one of the very first casualties of world order legislation.

We have already had a law against so-called hate crimes passed in the United States Congress. The new world government would have to have a law against world hate crimes where the politically correct speech of the college campuses would be magnified a thousand times. No one could speak out against the beliefs of a Muslim, a Hindu, or an animist, or against the beliefs of a communist or a socialist. Christians could not speak out against the sin of homosexuality or pedophilia. What we know as the freedom of religion would be taken away, and Christians would be muzzled.

Equality of all religions, races, sexual practices, and belief systems would be considered paramount, and anyone found guilty of stepping over the line would have to be publicly penalized by the world government. Remember, a court in the District of Columbia has already held that the right to forbid discrimination on the basis of sexual preference overrides existing American First Amendment rights of religious liberty.

UNPRECEDENTED VIOLATIONS

The court clearly violated religious freedom in Washington, D.C., when it forced a Catholic school, Georgetown University, to provide facilities for homosexual groups, even though homosexuality is specifically and historically proscribed both by the university and the tenets of the Christian faith.

The court decided the university would have to give the homosexual groups an office with telephones, access to mailing lists and other services, all free of charge. In essence, the Roman Catholic Church has been forced to subsidize homosexuality, even though this practice is a blatant violation of the essential doctrines of its faith. As educators, Georgetown University cannot choose conduct it considers to be biblical, or reject what is nonbiblical. The school must comply with government-mandated sexual-orientation guidelines or face severe penalties.

I asked Cardinal John O'Connor of New York why the governors of Georgetown University didn't appeal that case to the higher courts. He said that he personally would have shut the university down before compromising the faith in that way. That decision has now set a tragic precedent, undermining freedom of religion and religious conviction, in essence compromising in a measure the rights of Christians everywhere.

If there has been a gross abuse of liberty in Washington, the seat of our government under the Constitution, you can be certain that those without our values will do it worldwide. Whatever violation of freedom has taken place here will take place in a world body, only in a more blatant fashion. They are not going to be less restrictive or more permissive in the world body about Christian values than we are here in the United States.

Even if they don't go beyond what we have done, they will certainly go just as far. Remember that the collapse of morality in Europe in the past thirty years is absolutely staggering. So if Europe plays a major role in world government—which it most certainly will—then we can finally expect moral standards to drop even lower than we know here, and the freedom of religion will be severely limited.

At some point there will be a law of world religion. Instead of the First Amendment concept, which says that the government shall not establish a religion or prohibit the free exercise of religion, the new law would recognize the universal character of religion and probably adopt a syncretistic religion based on the "New Age." The meditation room at the current United Nations headquarters sets the stage for what they have in mind.

CONTROL OF RELIGION

It does not call for much imagination to see that there could be a formal recognition of the universal spirit, a theology that pays lip service to all religions but ends up as a New Age belief. This is the sort of thing that appeals to Buddhists, Hindus, and even some who claim to be Christians. It is like a religion of mankind, based on what they think is humanism and open-mindedness. But at some point, the world body would of necessity make evangelism and active conversion to a set of beliefs so doctrinaire as Christianity undesirable, then severely restricted, then unlawful.

With that kind of system in place, there would also have to be a law of world indoctrination and thought control. The world government wants a law of the press, regulating what criticism of the central government would be allowed in the media, then a muzzle on free speech with restrictions on public and even private expressions of disapproval.

Third World nations have introduced such proposals over and over again in the United Nations, trying to regulate the world's press. Only strong resistance from a powerful, independent United States has kept these measures from passing. But press control has been dear to the hearts of the Soviets and the Third World dictators. They don't want a free, unfettered press.

In 1991, Mikhail Gorbachev, once praised as the champion of democratic reform, convinced the government to tighten the screws on the press and to set up a new government bureau to use its powers of censorship to crack down on criticism of Gorbachev and the Soviet government. Ultimately this law was never implemented, but the intent was clearly there.

When expression is controlled, then there can be public indoctrination. There will be required courses in world citizenship at all levels of society, teaching the rights and obligations of citizens of the world. That is what Plato called for. That is precisely what happened in the Soviet system and in Germany, and isn't that what is happening right now in the public schools of America?

All over this country, children are being indoctrinated as world citizens, with reverence for the earth, the environment, the animals, and for people of all ethnic, religious, and sexual orientations. This would be carried forward with massive indoctrination paid for by the world government.

It would be a type of brainwashing, and that is only a short step from the Orwellian newspeak concept. Only what's good about the leader can be printed. Everybody is indoctrinated with a uniform set of ideas and beliefs. Think of mass meetings of the world on satellite television, where cheering throngs extol the leader and say what a great man he is and how wonderful it is to live in his new world order.

COMPUTER TECHNOLOGY

Those who speak glibly about the benefits of a world government overlook one alarming development of modern-day technology—the new microchips and the supercomputers. In the old days, with population records maintained by hand, there was no practical way to control all of the people. To be sure, totalitarian governments could exercise enormous control over the bulk of their populations, but people could always hide themselves or their money in some way from the authorities. Escape was possible from tyranny to a free country. Revolt was possible with aid from outside.

Under a totalitarian one-world government there will be no island of freedom. No large power like America holding forth democratic ideals.

Every citizen could be given a number, coded with his nation, his religion, and his personal identity. Now in the United States parents are forced to obtain social security numbers for their infant children, generally at birth, or lose out on tax deductions.

Super high-speed mainframe computers coupled with modular file-servers hooked together in wide-area networks can hold and process trillions of bits of information with lightning speed and accuracy. There is absolutely no doubt that a world government, for the first time in history, would have the ability to build and recall, in microseconds, the complete vital statistics and life record of every citizen in the world.

If we went to a world currency, then a so-called checkless, cashless society, it would be possible to monitor and control all wealth, other than primitive barter transactions. At some time it would be possible to tax the wealth stored in computers under law, or given a dictatorial environment to freeze the accumulated wealth of any individual or any class of individuals just by simple instructions to a computer.

With existing technology it would be simple to limit the types of purchases that certain people would be permitted to make, or to prohibit all purchases. Never before has our world known a time when the words of the Book of Revelation could be literally fulfilled "that no man could buy or sell without the mark of the beast." The supercomputer in Brussels handling worldwide bank clearings at the Society for Worldwide Interbank Financial Telecommunications (SWIFT) has already been nicknamed the "Beast."

But there is more. Monitoring mechanisms could be put in place and linked by global satellites to monitor the physical movements of every citizen around the world. All that would be necessary would be a cardreader located at permitted points at home and work. If the individual did not check in at the appropriate places at appropriate times, alarm bells would go off and a search would be made, much like that for a convict escaping from prison.

I know that this all sounds too much like a science fiction horror story, but the loss of United States sovereignty opens up the very real possibility that some day in the future a demonized madman like Hitler could seize control of a worldwide, homogenized government and then employ currently existing technology to turn the entire world into a giant prison.

COMPLEX INTERDEPENDENCE

In an agrarian society where each family was essentially self-sufficient, this type of control would have been impossible. Simple organisms are by their nature more resilient than highly interdependent complex ones. If every home has candles for light and wood for heat, it is not nearly as dependent on exterior support as a large city tied into a six-state electric power grid. Remember the panic that hit New York City when its regional power grid failed? Lights went off, subway cars trapped their riders underground, elevators stopped in-between floors in skyscrapers, street lights and burglar alarms went dead, and panic set in as street gangs began widespread looting under cover of darkness.

People in that complex situation were helpless. In a simpler setting, the loss of electric power is easily surmountable. In industry, in distribution, in finance, and in politics, the simpler, more independent systems are always more resilient to disruption and disaster. Obviously the more complex, interdependent systems are more efficient and less costly, but they are much more dangerous.

The globalists see the economies of scale of so-called transnational corporations, universal credit systems, and world banking and currency. They stress global interdependence almost as if it were the holy grail. We must remember what happened during the power failure in New York City when our leaders urge more and more complex global interdependence controlled by a one-world government, instead of our present system of dispersed power and local independence.

It is no secret. Allen Bloom said this year ago. The agenda of the Back-to-Basics movement has been to erase the slate, to erase the minds of the students, to tell them that everything is relative and everything is equal. American values, Judeo-Christian values, the values of Western civilization are no more important than the values of an aborigine in Australia or a communist cell leader in Red China. Consequently, entire generations of American students are perfectly prepared to accept any dominating theory that is presented as truth. They have no relative value system to use as a yardstick for critical analysis of right and wrong, good and evil.

Traditional values are old-fashioned and meaningless; new ideas and new beliefs are okay. The slate is clean, the door of the mind is standing ajar, and any slick, high-gloss, Madison Avenue fad can be pumped in without resistance.

It has been like a machine. For thirty years the minds of our children have been vacuumed and sanitized, leaving them open to anyone capable of exploiting their trained biases, their materialistic desires, and their programmed gullibility. The model is not universally true—particularly for children who have been taught a value system at home—but you don't have to look far to see just how pervasive this model has become.

Our young people are being taught that the American way, the Christian lifestyle, the standard of living of America, along with all the glorious chapters of our history are tainted with oppression and racism and sexism, and we are no better or no more capable than anybody else. Just read the propaganda against Columbus and the white settlers as we prepare for the five hundredth anniversary of his epic voyage of discovery.

This is, of course, conditioning for the new world. You have got a blank slate, young people with no concept of the history of America, no concept of the struggle for freedom or what the relative values are of our ways versus other ways. They are ready pawns for a value-neutral way of thinking.

This kind of brainwashing is incredibly strong in the university setting. You don't dare say America or Christianity is a better way of living. When I said during my presidential bid that I would only bring Christians and Jews into the government, I hit a firestorm. "What do you mean?" the media challenged me. "You're not going to bring atheists into the government? How dare you maintain that those who believe the Judeo-Christian values are better qualified to govern America than Hindus and Muslims?" My simple answer is, "Yes, they are."

STANDING ON PRINCIPLES

Both John Locke and Thomas Jefferson refused to allow atheists into their governments because atheists would not keep oaths. Oaths have to be sworn before God, and since atheists acknowledged no God, Locke and Jefferson maintained that they could not be trusted. If anyone understood what Hindus really believe, there would be no doubt that they have no business administering government policies in a country that favors freedom and equality.

Hindu concepts are totally foreign to our system of values. The practice of *suttee,* abolished by the Christian British, required that a Hindu woman whose husband died first had to be cremated alive on her husband's funeral pyre. Hindus have an entire class of people that is considered "untouchable," supposedly cursed by God and given a bad *karma* (a debt of suffering to repay with their lives). Efforts to help the poor out of their misery are nullified by this religious belief. Hindus let people starve rather than kill rats who breed disease and eat the people's food, because they believe rats are reincarnated people.

Can you imagine having the Ayatollah Ruhollah Khomeini as defense minister, or Mahatma Gandhi as minister of health, education, and welfare? The Hindu and Buddhist idea of *karma* and the Muslim idea of *kismet,* or fate, condemn the poor and the disabled to their suffering. If a child is lame and starving to death with flies all over his faced, there is no need to help him. It's the will of Allah. These beliefs are nothing but abject fatalism, and they would devastate the social gains this nation has made if they were ever put into practice.

Obviously, we wouldn't want that, but once we believe that the Christian tradition is no better than any other, and once we believe there is no distinction between our systems and those of India, Sri Lanka, China, the Congo, or the Soviet Union, then we will be ready to surrender anything we have.

During the entire history of modern society, since at least the Elizabethan era, the university campus has always been the haven of the intellectual whose primary right is the freedom to think whatever he likes, to learn from any source he chooses, and to come up with his own conclusions and state those in a public forum without restraint. Today that right no longer exists on the college campuses in this country. Students and professors are not free to think what they like or speak openly in a public forum.

You can see how higher education has changed. It began as a system, with a Christian world-view, where a professor or student could openly debate the nature of God and how the principles of science and the mind were supposed to work in relation to Him. Higher education has since become a system where one can deny the existence of God and openly advocate atheism. Now it is heading toward a system where one has no freedom at all, except the freedom to accept the politically correct doctrines of the current fad.

If the new world order must coerce life and thought into its mold, we are suddenly back to communism. The new world order must inevitably become what communism has been, only without any place on earth where freedom can flourish.

FROM ANARCHY TO SLAVERY

For most of the last fifty years the advocates of socialist and liberal institutions have been the most vocal opponents of capital punishment. Ironically, in the world to come they are going to need something like capital punishment to carry out their agenda. Don't be surprised to see some of these people switch sides on this issue in the very near future.

Capital punishment was common in the Soviet Union, and it reached barbaric heights under Adolf Hitler. A dream that is large and unrealistic—which any utopia must be—must be enforced through coercion and intimidation. Carried to its extreme, coercion becomes assassination, and intimidation becomes murder.

Arguments for reinstatement of capital punishment are already coming from the left. For years liberals had no problem with alcoholism; now arguments against alcoholism are coming from the left. These are the old arguments of the Christians—it's like a slow echo—except that we know the only way to change drug abuse and alcoholism is by faith in God to change the hearts of the people.

The way to transform murderers and other criminals into responsible citizens is not by penal reform. Our 85 percent recidivism rate proves that. The only thing that really works is the transforming power of Jesus Christ, working from within the human heart. The coercive utopians are saying, "No, we will force them to follow our way."

Margaret Sanger, in founding Planned Parenthood, advocated unrestrained sexuality, particularly among teenagers. But once they started engaging in widespread promiscuous sex, her solution was sterilization and abortion.

Sanger had an agenda. She wanted unrestrained licentiousness so that she could bring on involuntary sterilization. Perhaps one of the reasons she was so heavily funded by the Rockefeller and Ford Foundations was that Sanger wanted what is called eugenics or "good genes" by which an elite group under her leadership could cull out the undesirables and create a master race. Increased sexuality was a means of getting there, because the only solution to the problem of runaway illegitimacy is through sterilization and abortion. Sanger advocated sterilization of blacks, Jews, Southern Europeans, fundamentalist Christians, mental defectives, and the relatives of mental defectives. Her monograph published in 1920 called *Breeding the Thoroughbred* is a real eyeopener!

Now proponents of the new world order are working under various ruses and pretexts. To achieve ultimate authority over people, they now encourage a full expression of their baser instincts until a time when society rises up against them. Then to counter the anarchy and runaway evil, these manipulators can appear to be public heroes by advocating and implementing oppressive laws that restrain not only perceived anarchy, but the basic freedoms of all the people.

DISTURBING PRECEDENTS

One of the most disturbing precedents for the new world system of coercion is the recent outcry of liberals and humanists for congressional passage of the United Nations Treaty on the Rights of the Child. Citing the 135 heads of state who had already adopted the treaty, politicians like Connecticut Senator Christopher Dodd said that our government's delay was shameful, reprehensible, and irresponsible.

Even Senators Robert Dole of Kansas, Richard Lugar of Indiana, and Mark Hatfield of Oregon expressed official "concern" that the president could not pull the Senate together to support this bill that had already become law in such enlightened nations as Iran, Iraq, Libya, Ethiopia, and South Africa.

What does this controversial measure promise? It would grant freedom of expression to children, without restriction. It would guarantee children freedom of "thought, conscience, and religion." It would prohibit any restriction of the child's freedom of association. It would grant children the absolute right of privacy, including privacy from their own parents.

This is only a partial list of the "protections" the lawyers and sages of the United Nations have prescribed for children. A key provision is the right of each child to "mass media" intended for his or her social, moral, or intellectual good. This "right" would prevent parents from prohibiting their children from being indoctrinated by government-sponsored mass media—an alarming precedent. This tactic has always been uppermost in totalitarian regimes. Strip children from their parents, then propagandize them by the state, so that children become agents and informers against their parents.

It is not hard to imagine what sort of character such laws would promote. Nor is it hard to imagine what use clever manipulators will make of young people emptied of the values and instructions of their parents. This law strips away morality and posits a godless law of the jungle.

The idea that mass media can educate and inform the moral and mental health needs of children is really the ultimate farce. Just look at what the mass media offer our children today! Popular television is flooded with filth and violence; MTV, VH-1, and pop radio stations are sewers of obscenity, rebellion, and violence; pop magazines promote the vilest forms of pornography and a form of materialism, selfishness, and greed that has fallen to the lowest levels in human history. Are these the custodians of morality and mental hygiene?

But this is the era of the antifamily, anticommunity, antination new world order. The Rights of the Child Treaty is the law before the current United Nations, the body that is planned to guide us into the future. If a man beats up his fiancé before they are married, rest assured that she will become a battered wife. If the one-worlders are trying to ram the antifamily Rights of the Child Treaty down our throats now, just think what is coming after the wedding! The new world order will not be a promise of hope but a bitter, cruel hoax!

11

The Words of the Prophets

INSCRIBED OUTSIDE THE United Nations building on the East River in Manhattan are the words of the Prophet Isaiah, who wrote in 720 B.C., some 2,711 years ago, about a time in the future when,

> They shall beat their swords into plowshares,
> And their spears into pruning hooks;
> Nation shall not lift up sword against nation,
> Neither shall they learn war anymore.
> Isaiah 2:4

Obviously those who founded the United Nations believed in the lofty words of the prophet. Or at least they believed that the organization that they were establishing would be the human instrument of peace. Implicit in the message of the United Nations was a promise to disarm, to use the resources of war for peace, and to establish a world order in which the nations of the world would not go to war against one another—in fact they would not even study military science and strategy anymore. The great minds that had created atomic weapons, warplanes, tanks, and artillery would now be devoted to the betterment of mankind.

So far I have pointed out some of the dark sides of the new world order, but to be fair there are some in Establishment circles who sincerely and earnestly wanted the blessing to mankind that world peace would bring. As former Secretary of State Dean Acheson said, they embraced the United Nations "with evangelical fervor," only to have their hopes dashed by forty-five years of military confrontation, communist subversion, and countless wars and revolutions.

No, the United Nations founded in 1945 under the words of the prophet did not bring a time when swords became plowshares and spears became pruning hooks. The reason is simple. God and His prophets never promised world peace to mankind through a human world government.

Here are the words of the prophet which precede those carved at the United Nations:

> Now it shall come to pass in the latter days
> That the mountain of the LORD's house
> Shall be established on the top of the mountains,
> And shall be exalted above the hills;
> And all nations shall flow to it.
> Many people shall come and say,
> "Come, and let us go up to the mountain of the LORD.
> To the House of the God of Jacob;
> He will teach us His ways,
> And we shall walk in His paths."
> For out of Zion shall go forth the law,
> And the word of the LORD from Jerusalem.
> He shall judge between the nations,
> And shall rebuke many people;
> They shall beat their swords into plowshares,
> And their spears into pruning hooks.

First, the prophet makes it quite clear that peace will come to the earth "in the latter days." As much as we would like to hurry it up, it will come as was said of the coming of Jesus Christ, "in the fullness of time."

Second, peace will come when "the mountain of the Lord's house shall be established on the top of the mountains." There will never be world peace until God's house and God's people are given their rightful place of leadership at the top of the world. How can there be peace when drunkards, drug dealers, communists, atheists, New Age worshipers of Satan, secular humanists, oppressive dictators, greedy moneychangers, revolutionary assassins, adulterers, and homosexuals are on top? Under their leadership the world will never, I repeat never, experience lasting peace.

TRUE, LASTING PEACE

Peace will only come when its source is flowing from the benign influences of Almighty God, through the people given to His service who comprise "His house." As long as the cynical politicians and equally cynical media continue to deny God's people their rightful place in God's order for the world, they are condemning their world to violence, turmoil, oppression, and war.

Adolf Hitler once commented on the efforts of German evangelical clergymen to oppose his programs. "Their task is to prepare men's souls for heaven; they must leave the earth to me," he said. What a job he did on earth without their advice.

In America, a crescendo has been rising for decades, backed up by the power of the liberal members of Congress, the federal courts, and the Internal Revenue Service, to ensure that evangelical Christians stay in their churches, concern themselves with heaven, and leave the earth to them. Although I agree that it is unwise for the organized church as an institution to get itself entwined with government as an institution, there is absolutely no way that government can operate successfully unless led by godly men and women operating under the laws of the God of Jacob.

Yet when God's house is exalted, peace and prosperity will follow. The people of Guatemala recently elected, by an overwhelming majority, my friend Jorge Serrano as their president. Jorge is a dedicated, spirit-filled, evangelical Christian. Hardly was he inaugurated when he successfully concluded negotiations to end the guerrilla insurgency in Guatemala so the land could have peace. Serrano has placed godly people in high positions in his cabinet, and I am convinced that if they are free from outside mischief, they will bring their country to stability and prosperity.

Serrano continues the enlightened leadership of his patron, former President Rios Montt, who insisted on honesty in government and then had every key official sign a pledge that read, "I will not steal; I will not lie; I will not abuse." I was in Guatemala City three days after Rios Montt overthrew the corrupt Lopez Garcia government. The people had been dancing in the street for joy, literally fulfilling the words of Solomon who said, "When the righteous are in authority, the people rejoice."

Third, the Prophet Isaiah tells us that world peace will come when "many people say, 'Come, and let us go up to the mountain of the Lord, to the house of the God of Jacob; He will teach us His ways, and we will walk in His paths.'"

In other words, world peace will come when the people of the world finally reject the hypocritical lies that have been foisted upon them for centuries, whether by utopian dreamers, hot-headed revolutionaries, greedy, power-hungry politicians, or demonic madmen and then turn to the house of the God of Jacob for help.

Notice two elements of the prophetic message. First, the desire of the nations for help is totally voluntary. The philosophy of Thomas Jefferson, who drew up the landmark Virginia Statute of Religious Liberty, made it clear that the duty a man owes his Creator cannot be coerced by the state. The attitude that brings people's hearts into compliance with God's laws and therefore peace with their neighbors is always voluntary. No army and no civil service can compel it, and none should ever try.

Government can only accomplish its task by compulsion and coercion. Every theory of world order being put forth today always includes the force of arms. And every time government tries to bring on utopia by force of arms, it degenerates into the nightmare of Soviet communism or Hitler's Nazism.

LEARNING GOD'S WAYS

We will not have world peace until people begin to come to God or His representatives on earth and say, "Teach us your ways."

This very thing is happening now in many nations. The Soviet government's television network has requested the Christian Broadcasting Network to provide animated Bible stories to teach their children moral values. Our Soviet representative placed a brief spot announcement in the midst of our Russian language version of the popular "Superbook" and "Flying House" programs.

To those who answered three questions—"Where did people come from?" "What is one of the Ten Commandments?" and "Who is Jesus Christ?"—a little, colored, Bible-story book was sent. Imagine our delight when our Moscow office received more than 2 million handwritten letters from Soviet children and their parents, some containing absolutely beautiful hand-colored pictures of Bible stories.

Of special interest to us was the fact that after years of indoctrination in atheism and evolution, over 90 percent of the people responding said that human beings were created by God, not evolved from apes.

I was told by a distinguished pastor from an Eastern European country that the Soviet Academy of Science welcomed a series of lectures on Creationism and then requested further literature and a series of regional lectures to show that Creationism is more valid than the theory of evolution.

In the same vein, a delegation of the leaders of the Rumanian national television network visited our headquarters in Virginia Beach to request religious and family-oriented television programs for their nation. They will begin airing our Bible stories five nights per week at 7:30 P.M. across their entire nation in order to instruct their children in the ways of God.

The Rumanian government has now approached the churches of their land to send teachers of the Christian religion into their schools to instruct their children in the moral and ethical values that had been taken away from them during communism. To help meet the needs of the Christians in Rumania to learn the principles of government in God's kingdom, we had two hundred thousand copies of my book, *The Secret Kingdom,* translated and distributed throughout the country.

More recently, a member of the diplomatic corps from Zaire came to our headquarters at the direction of President Sese Mobutu with an invitation to me to come to his nation to teach the principles of government according to God's laws to his people, including the pastors as well as members of his government. Not only did I enjoy a successful visit, but we are now planning extended television broadcasts this fall on the national television network of Zaire to teach God's laws to all the people.

As more and more governments acknowledge their failures and come to "the house of the God of Jacob" for teaching, there will be increasing peace and prosperity. The natural process foretold by the Prophet Isaiah is beginning to take place, little by little, around the world. I know this because I have been privileged to be a part of it. My fervent prayer is that the big boys, with their weapons, money, and misguided plans for social reform, will not try to wreck what is springing spontaneously from a heartfelt need.

The prophet says that the nations will come not just to "religion," but to the God of Jacob. We read in the Bible that a woman of Samaria, who held a bastardized version of Judaism imposed on her people by the Assyrians, met Jesus Christ at Jacob's Well in Samaria. After some discussion about religious matters, Jesus made an amazing statement to the woman, "You do not know what you believe, for salvation is of the Jews."

Today's open-minded, anything-goes syncretism will not bring world peace. What I am saying may jar some sensibilities, but only the teaching that comes forth from the house of the God of Jacob will bring world peace. The gods of the animist tree worshipers, the gods of the ancestor worshipers, the million gods of the Hindus, and the Allah of the Muslims are not the God of Jacob. The revelation of the one true God came from Abraham to Isaac to Jacob to David and to Jesus. Then Jesus made the bold statement: "I am the way, the truth, and the life. No one comes to the Father but by me."

THE WAY OF THE WORLD

The new world order will have as its religion a god of light, whom Bible scholars recognize as Lucifer. Nations who walk in Lucifer's ways will find only suffering and heartache, but never peace!

We should note well that the prophet tells us that world peace will come when the nations not only come to the house of the God of Jacob to learn His ways, but when they agree to walk in His paths. Obviously it would do no good for the people of Zaire who heard me teach the ways of God to them on television if they refused to reorder their lives after the teaching. First there must be revelation, then obedience. Always voluntary, always from the heart, always on the basis of truth, never coerced, and never for purely selfish motives.

How revolutionary it would be if the nations of the world truly walked in the ways of the God of Jacob. The voluntary application of just one of His principles, called the Golden Rule, would cause air and water pollution to cease, crime to cease, divorce and child abuse to cease, economic exploitation to cease, the narcotics traffic to cease, human rights abuse to cease, and war to cease. The potential savings in national budgets from the elimination of police, criminal courts, standing armies, pollution control agencies, drug enforcement, and many poverty programs is almost beyond calculation.

What is this revolutionary law of God? It is one that many children learned in Sunday school: "Do unto others as you would have them do unto you." That is not utopianism, I might add, but reciprocal self-interest. If you don't want pollution dumped on you, don't dump it on someone else. If you don't want your property stolen, don't steal from someone else. If you don't want to be raped, don't rape someone else. If you don't want your country invaded by armies, don't invade someone else's country. If you want someone to help you when you are poor, then help someone else when he is poor.

It is all so simple. So inexpensive. So very practical. The world works because people at every level live out the Golden Rule and make it work. When they do, there is peace, and no huge money machine called the new world order is necessary.

Fourth, the prophet tells us that peace will come when "out of Zion shall go forth the law." In the United States today we have the highest voluntary income tax compliance of any nation on earth. If the American people ever become persuaded that the Internal Revenue Service is incompetent, corrupt, unfair, or ideologically biased, voluntary compliance would plummet and the government would not be able to place enough revenue agents throughout the country to collect the tax revenues due it. Americans voluntarily comply and pay taxes because, despite misgivings, we still trust our government. When the bond of trust is severed, the government will fall apart.

In Zaire, people do not trust their government. Cheating on taxes is pandemic, and the government is in crisis. Trust is an absolutely essential ingredient for successful government.

Think of a world with a tribunal so wise and so fair that all parties in a dispute would obey its decisions without conflict and without coercion. Then there would be no cause for war. Individuals and nations would submit their disputes to a tribunal that they trusted implicitly. Again it should be emphasized that compliance is not coerced. Compliance is voluntary because the law involved is clearly for the good of mankind, and its wisdom commends itself as being in accord with the nature of man and the nature of the universe.

After all, neither the law of gravity nor the law of thermodynamics requires standing armies and security police for enforcement. These laws enforce themselves by the very action of the universe itself. People who "break" the law of gravity injure themselves.

People who "obey" the law of thermodynamics build pumps, and motors, and vehicles. The physical laws are there for our benefit if we are willing to obey them. The moral laws of the God of Jacob are also there for our benefit, if we are willing to submit ourselves to them. As in the case of the physical laws, God's moral laws do not require armies to enforce them. They are self-enforcing. People and societies that break them destroy themselves.

THE UNIVERSAL MORAL LAW

Through the history of what has been called Christian civilization, the Ten Commandments, given directly by the God of Jacob thirty-four hundred years ago to a great leader of the family of Jacob, named Moses, have been considered the heart of the universal moral law.

In one of the great tragedies of history, the Supreme Court of the supposedly Christian United States guaranteed the moral collapse of this nation when it forbade children in the public schools to pray to the God of Jacob, to learn of His moral law, or even to view in their classrooms the heart of the law, the Ten Commandments, which children must obey for their own good or disobey at their peril.

It is one of the supreme ironies of history that the former communist bloc nations are desperately seeking to repair the moral wreckage brought upon their nations by an official policy of atheism, while irreligious liberal groups like the American Civil Liberties Union, People for the American Way, the American Jewish Congress, Americans United for Separation of Church and State, the National Organization for Women, and the liberal media are doing everything in their power to drive the United States into the same moral abyss that the Eastern Bloc countries are clawing their way out of.

The Ten Commandments are for our own good. As Jesus Christ put it, "The Sabbath was made for man." How do these commandments relate to the world?

The utopians have talked of world order. Without saying so explicitly, the Ten Commandments set the only order that will bring world peace—with devotion to and respect of God at the center, strong family bonds and respect next, and the sanctity of people, property, family, reputation, and peace of mind next.

All of the utopian societies that we have examined operate under a cloak of secrecy and a cloud of lies—every single one! They are furtive and conceal from view their real leaders and their real agenda. Each one has a series of concentric circles of order—from the key few to the enlightened initiates, to a larger front organization, to the agencies that they can manipulate.

Not one places God or the Bible at the center of its world schemes. When someone offers us a new social order, you would think we would have a clear right to ask, "If what you are offering is so good for us, why are you trying to sneak it by us the way you did the Federal Reserve Board?" God did not deliver His plan for world order in secret. He announced it from a smoking mountaintop and has subsequently caused hundreds of millions of copies of the law to be printed in virtually every known language on earth.

The first commandment is key to all the others, **"You shall have no other gods before Me."** Money, power, success, and utopian dreams all can become gods who have baser standards than the God of Jacob. Serving the lesser gods permits ethical lapses under the broad heading, "the end justifies the means." If our god is a Marxist paradise, then killing 60 million human beings is justified, if that is necessary to bring about paradise. If our god is financial success, then wiping out competitors by unethical means is permissible. To have the God of Jacob as the preeminent deity means to gain success that all of his ethical standards must be observed along the way.

CASTING DOWN IDOLS

The next point in God's world order, **"You shall not make for yourself any carved image, . . . you shall not bow down to them nor serve them,"** prohibits false religious worship. Idolatry sprang from the worship of the sun, moon, snakes, cows, certain mythical creatures, or Satan. The idol was created by man, and therefore the creators of the idol and its priests could change the rules of the idol to suit themselves.

In the Roman Empire, in the Soviet Union, and in Red China enormous statues and portraits of the leaders were displayed everywhere. Wherever the citizenry looked, they saw these bigger-than-life likenesses of Marx, Lenin, and Mao Tse Tung. Once these men were dead, their followers—

the priests of their temple—made up any stories they wished about the real meaning of "pure" Marxist-Leninist thought.

In Third World countries that practice idolatry, the idols are representatives of demonic power, and their worship often involves actual demon possession. The barbaric acts that have been committed in the name of idols range from the assassinations committed by worshipers of Kali in India, to the human sacrifices by the Mayans in Mexico, to the sacrifices to the volcano god in Polynesia, to the sacrifice of children to the Canaanite fire god Molech.

The Bible warns us that in the end times a world dictator will arise whose enormous statue will be energized by Satan in league with a false religious system to do signs and wonders. But if people engage in idolatry, there can be only delusion and manipulation in the name of the idol by the "priests of the temple," but never happiness or world peace.

The third commandment establishing God's world order, **"You shall not take the name of the Lord your God in vain,"** means two things. First, those who are serving Him must understand the full extent of His power, and in turn must not appear to be His followers when in truth they are not.

The name of the Lord means "I am." In history He has showed Himself as provider, healer, victor, wisdom, righteousness, shepherd, peace, and savior. When people and nations come to Him to learn His ways, He wants them to look to Him for the supply of all their needs. He wants them to realize it is not necessary to rob, lie, oppress, cheat, and steal in order to receive His bountiful supply.

God's order for the world requires that people look to God directly to meet their needs, not to government, social programs, or conduct that injures others and violates His laws. And when people claim to know Him, He insists that they live according to their profession. For the United States to write "In God We Trust" on its currency while denying public school children the right to pray is not only hypocritical, it breaks the third commandment.

The next obligation that a citizen of God's world order owes is to himself. **"Remember the Sabbath day, to keep it holy,"** is a command for the personal benefit of each citizen. Our minds, spirits, and bodies demand a regular time of rest. Perhaps God's greatest gift to mankind's earthly existence is the ability to be free from work one day a week. Only when people are permitted to rest from their labors, to meditate on God, to consider His way, to dream of a better world can there be progress and genuine human betterment.

SELF-INFLICTED WOUNDS

Galley slaves and coolies forced to work seven days a week became no better than beasts of burden. Higher civilizations rise when people can rest, think, and draw inspiration from God. Laws in America that mandated a day of rest from incessant commerce have been nullified as a violation of the separation of church and state. In modern America, shopping centers, malls, and stores of every description carry on their frantic pace seven days a week. As an outright insult to God and His plan, only those policies that can be shown to have a clearly secular purpose are recognized.

What idiocy our society has indulged in by refusing to acknowledge the wisdom of God. Before our eyes we watch the increase of chronic burnout, stress breakdowns, nervous disorders, and mental and spiritual exhaustion cauterizing the souls of our people. We consume billions of tranquilizers. Marriages fall apart, and the business of psychologists is booming. Psychosomatic illnesses make up 70 percent of our medical problems, yet we ignore the clear wisdom and will of God. The answer in God's world order is so easy to find. It is not a mystery. A loving God has made His way so simple, even a child can understand it.

I never gave the issue of a day of rest much thought until I read God's Word spoken through the Prophet Isaiah on the subject:

> If you turn away your foot from the Sabbath,
> From doing your pleasure on My holy day,
> And call the Sabbath a delight,
> The holy day of the LORD honorable, . . .
> [Not] finding your own pleasure,
> Nor speaking your own words,
> Then you shall delight yourself in the LORD;
> And I will cause you to ride on the high hills of the earth,
> And feed you with the heritage of Jacob your father.
> Isaiah 58:13–14

Since exaltation and promised rewards came from one day of rest and worship, I determined to remake my Sundays according to the biblical model. When I did, concepts began to flow, my strength and vigor during my workdays jumped dramatically, and along with them came the resulting productivity and resulting benefits. Indeed the Sabbath was made for man. If you don't believe me, try working thirty days nonstop with no weekend breaks, then gauge your mental acuity and productivity.

GOD'S UNIT OF ORDER

The basic unit of social, local, national, and international organization in God's world order is the family. As William Bennett, former secretary of education, said so eloquently, "The first Department of Health, Education, and Welfare is the family."

The basic responsibility for child rearing, social, and moral education belongs to the family. Every attempt at institutional child care has proved a miserable failure. Experiments with primates and human beings have shown beyond any chance of contradiction that the social and intellectual development of young children depends on extended personal nurturing by their mothers.

Furthermore, landmark studies by the World Health Organization, cited by Professor Armand Nicolai of Harvard University, showed that the prolonged absence of either parent had a dramatically negative impact upon young children, who then grow up lacking in drive, susceptible to peer pressure, and mediocre in studies. Although these clear findings are known and available, they are suppressed because women either must work or find personal fulfillment in work. Children are often ignored in the rhetoric of the feminist movement, which for so long denigrated motherhood and exalted the role of women in professions, in manual labor, and more recently in armed combat.

Virtually every recent pressure in society has been antifamily. We have brought in no-fault divorces. We have raised the tax burden on families by an estimated 226 percent. We have subsidized illegitimate births. We have permitted teenage abortions without parental consent. We have opened sex clinics in schools to teach illicit sex and to pass out contraceptives.

The National Education Association actually prints literature to show teachers how to subvert parental rights. More than anything, the number of working mothers has skyrocketed from 32.8 percent in 1948 to 66.6 percent in 1990, much of that caused by government-induced inflation and the resultant drop in the real incomes of male head-of-family wage earners.

The fifth commandment says, **"Honor your father and mother, that your days may be long upon the land."** Under God's order there is to be a family unit of mother, father, and children. The norm is the nuclear family, where both mother and father supply the material needs and give the appropriate education and discipline to the children. The family is to transmit the culture and traditions of the society to the children.

Children in turn are to respect and obey their parents because parents are God's representatives to them. When parents become elderly and unable to work, the honor due them includes material care. As one person said so poignantly to me, "If a mother and father can afford to care for four children, why can't four children afford to care for their mother and father?"

Instead, in our society we have cut the link given in God's order. We encourage childlessness and abortion that removes younger wage earners to care for the elderly. Then we, through social security, Medicare, Medicaid, and a host of other impersonal government assistance programs, have effectively cut the lifeline between children and their elderly parents. Instead of old age being a time of honor, it is often a time of destitution, as the enlightened humanists of the new world order look for government-funded nursing homes and ways to advertise the Hemlock Society and more efficient euthanasia.

KNOWING GOD

God's world order builds upon a proper relationship with Him, then respect for man made in God's image, and then the nuclear family as the basis of a healthy clan, which naturally makes for a healthy nation and, in turn, a healthy world.

Every healthy society in our world today stresses the importance of healthy cohesive families, loving parents, obedient children, strong traditions, quality education, respect for hard work and thrift, individual self-reliance, and ethnic pride. Every one of these virtues are under attack by the politically correct apostles of the new world order who have been trying to undermine America so it will surrender its sovereignty and willingly enter into a world government.

Once people in the world are in direct contact with God, have rejected satanic counterfeits, have recognized that God can supply all their needs, have established their own dignity and self-worth, and have come to the proper order in their families—then and only then are they in a position to take care of their fellow man.

The Apostle Paul wrote that the next five commandments are summed up in one phrase, **"You shall love your neighbor as yourself,"** because love does no harm to other people.

The sixth commandment in God's order guarantees respect for life: **"You shall not murder."** Human life has been created in God's image, and it is to be inviolate. The founders of the American republic recognized that God had created all men equal in His image and had endowed each of them with the inalienable rights of life, liberty, and the pursuit of happiness.

The basic rights of people in God's order are guaranteed by God Himself and cannot be taken away by any government. In the communist order, people only have the rights that were given them by the state. Under the United States Constitution, the state receives only that portion of the God-given rights which the people, by contract, cede over to it.

If God is removed from the equation, and if human life is not uniquely created in His image, then people can be treated like cattle for the benefit of their masters. Any new world order based on atheism or syncretism will downgrade the right to life of every human being. The unborn may be aborted, the unfit may be eliminated, and the elderly may be given lethal injections. Hitler in his new order called these people "useless eaters" and not fit to live. In the name of humanism, they downgraded the basic rights of human beings.

In God's order, no one has to fear for his life. He is to be safe from murder in his home, his job, and in his travels. Neither private individuals, mobs, nor the state are permitted to murder.

THE MARRIAGE BOND

In some utopias, all children are to be raised in common. In some, as in Nazi Germany, certain women are used like broodmares to bear the master race. In some, family life is forbidden except for the procreation of communal children. In today's view of utopia, unbridled sex between men and women, men and men, and women and women in whatever grouping, technique, or circumstance seems desirable. In God's order, sexual relations outside of marriage are forbidden, and marriage is to be for life. The marriage bond is to be so strong that neither partner is to engage in extramarital sex with another, nor is a single man or woman permitted to have sex with a married person.

In God's order, every spouse is to feel secure in the love and fidelity of the other spouse. Every father will know that the children his wife had born within their marriage are his. Every wife is assured that her husband is not sharing what belonged to her and her children with another woman and her children.

Each partner in a marriage is able to rest assured that the life they have built together will not be shattered by some fleeting liaison with someone outside the marriage. A godly marriage is a lifetime investment by both partners, and neither spouse should have to fear that investment will be squandered by the other. At the same time, neither spouse has to worry that a mate is bringing a deadly disease to their marriage bed. Children are to rest assured in the love and fidelity that their parents share and in the stability and honor of their home. The seventh commandment is clear, **"You shall not commit adultery."**

In God's order, the energy of the people is to be directed toward creating a just and happy world. History shows that every civilization in which the creative energies of people were dissipated by sexual promiscuity and drunkenness has quickly gone into decline. Without trust, fidelity, and discipline, families fail and nations fail.

RESPECT FOR PROPERTY

God's order recognizes the sanctity of private property. The eighth commandment, **"You shall not steal"** means that the God of Jacob forbids a citizen to take what belongs to another citizen. He did not permit a Robin Hood to take from the rich and give to the poor, or the greedy rich to steal possessions of the poor. What a man had accumulated was his. In God's order there are no schemes of wealth redistribution under which government forces productive citizens to give the fruit of their hard-earned labors to those who are nonproductive.

Opportunity was to be equal for all citizens. Those who were rich were instructed in order to receive God's blessings to give generous voluntary gifts to the poor, and sufficient gleaning was to be set aside so that the poor would have an opportunity to earn a living for themselves.

We hear in today's political jargon that there is a difference between human rights and property rights. This is nonsense. Without property of some sort it is impossible to obtain food, clothing, and shelter. It is certainly impossible to obtain recreation, education, books, music, art, travel, and worry-free retirement—the things that are considered the benefits of civilization.

When the framers of the U.S. Declaration of Independence spoke of the pursuit of happiness, they obviously had in mind the ability to work, to accumulate private material possessions, and to pay for the type of life-style such possessions made possible. Remember, though, our founders guaranteed the pursuit of happiness, not happiness itself. No government has the wealth or power to guarantee happiness, but any government can ensure the opportunity of all citizens to pursue their own destiny under God.

Every single utopian vision of world order requires a severe restriction on people's ownership of property and the enjoyment of its fruits. God's world order says that every man should be free to own private property free from the fear of theft by his fellow citizens or confiscation by a greedy government.

FALSE ACCUSERS

In the communist countries, a regular part of life for the citizens was the false trials and perjured accusations before kangaroo courts. Judges were corrupt, prosecutors were corrupt, witnesses were corrupt. In the United States, although there are occasional cases of defendants falsely accused, the only true counterpart of the communist legal system is found in America's liberal press.

Private citizens and public officials are slandered and convicted in the press by so-called investigative reporters who act as prosecutor, judge, and jury. The accused has no ability to question evidence brought against him, no appeal to an impartial tribunal, and no ability to review the accuracy of the indictment against him. Under the U.S. Supreme Court decision of *Sullivan v. The New York Times,* the burden of proof in proving press libel is so onerous that few of those victimized by the press have any option than to suffer in silence the loss of their reputations.

The price that the vicious, sensational press exacts of public officials is so great that good citizens of ability are increasingly reluctant to enter into any type of public service. After thirty years of being the recipient of libel and scorn at the hands of the print media, I have become a bit more hardened to their tactics. But I often wonder who gave these people the right to destroy, humiliate, and damage the reputation of another human being living at peace with them?

The liberal press has tried repeatedly to take away from Christian people in America the right to run for office, to support candidates, to protest government abuses, or to protect themselves in court. Whatever ultimate victory Christian candidates may win is usually nullified by the torrent of unwarranted vituperation they have to experience in the press. With very few exceptions in America, it is absolutely impossible for an evangelical Christian to receive a fair story in the liberal press when he or she is involved in any unfavorable encounter with a government agency at any level.

Regardless of government abuse, the evangelical knows that the government agency will be portrayed in a favorable light and he will be portrayed unfavorably. In one case in which I was a party, my Jewish attorney could not convince the liberal press that I had been proved completely blameless of the slander that had been brought against me. This was the comment from my lawyer, who has represented worldwide clients and several Israeli government agencies: "I have never encountered such press hostility in my life."

The liberal press represents the Establishment in the United States and Europe. The Nazis used the press to vilify the Jews and make association with them shameful. The communists used the press to undercut their enemies prior to their trial and punishment. In the new world order we can rest assured that those who stand in the way of the Establishment plans will become, like Margaret Thatcher, the victim of unremitting character assassination by the press.

FREEDOM FROM FEAR

In God's world order, libel and slander are not permitted. The ninth commandment, **"You shall not bear false witness,"** is meant to protect the reputation of every person. People are to be secure against false trials and lies brought against them in court. But they also are to be free from damage to their reputations brought by lying neighbors, lying officials, or lying reporters.

You see, in God's order, people are to live without fear of any kind. Fear for their lives, fear for their property, fear for their marriages, or fear of losing their reputations because of false accusations.

But no man is truly free from fear as long as someone else is looking longingly at his job, his wife, his home, his money, or his reputation. The welfare state and the socialistic systems are based on the politics of envy. The poor are envious of the rich and therefore will use government power to take their riches away from them. Liberal congressmen always define "rich" as anyone who makes more money than they do. Despite objections to congressional pay increases, it is much safer for the middle class when congressional salaries go higher, for we know they will not enact punitive taxes against themselves.

But the new world order promises to elevate the politics of envy and covetousness to a new level, once the Third World nations find the mechanism to loot the accumulated wealth of this nation. Few citizens are without fear in the United States now when faced with the sanctions of the IRS, their state taxing authorities, and local tax assessors. Think of the fear that will come over you when you contemplate two continents of people coveting your possessions and no way to keep them from taking what is yours.

In God's order, the last commandment makes all the others possible. God addresses something that no government can regulate, the power of the human heart. God effectively nips the root of murder, theft, adultery, and slander when He commands, **"You shall not covet."** In God's order, people may have all that they can get morally and ethically from the resources available to all the people, so long as they worship God and not possessions, and give generously to God and those less fortunate. But they cannot even desire what belongs to their neighbor. What is his, is his, sacred, inviolate, protected by the solemn decree of the God of Jacob.

The socialists, communists, and advocates of a managed welfare state all want government to solve the perceived problems of society. Their solutions invariably involve government regulation, government spending, increased government taxes, and stricter sanctions to enforce their decrees. Government for them takes the place of God, and their constituents increasingly look to government to carry them from birth to death. In America today more than 50 percent of the people, from the rich to the poor, receive some financial payment from the government, and therefore, absent a miracle or a political revolution, the process is virtually irreversible.

GOVERNMENT AS GOD

With the government as god, the major crimes in society involve breaking government regulations. Morality becomes whatever a majority in Congress or the Supreme Court says it is at any point of time. The litany of government-sponsored crimes includes failure to pay income taxes, lying to the government, operating your affairs against regulations, failure to make full disclosure to a state or federal agency, violating securities laws, speeding laws, parking laws, zoning laws, pollution laws, fishing laws. In a poll taken by *Seventeen* magazine, parking in a parking space reserved for handicapped people was rated as a worse moral offense than sexual relations out of wedlock.

The moral order at the heart of the universe is broken daily by blasphemy, adulterous sex, lying, disrespect for parents, and coveting. Society in fact encourages, where possible, every imaginable conduct to violate the true moral law, while defending petty regulations against the citizens as if *they* had been handed down on tablets from Mount Sinai, instead of from "Gucci Gulch," as the lobbyist-filled corridors of power in the United States capital are derisively called.

Yet the Apostle Paul tells us that love is the fulfilling of the moral law. Against the one who loves his neighbor, "there is no law." Marx fantasized about a classless, stateless society where government had faded away. His was a pipe dream. But in God's order that is precisely what will happen—government and its wasteful laws and regulations will be unnecessary. All that would be necessary would be an association of the citizens to accomplish tasks in common, such as road building and traffic control, which no individual family could do for itself.

Thomas Jefferson described it well when he said, "That government governs best which governs least." The founders of America—at Plymouth Rock and in the Massachusetts Colony—felt that they were organizing a society based on the Ten Commandments and the Sermon on the Mount. They perceived this new land as a successor to the nation of Israel, and they tried their best to model their institutions of governmental order after the Bible. In fact the man who interpreted the meaning of Scripture to them, the pastor, was given a higher place than the governor of the colony. These people built an incredible society because they exalted "the mountain of the Lord's house" above the other mountains.

THE MISSING INGREDIENT

There is no other way to explain the success of this experiment in liberty other than to realize that for almost two hundred years prior to our Constitution, all of the leadership of this nation had been steeped in the biblical principles of the Old and New Testaments. Their new order was a nation founded squarely on concepts of the nature of God, the nature of man, the role of the family, and the moral order as established by the God of Jacob.

They also knew that, although a few Christian settlers had received a change of heart to obey God's laws fully, there was no guarantee that a larger population at a later time would be so inclined. So they anchored their government with strong chains to keep it from acting rashly or in an arbitrary or dictatorial fashion. The wisdom of our biblically based Founding Fathers gave the United States of America the finest concept of ordered liberty the world has ever known.

It is this "Christian order" which the new world order seeks to replace!

The prophets tell us that there will be a time when the missing ingredient to complete God's world order will take place—the hearts of mankind will be changed to want to live a life of love with their fellow man. When that happens, not only will men be at peace with one another, the wild animals will be at peace as well. Instead of the Lex Talionis, the law of the jungle, there will be the law of God's love. Instead of an outward law, there will be an inner law of the heart.

Here is how the prophet Jeremiah related it:

> I will put My law in their minds, and write it on their hearts; and I will be their God, and they shall be My people.
>
> Jeremiah 31:33

When men's hearts have been changed, when from their hearts they want only good for their fellow men, and naturally, as if by instinct, they obey God's laws, then there will be world peace, a universal brotherhood of man, the sharing of wealth, and a paradise on earth.

Until that happens by the sovereign intervention of God's Spirit, any attempt to create a government structure with no godly values and based on corrupt and venal men will either lead to the foolishness and impotence of the current United Nations or, much worse, to a worldwide dictatorship more horrible than anything the world has yet known.

GOD'S NEW WORLD ORDER

But God's new world order is coming much nearer than we believe. Jesus Christ said that "the kingdom of God is at hand." At the present time the kingdom of God is not visible, but it is growing every day, day by day, as hundreds, thousands, millions, and tens of millions are coming to Jesus Christ, receiving His forgiveness for their sins, and being born again by the sovereign action of God Almighty into God's kingdom.

These people are called the sons of God. They are everywhere among us. In the lowest tasks, in the highest. People of no learning, some with great learning. Some with no wealth, others with fabled wealth. Some with no political power, others holding high government office. Some with no athletic ability, others world-class champions. Silently, steadily, they are being prepared for their place in God's coming world order.

The world can recognize them by their lives. Other than that, their nature is invisible. They appear on the surface to be just like everyone else. But they are being kept in waiting until the time that God sweeps away the pretense of the satanic and man-made counterfeits and announces His new world order and His anointed leader, Jesus the Messiah.

Then will come the unveiling of the sons and daughters of God to the world. Then these people, who have often been so ridiculed and despised by the world, will be revealed as what they really are and given their place in God's world order. Then, and only then, will the world be at peace.

The Apostle Paul put it this way in his letter to the church at Rome:

> For the earnest expectation of the creation eagerly waits for the revealing of the sons of God. For . . . the creation itself also will be delivered from the bondage of corruption into the glorious liberty of the children of God.
> Romans 8:19, 21

Therefore, do not be anxious. God's work is right on schedule. The company of the sons of God is almost complete—perhaps this very decade may finish the task. God sometimes seems to be slow, but He is never late. In the fullness of time, He will announce His kingdom on earth. I do not believe that we have much longer to wait!

12

The Great Divide

MODERN IRAQ NOW occupies the land at the mouth of the Tigris-Euphrates Rivers, where civilization began. Although modern-day Iraq is a creation of Winston Churchill as colonial secretary of Great Britain on August 23, 1919, its roots trail back into mystery and legend.

The first known urban civilization was located in Sumer near modern Basra, then farther north to Accad. Around the year 2000 B.C., a man called Abram, whose name was changed by God to Abraham ("father of a multitude"), was born in Ur of the Chaldees near the mouth of the Tigris-Euphrates River and near the site of ancient Sumer.

Abraham journeyed with his family from Ur to nearby Syria, and from there he went out under the command of Almighty God to receive the land we now know as Palestine, or Israel, as his permanent possession. From Abraham came two sons. One was born, as if by a miracle, when Abraham was a hundred years old and his beloved wife, Sarah, was ninety years old and past all natural childbearing ability. This child was named Isaac, which means "laughter." The other son, his first, was born to Sarah's servant girl Hagar. The boy was named Ishmael, which means "God hears."

God had promised Abraham that his descendants would be as numerous as the stars of heaven, and indeed they are. Ishmael was the progenitor of the Arab people, who number in the hundreds of millions. But God made an even greater promise to Abraham when He assured him that through his seed all the families of the earth would be blessed. The promise of blessing was transmitted not to Ishmael, but to Isaac, and then to Isaac's son Jacob, and then to Jacob's son Judah, and then to Judah's descendant, King David, and to King David's descendant, Jesus of Nazareth.

The law of the God of Jacob was preserved by the Jewish people, who were the descendants of Jacob's twelve sons, as the true rule of order for all the nations. The salvation offered to all the families on the earth, as foretold by the Jewish prophets, was to be through the person whom the Jews came to call the Messiah, which in Hebrew means "the anointed one of God."

THE ANOINTED ONE

For Christians and many others, the literal personification of the Messiah is Jesus of Nazareth, a lineal descendant of Abraham, Isaac, Jacob, Judah, and David, who for the past two millennia has been called *Christos,* which is the Greek word translating the Hebrew word, *Meshiach,* or Messiah. Jesus Christ is the final expression to all mankind of the faith of Abraham. He was a truly perfect man, totally yielded to the purposes of God.

His complete obedience even to death and His subsequent resurrection from death made Him the first of the ever-swelling multitude of those who are preparing for God's new world order of peace and justice. The time of this glorious paradise on earth under the divinely conceived Messiah and His chosen people is termed the Millennium, the thousand-year reign.

Those who have submitted themselves to the lordship of the Messiah and invited Him to live within their hearts eagerly look forward to the establishment of God's new world order when evil, hatred, sickness, poverty, and war are taken from the earth. The Apostle Paul calls the millennial kingdom "the blessed hope and glorious appearing" of our Lord Jesus Christ. The closing words in the Holy Bible, written nineteen hundred years ago, are a fervent prayer for the commencement of God's world order: "Even so, come, Lord Jesus!"

THE SEAT OF REBELLION

Another stream of human life was birthed in Mesopotamia, the cradle of civilization, that was completely opposite to the stream of life flowing from Abraham and his descendants. These people based their lives on human potential, human ability, and human rebellion against God and His order. Abraham was the father of all those on earth who believe that God exists, that His ways are beneficial for mankind, and who are therefore willing to follow Him even to the point of personal sacrifice so that His kingdom can come and His will be done on earth as it is in heaven. The other Mesopotamians rebelled against God and turned their worship to animals, heavenly bodies, demons, and other human beings.

Near the seat of the ancient Babylonian Empire along the Tigris-Euphrates River, people came together from ancient Accad, Babel, Erech, and Calneh to assert their humanity. They believed that a people united could effectively challenge God, and they set out to prove it. United in their labors, they started building a city and a tower "whose top is in the heavens." Their stated purpose was "to make a name for ourselves, lest we be scattered abroad over the face of the whole earth."

To put it another way, these people used their combined energies to exalt themselves for mutual self-defense while they showed themselves the equals of heaven. Nothing in their plans included faith in God or submission to Him. This early experiment in world government was built on pride, self-exaltation, and what the people considered mutual self-interest.

God's reaction is interesting. He acknowledged the power of combined humanity, even in rebellion against Him. His appraisal is fascinating:

> The people are one and they all have one language, and this is what they begin to do; now nothing that they propose to do will be withheld from them.
> Genesis 11:6

God knew that this first attempt to build a new world order, if allowed to continue unhindered, would succeed beyond the wildest dreams of its founders. The danger of such a plan to future generations and the threat of this man-made order to the people of faith was so great that God determined to stop it at its inception.

Therefore, God confused the speech of the participants and scattered them over the face of all the earth. In the words of the Bible, "they ceased building the city." God took away from them the key ingredient to success—harmony. If they could not communicate successfully with one another, they could not successfully build an embryonic world order. From that day unto this the nations of the world have never been in unity on anything, ever.

REUNITED AT BABYLON

The significance of the Persian Gulf War transcends Kuwait; it even transcends the concept of a new world order enunciated by George Bush.

The Gulf War is significant because the action of the United Nations to authorize military action against Iraq was the first time since Babel that all of the nations of the earth acted in concert with one another. I find it fascinating to consider that this union took place against the very place where the nations had been divided, the successor nation to ancient Babel.

It is as if some power reached out from Babel, where the first world rebellion against God was quashed, and once again called the nations of the world to unity. And on the very day the unity of nations was consummated, General Brent Scowcroft, national security adviser to the president of the United States, longtime Council on Foreign Relations member, and former aide and business associate of Henry Kissinger, announced, in an interview with Charles Bierbauer of CNN, the beginning of a new world order.

Once a new world order without God and based on human potential is established, sooner or later the present players will be moved out of the way. Whatever their motives, whether noble or venal, the present one-world crowd of monied aristocrats will find out, as the wealthy Duke of Orleans discovered in the French Revolution, that they were merely expendable pawns being used by a much greater power. Adolf Hitler used the monied industrialists of Germany so long as they served his purposes, then they were cast aside to make way for his demented inner circle.

The silly so-called intellectuals of academia who are spouting their politically correct foolishness will find themselves considered first irrelevant and then expendable when the real power begins to operate.

The danger to the world is not the plan of monied people to establish a world in which it is easier to make more money. The greatest danger is not even that the poor nations of the earth will use their influence to reduce America to poverty.

The real danger is that a revived one-world system, springing forth from the murky past of mankind's evil beginnings, will set spiritual forces into motion which no human being will be strong enough to contain.

In the Book of Revelation there is a cryptic reference to "four angels who are bound at the great river Euphrates." Is it possible that at the Tower of Babel, Almighty God not only confused the language and scattered the people, but He bound the demonic powers that had energized the earliest form of anti-God world order? Our movie screens have been full of stories of explorers who delved beyond the limits permitted to man, and in the process unloosed dreaded forces upon themselves. These plots are obviously fictional, but the Holy Bible is not fiction.

Here is what the Bible says:

> Then the sixth angel sounded: And I heard a voice from the four horns of the golden altar which is before God, saying to the sixth angel who had the

trumpet, "Release the four angels who are bound at the great river Euphrates." So the four angels, who had been prepared for the hour and day and month and year, were released to kill a third of mankind.

Revelation 9:13–15

This world horror would be motivated by demonic spirits and would be all consuming. The "angels" or demons had been bound by spiritual commandment from sometime in the early days of history until the precise hour, day, month, and year for them to be released. The result of their release would now cost the lives of some 2 billion people.

FULFILLING PROPHECY

As ghastly as it may seem, there are New Age advocates of a new world order who have openly advocated recently that up to 2 billion people need to die in the world in order to cleanse it in preparation for the reign of their Messiah—the Lord Meitreya or the Buddha. It is highly unlikely that these demonized people have been reading the Book of Revelation. Yet their ghastly conclusion accords with the activity of the four angels bound in Iraq at the Euphrates River. What power has been putting such macabre thoughts into their souls?

In a slightly different context, the Book of Revelation also speaks of a Dragon, who is the Devil, or Satan, being cast out of heaven and thrown to earth. He is the one we are told "who deceives the whole world." When he is cast down to earth from heaven, he is very angry "because he knows that he has a short time."

According to the biblical account, when the Dragon is near, he begins to persecute a woman who symbolizes the nation of Israel. When he is only partially successful in injuring Israel, the Dragon then begins mass persecution of the spiritual descendants of Israel, the Christians of the world. We are told the method to be used by Satan to fulfill his plans is to energize a world leader, one who arises from among the common people.

To this leader will be given what the Dragon had two thousand years earlier offered to Jesus—"his power, his throne, and great authority." The Bible tells us further that this world leader will be given authority "over every tribe, tongue, and nation. And all who dwell on the earth will worship him, whose names have not been written in the Book of Life of the Lamb."

This powerful world leader will not only be brutal toward people, but he will be totally and absolutely opposed to God. We are told, "he opened his mouth in blasphemy against God, to blaspheme His name, His tabernacle, and those who dwell in heaven."

Just as Jesus Christ, the Son of Man and Son of God, was the consummate example of a man baptized in God's Holy Spirit, yielded to God, and empowered by God; even so this world leader will be the consummate example of a man totally energized by the power of Satan, raging in blasphemy against God and His angels, filled with hatred against the people who are made in God's image. This world leader, who has come to be known as the Antichrist, will be more terrible than any human leader in history. Hitler, Stalin, Genghis Khan, and Caligula are all types of this leader, but no figure from history can match him for utter depravity and evil. Despite his evil, the world will be so caught up in satanic deception and delusion that it will worship the Antichrist as a god.

The good news for us all is that the world dictator is allocated only forty-two months to swagger on the world's stage. Then in the real mother of all battles, Jesus Christ, His holy angels, and all of the sons and daughters of God will fall upon him and will cast him and his followers into the lake of fire reserved for the Devil and his angels. Then the Devil will be bound for a thousand years, and the world will enjoy a time of peace and happiness and health and freedom and prosperity that is more wonderful than any human mind can conceive.

As Handel's exquisite *Messiah* proclaims: "The kingdoms of this world will become the kingdoms of our Lord, and of His Christ, and He shall reign forever and ever." Then and only then, God's new world order will officially begin, as the sons of God take their proper places in the new world.

THE BATTLE AHEAD

How does the word of the Bible relate to the events of today? It is clear that the counterfeit world order will be waiting for the satanic dictator. It just doesn't happen spontaneously. Therefore, it must be prepared for him in advance by someone. The next conclusion is inescapable. Satan knows that a world government must soon be prepared for the man whom he is preparing to receive his particular empowerment and authority.

Such a world government can come together only after the Christian United States is out of the way. After all, the rest of the world can federate any time it wants to, but a vital, economically strong, Christian United States would have at its disposal the spiritual and material force to prohibit a worldwide satanic dictator from winning his battle. With America still free and at large, Satan's schemes will at best be only partially successful. From these shores could come the television, radio, and printed matter to counter an otherwise all-out world news blackout. An independent America could point out Satan's lies. If America is free, people everywhere can hope for freedom. And if America goes down, all hope is lost to the rest of the world.

It is also clear that Satan's strategy will include a frontal assault on Israel. Rest assured that the next objective of the presently constituted new world order, under the present United nations, will be to make Israel its target. The precedent has been set by the action against Iraq.

A recalcitrant nation whose action does not accord with United Nations policy may be disciplined by military force. That is the newest law of world order. The United Nations General Assembly has already voted to brand Zionism as racism. Surely we can expect, sooner or later, an unreasonable demand for Israel to vacate control of the West Bank and the half of her capital city in East Jerusalem.

Although Israel may be reluctantly conciliatory in regard to some territory, it is absolutely adamant about not surrendering the city won by Kind David almost three thousand years ago, then won again by modern Israel in 1967. And if Israel refuses to vacate the Holy City, there will be war—under the world order as it is even now constituted.

Beyond that, Satan will launch a war against the Christian people. The Book of Revelation speaks of a flood of water coming after Israel and its seed. I see that as false propaganda, ridicule, and demeaning comments—anything to ruin the influence of Christians and their ability to block Satan's plans. The Nazis used this technique against the Jews in Germany. First, they were ridiculed and blamed for the economic collapse of Germany. Then they were denied a few rights of citizenship. Then they were crowded into restricted ghettos. And finally their property and their lives were taken from them.

Above all, the propaganda was intended to make ordinary Germans uncomfortable and afraid to associate with the Jews, then suspicious of them, then hostile toward them, and then glad to be rid of them. This very technique is being used already against Christian people. It will intensify in years to come as the spiritual battle becomes more intense.

THE GATHERING OF FORCES

I believe that the Persian Gulf War has now brought into sharp focus the great cleavage that has existed in the human race since the early beginnings of civilization in the Tigris-Euphrates Valley. On the one side are the beliefs of a portion of humanity that flowed from Abraham to the Jewish race and to the Christians of the world. These are the people of faith, the people who are part of God's world order.

On the other side are the people of Babel—those who build monuments to humanity under the inspiration of Satan. Their successors in Babylon included worshipers of the goddess Astarte and the god Baal. These are the people whose religious rites included the worship of sex with cult prostitutes and cult sodomites, whose temples were adorned with eggs and phallic symbols. These are the people who began the Babylonian mystery religions that swept the Roman Empire. Their pursuit of the occult was so intense that even the name of their region, Chaldean, came to be the identification of a person who was found in the company of conjurers, magicians, sorcerers, and soothsayers.

The people were famous for their astrologers, their signs of the Zodiac, and the monthly prognosticators. They worshiped the planets and consulted demonic spirits. Never in their entire history did they arrive at a higher form of monotheism. In fact, the Bible refers to "Mystery Babylon, the mother of harlots." It is this stream of humanity that asserted itself in the French Revolution, in Marxist communism, and now appears again in world order planning.

So long as the nations were separated by language, customs, and geography, the opportunity did not present itself for all of the people of the Babylonian humanistic and occultic traditions to unify against the people of the Abrahamic, monotheistic tradition. If, however, a one-world order comes forth, it will assuredly come under the control of the humanistic-occultic branch of humanity. When that happens, the humanistic-occultic leaders will then use the power at their disposal to eliminate the influence of the people of faith.

This means very simply that the world government of the new world order will one day become an instrument of oppression against the Christians and Jews around the world.

None of us should suddenly become philosophical determinists or fatalists. The plan to impose world government on us is well funded and far advanced. However, there is power in truth that is greater than money. What the secret planners of the Establishment fear most is the full spotlight of truth. If the full ramifications of what is being planned for every family in America comes out, their house of world order will splinter apart like so many match sticks.

Therefore it is necessary to bring the truth out in every church, in every synagogue, in every piece of literature, in every meeting. All of us must ask the hard question of our leaders: "What are the consequences of the course of action you are asking us to take?"

Whatever happens in world events, the average American, whose instincts are usually very good, should not be intimidated by "experts" on foreign relations. My wife, Dede, was born in the Midwest and raised as a Taft Republican. Her comment on foreign affairs a few years ago was very perceptive: "I don't trust anyone running the foreign affairs of America who speaks with a foreign accent." In fact, how can anyone who spent most of his life in Germany or Poland fully understand the family life, the shared values, the history of free enterprise and free speech, and the intense patriotism of people born in Columbus, Ohio?

For that matter how can a native-born American, educated at Groton, Harvard, and Oxford, who then goes to work on Wall Street, understand what goes on in the hearts of people in Iowa, Nebraska, Texas, or Florida? The Atlanticists on Wall Street may be willing to sell out America, but Main Street wants no part of their plan. It is these people who must hear what is being planned for their America. Then they must act to stop it.

TACTICS AND STRATEGIES

The American people were overwhelmingly opposed to the giveaway of the Panama Canal by Trilateralist Jimmy Carter. Twenty senators who voted to ratify that ill-advised treaty were voted out of office in subsequent elections.

Since treaties are ratified in the U.S. Senate, they also can be stopped in the Senate. The key is to make every candidate for election to the Senate declare himself in advance on the issues of surrendering the sovereignty of the United States into a world government, on unilateral disarmament of America, on arming the United Nations, on giving the United Nations power over American citizens, and on the role the Federal Reserve Board has in global banking.

Then it is necessary to print hundreds of thousands of leaflets giving the stand of each of the candidates on these and other key issues, and distribute them to every church member and registered voter in every community in America. The average voter may not understand all of my concerns about religious issues, but he or she will certainly understand having his or her money drained away by a world government. And I believe he or she will vote correctly if given the choice.

The effectiveness of leaflets comparing the stands of two candidates for the United States Senate was dramatically underscored in a recent election in North Carolina.

Before the election, the conservative incumbent, Jesse Helms, was trailing his liberal opponent, the black mayor of Charlotte, Harvey Gantt, by as much as eight percentage points in public opinion polls. On the two Sundays prior to the election, a public interest issues group that I had formed, the Christian Coalition, distributed 750,000 church bulletins listing the stands of the candidates on a number of major election issues. When the ballots were counted, Jesse Helms was ahead by almost the same percentage as he had previously been behind. I believe educating the people on the issues affecting them made the difference in that psychologically vital senatorial election.

Recently, evangelical voters have been very limited in their election preferences. They are known as single-issue voters. Their issues, both of which are usually decided by courts and not by elected officials, are school prayer and abortion. Beyond these things, they are not very discriminating about a whole range of issues from tax increases and deficit spending, to national defense and foreign policy.

If you are sensitive about the dangers of one-world globalism, you can make your senator sensitive, too. Most of them are harried, pressured, and completely unable to grasp the details of the hundreds of pieces of legislation that come before them. As a result they hide behind a safe party vote or a vote that the president has done a good job of selling to the public.

However, if they are sure that a vote is so unpopular with their constituents that it will cost them their jobs, then they will listen to the people. A former secretary of the interior told me that the most effective way to lobby a congressman would be to have three or four farmers or factory workers in their work clothes approach him at a political meeting to register their opinion on an upcoming vote. This man has been trained to react to well-dressed paid lobbyists, but he believes that those working people are speaking for thousands of average voters who will react in the same manner. A few such instances will be sufficient to convince him.

THE CHRISTIAN AGENDA

The Christian Coalition is launching an effort in selected states to become acquainted with registered voters in every precinct. This is slow, hard work. But it will build a significant database to use to communicate with those people who are regular voters. When they are mobilized in support of vital issues, elected officials listen. Richard Gardner, the former State Department official, spoke of "building the house of world order" from the bottom up. We must rebuild the foundation of a free, sovereign America from the grassroots, precinct by precinct, city by city, and state by state.

This decade will decide the outcome. Events are moving swiftly, but there is still time. My goal is to see a pro-freedom majority in the United States Senate in 1992, and a reversal of leadership in the House of Representatives by 1996. My associates are now publishing a newspaper called the *Christian American*, which is slated for a circulation of 10 million during this decade. Since in most congressional or senatorial elections a 5 percent swing in the vote means victory or defeat, the power of the concept of a free, sovereign America is so strong that, if properly presented, it can sweep the one-worlders out of contention in the public policy arena in a short time.

No group controlled by a narrow spectrum of internationalist money interests, however enlightened they may be, should be allowed to control in perpetuity the foreign policy, the treasury policy, and the defense policy of a great free nation.

The people need to receive a pledge from presidential contenders that they will go outside the Rockefeller-controlled Council on Foreign Relations and Trilateral Commission for their key appointments. Surely out of 250 million people we can find five thousand men and women for high-level presidential appointments who are not part of the ruling Establishment.

Perhaps the people could take control of both of the political parties and insist on party platforms and candidate pledges that will result in a more open appointment process.

People for the American Way and other ultraliberal lobby groups have had extraordinary success in preventing anyone with conservative Christian values from being confirmed to an appointed position in the government. The *Washington Post* is incredible in the character assassinations it makes against non-Establishment candidates for appointive office.

ESTABLISHMENT BIAS

This example of bias occurred after the 1988 election. The former United States ambassador to the Organization of American States, Richard McCormack, was under consideration for the post of under secretary of state for economic affairs. McCormack had worked in the Nixon White House, had been a Republican candidate for Congress from Pennsylvania, and in addition to being an absolutely brilliant student of international finance, possessed a blameless record of distinguished public service. He happens also to be a dedicated Christian. I joined a number of others in strongly recommending his appointment to the president.

After he was nominated for this key foreign policy post, and while he was awaiting confirmation before the Senate, an article appeared in the *Washington Post* about him. I could not believe my eyes as I read how lacking in experience he was, how he failed to meet the minimum expectations required for this position. Line after line poured out denigration against this outstanding man, and praising the qualifications of CFR member Robert Hormats, who is now a vice chairman of the Wall Street investment banking firm of Goldman Sachs.

I was astounded at the blatant misrepresentations in this story, but I did not say anything about it to Richard McCormack. He went on to win confirmation and to serve as the key economic adviser to President Bush at the various economic summits. When he recently resigned, he received a letter from the president filled with gratitude and praise for his service.

Recently over dinner, I told him of my shock at the *Washington Post* attack on him. He smiled and said that after his appointment, the reporter who wrote the story apologized and confided that he had been ordered by his editors to attack McCormack and to defeat his confirmation.

Have no doubt: Press objectivity about foreign policy does not exist in the two or three key Establishment papers. They are propaganda organs attempting to control and subvert United States policies in order to further their globalist collectivist plans. Therefore it is essential that nominees from the Establishment for key appointive positions receive the same scrutiny that is given on Capital Hill to pro-American conservatives. Action of this type will entail grassroots campaigns to stop the CFR domination of the most powerful branches of our government.

Such a program requires a modest research center to screen key federal appointees to determine, from their speeches, writings, and actions whether or not they support the CFR program of a one-world collectivist government along with a drastically diminished role for United States sovereignty.

There then needs to be a telefax network to activists all over the nation who can relay the truth about the mind-set and plans of those selected for high government office to the senators responsible for their confirmation.

Anyone who gets involved in the struggle for freedom can be assured of being branded by the Establishment as being narrow-minded, provincial, obstructionist, a defender of fortress America, out of touch with the global realities, unskilled in foreign policy and, of course, the usual "bigoted, fundamentalist Christian, right-wing zealot."

THE COURAGE OF CONVICTION

Like it or not, this is an epic struggle for the future. If it were not important, the Establishment would not have committed the better part of a hundred years of labor and billions of dollars of their resources to bring it about. Are the preservation of faith in God throughout the world and the future of our own families not just as important to us as the one-world agenda is to the global planners?

The time has come to mount an all-out assault on the ultimate power of the Establishment—the ability to elect or destroy political leaders through the control of the money supply. In my opinion a privately owned central bank in control of our nation's money is a clear subversion of the United States Constitution. It not only violates the letter of the Constitution, it also violates the clear spirit of the Constitution.

The Federal Reserve System has survived a half-hearted legal attack on its constitutionality. What is needed now is to produce a legal climate of opinion by law journal articles, learned papers, and historical analysis to show that the United States central bank is, like Russian communism, a relatively recent development that rose up at one time and can be put down at another. Its violation of the framework of constitutional government must be made crystal clear. Then a court campaign should be undertaken before judges who would understand the issues involved.

The Federal Reserve System could be abolished by a simple majority vote in the Congress, or a two-thirds vote if the president vetoed the legislation. If a court challenge fails, all that is needed is the political will to sway 51 senators and 218 representatives. The task is not easy, but with education it is not impossible either.

If the Federal Reserve System were abolished, all of the bank-clearing functions could be transferred to the treasury. The power to "coin money and regulate the value thereof" could be placed once again where the Constitution put it, in the hands of Congress.

A TRAGIC ASSASSINATION

President Abraham Lincoln arrived at the very simple concept that it was not necessary under our government to borrow any dollars from any bank. The government, in fact, has the authority to issue money that is in turn backed up by the taxing power of the federal government. Congress could mandate a percentage growth rate of the economy each year, and authorize the treasury to issue enough funds to permit a modest rate of growth in the various indexes of money supply.

Under this system, the government would pay no interest at all, could easily balance its budget, and then create reserves of gold, silver, and other assets to back its paper. In the event of rising inflation, a simple tax increase could sop up excess currency. Given an approaching recession, the people's representatives could increase the supply of money available for the national economy. Banks would operate under treasury regulations with strict limits on excesses in the use of fractional reserve banking. There would be no "discount window" where banks could pick up cheap taxpayer money to loan out at higher rates, and there would be no "open market" operations constantly manipulating the money supply up and down, and in turn bringing periodically painful swings in the economy.

Beyond all else, if Congress and the treasury did not do a good job, every two years we could vote them out of office. No longer would we be voting for or against public officials on the strength of actions taken by a quasi-private agency over which they have no control.

The European bankers and money lords of America do not want interest-free government loans, nor do they want to relinquish the power they now hold over the economic and political destiny of America. Lincoln's plan to print interest-free currency, called "greenbacks," during the Civil War—instead of issuing bonds at interest in exchange for bank loans—was so revolutionary that it would have destroyed the monopoly that European bankers exercised over their nation's money. There is no hard evidence to prove it, but it is my belief that John Wilkes Booth, the man who assassinated Lincoln, was in the employ of the European bankers who wanted to nip this American populist experiment in the bud.

While still in office, Lincoln saw clearly what would happen after his time; here are his words:

> The money power preys upon the nation in times of peace and conspires against it in times of adversity. It is more despotic than monarchy, more insolent than autocracy, more selfish than bureaucracy. I see in the near future a crisis approaching that unnerves me and causes me to tremble for the safety of my country. Corporations have been enthroned, an era of corruption in high places will follow, and the money power of the country will endeavor to prolong its reign by working upon the prejudices of the people until the wealth is aggregated in a few hands and the republic is destroyed.

Are these the ravings of a lunatic? No, they are the judicious and heartfelt words of a patriot, a friend of the people, a man of faith who dreamed great things for America and suffered profoundly over its pains.

Except for a brief interlude, the United States operated without a true central bank from the time of its founding under the Constitution in 1789 until 1913, a period of 124 years. We have only operated under a central bank for 78 years, a relatively short time.

Lincoln's plan would be more practical now than it was after the Civil War, because the United States dollar is the reserve currency of the world. A direct issue of our money, given political discipline and restraint, could be as good or better than the present Federal Reserve notes issued to fund government debt evidenced by interest-bearing Treasury bills, notes, and bonds.

For the average person, central banking is very complex. Many feel that it should be left, like foreign policy, "to the experts." I was amazed to learn that Walter Mondale, a lawyer, a former United States senator, a vice president of the United States, when he became the Democratic presidential candidate said, "I think I have finally figured how the Federal Reserve Board works." Obviously when someone is stealing you blind, he is not anxious to let you in on how he's doing it. Few, if any, even those on the inside of government, know how the Federal Reserve Board works. I have in my library a book by Maxwell Newton, the financial editor of the former *New York Post* and a prize winner in economics at Cambridge

University. On the jacket of the book published by New York Times Books is the title, *The Fed*, then this line, "Inside the Federal Reserve, the *Secret Power Center* that controls the American Economy." (Emphasis added.)

TOWARD A BETTER WORLD

We do not need a secret power center controlling our economy. We need our economy controlled by action of a free market under regulations laid down by those whom we vote into office by free and open elections to serve as our representatives. Nothing else is acceptable in a free society!

Obviously those who believe in freedom and American sovereignty must work toward a better world. We need cooperation with our trading partners and the lowering of barriers to free trade. We need a forum to exchange ideas. We need some world body to handle global weights, measures, and standards; allocation of spectrum space; designation of air corridors; postal regulations, etc.

It is helpful to have a World Health Organization working globally on immunizations, communicable diseases, infant mortality, and similar health concerns. It is helpful to have world libraries for the recording and dissemination of scientific discoveries of benefit to all mankind. Particularly the developed nations need coordinated plans to counter terrorism, the international drug trade, and global conflicts. We clearly need a coordination among the developed nations to alleviate poverty, plant forests, purify water, and stimulate domestic agriculture in Third World nations.

Cooperation to protect the world's air, water, vegetation, and wildlife is vital. In truth, the misuse of these resources damages all and should be protected in some reasonable way by all. Global cooperation of this nature is essential and may be accomplished by mutual limited accords between nations that preserve their own national identity, national beliefs, and national sovereignty. Obviously we must all try to find mechanisms to enable us to live together in peace on Planet Earth.

However, to accomplish all these worthwhile goals does not require the undermining of America economic and political power, nor does it require us to embrace some overarching utopian world vision in which all "become as one." This is where the danger lies, and we must resist every single day the sales pitch trying to lure this nation into a global trap.

Whatever the long-term political and emotional consequences for Mikhail Gorbachev, the failure of the August 1991 "coup" will dramatically reinforce the Establishment's goal of bringing about a new world order. The defeat of the "coup" seemingly eliminated certain threats, but it also signaled the beginning of a new, more volatile stage in Soviet-American relations.

I am reminded of Winston Churchill's words on learning of the British victory over the Nazis in North Africa, at El Alamein. He said, "This is not the end; it is not even the beginning of the end. But undoubtedly, it is the end of the beginning." The August "coup" adds an incredible new dimension to the plans for a globalist state. In the months and years ahead we will no doubt see these plans unfold. Only God knows where they will lead.

Finally, let us remember that the triumph of God's world order is certain. Those who believe in Him have truth and power within them which is "greater than that which is in the world." This is the decade of opportunity for the church of Jesus Christ, a decade in which at least 1 billion people will come to faith in Christ. Especially let us not forget the miraculous power of concerted, believing prayer to alter world events.

Indeed, there will be a struggle between people of faith and people of the humanistic-occultic sphere. But as we think of the new world order let us remember the words of Jesus Christ, who said:

In the world you will have tribulation; but be of good cheer, I have overcome the world.

John 16:33

Bibliography

Aaron, Henry J., ed., *Setting National Priorities: Policy for the Nineties*. Washington, D. C.: Brookings Institute, 1990.

Aliano, Richard A., *The Crime of World Power: Politics Without Government in the International System*. New York: G. P. Putnam's Sons, 1978.

Allen, Frederick Lewis, *Only Yesterday: An Informal History of the 1920s*. New York: Harper & Brothers, 1931. Revised 1962.

Baldwin, Hanson Weightman, *The Price of Power*. New York: Harper & Row for the Council on Foreign Relations, 1948.

Ball, George W., *Diplomacy for a Crowded World: An American Foreign Policy*. Boston: Little, Brown and Co., 1976.

Billington, James, *Fire in the Minds of Men: Origins of the Revolutionary Faith*. New York: Basic Books, 1980.

Boller, Paul F., Jr., *Presidential Anecdotes*. New York: Penguin Books, 1982.

Brooke, Tal, *When the World Will Be As One: The Coming New World Order in the New Age*. Eugene, Oreg.: Harvest House, 1989.

Brown, Seyom, *On the Front Burner: Issues in U.S. Foreign Policy*. Boston: Little, Brown and Co., 1978.

Capra, Fritjof, *Uncommon Wisdom: Conversations with Remarkable People*. New York: Bantam Books, 1988.

Carpenter, Galen Ted, ed., *Collective Defense or Strategic Independence? Alternative Strategies for the Future.* Washington, D. C.: Cato Institute, 1989.

Chandler, Russell, *Understanding the New Age.* Dallas: Word Publishing, 1989.

Commager, Henry Steele, "Misconceptions Governing American Foreign Policy" in *Perspectives on American Foreign Policy.* Edited by Charles W. Kegley and Eugene R. Wittkopf. New York: St. Martin's Press, 1983.

Cord, Robert L., *Separation of Church and State: Historical Fact and Current Fiction.* New York: Lambeth Press, 1982.

Cousins, Norman, *The Celebration of Life: A Dialogue of Hope, Spirit, and the Immortality of the Soul.* Revised edition. New York: Bantam Books, 1991.

Cromartie, Michael, ed., *Evangelicals and Foreign Policy: Four Perspectives.* Washington, D. C.: Ethics and Public Policy Center, 1989.

DeBeus, J. G., *The Future of the West.* New York: Harper & Brothers, 1953.

Deutsch, Karl W., *Tides Among Nations.* New York: Free Press, 1979.

Falk, Richard A., *The End of World Order.* New York: Holmes & Meier, 1982.

————. *A Global Approach to National Policy.* Cambridge, Mass.: Harvard University Press, 1975.

————. Samuel S. Kim and Saul H. Mendlovitz, *Toward a Just World Order.* Volume 1. Boulder, Colo.: Westview Press, 1982.

————. "The Trend Toward World Community: Issues" in *The Search for World Order.* Edited by Albert Lepawsky, Edward H. Buehrig, and Harold D. Lasswell. New York: Meredith, 1983.

Finder, Joseph, *Red Carpet.* New York: Holt, Rinehart, and Winston, 1983.

Fowle, Eleanor, *Cranston.* Los Angeles: Jeremy Tarcher, 1984.

Friedman, Thomas L., *From Beirut to Jerusalem.* New York: Doubleday, 1990.

Gill, Stephen, *American Hegemony and the Trilateral Commission.* Cambridge: Cambridge University Press, 1990.

Goldwater, Barry, *With No Apologies: The Personal and Political Memoirs of United States Senator Barry M. Goldwater.* With Barry Morris. New York: William Morrow, 1979.

Golitsyn, Anatoliy, *New Lies for Old: The Communist Strategy of Deception and Disinformation.* New York: Dodd, Mead, 1984.

Groothius, Douglas R., *Unmasking the New Age.* Downers Grove, Ill.: InterVarsity Press, 1986.

Halberstam, David, *The Best and the Brightest.* New York: Random House, 1972.

Heatherly, Charles, L., and Burton Yale Pines, *Mandate for Leadership III: Policy Strategies for the 1990s.* Washington, D. C.: Heritage Foundation, 1989.

Henkin, Louis, *How Nations Behave: Law and Foreign Policy.* New York: Columbia University Press for the Council on Foreign Relations, 1979.

Higham, Charles, *Trading with the Enemy: An Exposé of the Nazi-American Money Plot, 1933–1949.* New York: Delacorte Press, 1983.

Hoffman, Stanley, *Primacy or World Order: American Foreign Policy since the Cold War.* New York: McGraw-Hill, 1978.

House, Edward Mandell, *The Intimate Papers of Colonel House.* Arranged by Charles Seymour. Boston: Houghton Mifflin, 1926–28.

————. *Philip Dru: Administrator; A Story of Tomorrow, 1920–1935*. New York: B. W. Huebsch, 1912.

Isaacson, Walter, and Evan Thomas, *The Wise Men: Six Friends and the World They Made*. New York: Simon and Schuster, 1986.

Jaguaribe, Helio, "World Order, Rationality, and Development" in *Conditions of World Order*. Edited by Stanely Hoffman. Boston: Houghton Mifflin, 1968.

Johnson, George, *Architects of Fear: Conspiracy Theories and Paranoia in American Politics*. Los Angeles: Jeremy Tarcher, 1983.

Johnson, Paul, *The Birth of the Modern World Society, 1515–1830*. New York: HarperCollins, 1991.

Koch, Adrienne, and William Peden, *The Life and Selected Writings of Thomas Jefferson*. New York: Random House, 1944.

Kennedy, Robert F., *To Seek a Newer World*. New York: Doubleday, 1967.

Kurtz, Paul, and Edwin H. Wilson, *Humanist Manifesto* (1933) and *Humanist Manifesto II* (1973). New York: Prometheus Books, 1984.

Ledeen, Michael A., *Grave New World*. New York: Oxford University Press, 1985.

Lemesurier, Peter, *This New Age Business: The Story of the Ancient and Continuing Quest to Bring Down Heaven on Earth*. Moray, Scotland: Findhord Press, 1990.

Levinson, Charles, *Vodka Cola*. London: Gordon and Cremonesi, 1978.

Mann, Thomas E., ed., *A Question of Balance: The President, the Congress, and Foreign Policy*. Washington, D. C.: Brookings Institution, 1990.

McCormick, Thomas J., *America's Half Century: United States Foreign Policy in the Cold War*. Baltimore: Johns Hopkins University Press, 1989.

McHale, John, *The Future of the Future*. New York: George Braziller, 1969.

Mehring, Franz, *Karl Marx: The Story of His Life*. Ann Arbor: University of Michigan Press, 1962.

Methvin, Eugene, *The Rise of Radicalism*. New Rochelle, N.Y.: Arlington House, 1973.

Miller, Elliot, *A Crash Course on the New Age: Describing and Evaluating a Growing Social Force*. Grand Rapids, Mich.: Baker Book House, 1989.

Miller, Merle, *Plain Speaking: An Oral Biography of Harry S. Truman*. New York: G. P. Putnam's Sons, 1974.

Mullins, Eustace, *Secrets of the Federal Reserve*. Staunton, Va.: Bankers Research Institute, 1983.

National Center for Constitutional Studies, *The Real Thomas Jefferson*. Washington, D. C.: NCCS, 1983.

Neuhaus, Richard John, and Michael Cromartie, eds., *Piety and Politics: Evangelicals and Fundamentalists Confront the World*. Washington, D. C.: Ethics and Public Policy Center, 1987.

Nisbet, Robert, *The Present Age: Progress and Anarchy in Modern America*. New York: Harper & Row, 1988.

Padover, Saul, *Karl Marx: An Intimate Biography*. Abridged. New York: New American Library, 1980.

Perloff, James, *Shadows of Power: The Council on Foreign Relations and the American Decline*. Appleton, Wis.: Western Islands, 1988.

Pfaff, William, *Barbarian Sentiments: How the American Century Ends*. New York: Hill and Wang, 1989.

Pike, Albert, *Morals and Dogma of the Ancient and Accepted Rite of Scottish Freemasonry*. Richmond, Va.: L. H. Jenkins, 1871, 1921.

Pryce-Jones, David, *The Closed Circle: An Interpretation of the Arabs*. New York: HarperCollins, 1989.

Quigley, Carroll, *The Anglo-American Establishment: From Rhodes to Cliveden*. New York: Books in Focus, 1981.

————. *Tragedy and Hope: A History of the World in Our Time*. New York: Macmillan, 1966.

Ravenal, Earl C., "The Price of Defense" in *An American Vision: Policies for the 90s*. Edited by Edward H. Crane and David Boaz. Washington, D. C.: Cato Institute, 1989.

Reich, Robert B., *The Work of Nations: Preparing Ourselves for 21st Century Capitalism*. New York: Alfred A. Knopf, 1991.

Reichley, A. James, *Religion in American Public Life*. Washington, D. C.: Brookings Institution, 1985.

Roberts, Paul Craig, and Karen LaFollette, *Meltdown Inside the Soviet Economy*. Washington, D. C.: Cato Institute, 1990.

Robison, John, *Proofs of a Conspiracy*. 1798. Boston: Western Islands, 1967.

Russett, Bruce, and Harvey Starr, *World Politics: The Menu for Choice*. San Francisco: W. H. Freeman and Co., 1981.

Schlafly, Phyllis, and Chester Ward, *Kissinger on the Couch*. New Rochelle, N.Y.: Arlington House, 1975.

Schleicher, Charles P., *Introduction to International Relations*. New York: Prentice-Hall, 1953.

Schulzinger, Robert D., *The Wise Men of Foreign Affairs: The History of the Council on Foreign Relations*. New York: Columbia University Press, 1984.

Shoup, Lawrence H., and William Minter, *Imperial Brain Trust: The Council on Foreign Relations and United States Foreign Policy*. New York: Monthly Review Press, 1977.

Sklar, Holly, ed., *Trilateralism: The Trilateral Commission and Elite Planning for World Management*. Boston: South End Press, 1980.

Skousen, Cleon, *The Naked Communist*. Salt Lake City: Ensign, 1961.

Solzhenitsyn, Aledsandr, "Difficulties in the West with the Study of Russian History" in *Thinking About America: The United States in the 1990s*. Edited by Annelise Anderson and Dennis L. Bark. Stanford, Calif.: Hoover Institution, 1988.

Steinbrunner, John D., *Restructuring American Foreign Policy*. Washington, D. C.: Brookings Institution, 1989.

Still, William, *New World Order: The Ancient Plan of Secret Societies*. Lafayette, La.: Huntington House, 1990.

Sutton, Anthony C., *Wall Street and the Bolshevik Revolution*. New Rochelle, N.Y.: Arlington House, 1974.

Thompson, William Irwin, *Evil and World Order*. New York: Harper Torchbooks, 1980.

Tinbergen, Jan, Antony J. Dolman, and Jan van Ettinger, eds., *Reshaping the International Order: A Report to the Club of Rome.* New York: E. P. Dutton, 1976.

Toms, Michael, *At the Leading Edge: New Visions of Science, Spirituality, and Society.* Burdett, N.Y.: Larson Publications, 1991.

United Nations, *Global Outlook 2000: An Economic, Social, and Environmental Perspective.* New York: United Nations Publications, 1990.

Von Daniken, Erich, *Gold of the Gods.* Translated by Michael Heron. New York: G. P. Putnam's Sons, 1973.

Webster, Nesta, *Secret Societies.* New York: E. P. Dutton, 1924. Republished in a book club edition for Christian Book Club of America.

Wien, Barbara J., ed., *Peace and World Order Studies: A Curriculum Guide.* Fourth edition. New York: World Policy Institute, 1984.

Wormser, René, *Foundations: Their Power and Influence.* Second edition. Hollywood, Calif.: Angriff Press, 1977.

Wurmbrand, Richard, *Marx and Satan.* Westchester, Ill.: Crossway Books, 1986.

JOURNALS: SELECTED LIST

"New World Order." Special Issue, *New Perspectives Quarterly.* Published by the Center for the Study of Democratic Institutions, Spring 1990.

Blumenthal, Sydney, "April's Bluff." *The New Republic,* August 5, 1991.

Brooke, Tal, "The Emerging Reality of a New World Order." *SCP Journal,* Summer 1991.

Brookhiser, Richard, "Two Centuries of New World Orders." *Time,* May 6, 1991.

Foreign Affairs (Journal of the Council on Foreign Relations). Volumes 1–5. April 1974–Spring 1991.

Gerson, Michael, and Gary North, Debate. "George Bush's Vision of New World Order: International Stability or Another Babel?" *World* magazine, February 5, 1991.

Global 2000 Report to the President: Entering the Twenty-First Century. Volume 1. Summary Report. Washington, D. C.: U.S. Government Printing Office, 1980.

Kondracke, Morton, "The Fine Print." *The New Republic,* February 25, 1991.

Kraft, Joseph, "School for Statesmen." *Harper's* magazine, July 1958.

Novak, Jeremiah, "The Trilateral Connection." *Atlantic Monthly,* July 1979.

Roper Organization, "The Two World Orders." *The Public Pulse,* June 1991.

Russett, Bruce, and James S. Sutterlin, "The U.N. in a New World Order." *Foreign Affairs* (Journal of the Council on Foreign Relations), Spring 1991.

U.S. Congress, House Committee on Foreign Affairs, Res. 211, the 99th Congress, "U.S. Policy in the United Nations: Hearings and Markup Before the Committee on Foreign Affairs and Its Subcommittee on Human Rights and International Organizations." Volume 3. Washington, D. C.: United States Government Printing Office, 1986.

Volume Three

The
Secret
Kingdom

Then He said to them, "These are the words which I spoke to you while I was still with you, that all things must be fulfilled which were written in the Law of Moses and the Prophets and the Psalms concerning Me." And He opened their understanding, that they might comprehend the Scriptures.

Luke 24:44–45 NKJV

Contents

Preface   519
Introduction to the First Edition   522

Part I
Two Domains

1 The Visible World   529
2 The Invisible World   542
3 Seeing and Entering   553
4 How God's Kingdom Works   567
5 Progressive Happiness   583
6 Upside Down   593

Part II
Laws of the Kingdom

7 The Law of Reciprocity   603
8 The Law of Use   618
9 The Law of Perseverance   633
10 The Law of Responsibility   642
11 The Law of Greatness   652
12 The Law of Unity   662
13 The Law of Fidelity   671
14 The Law of Change   676
15 The Law of Miracles   685
16 The Law of Dominion   698
17 The Coming King   709

Notes   721

Preface

DURING THE STEAMY hot first days of August 1992, I found myself in an airport lounge at the British Airways terminal at Kennedy Airport in New York preparing to board a flight to London. I would make a connection there to my destination, Lusaka, Zambia, which is located at the center of one of the most savage droughts in the history of southern Africa. Hundreds of thousands of people in that troubled land have been experiencing dire poverty and possible starvation.

The scene at the airport was much as it was ten years ago when *The Secret Kingdom* was first published. Businessmen were intent on making deals in Europe. Families were ready for the vacation of a lifetime. Students were on their way to school. Tourists—replete with cameras, dark glasses, and polyester pants—were getting ready for the sights and sounds of the Old World.

Then I glanced at the front-page headlines of the day's *New York Times*. From left to right here were the day's headlines: SHELLING BY SERBS POUNDS SARAJEVO . . . TERRORIST BOMBS STRIP LIMA OF UTILITIES . . . 200 KILLED IN ASIA IN TWO PLANE CRASHES . . . LATIN DEBT LOAD KEEPS CLIMBING . . . DRUG RESISTANT TB IS SEEN SPREADING WITHIN HOSPITALS.

I asked myself, had the world improved in the ten years since *The Secret Kingdom* first appeared? The answer is both yes and no. On the one hand, Communism has collapsed. The Berlin Wall has fallen. On the surface it appears that a superpower nuclear confrontation is no longer a threat to mankind.

Yet the world seems no better. Active, small-scale wars now total forty or more around the world. The debt load of the United States and its Western Allies has not abated, but accelerated wildly. From Somalia to Afghanistan, from Burma to Brazil, from Moscow to the Cape of Good Hope, there is crushing debt, unemployment, poverty, disease, political unrest, crime, ethnic tension, war, and now there has arisen a plague virtually unknown in 1982, the greatest killer since the Black Death, AIDS.

AIDS is a disease transmitted primarily by homosexual relations, extramarital heterosexual relations, and intravenous drug use. A shocking study printed in the July 27, 1992, issue of *U.S. News & World Report* indicated the potential by the year 2000 for 100 million deaths from AIDS, an annual cost for AIDS treatment between $81 to $107 billion in the United States, with that figure leaping to $356 to $514 billion worldwide.

Not only will all of the material progress of the developing countries during the past twenty years be drained by the AIDS epidemic, but a significant percentage of their key middle-level technicians and executives will be dead. In Zambia, for instance, where AIDS infection has touched 30 percent of the population, I was told by a high-ranking government official that Barclay's Bank is losing so many middle managers to AIDS that they are forced to hire two people for every job. Despite a veneer of extraordinary wealth in the United States, Western Europe, and Asia, there is an underlying fear that things are not right in our world. We see the meltdown of the enormously inflated Japanese stock market and the companion Japanese real estate market, and we realize that the accumulation of the wealth of a lifetime can vanish in a few months or even a few days of market panic.

We are in the most sexually liberated generation in modern history, yet this liberty has brought with it tragically shattered marriages and a holocaust of abortion which exceeds the worst barbarities of recorded history. The generation of children who remain—those we have permitted to live—are permanently scarred by divorce, neglect, and abandonment; by physical, mental, and sexual abuse; and by a pandemic rise in sexually transmitted diseases of all sorts.

In the United States, our elites have replaced God's clear moral law with their version of what is "politically correct." Situational ethics have replaced God's absolutes. The courts have so restricted religious instruction in the public schools of the United States that a legal challenge has been mounted against a family life sexual education curriculum in

Jacksonville, Florida, by Planned Parenthood, on the grounds that teaching premarital sexual abstinence to young teenagers is a "religious doctrine" which violates the "separation of church and state."

It is now asserted that the practice of homosexuality is not the sinful abomination which the Bible declares it to be, but a protected civil right. Fornication and adultery are not only condoned but encouraged by countless subtle media messages. The message reaching most Americans in the 1990s is that nothing is morally wrong except lying to the press or the government, failing to pay income taxes, making racial slurs, or denigrating the open expression of homosexuality and lesbianism.

We do this in the name of pluralism, yet men's hearts cry out for *values* to give stability to their lives and conduct. Someone has defined pluralism as the name we give the transition from one orthodoxy to another. Without clearly defined values, people are confused, restless, and fearful. They lose hope, for to them the events of their lives and those around them seem to have lost their meaning.

To quote columnist Erma Bombeck from the August 12, 1992, edition of *USA Today,* "People are going crazy because there's no stability here anymore in our lives. There's no anchor. No center. People don't seem to have something they can hang onto and believe in anymore. People are really confused and they've lost their way."

But there is hope. God has given us a clear framework for our lives. His kingdom is not diminished by men's mistakes. In fact, it glows brighter in the darkness. In the first edition of *The Secret Kingdom* I laid out a set of principles given by Jesus Christ which hold the answer to success in international relations, in national government, in business, in families, in personal life, and in the church. Now *The Secret Kingdom* has been revised to show how the timeless principles of God's eternal kingdom can dramatically touch the lives of those who face the problems of the 1990s. In addition I have added and illustrated two more key laws of the kingdom, the Law of Fidelity and the Law of Change.

In the words of Jesus Christ, "The time if fulfilled, and the kingdom of God is at hand. Have a change of mind and believe in the good news" (Mark 1:15, literal translation). Indeed at this very moment "the kingdom of God is at hand!" May its principles revolutionize your life as they have mine.

Introduction
to the First Edition

THE YELLOW MOON hung low over the Atlantic. Two hundred feet from the narrow beach the surf boomed and crashed, streaking white in the crystal moonlight. Beyond the breakers a hundred sea gulls settled for the night, rising and falling in the dark swells.

I turned and looked north. Cape Henry, shadowy under the soft sky, stretched before me, a gathering of sand dunes named after the eldest son of King James I of England. It was utterly peaceful, clutching to itself a history little noticed as the noisy twentieth century raced toward conclusion. For that gentle corner of the Chesapeake Bay's great mouth had been the stage for a small drama of unusual significance to America.

On April 26, 1607, a small band of settlers arrived from England to lay claim to a new world, stepping from their boats into the fine sands of the cape, anxious and weary. Three days later, amazed by this big fresh land, they carefully carried ashore a rough, seven-foot oak cross and plunged it into the sand. As they knelt around it, their spiritual leader, an Anglican clergyman named Robert Hunt, reminded them of the admonition of the British Royal Council, derived from the words of the Holy Scripture: "Every plant, which my heavenly Father hath not planted, shall be rooted up."[1]

With face turned toward heaven, the priest then dedicated the vast new land and their future in it to the glory of Almighty God.

Revived, eager, and joyful, these brave pioneers reboarded their tiny ships and sailed around Cape Henry and into the mouth of a river they named in honor of their monarch, James. Before long they sighted an outcropping along the banks that seemed entirely suitable to their immediate needs and on May 3 founded Jamestown, the first permanent English settlement on the North American continent.

Their "plantation" was indeed not "rooted up." From it and later settlements in Massachusetts, Rhode Island, Pennsylvania, New York, and Maryland grew the most prosperous nation in humanity's history. Unparalleled freedom and creativity burst upon the earth.

As I surveyed that historical site and looked eastward at the Atlantic beneath that dazzling moon, I was gripped by the renewed realization that a dread disease had fastened itself upon the lands sending forth our forefathers. As I turned westward toward my car, my mind's eye swept across the huge country that lay before me. And I mourned more deeply because the same sickness was fastening itself upon my land, the New World so sincerely dedicated to God 375 years ago.

Yes, the disease seemed epidemic throughout the earth. Could it be fatal? Was an "uprooting" to come?

So great are our problems that to think of them as incurable is not unreasonable. Thoughtful men frequently compare the recent course of Western civilization with the collapse of the ancient Roman Empire. Everywhere scholars, politicians, industrialists, financiers, sociologists, and futurists see grave trouble ahead. Yearningly, they look back to the optimistic beginnings of our country and the whispers seep from their pursed lips, "What went wrong?" "What happened to the hopes and aspirations of the pioneers?" "Were their brave struggles in vain?"

The thoughts accruing from many months of reading and meditation poured in upon me that night when I looked upon the Atlantic where the American dream had begun. I, like other concerned persons, seemed to have nothing but questions. Is our nation—our world—faced with collapse? Can we survive? Is our only choice between anarchy and dictatorship? Or is there an alternative?

More than any time in my life, I knew that night that we must urgently seek a third choice. I knew we would have to reach into the invisible world that has been there all along, a world far truer than any civilization in history. We have wasted too much time, decades of delay and doubt.

The challenges of my contemporaries rang in my ear: Is there truly an invisible world of the spirit? Is it possible to draw help from that invisible world? Can there be, as Presidents Carter and Bush have promised, a new world order?

Yes. It will not be a secular order but a divine one, ordained by God and conforming to the timeless principles of His kingdom.

This book comes from convictions about these questions. Its purpose is to foster understanding of the invisible world, better described as an invisible kingdom, the kingdom of God. It has principles. They can be learned.

My recognition of this has come slowly, spanning several years, and is still expanding. First was a prayer for wisdom, spoken quite naively, perhaps in the manner of King David's son Solomon. I desperately wanted to understand—God, the world, the present, the future, the working of things.

Oddly, or so it might seem, my first awareness of the possible answer to that prayer dawned as my interest became fixed on the words of John the Baptist in the early pages of the New Testament: "Repent, for the kingdom of heaven is at hand."[2]

I was struck by the words "at hand." What did they mean? Eventually my mind recalled similar words of Jesus, spoken the night of His betrayal as Judas approached with his rowdy gang: "the one who betrays Me is at hand!"[3]

In this case, the meaning was obvious. Judas had arrived; he was there. John the Baptist, using the same words, had obviously meant the same thing. The kingdom had arrived; it was there, at hand.

This was revolutionary understanding, as simple as it may seem these six or seven years later. I had been instructed to regard our time as the age of the church, and it is that in a very real sense, but John the Baptist and later the Lord Jesus Christ declared the arrival of the kingdom of God. Somehow I had failed to take seriously the fact that the kingdom of God is the central teaching of Jesus. He began His earthly ministry by declaring the arrival of the kingdom,[4] and He ended it when "he spoke to them about the kingdom of God."[5] Indeed He described such teaching as His ultimate purpose: "I must preach about God's kingdom to other towns, too. *This is why I was sent.*"[6]

That the kingdom of God was at the heart of the Lord's work is obvious, and furthermore he spoke of it as existing then and now, not to arrive at some far-distant time and place. The kingdom of God is in our midst.[7]

My constant prayers for wisdom brought additional insight over the weeks, months, and years, and I gradually perceived that Jesus had spoken quite precisely about how this kingdom worked. He was far from theoretical. He actually laid down specific principles, so sweeping that they might be better considered as laws, even at the risk of offending those who cringe at the merest hint of legalism. Jesus quite bluntly said, "If you do this, then this will happen." When He added no restrictions as to time, place, nationality, and the like, then they were laws, in the same sense as the natural laws established by God—those governing motion, gravity, sound, and such. They simply work.

Sitting in a big stuffed chair morning after morning in my living room, poring over the Scriptures, praying, thinking, making notes on a yellow legal pad, I uncovered one, then two, and three, and more of these major principles. But, equally important, I put them to work in my life, my family's life, and the life of the Christian Broadcasting Network. I wasn't interested in abstraction. I wanted to determine if they worked.

They did. And they do. They, and they alone, can alter the world's slide into anarchy or dictatorship. They offer a third choice.

Part I

TWO DOMAINS

1

The Visible World

THE MODERN WORLD is in crisis. Many people have the feeling that unless drastic changes are made quickly in the way this country is being run, the United States may not last out the century as the number-one superpower. We are moving rapidly into a state of social, intellectual, economic, and moral decline. Anywhere you look today you can see the evidence of looming disaster; you can hear urgent cries for change. Where can we turn for stability in our life? Is there anything or anyone to help us? The world as we know it is in chaos.

It is clearer each day that the world is hurtling toward some type of catastrophe. The upheavals in Eastern Europe and problems with the political process in the United States are ongoing concerns. The federal budget deficit is out of control, and the worldwide debate over ecology and the environment is escalating as never before. Anyone can see that our problems are only getting worse, and the people of America and the entire world are reaching the point of desperation. Some people are apparently willing to try solutions that are not well thought out or well reasoned, just to make a change.

Recently we saw what could happen when, in similar circumstances, a new president came into power virtually overnight in Peru and took drastic measures to restore order and balance in his country. The reformer, President Alberto Fujimori, effectively abandoned the democratic process. He could see that the system had grown corrupt, crime was out of control, and the entire nation was seemingly in peril, so he simply took matters into his own hands and the people went along with it. That is a potentially dangerous precedent. Yet, despite his dramatic action, months later terrorists were bombing the utilities of Lima, the capital city of Peru.

In this country we need only pause to consider what happened in the spring of 1992 in South Central Los Angeles. As a result of the unpopular jury decision in the Rodney King case, angry protesters took part in riots that cost more than forty lives and more than $1.5 billion in property damages. There is unrest and bitterness in the black community and a splintering of society. There is a deepening decline in moral values. What have we left to build upon? Everywhere people are crying out for something better.

In my book, *The New World Order,* I surveyed the conditions driving the world toward chaos. We don't hear as much about the government's world order agenda these days, but the conditions are still there, and, if anything, they are intensifying. Looking at the economic trends of the 1990s, it is clear that the exponential compounding of debt has taken us to the brink of economic collapse. Today there is a very real possibility of a money crisis to be followed by ruinous inflation.

During 1991 and '92 I was invited to go to Zaire and develop agricultural and economic programs to help aid that faltering economy. Zaire is an example of a rich, productive economy that collapsed under decades of mismanagement. Today anyone can see the results of the breakdown there. The currency has inflated from one zaire-to-three dollars to eight hundred thousand zaires-to-one dollar.

Nothing works properly. Airlines fly erratically; telephone service is not available; the roads are impassable; the hospitals have no medicine. Once an exporter of food, there is now not enough food for the people. Seventy percent of the people are unemployed. Forty percent of them have AIDS. There is catastrophe everywhere. Conditions for Zaire and other nations of Africa have plunged precipitously in the ten years since I first wrote down the principles of the secret kingdom.

RICH AND POOR

In many parts of the world there is a heightened sense of uncertainty amid what seems to be incredible prosperity. The wealthy are very wealthy; those with access to capital have never had it so good. The wealth available to them is simply staggering. The statistics in various news magazines indicate that the percentage of wealth controlled by the top 1 percent of the population continues to grow while the bottom 63 percent of wage earners have experienced only marginal growth in income over the past decade.

Of course the economic structure is not totally frozen: Some people have been able to move from middle-income levels into the upper-income brackets—there is still some economic mobility—but there is no question that the total share of wealth to those in the upper-income categories has grown more rapidly than the other segments of society.

Over the past ten years CBN News has tracked the social and moral conditions of this nation, and the reports I have seen are shocking. The educational crisis is appalling. This country is becoming a nation of illiterates. We have also done story after story on crime, addiction, divorce, the collapse of the family, and other issues, and the situation is not getting any better. We don't see any signs in this country that things are improving.

Ironically, in the former Soviet Union moral conditions are no worse and potentially much better than here. At least there is a genuine hunger for moral and spiritual values, and that is the absolutely essential first step to recovery. It is ironic that while America is moving away from the heritage which made us great, the former Communist nations are seeking after God.

The key words in any description of our plight are economy, energy, crime, poverty, morality, education, hunger, and pollution. Volumes are written on each. And each carries the same deterioration theme—deterioration and danger. The great cosmic clock appears to be winding down.

All about us we see "fear in a handful of dust," in Eliot's words, as man stares horror-stricken at,

> A heap of broken images, where the sun beats,
> And the dead tree gives no shelter, the cricket no
> relief,
> And the dry stone no sound of water.[1]

Even starker are the images from the Book of Isaiah in which the Old Testament prophet speaks of the darkness that descends upon a people when they have been disobedient to the will of God. Isaiah writes:

> We grope for the wall like the blind,
> And we grope as if we had no eyes;
> We stumble at noonday as at twilight;
> We are as dead men in desolate places.

We all growl like bears,
And moan sadly like doves;
We look for justice, but there is none;
For salvation, but it is far from us.
For our transgressions are multiplied before You,
And our sins testify against us;
For our transgressions are with us,
And as for our iniquities, we know them.[2]

Just as Isaiah predicted, the world is crying out for solutions to problems that are too big for us. Our governments are on the verge of collapse; our finances are in desperate condition; the environment is polluted; millions die of starvation in Third World nations where the population is skyrocketing and industry is collapsing. Underlying fear is covered by a thin veneer of affluence. "'There is no peace,' / Says my God, 'for the wicked.'"[3]

Our condition is not difficult to understand. And the purpose of this book is not to dwell on that condition, but rather to explore reliable remedies. Nonetheless, to understand the encompassing nature of those remedies, we should take a few moments to set the stage of the visible world. We need only trace a few strands of the hangman's noose that seems poised over our heads, beginning with the most immediately destructive, the threat of nuclear holocaust.

THE AGE OF TERROR

Let us go back to 1940. Three physicists—Enrico Fermi, Leo Szilard, and Eugene Wigner—working in a makeshift laboratory in a handball court under the grandstand at the University of Chicago, split the atom and thereby confirmed the theoretical formula of Albert Einstein: $E=mc^2$. The split, or fission, caused a multiplication of energy in the order of 6 million-to-one.

At last man had found a source of cheap and abundant energy for the world forever. A new industrial revolution was at hand. Age-old territorial disputes would end. Wars would cease. The poor could be warmed, sheltered, fed. No nation need be without.

History records a different outcome. The work of those three deeply religious men evolved into an age of terror, not an age of abundance. There was Hiroshima. Then Nagasaki.

That was only the beginning. Physicists quickly perfected nuclear fusion and a release of energy of 50 million-to-one. Utilizing hydrogen, a fuel as abundant as the waters of the seas, this process held promise as the energy source of the millennium. There need be no fossil fuel shortage, no air pollution, no fabulously wealthy OPEC oil cartel, no desperately poor Third World.

The utopia did not come. Instead we have hydrogen bombs rated in millions of tons of TNT. The superpower nations, during the fifties and sixties, built arsenals capable of destroying all life on earth. A balance of terror developed between the United States and the Soviet Union bearing the terrifying acronym MAD—Mutual Assured Destruction.

Then came the seventies. The United States, wearied by its struggle in Southeast Asia, gradually dismantled its military capability, delaying the start of weapons systems commensurate with advanced technology. The Soviet Union, meanwhile, pushed its flagging economy to the breaking point to build the most awesome array of weapons ever assembled by a nation in peacetime.

Instead of balance, the world of the 1980s was faced with an imbalance of terror in favor of a malevolent dictatorship bent on world domination. Ultimately it was the inherent weaknesses of the Soviet system which brought that giant colossus to its knees. Its economy was in such terrible decay after years of godless socialism, collapse was inevitable. Even though I had predicted the collapse of the Soviet Union as early as 1969, it was stunning to see that event fulfilled in 1989 and 1990.

Today it is clear that Marxism was a failure from the very beginning. Its leadership was corrupt. The people lacked incentive to work; moral decay destroyed the sanctity of the family. Faith in God was prohibited, thus the souls of the people grew pale and desperate. Some kind of change had to come about.

Today Russia and the Commonwealth of Independent States (CIS) are looking to the West for help. Having endured a long string of upsets, complicated by hunger, a shocking coup attempt, and general disarray, the leaders of these fifteen former communist nations are more open-minded now than ever. But we should never forget that the majority of the former Soviet nuclear capability is still intact, and the possibility of a hardline pro-communist coup is very real indeed.

And nuclear weapons have found their way to Iraq and Iran. Nuclear and chemical technology rests with the madman Saddam Hussein. Mohamar Qaddafi of Libya and Syrian President Hafez al Assad are still very real threats to peace. The nations controlling Middle East oil are often ruthless, as we witnessed in the Iraqi invasion of Kuwait and the events of Operation Desert Storm in the spring of 1991. Despite the apparent peace in the Middle East, our age still retains the potential to touch off World War III. "Age of terror" is an apt description. But there is a solution, as we will see.

THE STRUGGLE FOR ENERGY

Intertwined with the age of terror is the concern for sufficient energy to satisfy the mushrooming demands of our planet. Scientists believe the demand for energy may be as ominous as the nuclear threat, despite the deceptive ebb and flow in short-range supply and demand.

In 1950 there were 2.51 billion people in the world. By 1980 the figure soared to 4.41 billion. The demand for everything from food to factories skyrocketed. Today we have a worldwide population of nearly 6 billion people, and unless interrupted by drastic changes or some terrible catastrophe, by 2010 the population will exceed 8 billion men, women, and children. With a birthrate of 100 million per year and a death rate of 50 million, the population of the world is growing with unbelievable speed.

But nothing exploded like the demand for energy. In 1950 the world used the equivalent of 2.66 billion metric tons of coal. In 1980 consumption was 9.5 billion metric tons. Today the world consumes the equivalent of 14.5 billion metric tons of coal, and the demand continues to grow.

In thirty years the population had not quite doubled; yet energy use had more than tripled. We were running wild with everything that required fuel.

This massive growth presented a simple truth as the decade of the eighties got under way: The planet does not contain enough nonrenewable and renewable sources of energy to supply indefinitely the basic needs and growing aspirations of a world population that continues to explode.

It seems clear that if some sort of solution is not forthcoming, we face the following perilous prospects:

• Those possessing dwindling energy sources will extract ever-increasing prices. This trend will hold true in the long run, even when temporary conditions cause occasional price drops that give the world a false sense of security. If recent patterns continue, the cost of energy will place such insupportable burdens on world-wide industry and financial markets that money supplies will be imprudently increased. This could set off hyperinflation and lead to worldwide financial collapse.

• To prolong high-energy lifestyles, the developed nations may use military force to seize dwindling resources. The war in the Persian Gulf was after all not so much an exercise to support the rights of the oppressed as it was a move to protect our continued access to Middle East oil.

• As oil import costs continue to mount, industrially developed nations will show more and more strain as they try to maintain a balance of trade.

Aggressive financial actions, including punitive trade measures, seem certain and will heighten world tension.

• The prognosis is even worse for the weaker nations. They simply do not have the money to buy oil and pay interest on their huge debts at the same time. Many face bankruptcy already. Such default by any of several nations can cause suffering internally and global economic confusion externally. It could trigger a worldwide bank collapse, for example, unless the United States is willing to bail out the country in trouble.

• America's cities pose a unique danger that has wide-ranging potential, traceable in large part to energy consumption and high costs. The mammoth office buildings, shopping centers, and apartment houses of New York, Detroit, Chicago, Cleveland, Boston, Philadelphia, and other cities are energy gluttons. The rising operating costs have been staggering. Compounding this financial burden is the fact that the physical plants of these cities—the sewers, water lines, and other underground support utilities, plus the roads, bridges, and other systems above ground—have far exceeded their life expectancies. The cities don't have the money for proper maintenance and replacement. Time bombs are ticking away both above and below ground. Should they begin to explode, the cities will be brought to their knees. The social and economic consequences nationally and globally will be staggering.

• Imprudent substitution of hazardous, untested energy sources in the face of diminishing traditional sources could present the world with intolerable environmental problems affecting all of life. Yet rigid regulation could inhibit exploration, discovery, and creativity needed to overcome shortages. The dilemma breeds deep strife.

• The reluctance and/or inability of car manufacturers to respond to worldwide energy problems threw a major portion of American industry into a tailspin that threatened the wider economy. By the early eighties, foreign car manufacturers, led by the Japanese, had seized 28 percent of U.S. domestic auto business. Today, including foreign transplant operations, that figure has grown to 30 percent. Many major American industries, in fact, have been badly hurt in recent years by foreign competition and trade practices. Anger and discontent are mounting, with a crescendo of protectionist threats all around us.

The struggle for energy and the manifold ramifications of that struggle have propelled the world to the brink of upheaval. Even the tiniest of international movements has the potential for escalation. We will see, however, that there are alternatives.

ECONOMIC DISASTER

Picking up another related thread, we learned that the lesser-developed nations of the world owed more than $500 billion to banks and wealthier nations early in 1981. Annual interest on those loans approached $100 billion, which was $35 billion more than the total debt of those nations only eight years earlier. Now, by 1992, just the Latin American nations have a combined debt of $442.7 billion. Tragically, they are being forced to borrow simply to pay their interest charges. A number of loans are being refinanced so the nations do not appear to be in default.

During this period, Poland was in the news as its people suffered the penalty of reaching for freedom from Soviet-led repression. That country's disastrous financial condition is typical of many other countries of the world. In 1982 it owed $24 billion of the total $89 billion owed to the West by Russia and the Eastern Bloc countries. By 1987, Poland's debt had soared to more than $40 billion. An agreement by foreign creditors arranged by the Paris Club in 1991 to write off nearly half that amount has given them some leverage, but current debt remains at more than $25 billion, and today the hopes of the Polish people for democracy and privatization remain in doubt.

It seems certain, with so many countries in a condition like Poland's, that one day a scene similar to the following will be played out.

A sweaty-palmed finance minister from Russia or Brazil or Poland will sit in a room in Switzerland or Germany or France and be told by several dignified bankers that his country's loans are in default. No more money is available. When word leaks out, the canny finance minister from oil-rich Kuwait, Abu Dhabi, Saudi Arabia, Iraq, or Libya could quietly withdraw his country's deposits from the banks in question. When word of this withdrawal is circulated, a wild scramble to get cash out of weakening banks could result.

Major institutions could fall like dominoes overnight. Euro-dollar certificates of deposit could be wiped out, along with other large domestic certificates. Broad-based money market funds could lose virtually all their bank assets. There would very possibly have to be a nationwide freeze on bank withdrawals in this country to prevent a collapse of the banking system. Bonds, stocks, gold, silver, and jewels would fall like stones. Trade and commerce could be brought to a standstill.

Only a multinational effort to print a trillion or more dollars could stave off fiscal disaster. And this rescue would merely accelerate post-World War I, German-style hyperinflation, followed eventually by a worse crash.

In 1974–75 the world economy lurched, and several big banks and real estate operations failed, but the system held together. In 1980 it lurched again. That time silver crashed and the bond market lost $300 billion. Many financial institutions became technically insolvent as the market value of their bond and mortgage portfolios plunged in the wake of a 21 percent prime interest rate. One major bank failed and Chrysler became a government ward, but the system survived.

It lurched again with the savings and loan collapse, but was saved by a $500 billion federal bailout. Despite high profits, banks and insurance companies have neither restored liquidity as they did after the mid-seventies problem, nor have their portfolios improved as much as desired. Nonbank businesses are still illiquid and overextended despite recent dramatic drops in short-term interest rates.

Furthermore, the U.S. government continues to borrow to cover budget deficits. The federal deficit is a record $400 billion and the direct debt is a mind-boggling $4 trillion. Inflation, although dipping at least temporarily, can still come alive quickly. It seems built into the system at every level. Prices do not actually fall; their rate of increase merely slows.

Questions are inevitable. Are major business and financial institutions, as well as individuals, bound for bankruptcy? Will this trigger the sort of doomsday scenario described above?

There are options, as we will see.

A TAILSPIN IN MORALITY

As the nineties unfold, nothing portrays our world crisis more clearly than man's internal and moral condition. The unmistakable scent of what the Bible calls the antichrist spirit is in the air. It was present at the tower of Babel and at Sodom and Gomorrah. It was present in the French Revolution and in Nazi Germany. And it is present in Europe and the United States today. The signs of this spirit are clear. They emerge in this fashion: A significant minority, then an actual majority, of the people in a society begin to throw off the restraints of history, then the restraints of written law, then accepted standards of morality, then established religion, and, finally, God Himself.

As the rebellion gains momentum, the participants grow bolder. Those practices that once were considered shameful and unlawful move into the open. Soon the practitioners are aggressive, militant. As each societal standard falls, another comes under attack. The pressure is relentless. Established institutions crumble. Ultimately the struggle that began as a cry for freedom of expression grows into an all-out war against the rights of advocates of traditional morality. The latter are hated, reviled, isolated, and then persecuted.

Honor, decency, honesty, self-control, sexual restraint, family values, and sacrifice are replaced by gluttony, sensuality, bizarre sexual practices, cruelty, profligacy, dishonesty, delinquency, drunkenness, drug-induced euphoria, fraud, waste, debauched currency, and rampant inflation.

The people then search for a deity that will both permit and personify their basest desires. At Babel it was a tower—man's attempt to glorify himself. In ancient Mediterranean cultures, like those of Sodom and Gomorrah, it was a god or goddess of sex. In France, it was the goddess of reason; in Germany, Hitler and the Nazi party; in Europe and especially in the United States, the god of central government under the religion of secular humanism.

The pattern is always the same. So is the result. No society falling under a grip of the Antichrist spirit has survived. First comes a period of lawlessness and virtual anarchy, then an economic collapse followed by a reign of terror. Then comes a strong dictator who plunders society for his personal aggrandizement; he dreams of a worldwide empire and storms into war. Eventually come defeat and collapse.

In some cases God intervenes directly to destroy the Antichrist society before it reaches full flower. In others, the society destroys itself. Sometimes a righteous nation takes action; in others the task is performed by stronger barbarians. But always there is destruction.

In the United States, trends, also reflected in other countries, are well defined:

• Organized crime is the largest industry in the land. With gross revenues of $150 billion, the profits of crime eclipse the profits of the American oil or auto industries, producing power and influence that compromise and corrupt the fabric of society. The impact of illegal drug use, as only one example, is staggering. In 1981 cocaine grossed $35 billion and marijuana $24 billion, establishing that Americans spent more on those two illegal drugs than they contributed to all charities, education, and religion combined. By 1991, there were 6.3 million users of cocaine in the United States and 19.5 million users of marijuana, and national spending on drugs continues to climb.

• The sexual revolution has snaked its way into the schools, the homes, and virtually all of society. Traditional standards regarding nudity, fornication, adultery, homosexuality, incest, and sadomasochism have been under fierce attack and many are crumbling. Educators deluded by humanism are offering sex education without moral standards to children; some courses appear to advocate masturbation, premarital sex, and homosexuality. Motion pictures, television, and the publishing industry pour the excesses of unbridled gratification into communities and homes.

• From this rampant hedonism has emerged permission to minimize the inconvenient side effects of sexual pleasure. The Supreme Court ruled that the thing conceived through sexual relations between two humans is not itself a human and therefore may be destroyed prior to the fourth month of pregnancy. The killing of unborn infants through abortion has thus proceeded at the rate of 1.5 million a year.

• At the same time, family life has been battered. In the decade of the seventies, the number of couples living together outside of marriage doubled, and divorce reached a rate of one for every two marriages. But data were not crystallized for the marred lives of children caught in the breakup of families, for the suicides of young and old unable to survive the trauma of sudden rootlessness, for the wasted lives of despair.

Financial morality has been corrupted as the government, exalted by humanist philosophy, has become god and provider. In 1941 the population of the United States was 133.7 million; government spending was $13.6 billion. Forty years later the population had grown by 72 percent, to 229.3 million; federal spending had grown by 4,762 percent, to $661.2 billion. By 1992 the population had grown to 250 million, an increase of 92 percent over 1940, yet the spending of the federal government had grown an astounding $1.5 trillion, an increase of 10,929 percent over 1940. We have already touched on the result: federal debt nearing $4 trillion, ever-increasing inflation, and domestic and world economics in danger of collapse.

• As self-restraint and regard for God rapidly diminish under the assault of secular humanism, a new rule of law has been emerging. Judges are less inclined to make decisions based on the Bible, the Constitution, natural laws, or precedent. Instead, they often impose as a rule of law whatever seems sociologically expedient or whatever reflects the prevailing sentiment of the ruling elite. As Justice Charles Evans Hughes declared early in the century, "The Constitution is what the judges say it is," pointing to a trend in which a government based on men's opinions would supersede a government based on laws. Lawlessness has thus come a long way.

But we will see that there is a remedy.

REVOLT AGAINST GOD

Underlying all the threads we have examined as integral to the deepening crisis coming upon the world—and we have examined only a fraction of them—is one that transcends all others. It is the increased disregard for the Creator of the world.

Shortly after the turn of the century, a false view of reality began to take hold in America. Although its name did not become well known immediately, humanism spread into all aspects of life and became the dominant philosophical view about the time of World War II. Today millions of people openly embrace it, and many millions more follow along under its influence.

Francis A. Schaeffer, the Christian philosopher-theologian, described
humanism's influence this way:

> . . . the humanist world view includes many thousands of adherents and
> today controls the consensus in society, much of the media, much of what is
> taught in our schools, and much of the arbitrary law being produced by the
> various departments of government.
>
> The term humanism used in this wider, more prevalent way means Man
> beginning from himself, with no knowledge except what he himself can
> discover and no standards outside of himself. In this view Man is the
> measure of all things, as the Enlightenment expressed it. . . .
>
> Since [the humanists'] concept of Man is mistaken, their concept of society
> and of law is mistaken, and they have no sufficient base for either society or
> law. They have reduced Man to even less than his natural finiteness by
> seeing him only as a complex arrangement of molecules, made complex by
> blind chance. Instead of seeing him as something great who is significant
> even in his sinning, they see Man in his essence only as an intrinsically
> competitive animal, that has no other basic operating principle than natural
> selection brought about by the strongest, the fittest, ending on top. And they
> see Man as acting in this way both individually and collectively as society.[4]

Thus, for a vast number of people, God has been removed from the
center of things, and man has taken His place. All things exist for man
and his pleasure.

In a church-state dialogue sponsored in 1981 by the Virginia Council of
Churches, a professor of humanistic studies summed up the direction of
American leadership most clearly: "We must throw off the tyranny of the
concept that the Bible is the Word of God. We must be freed from the
tyranny of thought that comes from Martin Luther, John Calvin, [Ulrich]
Zwingli, and John Knox."

He discarded the Bible as the authoritative guide for faith and conduct,
casting with it such long-accepted truths as the doctrine of man's
sinfulness, the doctrine of eternal reward and eternal punishment, the
necessity for repentance and justification by faith in Jesus Christ, and the
necessity for holy living to please God. Such astounding recommendations can only be grasped when one recalls the words of *Humanist
Manifesto I* and *II* (produced in 1933 and 1973), which denied the
"existence of a supernatural God who hears and answers prayer."

With all standards and yardsticks removed, society first eased, then
rushed toward the extremes of hedonism and nihilism, with increasing
numbers finding fulfillment in "doing their own thing."

"If it feels good, do it," comes the advice of everyone from parents to
psychologists. This, they say, is freedom. Meanwhile, as we noted earlier,
nothing works. Bodies wear out early as sickness and disease soar. Never
has there been so much cancer, so much heart disease. Brains, too, wear

out. Never have emotional and mental breakdowns run so high; never have suicides reached such levels. Schools fail; businesses fail; governments fail.

Yes, humanism and its society are failing, although seemingly few have perceived the depth of that failure. Most see only symptoms, not the underlying sickness.

Perhaps the bright spot for those of faith is that the collapse of the Soviet Union showed the world the stark and terrible failure of a social and political system founded on humanism. Despite its seemingly unassailable grip on the power centers of Western society, humanism has clearly been exposed as a failed system that cannot withstand the assault of resolute faith. In the 1990s and beyond, the battle is not going to be fought much longer between Christianity and atheistic humanism, but between Christianity and satanic-inspired Eastern religions. In truth the collapse of communism has opened up for the Soviet Union, the Eastern Bloc countries, and the so-called Third World the greatest religious revival in the history of mankind.

INEVITABLE CONCLUSIONS

The fear has become widespread that our society—and the world's—is beyond repair. There is confusion everywhere. At times the confusion approaches chaos. It seems clear that we will slide further into chaos, the jungle of anarchy: "I've got mine; to heck with you"—"do unto others before they can do unto you"—"every man for himself," or in desperation we will yield to dictatorship. Which will it be?

It matters not that both of the prevailing philosophies of materialism have been proven corrupt and ineffective. communism said materialism is the goal but the state should control it. Now communism has fallen. Emerging democracy and capitalism go hand in hand. But unbridled capitalism strives for materialism and the strong control of it. Both systems without a biblical balance will move toward dictatorship, either oligarchical or individual.

Eventually a strong man will be chosen if secular, capitalist materialism fails—unless we turn to the third choice that is available to us.

What will we do?

2

The Invisible World

THROUGHOUT HIS EARTHLY ministry, Jesus Christ preached the good news of the kingdom. He said, "The time is fulfilled, and the kingdom of God is at hand. Repent, and believe in the gospel."[1] That was His central message. He instructed His followers to go out and teach the people and to tell them that "The kingdom of heaven is at hand."[2] For when Christ came as Messiah, He was the fulfillment of Old Testament prophecy and the realization of the promises of God toward His people. That is the central truth of Christianity.

Jesus brought the kingdom with Him, and He left tangible and very real evidence of the kingdom in our hands when He was taken up into heaven. When Christ went ahead to prepare a place for us, He fully expected us to claim the rights and privileges of our citizenship from that moment on.

Jesus taught that the kingdom has two dimensions: the immediate and visible, which we see, and the invisible kingdom, which we do not see now but which will be fully revealed at the close of this age. From beginning to end, the Bible teaches that these two dimensions are real and very powerful.

True enough, the people of His own day wanted tangible evidence of God's power. They wanted to see signs and miracles; they wanted physical bread and wine; and they wanted assurances that their king would be either a great conqueror or a great provider. In teachings such as the Sermon on the Mount and the Beatitudes, Jesus made many promises about the kingdom to come, but He also taught them to live in the kingdom of God's present revelation. He told them to trust in God not only for their spiritual food, but for their earthly needs as well. He said:

> Therefore do not worry, saying, "What shall we eat?" or "What shall we drink?" or "What shall we wear?" For after all these things the Gentiles seek. For your heavenly Father knows that you need all these things. But seek first the kingdom of God and His righteousness, and all these things shall be added to you. Therefore do not worry about tomorrow, for tomorrow will worry about its own things. Sufficient for the day is its own trouble.[3]

The truths of Christ's teachings were not merely comforting ideas, pious meditations, or convenient philosophies. Jesus taught that these principles were to be understood in all their reality by anyone who would truly listen to what He was saying. "For there is nothing hidden which will not be revealed, nor has anything been kept secret but that it should come to light. If anyone has ears to hear, let him hear."[4]

The principles of the invisible kingdom in our midst do not change. They apply to all people in all situations, everywhere, equally. I have seen rapt attention to them recently in Zaire among those looking to become successful leaders. I've seen families that give them the same kind of attention. These principles have applications in every situation. And even while the world seems to be in constant change around us, the principles are faithful and true.

I firmly believe that the principles of the kingdom are God's answer for the world in which we live in the 1990s and the coming new millennium. Their insights into the workings of the kingdom can offer powerful solutions to the problems of this or any other time.

CALM AMID THE STORM

Fortunately, a Voice speaks steadily and clearly into the turmoil and dread of the day, a Voice that contradicts our finitude and limitation and restriction. It says, "But seek first His kingdom and His righteousness; and all these things shall be added to you."[5]

Obviously the words are those of Jesus, climaxing a teaching about food, clothing, shelter, and all the "things" needed for life. God, His heavenly Father, was able and eager to provide the necessities for happy, successful living on Earth if the people merely turned to the right place—His kingdom.

His point immediately established a fact that the world has in large measure refused to consider—the fact that an invisible world undergirds, surrounds, and interpenetrates the visible world in which we live. Indeed, it controls the visible world, for it is unrestricted, unlimited, infinite.

The problem of the world, and of many Christians, has not been simply refusing to acknowledge the possibility of such a kingdom, but failing to perceive that it exists right now, not in some far-off time or far-off place called heaven. This is so strange because Jesus spent virtually all of His earthly ministry telling people that the kingdom of God had come and then explaining its workings.

For reasons that are beyond our comprehension, even we Christians missed it as we soaked up the good news of salvation, the fullness of the Holy Spirit, the fellowship of the church, and the future millennium. In fact, it is embarrassing today, as we begin to glimpse the core of what Jesus was doing, to note that practically everything He said pertained to the "kingdom." For example, His first utterance in His public ministry, according to Matthew, was: "Repent, for the kingdom of heaven is at hand."[6]

Each of the Gospel writers said it similarly. "The time has come," Jesus declared, in essence. "The kingdom is here, and I've come to open it to you and to show you how it works."

His pattern recalls the days following the anointing of Saul as Israel's first king when it became necessary for the prophet Samuel to teach how things should work: "Then Samuel told the people the manner of the kingdom, and wrote it in a book, and laid it up before the LORD."[7]

Jesus did much the same, teaching His followers "the manner of the kingdom," but leaving it to others to put it in writing.

Many of us are now discovering this central purpose of our Lord, perceiving that the kingdom of God, though invisible, is right now nonetheless real, nonetheless powerful. We are much like the servant of Elisha who went outside the tent one morning and saw Syrian troops ready to close in on them from every side.

"We're surrounded!" he yelled.

But Elisha calmly asked the Lord to open the young man's eyes. Then he saw into the invisible world. Chariots of fire, the heavenly host, were everywhere about them, protecting Elisha. As the prophet had said, "those who are with us are more than those who are with them."[8]

THINGS THAT ENDURE

Yes, the kingdom of God is here—now. And the message of the Bible is that we can and should look from this visible world, which is finite, into the invisible world, which is infinite. We should look from a world filled with impossibilities into one filled with possibilities.

We should do more than look, however, if we believe the Scriptures. We should enter. We should reach from the visible into the invisible and bring that secret kingdom into the visible through its principles—principles that can be adopted at this moment.

"The kingdom of God is like this . . . ," Jesus said, in effect. "It operates this way . . ." "If you want this, then do this . . ." Over and over.

So real is this invisible world, that when Jesus comes to Earth the second time, things will be turned inside out, through a sort of skinning process, you might say—and the invisible will become visible. The kingdom of God and its subjects will be manifested—unveiled. In the language of Paul's letter to the Romans: "The creation waits eagerly for the revealing of the sons of God."[9] It "groans and suffers"—"standing on tiptoe," according to J. B. Phillips's translation—as it yearns for that unveiling.

The apostles had a foretaste of the inside-out effect during their days with Jesus. First came a statement by the Lord that has puzzled many Bible readers through the centuries: "Truly I say to you, there are some of those who are standing here who shall not taste death until they see the Son of Man coming in His kingdom."[10]

A most marvelous event occurred six days later. We refer to it as the Transfiguration. Taking Peter, James, and John with Him, Jesus went to a high mountain.

> And He was transfigured before them; and His face shone like the sun, and His garments became as white as light. And behold, Moses and Elijah appeared to them, talking with Him. And Peter answered and said to Jesus, "Lord, it is good for us to be here; if You wish, I will make three tabernacles here, one for You, and one for Moses, and one for Elijah." While he was still speaking, behold, a bright cloud overshadowed them; and behold, a voice out of the cloud, saying, "This is My beloved Son, with whom I am well-pleased; hear Him!" And when the disciples heard this, they fell on their faces and were much afraid. . . . And lifting up their eyes, they saw no one, except Jesus Himself alone.[11]

The Lord became like lightning, shining white, and what had been invisible within Him became visible. The inside became the outside. The Law (Moses) and the prophets (Elijah) were fulfilled, and the Son of Man (Jesus) came visibly in His kingdom, in power and glory.

The disciples had a taste of what the kingdom will be at its manifestation. But what they saw at that moment had been resident in Jesus all the time. It had merely been invisible, but no less real and powerful. And that is what the Lord was telling His followers to lay hold of when He instructed them to seek the kingdom first so that all of their needs would be met.

"Reach into the invisible and apply it to the visible," He said, in effect. "For all things are possible with God."[12]

THE UNLIMITED WORLD OF JESUS

Almighty God has been warning for thousands of years that because of our foolishness we will face crises. We are face to face with nuclear terror, a massive energy shortage, an insoluble economic crisis, debilitating moral bankruptcy, and other impossible difficulties. But Jesus explained that we are limited in our ability to cope with such problems only because we insist on living according to the ways of a world that is limited.

In effect he has said, "That need not remain so. An unlimited world surrounds you.

"You are finite; it is infinite.

"You are mortal; it is immortal.

"You are filled with impossibilities; it is filled with possibilities."

That was the world of Jesus, even when He came as a man to live on this finite earth. He was careful to say, "the Son can do nothing of Himself, unless it is something He sees the Father doing; for whatever the Father does, these things the Son also does in like manner."[13]

The invisible world of His Father was Jesus' world throughout His incarnation. It was a world where everything was beautiful. And He became upset when His disciples failed to follow His example.

Once, when they were in the middle of the Sea of Galilee on a boat journey Jesus had instructed them to make, a storm arose and their mission was near failure as their little vessel was swamped and showed signs of sinking. They rushed to wake Him from a much-needed nap. He was visibly perplexed. Why hadn't they been able to cope with the situation? They had failed to see into the invisible world where there were no impediments to the Lord's mission, and they had allowed themselves to be limited by world conditions.

So Jesus Himself arose and spoke to the storm, calming it. He then asked a rather humbling question: "Why are you timid, you men of little faith?"[14]

They had refused to reach into the world of the possible. And Jesus was angry, frustrated by the unwillingness of those He loved to accept the truth of what He had told them. One cannot help but wonder about His frustration as His followers seem so impotent to overcome the visible world today.

A MAJOR LESSON

The Gospel according to Mark contains one of the Lord's most compact, yet most comprehensive, teachings about how to manifest the power of the invisible world in the visible today. Although we will be exploring the passage in more detail later, it is so significant for our initial understanding of the kingdom that we need to look at it in part now.

Jesus set the stage for the teaching when, on the way with His disciples to the temple to deal with the mockery practiced there under the guise of worship, He walked up to a fig tree in leaf, examined it for fruit, found none, and said: "May no one ever eat fruit from you again."[15]

We must understand immediately that Jesus was not being capricious or petulant. He didn't simply lose His temper. The fig tree, as is so often the case in Scripture, symbolized Israel in biblical times. When He cursed it, he was symbolically addressing a religious system that was often outwardly showy and inwardly fruitless. It was a system that practiced money changing and the selling of doves for sacrifice within the temple walls but gave the people little to feed their souls. He cursed that practice, too, as the Scripture goes on to report, and drove the money changers from the premises: "It is written in the Scriptures, 'My Temple will be called a house for prayer for people from all nations.' But you are changing God's house into a 'hideout for robbers.'"[16]

No, He was not showing off. As with everything in His brief time on earth, the Lord made a point of tremendous significance. The next morning it came to light.

Jesus and His disciples passed the fig tree on the way back into Jerusalem and it had died, withered under His curse. Still failing to perceive the invisible world but yet observing its effects, Peter blurted out, "Look, the fig tree you cursed is all dried up!"

Then came the simplest insight into the deepest phenomenon: "Jesus answered, 'Have faith in God.'"[17]

Those four words burst through the frontiers of heaven, laying bare the invisible kingdom. *Have faith in God*. We must totally believe in and trust Almighty God. We must know that One sits on the throne of the universe, as John saw in his great vision in the Book of the Revelation.[18] He controls everything to the uttermost. He is without peer. He is omnipotent, omniscient, and omnipresent—the only free, unrestricted being in the universe.

Kathryn Kuhlman often said during her powerful ministry, "I sometimes think we're too familiar with God." She was right. Many times it seems we are trying to make Him into a toy that we can wind up and get to do our bidding. We sing Him little songs and utter all manner of things that threaten to demean His utter sovereignty. Kathryn's point was that God is God Almighty, the Great I AM. He created the sun and the moon and the earth and the solar system. It is staggering! He merely said, "Let there be light,"[19] and the power of a billion hydrogen bombs began to move, rolling from one end of the solar system to the other. The distances and the energy are awesome. And they clearly illustrate the truth that a power exists in the universe transcending anything finite man's tiny mind can imagine. Paul the apostle put it into words, but even they are inadequate: "Now to Him who is able to do exceeding abundantly beyond all that we ask or think . . ."[20]

That is God. And Jesus said, "Have faith in Him." Touch Him, He said, and anything is possible.

THE LIVING PRESENCE

The Lord wants us in league with His Father. His teachings make it plain that total faith and trust in God—for every breath and every second—are to produce a oneness with Him. We are to see with Him, think with Him, as Jesus did, so that we can say along with Jesus that we do only what we see the Father doing. That way, we will reach into the invisible world even though living in the visible.

In the fig tree episode, Jesus went on to explain another point that will be dealt with fully in another chapter, but for now we will simply reflect on it:

> Truly I say to you, whosoever says to this mountain, "Be taken up and cast into the sea," and does not doubt in his heart, but believes that what he says is going to happen, it shall be *granted* him. Therefore I say to you, all things for which you pray and ask, believe that you have received them, and they shall be granted to you.[21]

In short, Jesus told His disciples that if they truly had faith in God, believed in His absolute sovereignty and mighty power, and entered into league with Him, they would become participants in the same energy and power that prevailed at the Creation. They would work as God works, be fellow workers with Him, in the words of Paul.[22]

Yes, Jesus said, there is an invisible world, but we can see into it and touch it—here, now. God works; He wants us to work.

The great book of the Bible dealing with the early church, the Book of Acts, doesn't have a conclusion. It just stops with the apostle Paul in his own rented house, receiving all who came to see him in Rome. That was the end of the account. Some of the Gospels indicate that they are the good news of what Jesus began to do and to teach. Jesus told His disciples that they would do the things that He did and greater things because He was going to be with His Father and would send the Holy Spirit to guide them.

There has never been any thought in the Christian church until very recently that the miracles of Jesus stopped. In fact, in the Third World in particular, we are seeing an explosion of miraculous activity. We are receiving astonishing reports from Africa where there are healings of every known malady. People who were dead are actually being raised again. There are miraculous provisions of food. There have been storms that have been stilled, and large rain clouds have been dispersed over the open-air evangelistic meetings.

It just seems that in the world today the fastest growing segment of Christianity is what is called the charismatic group. Those numbers have been estimated at anywhere between 160 million and 360 million people. Now, for these believers, miracles are an article of faith: They are taken as part of what they receive when they become Christians.

At CBN we have seen tens of thousands of answers to prayer. I recall one dramatic instance that occurred when I was campaigning for the presidency of the United States in 1987. I had addressed a Republican party luncheon in Huntington, West Virginia, accompanied by a reporter for the *New York Times*. As I was leaving the luncheon, a young man came up to me and said, "Mr. Robertson, I've got to talk to you." So I listened. He said, "I was blind, and I was watching 'The 700 Club,' and after prayer I began to see." I said, "Well, thank you very much." But he stopped me again and said, "But you don't understand. I was blind and now I can see!" He wasn't exaggerating; he was thrilled because God had performed a miracle in his life, and he was changed.

This kind of thing has been repeated over and over again. I meet people who were dying of cancer, and they say that because of prayer they were completely restored to health. On many occasions women with little children in their arms have come up to me and said, "My husband and I were barren; we couldn't have children. After prayer with the people on your program, we conceived a child."

I will never forget the Jewish man who lived in Nazareth, the hometown of Jesus. He was paralyzed from the waist down, and was watching from a wheelchair our "700 Club" program being broadcast through our station in Lebanon called Middle East Television. On that broadcast, our co-hostess, Danuta Soderman, during a time of prayer received a word from God that someone in the audience who was paralyzed was being healed. She spoke this word, the program was recorded, and the Israeli man in Nazareth watched the tape replay. He went to bed totally paralyzed, but when he woke up the next morning there was feeling in his feet and legs.

For the first time in years he stood up without a brace and walked. When our film crew recorded him some months later, he was jogging around the streets of Nazareth. He now has a vibrant testimony of his faith in Jesus as his Messiah. That is just one of the tens of thousands of miracles that have been reported to us concerning prayer offered on our program.

George Gallup told me several years ago of his findings that at least 7.5 million Americans have reported some kind of miraculous answer to prayer, primarily in relation to physical healing.

PRINCIPLES OF THE KINGDOM

Having been trained and surrounded by Christians who did not concern themselves especially with the Lord's teachings on the reality of the kingdom here and now, I didn't begin to catch glimpses of this reality in any meaningful way until the mid-seventies. I, too, had dwelt pretty much on the good news of salvation and the work of the Holy Spirit in believers' lives, and that truly is good news. But there is much more.

By mid-decade, I was wrestling with John the Baptist's insistence that "the kingdom of heaven is at hand."[23] As I have said, I soon saw he was reporting that the kingdom was here—here on earth—obviously because Jesus Christ was here.

I mused over this for many weeks and months, tracking through the Scriptures, praying for wisdom, and talking with one or two friends. As I badgered the Lord for wisdom, I began to realize that there are principles in the kingdom as enunciated by Jesus Christ and that they are as valid for our lives as the laws of thermodynamics or the law of gravity. The physical laws are immutable, and I soon saw that the kingdom laws are equally so.

How can we determine those principles? They are found in the Bible. When we see a statement of Jesus that is not qualified as to time or recipient, then we have uncovered a universal truth. If He uses the terms "whosoever" or "whatsoever" or some other sweeping generalization, we should be especially alert. He is probably declaring a truth that will apply in every situation, in every part of the world, in every time.

It sounds so simple, and it is. Not every word spoken by the Lord had direct application for everyone; some were restricted. But others were without restriction—a "house divided against itself shall not stand,"[24] for example.

Once we perceive this secret, we realize anew that the Bible is not an impractical book of theology, but rather a practical book of life containing a system of thought and conduct that will guarantee success. And it will be true success, true happiness, true prosperity, not the fleeting, flashy, inconsistent success the world usually settles for.

The Bible, quite bluntly, is a workable guidebook for politics, government, business, families, and all the affairs of mankind.

There are dozens of these principles sprinkled throughout, and they are all marvelous. But there are several broad, overriding ones that I like to think of as "laws" of the kingdom. They span all of life, often overlapping and supplementing one another, but never contradicting. We will be probing into those major ones that hold special potential for revolutionizing our time and world.

They give us an alternative in our current world dilemma.

NOW IS THE TIME

Think for a moment about those strange words of Jesus, "seek first His kingdom and His righteousness; and all these things shall be added to you."[25]

So many of us see the words and are conscience-stricken. But for the wrong reasons.

We say, "Oh, if I could only bring myself to pray a lot and read the Bible and go to church every day, then God would like me and I would be His, and He would send His blessing to me."

We are not even certain we understand what we mean when we say "blessing."

Jesus was much more concrete than that. He was saying, "The kingdom of God rules in the affairs of men. It has principles for living, and they will bring success." Indeed, they will bring forth the kinds of things the world needs so desperately—the food, the shelter, the clothing, the fuel, the happiness, the health, the peace.

"But you shouldn't spend all your time and concentration seeking those things," He said in effect. "Seek the kingdom, understand the way it works, and then, as day follows night and as spring follows winter, the evidences of earthly success will follow you."

If we press this through to its logical conclusion, possibilities for life will rise up that we long ago relegated to the musty, unused portions of our Bibles, thinking of them as those promises made for a future time referred to as "the millennium." We will see that many of those conditions—those blessings we feared might turn out to be lofty Bible language that would pass us by—can be experienced in large measure right now. For they exist in the kingdom now. And we are speaking of reaching into that kingdom and letting its principles govern us right now.

Only God will inaugurate the visible reign on earth of His Son and those who will rule with Him,[26] but His word for the last two thousand years has been to "prepare the way."[27] His purpose is that His people know Him and learn how His secret kingdom functions. For the most part, we have fallen far short. But the word persists, and we can readily expect the willing fulfillment of some of the millennium blessings, like those foreseen by the prophet Isaiah, if we will follow His instructions:

> They will not hurt or destroy in all My holy
>   mountain,
> For the earth will be full of the knowledge of the
>   Lord
> As the waters cover the sea.[28]

> . . . they will hammer their swords into
>   plowshares, and their spears into pruning
>   hooks.
> Nation will not lift up sword against nation,
> And never again will they learn war.[29]

There *can* be peace; there *can* be plenty; there *can* be freedom. They will come the minute human beings accept the principles of the invisible world and begin to live by them in the visible world.

Can mankind do that? We will see how.

3

Seeing and Entering

W<small>HY IS THERE</small> so much controversy about the divinity of Jesus Christ? If Jesus were only a historical figure with no importance in this modern world, why is He constantly in the news? Why is He the subject of books, films, speeches, debates, sermons, plays, documentaries, television specials, court cases, public hearings, and articles of every kind? If Jesus were only a good man, why is He still a figure of such heated debate?

During the past several months, the Dead Sea Scrolls have been in the news a great deal. Even though the scrolls were discovered by a group of Arab shepherds in a Jordanian cave in 1947, it was not until late 1991 that authenticated photographs of the ancient texts were circulated among scholars and researchers. That event precipitated another round of conjecture and debate.

Doubtless there were many reasons for keeping these important documents under wraps. Harvard University Professor John Strugnell, an Oxford-trained specialist in ancient Semitic texts and a renowned Bible scholar, told reporters he had hoped to produce an exact and reliable translation before releasing any preliminary fragments of the scrolls.

After all, there are dozens (actually hundreds) of scrolls and fragments to be reviewed. However, by 1991, portions of the scrolls were made public, and eventually a series of photographs prepared for the Huntington Library was distributed covertly to archaeologists and scholars.

Why did Strugnell and his colleagues keep such secrecy? One answer is that the editors felt that the degree to which the texts verified the Holy Scriptures and confirmed the reality of Jesus Christ as the Jewish Messiah could be controversial and inflammatory. Indeed, Strugnell's candid comment to a *New York Times* reporter that the scrolls proved modern Judaism to be a Christian heresy sent shock waves through the religious community. Strugnell was excoriated by the media, by the Jewish community, and by the liberal church, and he was summarily fired from his post.

But this is only the latest flareup. Throughout history the deity of Jesus Christ has been a matter of intense debate. True believers openly declare their faith in Christ as the Son of God and the only hope for a fallen world. While there are cults and religious groups claiming to be Christian which deny the divinity of Christ—and churches which deny the significance of the redemption He offered through His death on the cross—it is impossible to be a follower of Christ unless one believes His essential teaching; namely, that Jesus Christ is the only begotten Son of God who came to save the lost and to usher in the kingdom of heaven.

A RULER OF THE JEWS

In New Testament times, there was a man who perceived there was more to Jesus than met the eye. He may have heard John the Baptist refer to Him as one who "existed before me."[1] The strange prophet, who lived alone in the desert, had even called Him "the son of God."[2] Jesus of Nazareth was real and down-to-earth. Yet there was something other-worldly about Him. He spoke with authority, like the authority of Jehovah written about in the scrolls.[3] He must have been sent from heaven.[4]

One night this man, Nicodemus,[5] a ruler of the Jews, found Jesus alone and managed to talk with Him, which was hard to do because of the crowds. He may have been glad no one would see him.

He fumbled a bit for something to say and then blurted out: "Rabbi, we know You've come from God as a teacher, for no one can do the signs You do unless God is with him."

It was an awkward start, but it summarized what he was feeling. Nicodemus wanted to know God, and he instinctively realized that Jesus could give him teaching that would lead directly to God.

The Lord skipped small talk and went to the heart of Nicodemus' concern, preserving for all generations an understanding of the indispensable initial step toward life in an invisible world that governs all else. The kingdom of God is not really a place—at least not yet—but rather a state of being in which men, women, and children have yielded all sovereignty to the one and only true sovereign, Almighty God. It is the rule of God in the hearts, minds, and wills of people—the state in which the unlimited power and blessing of the unlimited Lord are forthcoming.

The natural eye cannot see this domain, and Jesus quickly explained that. He probably spoke softly, but distinctly. "Unless one is born again, he cannot *see* the kingdom of God."[6]

Nicodemus was startled. What kind of a remark was that? So, getting bolder, he answered back more directly than he had begun: "How can a man be born when he is old? He cannot enter a second time into his mother's womb and be born, can he?"[7]

The poor man had wanted to glimpse the invisible world and had been told how, but it went right by him, as it probably would have most of us. But Jesus really had told him how to peer into the throne room of God, from which the universe is directed. It should be noted, however, that He referred first to "seeing" the kingdom. Next, He took it a step further: "Unless one is born of water and the Spirit, he cannot *enter* into the kingdom of God."[8]

Jesus knew His man. Nicodemus wanted it all. He had suspected this very special rabbi, although visibly a flesh-and-blood man, was somehow living at that moment in contact with God. So Jesus laid it out for him.

God is spirit. Those who would know Him—who would worship Him—must do so in spirit.[9] Since the Fall left man spiritually dead,[10] we must be reborn. Flesh begets flesh and spirit begets spirit,[11] so this rebirth must be accomplished by God the Holy Spirit. After that, being children of God,[12] we are able to engage in communion and fellowship with Him, as Adam did in the original kingdom in the Garden of Eden.[13]

YOU MUST BE BORN AGAIN

Nicodemus' amazement soared, so Jesus pressed on with many deep things of the spirit—the things that men and women everywhere must make a part of themselves if they are to begin to deal successfully with our world in crisis:

> "Do not marvel that I said to you, 'You must be born again.' The wind blows where it wishes and you hear the sound of it, but do not know where it comes from and where it is going; so is every one who is born of the Spirit." Nicodemus answered and said to him, "How can these things be?" Jesus answered and said to him, "Are you the teacher of Israel, and do not

understand these things? Truly, truly, I say to you, we speak that which we know, and bear witness of that which we have seen; and you do not receive our witness. If I told you earthly things and you do not believe, how shall you believe if I tell you heavenly things? And no one has ascended into heaven, but He who descended from heaven, even the Son of Man. And as Moses lifted up the serpent in the wilderness, even so must the Son of Man be lifted up; that whoever believes may in Him have eternal life. For God so loved the world, that He gave His only begotten Son, that whosoever believes in Him should not perish, but have eternal life."[14]

The New Testament evidence is that Nicodemus did eventually believe,[15] accepting entry into the secret kingdom even while coping with the trials of the visible one.

Like millions and millions of others, this once-timid man received Jesus into his life, accepting Him for who He was—God incarnate, the Word become flesh, Savior of the world, Lord of all. Forgiven for his sins, he was reconciled to God Almighty and enabled to perceive the "heavenly things" Jesus had spoken of, to gain access to the kingdom of God.

He was, in short, born again—born from above, as some translators prefer, born of the Spirit. He could say with Paul the apostle who later wrote:

Now we have received, not the spirit of the world, but the Spirit who is from God, that we might *know the things freely given to us by God*, which things we also speak, not in words taught by human wisdom, but in those taught by the Spirit, combining spiritual thoughts with spiritual words.[16]

Both Nicodemus and Paul discovered that the kingdom of heaven is based on an invisible, spiritual reality, capable of visible, physical effects.

This is the reality that the world craves so badly.

A MATTER OF AUTHORITY

Unhappily, evangelical Christians have for too long reduced the born-again experience to the issue of being "saved." Salvation is an important issue, obviously, and must never be deemphasized. But rebirth must be seen as a beginning, not an arrival. It provides access to the invisible world, the kingdom of God, of which we are to learn and experience and then share with others. Jesus Himself said it clearly before His ascension:

All authority has been given to Me in heaven and on earth. Go therefore and *make disciples* of all the nations, baptizing them in the name of the Father and the Son and the Holy Spirit, *teaching them to observe all that I commanded you;* and lo, I am with you always, even to the end of the age.[17]

The commission was to make followers and learners—converts—and to *teach* them the principles of the kingdom. Entry into the body of believers was not enough. They were to learn how to live in this world, although their residence was in the kingdom. The invisible was to rule the visible. Christ has authority over both.

We have fallen short. Occasionally we have perceived God's hand at work in the world. But we have not striven to understand how the kingdom functions nor have we fully participated in its manifestation on earth.

We *must* hear this before it is too late: Jesus has opened to us the truths of the secret world of God! He has given us entrance into a world of indescribable power.

The atom gives us a clue as to what we're dealing with. We can't see an atom—solid matter looks like solid matter. But atomic theory convinces us the atoms are there, pressed together into material substance at some point in time. And with Einstein's $E=mc^2$, we have discovered that this means matter is energy—sheer power capable of blowing up the world. Yet all we see is the matter, even though the energy controls the matter.

Now this terribly great power is a tiny fraction of what we touch when we touch God's power. And it, too, is unseen—totally undiscerned—by one who has not been born again. The unspiritual man or woman regards such possibilities as foolishness.[18] And even many who have been born anew by the Spirit, though possessing the internal eyesight to see and believe in the invisible realm, refrain from appropriating its power for their daily lives. Having "seen" the kingdom, but not having fully "entered" in, they allow the conditions of the world to dominate them, contrary to the instructions of the Lord. The rebirth should give us the power to prevail over circumstances surrounding us.

Jesus gave us an additional piece of insight on this score. If we are to enter into the kingdom, taking full hold of that which is available, then we must "become like children," He said.[19] That is hard for our sophisticated generation, for it requires simple trust. A child is willing to leap ahead and seize any opportunity his father lays before him. So it must be with Christians and their heavenly Father, who gladly offers them the inexhaustible riches and power of His kingdom.[20] Indeed, He is pressing them upon us, if we will only respond confidently, joyfully, exuberantly—like little children.

YOU SHALL KNOW THE TRUTH

In light of the critical condition of the world, we need to examine even more philosophically why we are falling short in the matter of entering into the kingdom after rebirth. For if Christians miss the mark, how will the *world* learn?

Let's look at the logic of the problem. It leads us right into the issue of truth, and if there is anything the people of the world are looking for, it's truth.

First, we should recall the teachings of the Lord delivered through His encounter with a woman of Samaria. It is remarkable that this discourse, containing spiritual instruction with practical physical efforts, involved one from the despised Samaritans, a people of mixed Assyrian and Jewish blood resulting from the Assyrian invasion of the Israelites' land centuries earlier. The Lord, a Jew, obviously wanted to show that His message extended to all people. We pick up the conversation in the middle of profound insights into the Holy Spirit, eternal life, adultery, worship, and ministry to the world, with Jesus speaking:

> An hour is coming, and now is, when the true worshipers shall worship the Father in spirit and *truth*; for such people the Father seeks to be His worshipers. God is spirit; and those who worship Him must worship in spirit and truth.[21]

That alone sounds right and good, but how does one practically do it?

Fortunately Jesus also said the following in a discussion with His disciples: "I am the way, and the *truth*, and the life."[22]

Putting those two revelations together, we see that we are to bring ourselves into line with a standard that is true. Jesus is the *truth*, so, being born of His spirit, we are to conform to Him. We are to walk in His will. Only then can we worship God in spirit and truth. Only then can we move in truth. Note how essential He said this was: "Not every one who says to Me, 'Lord, Lord,' will enter the kingdom of heaven; but *he who does the will of My Father* who is in heaven."[23]

We need to be clear on this. Truth is the very centerpiece of the kingdom and its principles. We must be certain of the essential rightness of the principles, as opposed to other views. They lead to a new system of life that is better than any other system, the most practical possible, providing peace of mind, health, happiness, abundance, joy, and life everlasting. But we believe them because they are *true*.

Consider the following dialogue between Jesus and Pontius Pilate, the Roman governor at the time of the Lord's arrest and crucifixion:

> Then Pilate went back into the palace and called for Jesus to be brought to him. "Are you the King of the Jews?" he asked him. "'King,' as *you* use the word or as the *Jews* use it?" Jesus asked. "Am I a Jew?" Pilate retorted. "Your own people and their chief priests brought you here. Why? What have you done?" Then Jesus answered, "I am not an earthly king. If I were, my

followers would have fought when I was arrested by the Jewish leaders. But my Kingdom is not of the world." Pilate replied, "But you are a king then?" "Yes," Jesus said. "I was born for that purpose. *And I came to bring truth to the world. All who love the truth are my followers.*"[24]

THE KINGDOM OF HIS TRUTH

Yes, there is a kingdom. Jesus said it is founded on truth. He, the Truth, is king of it. Everyone who loves the Truth—Him—and wants to follow the Truth is a member of that kingdom.

He who sent Me is true; and the things which I heard from Him, these I speak to the world. . . . If you abide in My word, then you are truly disciples of Mine; and you shall know *the truth,* and *the truth shall make you free.*[25]

Not only is He true, the Lord said, but the things He teaches are true. And if we accept and practice these truths, we will be free, another condition the people of the world so desperately seek. I want to emphasize what it is that makes us free. It is not merely the acceptance of Jesus and His atonement, but *the doing of the truth*—putting into practice the principles of the kingdom.

As I said, we too often stop short. We must start with the crucifixion and the resurrection, but we must follow through with the practice of the principles, the laws of life. For God said thousands of years ago:

I will give you a new heart and put a new spirit within you; and I will remove the heart of stone from your flesh and give you a heart of flesh. And I will put My spirit within you *and cause you to walk in My statutes, and you will be careful to observe My ordinances.*[26]

He has gone to great lengths over many centuries to plant within our hearts His ways, His truth, His principles. What He has done surpasses the old covenant of law and regulation handed down to the people of Israel at Mount Sinai. Jesus has fulfilled the written law, placing it within His subjects, but they must live out the principles.

Applying this to our personal conduct, we see that speaking the truth is central. Its importance must never be minimized. Just as Jesus is the King of truth, the Holy Spirit (the Lord and giver of life) is called "the Spirit of truth."[27] Where He abides there is truth. At the same time, Satan (the adversary) is described as "the father of lies."[28]

Although true speech is only a part of ultimate truth, it is no mere coincidence that the apostle John tells us God's final heaven will exclude anyone who "maketh a lie."[29] "All liars," he declares, "shall have their part in the lake which burns with fire and brimstone."[30] Telling the truth is a serious matter! In the world we see conduct that flies flagrantly in the face of these warnings. The now defunct Soviet Union was an atheistic society which traded in and survived by "disinformation"—that is, the systematic spreading of lies through the free press of its adversaries. While communism and Soviet tactics have been discredited in the eyes of the world, many of their practices survive in the United States today, in some cases turning our institutions of higher learning into socialist disinformation factories.

BIG BROTHER RETURNS

The "big lie" has become so frequent, and perhaps even so necessary, in dictatorial societies that George Orwell, in his book *1984*, portrayed the ultimate dictatorship as one in which there was no truth, only a reordering of facts. History books were burned and the facts were rewritten to suit the lie. The people learned to use "truth" selectively, in a language of convenient lies called "newspeak."

Ironically, this is precisely what is happening in our colleges and universities. Campus gurus and thought police have attempted to strip from our society all references to our Christian heritage, to the faith of our fathers, to the artistic and literary achievements of Western Christian civilization. They have discarded the venerable political thought of great thinkers such as Hugo Grotius, John Locke, and Thomas Hobbes, who wrote the political treatises from which our forefathers learned.

Many of those pioneers, if not all of them, were profoundly Christian in orientation. But the revisionists have ignored the truth; they are rewriting history as fast as they can to favor the plight of the so-called oppressed classes in a struggle for minority rights, women's rights, and others such as homosexual and lesbian rights, which have never been tolerated in civilized societies throughout recorded history.

I can't help but recall Prime Minister Lloyd George's remark when asked if he would like the British government to recognize the Bolsheviks in Russia. He said they might as well legalize sodomy as recognize communists. Both were anathema to civilized peoples just seventy years ago. And now, at the end of the century, we are seeing sodomy go from a crime to a protected right! Homosexuals have proclaimed themselves a protected class, and they are staging marches outside of Christian churches protesting Christianity as being a religion of bigots and "homophobes."

Even worse, in the spring of 1992 we saw militant lesbians and gays desecrating churches and violating the freedom of religion, which is protected by the Constitution. I believe such people have proved why the Bible calls their practices "abominations." When homosexuals invade churches and cathedrals, as they have done in this country, screaming blasphemies at priests, pastors, and worshipers, defiling the very house of God, they have reached the depths of depravity.

A group of homosexuals from the organization called Queer Nation picketed the Founder's Inn Hotel and Conference Center at our CBN headquarters in Virginia Beach in early 1992. I publicly said that I felt that homosexuals are "hurting" and that they are "sinners." They said such statements were examples of "hate crimes." They and their allies are asking the government to track similar "hate crimes," and then establish a procedure like the one in Canada to punish free expression. Needless to say, this is beyond belief; even Big Brother in Orwell's epic might have been shocked by such behavior.

Even more shocking, however, is the news that parts of the government, the media, and the liberal establishment are very supportive of homosexuality. Recently CBS broadcast a prime-time documentary about homosexuals and lesbians adopting children. The only editorial comment was that this is a growing new trend.

There was not one word of criticism; not one indication of the sin such practices represent in the eyes of a righteous God. No one pointed out that every healthy society has always, from the beginning of time, condemned such practices. We can only wonder what judgment God will visit upon a nation that would tolerate, and even praise, such behavior.

NEWSPEAK ALL OVER AGAIN

Now that the Soviet Union has come unraveled, we can see the hypocrisy and the absurdity of communism for what it was. We see the sham and the fraud that was partially hidden by lies. Yet in the past few years we have begun to see Orwell's dire prophecies matched and even exceeded by the promoters of the socialist agenda in this country. Consider, for example, the ongoing controversy over "politically correct thinking."

The biggest upset for liberal faculty members and the new generation of would-be revolutionaries on America's college and university campuses in recent months has not been the collapse of communism, the attempted Soviet coup, or the Iraqi invasion of Kuwait, but the news that responsible Americans are offended by the foolishness of "political correctness" ("PC"). Like a new wave of Leninists or Nazi secret police marching against Western Christian values, the campus liberals have tried to rewrite the dictionary and redefine what is acceptable and unacceptable speech.

But the American people are upset for very good reason, since "PC thinking" sets out to reinterpret history and ideas through the vocabulary of radical feminism, virulent racism, belligerent homosexuality, and bizarre social ideas that are flagrantly anti-democratic.

Dinesh DeSouza's bestselling book, *Illiberal Education: The Politics of Race and Sex on Campus,* helped to bring this phenomenon to light. The book generated heated debate on and off campus and generally helped to discredit the types of mind control advocated by the latent Marxists and sociophobes who dominate higher education in the 1990s. DeSouza points out that the term "politically correct" was first used by Marxists in the early part of this century to classify ideas which aided their socialist and deconstructionist agenda. The term disappeared for a while but, predictably, reappeared on campuses in the 1960s, associated with feminism, racism, environmentalism, and other politicized issues. By and large, the leaders of the movement are activists, abetted by junior faculty members and compliant administrators, who have a sinister social agenda. "Like the Stalinists and Trotskyists of an earlier day," says DeSouza, "contemporary campus activists maintain that 'everything is political' and thus it seems quite proper to insist that classroom lectures, the use of language, and even styles of dress and demeanor reflect the P.C. stance of the new generation of professors and administrators—products of the counterculture of the 1960s—who are coming to power in American universities."

Newsweek's cover story on the thought police helped alert the general public to PC thinking. Major articles in the *New York Times, New York* magazine, and other publications also helped demonstrate the absurdity of PC logic. Suddenly we became aware of such neologism as "multiethnic," "multicultural," "developmentally challenged," and even the ludicrous description of short people as "vertically challenged."

DANGEROUS ILLUSIONS

The real irony is that a movement which marches under the name of "diversity" and "pluralism" is actually one of the most closed-minded, judgmental, condemning, and potentially dangerous -isms since the rise of Nazi Germany. Politically correct thinking denies the value of a canon of great literature because it reflects the biases of "dead white European males." History, too, is colored by imperialism, greed, and racism. The recent attacks on Christopher Columbus and the founding fathers of the

United States reveal the types of hostility and divisiveness that underlies such views.

In a July 1991 article in the *Reporter Dispatch*, Louis Ruckeyser spoke out against the radicals who claim that America's place in history is tarnished by a heritage of bigotry and greed. Their charges are absurd at best and anti-American at worst, he said, "Yet that is the message behind the current nonsense that holds that celebration of America's place in history is nothing more than a paean to racist, sexist, dead white European males."

"Spare me," says Rukeyser. "Those who pursue this sort of demagoguery are cheaply inflaming group bigotry. Worse, they are endangering this nation's ability to compete and flourish in the 21st century."

As a respected broadcaster, author, and Wall Street analyst, Rukeyser recognizes the liberals' appeal for "diversity" as a thinly disguised attempt to split America into radical factions and, thus, to destroy the unity and the spirit of cooperation upon which this nation was founded. "In fact," he says, "it is tribalism—one of the planet's oldest and most destructive tendencies. Human progress in general and the American experience in particular have sought assiduously to overcome it."

The fact that there are still social and racial problems in this nation, the writer argues, "is scarcely reason to abdicate to the apostles of division. On the contrary, it is reason to rededicate ourselves to making the American dream a reality for all our citizens."

Clearly Rukeyser is right and perhaps most perceptive in his observation that, "Exclusionist, paranoid ethnicity is alien to American instincts." From the very beginning, this was a country of widely different peoples assimilated as a nation by a unique experiment in cooperation. The radicals who espouse "diversity" and politically correct thinking are, once again, trying their hardest to split us apart. Their objective is insidious and dangerous; ultimately it is the work of the deceiver.

But Dinesh DeSouza points out another dangerous trend in the PC movement; namely, the growing backlash among those groups who resent and resist the labels being put on them by advocates of PC. In reaction to Black Studies, Women's Studies, and Gay and Lesbian Studies programs on some campuses, there is an outcry for White Studies, Men's Studies, and the like. PC thinking has, in fact, reawakened a warfare between the races, encouraged a degree of hostility between the sexes, and incited deeper resentment between all classes of people by virtue of its twisted judgments and perverse logic. It has awakened angers and resentments that are unprecedented in this culture. People who have never held racist or sexist emotions of any kind are suddenly enraged because they have been condemned and discredited for simply being born.

THE FIFTH COLUMN

The vocabulary of the activists condemns traditional or historical orthodoxy in favor of an untested and potentially dangerous new orthodoxy. I call these revisionists the fifth column, for like the saboteurs and collaborators of wartime, their very purpose is to destabilize and undermine American society from within and ultimately to destroy our Western heritage from the ground up. They will use any means, employ any weapons, and assault any sacred traditions that suit them in order to accomplish their goals.

If the problems on the university campus were not enough, an article in *The New Republic* by Kay Sunstein Hymowitz tells about the PC invasion of kindergarten. For example, a new handbook for teachers, entitled the *Anti-Bias Curriculum,* alerts teachers to the dangers of such classic stories as Hansel and Gretel, Cinderella, Babar, and others.

Among the dangers noted by the PC adviser is the negative stereotyping of the witch in Hansel and Gretel, identified as an old hag, when in fact witches are "actually good women who used herbal remedies to help people." Elsewhere, the director of a politically correct child studies center in South Hadley, Massachusetts, claims that Babar (including all the books in this famous series) is unacceptable for children since it "extols the virtues of a European middle-class life-style and disparages the animals and people who have remained in the jungle."

I have heard that there are councils and companies that do nothing but rate books for children on the basis of racism, sexism, ageism, handicapism, and other "anti-human values." Children are thus taught from infancy to distrust their culture, to repudiate traditional values, to disavow the role of father as principal provider and mother as homemaker and nurturer of children. In one series of books being promoted by women's studies programs, the little girl who is the main character of the stories finally achieves ultimate maturity and wisdom when she grows up to disavow motherhood and childbearing.

What troubles me most of all in this movement is that the freedom of childhood fantasy has been politicized and violated to such an extent through overt demagoguery and socialist ideologies. What will become of such children? What happiness can they look forward to? What hope is there for a nation whose children (at least those who manage to survive the legal assault on pregnancy and childbearing) are routinely subjected to this kind of relentless and hostile programming in the nursery?

Where will it end? Dinesh DeSouza observes wisely, "The current revolution of minority victims threatens to destroy the highest ideals of liberal education," and he adds that "liberal education is too important to entrust to these self-styled revolutionaries." He is absolutely right.

What an obvious tragedy exists when those who lead our society first repudiate the One who is the way, the truth, and the life, then turn their backs on the Spirit of truth, and finally set out to destroy the historical record of truth which underlies our entire society. However, in the United States, regard for truth still exists in some quarters, although it is clearly diminishing along with regard for absolute values. Perjury—the willful telling of a lie while under lawful oath—is a felony and stands as a secular affirmation of the kingdom's demand for truth. One wonders when a liberal group will bring a suit against perjury laws as an "establishment of religion" because they reflect the ninth commandment, "Thou shalt not bear false witness against thy neighbor."

HIS WAY IS TRUE

Since the kingdom of God is the kingdom of truth, how sad that in some instances we find people in the church who believe they can further God's kingdom by the use of falsehoods and building up with one hand but tearing down with the other. Exaggeration, embellishment, and even fabrications have become instruments of evangelism in some quarters. Christians must understand that the Lord does not need our embellishment to accomplish His purpose or to glorify His name. We do Him and ourselves a disservice when we depart from the truth.

Jesus and His Ways are true. As the One by whom and for whom all things were created,[31] He understands precisely how the world works. His teachings, which so many in the world have tried to relegate to the categories of goody-goody daydreaming or pietistic navel-gazing, are functional.

The world yearns for peace; He can provide it. The world wants love; He has the formula. The world wants riches, honor, and full life; He promises them all.

But there are requisites. One must be born again by accepting the free gift of salvation that He alone provides, learn from Him, and put His principles into practice.

What are the key laws or principles that govern the deepest desires and needs of mankind? They embody the truths that we will be examining and illustrating in detail in the following chapters, along with the virtues and subprinciples flowing through them.

We will see that the truths of Jesus have the characteristic of the "truths" of the American Declaration of Independence—they are "self-evident." We will begin to understand why a society that abandons these laws, which are self-evident, will collapse. And equally evident will be the reasons why a society that voluntarily adheres to such laws can be expected to prosper.

Do not forget: The One proclaiming the laws created and controls both the visible world and the invisible kingdom. He knows how they both work!

4

How God's Kingdom Works

To UNDERSTAND HOW the kingdom of heaven works and how it holds sway over the visible world, we must place two facts in the brightest light.

First, there is absolute abundance in the kingdom of God.

Second, it is possible to have total favor with the ruler of that abundance.

On the first point, Jesus, telling His disciples that they were being permitted to know the secrets of the kingdom,[1] set forth the truth of abundance with a parable about a sower.[2] The seed that fell on good ground, He said, yielded crops of thirtyfold, sixtyfold, and a hundred-fold. *That* is abundance—returns of 3,000, 6,000, and 10,000 percent. You see, there is no economic recession, no shortage, in the kingdom of God.

Throughout our forests, we see this truth touching the physical world. Consider the profusion of seed that comes from a maple tree. Look at the multiplicity of colors in a sunset; there are more hues than we can name. Plant life, marine life, bird life—there is no end, almost as though God had sent abundance into the universe as testimony to His own infinitude.

Because He is the only truly free being in the universe, His kingdom is a sphere of total possibility. Jesus emphasized this when He multiplied the loaves and fishes, taking a little boy's lunch and feeding more than five thousand hungry people.[3] God is never diminished by circumstances.

Neither is He limited by His own universe or the natural laws He Himself established. Some of the new environmentalists, who are actually New Age pantheists, attempt to convince us that God is merely *in* nature. But were that true, He would be limited. No, He is above the laws of nature and any restrictions that those laws might try to impose. He can create from nothing, or He can take existing matter and transform it. His is a total world—total health, total life, total energy, total strength, total provision.

In the matter of favor, Jesus, of course, was our perfect illustration of God's provision: "And Jesus kept increasing in wisdom and stature, and in *favor* with God and men."[4]

Within a few short years, God presented the supreme token of this grace at the time of the baptism of Jesus in the River Jordan: "And immediately, coming up from the water, He saw the heavens parting and the Spirit descending upon Him like a dove. Then a voice came from heaven, 'You are My beloved Son, in whom I am well pleased.'"[5]

This, God the Father was saying, was the One He had spoken of and promised for centuries. He was going to pour out His grace and blessing on His only begotten Son and on those who belong to Him.

First, we need to recognize that when the Bible speaks of God's "grace," it is speaking of His "favor." In the New Testament, the Greek word for grace is *charis*, perhaps best defined as "the unmerited favor of God."

BEFORE HIS THRONE

This favor, the apostle Paul said, allows us to stand before God Himself.[6] It is our sole means of access to the throne of the kingdom.[7] Think of it: If we have access to the Father, standing before Him in His favor, then we have the prospect of continuous blessing. Indeed, Paul wrote that the prospect was for *increasing* blessing:

> But God, being rich in mercy, because of His great love with which He loved us, even when we were dead in our transgressions, made us alive together with Christ (by grace you have been saved), and raised us up with Him, and seated us with Him in the heavenly places, in Christ Jesus, in order that *in the ages to come He might show the surpassing riches of His grace* in kindness toward us in Christ Jesus.[8]

Now when God blesses us and keeps us, and lets His face shine upon us, and is gracious to us,[9] then before men we appear in a light that far transcends any of our natural abilities. He can cause our plans to succeed. He can cause people to like us. He can cause us to be preferred and chosen above others of equal talent. He can protect our children. He can guard our property. He can cause His angels to aid us.

How well I remember the day in the late sixties when God showed forth this favor in my life in a practical, workaday manner. CBN was in urgent need of $2.3 million worth of modern equipment that would allow us to broadcast with the power and quality needed if we were to do what the Lord had called us to do. With absolutely no worldly credentials or the support that would normally be required to do business at this level, I began negotiations with one of the world's leading electronics manufacturers. There was no reason to expect a successful outcome.

But God had other plans. In the most remarkable, yet smooth and calm manner, I received total favor from this giant company and arranged for our equipment needs to be met for a period of years at the finest terms imaginable. Others in the industry were envious, for I had received every concession in price, down payment, and credit terms that it was possible to get.

You see, God had let His face shine upon us and was gracious to us. We had favor with Him in the invisible world, and since He ruled even the visible world that tried to ignore Him, He gave us favor there as well.

With those two truths of abundance and favor established, we are ready for the fact that God had entered into a partnership with redeemed man. He has given us the potential of cooperating with His Spirit in the whole work of the kingdom.

Prayer is the link between finite man and the infinite purposes of God. In its ultimate sense, prayer consists of determining God's will and then doing it on earth. It does *not* consist merely of asking for what *we* want. To pray in the truest sense means to put our lives into total conformity with what God desires. We make ourselves available to God.

We begin this process by dropping our own preconceived ideas and entering His presence by grace to wait upon Him. Our thought should be: "Lord, what do *You* want? What are *You* doing?" As George Mueller, the great British man of faith, said, "Have no mind of your own in the matter."

THE POWER OF SPEECH

The Lord's chastisement of the false prophets, recorded in the Book of Jeremiah, illustrates the importance of this. Warning the people against those prophets who were speaking visions of their own imaginations and not from the mouth of God, He asked: "But who has stood in the council of the LORD,/That he should see and hear His word?/ Who has given heed to His word and listened?[10] They were to be alone with the Lord, to see and to hear what He was doing. They were not to put their own ideas first.

So it should be with us when we pray. We should stand in the Spirit in the invisible kingdom; there we will see and hear, and our role in the partnership can become active.

If we turn again to the account of Jesus and the fig tree as recorded in Mark's Gospel, which we touched on in chapter 2, this becomes clear. We should recall that Jesus, discussing the power that withered the tree, said that the first thing required was "faith in God," absolute trust and confidence that He is God Almighty, unlimited and infinite. Implied was the fact that He speaks to His people, revealing what He is doing. Then Jesus said this:

> For assuredly, I say to you, whoever says to this mountain, "Be removed and be cast into the sea," and does not doubt in his heart, but believes that those things he says will come to pass, he will have whatever he says. Therefore I say to you, whatever things you ask when you pray, believe that you receive them, and you will have them.[11]

If we fully believe God and have discerned His will, Christ said that we may translate that will from the invisible world to the visible by the spoken word. In short, God uses the spoken word to translate spiritual energy—sheer power—into the material.

The most vivid illustration, of course, was the creation of the world. God spoke to the void and said, "Let there be light,"[12] and there was light. The same with the firmament and the waters and the dry land; the same with everything that was created.[13] All things were made by the Word.[14] And that which was spoken was energized by the Spirit, moving upon the face of the waters,[15] shaping matter, which is itself energy, into God's predetermined patterns.

In like manner, our partnership with God is fulfilled when we speak His word in the power of the Holy Spirit. As Jesus taught: "So I tell you to believe that you have received the things you ask for in prayer, and God will give them to you."[16] Thus He took us right back to where He began. Have faith in God, know who He is, know what He is doing, trust His favor upon us, participate with Him. What we say in His name should then come to pass.

THE MISSING LINK

For the vast majority of Christians throughout history, the "speaking" has been the missing link between what we believe and what we do. We have lost the understanding of how God Almighty works, how His Son works, and how we are to work once we enter into the unobstructed view of God that Jesus provides in the kingdom.

The thing that clouds our view is sin. But once the sin is forgiven, we are to enter bodily into the throne room of grace and commune with God by His Spirit, who communicates with our spirit. It's a bit like tuning in to a radio or television station. You get on the right frequency and you pick up a program. So it is with listening to the Lord. He is speaking constantly, but we are often on the wrong frequency.

Once He has spoken to us, we are to speak after Him. If we do, miracles occur. If we don't, usually nothing will happen. For, in the material world, God has chosen to enter into partnership with us, his co-laborers, whom He is grooming for the perfect, visible establishment of His kingdom on earth.

Right now, in this life, He would have us stop cajoling and begging. He would have us live in the kingdom, in harmony with Him, receiving His thoughts by the Spirit. As the apostle Paul said, "We have the mind of Christ."[17] So speak that mind, Jesus was saying in the fig tree episode. Speak His thoughts. Don't be afraid. Don't doubt. "For God has not given us a spirit of timidity, but of power and love and discipline."[18]

We must see that, by living in the kingdom now, we enter back into what man lost in the Garden of Eden. We return to the authority God gave us at the creation. Like Adam, we hear the Lord's voice revealing the secrets of the world. And, as He speaks, we speak after Him in the manner of Ezekiel in his vision in the valley of dry bones.

> Again He said to me, "Prophesy over the bones, and say to them. 'O dry bones, hear the word of the Lord.'"[19]

The prophet listened as the Lord said He intended to give the bones life, sinews, flesh, skin, and breath. Then it was Ezekiel's turn.

> So I *prophesied* as I was commanded; and as I *prophesied*, there was a noise, and behold, a rattling; and the bones came together, bone to its bone. And I looked, and behold, sinews were on them, and flesh grew, and skin covered them; but there was no breath in them. Then He said to me, "Prophesy to the breath, prophesy, son of man, and say to the breath, 'Thus says the Lord GOD, "Come from the four winds, O breath, and breathe on these slain, that they come to life."'" So I *prophesied* as He commanded me, and the breath came into them, and they came to life, and stood on their feet, an exceedingly great army.[20]

In this Old Testament episode, Ezekiel learned what I call the word of faith, which didn't receive full development until the New Testament was written. The lesson was this: Through our words, we translate the will of God in the invisible kingdom to the visible situation that confronts us. We speak to storms, and they cease. We speak to money, and it comes. We speak to crops, and they flourish.

Although I will discuss this miraculous phenomenon in detail later, the simple truth is that God's word, spoken into a situation, will perform His purpose: "So shall My word be which goes forth from My Mouth;/It shall not return to Me empty,/Without accomplishing what I desire,/And without succeeding in the matter for which I sent it."[21]

THE WAY IT WILL BE

Some day, when the kingdom is fully manifested, the speaking will not be necessary. The thought will become the deed, as it is in heaven today.

On my television program, "The 700 Club," I did an interview with Dr. Richard E. Eby, a well-known California obstetrician and gynecologist, that illustrates the point vividly. In 1972, Dr. Eby said he fell from a second-story balcony and split his skull. He told me that he died (whether for minutes or hours, he doesn't know) but miraculously returned to life and at the time of the interview was perfectly healthy and normal. During the experience, Dr. Eby related, his spirit left his body and apparently went to heaven, or paradise. As one would expect, he found it to be a most beautiful place. At one stage he entered a field of flowers and as he walked along, he was overwhelmed by their beauty. "Wouldn't it be wonderful if I had a bunch and could smell them?" he thought. But as he started to bend over, he looked at his hand, and it was already full of flowers.

At another point, he was thinking how good it would be to go to a distant valley, and suddenly he was there.

As a scientific man, he naturally analyzed these experiences carefully and concluded that in heaven the mere thought produces the action. As the psalmist declared: "Delight yourself also in the LORD,/ And He shall give you the desires of your heart. / Commit your way to the LORD,/ Trust also in Him,/ And He shall bring it to pass."[22]

In his brief visit to heaven, Dr. Eby was delighting himself in the Lord, doing His perfect will, and the yearnings of his heart were immediately fulfilled. He didn't have to speak them. On earth a translation is required, but not so in the ultimate kingdom. One day we will not need telephones, mass transit, or computers; the speed of thought exceeds the speed of light. But now we need the spoken word.

WHAT IS FAITH?

As we have emphasized several times, the covering statement for the entire matter of how the kingdom works is "Have faith in God." Faith governs all. But it is frequently misunderstood.

The Bible says bluntly:

Now faith is the substance of things hoped for, the evidence of things not seen. For by it the elders obtained a good testimony. By faith we understand that the worlds were framed by the word of God, so that the things which are seen were not made of things which are visible. . . . But without faith it is impossible to please Him, for he who comes to God must believe that He is, and that He is a rewarder of those who diligently seek Him.[23]

The Living Bible's paraphrase is helpful:

What is Faith? It is the confident assurance that something we want is going to happen. It is the certainty that what we hope for is waiting for us, even though we cannot see it up ahead.[24]

Said another way, faith is the title deed to things we can't see. When we buy property, we meet with the seller and papers are drawn up. We receive a deed, and it says we own a stated piece of property. The minute it is signed, we own the property. We don't have to go to it; we don't have to see it. It is ours. We have a title deed.

It is the same with faith. We have a title deed to what God has promised. Our role is to believe in our hearts that it has been accomplished, according to what God has given us the deed to, and then to speak it. We can't force it. We can't sit around a room with a group and work it up. We can receive it only from God. The Bible says: "So then faith cometh by hearing, and hearing by the word of God.[25]

We hear the Lord's Word; it builds in our hearts, and the light goes on. "It's mine!" Deep down inside, there will be no doubt. That is what the Lord meant in the fig tree episode when He referred to the one who speaks to the mountain and "does not doubt in his heart." The mountain will move if the Lord has spoken.

The Bible also cautions about double-mindedness:

. . . let him ask in faith without any doubting, for the one who doubts is like the surf of the sea driven and tossed by the wind. For let not that man expect that he will receive anything from the Lord, being a double-minded man, unstable in all his ways.[26]

There can be no equivocating, no going back and forth. So many of us hear something from the Lord, we believe it briefly, but the wind blows and the storm pounds and our faith in what God said vanishes like the mist. We need to counter by speaking the word God has given and then simply accepting it.

I must add a word, however, to drive home a subtle point. Our faith throughout all of this must be in the Lord—"have faith in God," Jesus said—and not in our ability, not in our stubborn strength. Our faith is not to be *in our faith:* "Trust in the LORD with all your heart,/ And lean not on your own understanding;/ In all your ways acknowledge Him,/ And He shall direct your paths."[27]

While structuring most of His dealings with man around the point of faith, the Lord made plain that His insistence on faith was not quantitative, but qualitative. He said that we would move mountains even if our faith were no larger than a mustard seed.[28] We don't need a mountain of faith to move a mountain of dirt or even a mountain of world problems.

The object and reality of the faith are the issues. We don't need stubbornness, but confidence.

. . . this is the confidence which we have before Him, that, if we ask anything according to His will, He hears us. And if we know that He hears us in whatever we ask, we know that we have the requests which we have asked from Him.[29]

THE IMPORTANCE OF RIGHT THINKING

We begin to see that in the kingdom:
• Spirit controls matter.
• Lesser authority yields to greater authority.
• The mind is the ultimate conduit of the spirit.
• Speech is the intermediate conduit between spirit and matter and between greater and lesser authority.

That which the writers of the many "success" books call "positive mental attitude," or PMA, is indeed important. Because our minds are the agents our spirits use in influencing the world around us, it is patently clear that negative attitudes can weaken our most valiant attempts. Conversely, positive thinking will more often than not lead to successful action.

Unfortunately, people such as Napoleon Hill, author of the book, *Think and Grow Rich,* attempt to trade on the truth of the kingdom principles without first obtaining their citizenship in the kingdom. Positive thinkers in the secular world, whatever their stripe, have gleaned only a few of the truths of the kingdom of God. Nevertheless, they try to gain the kingdom without submitting themselves to the King. There are inherent dangers with that approach.

Some of the metaphysical principles of the kingdom, taken by themselves, can produce fantastic temporal benefits. But without the lordship of Jesus Christ, these benefits are both transitory and harmful. In fact, many of the advocates of mind over matter ultimately end up involved in spiritism. Jesus warned, "For what will it profit a man if he gains the whole world, and loses his own soul? Or what will a man give in exchange for his soul?"[30]

Many sincere followers of Jesus destroy their effectiveness in this world because they do not understand the laws of spiritual authority and the way this authority is transmitted. They especially are not aware of the power of what they say.

Solomon wrote: "From the fruit of a man's mouth he enjoys good."[31] In other words, when you confess blessing, favor, victory, and success, those things will come to you.

But the majority of Christians ignore this truth. "How do you feel?" we ask someone.

"I feel terrible," he replies, not realizing he has commanded his body to be sick.

"Can you do it?" we ask.

"I can't do that," he replies, not knowing he has limited God and himself by his words.

"I can't get out of debt," someone says. He has just commanded his debt to continue.

We call such negative assertions, "realistic appraisals" of the situation. But they aren't realistic, for they ignore the power of God, the authority of the invisible world of the spirit, and the grant of power made by God to His children.

A much more realistic assertion was made by the apostle Paul when he boldly declared: "I can do all things through Him who strengthens me."[32]

SEEING THE POSSIBLE

Pettiness, overemphasis on minutiae, fear of failure, constant complaining, murmuring—all inhibit the realization of kingdom conditions. As a man thinks in his heart, so is he.[33]

Many athletes have realized this principle. Golfers, from Ben Hogan to Jack Nicklaus, have long made this technique a part of their game. As they approach each shot, in their mind's eye they see themselves swinging the club and the ball traveling in a perfect arc, landing in a particular spot. By visualizing the perfect shot, they set the pattern in the mind, and then they simply follow through with the body. Clearly, their success with this technique has been spectacular.

The same has been true with runners and jumpers. God has given us minds and bodies that work that way. Our bodies will obey our minds, for the most part. Added to that is the fact that our spirits can be in touch with God. Now if our spirits govern our minds and our minds govern our bodies, then God in the invisible world governs us in the visible world.

At the same time, the Lord has called for us to be honest and truthful in the innermost being,[34] so we are not to delude ourselves and to say something is true when it is not. We are not to engage in superstition or silliness. We merely are to have confidence that with Him all things are possible.

Perhaps the most dramatic example of proper thinking, speaking, and doing came to my attention through "The 700 Club." It involved Leslie, May, and Joe Lemke and an extraordinary true-life story of love.

The story began in 1952 when May, a nurse-governess with a reputation for unusual ability with children, was asked to take care of a six-month-old baby named Leslie who was retarded, who had cerebral palsy, and whose eyes had been removed because they were diseased. Leslie was not expected to live long.

The Lord gave May a great love for Leslie, and she began to treat him like a normal baby. She taught him to feed from a nursing bottle by making loud sucking noises against his cheek. Soon she gave up everything else to take care of the child. "I have a job to do for Jesus now," she said, "and I'm going to do it."

By the time he was ten, Leslie could move only a hand and friends advised May that she was wasting her time. But she refused to concede. "I'm doing something for an innocent boy who will be something some day," she said. "I believe in God, and He will do it."

She carried the boy around and spoke her love into his ear, holding him and squeezing him, continuing to treat him like a normal child. Eventually he learned to stand by holding onto a fence and then to walk by following it.

Throughout it all, May prayed constantly for Leslie. Before long, she added a thought to her petitions, repeating it to the Lord several times a day: "Dear Lord, the Bible says you gave each of us a talent. Please help me find the talent in this poor boy who lies there most of the day and does nothing."

May noticed that the boy seemed to respond to musical sounds like the plucking of a string or a cord. So she and her husband, Joe, bought a piano, and she played him all kinds of music, using the radio and records. Leslie listened for hours, seemingly in deep concentration.

After four years of praying for the boy's "talent" to be revealed, May and Joe were awakened at 3:00 A.M. one night by the sound of piano music. They found Leslie sitting at the piano playing beautifully, like a trained musician. He was sixteen years old.

Over the next ten years, the boy learned dozens of songs—classical, popular, jazz—and has even learned to sing with the playing. His talent was fully manifested through May's constant love and confession that nothing is impossible with God. She discerned God's purpose and spoke it into being, thoroughly rejecting negativism.

NECESSARY INGREDIENTS

Perhaps history's biggest roadblock to the effective demonstration of the invisible kingdom is found in negativism. For in the final analysis, it reveals the absence of *unity*, about which I will have more to say in conjunction with the other principles. But at this point, we need to see that the kingdom of God works through the phenomenon of harmony.

To begin with, entrance into the kingdom, totally dependent upon grace and not upon any kind of status or merit, immediately establishes a basic equality among people. No one can say, "I've earned a better place than you." Growing from that, logically, is a new relationship between individuals. It is one based on the will of the Father, surpassing existing national, racial, familial, or church relationships. The Lord Jesus was precise on this: "My true brother and sister and mother are those who do what my Father in heaven wants."[35]

That statement transcended the Lord's own family relationships, and it transcends ours. The kingdom thus is a family. Jesus is our elder brother; His Father is our Father. That cuts across all lines. My mother can be a black woman who does the will of the Father. My brother can be a Chinese who does likewise, or a Jew, or an Arab.

How we need to see this! All strife and turmoil in the world can be eliminated simply by its fulfillment. The Middle East can be at peace. Latin America can be at peace. The aged and the young can be at peace.

This wholly unique concept of love and family relationships can produce that which has escaped man's grasp from the beginning. But peace will not be the only fruit of such transferal of kingdom life to this world. Paul the apostle wrote of the "fruit of the Spirit" that would grow in a climate of unity—"love, joy, peace, patience, kindness, goodness, faithfulness, gentleness, self-control."[36] Against such characteristics there is no law, Paul added. None is needed.

The Scripture's classic illustration of the transfer of kingdom power to the visible world when there is unity comes in a well-known but underutilized portion of Matthew's Gospel.

Also, I tell you that if two of you on earth agree about something and pray for it, it will be done for you by my Father in heaven. This is true because if two or three people come together in my name, I am there with them.[37]

The full implication of the point is that when there is no unity of purpose, no crossover of barriers, then the power is not activated.

PROSPECTS FOR IMPROVEMENT

I am confident that we will see the kingdom of God working more in the visible world as the Lord continues to bring people to Himself. Should the world experience the great revival of faith in Jesus Christ that I am expecting, then it would be reasonable to see an increase in the exercise of these truths of the kingdom. This, I am sure, will enable the world to transcend many of the limitations we are experiencing now.

For example, it is important for us to continue to develop new sources of energy. The panic of the 1970s' "energy crisis," as it turns out, was largely false. Industry analysts have told us that the endless string of crises during the time of Jimmy Carter's administration were actually fabricated in order to justify a variety of expensive government programs and to justify increased taxes and reduced supplies. In reality, there never was an oil and gas shortage.

But even if research should prove that we can't keep burning up our energy resources forever, it is just as true that we are surrounded by oceans, and sea water contains hydrogen. Someday God may give to one or more of His people a concept for running cars on hydrogen produced from this untapped source. Perhaps he will allow some privileged man or woman a peek into the invisible world to see His purpose. Then a faithful one will speak and act according to the revelation, and the concept will take life.

I believe we can expect this in the area of building materials, perhaps to replace steel and other items in short supply. I am sure there will be foodstuffs we haven't dreamed of, perhaps new living space to accommodate vast populations. The limits are not found in what we see, feel, and taste. They are in our hearts and our willingness to stand in that place where we have an unclouded view of what the Lord is doing.

Thoughts like these invariably cause concern about whether someone who is not prospering or indeed is suffering in slums and poverty is violating the truths of the kingdom. Such questions must not be dismissed hastily. For there is suffering in the world and there are, of course, many Christians who are living short of the ideals we are discussing in this book.

So what does this mean? Are the principles in error? No, on the contrary. I am convinced that if a person is *continuously* in sickness, poverty, or other physical and mental straits, then he is missing the truths of the kingdom. He has either failed to grasp the points we have been making in this chapter about the operation of the kingdom or is not living according to the major principles we will be exploring. He has missed the prosperity I believe the Scripture promises.

SUFFERING AND POVERTY

Obviously there will be times of suffering for God's people, times that are given us by the Lord to bring us closer to Him. The apostle Peter says, "he who has suffered in the flesh has ceased from sin, that he no longer should live the rest of his time in the flesh for the lusts of men, but for the will of God."[38] So suffering, trial, and tribulation have a very real and worthwhile role in bringing us near to Jesus. But John, in his third letter to the believers, said, "I pray that you may prosper in all things and be in health, just as your soul prospers."[39]

The normal condition for God's people is spoken about in the book of the law, in Deuteronomy, where Moses tells the people of the blessings God has ordained for them so long as they follow His commandments. He said:

> And the LORD will grant you plenty of goods, in the fruit of your body, in the increase of your livestock, and in the produce of your ground, in the land of which the LORD swore to your fathers to give you. The LORD will open to you His good treasure, the heavens, to give the rain to your land in its season, and to bless all the work of your hand. You shall lend to many nations, but you shall not borrow. And the LORD will make you the head and not the tail; you shall be above only, and not be beneath, if you heed the commandments of the LORD your God, which I command you today, and are careful to observe them. So you shall not turn aside from any of the words which I command you this day, to the right or to the left, to go after other gods to serve them.[40]

Of course, we must not forget that God also gave the children of Israel a stern warning. He said that the commandments He gave through Moses were inviolable. Moses told them: "But it shall come to pass, if you do not obey the voice of the LORD your God, to observe carefully all His commandments and His statutes which I command you today, that all these curses will come upon you and overtake you."[41] The litany of curses was awful, but much of the Old Testament turns out to be a record of the ways in which the people, in fact, turned their backs upon God and how

God brought destruction upon Israel, drove them out of the land, and scattered the people all over the globe.

The concept of God's people being bankrupt and always needy and begging from the world for subsistence is not a scriptural concept. There are times when God's people have to be fed by manna and go through extraordinary trials, but we have probably interlarded a medieval monasticism with Judeo-Christian thought that is not necessarily biblical.

It is more like what Paul was warning about in Colossians: "It has a show of will worshiping and neglecting the flesh," but that really isn't what God is interested in: He's interested in a pure heart.

BY DEDICATED EFFORT

On the other hand, the Name-It-and-Claim-It school that says, "I want a new Cadillac, and I think good thoughts, and I speak to get a Cadillac, and I pray . . . ," is not what we're talking about. The principles of God, if put to work will result in prosperity. People will give money, they will save money, they will work hard, they will be sober, they will bring up families in the knowledge and admonition of the Lord, they will work heartily as unto the Lord, they will gain new skills and abilities, and if they invest their money and it builds up with compound interest, after a while they will have more. It is just that simple.

This isn't instant riches, nor is it some kind of flashy conspicuous consumption. It's just that the normal consequence of godly, frugal living and generosity is to have more. The religious hucksters of this world, like those we see in the news, are teaching some kind of miracle rabbit's foot where people send them $100 and all of a sudden begin receiving bucketloads of money. It just does not work that way.

But Jesus did say, "Give, and it will be given to you: good measure, pressed down, shaken together, and running over will be put into your bosom. For with the same measure that you use, it will be measured back to you."[42] If you give love, you will get love; if you give good service, you will get good service. If you give money to people and to the Lord, money has a way of coming back to you. That's just one of the fundamental laws of the kingdom, and we will discuss each of its facets in greater detail in subsequent chapters.

It is important, however, that we not try to equate scriptural prosperity with riches. We are speaking of the Lord's blessing, not great material wealth. Some people are not capable of handling money or other wealth. Some would be destroyed by pride. So God prospers according to His wisdom, according to the true need of those involved.

Nonetheless, I believe Christians can escape any ghetto to which they have been confined, real or imagined. God will make a way. He will provide methods with which to reverse conditions and attitudes. Shortage will turn to abundance, hostility to favor.

When I look at the problems in our inner cities and in the pernicious pockets of poverty in this country, I realize that those places are ready for the hand of God to bring change and hope and renewal. Look at the problems that surfaced in South Central Los Angeles. If we could be free from the mocking scorn of the liberals and the humanists to teach God's principles to everyone, entire communities could be changed.

By the proclamation of new life in Christ, by teaching people the principles of God and how to follow them, and by teaching the principles of marriage and the family, the explosive situation in these pockets of poverty would be eliminated.

FEEDING ON THE POOR

The problem is that the liberals in government, the media, and the education establishment do everything they can to discredit the efforts of those who know God's solutions to social problems. Often they hinder rather than help. The people in the ghettos, in the slums, along with the disenfranchised and the unhappy people in our cities make up their power base. They have built their power on poor people, and if anyone were to come in and clean up the mess and help restore the values that lead to prosperity, contentment, and peace, the liberal bureaucrats would have lost their constituency. They would be out of a job.

In all fairness, I suppose some of them actually feel that their concepts are right. They can't see that their concepts are abysmal failures. So they demand more money to spend on more of the things that do not work.

Over the years I have tried to set a standard of at least the Old Testament concept of tithing, which to me is a triple tithe, and the Lord has honored it. And I think He will honor anybody who abides by these precepts. But the Bible also says the borrower is the servant of the lender. Yet millions of Christians are slaves to debt; facing 18 to 22 percent interest rates. "Easy credit" is literally stifling their lives.

God spoke through the prophet Hosea: "My people perish for lack of knowledge." If they were to follow the principles of the kingdom they would understand the necessity of paying off debt and then letting their savings work for them.

Debt is not only a form of slavery, it leads to poverty, as does drunkenness, dissipation, divorce, and lack of education. Some people have tragedy thrust upon them, but it is certain that a drunkard, a drug addict, a person who refuses to save or exercise self-control, or a person who refuses to study and learn is going to be poor.

That does not mean that everybody who is poor is cursed by God. It doesn't mean that being poor or having financial difficulties is a sin. But sloth, which is cursed by God, and ignorance will always lead to poverty. Virtually anyone who wants to break the cycle of debt and poverty can do so with the power and blessing of God.

As for tragedy and seemingly inevitable mishap, the Bible says:

> The steps of a good man are ordered by the LORD: and he delighteth in his way. Though he fall, *he shall not be utterly cast down:* for the LORD upholdeth him with his hand.[43]

Furthermore, it says that when the wicked will try to harm the righteous, "the LORD will not leave him in his hand."[44] There may be difficult days and even stumbling, but God's arm will be there to deliver those who faithfully obey His commandments.

5

Progressive Happiness

As WE HAVE seen, the kingdom of heaven exists now, here. Although it is spiritual and invisible, it governs the material and visible. It is inhabited by people who have been born again spiritually. It operates in a specified manner.

Now we see that it also has a constitution, a system of fundamental principles and virtues to determine the quality and conduct of life. That constitution is contained in what has come to be known as the Sermon on the Mount, presented by Jesus quite early in His public ministry, probably within the first year.

This constitution of the kingdom has no amendments; it was set down perfectly and with divine insight. It clearly sums up a new way of life. It demands an inner revolution of attitude and outlook. It turns ordinary ideas upside down.

In early 1991, President George Bush said that the unity of purpose demonstrated by the nations allied against Iraq in the Persian Gulf crisis set the stage for a *new world order*. The fact is, politicians and intellectuals have been formulating a secular new world order for decades. In my book on this topic I reviewed the origins of the term in great depth.

However, Jesus Christ announced His program for a new world order more than nineteen hundred years ago, and His constitution and bylaws are eternal in consequence and application. This constitution has a preamble. We label its eight points as the Beatitudes, which is fitting since they truly do guarantee "blessedness" or "happiness." Happy are those who live by them, but more importantly, those who live by them are blessed by God.

The Beatitudes also show us a lot about the nature of God, the one ruling the kingdom.

Complemented by principles and virtues set forth throughout Scripture, they provide the underpinning and framework for our lives, even during a time of transition from the old, discredited order into the emerging future.

As we explore these well-known, yet still-alien words, we should peer between and behind them to perceive the Lord Himself. For the Beatitudes demonstrate the nature of God in a sweeping foundational way.

We should start by remembering that God's name, Yahweh, is no mere label but is significant of the real personality of the One bearing it. It stems from the Hebrew word for "to be," and some authorities believe it may be the so-called *hiph'il* tense, which would mean "He who causes everything to be."

At any rate, He revealed Himself to the covenant people as "I AM."[1] It was almost like a blank check. God said, "I AM _____," and His people were to fill in the blank according to their need. If they needed peace, He was Jehovah-shalom ("I am your peace").[2] If they needed victory, He was Jehovah-nissi ("I am your banner, your victory").[3] If they needed help of any kind, as Abraham so desperately did when he was being tested regarding his son, Isaac, then He was Jehovah-jireh ("I am your provider").[4]

The point we should remember, which is the one the Beatitudes demonstrate so simply, is that God revealed Himself, His nature, His power, and His will at the point of the need. The people had to recognize and acknowledge their need.

This is an overriding lesson of the Beatitudes, which is essential to life in the kingdom. The one who feels he has need of nothing *will receive nothing*. He will never experience the full name and nature of God. He will never know His peace and comfort; he will never know His victory; he will never know His provision of every need of life. Indeed, he will never know His salvation and experience the name God gave to His Son—Jesus, which means "I Am Salvation."

No, the self-sufficient, the self-righteous will not experience the kingdom of heaven. The void within them will not be filled if they do not cry out, "God Almighty, come and meet the deepest need in my life."

Let's look at the Beatitudes themselves,[5] taking note of their progressive nature in the working of an individual's life.

SPIRITUAL BEGGARS

Blessed are the poor in spirit, for theirs is the kingdom of heaven.

As with each of the points, the Lord began with a word that is preserved for us in the New Testament as *makarios*, which we render usually as "blessed" or "happy." Therefore, each of the points contains a guideline to happiness, which our world desperately craves.

"Happy are the poor in spirit." What a contradiction this seems! But upon closer examination it becomes clear. First, we must understand that the Lord meant more than merely "poor." His words conveyed the meaning "beggarly." Happy are the beggars in spirit, the spiritual beggars, those who know they are needy and are not afraid to say so, as we noted above.

The Lord's teaching at another time made the point most dramatically. Contrasting a shame-stricken publican (or tax-gatherer) with a proud Pharisee, He revealed a man who was poor in spirit.

> And the publican, standing afar off, would not lift up so much as his eyes up to heaven, but smote upon his breast, saying, God be merciful to me a sinner. I tell you, this man went down to his house justified rather than the other: for every one that exalteth himself shall be abased; and he that humbleth himself shall be exalted.[6]

He was exalted right into the kingdom, into perfect happiness. He had been empty, but he was filled, simply because he was ready to acknowledge that he needed God and was willing to beg for help. The kingdom was his, right then—"theirs *is* the kingdom." He had taken the first step in the progression demonstrated in the Beatitudes.

THE INTERCESSORS

Blessed are those who mourn, for they shall be comforted.

This contradiction seems more extreme than the first. Happy are those who mourn. How can it be?

We find help from the writings of Paul, in which he told of a "godly sorrow" that works repentance.[7] This is what Jesus was pointing to. For "repentance" means "afterthought" or "reconsideration." A man is to be repentant, to have an afterthought, to reconsider. He is to be sorry for his sins; he is never to be self-satisfied. As the psalmist wrote:

> The sacrifices of God are a broken spirit;
> A broken and contrite heart, O God, Thou wilt
>   not despise.[8]

So the Lord's message in this second Beatitude was, in essence, "If you want the comfort of God surrounding you, you must come to a place where you mourn for your sins." But He pressed it beyond that; He wanted us to mourn for the sins of people around us, too. The world does not want to mourn; it wants to laugh all the time. But rather than thumbing our noses at the world, we are to mourn, to hurt, to cry out for the lost.

We have the biblical account of Lot in Sodom and Gomorrah, where greed, drunkenness, homosexuality, and corruption were rampant. Lot, a "righteous man," was not merely angered by the filthy deeds of the wicked; he was "vexed" and "tormented" in his soul.[9] He mourned over their deeds. And God comforted him by sending angels to preserve him when those cities were destroyed.[10]

Do you see the progression? The kingdom becomes ours; we are in it. Immediately, the magnitude of our sins fall upon us, even though the Lord has forgiven us. In quick succession, we then see the sin of others—our relatives and friends who are not saved, indeed, the whole world. We are burdened with concern for others. We mourn. We become intercessors.

A philosophy has swept the earth that says, in effect, I'm OK; you're OK." Without Jesus' salvation there is no room in His kingdom for such thinking. Complacency is an abomination. We have only to recall the lesson He gave when speaking of His second coming. It will be just like the days of Noah, He said:

> For as in those days which were before the flood they were eating and drinking, they were marrying and giving in marriage, until the day that Noah entered the ark, and they did not understand until the flood came and took them all away; so shall the coming of the Son of Man be.[11]

He deplored the people's complacency over the condition of the world. In the kingdom, this must give way to concern and mourning. Then we can expect the fulfillment of Jeremiah's prophecy: "For I will turn their mourning into joy, / And will comfort them, and give them joy for their sorrow."[12]

A MATTER OF CONTROL

Blessed are the gentle, for they shall inherit the earth.

This next step in the progression is one of the most misunderstood verses in the Bible. It has convinced many that Jesus wanted His people to be dull, obsequious, spineless, and stupid. This, of course, runs contrary to everything we find about the men and women of God in the pages of Scripture. They were strong, vocal, and often brilliant.

Our problem has been with the word *meek* in the King James Version. It *does* mean "humble" and "gentle," even "docile." But the definition cannot stop there. Biblical meekness does not call for the abject surrender of one's character or personal integrity. It calls for a total yielding of the reins of life from one's own hands to God's hands. But it doesn't stop there either. The meek exercise discipline, which results in their being kept continuously under God's control.

Thus, a meek man is a disciplined man who is under the control of God. He is like Moses, a strong, bold leader who at the same time was described as the meekest man on earth.[13] Having seen his sin and that of others, the meek person takes the next step and places himself under God's control and discipline. He serves God. But, remember, God will not seize control. He will govern a life only if it is constantly yielded to Him, and that requires constant discipline. God is not interested in building robots.

Happy is the man who is under control—of God and of himself. Earlier I mentioned Paul's reminder to his beloved Timothy that they had received a spirit of "power and love and *discipline* [or self-control]," not of "timidity."[14] This is what the Lord was talking about. One with this virtue will inherit the earth.

So often Christians have been misled into thinking that once they are born again, nothing is required. This, as we will see, is damaging. The Lord and all those who wrote of Him made clear that rebirth was only the beginning, to be followed by discipline, work, and suffering. Obviously the drunk, the drug addict, the lustful, the slothful do not have the discipline to rule the earth and to correct its evils. No, it is for the meek, the disciplined—those who are controlled by God, who follow His Son, who struggle to inherit the earth and govern it.

Remember these powerful words: "from the days of John the Baptist until now the kingdom of heaven suffers violence, and violent men take it by force."[15] Zealous men force their way in. That's what it means. Though weaklings and wimps will fall by the wayside, God's meek men and women will inherit the earth; the undisciplined and the profligate will lose it.

HUNGER AND FULLNESS

> Blessed are those who hunger and thirst for righteousness, for they shall be satisfied [filled].

God is righteousness. To be righteous is to be Godlike. Jesus said we should hunger and thirst after righteousness. It is a free gift,[16] but we must seek it. We should desire in every fiber to be Christlike in nature. For such can be ours. According to the Bible, God planted the Spirit of His Son within us when we received Him, not being satisfied that we merely be adopted children, but that we also have Christ's very nature *within* us.[17]

Setting our life's course in pursuit of Him, we must yearn for this nature, this righteousness and holiness, to flood us. Having had the righteousness of Jesus *imputed* to us, we now should desire to have that righteousness *imparted* to us, actually living it out. If we remain unrighteous, the Bible says, we will miss the kingdom.

> Or do you not know that the unrighteous shall not inherit the kingdom of God? Do not be deceived; neither fornicators, nor idolaters, nor adulterers, nor effeminate, nor homosexuals, nor thieves, nor the covetous, nor drunkards, nor revilers, nor swindlers, shall inherit the kingdom of God.[18]

"I want to know more of God"—that should be our cry. "I want His Spirit to possess more of me. I want to be more effective. I want to see His kingdom come on earth."

With that cry of hunger and thirst for God, for more of His power, we in fact are crying out for an anointing of the Holy Spirit for service, which the Bible calls baptism in the Holy Spirit. This actually fulfills the next step in the progression of development revealed in the Beatitudes, providing an empowerment for serving God.

Jesus described it this way: "You shall receive power when the Holy Spirit has come upon you; and you shall be My witnesses both in Jerusalem, and in all Judea and Samaria, and even to the remotest part of the earth."[19] You will indeed be effective—being filled with the miraculous power of God Himself—simply because you hungered and thirsted for Him.

Yes, Jesus said, you will be filled and satisfied. Interestingly, the Greek word that we translated "filled" is *chortazo,*[20] which carries the implication of "gorged." We won't merely have a little, the Lord said; we will be gorged with righteousness, power, and everything good in the kingdom. This obviously is the perfect fulfillment of "seek, and you shall find."[21]

THE FLOW OF MERCY

Blessed are the merciful, for they shall receive mercy.

Most of us grasp this one, but we may fall short in seeing its magnitude.

The root Greek word for mercy is *eleos*, containing the sense of compassion and tenderness, of kindness and beneficence. It flows from the greater to the lesser: God is merciful to man; a wealthy man is merciful to a poorer man.

Thus we see a further progression in the Beatitudes. We begin to think toward men as God thinks toward us, extending our work out into the world. Having received mercy from One greater than we are, we are to give mercy to those we are in a position to favor.

Although our motivation should be purer than this, the fact is that as we show compassion to someone below us, there is always someone upstream to do the same for us—either men or God Himself. Behind this is a broader law that we will examine at greater length.

ULTIMATE HAPPINESS

Blessed are the pure in heart, for they shall see God.

From the Middle Ages came the idea that "the highest good," the *summum bonum*, was the "beatific vision." The ultimate happiness was to see God. There could be nothing greater. It was its own reward—an end, not a means.

In this Beatitude, Jesus showed the way for the fulfillment of that truth, elevating to its climax the progression of experience we have observed in these teachings.

If the highest good, the supreme happiness, is to see God—and it is—then purity in heart is required. Again, we grasp this simple statement rather quickly, but frequently its greatness passes over our heads.

In the Bible the word "pure" often means clean and untainted, but it is also used to describe gold that is without alloy or unadulterated. So the Lord was saying more than "blessed are those who have clean hearts." He was additionally saying "blessed are those whose hearts are single and undivided, whose devotion is without mixture."

As for the word *heart*, it means the center of our being, the core of our spirituality and deepest motivations. It is the real person.

It is not uncommon for people to want God, at least part of the time or with part of themselves, while at the same time wanting money and fame and all the world has to give. That won't do if you want to see God and receive the ultimate happiness, Jesus said.

Again, we need to see the insistence on unity and wholeness that filled the Lord's ministry. If your eye is unclear or dark, then your whole body will be full of darkness, He said, adding: "No one can serve two masters; for either he will hate the one and love the other, or he will hold to one and despise the other. You cannot serve God and mammon."[22]

We must focus on heaven or on earth. If it is the former, we will find the highest good.

CHILDREN OF THE KING

Blessed are the peacemakers, for they shall be called sons of God.

Most of us would indeed be happy were we the children of a reigning monarch with power to act in his name and eventually to rule. Well, that can be the case, and the monarch is known as the "KING OF KINGS"[23] whose realm is all of creation.

Now a child of God is an heir of God,[24] the recipient of authority, possession, wealth, and even the kingdom itself. In short, he is the inheritor of everything that exists.

But, Jesus said, to progress to that status you must be a "peacemaker." And that is one who stops conflict and war.

The Lord Himself was the unique peacemaker, bringing peace between man and God.[25] In His name we are to do the same. We are to be going throughout the earth saying to all men, "Your sins are pardoned. You can be reconciled to God." As Paul taught:

All this is from God. Through Christ, God made peace between us and himself, and God gave us the work of telling everyone about the peace we can have with him. God was in Christ, making peace between the world and himself. In Christ, God did not hold the world guilty of its sins. And he gave us this message of peace. So we have been sent to speak for Christ. It is as if God is calling to you through us. We speak for Christ when we beg you to be at peace with God.[26]

Indeed, we as peacemakers should be *begging* people to accept that which God has already done, since reconciliation is a two way street requiring a response from both parties. For the world still echoes with the song of the heavenly host on a quiet night two thousand years ago: "peace, good will toward men."[27] Each Christmas Eve, even the hardest hearts quiver at the prospect. Man craves God and peace from his deepest recesses.

However, the sons of God, the peacemakers, do not stop at the point of peace with God. They work for peace between men. They themselves are not warriors, and they counsel others to stop fighting among themselves. Their goal is peace among individuals and among nations as they constantly strive to bring conflicting groups together and seek harmony and love, not at the expense of godly principle, but through godly relationships.

These will be blessed, for they do the will and the work of the Father, as sons and daughters. They will mature as heirs, and they will inherit their Father's estate, the kingdom.

PERSECUTION WILL COME

Blessed are those who have been persecuted for the sake of righteousness, for theirs is the kingdom of heaven.

Blessed are you when men cast insults at you, and persecute you, and say all kinds of evil against you falsely, on account of Me.[28]

A new world order is coming. It will not be the synthetic secular order promised by the United Nations or the Council on Foreign Relations. No, it is called the eternal kingdom of heaven, to be brought about by God Almighty. Only certain people will live in it. And it is the Lord's intention that those people practice living in it right now, doing His will and experiencing the blessings at this time.

As they do so, however—bringing every thought captive and exercising the authority of the kingdom—they will become visible for who they are, and opposition will mount. Abuse will come. It came to Jesus; it came to the early saints.

But, this Beatitude says, they will be happy as they continue in their remarkable realm. Indeed, wrote the apostle Peter, they will be experiencing genuine maturity: "If you are reviled for the name of Christ, you are blessed, because *the Spirit of glory and of God rests upon you.*"[29] The blessing can hardly be greater than that in this life.

Many people innocently ask, "But why would anyone want to persecute people if they're loving and kind?"

The answer lies deep in the innermost parts of unregenerate man. He is offended by the goodness of others, by their brightness, their happiness, their prosperity. He prefers a dark, worried countenance over a clear, carefree one. He simply loves darkness more than light, which is a specific disclosure of Scripture.[30]

The Bible says those who are following Christ bear a fragrance that is distinguishable both to the believer and the unbeliever. To one, it is the sweet aroma of life; to the other, the stench of death.[31] Such a person produces either appreciation or offense. The offense has at times turned to rage and persecution.

The Greek root behind the word we translate "persecute" means "to pursue" in the manner one would chase a fox or rabbit in a hunt, and pursuit is sometimes what results from the world's rage and persecution. "We must drive them from our midst," people roar. "We must search them out and destroy them." Before his conversion Paul the apostle did the same thing to the Christians as his offense turned to fury.[32]

But whether it be rage or merely rudeness, Jesus said we would be happy. "When men lie about you, when they curse you, when they throw you into prison because you remind them of God," He said, "be glad, rejoice, jump up and down, for the kingdom is yours. It is already yours."

But now the progression has reached fullness.

6

Upside Down

Fʀᴏᴍ THE CONSTITUTION of the kingdom of God, which so clearly reverses normal world thinking, we see that one virtue comes ahead of all others in the invisible realm. It is humility.

How can humility underlie happiness, prosperity, and fulfillment?

In my own case, the deep significance of this virtue unfolded in my constant search for wisdom from God. For, as we will see, wisdom and humility are thoroughly intertwined.

At one point, the following words sprang to life in my spirit: "God *resisteth* the proud, but giveth grace unto the humble."[1] The power of those words is devastating if you trace the logic. Not only does God help those with genuine humility, but also He actively *opposes* those who are proud.

Of course, the definition of humble that is easiest for most of us to grasp is that it is the opposite of proud. Most of us seem to know what pride is. God insists that we be the very opposite if we are to receive His favor and blessing; otherwise He is against us.

Thus it became clear to me that if we desire to live in the kingdom of God, to receive God's favor, we must make humility the number one virtue. It is foundational. Jesus, the very Son of God, existing in the form of God, took on the likeness of man without diminishing His deity and "humbled Himself by becoming obedient to the point of death, even death on a cross."[2] And His Father *favored* that humility in this manner. "Therefore also God highly *exalted* Him, and bestowed on Him the name which is above every name."[3]

The Old Testament prepares us for such a consequence with words like: "The reward of humility and the fear of the LORD / Are riches, honor and life."[4]

Those humble before God, obedient and reverent toward Him and His will, are the victorious ones, the ones elevated to the rewards that the world scrambles after—riches, honor, life. Just consider the competition, the greed, the worry, the abuse, the killing expended in the race for those benefits. People worldwide want (1) enough to live on, (2) recognition and approval of what they do, and (3) good health and long life. To the humble and obedient, these blessings come naturally.

THE PATH OF PRIDE

The path of the proud is perfectly clear from Scripture, for without question pride is the greatest sin there is in the eyes of God. It thwarts His goodness toward man.

The proud man says, "I'll do it my way. I'm sufficient. I can control my destiny. I'm the captain of my soul, the master of my fate." There is nothing spiritually beggarly about him, nothing regretful about his inner condition, nothing hungering to be Godlike. In short, he lacks humility, and he receives nothing from the Lord, as we saw in discussing God's nature. His rewards, which are from men, are like vapor; they vanish suddenly, imperceptibly. For the wisdom of the Scripture says, "Pride goes before destruction, / And a haughty spirit before stumbling."[5]

Where there is pride, there will always be a fall. It is inevitable. We see it all about us, on a large scale and on small. Nations and individuals are slipping. They become arrogant; they cut off advice from old and respected friends; they go alone, and they fall.

As we strive to look into the invisible world to see God, to hear what He is saying, it is essential that we always bear in mind that our knowledge of that world comes primarily through His disclosure. *He* must reveal. Otherwise, we cannot see. Remembering that should keep us humble, even though our confidence rests in the fact that He said He would be found by those who diligently seek Him.[6] The proud, however, cannot bring themselves to seek, for that requires coming in from a lower position, and they have been conditioned otherwise.

As I said, humility is closely entwined with wisdom, which was the object of my diligent search years ago. I had been impressed with Solomon's reply to the Lord's offer one night following King David's death, "Ask what I shall give you."[7]

Can you imagine how most of us would have replied? But the Bible shows that Solomon revealed great humility in even approaching God, describing himself as a little child. "I do not know how to go out or come in," he said.[8] "Give me now wisdom and knowledge . . . for who can rule this great people of Thine?"[9] The Lord's response laid bare the pattern prevailing in the kingdom of heaven.

> Because you had this in mind, and did not ask for riches, wealth, or honor, or the life of those who hate you, nor have you even asked for long life, but you have asked for yourself wisdom and knowledge, that you may rule My people, over whom I have made you king, wisdom and knowledge have been granted to you. And I will give you riches and wealth and honor, such as none of the kings who were before you has possessed, nor those who will come after you.[10]

Echoing throughout were the words of Christ centuries later. "Seek first His kingdom and His righteousness; and all these things shall be added to you."[11]

I have become convinced that wisdom is the key to the secrets of the kingdom of God. It leads to favor. But the starting point is humility, as Solomon knew. For humility reveals fear of, or reverence for, the Lord.

The Book of Proverbs reveals the next step: "The fear of the LORD is the beginning of wisdom, / And the knowledge of the Holy One is understanding."[12]

SOLOMON WAS RIGHT

The cycle is complete—from humility, to fear of the Lord, to wisdom, to knowledge of the Holy One.

Wisdom, or spiritual understanding, *is* knowledge of the Holy One. And that is what we are seeking—knowledge of God, knowledge of His will and purpose, knowledge of the invisible world and how it works, knowledge of how to reach into it and bring its blessing and prosperity into our visible world.

In its ultimate sense, wisdom is understanding that an action taken today will be proven in the future to have been a correct one. And God provides that understanding.

To the people of Israel, God presented a body of Law that was to be their wisdom, an external expression of His will. If they followed those rules and principles in their society, then many years later people would look back and say that they had acted wisely. Unfortunately, they were inconsistent and often improperly motivated, and God's wisdom was not fully realized in their lives.

Through the incarnation of Christ and the coming of the Holy Spirit to dwell within believers, the wisdom of God took on an internal expression, with which we are now dealing. Obviously, like the Israelites, we have not been consistent or sincere in all of our efforts to manifest it.

But this wisdom from God is still available. Knowing that He governs all things, present and future, we can approach Him with pure hearts and say: "Show me how to run my life. Show me how the world works. Show me Your ways, Your principles, for running this enormously complex universe. I want to conform to what You do, to Your will, Your purpose, Your plan."

At that point we are seeking truth, and He will grant us wisdom for that. His entire purpose is to have us conform to truth. His wisdom will come; His principles will work. We will act, and the future will bear us out. People will say, "My, wasn't that man wise? Where did he get such wisdom?"

And all the while, it came from God.

LESSON FROM THE GARDEN

It is helpful to recognize that the entire point of conflict in the Garden of Eden came from God's attempt to teach Adam and Eve wisdom. It was not that God wanted to prevent them from obtaining knowledge by forbidding them to eat from the tree of the knowledge of good and evil. His purpose was that they would gain wisdom by obeying Him. Day after day they were to pass that tree, saying, "If I eat the fruit from there, that will be evil; if I refrain from eating it, that will be good." They were to learn good and evil simply from having that tree in their midst.

We know that they ate, did evil, and failed to obtain what God intended. For good is doing what God wants; it reveals wisdom. Evil is doing what He does not want; it reveals foolishness.

God was, and still is, looking for people who will do what He wants, people with wisdom, that He may enter into their lives, their visible world, and favor them. No problem, no shortage, no crisis is beyond His ability.

But instead He encountered, and still encounters, foolishness fed by pride.

THREE CARDINAL VIRTUES

The three cardinal virtues in the kingdom of God are *faith, hope,* and *love.* We've already spoken of the centrality of faith in seeing, entering, and experiencing the kingdom, but it is also interwoven with the virtues of hope and love. Paul the apostle more than once put them together in describing the Christian life and ministry: "So these three things continue forever: faith, hope, and love. And the greatest of these is love."[13]

Faith is essential to the functioning of a civilization. We daily reveal faith in the laws of the creation. How could the world function if it didn't have faith that there would be a tomorrow? How could medical doctors and scientists function without faith in an orderly universe? How could we exist without faith, to some degree, in other people? How could we conduct business without faith in the marketplace and the rules of commerce? Nothing would work without some kind of faith.

Since we as spiritual beings are saved by the grace of God "through faith,"[14] it is obvious that faith is indispensable in any relationship with the Lord. Without it, we don't even know God exists. We are lost in our sins and are unable to see or to enter the invisible world, let alone transfer its blessings into this visible one.

As for hope, we need to make a distinction between it and faith. Hope is the ability to transfer our reliance from ourselves to God. It is founded on the sovereignty of God, His total independence of circumstances, His limitlessness.

It does not develop in us until our faith is tried, until under pressure we realize there is a Creator who will work things out for those with whom He is pleased. The apostle Paul described the progression:

> Therefore having been justified by faith, we have peace with God through our Lord Jesus Christ, through whom also we have obtained our introduction by faith into this grace in which we stand; and we exult in *hope* of the glory of God. And not only this, but we also exult in our tribulations, knowing that tribulation brings about perseverance; and perseverance, proven character; and proven character, *hope*[15]

God's purpose is that our faith be tested, expressly to refine and strengthen it. Our endurance purifies and toughens our character; resolute hope in God and His plan results.

Note how Paul concludes the development of his thought: "and hope does not disappoint."[16]

Why is this true? Because hope shaped on the anvil rests in Him and in the moral rightness of His ultimate purpose—that the wicked will fall and the righteous will be rewarded.[17] Any expectation of the transfer of the blessings of the kingdom into our lives depends on it.

Finally, there must be love, which Paul described as the greatest of the trinity of virtues. Interestingly, it grows out of the other two. Hope grows out of faith, and love grows out of hope.

THE ABILITY TO LOVE

When a person has hope, when he knows that his future is assured, he stops struggling to maintain his own sphere of dominance; he stops fighting other people. He is willing to let the moral law of God work to defend his place. Then he is free to have concern for the well-being of others. He is no longer threatened and can give himself, his possessions, his life to someone else and know that God will make it right.

This process—and it usually is a process rather than an immediate change—was radical in my life. Stepping from the role of aggressive, competitive young lawyer who was just beginning the climb up the power ladder in a major international corporation, to the role of a man whose hope is secured by Almighty God completely altered my life and lifestyle. That hope released my ability to love—to love *real* people in *concrete* ways, not merely abstractly. Those in corporate halls were no longer shallow faces; folks in the hard, dirty streets of New York City were no longer the masses. They were people. I had been set free to express my concern for them, which eventually led my family and me to share our lives—our food, our clothing, our shelter—with others in one of the most wretched sections of New York. Our concern took on visible expression.

The Lord's experience with the cross was the ultimate expression of hope and love, of course. He had no visible assurance that He wouldn't be found absolutely foolish. He could have turned out to have been the most tragic figure in history, but He had hope in the rightness and goodness of His Father. He was free to love His people and to die for them. Hope and love are what we must have, Paul said, if we are to experience the power of God in the world today. Love is the strongest force possible. The reason is simple: God *is* love. No negative can overcome that positive. The perpetrators of hate and darkness have tried since the beginning but the light from Him has prevailed.[18]

Love is so overwhelming that it nullifies the physical principle under which every action produces an opposite, equal reaction. If someone pushes someone else, the latter will push hard in return, and escalation develops, usually to the point of violence. But Paul advised, "Absorb the push. Break the cycle. Overcome evil with good."[19]

We need to see that He wasn't advocating merely defense, but rather the perfect offense with the only weapon capable of absorbing and defeating evil. If someone demands you to go one mile, you can fight him; you can go sullenly and curse him all the way, feeling beaten and rejected. Or you can go on the attack and follow the charter of the kingdom: "If someone forces you to go with him one mile, go with him two miles."[20] Love will thus heap burning coals on his head, and the conviction of the Lord will work in His life for good.[21]

Yes, any of us who yearn to see our world changed and have been disappointed by the relative importance of the people of God must examine ourselves regarding the virtue of love. For the picture painted by Paul in one of his most famous discourses has to convince us that, were love to underlie all of our thoughts, words, and deeds—our use of the principles of God—then the world *would* be changed.

> Love is patient, love is kind, and is not jealous; love does not brag and is not arrogant, does not act unbecomingly; it does not seek its own, is not provoked, does not take into account a wrong suffered, does not rejoice in unrighteousness, but rejoices with the truth; bears all things, believes all things, hopes all things, endures all things. Love never fails.[22]

Eventually, Paul said, all else will pass away. The special gifts and talents, the wonderful endowments from on high—they will all run their course. But love endures forever, bridging eternity.

HOLY PARADOXES

I trust it is abundantly clear that the constitution of the kingdom of God (the priorities of anyone who would experience the power and blessings of life there) is riddled with paradox. One can almost hear the Lord chuckle as the world looks in disbelief at what would appear to be anti-principles, in light of the way most people and nations conduct their affairs.

The world says hate your enemies. The kingdom says love your enemies.

The world says hit back. The kingdom says do good to those who mistreat you.

The world says hold onto your life at any cost. The kingdom says lose your life and you will find it.

The world says a young and beautiful body is essential. The kingdom says even a grain of wheat must die if it is to have life.

The world says push yourself to the top. The kingdom says serve if you want to lead.

The world says you are number one. The kingdom says many who are first will be last and the last first.

The world says acquire gold and silver. The kingdom says store up treasure in heaven if you would be rich.

The world says exploit the masses. The kingdom says do good to the poor.

Sadly, the church itself has often been a leader among those blinded to the paradoxes of the kingdom of God. So many times congregations have fled from the inner city, where they are so desperately needed, to comfortable suburbs, where they could luxuriate and not have to face the poor and their problems. Or they have served a political or social movement rather than the needy. Or they have embraced the management techniques of corporations rather than the government techniques of God. In short, they lost the sound of truth.

The temptations of worldly thinking are great, but they must be resisted even at the cost of appearing foolish by embracing truths that are paradoxical to conventional wisdom.

You see, one major paradox that we must accept as we try to change the world is this: The people of God are to live out the Beatitudes and the virtues of humility, wisdom, faith, hope, and love while at the same time becoming leaders.

"You are the light that gives light to the world," Jesus said.[23] In darkness, the man or woman who carries the light does not follow; he or she leads the way.

Yes, the humble, the disciplined, the wise, the faithful, the hopeful, the loving—they are to lead. *That* is the holy paradox.

And how will it be brought to pass? The laws of the kingdom in the following chapters will show us.

Part II

LAWS
OF THE KINGDOM

7

The Law of Reciprocity

ONE SIMPLE DECLARATION by Jesus revealed a law that will change the world: "Give, and it will be given to you."[1]

Eight words. They form a spiritual principle that touches every relationship, every condition of man, whether spiritual or physical. They are pivotal in any hope we have of relieving the world's worsening crises.

Jesus expanded the universality of this theme throughout His ministry, varying subject matter and application. His point was so encompassing that it demanded many illustrations. In the discourse from which we get the eight words, we find this expansion: "just as you want people to treat you, treat them in the same way."[2] And from that, of course, came what the world describes as the Golden Rule: "Do unto others as you would have them do unto you."

Jesus went on, putting a frame around the eight key words in this manner:

> Be merciful, just as your Father is merciful. And do not pass judgment and you shall not be judged: and do not condemn, and you shall not be condemned; pardon, and you will be pardoned. Give, and it will be given to

you; good measure, pressed down, shaken together, running over, they will pour into your lap. For whatever measure you deal out to others, it will be dealt to you in return.[3]

By putting this together with the world's greatest teaching on love, repeated from the Old Testament by Jesus as the heart of God's will, we establish the perfect "law" for conduct: "You shall love your neighbor as yourself."[4]

A UNIVERSAL PRINCIPLE

The *Law of Reciprocity*, a kingdom principle revealed in these teachings of the Lord, is relatively easy for us to identify since it is so visibly pervasive in the physical world. As we noted in the previous chapter, a basic law of physics says that for every action there is an equal and opposite reaction. The jet age in which we live is founded on it.

Scientists some years ago must have said, "If we can push a jet of hot air out the back end of an engine, there has to be an equal and opposite reaction going forward. Now, if we can attach this to an airplane, the thrust will be unprecedented."

Of course the logical, parallel step produced rocket engines able to generate enough backward thrust to provide forward speeds necessary to break the hold of gravity and send machines and men into outer space.

In the interpersonal realm, we find the same principle prevailing. If you smile at someone, he most likely will smile back. If you strike someone, the chances are he will hit you back. If you express kindness, you are almost certain to have someone express kindness in return. If you are critical of everything and everyone, you can expect to receive critical judgment from others.

A number of years ago, not long after our family moved to the Tidewater area of Virginia to begin the Christian Broadcasting Network, I remarked to my uncle, a man of admirable maturity, "The people in Tidewater are so very nice, far more so than I had even expected."

My uncle's eyes twinkled and he spoke a powerful, homespun version of the Law of Reciprocity that I hope I never forget: "I tell you what, young man, you will find nice people anywhere you go if you're nice to them."

It is a principle built into the universe. Even international relations respond to it. We Americans saw it at work from the earliest days of the conflict that escalated into the Vietnam War. The escalation was gradual at first. The North Vietnamese and Viet Cong would push at our allies and us. And we would push back, a little harder. They would retaliate, harder, and then back we would come. In such fashion, the United States participated in a dragged-out war that sapped its resources and resolve, simply because of an unwillingness on either side to break the cycle.

This should have been done in one of two ways.

First, we could have loved the enemy and all Southeast Asians, giving them food, clothing, and housing, and doing everything possible to establish them in freedom and the love of God. Love is able to absorb evil actions without fighting back, thus disrupting the cycle of tit for tat. Great faith and courage would have been required while awaiting reciprocal love.

Second, we could have hit the enemy so fast and so devastatingly as to nullify reciprocal action. Because of the ultimate infallibility of the Law of Reciprocity, however, it seems almost certain that the latter course would have at a point in history, perhaps distant, produced reciprocity from some source. Recall, for instance, the low estate to which Babylon fell from its days of great, but frequently cruel, empire. Consider how even today, as by the recurrence of an ancient debt, the modern nation of Iraq continues to incur the wrath and scorn of both God and man. The Persian Gulf War was just one more stage in a longstanding chain of repercussions arising from the laws of God.

The point, however, is that the Law of Reciprocity functions in international relations—for good or for evil. It is immutable.

THE INDIVIDUAL LEVEL

I want to look first at the personal level, for that is where our walk with God must begin. The Christian faith is personal, although it quickly spreads to the interpersonal, the national, and the international. It is rarely private for long.

Nonetheless, individuals today are in crisis, and the Law of Reciprocity is important to them.

Jesus, as we have seen, said, "Give, and it shall be given unto you; good measure, pressed down, and shaken together, and running over, shall men give into your bosom."[5] What words for those today who are suffering economically, threatened with unemployment or foreclosure! They, quite bluntly, need money. The stories are much the same: "What do I do? I'm using everything I have, and still my bills aren't paid. It seems I've been in debt forever."

As simple as it might look, the Law of Reciprocity is the solution. The world sees such thinking as foolishness, but the Lord says it is wisdom—because it is founded on truth.

As we hear Christ's words, "Give, and it will be given to you,"[6] they take us immediately to His commandment to "seek first the kingdom of God and His righteousness, and all these things shall be added to you."[7] We saw that "all these things" means whatever is needed to provide what we need to live fruitful and productive lives.

Giving is foundational. You have to give of yourself. You have to give of your money. You have to give of your time. And this foundational truth works in both the invisible and the visible worlds.

It is not complicated. If you want a higher salary in your job, you have to give more. Those with good salaries are not people who sit back and scheme and spend all their time thinking of ways to promote themselves. The people who are recognized in an organization are those who work harder, think more creatively, and act more forcefully in behalf of the enterprise. They give. They are rewarded.

So many people in our age go for a job with one thought in mind: "What will I get out of it?" Their only concerns are salary, fringe benefits, and title. They are takers, not givers. And takers do not go to the head of the list. The top people are those who say, "I want to do this to help you. Your company has a product that I can help make successful. I have a plan that I'm certain will work." They are givers.

We tend to justify our shortcomings in comparison with these people by hinting at "lucky breaks" or "knowing the right people." But we're wrong. Invariably, those who give concepts, extra time, personal concern, and the like are the receivers. They are giving to an organization—and, indirectly, to individuals in that organization—and they are bound to benefit.

The hard work and overtime must also be accompanied by a proper attitude, of course. Those who give meanness or anger or trouble will get it back. "Do not judge lest you be judged,"[8] the Lord said, which drives directly at attitudes. Anyone who is critical, constantly faulting others and cutting associates, will not rise to the top. He will get back what he gives. The one who makes his department look good, including his boss, is the one who will get the salary increase he needs. "The way you give to others is the way God will give to you."[9] That's a law.

THE ISSUE OF GIVING

We cannot talk about a need for money without running headlong into the matter of giving to the Lord. Since everything in His—the cattle on a thousand hills, silver, gold, governments—He obviously is the one we should be turning to in our need. "Give, and it shall be given to you," Jesus said. And that includes our dealing with God Almighty.

The prophet Malachi was precise in speaking the thoughts of the Lord regarding such dealings.

> "From the days of your fathers you have turned aside from My statues, and have not kept them. Return to Me, and I will return to you," says the Lord of hosts. "But you say, 'How shall we return?' Will a man rob God? Yet you are robbing Me! But you say, 'How have we robbed Thee?' *In tithes and contributions.* You are cursed with a curse, for you are robbing Me, the whole nation of you! *Bring the whole tithe* into the storehouse, so that there may be food in My house, and *test Me now in this*," says the LORD of hosts, "*if I will not open for you the windows of heaven, and pour out for you a blessing until there is no more need.*"[10]

The passage shows how seriously the Lord God takes the matter of giving. Obviously, He owns everything. He doesn't really need our tithes and offerings, but He has gone to great lengths to teach us how things work. If we want to release the superabundance of the kingdom of heaven, we must first give. Our Father is more than ready to fulfill His side of the Law of Reciprocity. One can almost imagine His heavenly host standing on tiptoe, brimming with anticipation, gleeful, awaiting the opportunity to release the treasures so badly needed in our visible world.

Note the promise of abundance in Malachi's words. Some translators render the promised blessing as "so great you won't have enough room to take it in!"[11] In the world, we measure return in percentages of 6 or 8 or 10, and sometimes 15 and 20. In the kingdom, as we noted earlier, the measures are 3,000 percent, 6,000 percent, and 10,000 percent—thirty, sixty, and a hundredfold.

That is a beautiful promise for those facing economic distress today. "Test Me," says the Lord. "Prove Me."

I am as certain of this as of anything in my life: If you are in financial trouble, the smartest thing you can do is to start giving money away. Give tithes and offerings to the Lord. Give time. Give work. Give love. That sounds crazy. But we have seen how the plan of God is filled with paradox. If you need money, then begin to give away some of whatever you have. Your return, poured into your lap, will be great, pressed down, and running over.

A CASE IN CHILE

A missionary to Chile shared some insights into this law of the kingdom some time ago. As pastor of a group of extremely poor peasants, he did everything he could to minister to their needs. He revealed what he considered to be the full counsel of the Lord, teaching the Bible as the

Word of God and leading them into many significant and deep under-
standings. But one day the Lord spoke as clearly as if He had been
standing face to face with him. "You have not declared My whole truth to
these people," He said.

"But Lord," the missionary replied, "I don't understand. I've taught
them about justification by faith and forgiveness of sins and baptism in
the Holy Spirit, about miracles and walking in Your power. I've taught
them about the church, about history, about doctrine. I've taught them
about godliness and holy living, about the Second Coming.

"What, my Lord, have I failed to teach them?"

He waited a moment. The voice was very clear. "You have not declared
My tithe to them."

The missionary was stunned. "But Lord, these are very poor people!
They hardly have enough to live. I can't ask them to tithe. They have
nothing."

Again, a silent moment. "You must declare to them My tithe."

He was a faithful, obedient man. And the debate ended.

The next Sunday morning, with heavy heart, he stepped into the pulpit
of the little rustic church in that poor, backward community, took a deep
breath, and began.

"My beloved brethren," he said, looking into the open, uplifted faces of
his flock, "God has shown me that I haven't been faithful in declaring to
you His whole counsel. There is something you have not been doing that
I must tell you about. You have not been tithing to the Lord."

And he began a trek through the Scriptures with them that lasted
nearly an hour. He explained everything, including the Malachi portions
urging that the Lord be proven on the matter.

The next Sunday, it was their turn. In they came, obedient to the Word.
They didn't have money, so they brought eggs, chickens, leather goods,
woven articles, and all manner of things from their poor peasant homes.
The altar area was heaped high.

The missionary felt badly about taking the gifts, but he too was faithful,
so he sold some and used the money for the work of the church. He
distributed some of the gifts to the destitute in the neighborhood and kept
some for his own sustenance, in lieu of income.

The same thing happened Sunday after Sunday. The people tithed.

It wasn't long before the effects of drought were seen throughout the
countryside. Poverty gripped the people of the land worse than ever.
Crops failed; buildings deteriorated; gloom covered everything.

But, miraculously, this was not so with the members of that little
church. Their crops flourished as though supernaturally watered. But
more than that, the yields were extraordinary, bounteous, healthy, flavor-

ful. Their fields were green, while those around were withering. Their livestock were sleek and strong. Relative abundance replaced abject poverty.

They even had an overflow of crops and goods that could be sold, and before long their tithes included money. They were able to build a much-needed new meeting house.

Despite his misgivings, the missionary and his people had learned that no matter how desperate the situation, no matter how deep the impoverishment, the principles of the kingdom can turn deprivation into abundance.

They touch the visible world.

WHAT IS A TITHE?

Lest we become rigid and legalistic, we need to understand the tithe quantitatively. The word, of course, means a "tenth." People quibble over such questions as whether it is before or after taxes, whether it should go to a single ministry, whether it should be put ahead of absolute necessities, and the like. Such niggling misses the point.

The Lord cherishes a ready giver whose heart puts Him and His service ahead of everything. The apostle Paul had a lot to declare on this point:

> Now this I say, he who sows sparingly shall also reap sparingly; and he who sows bountifully shall also reap bountifully. Let each one do just as he has purposed in his heart; not grudgingly or under compulsion; for God loves a cheerful giver. And God is able to make all grace abound to you, that always having all sufficiency in everything, you may have an abundance for every good deed. . . . You will be enriched in everything for all liberality.[12]

According to the dictionary, the original definition of tithe was one-tenth of the annual produce of one's land or of one's annual income. According to the Bible, that is merely the *starting place* of giving to the Lord. The Malachi passage refers to "tithes and offerings." One might say, then, that there is no offering until the tithe has been paid; it is the expected, minimum amount.

So a lot of people who practice this critical spiritual law give far more than 10 percent of their income to the Lord's work. It's all His anyhow, they recognize. King David voiced his when he said:

> Both riches and honor come from Thee, and Thou dost rule over all. . . . But who am I and who are my people that we should be able to offer as generously as this? For all things come from Thee, and from Thy hand we have given Thee.[13]

He also wrote in one of his great psalms:

The earth is the Lord's, and the fulness thereof; the world, and they that dwell therein.[14]

Therefore, many people ignore any 10 percent cutoff and give out of the abundance of their provision. I know one New Jersey florist who had been thoroughly blessed by the Lord as he exercised the principles we are exploring in this book, and he frequently gave 90 percent of his annual income to the service of God. And the prosperity simply mounted. He was not able to outgive the Lord. That law is built into the kingdom. It never changes.

One of the saddest things that can happen to people comes about so naturally. When hard times come, when they are thrown out of work or inflation runs wild, the first place they cut is often their tithe. Usually their intentions are good. "I'll make it up next week," they rationalize. And God lets them go. He does not pressure. But that is the worst thing they can do. That, I believe, is the time to step up your giving. That is the time you need something from God. "Prove Me," the Lord says. "Give, and you will receive."[15]

THE FRUITS OF NEGLECT

One of the many men who served the Lord in the rescue missions and other street ministries during the Depression of the thirties has reported very moving accounts about those who would pass through the soup kitchen—broken, smashed men, virtually destroyed—where he would often ask them about their spiritual lives.

"Tell me, friend, were you faithful to the Lord with your tithes?" he would inquire.

And the man would shake his head no, clutching his cup and plate in front of him, staring vacantly ahead.

And he'd ask the next one, "When you were prosperous and all was well with you, did you give to the Lord? Were you faithful with your tithe?"

The man would shake his head no.

Never once, this worker reported, did he find a man living in poverty who had been faithful to the Lord and His principle of giving. And that fits exactly with what David said thousands of years ago: "I have been young, and now I am old; / Yet I have not seen the righteous forsaken, / Or his descendants begging bread."[16]

We must not misunderstand any of this to say that should there be a general economic collapse, we will see Christians riding in Rolls-Royces, wearing big jewels and rich furs, and living in mansions while everyone else lives in poverty. That would be contrary to the nature of God. It merely means that, if we have been faithful to the Lord, given to Him, given to the poor, given to our neighbor, then we will receive according to the prosperity of the Lord, not the prosperity of the ungodly.

We will experience the fulfillment of seeking first the kingdom of God and having the things necessary for life given to us additionally, even matter-of-factly, if you will.

Those who ignore God's principles, on the other hand, can be expected in a moment, a flash, to find themselves totally stripped of what they thought was theirs.

Yet a little while and the wicked man will be no
    more;
And you will look carefully for his place, and he
    will not be there.
But the humble will inherit the land,
And will delight themselves in abundant
    prosperity.[17]

NEGATIVE RECIPROCITY

As we have noted, the Law of Reciprocity works in all the affairs of men. It can work for our good, or it can work for our harm. Americans saw it fulfilled in racial relationships, with roots going back to the days of slavery.

In one of the horrors of history, our representatives went to Africa, seized human beings, stored them in ships, and brought them here to treat like property. We sold them and put them out as forced labor, mistreating them, breaking up families, and ignoring their rights and dignity as people created in the image of God.

"Give, and it will be given to you . . ."

It took a hundred years, but our land has been reaping what it sowed. In many cases, blacks were forced into a matriarchal society as men were totally destroyed emotionally, psychologically, and spiritually. Women struggled to put bread on the table for their children, who soon perceived the cause of their suffering and were ripe for hatred.

Guilt and resentment often overtook the whites. The sides of conflict were locked in. And it came. A good nation was battered, its regions divided, its people torn.

Even though education has been improved, rights defended, and poverty relieved, the suffering continues. The government itself teeters under the threat of bankruptcy as it is unable to meet the demands of sickness, unemployment, welfare, inner-city redevelopment, and other social distress, much of it traceable to the deprivation of the black man centuries ago.

Signs of a possible turnaround through proper use of the Law of Reciprocity, which again identifies slavery as the cause of much that went wrong in America, can be seen in the economic recovery of the South. For many years, the Southern economy foundered, hostage to the Northern banking and commercial interests, because the region did not have properly trained and educated people capable and desirous of working in factories and offices. Without these wage earners, there were also few customers for Southern manufacturers, and prosperity eluded all.

But once the South began to give freedom to the black people, providing education and taking other steps to lift their standard of living, the economy edged upward and soon reached boom level in many places. The South prospered as it never had.

Quite simply, the society had cursed itself. But the Law of Reciprocity, still lacking in many dimensions of life, had made it possible to reverse the curse.

GETTING BACK IN KIND

I saw the very opposite of the national racial experience unfold on the streets of Portsmouth, Virginia, one day in 1960, only to be snuffed out, all through the working of the reciprocity principle.

A friend, Dick Simmons, was visiting shortly after my family and I had moved to Tidewater, and he asked if we could go preach on the streets in some of the poor sections of the city. We ended up going to a shopping center in the middle of an area of recent racial violence.

We began by engaging a number of black youths in conversation, and before long several dozen had gathered. Dick preached to them about Jesus. The Holy Spirit moved upon all of us, and after a few minutes Dick said, "Now if you want to meet Jesus, the One I'm talking about, you can do that right here, right now. You bow your head and kneel right here on the sidewalk and pray and ask Jesus to come into your life."

What a unique gathering that was! In the middle of one of the city's tensest areas, where violence had already erupted, love and peace and beauty descended. Here were two white men giving love and knowledge and experience—giving the truth of the gospel—to a group of deprived, volatile black youngsters, and what did we get in return? We received love and kindness and warmth back from them.

In an instant, even as the youngsters were praying the sinner's prayer and lives were being changed, everything exploded into a surrealistic movie scene. Two cars of police with trained dogs wheeled to a stop. Men and dogs piled out and charged the kneeling black youngsters. The policemen had jumped to a hasty conclusion, prompted by a phone call from a bystander, that a racial protest was mounting, and they intended to break it up. They chased the youngsters across the street as growls and yells filled the air.

In a twinkling, the Law of Reciprocity set in. The youngsters began to throw rocks at the policemen. Yells turned to curses. And the violence escalated, with all the potential of the devastation that shattered American cities in the sixties.

Dick and I had given love; we had received love. The police had given harshness; they had received harshness. Unhappily the latter pattern prevailed through most of the land.

POTENTIAL FOR THE WORLD

Convinced that the Law of Reciprocity could bring relief, if not total solution, to the major problems of the world, I began shortly after dawn one morning early in the decade to make notes on these problems. In less than an hour I had covered the spectrum: The Law of Reciprocity without question affects the way people and nations live with each other. It has the potential to bring peace to the world.

Following are merely a few of the issues I jotted down, but they are widespread enough to make the case. Remember, under the Law of Reciprocity, men everywhere would operate under the principle of giving what they expect to receive, treating others the way they want to be treated, and loving their neighbors as themselves.

War. The need for standing armies would be removed as nations give as they receive and love their neighbors as themselves. The threat of invasion would be gone. Defense appropriations would be unnecessary. Huge governmental spending and the cruelty of high inflation and high taxes would be relieved.

Trade. There would be no need for tariff barriers because nations and companies would not be dumping products and damaging domestic industries. Trade would occur as needed and desired, fostered by healthy, imaginative competition, uninterrupted by runaway greed. Terms like "Third World" would become meaningless.

Injustice. Incredible extremes of wealth and poverty would be evened out simply by human kindness and generosity. The unjust privileges of wealth and other types of status would diminish, melting away envy, jealousy, greedy ambition, and perverted competitiveness.

Crime. Burglary, theft, and vandalism would vanish, along with personal assaults, murder, rape, and kidnaping. Narcotics usage and traffic would cease. Business and securities fraud would pass, cheating at every level would fade, along with price fixing, monopoly and cartel abuse, and influence peddling. International terrorism would end. Prisons would become obsolete.

Pollution. Air, water, and land could be cleaned up. There would be no more factories belching acid smoke into the air and draining chemical waste into rivers. Beer cans, bottles, and garbage would vanish from the roadsides and campsites. Parks would retain their beauty. Wildlife would flourish.

Productivity. As the Japanese have learned from their change of heart after World War II, moving from a people known for cheap merchandise to one prospering from excellence, nations would see their economies improve radically through increased productivity in every sector. Employers and employees alike would see sharp changes in their motivation, satisfaction, and collective prosperity. There would be no more shoddy products, no more dangerous construction in which buildings collapse and hundreds are injured or killed, no more unsafe toys to maim children.

Government. Huge governmental bureaucracy would disappear as overdrawn, rigid regulation and enforcement becomes unnecessary, along with most of the social services. As men begin to treat one another as God intended, the governments could concentrate on those relatively few things that must be done collectively.

THE FOUNDATION OF SOCIETY

The Law of Reciprocity is the fundamental principle of social development. It is the foundation for development between people and communities. Great things happen when people follow this principle, but devastation comes when it is ignored. Consider, for example, the crisis of the family and all the aftermath that follows the breakup of the home in our culture.

We see the repercussions of disobedience of this law in international affairs as well. When Saddam Hussein went up against a defenseless neighbor and did to those people what was unjust and unfair, the nations of the world came against him. As a result, there was great suffering; there always is when somebody violates the fundamental law which says, "Do unto others as you would have them do unto you."

In the troubled economy of the 1990s we can see better than ever that this principle is the real reason for Japan's emergence as a world leader in industry and technology. When I wrote the first edition of *The Secret Kingdom,* the Japanese were not the power they are today. True, they were coming, but they had not yet reached the levels they would eventually attain. They had not yet become America's rival, dominating several key high-tech industries worldwide.

But what the Japanese discovered through the guidance of the brilliant American teacher, W. Edwards Deming, was the principle of the Golden Rule. The strategic factor behind Japan's success involves the whole idea of service; it is a combination of the Law of Greatness and the Law of Reciprocity. They found that in order to win, they had to give service. If they served their customers, the customers served them in return. If they served their employees and gave employees a voice in decision making, the employees worked even harder and helped the company to grow.

Jesus said, "Give, and it will be given unto you." And He said to the disciples, "Let he who would be greatest among you be the servant of all." Companies, individuals, and nations who follow His guidance will attain prosperity.

In his celebrated books, *In Search of Excellence* and *Thriving on Chaos,* author Tom Peters explored the factors that contribute to the success of America's greatest, most prosperous companies. What he found was that the industry leaders in virtually every case made, in effect, a fetish out of customer service. In *Thriving on Chaos,* Peters makes a strong point that the top companies have virtually a fanatical desire to serve their customers at any cost. Successful companies, here or anywhere else, do everything they can to serve the customer.

GENUINE CONCERN

Stores he pointed out, like Nordstrom's, which is famous for its service, ranked at the top of their industry. And the example can be extended in many areas, not just businesses. We work very hard to do the same type of thing at CBN. For instance, we have a telephone ministry where we call people and simply ask how we can serve them. Counselors ask, "How can we pray for you? How can we help you?" People are sometimes surprised by this type of service. They ask, "Where's the pitch?" But there is no pitch. We tell them, "We just called to see if we can be of help to you in some way." What has pleased us is the bonding this kind of personal service produces. When people feel that you genuinely care, they respond. And in this cold, impersonal world, people are so desperate to have someone care for them.

It is such a tragedy that in this densely populated, highly social nation, we have the loneliest people who have ever lived. In an age that has produced miracles in communications technology, there is little communication on the human level, or personal contact, or touching, or genuine love. History shows that caring attention and service is the way to bridge the emotional gap between people. It says that when you give personal service, you always win. But somehow that message has to be understood and adopted on a much greater scale.

When you contrast the incredible debt and lingering recession of the United States with the incredible prosperity and financial achievements of Japan, you eventually have to realize that the Japanese are simply practicing what we used to preach. As a result, they have built an economic colossus on this one principle.

In the past few years Japan has made some mistakes, grown too fast, leveraged too much. But even if the recent problems in their economy were to lead to some kind of collapse, the fact remains that they built their success on service. The Law of Reciprocity was the underpinning of their achievement, and when it is followed faithfully, it will always bring positive results.

I have pushed and tested these principles for many years now, and they work in every situation. It's just a matter of having our minds open to see the correlation between current events and God's Word and how they fit.

RENEGADES EXCLUDED

Many people rightly ask, "Can this law be made to work in the world today? Can we simply begin to live this way?"

I believe the answer is yes, with an exception.

The Law of Reciprocity when practiced by law-abiding people and nations will not work with a totally lawless renegade. To begin to practice this principle with one such as that is extraordinarily dangerous, and a distinction must be made.

However, if you analyze it, you will see that even this exception is a fulfillment of the reciprocity principle. As the renegade gives (living outside law and decency) so will he receive from the entire society, in force. He will be ostracized. That, in a sense, was God's answer to the problem when He called forth His people, Israel. They were not to temporize—to try to disregard God's principles because of convenience or expediency. The renegade was removed from society and rendered incapable of such conduct through very harsh punishment.[18]

For us, the example is found in the New Testament. Jesus did not turn the other cheek to the devil or anyone governed by the devil through His ministry. Instead, He exercised His authority. As James said: "Stand against the devil, and the devil will run from you."[19] Oppose him and those belonging to him. They are renegades.

It should be noted that the need to act quickly against the renegade in our society explains why the Law of Reciprocity does not encompass pacifism. For domestic tranquility, there must be a police force and a system of justice capable of bringing sure and swift punishment upon those who rebel against society. Injustice in the administration of the law will bring on revolution. But lack of diligence in the punishment of crime will promote anarchy.

So also in the international realm, the family of peace-loving nations must be able to protect itself against renegades. The Law of Reciprocity would forbid two equals from beginning a fight to settle a dispute. However, a miscreant is not the equal of law-abiding persons. A rogue nation is not the equal of the family of nations. A rebellious child is not the equal of his parents. In each of these cases, the lawful and just application of discipline or restraint does not violate the Law of Reciprocity. Such discipline is in fact a God-given, albeit temporary, method of dealing with evil in a still imperfect world.

But in all other cases, I believe we should exercise the Law of Reciprocity to the fullest, even among those not yet committed personally to God Almighty. For it is a principle that will work in the visible world—now.

8

The Law of Use

THE NEXT SEVEN years are going to be absolutely critical for Western civilization and the United States. If our culture continues the present, accelerating moral decline, the demise of our society seems virtually inevitable.

In Western Europe and the United States large numbers of people have forsaken the principles of the kingdom of God while their elites have exerted every effort to undermine the organizing premise of this society. The media, the intellectual community, government officials—those responsible for policy at every level—from the local school boards to the United States Supreme Court—seem determined to subvert and under-mine the Christian principles and traditional family values that have upheld this society from its beginning.

On the global scale a concerted effort has been launched to establish a new world order based on a vague amalgam of socialism, humanism, and religious syncretism of values, while the traditional Western Christian heritage is abandoned. During the past fifty years these utopian dreamers have all but destroyed public education in America while they have fastened upon our nation a wasteful and profligate governmental system.

But instead of acknowledging their failures, these liberal manipulators and demagogues are stepping up their demand for more of the same. They want more failed polices instead of fewer; they seem not to have understood the lessons we have just learned from the fall of communism.

I believe all this gives a great sense of urgency to the issues being discussed in this book. But when you look at the approaching financial collapse that may well be upon us—either a deflationary collapse or a hyperinflationary blowout—you have to see that we are in very real danger of destabilizing governments worldwide.

Anarchy, a revolution, emerging dictatorship, or worse, a worldwide dictatorship could well emerge from such an extraordinarily serious debacle. Most of the problems we have in the world today could be solved if we would simply adopt and implement God's principles of success. But short of a powerful spiritual revival and the concerted effort of America's Christians to bring about dramatic moral and political change, the future is not promising.

There is hope for a bright future, but we must act now! If we are to survive this momentous time in our nation's history, we must return to the laws of the kingdom or it will be too late for all of us. The secular world as presently constituted will not do it. The task is the responsibility of Christian people. Christians must boldly proclaim the truth of the kingdom, then as citizens of this world insist that the common-sense principles of God's kingdom be reflected in public policy for the good of all.

The term "from Christ to chaos" expresses our current dilemma. Surely, unless we adopt the wise principles of the Bible to bring order to our government and our lives, we are going to see the unavoidable collapse of what has been called Western Civilization. It will follow moral collapse as surely as night follows day.

CHRIST'S SENSE OF URGENCY

But we must not lose hope; great things can be done out of a sense of urgency. An exceptional urgency seemed to have gripped the Lord's ministry by the time He reached the teaching I wish to examine in this chapter. He had so much to impart and seemingly so little time to do it. Everything was speeding up.

In the midst of rapid-fire teachings about the kingdom of heaven, He began this story:

For it is just like a man about to go on a journey, who called his own slaves, and entrusted his possessions to them. And to one he gave five talents, to another, two, and to another, one, each according to his own ability; and he went on his journey.[1]

Then unfolds the development of what I have come to call the **Law of Use**. To me this is the most important principle for human growth and development to be found in our world. It touches every facet of personal and communal life. We follow it to our benefit; we ignore it to our peril. Here is the setting.

Servant number one received five talents. The parable says he went out and "traded with them." We can imagine what happened. Perhaps he bought some commodities, sold them at a profit, and reinvested the entire amount. Or perhaps he took a journey and returned with valuable goods, and he added to the value of those goods through work he or someone else did to them. Regardless, he worked with his master's money and eventually doubled it.

The man with the two talents acted similarly. He may have bought wool, handed it over to a weaver, and then sold the woven cloth at a profit, only to quickly reinvest it and keep all the money working. Eventually he had doubled the amount left with him.

The third slave acted differently, however. The parable says he took the single talent, dug a hole, and buried it. He was afraid, Jesus said—afraid that if he went out and bought wool or oil or some such item, a depression would come and he would lose the money. Or maybe robbers would steal it. Or maybe someone would outsmart him or cheat him, say, at the weights and balances. Perhaps he would make a wrong decision. So, impotent with fear, he preserved his lord's investment by hiding it in a safe place.

After a long time, the lord returned and called the slaves to him. "Tell me," he said after a brief exchange, "how did you do with my money?"

The first servant quickly replied, "Master, I took the five talents and I traded with them. I bought and sold, and leveraged your money, but I made five more talents. Here is the original and five additional."

He had covered his overhead and still doubled the amount.

The master was pleased: "Well done, good and faithful slave; you were faithful with a few things. I will put you in charge of many things; enter into the joy of your master."

The next servant stepped forward and reported: "Lord, I took your two talents, and I went out and bought and sold. I entered into some business transactions, and I took some risks, but I made money. I've got two more talents. Here are the two you gave me and two additional."

The lord replied in the same way he had to the man with five talents.

Then it was the third man's turn. "Tell me what you've done with my money while I've been gone," the master said.

"Lord, I knew you were a hard man," he began. "You reap where you don't sow. You gather where you don't even plant. So I was afraid. I figured the best thing to do was play it safe, so I wrapped the talent up nicely and hid it. Here it is; I didn't lose anything."

Most of us today can sympathize with this fellow. After all, if you're a trustee over somebody else's property, you have to be careful. You can't take risks. It's even worse in an economically volatile world like ours.

What did the master do in this illustration to prepare us for the kingdom?

> You wicked, lazy slave, you knew that I reap where I did not sow, and gather where I scattered no seed. Then you ought to have put my money in the bank, and on my arrival I would have received my money back with interest. . . . Cast out the worthless slave into the outer darkness; in that place there shall be weeping and gnashing of teeth.[2]

The man was considered wicked and sinful, given to evil, and because he refused to take what his lord had given him and put it to work, improving upon it.

Note that quantity wasn't the key. Their use of what they had been given was what mattered. Proper use gave them entry into the place of joy. Improper use barred the third man.

However, the startling point of the parable is the following conclusion: "to everyone who has shall more be given, and he shall have an abundance; but from the one who does not have, even what he does have shall be taken away."[3] During my extended time of seeking wisdom from God, the magnitude of that sentence crystallized for me. I perceived that it presented a principle, a law, that was as important for day-to-day life as any there is.

"To everyone who has shall more be given." It seems shocking, particularly to those tending toward a welfare state or socialism, as so many in the world do today. We have a poor man with only one talent and another who has improved his lot, and we take the one away from the former and give it to the one who already has ten. It goes against the grain, simply because we have failed to see how important God views our use of what He has given us.

USE IT OR LOSE IT

Despite our preconceived attitudes toward social justice, God's Law of Use controls the ultimate distribution of wealth. We must be willing to take the world as He made it and live in it to the fullest. For He says, in fact, that if we are willing to do that—if we are willing to use what He has given us—we will have more. But if we are not willing to use what He has given us, we will lose it.

As we will see, this is not mean or unfair. It is the way *God* wants the world to be. And as we begin to understand the Law of Use, we will soon realize that this is the only way it can be.

Our bodies give us a perfect illustration of the working of the Law of Use. For instance, let's say you would like to learn to do push-ups. Perhaps you've never been able to do them well.

I will assume the Lord has given you the strength to do one, perhaps only the kind from the knees, but you can do that. And so you take what you have, and you put it to work. Do one a day for a week or two and before long you'll find it's not hard. Then go to two, and do two for a week or two. They'll get easier, and then you can move to three, and so on. Before long you'll be doing ten, and you'll start to wonder, "Why did I think these were so hard?"

Do you see the same principle? To everyone who has, and who uses what he has, more shall be given.

Now, you could do the very opposite. You could take what you have, refuse to use it, and ultimately lose it. For instance, you could tape your hand to your side in such a way that you would be unable to move it. If you left it there, totally unused, for six months, the muscles would wither and an arm that had had unlimited potential would be useless. Even what you had would have been taken away.

The same would hold true for the development of your mind and resultant skills. If you were a doctor and wanted to master a particular type of treatment, you would begin simply with the knowledge you had. You could study everything available, and you could practice your knowledge, simply at first, perhaps under close supervision. You could stay at it for a year or two and before long, you would master the subject. You would have expertise and a specialty that others would covet, all acquired through using what you already had.

Of course, if you thoroughly neglected study and abstained totally from practice, you would gradually reach a point of deterioration and incompetence where no one would want to trust himself in your hands. You would lose what you started with.

So also in our spiritual lives. If we pray, read the Bible, and exercise the understanding we already have, we will grow. If we don't, we will weaken and diminish in effectiveness.

CARVER AND THE PEANUT

One of the geniuses of our country was the son of a slave, a black educator and botanist named George Washington Carver. He perfectly illustrated the Law of Use in a different fashion.

Carver was an agricultural chemist and researcher, and he suspected that there were many wonderful treasures still hidden in God's kingdom. So, the story goes, one day Carver went before the Lord in prayer and said, "Mr. Creator, show me the secrets of Your universe."

It was a big request, but he believed in asking boldly.

He received a bold answer, although it might not have seemed so at first.

"Little man," God said, "you're not big enough to know the secrets of My universe."

One can almost feel the sense of repudiation. However, God was not finished with His reply. "But I'll show you the secret of the peanut."

From the universe to the peanut! "Take it apart," God said.

Undaunted and obedient, Carver did just that. He took the peanut apart and discovered several hundred elements in that little seed and its shell.

Still God wasn't finished. "Start putting it back together again, in different form," the Lord instructed.

He did. And from that work came food of many kinds, plastics, paint, oil, and seemingly endless products. He revolutionized Southern agriculture and industry just by using what God had given him—boldly, creatively, patiently.

THE EXPONENTIAL CURVE

Working hand in hand with the Law of Use is a mathematical phenomenon known as the exponential curve. Actually Jesus set forth the first step in such a curve when He told the parable of the talents. It fits perfectly into our principle. The Lord told how two of the servants doubled what had been given to them. Had they done that at regular intervals, such as annually, then their increases, placed on a graph, would have established an exponential curve that would have proved astounding.

For example, if they began with $100 and continued to double the amount each year, the graph would proceed along a rather ho-hum level for a few years and then it would skyrocket. At the end of twenty years, the $100 would have grown to $50 million. In just five more years, it would have soared to $1.6 billion. By the thirty-five-year mark, it would be $1.6 trillion, and at the end of fifty years, it would be $12.8 quadrillion, which is more money than exists in the world.

This shows dramatically what can happen through a joining of the Law of Use with the exponential curve, simply accomplishing at a set rate what Jesus was teaching in the parable.

Of course, such 100 percent increases are not necessary for the exponential curve to be effective with this law. Take the $100 and compound it at 6 percent for fifty years and it is transformed into nearly $2,800. Increase the percentage to 15 or 20 percent and you end up with several hundred thousand dollars.

So phenomenal is this principle that Baron Rothschild, the financier, once described compound interest as "the eighth wonder of the world." Bankers throughout history have enriched themselves enormously by way of this "wonder." The key is consistency and longevity, to the point where the exponential curve makes its sharp upward turn, and the escalation defies the imagination.

I was in Zaire in June 1991, addressing a group of government leaders. I wanted to explain these principles as clearly and as memorably as possible, so I took hundred dollar bills and gave one to each member of the cabinet. I told them, "You now have in your hand the wealth of the world." Then I explained to them how it works. I said that at the end of fifty years, if the money in their hands doubled every year, they would have $12.8 quadrillion.

"You'll have more money than there is in the world today," I told them. "On the other hand, I said, if you start out with all the money in the world and continue to live under 230 percent inflation, you'll be back to a hundred dollars in just thirty-two years. You can take all the money in the world and reduce it to a hundred dollars if you allow the economy to stagnate. If you tolerate the kind of inflation you have in this country today, the only possible result is absolute and total collapse."

I am sorry to say that they didn't listen to me. I said, "If you don't stop printing money, you're going to have riots, looting, and violence in the streets." Within three months inflation had gotten so bad that the army revolted and did more than a billion dollars' worth of damage. There was killing, bloodshed, and devastation, and it all came, just as I had said, within three months.

DEALING WITH REALITY

But we need to understand that the secret of growth applies in every area. It applies in areas such as church growth just as much as it does to individual, family, corporate, or any other kind of growth. These laws apply wherever people work for specific goals.

It says, "unto him who has, more will be given." The principle exploded for good with our Project Light initiative. I had visited Nicaragua, El Salvador, and Guatemala. I saw the beginning of a powerful spiritual revival. Then I realized the mass communications expertise our organization had accumulated during thirty years of intensive use. We were experts in television, radio, film, arts, billboards, printing, and mass marketing.

So I challenged our staff to assemble all of these skills for one massive media blitz in Central America. We called it *Projecto Luz* ("Project Light"). And blitz we did. As a result we had the largest television audience in the history of those nations, and 3 million people made decisions to accept Jesus Christ as their Savior. It was amazing, and it was thrilling, but it was the result of the application of the Law of Use. We had worked with what we had, allowing God to multiply our efforts.

As I have said before, I only had seventy dollars in my pocket when we started CBN. But I used what I had, and God blessed it beyond measure. Now we operate in seventy nations, and just one division, Operation Blessing, has had the joy of giving $340 million to the poor and needy over the past fourteen years. This is no boast; it is merely evidence that we have discovered, firsthand, that God's law of growth and development really works!

Certainly, the Lord Jesus did not intend to lay down for us a principle whose purpose was to allow the rich to get richer and the poor to get poorer. No, He was showing how the world works and how, through the diligent, patient exercise of the gifts He is constantly bestowing, we can enter into the prosperity and abundance of the invisible world.

We need to see that the truths He disclosed are available to everyone—now. The sad fact is that not everyone—not even those committed to Him—will enter in. We are too much like the servant who took his talent and buried it.

THE POLITICS OF ENVY

The problem often is that we will look at someone who's successful in a field where we would like to be, and we say, "I wish I were like him." We want to have the success without having applied the Law of Use and the exponential curve. We want to go from obscurity and poverty to fame and riches in one quick jump, without realizing that we have to first take what God has given us and then multiply it, steadily and patiently. If we do in accordance with His will, success will come.

To want full accomplishment immediately is lust. It is a sin and calls for a violation of the pattern of God. It is wanting something for nothing. Socialism and communism feed on such lust, calling for taking from the rich and giving to the poor, for leveling society in such a way as to deprive individuals of the learning and maturity necessary to handle abundance. It is characterized by demagoguery and the politics of envy.

So many well-meaning people have in fact done harm to individuals and indeed to nations by short-cutting God's plan and short-circuiting the blessings intended. They want to give everything to everyone immediately, not only stirring up lust, but also fulfilling it, and ultimately harming those they want to help.

FROM SMALL SEEDS

God's way is the way of gradual, sure growth and maturity, moving toward perfection. It can be compared to an airplane during takeoff. If the trajectory is too low, then time will overtake it; the plane will run out of runway and crash, or it will get a few feet off the ground and not rise fast enough to avoid the trees or buildings.

People are the same. If their goals are too low, too stretched out and easy, they will never rise to any significant potential before time overtakes them.

On the other hand, if the pilot sets his angle of climb at takeoff too high and the plane rises steeply too soon, it is likely to stall and crash.

The same is true with people. Set your economic growth too high, and you will stall; try to make your child learn too much too fast, and he will become discouraged and give up; try to do fifty push-ups without practice, and you will encounter agony.

Thus, although there is nothing but abundance in the kingdom of heaven and nothing is impossible with God, the Lord's plan is for us to set realistic goals with what He has given us. He wants us to have goals that are demanding enough to keep us occupied, but are not overtaxing, and to stick with them long enough for them to come to fruition. The key is to set a percentage to add to your performance each day, week, month, or year and then let God's Law of Use take you to undreamed of heights of achievement and blessing.

We find clues to this in other parables of the Lord.

> Then Jesus told another story: "The kingdom of heaven is like a mustard seed that a man planted in his field. That seed is the smallest of all seeds, but when it grows, it is one of the largest garden plants. It becomes big enough for the wild birds to come and build nests in its branches."

The black mustard of the East starts with the tiniest seed imaginable, but from that tiny beginning comes a strong plant often running to heights as tall as a man on horseback. The grown plant is tens of thousands of times as big as the seed from which it began. Remember the Christian church, which started with just one tiny baby in an obscure stable, now numbers nearly 2 billion members.

Similarly Jesus told of what might be called unconscious growth from small beginnings:

> Then Jesus said, "The kingdom of God is like someone who plants seed in the ground. Night and day, whether the person is asleep or awake, the seed still grows, but the person does not know how it grows. By itself the earth produces grain. First the plant grows, then the head, and then all the grain in the head. When the grain is ready, the farmer cuts it, because this is the harvest time."

We must never despise or be impatient with small beginnings. The increase will come, almost unconsciously, imperceptibly, in the early stages, but suddenly there will be a burst of growth as the exponential rate takes hold and reaches maturity. Before long, it's harvest time.

Remember, everyone has some talent. With some, it's music. With some, it's athletics. With some, it's technical skill. Even a quadriplegic confined to bed cannot feel left out of this marvelous principle. Perhaps more important than anything else, he can consistently exercise the great gift of prayer, maturing to remarkable spiritual depths and affecting the entire world.

TOUCHING THE FAMILY

Families in the world are in crisis, but an understanding of the Law of Use can help dramatically.

One of the most serious problems confronting families is the lack of even growth and shared interests between spouses. Many couples begin life fresh out of school and with few material possessions. Then one spouse, typically the husband, begins to grow intellectually, profession- ally, and financially. His interests and scope grow little by little until after ten or fifteen years he is a different person. His wife, on the other hand, does not read, does not learn, and does not grow intellectually or socially. She is still the sweet girl he married, but he is no longer the young man she married. He wants to share his life with her, but she is now incapable of doing so. Often she will become jealous and resentful of her husband's new interests and circle of friends. As she becomes withdrawn and hostile, he begins to seek companionship with someone more compatible—with a physical relationship that is often the consequence of such shifts in interest. We say that they have grown apart. Indeed they have. Separation and divorce are often not far behind.

In today's world, women often become the professional achievers and grow ahead of their husbands. The same problems develop, but the roles are reversed.

Both spouses must exert an effort to grow spiritually, intellectually, and socially during their marriages. Each must ensure that he or she, in addition to his or her own personal role, keeps up with the interests and growth of the mate.

This is not an invitation to competition and rivalry, but an admonition to complement one another. Marriage is a shared life between two people. To build a life together, they must grow as individuals so that they can grow together as a couple.

Financial pressures are second only to the lack of communications in undermining marriages. Couples must establish early on in their marriage the Law of Reciprocity and the Law of Use. If they are faithful in giving to God's work, not only will He "open the windows of heaven and pour them out a blessing," but He will also "rebuke the destroyer" for their sake. In other words income will come, and the tragic outlays caused by accidents and sickness will not come.

Second, they must establish a budget that not only causes them to live within their income but also contributes to a modest and regular program of savings and investment. Then their marriage will not be torn apart because they are having to work and slave to pay usurious interest rates to credit card companies and merchants. Instead, they will have the shared joy of knowing that their little nest egg is growing at an exponential rate which will either permit a comfortable retirement or the acquisition of things that will enrich their lives and the lives of their children. Instead of working for money, they will have money working for them.

Not only will such stable families help stabilize our nation by reducing health costs, welfare costs, and delinquency, this pool of savings brought about by a nation of savers rather than a nation of consumers will enable businesses to find capital at lower rates to create jobs, which in turn will create more revenues so that we can have government services without crippling deficits.

It is all so simple, but it is true because it comes from God, and it works.

WRONG SIDE OF THE CURVE

Human tragedy occurs when people get on the wrong side of the exponential curve, which can work against us as well as for us. Both individuals and nations can be its victims.

The United States and many of its citizens are prime examples. Singly and collectively we have allowed the exponential curve to plunge us into enormous debt. In most cases, the beginnings were innocent, but the exponential rate is merciless if it's working against you. It can destroy people who borrow money at high interest rates. Obviously, vast numbers of Americans are caught in such debt traps right now, and our government is the worst offender.

Consider the facts. From our early beginnings as a nation until 1981, a period of 205 years, the United States accumulated a debt burden of $1 trillion. Then as exponential compounding kicked in with a vengeance, the total jumped to $2 trillion in just 5 years, then $3 trillion in 4 years, then $4 trillion in a bit more than 2 years. Think of it: in 11 years we have accumulated three times the debt accumulation of the preceding 205 years of our history. At those rates our total stated national debt will be $10 trillion by the year 2000 and interest alone at that time may well approach $1 trillion every year! It doesn't take a genius to determine that our currency will lose its value, prices will skyrocket, and somewhere there will either be a dramatic crash or a massive repudiation of debt. All because as a nation we violated God's Law of Use.

Private and public debt usually comes from an inability to defer gratification. It comes from lust and covetousness, the insistence on having everything now. "I want my furniture now," the housewife cries. Meanwhile her husband demands his new, bigger car—now. Neither wants to await the accumulation of the resources necessary to avoid sending compound interest careening into action. On a wider scale, our national attitude views many luxuries as necessities. We override the Law of Use when we attempt to put the biggest, most modern television sets and gadgetry in every house and apartment through consumer debt or even through welfare laws. The national debt soars, credit card bills reach astronomical heights, and the exponential curve zooms upward to hopelessness and collapse.

Jesus Himself, coming in the flesh as man and suffering temptation just as we do, ran into a test on this score early in His public ministry. It came during His temptation in the wilderness: "Again, the devil took Him to a very high mountain, and showed Him all the kingdoms of the world, and their glory; and he said to Him, 'All these things will I give You, if You fall down and worship me.'"[6]

Satan, described in the New Testament as "the ruler of the world" (although destined to be cast out),[7] promised Him everything, right then, if He would just do it his way. But the Lord said He would do it God's way—gradually, the way of sacrifice and suffering, the way of work, the way of the cross.

The law of Satan's kingdom is: Have it now, with a splash. Quick money, quick things, quick success.

THE KEY TO SECURITY

In God's kingdom, the Law of Use governs, providing genuine and lasting security, genuine and lasting prosperity.

Because of the power of the Law of Use and the exponential curve—along with man's seemingly incurable weaknesses—God many centuries ago established two rules for the people of Israel of which we should be aware.

First, He decreed that the Israelites were not to take usury of one another: "You shall not charge interest to your countrymen: interest on money, food, or anything that may be loaned at interest."[8]

They were permitted to charge interest to foreigners, which would agree with the parable of the talents in the New Testament, apparently because the Lord intended to give the Jews dominance over other nations: "For the LORD your God shall bless you as He has promised you, and *you will lend to many nations*, but you will not borrow; and *you will rule over many nations*, but they will not rule over you."[9]

Modern experience has shown that usury ultimately leads to subservience, and God did not want that for His people, but rather intended for them to rule.

Second, God set up a year of jubilee for His people to counteract the fact that through the compounding of debt a few eventually gain control of all wealth and land. In short, He directed that every fifty years all debt be canceled, all accumulated property be redistributed, and the cycle of use begin again.

It was part of His marvelous plan under which the land would have a sabbath year to the Lord. For six years, the land would be worked, "but during the seventh year the land shall have a sabbath rest, a sabbath to the LORD."[10] Then He laid out the jubilee plan:

> You are also to count off seven sabbaths of years for yourself, seven times seven years, so that you have the time of the seven sabbaths of years, namely, forty-nine years. You shall then sound a ram's horn abroad on the tenth day of the seventh month; on the day of atonement you shall sound a horn all through your land. You shall thus consecrate the fiftieth year and *proclaim a release through the land* to all its inhabitants. It shall be a jubilee for you, and each of you shall return . . . to his family.[11]

The "release" or "liberty" was multifaceted and touched much of the life of the Israelites, specifically through the cancellation of indebtedness. It was as though God said to a man who perhaps was twenty at the beginning of the cycle and who is now seventy: "You had your day in the sun, your time of opportunity, so now you should step aside, cancel the debts, and let people start over again."

I believe it is quite possible that the year of jubilee will be the only way out, short of collapse for our world in its current economic slide. The United States government, and indeed all governments, have gotten on the wrong side of the exponential curve and the Law of Use and have reached the point of insupportable debt. Trying to meet the demands of the people who are screaming "We want it now!" the governments, along with individuals, are running major deficits, borrowing huge sums of money, always at compound interest. By 1991, the estimated worldwide total of public and private debt was in excess of $25.6 trillion. In fact, I observed in the *Weiss Money & Markets* a 1992 estimate of an astounding $50 trillion debt worldwide. Interest payments have reached the point where some nations can no longer meet them.

Notwithstanding the sneers of many in the banking community, it may be that God's way will be the only one open to us—a year of jubilee to straighten out the mess.

We should also be fully aware of the fact that finance is not the only area in which the exponential curve can work against us. We need only look at the snowballing evils of pornography, adultery, divorce, alcoholism, and drug addiction to grasp this. Such evil began small and steadily increased, almost unconsciously it seems, until the unprecedented surge of recent years and today's raging flood tide.

THE MOST POWERFUL PRINCIPLE

In the previous chapter, I said the Law of Reciprocity was probably the most encompassing of the kingdom principles, virtually undergirding every aspect of life and revealing a course of conduct that could change the world.

The Law of Use, meanwhile, coupled with the exponential curve, is probably the most powerful of the principles in terms of day-to-day life. It is the fundamental law for the growth and development—or the decline—of all organizations and societies in both the invisible and the visible worlds. Beginning with the cradle, it touches everything—child development, intellectual development, professional development, physical development, social development, and on and on.

Together the Law of Reciprocity and the Law of Use are the core of the way the world works, the invisible world and the visible one.

We have already explored major areas touched by the Law of Use and the exponential curve, but we need to see the never-ending, ever-increasing potential. There is, in fact, a principle of increasing opportunity. For example, the man with $100 has certain vistas of opportunity before him. By applying the Law of Use, he can increase that sum to $1,000, and immediately his opportunities for expanded use of the law are increased. Quite simply, the man with $1,000 has more clout than the man with $100.

If he presses on with the Law of Use, he will rise to the $10,000 level and his vistas widen; then $100,000 and he finds bank doors and credit open to him that he hadn't dreamed of. A million dollars opens an entirely new class of opportunity, and so it goes—never-ending opportunity for the person involved in the Law of Use.

I found that the broadcasting world follows the same principle. To him who is faithful in a little will more be given. When we owned five stations we had a far easier time acquiring a sixth than the person just starting out has in acquiring his first. A five-station owner is experienced and knowledgeable. He knows when and how to move. He has access to money markets that the inexperienced, struggling beginner lacks.

So it is with people in science. The one who has mastered fundamental and intermediate theorems is far more capable of going on to an advanced theorem than is the youngster who hasn't had his first high school science course.

In politics, the person who has successfully run for a city council seat is more likely to succeed in a race for mayor than someone who is unknown and untested. The mayor is then in a stronger position to move to the state legislature than the beginner, and on up the line to governor, senator, and perhaps president.

The same holds true for spiritual life. The opportunities steadily increase as we move from one level of understanding and maturity to the next. Mastery of one small principle of faith opens up new horizons for even wider growth. Prayer and intercession for our families build us up for prayer and intercession for our church, and then our town, our state, and our nation. Similarly, public ministry to fifty people will open opportunities for ministry to one hundred. We are then far better prepared to minister to one thousand, then ten thousand, then twenty thousand.

No, we are not to despise small beginnings, but rather to exercise the eternally established Law of Use.

I am convinced that this law—put to work with the commitment, the virtues, and the accompanying subprinciples—can produce giant steps toward easing and ultimately removing the crises that grip the world. It will touch world hunger, the economic quagmire, energy depletion, Third World needs, educational and social injustice, church evangelism, moral decadence, disease, and inadequate health care.

The only thing lacking is for us to hear with understanding the words spoken by God to Moses regarding the sanctuary Israel was to construct for the Lord: "According to all that I am going to show you, as the *pattern* of the tabernacle and the *pattern* of all its furniture, just so *you shall construct it.*"[12]

"Do it MY way," says the Lord. He has given a pattern for the secret kingdom. We merely need to follow it.

9

The Law of Perseverance

As WE MOVE on from the Law of Use, I want to be sure that we understand that success in this life comes through industry. By industry I mean those traits of character such as dedication, commitment, patience, self-discipline, and hard work that bring positive results—in short, perseverance. So to prepare the way for what follows, we need to examine this next principle, the *Law of Perseverance,* and how it relates to each of the other kingdom principles.

We caught glimpses of this law in previous chapters, but we need to see clearly that the ways of the universe yield to perseverance. God does not give the good things of this world to those who will not work. There are times when, in His grace, He may just hand us something, for whatever reason. Sometimes in His favor, God brings unexpected, perhaps even undeserved, blessings into our life. But no one who is successful can afford to stand around and do nothing while waiting for such a gift. God never rewards sloth and indolence.

When Jesus told his followers to "keep on asking," as we will see in the following pages, He meant that they were to be persistent in their endeavors. If we are persistent, if we keep on asking, and if we keep on knocking, the doors will eventually be opened. But we must keep on until they do.

Anyone working in sales can tell you that sometimes it takes five or six calls in order to close a sale. If you are doubtful, unprepared, and easily defeated, you will not make that sale. But if you are prepared and persistent, sooner or later you will succeed. So, in addition to all the other positive values needed for doing anything successfully, there has to be effort and perseverance.

We see this principle in the homey story of the chicken and the egg. The baby chick, still living in his shell, finds himself in a nice, safe environment, dark and quiet. For a period of time his home, the egg, keeps him warm and cozy; everything is more or less perfect.

Soon, however, the chick becomes aware that the shell keeping him so comfortable and safe is also circumscribing his life. He begins to feel restricted. He is growing by the hour, and the egg is not as pleasant as it once was.

You see, there is something in life that says, "I have to grow." Every living thing on this planet is designed to grow; that's the way we are made. Humans and animals have within them an inborn need to grow and develop their full potential.

So the little chick begins pecking at the shell. He doesn't understand it, but things have been set up so that he has to peck and peck and peck. He works very hard, gaining strength hour by hour from that God-ordained struggle. Before long, he has attained the strength and the endurance to cope with a new environment, and he breaks through the shell. He pecks some more, and soon he is free, ready for a new level of life.

People have tried to help little chicks speed the process of cracking the shell and opening it for them. But if they try to short-circuit God's process, they will kill the chicks. They are stillborn, unable to handle for even a few moments the rigors of their new environment.

POSITIVE SIGNALS

Supporting each of these various keys of the kingdom is the understanding that everything in this world is controlled by spirit. For God Himself is spirit, and through the spirit He controls everything that is. He created the earth, the universe, and everything that is in them. Paul tells us that Jesus Christ, the Son of God, was at work in the creation, and that He was the agent of creation. He says:

> For by Him all things were created that are in heaven and that are on earth, visible and invisible, whether thrones or dominions or principalities or powers. All things were created through Him and for Him.[1]

Spirit is the ultimate power of the universe. The spirit can transmit the messages of God, or your own messages, to the mind; and it is mind that controls the events of nature and the world around you. And as I said briefly in chapter 4, in such matters a positive mental attitude is absolutely essential.

The way you transmit the thoughts in your mind is twofold. First, we have, in effect, an AM/FM transmitter in our brains that can send out impulses around us. Second, we can also speak the word out of our mouths and transmit the voice of spirit into the material world. Does this sound incredible?

Admittedly, certain New Age teachers have attempted to appropriate some of these Bible truths and apply them to their own false doctrines. Over the years, a number of authors have written popular secular books on these ideas. But that does not limit their application and value for the believer in Jesus Christ. These truths are eternal laws of the kingdom, and even if New Age mystics and gurus attempt to pirate what rightfully belongs to God's people, we should not allow them to damage or discredit what is rightfully ours.

Still, if this sounds too metaphysical or strange for you, please recall the apostle's words when he wrote:

> . . . we do not look at the things which are seen, but at the things which are not seen. For the things which are seen are temporary, but the things which are not seen are eternal.[2]

In the creation, God had a creative thought transmitted and empowered by the Spirit. By the spoken Word God said, "Let there be light," and it was so. That's the way He brought the world into existence. He has given us a portion of this same power in our daily lives. Here's how it works. If you think failure, impossibility, and negative thoughts, then you will indeed forecast your own failure. You will have what you say and what you think. You transmit failure to yourself, to other people, and to the world around you. Furthermore, your negative message will be transmitted to angels and demons, which are very real (though unseen) beings in our midst. But if you transmit faith, hope, and love, you will be sending a very different message.

THE SOURCE OF POWER

Paul said, "I can do all things through Him who strengthens me."[3] He spoke positive words. He said: "we are more than conquerors through Him who loved us."[4] Paul's own spirit was indomitable; his mind was full of the thoughts of God; his voice spoke forth faith and conviction. "Be anxious for nothing," he said, "but in everything by prayer and supplication, with thanksgiving, let your requests be made known to God; and the peace of God, which surpasses all understanding, will guard your hearts and minds through Christ Jesus."[5]

Compare that to someone who says, "I just can't do it. I've tried everything and nothing works. I can't do mathematics; I can't make sales; I can't hold a job; I can't make a go of my family. The whole world is against me. It's not what you know, it's who you know that counts. I'm a born loser." How can anyone hope to succeed with such destructive attitudes? That kind of thinking is a self-fulfilling prophecy for failure.

On the other hand, enthusiasm is contagious, and if you believe in the future, if you have faith, and if you are enthusiastic about what is to come, other people will catch that spirit. They will want to participate. In reality, they sense the spirit of God within you, and suddenly the Red Sea begins to part, Pharaoh lifts you out of prison and puts you in charge of things, and miracles begin to happen because you are sensing God's favor; you have humbled yourself before the Lord, and you have followed the principles of the kingdom. Suddenly your mind is filled with unlimited possibilities.

This is the attitude you must have for financial success; this is how you begin to approach the world. If you know Jesus Christ as your Savior, you have the ultimate hope. Your spirit lives forever; you are, at this moment, a child of the kingdom, and you will not see death.

In Christ you have new life. Jesus said, "I have come that they may have life, and that they may have it more abundantly."[6] Jesus did not bring us a spirit of defeat or despair, but of victory and hope. Are you certain that you are living in this kingdom? Are you a child of God?

If you are not certain of your eternal hope in Christ Jesus, I would invite you now to claim Him by simple faith as your Savior. Trust Him now and be certain that you are a member of this dynamic kingdom. Its privileges and promises—and, yes, its demands—are yours as you enter into a new relationship with God and discover the new freedom He offers.

THE RISKS OF FREEDOM

These are elements of what I call the Law of Perseverance. It is critical to success in life generally and to life in the kingdom especially.

But certain risks go with new life and growth—the risks of freedom, we might say—but God prepares us for those risks, through perseverance and struggle, building our muscles, as it were, for each new phase. To refuse to struggle is to stand still, to stagnate.

Jesus taught the Law of Perseverance in a passage well known to most Christians:

> Ask, and it shall be given to you; seek, and you shall find; knock, and it shall be opened to you. For every one who asks receives, and he who seeks finds, and to him who knocks it shall be opened. Or what man is there among you, when his son shall ask him for a loaf, will give him a stone? Or if he shall ask for a fish, he will not give him a snake, will he? If you then, being evil, know how to give good gifts to your children, how much more shall your Father who is in heaven give what is good to those who ask Him?"[7]

We grasp His meaning more fully when we understand that the verbs "asks," "seeks," and "knocks" were written in the Greek present imperative and are to be understood in this manner: "*Keep asking,* and it shall be given to you; *keep seeking,* and you shall find; *keep knocking,* and it shall be opened to you." The Father gives "what is good to those who *keep asking Him.*"

He also said, as we have noted, that "the kingdom of heaven suffers violence, and violent men take it by force."[8] It does not come easily. The little chick we spoke of was violent, he had to be. Most of the secrets of God come forth with effort; the blessings of God are the same.

Some Christians have been taught that all one has to do to get things from God is to speak the word of faith, believe, and receive. That comes close to the truth, but it neglects the universal Law of Perseverance. God slowly yields the good things of the kingdom and the world to those who struggle. Jacob, for instance, wrestled all night with an angel before he became Israel, a prince with God. Abraham waited a hundred years before he received Isaac, the child of promise. The people of Judah waited and struggled seventy years in captivity before God brought them home.

THE NECESSITY OF FAITH

This does not negate the necessity for asking in faith, the believing, and the receiving. But many times those steps are only the beginning of the process. The fulfillment may take years.

Jesus gave this illustration of perseverance:

> Now He was telling them a parable to show that at all times they ought to pray and not to lose heart, saying, "There was in a certain city a judge who did not fear God, and did not respect man. And there was a widow in that city, and she kept coming to him saying, 'Give me legal protection from my opponent.' And for a while he was unwilling; but afterward he said to himself, 'Even though I do not fear God nor respect man, yet because this widow bothers me, I will give her legal protection, lest by continually

coming she wear me out.'" And the Lord said, "Hear what the unrighteous judge said; now shall not God bring about justice for His elect, who cry to Him day and night, and will He delay long over them? I tell you that He will bring about justice for them speedily. However, when the Son of Man comes, will He find faith on the earth?"[9]

Jesus knew men inside out. He knew our tendency to give up quickly, to become inconsistent and lackadaisical. Yet He pleaded with us to persist, in prayer and in all aspects of life.

And He said to them, "Suppose one of you shall have a friend, and shall go to him at midnight, and say to him, 'Friend, lend me three loaves; for a friend of mine has come to me from a journey, and I have nothing to set before him'; and from inside he shall answer and say, 'Do not bother me; the door has already been shut and my children and I are in bed; I cannot get up and give you anything.' I tell you, even though he will not get up and give him anything because he is his friend, yet because of his persistence he will get up and give him as much as he needs."[10]

Keep on asking, He said, keep on seeking, and keep on knocking. Don't be afraid even to make a ruckus. God prefers persistence much more than slothfulness and indolence. He wants people who will travail and perhaps stumble a bit, but keep on going forward, just like a toddler who's trying to learn to walk. The child builds muscles and learns. One day he will run.

STRENGTH THROUGH TESTING

In the early, trying days of the church, according to the Book of Acts, Paul and Barnabas traveled through Lystra, Iconium, and Antioch "strengthening the souls of the disciples, encouraging them to continue in the faith, and saying, 'Through many tribulations we must enter the kingdom of God.'"[11]

There was to be conflict, they said, using a word that most translators have rendered "tribulation" but which carries the idea of "pressure," especially pressure on the spirit. This pressure, or tribulation, was understood in New Testament times to build stamina and staying power, leading to fullness of character.

We are to remember that there is an adversary. He is called Satan. One of his favorite techniques is the unrelenting effort to trip the people of God to foster discouragement and depression. That is why the Bible says repeatedly that Christians are to be patient, to hold on, to persist.

Satan is continuously pouring into our ears such negatives as these: "You're not accomplishing anything. . . . You're on the wrong course. . . .

You don't have the necessary skill and ability. . . . Everyone else has failed so why do you think you'll succeed? . . . Those promises you thought were from God are nothing. . . . You're unworthy. . . ."

So we often grow discouraged and quit. Then the principles of the kingdom cease to function in our lives. And we fail.

The ultimate personal failure, of course, is suicide. It is the number two killer of our nation's youth, next to automobile accidents. So many people have given up in hopelessness, finding their problems overwhelming, the world a mess beyond repair, the possibilities of life too dark. And they slip into the horror of taking their lives, which truly are not theirs to take.

Even the great prophet Elijah reached such despair. Having experienced one of his great triumphs, the defeat of the priests of Baal through a powerful miracle of God, he obviously was exhausted mentally, emotionally, and physically. Jezebel was trying to kill him. He fell into gloom.

"It is enough . . . ," he cried out. "O LORD, take my life, for I am not better than my fathers."[12]

But God would not let him give up. Neither does He want us to quit.

Instead, we are to be constantly alert against discouragement and depression. We are to be aware of what our enemy is trying to do. We are to reject him and he will flee. God will not let trial and temptation overcome us if we will stand, but rather will make a way of victory for us.[13] He wants us to persevere and will make it possible.

Remember that the Law of Use and the exponential curve will bring wealth, physical strength, spiritual growth, expanded knowledge, organizational growth, and national prosperity. But none of these things will happen unless we persevere long enough for the blessing to be realized. How many overweight people begin a sensible weight-loss plan that is guaranteed to give them a slimmer body only to quit after three or four weeks? How many people began a modest savings plan that compounded could yield them a million dollars in thirty years only to withdraw their savings to buy a stereo or an automobile? How many gifted children with the potential to be leaders drop out of school or lack the perseverance necessary to work through college and graduate school? How many gifted musicians never progress because they refuse the daily discipline of practice? How many treadmills and exercise machines that would bring physical vitality and strength gather dust in spare rooms and garages because of lack of perseverance?

God's tangible blessings are there for all. But only those willing to persevere in their exercise will receive them.

LESSONS OF HISTORY

Had God given us no more insight than the Law of Perseverance together with the Laws of Reciprocity and Use, we would have enough to change the world. We need only think of examples from our own national history.

Consider Abraham Lincoln. He became one of the greatest governmental and moral leaders in American history. But the achievements didn't come until he had passed through many personal failures, including bankruptcies and endless humiliating labors to make ends meet. The struggles, the battles, the wounds—they equipped him for the environment in which he would make his greatest contribution.

Consider Thomas Edison. This greatest of inventors went through hundreds of experiments that were failures before he achieved success with the electric light. He attributed his incredible accomplishments to "2 percent inspiration and 98 percent perspiration"—a formula for struggle and perseverance.

Consider the Wright Brothers. On the lonely sands of North Carolina's outer banks, they battled the elements, the ridicule of men, the lack of resources. They built; they failed; they rebuilt and failed again. Finally, they flew, and the world was forever changed.

In my own life's work, through the grace of God, I learned the centrality of perseverance. In 1959 my family and I arrived in Tidewater with seventy dollars and a God-planted desire to establish a broadcasting ministry that would glorify the Lord. We went through two years of personal and corporate struggle before getting on the air with our first station. Them came ten more years of striving, anguish, and hardship before we obtained our second station. Steadily the growth increased as we persevered and learned the lessons of the kingdom.

In that pressure cooker, which in so many ways resembled the trials of the chick with the egg, we matured to the point of readiness for a worldwide ministry. With hindsight, it is amusing to note how the Lord forced us to use everything He had given us to its very limit before He provided something new. Before establishing us in our new Virginia Beach international center, He had us using every nook and cranny of space available to us. We had trailers lined up all over the land, jammed with people and activity. We had rented property all over Tidewater, taxing our ingenuity and patience daily. Through it all, we were getting ready for the next phase of our work; we were being strengthened for a new environment and new challenges. We were getting maturity the only way a Christian can get it.

In 1979, I examined CBN's history and found that in those twenty years, the Lord had taken our initial seventy dollars and caused it to double exponentially every year during that time. By sheer mercy and grace, He had led us in the Laws of Reciprocity, Use, and Perseverance.

Had He led us otherwise, dumping on us too quickly the responsibility for a worldwide ministry and budgets of tens of millions of dollars, we would have crumbled. But He is wise enough to lead His people according to His laws even before we are able to know and articulate them.

As the great Bible teacher Donald Gray Barnhouse put it, "God uses oak trees, not mushrooms." Are not perseverance and strength the great virtues of oak trees?

10

The Law of Responsibility

A PERSON, A business, a charity, or a nation that diligently and conscientiously applies the Laws of Reciprocity, Use, and Perseverance must succeed. There will be prosperity, strength, and blessing. The consequence of following the laws of the kingdom are inexorable. The results over time are nothing short of incredible.

But did God put His laws in the universe so that men might head up boundless riches for their own pleasure, or have muscles like Arnold Schwarzenegger for men and women to admire, or have wisdom like Edison to gain popular acclaim, or be a famous and powerful world leader for the purpose of controlling others? Of course not.

Jesus made it clear that with the blessings also come responsibilities. He summed it up succinctly: "unto whomsoever much is given, of him shall much be required: and to whom men have committed much, of him they will ask the more."[1]

Using a parable on watchfulness and preparation, He made clear that rejection of this law leads to suffering. Those who are given understanding, ability, goods, money, authority, or fame have a responsibility that the less favored do not bear; failure to fulfill it produces fearful punishment.[2]

Jesus was precise in showing that the parable was for the favored in every category, spiritual and physical, those living in the invisible world and those living in the visible.

Whatever level of opportunity is given to us, both God and man expect us to give a certain standard of performance. Favor carries with it responsibility. As the favor increases, the responsibility increases.

If, for example, I am the steward of $1,000 for someone, that person may expect a profit of some $100 on his money. But if I am the chairman of multi-billion-dollar General Motors and report a profit of only $100 to the stockholders, I would be forced to resign in disgrace.

If I am a weekend tennis player who manages to win a few games with friends, my friends and I will be satisfied. But if after years of training I have the skill to be ranked first in the world, I must beat the world's best lest the fans, my peers, and the press diminish my stature rapidly and I feel disgraced.

Artur Rubinstein, the great pianist, capsulized this principle when he remarked that should he fail to practice one day, he would know it; should he skip practice for two days, the critics would know it; but should that extend to three days "the whole world knows it." A part-time church pianist might get away with a bit of a let-down, but not an internationally acclaimed musician. More is required of the professional.

Harry Truman said it well when remarking on the burden of the presidency: "If you can't stand the heat, get out of the kitchen." The presidency of the United States carries heavy responsibilities, he related, and if one doesn't want to face the responsibilities, he should not seek the favor of the people in the first place. For, as he said at another time, "There is no end to the chain of responsibility that binds [the president], and he is never allowed to forget that he is president." The sign on his Oval Office desk said, "The buck stops here."

THE BURDEN OF FAVOR

At CBN, we have found the burden of favor to be a responsibility never to be forgotten and never to be neglected. In 1991 CBN telephone counselors received more than 1.5 million calls, most with prayer requests. Of those, 430,130 asked for prayer for healing; 205,343 needed help with finances; 388,913 were having family problems of one kind or another; and more than 3,000 were contemplating suicide. Most exciting was the fact that in the same year 27,000 people called to say they had prayed to receive Christ with the hosts of our "700 Club" broadcast, and another 33,000 prayed for salvation with our phone counselors.

In 1991, CBN International was overwhelmed by the incredible response from people seeking God in countries around the world. In the former Soviet Union, for example, where CBN programming in Russian went out to more than 103 million viewers, more than 20 million viewers prayed with the show's hosts to accept Christ as Savior. Throughout the Commonwealth of Independent States, more than 150 million men, women, and children watched these broadcasts, and more than 30 million accepted Jesus Christ.

Such news is thrilling to anyone who understands what God is accomplishing in the world. But it is also a burden to know that God uses our skills and talents in this way to build His kingdom. I recall my emotions a few years ago when we calculated that we had led seventy-five thousand people to faith in Jesus Christ through CBN. From that point on, there is no way we could be satisfied with leading one thousand people to the Lord. Indeed, one thousand decisions for Christ in one year is a wonderful achievement. But the Lord has given us equipment, personnel, and opportunity, and of those to whom much is given, Scripture tells us, much is required. So we are determined to be faithful to the high calling to which we have been called in Christ.

THE CHURCH MUST LISTEN

Leaders of the church should be especially careful to rise to the responsibility given to them, for the Scripture is so clear on this point as to be somewhat frightening. I am always stopped momentarily when I read the words of James regarding teachers: "Let not many of you become teachers, my brethren, knowing that as such we shall incur a stricter judgment."[3]

Those who have been shown enough to teach can be expected to practice what they teach, at the very least. The office carries a great responsibility.

Paul's letters to Timothy and Titus show the great expectations of God and man from those desiring to be overseers ("bishops" in the older translations).

> What I say is true: Anyone wanting to become an elder desires a good work. An elder must not give people a reason to criticize him, and he must have only one wife. He must be self-controlled, wise, respected by others, ready to welcome guests, and able to teach. He must not drink too much wine or like to fight, but rather be gentle and peaceable, not loving money. He must be a good family leader, having children who cooperate with full respect. (If someone does not know how to lead the family, how can that person take care of God's church?) But an elder must not be a new believer, or he might be too proud of himself and be judged guilty just as the devil was. An elder

must also have the respect of people who are not in the church so he will not be criticized by others and caught in the devil's trap.

He goes on to point out that those seeking the lesser office of deacon, while not required to measure up to the full responsibility of overseer or bishop, must nevertheless bear a burden greater than that of most, first being "tested" and found "beyond reproach."[5]

Christ's first disciples, especially the Twelve, carried extraordinary burdens and responsibilities, as the New Testament shows in detail. They had been "given the mystery of the kingdom of God"[6] by the Lord Himself while others heard only in parables. This great gift, in a sense, carried with it the load of the world, and those apostles paid a great price—ridicule, ostracism, persecution, martyrdom—for the opportunity of spreading the gospel. Their sense of responsibility was always before them. In his letter to the Romans, Paul summed up that responsibility with these words: "I am under obligation both to Greeks and to barbarians, both to the wise and to the foolish."[7]

Even the ordinary, little-known people who have received the inexpressibly rich gift of eternal life—by grace through faith—are called to a life far more responsible and demanding than they led before. Knowing the Lord, who is "the way, and the truth, and the life,"[8] sets a standard for us in the sight of God and people that we should always keep in mind. Paul referred to it as knowing how to conduct yourself "in the household of God, which is the church of the living God, the pillar and support of the truth."[9] It is a significant responsibility each Christian must meet. We need only look at the Great Commission given by Jesus to His people just before His ascension.

> All authority has been given to Me in heaven and on earth. Go therefore and make disciples of all the nations, baptizing them in the name of the Father and the Son and the Holy Spirit, teaching them to observe all that I commanded you.[10]

Even though He had said He Himself would build His church,[11] the responsibility for carrying that plan forward for the entire world was put into the hands of His people. *That* is responsibility.

RANK AND RESPONSIBILITY

Early in the nineteenth century, a French duke, Gaston Pierre Marc, wrote in a collection of *Maxims and Reflections* a two-word statement that has become part of our language: "*Noblesse oblige.*" Despite historical abuses, it expresses the essence of the Law of Responsibility. "Nobility obliges" or, better, "nobility obligates" states the obligation of people of high rank, position, or favor to behave nobly, kindly, and responsibly toward others.

The idea, of course, did not originate with the Frenchman. The ancient Greeks reflected such attitudes in their writings, as shown by Euripides— "The nobly born must nobly meet his fate"[12]—and by Sophocles— "Nobly to live, or else nobly to die, befits proud birth."[13]

Men have known almost instinctively that as accomplishment and position rise, so do responsibility and burden. With each achievement, society raises its expectation a notch.

With the British of the nineteenth century, the concept of *noblesse oblige* reached its zenith, sometimes for good, sometimes for not-so-good. Regardless of mistakes, the British nobility perceived that if they were to have their country houses and servants, their privileges and honors, they in turn had to be responsible for the working people.

In the case of Great Britain as a whole, she felt a responsibility for the entire world, a duty to Pax Britannia—the British peace—on every continent. She called it the burden of empire, sending young men and women to India and the four corners of the earth, challenging any she felt would disrupt the peace of the world.

In a pattern that would be repeated, Russia threatened to enter Afghanistan in the late nineteenth century as a move toward a warm-water port in the Middle East. The British, accepting the responsibility accompanying their position as the world's greatest power, challenged the Russians and prevailed. To them, it was *noblesse oblige*, protecting the people from invaders, pirates, and brigands. To others, it often was unadulterated colonialism, in which people were exploited, confined to subservience and poverty. Both views contained truth. Humility and purity, among other virtues, were lacking. Nonetheless, Victorian Britain instinctively realized that the Law of Responsibility was a foundational corollary to her preeminent position in the nineteenth-century world.

Having witnessed the Soviet invasion and occupation of Afghanistan— during virtually the entire decade of the 1980s—it is fascinating to see what consequences have ultimately befallen these nations. Many have said that, as Vietnam was a fatal stumbling block to American supremacy in the world, so Afghanistan was the ultimate undoing of the Soviet Union. In nine years, the Soviets lost fifteen thousand lives, untold millions of dollars' worth of armaments, equipment, and supplies, and ultimately their prestige and self-confidence.

The lesson of Afghanistan was a bitter and tragic pill for the communists. They did not come responsibly to build up and bring freedom, but to tear down. They gained nothing. The Afghan republic is still splintered and torn by civil war, and within months of the Red Army's retreat from

Kabul, their own government collapsed. God had given the Afghans a somber role in world history for they were, at least in current events, the straw that broke the Soviet camel's back.

THE UNITED STATES FALTERED

Contrasted with the British leaning toward *noblesse oblige* were the frequent failures of responsibility by the government of the United States during the second half of this century. To begin with, Americans during most of their history worked hard under the Law of Use. They were frugal, disciplined, and moral. Furthermore, they persevered, and following World War II became the strongest power on earth. With that stature came responsibility, especially, in my judgment, the responsibility to accomplish two goals: To order the world economy and to keep world peace.

On the first, we began to fail rapidly in the sixties, refusing to measure up to the responsibility. We were profligate in our spending, igniting the time bomb of inflation, which we exported overseas since every other currency was tied into the American dollar. We printed money faster and faster, sending more abroad than we got back through sales of our own goods, eventually reaching a point where more than $600 billion of our money was held in foreign banks. This showed little sense of duty, strength, courage, or determination.

In 1971, shirking our responsibility even more, we went off the gold standard, having little choice in light of overseas claims against our currency. Thus inflation exploded across the world.

Second, as the leader of the free world, we faltered in our duty to lead in keeping the peace. It became especially critical after the Vietnam debacle, in which our course cost us severely in morale, determination, economic strength, and lives of more than fifty-eight thousand valiant youths. From that point on, our neglect went on the downhill slalom. We neglected to keep the peace in Africa, allowing the communist-led world to take several countries in an unprecedented display of international burglary. We allowed similar conduct in Latin America and put up only token resistance as the communists came in to take over and destroy Nicaragua. They tried the same subversion in El Salvador, Honduras, and other countries throughout Central and South America.

All of this merely solidified a trend that had been building momentum since the end of World War II. Although as a nation we have been extraordinarily generous, for many reasons, we Americans seem to have no stomach for the full burden of leadership and responsibility demanded of someone to whom much has been given. We apparently want the position of power but not all the sacrifices of duty that accompany it. Because of historical and cultural factors, we have not developed a national fiber of *noblesse oblige.*

Yet God and man insist on it. The parable told by Jesus about the slave who was made steward over his master's possessions said this about failure to fulfill responsibility: "And that slave who knew his master's will and did not get ready or act in accord with his will, shall receive many lashes."[14]

Despite a certain euphoria over our success in the Persian Gulf, the apparent collapse of Soviet communism, and economic gains in foreign markets, we are experiencing the pains of our neglect and are beleaguered at every turn. We are plagued by insoluble tensions, a persistent recession, constant acrimony and bloody battles between liberal and conservative factions, and an electorate that has lost faith not only in the candidates for public office but in the elective process itself. In the 1990s, the ship of state in America is veering off course, listing under intolerable financial burdens, straining at the mercy of insensitive leaders, and drifting in angry seas because we first lost our moral compass and the *foundation* of our freedom.

THE ISSUE OF CAPITALISM

Although I believe communism and capitalism in their most extreme, secular manifestations are equally doomed to failure, likely to result in tragic dictatorship, at the same time I believe free enterprise is the economic system most nearly meeting humanity's God-given need for freedom in existence. The freedom of self-determination in an open economy is, in my view, an ideal system, but when greed and materialism displace all spiritual and moral values, capitalism breaks down into ugliness. In his instructive and provocative book, *Wealth and Poverty,*[15] widely circulated in the early days of the Reagan administration, George Gilder makes a convincing argument that capitalism at least *sets out* to fulfill generally what I am calling the Law of Responsibility.

"Giving is the vital impulse and moral center of capitalism," Gilder argues, adding:

> Capitalists are motivated not chiefly by the desire to consume wealth or indulge their appetites, but by the freedom and power to consummate their entrepreneurial ideas. Whether piling up coconuts or designing new computers, they are movers and shakers, doers and givers, obsessed with positive visions of change and opportunity. They are men with an urge to understand and act, to master something and transform it, to work out a puzzle and profit from it, to figure out a part of nature and society and turn

it to the common good. They are inventors and explorers, boosters and problem solvers; they take infinite pains and they strike fast.

Then the author drives to the heart of the criticism leveled at the capitalists—their preoccupation with money. But his answers are logical and need to be heard.

> Are they greedier than doctors or writers or professors of sociology or assistant secretaries of energy or commissars of wheat? Yes, their goals seem more mercenary. But this is only because money is their very means of production. Just as the sociologist requires books and free time and the bureaucrat needs arbitrary power, the capitalist needs capital. . . . Capitalists need capital to fulfill their role in launching and financing enterprise. Are they self-interested? Presumably. But the crucial fact about them is their deep interest and engagement in the world beyond themselves, impelled by their imagination, optimism and faith.

Gilder's assessment is on target, I believe. Capitalism satisfies the freedom-loving side of humanity. It has an inherent quality of giving, of breaking through into new levels of experience. It uses that which it has and fully exploits the exponential curve, and perseverance is one of its tested virtues.

RESPONSIBILITY GROWS, TOO

But what about responsibility? As success grows, the responsibility grows. Has the level of fulfillment of that responsibility kept pace? That is the problem.

Gilder's argument, while touching on "religious" factors, becomes muddy on the point of God and faith. He is imprecise, as in the case of the last word in the above-quoted passage when it comes to what precisely this "faith" is in. The fact is that everything else rests on that foundation. Ultimately, imprecision in this area will produce shakiness. Jesus said, "Have faith in God."[16] That principle was the umbrella for all activities.

If the faith is in God, then this quite naturally flavors the question of responsibility. Faith in God presumably will produce an acknowledgment of responsibility toward God—and an ongoing and rising responsibility toward men. This is where the capitalists most frequently stumble.

And they are not alone. Other conservatives have fallen short, too. This is exemplified by the evangelical Christians who so often find themselves in league with economic and political conservatives. They have been given great understanding, and often they have given much in return. However, they have concentrated almost exclusively on personal salvation, neglecting responsibility for intelligent public policy, international affairs, the poor, the oppressed. To whom much enlightenment has been given, much will be required.

We in the developed world—capitalists, evangelicals, everyone—will be held accountable for all that has been given. The people in Africa and South America will not be held to the same level of accountability simply because they have not received as much.

Just think of the Western world! Think of the revelations in law, justice, science, medicine, technology, religion. Think of the rewards that have come through capitalism and evangelical Christianity as merely two examples. Those revelations, those rewards, govern what is demanded of us—by God and by men.

The responsibility is great. And this may not be comprehended to the fullest by Gilder and his fellow conservatives and capitalists. We all need to hear Isaiah, who in his great prophecy spelled out this responsibility, mincing no words in reporting God's instructions. We will look at only one section of them,[17] for they alone are enough to set us in motion with the Law of Responsibility.

> Shout with the voice of a trumpet blast, tell my people of their sins! Yet they act so pious! They come to the Temple every day and are so delighted to hear the reading of my laws—just as though they would obey them—just as though they don't despise the commandments of their God! How anxious they are to worship correctly; oh, how they love the Temple services![18]

BEING DOERS OF THE WORD

The words echo throughout the New Testament. How God deplores those who hear His word and do not *do* it![19] They wonder why they don't see power in their lives. Isaiah looks at the kinds of questions they throw at God.

> "We have fasted before you," they say. "Why aren't you impressed? Why don't you see our sacrifices? Why don't you hear our prayers? We have done much penance, and you don't even notice it!" I'll tell you why! Because you are living in evil pleasure even while you are fasting, and *you keep right on oppressing your workers.* Look, what good is fasting when *you keep on fighting and quarreling?* This kind of fasting will never get you anywhere with me.[20]

No, the Lord says, your revelation carries a responsibility to Him and to people. He hits the point on workers hard.

> No, the kind of fast I want is that you stop *oppressing* those who work for you and treat them fairly and give them what they earn.[21]

Then He broadens it.

> I want you to share your food with the hungry and bring right into your own homes those who are helpless, poor and destitute. Clothe those who are cold and don't hide from relatives who need your help.[22]

Fulfill your responsibility at the level to which He has raised you, God says, and He will raise you even higher.

> If you do these things, God will shed his own glorious light upon you. He will heal you; your godliness will lead you forward, and goodness will be a shield before you, and the glory of the Lord will protect you from behind. Then, when you call, the Lord will answer. "Yes, I am here," he will quickly reply. All you need to do is to stop oppressing the weak, and to stop making false accusations and spreading vicious rumors![23]

From the beginning of the Scriptures to the end, a theme flows relentlessly: *God is the enemy of oppression.* So must His people be. In His behalf, Isaiah pounds at the issues even more boldly.

> *Feed the hungry! Help those in trouble!* . . . And the Lord will . . . satisfy you with all good things . . . and you will be like a well-watered garden, like an ever-flowing spring.[24]

Give and it will be given to you. Fulfill your responsibility at your current level if you would rise to a higher one. Blessing carries responsibility.

Unending commitment to the truth would advance the cause of capitalism and free enterprise immensely, carrying it perhaps past the dangers of anarchy and dictatorship. It would also advance the cause of evangelical Christianity, perhaps to the point of winning the world, a feat that has thus far eluded us.

11

The Law of Greatness

ALL PEOPLE DESIRE to be great.

Because of human frailty, however, this can turn out badly, especially if we think in terms of comparison with others, for that usually spells pride.

But we need to think more deeply than that. Pride is still a hazard, but one can set goals of accomplishing tasks rather than of performing better than someone else. It's a fine line, but it exists.

Jesus, pointing to that line, spoke of the possibilities of greatness—a purity of greatness, we might say. Indeed, He set forth a two-part principle that I have labeled the *Law of Greatness*. The world needs it desperately at this hour.

It is easy to forget that the people surrounding Jesus during His earthly ministry were just that—people. Plain, simple, ordinary people. They exhibited the frailties of all of us. For example, at one point, acting a bit like twentieth-century kids quarreling over who's the greatest shortstop in the American League, the disciples came to the Lord and asked, "Who then is the greatest in the kingdom of heaven?"

The answer was remarkable, flying in the face of everything we expect in our day.

Jesus called a little child to him and stood the child before his followers. Then he said, "I tell you the truth, you must change and become like little children. Otherwise, you will never enter the kingdom of heaven. *The greatest person in the kingdom of heaven is the one who makes himself humble like this child.*"[1]

At another time, they fell into a dispute over which of *them* was regarded as the greatest. They, like us, were very concerned about their status from time to time. But the Lord showed great patience with them.

And He said to them, "The kings of the Gentiles lord it over them; and those who have authority over them are called 'Benefactors.' But not so with you, but *let him who is the greatest among you become as the youngest, and the leader as the servant.* For who is greater, the one who reclines at table, or the one who serves? Is it not the one who reclines at table? But I am among you as *the one who serves.*"[2]

Every time the question arose, the answer was the same two-pronged directive: If you want to be great, become like a *child* and become a *servant.* And that answer reverberates down through human experience to our day, yet so few of us grasp it.

"Oh, that was OK for what He was doing then," we say, "but He didn't understand what it was going to be like in the modern world." Or we mumble something like, "That may be all right for church, but you'll get killed in the real world."

FACING REALITY

If you're honest, you have to admit those remarks seem true as the twentieth century winds down. Knowledge has exploded all over the planet and, through the space program, even onto other planets. Man is doing things never dreamed possible in earlier generations. Furthermore, we are in a life-and-death struggle for the hearts and minds of the next generation. It is what my friend, Dr. James Dobson, described in his book, *Children at Risk,* as a civil war of values. Greatness in this world will be measured by success on these fronts. Trying to live as a little child in this modern world, we tell ourselves, would be suicide.

We all rationalize that way. We argue with the things we learn from Scripture as if the Bible were no longer relevant to our world, and we are in a terrible mess as a result. We should look at what Jesus was showing us.

What is there about a little child that He wants us to copy? If they're very little, they cry a lot and seem to be pretty much governed by what their stomachs tell them. If they have pain, they cry; if they're wet, they cry.

As they grow, they're apt to be spoiled by their families. They may become extraordinarily self-centered; they may whine a lot. In time, they may become unruly and undisciplined. All parents know the pattern.

Is this what Jesus wanted us to be?

No. He had something else in mind. He spoke of three qualities that under normal circumstances predominate in little children: They are trusting. They are teachable. They are humble.

To begin with, little children trust their mothers and fathers. They have to. A baby relies upon his mother to feed him, trusting that she is not going to put poison in his mouth. As he grows, he believes in his parents, usually certain that his daddy is absolutely the greatest man in the world. We all know that many things can work to warp that trust, but basically all children, if treated the way God would have parents treat their offspring, will have incredible faith in their mothers and fathers. They won't worry about being fed, clothed, or housed. They will simply trust that their parents will meet their needs.

Such total trust in the provision and protection of God is the first giant step toward greatness.

As for being teachable, children, most significantly, will listen. They have voracious appetites for learning, and since they're starting from zero, they know the best way to feed those appetites is to listen. They may ask a lot of questions, but they listen to the answers. "Daddy, why is the grass green?" "Daddy, why are the birds flying?" "Daddy, why is the car running?"

It never stops. Their minds are set in the inquiry mode.

Too often parents become annoyed, but they need to understand that this is a mark of intelligence. It is desirable and pleasing to the Creator. A child between the ages of four and five will learn more in that one year than a student will in four years of college.

This teachableness has an interesting side effect that I'm sure Jesus had in mind. Children, hungry to learn, will experiment. They are quick to master new ideas, new languages, new techniques. Their minds are open. If we think of this in the context of God's instruction to Adam and Eve to master and subdue the earth,[3] we see the importance of such inquiry and openness.

They are steps toward greatness.

INNOCENT AS A CHILD

Then, little children are humble—at least until someone spoils them. You seldom see a young child vaunting himself as if he is something special. This virtue is eventually corrupted by a society that has become increasingly warped through the centuries, but in his very early years a child doesn't care if his dad is a prince or a pauper, highly educated or lacking in training. All he cares about is that this man is Daddy, and he loves him. Usually this carries over to attitudes toward others; he loves people as people, regardless of social status.

Quite simply, children love life, until we train this quality out of them. When you watch them play, they are free; they throw themselves into situations with abandon, even getting a little reckless. And they'll throw themselves into your arms with absolute delight. Their innocence is beautiful. While fully content in the fact that their parents are sovereign—it's so good and natural that they never even think to challenge it—they are free to be free.

They wear no masks. They're innocent, transparent, and genuine. Jesus says, become like them and you're on the road to greatness.

The New Testament is jammed with urgings toward humility, and we have noted the importance of this virtue in simply moving toward the kingdom of God. But we should observe that Jesus, in a parallel passage on greatness, reemphasized that insistence on humility. It is a virtue with more than passing importance. After having said that "the greatest among you shall be your servant,"[4] He continued: "And whoever exalts himself shall be humbled; and *whoever humbles himself shall be exalted.*"[5]

With that principle, Christ was pointing to a truth that Solomon had unfolded in a different way: "The reward of humility and the fear of the LORD / Are riches, honor and life."[6] Greatness, summed up as "riches, honor and life," is the reward of those who are humble, which is the necessary ingredient for fearing the Lord. And that, psychology confirms, is what men long for—financial reward, recognition, and a good, satisfying life. It all awaits the little child, epitome of the humble.

So, in short, Jesus said greatness begins with being trusting, being teachable, and being humble. The three traits go together—not merely in children, but in adults as well. The trusting person puts away criticism and skepticism, and becomes open. He doesn't have to be right all the time. Then he is able to learn—from God, from people, from circumstances. He'll listen; he'll try new things. And *that* is the humble person.

Do you see the circle? Trust. Teachableness. Humility. They run from one to another, backward and forward.

The businessman who becomes like a child in this regard will rise to greatness. So will the scientist. So will the minister.

LEARNING

In God's order it is the poor in spirit, the "spiritual beggars," who are given the kingdom of God. In God's order it is "little children" who make up the kingdom of God. In God's kingdom the servant becomes the greatest. Yet in the material world as well it is these very heavenly characteristics which, despite our preconceptions, make for success.

In politics the winner is usually the man or woman who goes door to door shaking hands, asking for votes, offering to serve the people. Those office-seekers who are too arrogant to "beg" for votes sooner or later lose.

In business, the most successful entrepreneurs are those who have a childlike curiosity and a childlike, contagious enthusiasm. They always want to learn more. How can they improve production and sales techniques? How can they streamline costs? What are the latest consumer trends and marketing techniques? What are their competitors doing? What ways can they find to copy, improve, extend? What better and more profitable uses can be made of existing product lines?

These successful men and women are always listening and learning. They listen to their customers, to their employees, to experts, to the man on the street. They and their companies will always defeat the man or company that says, "I know it all. My product is the best. My techniques have worked for years and they are the best. No one can teach me." The successful are innovative and adaptive. Whatever the business climate they will succeed. They become great. The other is rigid and autocratic. Their position and power will carry them for a time, but like dinosaurs in the Ice Age, when dramatic change comes, their pride and unwillingness to learn guarantees their defeat.

A DIFFICULT CONCEPT

In the second episode we examined at the beginning of this chapter, Jesus added another criterion for greatness. Quite paradoxically, He said the secret of greatness is service. If you reflect on it, you see that it fits well with being childlike, but it begins to rub. It goes against the grain of society.

That is why we should be serious and careful on this subject. We are dealing with a law that turns everything upside down. Little children soon yearn to grow up so they can "be somebody." But Jesus says, "Be a child if you really want to *be* somebody." Servants, meanwhile, usually hate their position, yearning to earn enough to have their *own* servants. But Jesus says, "No, become a servant if you wish to be truly great."

This pushes us into a corner where we have to ask, "Do I really want this?" We should weigh it carefully, for the Lord said to count the cost of the things we set out to do.[7]

If you're an average working man, you may have been striving all your life to escape any image of servanthood, trying to rise to the point, perhaps, where you work for yourself and not for someone else.

If you're a black man or woman, you have known the effects of the struggle against slavery all your life, and chances are one of the most disturbing facts you have lived with is the tendency to think of blacks as service workers. But what happens when a black man or woman works hard to get a good education and moves into one of the higher professions? Will the idea of being a "servant," as Christ commanded, have any appeal to him or her? Can we honestly expect anyone escaping from "servant" status to volunteer for servanthood in another form?

If you have ever been exposed to management-labor relations, you know that no manager has any true desire to be a servant of the labor ranks, and no union member will accept the slightest hint that he or she is a "servant" of management—or anyone else. That kind of thinking would be anathema to both sides.

If you're a politician, you smile indulgently when someone refers to you as a "public servant"; you really prefer the role of celebrity.

If you're a minister of the gospel, "successful" and well known on the speaking circuit or perhaps on television, the chances are very good that you are far more comfortable signing autographs and sitting at head tables than being a servant to the flock.

You see, there will be a cost if we seek true greatness. For our attitudes—wrong ones—are well solidified, despite the fact that we have had examples of true greatness over the years.

JUDGING GREATNESS

My generation considered Albert Schweitzer to be a great man, and most—even those who disagreed with his theology—would acknowledge that his was true greatness. Why? Because he became like a little child and like a servant. He gave his life for the sick and the oppressed. He was trusting, teachable, and humble. He was a servant.

A scientist, musician, philosopher, and theologian, Schweitzer left what the world would have considered to be the road to greatness in Germany and went to Africa to labor among primitive, underprivileged people in a remote, little village. Establishing a hospital, he lived his life out in full service to others, continually learning, continually enthusiastic, continually innocent.

Even the modern world came to understand that his greatness was somehow different from the greatness most men sought. Year after year, he was numbered at the top of the list of outstanding people.

Similarly, polls measuring the ten most admired women in the world place a remarkable Roman Catholic nun, Mother Teresa of Calcutta, at the top. This is a woman who has given up everything, in a materialistic world's terms, to go among the poor, downtrodden masses of India to feed them, clothe them, house them, and love them.

Hers is a role of a servant through and through, a refusal to lord it over anyone, and yet we somehow know she has achieved greatness.

Stepping back through history, we encounter Father Damien, the Belgian priest who gave himself entirely to service to the leper colony on the Hawaiian island of Molokai in the mid-nineteenth century. His was true greatness.

And there is Hudson Taylor, the missionary who turned away from a life of comfort in Britain to throw himself into service of the suffering and lost Chinese. His greatness still rings in the annals of missionary service.

And there was Florence Nightingale, the English nurse who served heroically in the Crimean War and became known as the founder of modern nursing.

These unusual humanitarians were among those who found the key to success through the Law of Greatness.

The business world, too, has produced greatness. And we need to understand that the principles set forth by Jesus are pragmatic and effective in the hard-nosed give-and-take of free enterprise.

Henry Ford was a good illustration. He wanted to make inexpensive, efficient transportation available to as many people as possible. So he came up with the Model T. Before long he was serving thousands with cheap transportation. The more he served, the more money he made, and the greater his business became. He became the greatest figure in the auto industry.

MANAGEMENT INSENSITIVITY

The Law of Greatness did not gain a permanent foothold in the American car industry, however. Confrontations gradually replaced service. Management and labor lost all semblance of unity, and the thought of serving one another became a joke. The industry also confronted the public, steadily losing awareness about changes in society, consumer economics, and fuel outlook. It designed cars the way *it* wanted them.

The early tolling of the death knell went largely unnoticed. While there has been a concerted effort in Detroit in the past decade to reverse this trend and to put the customer and the worker back in the driver's seat, it remains to be seen if the American auto industry can ever regain its position as the world leader in this field.

For a long time, the deterioration in the concept of service reached the point where car manufacturers decided that fully effective quality control at the factories was too expensive. Their surveys convinced them that they would be better off to repair mistakes at the dealership level.

So cars came off the assembly lines with little things untended. Buyers drove them a short while and things started going bad. When they took them back, the dealers made the repairs and sent the bill to the manufacturer. Almost inevitably something else would happen to the same car, and the process would be repeated. It was terribly inconvenient for car buyers, but it was less expensive for the manufacturer.

The tolling of the bell grew louder as the principle of service fell by the roadside.

Consider the kinds of arrogant and destructive self-interest that brought men like Ivan Boesky, Charles Keating, Michael Milken, and Donald Trump into the headlines between 1989 and 1992. Along with the virtual collapse of the savings-and-loan industry, the international BCCI banking scandal, and a litany of insider-trading scams and stock fraud cases, American industry has been shaken to its foundations. No longer were businesses looking after their customers' interests; they were catering to the personal fortunes of a few unscrupulous top executives.

This, as we noted in an earlier chapter, was not the case in the booming Pacific-rim countries like Japan. There, thoughts of service penetrated deeper into the industrial consciousness. Until the mid-1960s Japan was known only as a country of cut-rate merchandise and cheap knock-offs, but one day that situation came to an end. A desire emerged among Japanese managers and workers to end shoddiness and to give their customers the best products available. Industry would serve the people; and particularly in the automobile market, their achievement speaks for itself.

In Japan, following the teachings of W. Edwards Deming, management and labor began to work on the idea of becoming servants of one another. Companies took pains to instill in their managers the thought that they were servants of the workers. "We're here to make their jobs better, to improve their environment, to solve their problems," they repeated. Furthermore, they became like little children and listened to their workers.

"We want to learn from you," management said. Japanese automobile workers were each submitting eighteen and nineteen suggestions a year for improving their automobiles, and management was adopting at least 80 percent. While Japanese automobile companies led by servant managers were seeing stunning success, American managers remained autocratic and rigid. Here workers offered only two suggestions a year and only one of them was adopted by management.

Japanese employees, meanwhile, were constantly reinforced in their understanding, through attitudes and material rewards, that they were servants of the customers and the society. United States employees were locked in hostile confrontation with management.

PRINCIPLES THAT REALLY WORK

Serving is a concept that works at every level, even in an enterprise as massive as the automobile industry of a major, very prosperous nation. For, as the world knows, the Japanese auto industry overwhelmed everyone, even gaining a foothold in America that resulted in a major share of sales.

The principle works in other industries, too. J. C. Penney, for example, embraced the concept of giving a square deal to everyone—honest merchandise, honest measure, honest price. With that in mind, he developed a giant chain of stores across America, becoming a great man in merchandising. More recently Sam Walton, founder of Wal-Mart and Sam's wholesale stores, built one of the world's most prosperous retail chains by bringing mass merchandising and low prices to small towns and rural communities all across America that had never seen a discount store. His venture paid off in many ways, and at his death in 1992 Walton and his family were reportedly the richest in the world. So a life principle emerges. Those who serve others—whether in religion, philanthropy, education, science, art, government, or business—are the great ones. Indeed, the deeper the sacrifice or the broader the scope of service, the greater the individual becomes.

And rarely will our society award the status of greatness to those who lust for personal power and seek to exalt themselves. How often we hear applied to such persons the phrases "petty tyrant," "little Caesar," "self-seeking," "ruthless," "vain." And though occasionally these people rise to prominence, they never touch greatness. Invariably the Law of Reciprocity brings them down.

Looking around us in this last decade of the twentieth century, we would certainly find a consensus that if ever greatness was needed in the world, it is now. We have few statesmen of international stature; few political leaders we would trust in a personal relationship; few heroes in any field. Instead of greatness of spirit, more often we find meanness. Our vision is dim.

Frankly, we need leadership at every level, especially in the international realm. As Armageddon looms closer with each passing day, there is every reason to fear that the kinds of mismanagement and insensitivity we have witnessed during most of the past generation will lead us to the brink of catastrophe. We need men and women to lead our nation in taking on the responsibilities and the risks of serving other nations, helping them to achieve their potential, helping them with education, agriculture, and industry. We need to cast off the paternalism and exploitation that has passed for foreign relations.

We need to dare to live the Beatitudes at this level, to be trusting, teachable, and humble, to discover perhaps for the first time in history how a true servant can lead.

In addition to being spiritually and biblically sound, this course has a very practical result. The nation that does the most for others will be the one growing in greatness. That nation will be the one other nations, as customers, will turn to, the one whose products will sweep the world. That nation will be exalted, elevated, enlarged as the Laws of Reciprocity and Use take hold.

As with nations, so with all of us.

12

The Law of Unity

From THE BEGINNING of His revelation to mankind, God has held forth a difficult principle that flows naturally into and out of the concept of serving. Men have continually stumbled over it.

I call it the *Law of Unity.* It is simple to understand, and for some, difficult to obey. But it is essential to success. God has been trying to explain that to mankind for thousands of years, for unity is central to the working of the universe.

Perhaps the most powerful illustration of the creative power of perfect unity is found in God Himself. At the very moment of creation there was unity. "Then God said, 'Let *Us* make man in *Our* image, according to *Our* likeness.'"[1]

This the only part of the Creation where such language is used and, admittedly, we do not know with great precision what the Lord was inspiring the writer to communicate. He probably was referring to the Godhead, the Trinity, when He spoke of "Us." But He could have been speaking to the angelic court of God or perhaps even the multifaceted majesty of God. Regardless, there was some form of conversation involving more than one Person, and *there was unity.*

Although the passage presents many significant facts, this is the one we should see here: Within the Godhead (or the court of heaven) there was agreement and harmony. God moves in unity.

Thus, the principle is first stated: Great creativity occurs where there is unity. God's unfathomable power is released where there is harmony.

The early Genesis accounts add another piece of insight in this regard. After man had refused to obey God and live under His sovereignty, the half-truth of Satan, the liar and deceiver, came to pass: Adam and Eve became "like God."[2] We are not able to comprehend the seriousness of that moment. It was history's terrible tragedy. Man, the delight of God's heart, had fallen. And we read these words:

> Then the LORD God said, "Behold, the man has become like one of *Us*, knowing good and evil; and now, lest he stretch out his hand, and take also from the tree of life, and eat, and live forever"—therefore the LORD God sent him out from the garden of Eden.[3]

Judgment flowed from unity. Just as the magnificent power of creation had sprung from the perfect harmony of heaven, so had the dreadful power of judgment and justice come from the awesome unity of the Almighty.

The examples are clear. God moves in unity. Harmony is central to the unleashing of God's incredible power.

Furthermore, unity in the invisible world governs the visible world. If it works in heaven, it works on earth. "Thy kingdom come. / Thy will be done. / *On earth as it is in heaven*."[4]

This operation of the Law of Unity on earth was the point of one of the Lord's most-quoted statements:

> Again I say to you, that if *two of you agree on earth about anything* that they may ask, *it shall be done* for them by My Father who is in heaven. For where two or three have gathered together in My name, there I am in their midst.[5]

He was calling for agreement, but not merely for agreement's sake. He was calling for unity. Since He would be in their midst when they gathered to consider some issue, they would be expected to agree with Him. Their unity would be an external manifestation of their internal agreement. Since He was there, He would bring them to harmony if they genuinely laid aside their own preoccupations and centered on Him.

Then, and only then, would power flow, just as at the creation. For unity is the fountainhead of God's creative power.

There is a multiplication factor in that unity too. We see it in a song of Moses spoken to all of Israel as he approached the end of his life. One standing on the Rock, he said, would chase a thousand of the enemy, while two would put ten thousand to flight.[6] Unity does not cause a mere doubling or tripling of power; the progression explodes.

THE EARLY CHURCH

The biblical accounts of unity within the early church show the power of the Law of Unity. For example, the fledgling assembly (the *ekklesia*, or church) continued to stick together after Christ's crucifixion, resurrection, and ascension—still weak, still uncertain, still afraid. But an enlightening verse says, "These all *with one mind* were continually devoting themselves to prayer."[7] They were in accord in unity.

Then, the Bible says, power flowed through and from that unity. The Holy Spirit, the giver of life and power, was sent forth upon the people of God as never before. The church was on its way.

At another critical stage, as the people reached unity and harmony, we see the launching of the missionary outreach that was to change the world. This occurred in Antioch, where the Lord's followers were first called Christians.[8]

> In the church at Antioch there were these prophets and teachers: Barnabas, Simeon (also called Niger), Lucius (from the city of Cyrene), Manaen (who had grown up with Herod, the ruler), and Saul. They were all worshiping the Lord and giving up eating for a certain time. During this time the Holy Spirit said to them, "Set apart for me Barnabas and Saul to do a special work for which I have chosen them." So after they gave up eating and prayed, they laid their hands on Barnabas and Saul and sent them out.

The Lord acted in that setting of harmony, in which those great and diverse leaders centered in on Christ—"ministering" to Him, worshiping Him, turning their full devotion upon Him, feasting upon Him rather than upon ordinary food. He called out Saul, whose name was changed to Paul,[10] and Barnabas, the "Son of Encouragement" whose name had already been changed from Joseph, and sent them forth in power.[11]

We see in all of these reports evidence that people will not hear the voice of God clearly unless the unity of the Spirit is maintained. Disunity will cause the Spirit to flee.

If we need further support for the point, we have only to look at the recent history of the church. Division and disunity have been its most distinguishing characteristics, with the result that it has been impotent to move the world. It has lacked the power that flows from unity. It is small wonder that Jesus, on the night of His betrayal, prayed so movingly and powerfully for the harmony of His people, asking that they might be "perfected in unity."[12] He knew how critical it was.

FOR GOOD OR FOR EVIL

A fascinating aspect of unity is that it apparently generates a power that can work for good or for evil, at least for a time. We find this illustrated early in the Bible in the story of the Tower of Babel.

After the Flood, we read, "the whole earth used the same language and the same words."[13] The people were becoming gradually unified and beginning to work in harmony. They discovered the use of bricks and mortar, for example, and set out to build themselves a city with a great tower "whose top will reach into heaven." They wanted to make "a name" for themselves and to grow as a unified force.[14]

If we read carefully, we see that their motive reflected pride. Their plan actually constituted man's first effort to glorify himself. They wanted to build a memorial to themselves, a symbolic assault on heaven in defiance of God.

God viewed this as sin, and Scripture records His reaction as follows:

> "Behold, they are *one people,* and they all have the same language. And this is what they began to do, and now *nothing which they purpose to do will be impossible* for them. Come, let Us go down and there confuse their language, that they may not understand one another's speech." So the LORD scattered them abroad from there over the face of the whole earth.[15]

God Almighty saw that the people were of one mind and one language; they were unified. Nothing would be impossible for them, whether for good or for evil.

God's assessment is blunt: Mankind in unity becomes absolutely overwhelming. Here we must emphasize in the strongest terms possible what God is saying. To a group, a business, a church, a family, a nation that is of "one mind and speaks one language" *nothing will be impossible. Absolutely nothing.* Conversely, if a house or a kingdom is divided against itself, *it cannot stand. The lack of unity is destroying our families and the increasing lack of unity in America is guaranteed to destroy our nation!* Divided against itself, it cannot stand! Not "might not stand"—it "cannot stand."

There are those who might think God's action against Babel was harsh and unreasonable, so we must make sure we comprehend the truth of the episode. The Lord instantly understood that the people's intention was to unify in glorifying man, which meant the same thing as unifying in rebellion against God. The Bible, as we have seen, tells us that God resists the proud but gives favor to the humble. Indeed, He resists pride in any form. Any expression of rebellious pride, especially the pride of a unified group, wherever found, will ultimately draw opposition from Him.

It is noteworthy that pride, which leads to the glorification of man, continues in the world today in a subtler, yet similar manner. It goes under the label of secular humanism, which, in truth, is a religion of man. Its intention is to build great towers, as it were, to the glory of man. Moving slowly but persistently across the earth and capitalizing on the natural pride of man, it has been gaining adherents. Its final aim is the rejection of the centrality of God and the removal of religious freedom from society. The unity of its believers has given it unprecedented force in our time. It's ultimate goal is the establishment of a new world order in defiance of God that one day will, according to the Bible, be ruled by Satan's emissary on earth.

Bible believers draw confidence, however, from the fact that the Scripture announces that such forces as those gathered under the banner of humanism or those who rallied at Babel, as long as they remain in opposition to God, will be defeated. The Bible places them under the name of "Babylon," which is doomed to annihilation.[16] It is noteworthy that the presumed site of the Tower of Babel was at or near historical Babylon in modern-day Iraq.

The lesson we are to learn from all of this is that the Lord God takes the matter of unity very seriously. We, His people, should do no less.

UNITY OF QUEST

Unity must begin with the individual. If you are going to experience the power that can change the world, you must be unified within yourself. You must have internal harmony. In the Bible, James addresses this point specifically. A "double-minded man," he says, will not receive anything from the Lord.[17]

One mind believing or desiring one thing and in the same person another mind believing or desiring something else will not work. And there can be no doubting, James added, "Anyone who doubts is like a wave in the sea, blown up and down by the wind."[18]

Instead, the Bible says, you must be as Abraham was when, at a hundred years of age and sonless, he was told he would be the father of many nations. He did not "waver" regarding the promise, but remained fully assured that God would perform what He had said.[19]

Abraham had unified his quest in life. He did not fall victim to spiritual schizophrenia, which wracks so many in their walk with the Lord. People can be torn between the pursuit of worldly goals and the pursuit of the Christian life. They can't make up their minds which to put first, needing desperately to hear the words of David: "My heart is fixed, O God, my heart is fixed."[20]

The well-known story of Mary and Martha illustrates the problem.

> Now as they were traveling along, He entered a certain village; and a woman named Martha welcomed Him into her home. And she had a sister called Mary, who moreover was listening to the Lord's word, seated his His feet. But Martha was distracted with all her preparations; and she came up to Him, and said, "Lord, do You not care that my sister has left me to do all the serving alone? Then tell her to help me." But the Lord answered and said to her, "Martha, Martha, you are worried and bothered about so many things; but only a few things are necessary, really only one, for Mary has chosen the good part, which shall not be taken away from her."[21]

We must not interpret that passage as approval of laziness or irresponsibility. Jesus loved Martha and her willingness to serve, but He was concerned about her attitude, her internal unity. Mary had "chosen the good part"; her quest had been unified. If need be, she would sacrifice all else for it. But Martha wanted to be recognized as a follower of Jesus *and* as a good organizer *and* as a good cook. She wasn't single-minded, and she had no peace. She was "worried and bothered about so many things."

We cannot serve two masters.[22] We cannot put our spouse and Jesus first in our lives at the same time. We cannot put our job ahead of everything and service Jesus as Lord at the same time. Our problem is that we make a gap between the two, seeing them as two masters, and try to put each one first. That leads to schizophrenia and breakdowns.

The solution, of course, is to be single-minded. Put Jesus first, and then He will say, "Love your wife as I loved the church."[23] A spouse can get no greater love than that. Similarly, put Jesus first and He will say, "When you undertake a task, do it with all your might."[24] A job can get no more attention than that.

Single-mindedness is the solution to the internal desperation so many people regularly experience. It moves the terrible burden and dark heaviness that weigh upon the chest as they teeter on the fringes of nervous collapse.

A COLLECTIVE PRINCIPLE

The Bible is precise in showing that what is true for the individual is true for the family, the group, the organization, and the nation. When the Pharisees accused Him of being in league with Satan, Jesus countered with the following universal principle: "Any kingdom divided against itself is laid waste; and any city or house divided against itself shall not stand."[25]

His point was simple. Without internal unity in a group—whether a family, a business, or a political entity—that group will ultimately collapse. Vacillation and dissension will lead to tearing and destruction.

Jesus, in this verse, was talking about the kingdom of Satan, showing that such universal principles as the Law of Unity apply everywhere. They are broader than religion. Even works of evil will collapse unless the evil forces are unified.

Unity produces strength; disunity produces weakness. Obviously, this was not a New Testament revelation. The Lord's words quickly remind us of the teachings of the man credited with unimaginable wisdom, Solomon: "He who troubles his own house will inherit wind."[26] This proverb was thoroughly supported throughout biblical history. Houses of leadership would often fall to scheming and fighting among themselves, and then the leadership would crumble.

In my generation, the name of Kennedy immediately comes to mind when we consider the strength derived from unity within a house or clan. Working together and for the good of the family or for one of its members, the Kennedys of Massachusetts achieved remarkable political success. The power of the individual was geometrically multiplied by the harmony of the group. We have fewer and fewer examples of such family unity.

When any family is supportive in unity it can succeed even in a hostile environment. The husband and wife support each other. The children are together and honor their parents. All members work for the good of the family. It is this family unity that above all else accounts for the remarkable rise of immigrant Vietnamese, Korean, and Chinese in our society.

But consider the tragedy that comes when husbands and wives battle each other and seek to undermine one another. When children are neglected and grow up estranged, even hating their parents. The economic and social cost of the lack of unity in families is appalling. When families lack unity and cohesion, all society begins to suffer. The hatred engendered by disunity in marriages leads to racial, ethnic, and class warfare, which rips society apart and destroys cities, states, and nations. "A kingdom divided against itself cannot stand!"

CORPORATE DISUNITY

The same is true of the business world. We need only think of those businesses that have fallen on hard times because they abandoned a clear-cut unity of mission in favor of diversification. A great electronics company floundered because it tried to make large computers. A chemical company ran into trouble when it tried to be a land developer.

Successful organizations, as well as successful individuals, are those unified around a relatively simple statement of goals and mission. A double-minded man is "unstable in all his ways."[27] So is a double-minded business.

At the national level, the problem is just as great. Turning back into history we see the roots of modern-day Italy, whose turmoil may be greater than any developed country in the world despite its conspicuous marks of great civilization. Before, the time of Guiseppe Garibaldi's efforts to unify Italy in the nineteenth century, that land witnessed the struggle of little city-states to prevail over one another and maintain their autonomy. Garibaldi brought them together in a fragile alliance, but following the wars in our century and the conditions in modern Europe, Italy is probably best described as "the sick man" of the continent, owing almost exclusively to the absence of harmony.

The factions in that nation simply will not come together. The house is divided. Consequently, the economy is sick; the society with its unbelievable terrorism and crime is unstable; governmental services falter. Life is a shambles.

In the United States, the history is different and the symptoms vary, but the disease is the same. From its founding until about 1960, Americans were united by at least a common ethic. Essentially, the country had been founded as a Christian nation, adopting biblical principles and governing itself pretty much under biblical countenance. There was a work ethic and moral restraint based on an underlying philosophical system of honor and decency that prevailed even in the face of frequent and flagrant violations.

Today, the United States struggles under a social philosophy of "diversity" and "pluralism." There is no unified reality. Many disparate, frequently cacophonous voices echo from one shore to another. Unity is no longer the goal of secular society, but disparity, difference, and diversity. Consequently, confusion is triumphant.

A "700 Club" guest once asked a question typically heard in the current atmosphere: "Whatever happened to the concept that 'I am my brother's keeper?'"

The answer was easy. It vanished with the Christian ethic. Such concepts spring from a God-centered society, but we no longer have that unifying force. We are now fragmented, and each fragment spawns its own jealousy and self-concern. If this continues and the rival factions increase and strengthen, the country will fall quite simply from violation of the law of Unity.

UNITY WITH DISTINCTIVENESS

It is important we understand that unity springing from the truth of the kingdom of God does not insist on, or even desire, uniformity. Lessons from the Bible about the unity of the Godhead makes this abundantly clear. There is distinctiveness even with the oneness of the Trinity.

We see this point in the lives of Christ's disciples, too. They were unified in their quest, but they were a diverse lot, thoroughly nonconformist in several instances.

Paul the apostle taught on this in a spiritual lesson that has physical applications:

> Now there are *varieties* of gifts, but the same Spirit. And there are *varieties* of ministries, and the same Lord. And there are *varieties* of effects, but the same God who works all things in all persons. But to each one is given the manifestation of the Spirit for the common good.[28]

Variety is God's way, he said, even invoking the Trinity to make the point—Spirit, Lord, God. Variety and distinctiveness serve God's purpose, working differently but pointedly to arrive at the common good.

No, in families, businesses, churches, and nations, the Lord is not seeking a collection of robots. He is seeking people with varying personalities, talents, and styles who are unified in purpose and will work toward the common good.

Using His principles harmoniously, they can overcome the crises of our century.

Keenly aware of this the night before He was crucified, Jesus prayed to His Father in this manner:

> I do not ask in behalf of these alone, but for those also who believe in Me through their word; *that they may all be one;* even as Thou, Father, art in Me, and I in Thee, that they also may be in Us; that the world may believe that Thou didst send Me. And the glory which Thou hast given Me I have given to them; *that they may be one, just as We are one;* I in them, and Thou in Me, that they may be perfected in unity, that the world may know that Thou didst send Me, and didst love them, even as Thou didst love Me.[29]

He knew that the fulfillment of the purpose of God would require unity. Without it, there would be no flow of power to save the world and to perfect the people of God.

13

The Law of Fidelity

A WOMAN ONCE approached Billy Sunday, the great evangelist of the World War I era, with this question: "Reverend Sunday, tell me how I can stop exaggerating?" Sunday shot back, "Call it lying."

To many in our culture there are euphemisms to describe conduct that is prohibited by God's clear command. The woman in the story was lying repeatedly, but her conduct was somehow made acceptable by calling it "exaggerations" or "little white lies."

Unmarried men and women are not fornicating, they are "living together," "having an affair," or "making love." Homosexuals aren't sodomites. They are "gay." The killing of unborn babies is not murder, it is a woman's "freedom of choice." Looting and pillaging by ghetto youths is no longer theft, it is an act of "cultural deprivation." Workers do not steal tools and parts from their employers; they temporarily "borrow" or, in wartime jargon, they "liberate" them. We don't slander and gossip, we show "concern."

In each case we can then say we are truly "good" people, but, of course, we, like everyone else, are guilty of all of the "little" sins that don't really matter because everybody is doing them.

But in God's eyes there are no "peccadilloes" and "mortal" sins. Either we are living for God, or we are not. Either we are sinning, or we are not.

Jesus laid out the universal principle in what I call the *Law of Fidelity*. He said, "Whoever can be trusted with very little can also be trusted with much, and whoever is dishonest with very little will also be dishonest with much. So if you have not been trustworthy in handling worldly wealth, who will trust you with true riches? And if you have not been trustworthy with someone else's property, who will give you property of your own?"[1]

The story is told of a private dinner which found the witty and irreverent playwright, George Bernard Shaw, seated next to an attractive young actress from London. "Tell me," Shaw began, "would you consider sleeping with a strange man if he paid you a million pounds sterling?" The young lady thought for a moment and then coyly said, "Yes, I would." Then Shaw asked, "Would you sleep with a strange man if he paid you five pounds?" "Of course not," was the angry reply. "What do you take me for?" "I have already discovered that," said Shaw. "Now I am trying to determine the price."

A person who would resist a five-dollar bribe but yield to a million-dollar bribe is not honest. And conversely, if a man would steal one dollar from the company stamp drawer, he will also steal ten thousand dollars from a trust account if the opportunity presents itself.

If a worker will not work hard and conscientiously for ten dollars per hour, he will not suddenly become conscientious if paid a hundred dollars per hour. An employee who will lie on his résumé to get a job will lie about his performance in order to keep his job. A husband who cheats on his wife under extreme temptation will also cheat under more normal circumstances.

A MATTER OF DEGREE

Recently a New Hampshire-based manufacturer of hand guns dismissed a longtime employee because, when he found himself without change for the coffee machine, he took thirty-five cents from the desk of a fellow worker. Most people who heard of that action, including me, felt that the company had acted with excessive severity. Apparently there were other instances of petty theft concerning this worker which justified his dismissal. Nevertheless, knowingly or unknowingly, the company realized that a man who takes thirty-five cents will also take thirty-five dollars or thirty-five hundred dollars because that is the truth of the Law of Fidelity.

In our permissive society there is so much petty theft, shoplifting, insurance fraud, and tax cheating, that losses are considered an ordinary part of doing business. The New Hampshire incident is an aberration, not the rule in our society.

Nevertheless, the Law of Fidelity has much wider application for it speaks not just of isolated acts, but tendencies. And it really deals more with ultimate rewards in the kingdom of heaven than reward for conduct on earth. Jesus was contrasting material wealth with "true riches" and "someone else's property" versus "your own" property.

Here is the concept. Each of us is only a life tenant of the property we possess on earth. Whether we live ten years or a hundred years, whether we drink from a beggar's cup and live in a shanty or drink from fine crystal and live in a mansion we cannot take anything material with us to our permanent home in heaven. When we die, all of it is taken from us—stocks, bonds, bank accounts, insurance policies, pensions, farms, ranches, office buildings, houses, cars, boats, furniture, jewelry—everything is left behind. Then, we learn from the Bible, one day all of the material things will "melt with fervent heat." Nothing on earth will remain for eternity. All will be destroyed by fire. Every single thing!

Jesus is telling us that earthly possessions, including our life, our health, and our abilities, are on loan to us to determine what we will do with them. Will we lie and cheat to acquire them? Will we trample upon the rights of others to gain our success? Will we neglect and dissipate the stewardship of our earthly talents and resources? Will we hoard them selfishly for our own pleasure and glory? Will they become a source of arrogance whereby we exalt ourselves above those who have less than we?

Or will we consider ourselves as holding stewardship under Almighty God of whatever He places for a time in our hands? Remember the parable of the talents. The servant who used to the fullest that which had been temporarily entrusted to him in order to enhance his lord's estate was called "good and faithful." The servant who out of fear or indolence refused to use what had been temporarily entrusted to him was called "wicked and slothful." The faithful servant who created ten talents for his lord was given a permanent possession of ten cities. The servant who failed to use his one talent at all not only had that talent stripped away from him, he himself was "cast into outer darkness."

STARTING SMALL

Obviously the Law of Fidelity applies to the material world. The faithful employee in little things is entrusted with bigger things. Some years ago at the tender age of thirteen I was given the role of Sir Joseph in the Gilbert and Sullivan operetta *"HMS Pinafore."* The story that I had to sing was that the great Sir Joseph—the "monarch of the sea"—started in life as an office boy in an attorney's firm whose task it was to polish the handle on the big front door. Then the line, "I polished up the handle so carefully that now I am the ruler of the Queen's Navy."

"Pinafore" is a delightful spoof, but it reflects the clear-cut expectation in our material world that those who are diligent and faithful with small responsibilities will over time be entrusted with larger responsibilities.

But the material expectations are just a prelude to the true meaning of the Law of Fidelity which our Lord was careful to repeat in various contexts for emphasis.

The basis rule is this: Every person will be held accountable for whatever talent, ability, or opportunity that is afforded to him. All of these things are, like the talents, not our personal property but the property of the Lord. There will be an accounting at the end of each of our lives. For those who have been faithful in the "little things," such as the material world, they will be given "true riches" as a permanent, eternal possession. The measure of the scope of our responsibilities in the eternal and never-ending kingdom of God will be determined by our fidelity in managing our Lord's affairs here on earth.

To say that this is an awesome concept is a vast understatement. Henceforth, we cannot think that a tithe of money belongs to God and 90 percent belongs to us to do with as we please. None of it is ours; it is all, 100 percent, God's. We are merely its stewards who can use and enjoy it for His Glory. So also our time. We cannot think that one or two or three hours a week spent in church belongs to God and the rest belongs to us to use or waste as we please. All of our time is His. We are stewards of God's time to use and enjoy it for His glory.

NO SURPRISES

When the final judgment comes, those surprised by the outcome will comprise a multitude beyond reckoning. Many who have regularly been excused by society for "little sins" will find heaven's doors slammed in their faces. Revelation makes it clear, "Outside are the dogs [cult sodomites], those who practice magic arts, the sexually immoral, the murderers, the idolaters [those who worship the material] and everyone who loves and practices falsehood."[2]

Why is God being so harsh? Remember His law. Everyone who is unfaithful in the little things will be unfaithful in the big. Imagine what would progressively happen to the teller of "little white lies" during the first million years of existence in heaven. The monstrosity of the eventual falsehoods possible to him could rival those of Satan himself.

And think of those who will enter the kingdom of God by the grace of God because they have received Jesus Christ as their Savior and have been born again, yet they have done nothing with their lives or their talents or their material resources to extend their Lord's kingdom. If they have not been faithful with what belongs to another, who will give them "true riches"?[3] For them, the Lord says, "The servant who knows what his master wants but is not ready, or who does not do what the master wants, will be *beaten with many blows!*"[4] The apostle Paul put it another way when he wrote, "We all shall appear before the judgment seat of Christ to account for the deeds that we have done in our body."[5]

Of course, many will be surprised when they find that their stewardship of their meager possessions to feed the hungry, to clothe the naked, to visit the sick and those in prison, to intercede in prayer will open for them entrance into the true riches, "the joy of the LORD"![6]

The Law of Fidelity is at once a solemn warning and a promise of eternal blessing. Even as I write these words I am solemnly praying, "Lord, when it's over, will you say to me, 'Well done good and faithful servant. . . . Enter into the joy of your Master'?"[7]

14

The Law of Change

THE FRENCH HAVE a saying: *Plus ça change, plus c'est la même chose* ("The more things change, the more they remain the same"). The writer of Ecclesiastes expressed it this way, "What has been will be again / what has been done will be done again; / there is nothing new under the sun."[1]

God has said, "I am the LORD, I change not."[2] God is spirit, and spirit is changeless and ageless. My good friend, the late Father Dennis Bennett, put it this way, "We have sinned and grown old. Our father is younger than we."[3]

It is a sobering thought to realize that the One who is called the Ancient of Days is actually younger than I am. The earth is running down; our sun is gradually running out of energy; all stored energy in the universe is running down. In fact, all living things in the created universe experience a life cycle of birth, growth, and death.

Yet God, the Creator of all, is continually fresh, new, vibrant, and a source of life. According to the psalmist, He "will neither slumber nor sleep."[4]

We are told in the Bible that the "elements shall melt with fervent heat" and the "sky will be rolled up like a scroll."[5] Yet the invisible world of the secret kingdom and the laws that govern it will abide unchanged forever.

It is at this point that the parallels between the visible material kingdom and the invisible spiritual kingdom diverge. Although God never changes and His immutable laws never change—nor does His spiritual kingdom change—there have to be principles to govern existence in a world where there is an array of changing cycles—seedtime and harvest, birth and death, invention and obsolescence, flexibility and rigidity, enthusiasm and boredom, war and peace, wealth and poverty, revival and apostasy.

Here is the governing *Law of Change:* "No man puts new wine into old skins, lest the skins break and all be lost."[6]

What Jesus is telling us is that the spirit and message of the kingdom of God is always new, but that the receptacles prepared by human beings to receive it will age, become rigid and inflexible, and then must be replaced by receptacles that are new, pliable, and able to adapt. God is always the same; His plan is always the same. But the vehicles, the organizations, and the techniques of carrying out His program will always be changing.

A MANDATE FOR ACTION

Many examples come to my own mind. In 1959, I was moved by a clear direction from God's Spirit to leave New York City with my family and to journey to the seacoast area of Hampton Roads, Virginia, to purchase a run-down UHF television station for God's glory. I had neither the money nor the knowledge to operate a television station. But I had a mandate for action from the Lord of the secret kingdom.

At the time, I could not have conceived in my wildest imagination that what was to be brought into being would result in more than 50 million people accepting Jesus as Savior in more then seventy nations; a cable network with 55 million subscribers; a daily television broadcast to millions; a relief agency that has distributed over $340 million to needy people; a fully accredited graduate university training future leaders; the preeminent Christian public service law firm in America; a Christian coalition to mobilize America's Christians to resist the wasting secular trends in government; two large radio news networks; a motion picture company; and a personal run for the nomination of a major political party for the presidency of the United States.

I had within me new wine. God wanted to prepare a totally new wineskin to contain it. The old wineskins of the existing church structure were just not capable of what God had in mind. If I had tried to force it upon them, I would have brought about conflict, confusion, and failure. The new wine would have been lost and the old skins would have been destroyed.

I can still see the morning meeting of the Portsmouth, Virginia

Ministerial Association when I tried to share the excitement of God's vision to use the powerful medium of television to reach the city for Christ. They nodded, asked a few questions, then adjourned for a coffee break. I went to a pay phone in the lobby to make a call. Imagine my surprise when I heard two of the pastors talking. Here were the exact words: "If we can't stop it, at least we can disassociate ourselves from it."

I was listening to tired old skins whose day of service in God's kingdom was coming to an end. Change was on the way in God's kingdom, but God Himself would have to show me how to put together the new wine flask for the new wine He was preparing. Had I insisted, despite objections, that the new wine be forced into the local denominational church structure of that one small city I would only have succeeded in destroying what they had and losing completely what God had given to me.

WITH DUE DILIGENCE

Moving to the present, in the spring of 1992 I read that the venerable news service, United Press International, was in bankruptcy and was to be sold to the highest bidder at the Federal Bankruptcy Court in Rutland, Vermont. Since our organization had a considerable news presence already, I felt that a worldwide news service would prove a logical extension of our activities.

So I flew up to Rutland, and in the company of a very able local bankruptcy attorney submitted what I considered to be a modest bid. Imagine my amazement when my bid proved to be the only one offered, and I walked out with a contract to buy the eighty-five-year-old news service after a thirty-day period of "due diligence."

My bid was welcomed by the management and most of the staff because it meant that the company had been saved from extinction. With a few exceptions, I found delightful, courteous, and helpful people. So, with a team of accountants, lawyers, journalists, broadcasters, and financial advisers we plunged into the books and records of UPI. After a few days the accountants said, "Don't do it." After a few more days the lawyers said, "Don't do it." After a few more days the journalists said, "Don't do it."Nevertheless, I was hoping to find something to salvage for what seemed a bargain price.

As I wrestled with the decision, I asked my wife, Dede, to join me at our breakfast table to ask God for wisdom. As I prayed, the quiet voice of the Lord spoke to me from the Gospel of Matthew. I opened my Bible and read these words:

> Neither do men pour new wine into old wineskins. If they do, the skins will burst, the wine will run out and the wineskins will be ruined. No, they pour new wine into new wineskins, and both are preserved.[7]

I called my news director, and asked his opinion. His reply, "UPI is about as tired an old wineskin as you can find. I think we should pass." And pass we did with great reluctance.

But in retrospect, there is no question that this was the course of wisdom. Our news has been on the cutting edge of technology—chip cameras, digital tapes, computer graphics, etc. The wave of the future is the satellite delivery of compressed digital information to computers, with television having a decided edge over print journalism. Everything about UPI was antiquated—old methods, old technology, old distribution, and in some cases old people. We needed to invest our time, resources, and talent into building the technology of the future, not in trying to keep alive the technology of the past.

The Law of Change was working.

TIME FOR A CHANGE

In 1992 there is an incessant clamor for change at every level of government. People not only have a disrespect for government, in many cases they actually loathe it. Tell a room full of businessmen, "I am from the government. I want to help you," and they will burst out laughing. The secretary of health, education, and welfare needed no further discussion to condemn a national health care plan than to say, "It would have the efficiency of the Post Office and the compassion of the Internal Revenue Service."

The federal government as we now know it started on its present course in 1932 under the administration of Franklin D. Roosevelt and what was known as the New Deal. Roosevelt took office in the midst of a desperate recession when 25 percent of the work force was unemployed, when long lines of helpless men queued up at soup kitchens for something to eat, and when the potential collapse of our society threatened. Roosevelt ran over a compliant Congress to jam through dozens of pieces of emergency legislation to transfer control of the economy from private industry to federal bureaucrats.

In a brilliant and prophetic article written for the September 15, 1934 issue of *Saturday Evening Post* former president Herbert Hoover made this comment:

> These proposals necessitate that a larger part of leadership and managerial responsibility and authority in business and agriculture be taken from the hands of those who have risen in leadership . . . and placed in the hands of those who appear to merit political power. An enormous extension of bureaucracy is inevitable. . . . No one with a day's experience in government

fails to realize that in all bureaucracies there are three implacable spirits—self perpetuation, expansion, and incessant demand for more power.

Now after sixty years, the New Deal bureaucracy has grown even beyond the worst fears of Herbert Hoover. Each year it turns out more than sixty thousand pages of regulation to annoy and sap the vitality of the private sector. I recall reading one informal survey that placed the cost to the private sector of conforming to the bureaucratic regulation of the federal government at $450 billion per year.

Every four years, the American people vote for change, but nothing changes because the new wine is quickly lost in the old skins.

In the former Soviet Union, East Germany, Poland, Hungary, Czechoslovakia, and Romania, it became painfully obvious that no amount of *glasnost* or *perestroika* could cause communism to adapt to free-market economics and capitalism. When a little new wine of change came in, the rigidly inflexible old system suddenly collapsed. Only then did it become possible to begin building new structures to house the new liberties demanded by the people.

THE CHANGE MOVEMENT

In the United States a movement is under way to limit the terms of congressmen. But even if this initiative succeeds in a few states, it will not be adequate to remove the deeply ingrained habits of wasteful spending, the multiple committees, and the utter venality that has taken control of that body.

But even if a reform effort changes both the chief executive and the Congress, they are still stymied by an intractable bureaucracy of nearly 3 million government workers. The old bureaucratic skin will frustrate and waste any reform effort from either party that is poured into it.

As frustrations mount in America, it will become crystal clear that a revolution—peaceful or violent—will come to pass to break the gridlock of waste, ineptitude, and senseless regulation that has been strangling the productive energies of our nation. Vast changes are needed, including the wholesale elimination of federal programs, bureaus, agencies, and departments. Not only must the terms of congressmen and senators be limited, so also must the terms of bureaucrats be limited. Basically the structures of the New Deal, the Fair Deal, and the Great Society must be dismantled and replaced with a simple, efficient, service-oriented new wineskin into which we can pour a new birth of liberty in America.

The Bible says, "Where the Spirit of the Lord is, there is liberty."[8] Communism fell in Romania only after a protest when thousands of people jammed the streets of the city of Timisoara shouting, "God is alive!" Freedom came to East Germany directly as the result of prayer vigils in churches across the land. Christians around the world prayed for decades for the fall of communism in the Soviet Union.

Where God's Spirit is, there is truth, justice, compassion, wisdom, liberty, free enterprise, moral self-restraint, evangelism, and usually humble simplicity. When the structures men build in the material visible world—whether in politics, law, business, science, health, social relations, education, and religion—begin to depart from the principles that characterize God's Spirit, the eternal, invisible kingdom begins to work quietly and secretly in the hearts of men to bring them new structures.

Without a doubt the authors of the American Revolution were moved upon by God's Spirit when they appealed to the Creator God as the author of their liberty and then framed a unique experiment in democracy dedicated to the proposition that all men are created equal.

HOPE AGAINST HOPE

I recently returned from Zambia, where I visited at length with its new president, Frederick Chiluba. He is a fully committed, Spirit-filled Christian who was imprisoned by the tyrannical and corrupt regime of Kenneth Kuanda, the previous president. President Chiluba told me of a miracle that took place when God caused a man who was considered the most corrupt tyrannical judge in the service of Kuanda to dismiss all charges against him, even though this act later cost the man his judgeship.

Chiluba told me of God's intervention in his campaign for president, when the polls showed that he came from nowhere to defeat the powerful president of twenty-eight years. God put in his heart the ability to hope against hope and to believe for the electoral miracle that occurred.

Now a new structure exists in Zambia. President Chiluba declared it a Christian nation and then set about establishing freedom, cutting the bureaucracy, privatizing state-owned businesses, inviting foreign investors, and eliminating corruption. He plans to balance his nation's budget by the end of 1993, a feat that has steadfastly eluded our own government. The new government structure in Zambia can only lead to prosperity.

But to bring about this change, God was preparing a man, letting him suffer and grow, teaching him the Bible, giving him an understanding of the principles of the kingdom. Then with God's blessing, tyranny was overthrown; the old was swept away and the new began.

No one of us knows which people of the invisible kingdom are being prepared to change the visible kingdom. Someone reading this book my suddenly realize that he or she is God's agent for change. It may be a corrupt school board, an incompetent city government, a legislature controlled by selfish interests, or a church that has lost its vision of mission. Whatever the task, God is looking for people to say like Isaiah, "Here am I. Send me."[9]

Whatever changes may come about in institutions, God's principal mission is people. At the end of the eighteenth century, England was a cesspool of corruption, crime, drunkenness, and unattended poverty. Then God's Spirit moved upon several students at Oxford University who wanted their lives to stand for holiness, not debauchery. The leaders of this small band were two sons of an Anglican pastor and his godly wife, Suzanna Wesley. These young men moved deeper into the truths of the invisible kingdom until their hearts were on fire for spiritual revival in England.

They attempted to pour their new wine into the Church of England, but this particular old wineskin was a major part of the spiritual problem in the nation. Instead of receiving the changes God was bringing by Wesley, the church forbade him to preach the truth in their churches. He turned from them, declared "the world is my parish," and set out with a zeal to change the hearts of his countrymen and, in the process, to create a new structure, the Medthodist Church. Wesley, like John the Baptist in Jesus' day, called on men and women to repent—to have *a change of mind*—and be born again.[10]

Spiritual revival swept like wildfire throughout England and then jumped across the Atlantic. Tens of thousands of people turned out to giant open-air meetings to hear John Wesley or his contemporary, George Whitefield. England, which had been standing on the brink of moral collapse, moved to revival, public morality, and then a century of prosperity, while France was plunged into the horrors of the French Revolution and the excesses of Napoleon Bonaparte.

TARGETS FOR CHANGE

We can be sure that even now the corrupt, outworn, ineffective, or ungodly structures of the material world have been targeted for change by those special agents chosen by God to represent the invisible world of God's kingdom. To them and to us the words of the apostle Paul ring out, "Do not change yourselves to be like the people of this world, but be changed within by a new way of thinking."[11]

This is the reason that we should never be discouraged or despair when we are confronted with entrenched evil or dogged mismanagement. The clearest reference to just such despair is found in the biblical account of the great prophet Elijah.

According to the record, the nation of Israel was ruled by evil King

Ahab and his malevolent wife, Jezebel, and had virtually abandoned the worship of Jehovah and turned to the worship of Baal.

As a consequence God sent a severe three-year drought which brought the nation to its knees. Then God directed Elijah to approach the king and demand a showdown with the priests of Baal at Mount Carmel, which overlooks the Mediterranean port city of present-day Haifa.

In that encounter, Elijah boldly proclaimed his faith in Jehovah God, was vindicated above the hapless priests of Baal, and then personally slaughtered 450 of the priests. The representative of the secret kingdom had won a smashing victory and the oppressive false system was crippled.

But Elijah did not stop there. He boldly reached into the invisible world through earnest, repeated prayer and brought forth a deluge of rain upon the parched land. But even though he had won, he fled for his life to avoid being killed by the vengeful Queen Jezebel.

His flight took him to the Sinai desert, to Mount Horeb, which we call Mount Sinai. There his exhaustion and the seeming impossibility of ever overthrowing Ahab and Jezebel led him to thoughts of death. So, he prayed to the Lord in despair, "Lord, take away my life."[12]

Then God quietly showed him that the plan of His invisible world was right on schedule. Hidden among the population was a faithful remnant of seven thousand people who had never worshiped Baal and from whom the Lord could build a new society.

Then God reached from the invisible world to the visible and ordered HIs servant to anoint the next generation of leaders who would bring about and manage the change that was coming: Elisha was to be the next great prophet to take Elijah's place, Hazael was to be king over Aram (Syria) and Jehu was to be king of Israel in place of Ahab and Jezebel. The Lord told him that these three were to replace the leadership of the old system of rebellion against God and bring in complete change.[13]

Elijah was one of the greatest and best of the prophets, but even the best and strongest and most godly can grow weary and discouraged by entrenched evil. The lesson of Elijah should encourage us all. In times of discouragement we need to remember that God rules in the affairs of men. When things get darkest, suddenly, unexpectedly, dramatically, His plan for change will burst forth.

A PERSONAL CHALLENGE

I would be remiss at the close of this chapter if I did not clearly point out the personal ramifications of the Law of Change. As we grow as individuals, each one of us develops habits, thought patterns, and conscious and unconscious attitudes that become more and more shaped by the secular world in which we live. We are shaped by a world system around us, the inner desires from within us, and the incessant urgings of a spiritual adversary we call the devil.

The force of God's Spirit becomes progressively dim as we progress in age and worldly experience. Our spirit grows callous and insensitive to communion with God. At this point, whether it occurs at age ten or age fifty, we are old skins.

If we sit in church in that condition and hear sermons and exhortations to righteousness, they will pass right over us. Our own attempts to pour New Year's resolutions or solemn resolves or moral rearmament into our lives is a waste of time. If we take these moral homilies too seriously, as many do, they have an absolutely deadening effect—taking away the pleasures and pursuits of a worldly, sinful life without having the ability to give the vibrant life of God's Holy Spirit in exchange.

I know of nothing sadder than the hapless drones who have given up a worldly life to try to please God by physical, legalistic means. In the process they become part of some extreme rigorous cult that demands abstinence, sacrifice, and poverty to serve their version of God, but these groups never offer the transforming gospel of Jesus Christ. Often it is just such unhappily legalistic people who become the pattern for "Christians" in motion pictures and popular fiction.

It is impossible to reform a tired, cracked, wineskin to receive new wine. And it is impossible to reform our cracked, broken, sinful lives by religious exercises. That is why it is absolutely imperative that worldly persons who want God must first have a change of mind, turn from the old life, and then allow Jesus Christ to remake them into vessels suitable for the new wine of God's Spirit.

Indeed God changes institutional structures and nations, but the greatest change is in the heart of the individual. To quote the apostle Paul: "If any man is in Christ, he is a new creation. Old things have passed away. Behold all has become new!"[14]

God's plan for you and me is not re-formation, but transformation into a new creation in Christ. No amount of rigorous asceticism, personal neglect, strict legalism, or even an extended devotional life will suffice. Only a new creation by the power of God's Spirit.

It should go without saying that in the final culmination of time, God will not try to place His new heavenly kingdom into a universe filled with decay and death. No, He is planning "new heavens and a new earth, wherein dwelleth righteousness" to receive his new reborn humanity. Then the invisible kingdom will become the visible kingdom and all else will "melt with fervent heat."

15

The Law of Miracles

LITTLE BY LITTLE over the past dozen chapters we have seen how the kingdom works. We have looked briefly at how our physical world appears to be approaching the outer limits of survival through its violation of the laws of the spiritual world on which everything we know ultimately stands.

We have considered how the invisible nature of that spiritual world does not diminish its reality, but merely governs who will understand it.

We have spoken of reaching into that spiritual world, touching the truth and power of God, and transferring them into the physical world. This is possible even as we hurtle toward that moment when the kingdom of God will burst into visibility and supplant all the kingdoms and powers on earth.

It is this point of reaching into the invisible and seeing its effects manifest in the visible that we should examine more closely. There is a *Law of Miracles.* It governs the question of God's willingness to disrupt His natural order to accomplish His purpose. When He does disrupt that natural order, the result is a miracle, a contravention of the natural laws through which He usually works moment by moment. He overrides the way in which things normally operate.

Since God is almighty, the only absolutely free person in the universe, not bound even by His own creation, He is perfectly able at any time to change the way things are done. He can heal a body instantly; He can still a storm; He can move a mountain. Those are miracles. Even then, however, He works within principles, and they frame the Law of Miracles.

Because of the desperate condition of our world, we still need miracles today. That means we need to understand the law and act on it, for Jesus introduced a new order of normality at the Day of Pentecost. With the power of the Holy Spirit, miracles were to be normal. He expected His followers to do even greater things than He did.[1] After all, during His incarnation He rebuked them for failing to do miracles like walking on water and casting out demons. And He praised an outsider, a Roman centurion, who perceived Christ's spiritual authority and discerned the relationship between the spiritual and the natural. "Just say the word and my servant will be healed," the centurion declared. Jesus marveled at the Roman's understanding. "I have not found such great faith with anyone in Israel," He said.[2] That is what we must recover.

THE UMBRELLA OF FAITH

"Have faith in God."[3] In chapter 4, we saw that to understand how the kingdom works, we have to *begin* there. That was the umbrella given by Jesus in explaining the cursing of the fig tree. We have to *end* there, too.

Through the process of rebirth—by grace through faith—we are to see and enter into the kingdom of heaven, where the miraculous power resides. As the Lord explained to Nicodemus, this is the world of the Spirit, which is like the wind, invisible, yet frequently revealing its effects. We cannot see the wind itself, but we can see the things it moves. With the kingdom, we too observe its effects. Furthermore, we gain access to its power through our faith in Jesus Christ, through our rebirth.

We might think of ourselves as a people dying of thirst. But off in a distance there is a pool of water, a reservoir with a dam and beautiful pebble-lined banks. We can see the green trees and lush grass in its vicinity, but we can't see the reservoir itself. We desperately need to get to it.

By accepting Jesus, all that He is, all that He has done—by being born again—we gain access to this marvelous reservoir, this thirst-quenching pool of water, the kingdom of God. We are given access to an entirely new world, a heretofore invisible world—the secret kingdom.

"Have faith in God," Jesus said. Believe that God exists, trust Him, expect Him to enter into communion with you, to show you His will and purpose. Use the water in the reservoir. Remember that faith is the title deed to that pool of power.

It is all ours, if we know the *rules of miracles.*

First, *we are to take our eyes off the circumstances and the impossibilities and to look upon God and the possibilities.* We have good examples from the history of God's people for this. Remember Joshua and Caleb.[4] Representing the twelve tribes of Israel, they and ten others were sent as spies to determine if the people should enter the land promised to them by God. They stayed forty days and returned with reports of a marvelous land of milk and honey, but it was peopled with giants living in fortified cities.

"They are too strong for us," ten of the spies said.

But Caleb and Joshua, who were to figure prominently in Israel's future, were enthusiastic and eager to move ahead. "It doesn't matter how many giants there are. The Lord is with us." They looked at God and not at the circumstances, reflecting the attitude He expected of His people.

Yet the ten others prevailed, exploiting the fears of the Israelites existing since their flight from Egypt. They succumbed to their crisis, ignoring the principles of the miraculous, and failed to take what was theirs.

The biblical story of Jonathan, the son of King Saul, shows us how to focus on God rather than circumstances.[5] He and his young armorbearer, looking at a great field of enemy Philistine soldiers, put out a sign to see if God was with them. He was. So they moved to the attack, declaring that it was no harder for the Lord to win with a few than with many. Their refusal to be deterred by seemingly impossible circumstances led to an important victory by the entire army of Israel.

HAVE FAITH, NEVER DOUBTING

Second, *we are not to doubt in our hearts.* We have seen that spirit controls matter, that lesser authority yields to greater authority, and that the mind and the voice are the instruments by which the will of the spirit is transmitted to the environment.

For miracles to happen through us, God's will must first be transmitted by the Holy Spirit to our spirits. Then, Jesus declared, we must not doubt in our hearts. The inmost center of our beings—which the Bible alternately terms the "heart" or the "spirit"—must be focused on the objective. Our hearts must be fully persuaded, without any doubt. We must be like Abraham, who against all hope believed God would grant him a son by his wife Sarah. "He staggered not at the promise of God through unbelief; but was strong in faith, giving glory to God; and being fully persuaded that, what he had promised, he was able also to perform."[6]

In fact, the persuasion in our spirit must be so strong that it seems to us the desired result has already taken place. As Jesus put it, "Believe that you have received" and you will have what you say.

I experienced this extraordinary *present* possession of a *future* miracle before I acquired CBN's first television station. Although my available capital was only seventy dollars, and I was without a job, and although I did not own a television set and was without any knowledge of broadcasting, motion pictures, or theater, the purchase of a station became for me a present reality. Even now it is hard to describe my inner experience at that time. The persuasion in my spirit was so real that purchasing a station with seventy dollars seemed as possible as buying a bag of groceries at a supermarket.

As an official of RCA later told me, "You sounded so positive that we thought you had the money in the bank."

To those around me who could see only the *visible* reality, I was on a fool's errand. The things I was attempting were clearly impossible. But God had given me a measure of faith, and my spirit counted God's resources as part of my reality. As Jesus said: "This is something people cannot do, but God can. God can do all things."[7]

The tentative, the hesitant, the fearful, the overly cautious, the half-hearted, and the half-persuaded will never know miracle power. They will never experience success or victory in the visible or the invisible worlds. The goals they seek will always elude them, and they will never understand why. Never, at least, until they understand that their divided minds and spirits are actually projecting the seeds of failure into every situation.

THE TIME TO SPEAK

When Mark told in his Gospel of the cursing of the fig tree, he was careful to include the voice. Jesus *spoke* to the fig tree, and He told the disciples to *command* the mountain, which would do what they said if they didn't doubt in their hearts.

Scripture tells us further that Jesus stilled a storm by *speaking* to it,[8] raised three dead people by *speaking* to them,[9] cast out demons by *speaking* to them,[10] cleansed a leper by *speaking* to him,[11] and healed a Roman officer's servant by *speaking a word from a remote location.*[12]

Prayer for Jesus was communing with the Father, listening to the Father, watching the Father. What was the Father doing? What did He desire? Insight from the Father unified the heart and mind of the Son. Then, taking the authority that was His, the Son spoke the word of the Father. And the miracle happened.

So we see that miracles begin with certainty that God is present and that He has a purpose. Then we, His people, translate that purpose into the physical world by invoking His unlimited power. We do it with our mouths, speaking the word of the Lord to the mountain, to the disease, to the storm, to the demons, to the finances that God wants to send to us.

We do not pray further, unless the situation specifically calls for prayer. In one instance, Jesus said, "That kind of [unclean] spirit can only be forced out by prayer."[13] That means we pray in those cases. Jesus also prayed at the tomb of Lazarus, but He made it plain that He was doing so for the people to recognize that God was performing the miracle. Then He Himself approached the tomb and uttered the words, "Lazarus, come forth,"[14] executing God's will by speaking.

Prayer is extremely important, and we are never to neglect it. Jesus gave us example after example, going off by Himself to pray, often for hours, and the Scripture writers are relentless in their admonitions to pray. Paul went so far as to tell us to pray without ceasing.[15]

But once God's will is disclosed, then is the time to shift to speaking.

Because of the great power the Lord has given to speech, it is terribly important that we Christians not use our mouths to speak slander, profanity, lust, or foolishness. The last point is delicate. We are not to think that the Lord lacks humor or that we should not have fun. It means merely that we should avoid jokes and foolishness about sacred things, for that comes dangerously close to violation of the third commandment: "You shall not take the name of the LORD your God in vain."[16]

Why should the Lord be so deeply concerned about our use of His name that He would include the issue in the Ten Commandments? He was giving us insight into the power of speech. We have in our mouths the power to kill or to make alive. We must not take it lightly.

This significance explains why, on the Day of Pentecost when the power of the Holy Spirit came upon the disciples, an evidence of their anointing was their speaking in tongues.[17] Their voices were empowered by the Holy Spirit, a miracle that continues to be experienced by people of God today through what is known as the baptism of the Holy Spirit. From there, the disciples entered into ministry more miraculous than any they had known. They had been clothed with power from on high.[18] Their speech was a critical factor—again, not to be taken lightly.

THE MAJOR HINDRANCE

Having faith, seeing, refusing to doubt, speaking—all are critically important parts of the Law of Miracles. But Jesus made another point in the episode with the fig tree. Many people wish He hadn't.

> And whenever you stand praying, forgive, if you have anything against anyone; so that your Father also who is in heaven may forgive you your transgressions. But if you do not forgive, neither will your Father who is in heaven forgive your transgressions.[19]

With those few words, He set forth the major hindrance to the working of miracles in the visible world—the lack of forgiveness. Men and women, Christian and non-Christian, carry grudges. Any power of God within them is eaten up by resentment.

Is there any wonder that we see so little of the miraculous intervention of God in the affairs of the world?

We noted earlier that our initial view of God and our entrance into kingdom blessings depend on being born again and allowing the Lord to remove the cloud of sin between us and God. That unobstructed view must continue if we are to evidence the miraculous. Being born again merely sets the process in motion; we must then walk step by step in a state of forgiveness. John the apostle said it this way: "If we live in the light, as God is in the light, we can share fellowship with each other. Then the blood of Jesus, God's Son, [continuously] cleanses us from every sin."[20]

He went on to say that the one who hates his brother, who is not in a state of forgiveness with him, walks in the darkness and doesn't know where he's going. Thus walking in the light equates to living in proper relationships, which also means that we can be cleansed of our sins. The blood of Jesus does not cleanse in the dark or in a state of unforgiveness. Without forgiveness, our view of God and His kingdom is clouded. We will see no miracles.

In this matter, the Lord does not appear to be speaking of the loss of eternal salvation, for we have learned that this comes by grace through faith, not works. He is not saying a grudge will prevent you from ultimately going to heaven; He can be expected to deal with that at the proper time. Rather, He is declaring that if we want to experience now the miraculous power, say, of moving mountains, it is imperative that we live in a condition of forgiveness. Unforgiveness is not a characteristic acceptable in the kingdom of God. It contradicts the doctrine of forgiveness itself.

If all the law and all the prophets hang on loving God with one's entire being and loving our neighbors as ourselves,[21] then unforgiveness can shatter everything. It reveals, among other things, the horrible sin of pride. For only the humble can forgive—those who surrender anger, feelings, and reputation to the will of God.

NO SMALL MATTER

One well-known dialogue occurred with Peter right after a bit of instruction on unity: "Then Peter came and said to Him, 'Lord, how often shall my brother sin against me and I forgive him? Up to seven times?' Jesus said to him, 'I do not say to you, up to seven times, but up to seventy times seven.'"[22]

Increasing the impact of the lesson, the Lord went on to tell a parable about a nobleman's slave who was forgiven a debt of $10 million after coming close to being sold, along with his family, on the slave market to recover the money. The man turned around and seized another slave who owed him $100 and had him thrown into prison for nonpayment. Here is how Jesus concluded the parable:

> Then summoning him [the first man], his lord said to him, "You wicked slave, I forgave you all that debt because you entreated me. Should you not also have had mercy on your fellow slave, even as I had mercy on you?" And his lord, moved with anger, handed him over to the torturers until he should repay all that was owed him. So shall My heavenly Father also do to you, if each of you does not forgive his brother from your heart.[23]

It is no small matter, and I regret that the church through the years has not dealt more forcefully with it. As members of the kingdom, totally indebted to our loving heavenly Father, we must maintain an attitude and an atmosphere that promote harmony with our brothers. If we refuse to love our neighbors, we cannot receive blessings from our Father, and we block the flow of miraculous power.

Our principal weapon in the crisis we face in the world is love, and love operates only in a state of forgiveness and reconciliation. Pettiness must go, and jealousy and pride and lack of concern for others, and neglect of the poor and needy.

LETTING GO, LETTING GOD

I have a close friend, Demos Shakarian, the founder of the Full Gospel Businessmen's Fellowship, one of the outstanding ministries in the world, who told me a story from his own life that reinforces the reality of the Law of Miracles as well as any I know.

At death, his father left a sizable fortune in property. In that period of grief and legal confusion, a family friend stepped in and legally, yet questionably, took advantage of the grieving children to gain control of a part of the estate.

Demos, when he realized what had happened, became angry and a seed of bitterness took root in him. A deep and churning resentment grew, worsening as he reflected on the nature of a man who would take advantage of those who trusted him.

One day God showed Demos that if he was to please Him, he would have to deal with this resentment. He would have to forgive the man.

That was a difficult instruction from the Lord. The family friend was guilty. He had done something wrong to make money. Yet God said, "You must forgive him."

So, despite the spiritual struggle, Demos telephoned the man and arranged a meeting. I'm sure the man expected a confrontation and perhaps a shouting match; that's the way those things usually work out. But Demos, Spirit-filled and familiar with the purposes of God, followed through and said: "I want to ask your forgiveness. I've harbored resentment against you over what happened. I've actually hated you. But I've been wrong and I've repented before God, and I totally forgive you for anything you may have done. And now I ask your forgiveness."

It was more than the man could stand. He began to weep, and the uniqueness of the moment broke him internally. Someone he had treated badly was actually asking him for forgiveness! It was upside down.

Demos recalled that he immediately felt the flow of God's power in his own life. He was thoroughly free.

The two embraced and were reconciled.

In a matter of days, Demos received a call from an official of a corporation that owned a store on another piece of his property. The corporation had closed the store, and the future of the building and lease were unsettled. However, the official said, "You've been so nice to us that we're going to give you the store."

Again, things were upside down. That sort of thing simply was not done.

Without lifting a finger, Demos had overnight received a building worth far more than the disputed inheritance. There was no quarreling or legal fighting. God had moved miraculously once the roadblock of unforgiveness had been removed.

Furthermore, his ministry, which centers on the miracle-working power of God, is flourishing to this day. Continuous forgiveness and continuous love are the crucial ingredients in the Law of Miracles.

MIRACLES ARE AVAILABLE

If we would live in the kingdom of God today, by grace through faith, we would see far more miracles. We need only look at Paul's relatively compact, but nonetheless illuminating, instructions to the early Corinthian church to discover the miracle experiences that were considered normal.[24] He spoke of the "manifestations" that the unblocked presence of the Holy Spirit within God's people would bring forth, declaring that these were for the common good.[25] There was nothing elitist or abnormal about them.

> For to one is given the *word of wisdom* through the Spirit, and to another the *word of knowledge* according to the same Spirit; to another *faith* by the same Spirit, and to another *gifts of healing* by the one Spirit, and to another the *effecting of miracles,* and to another *prophecy,* and to another the *distinguishing of spirits,* to another *various kinds of tongues,* and to another the *interpretation of tongues.*[26]

These are the supernatural evidences of God's favor and grace. They are among the effects of the blowing of the Spirit in our lives that the Lord was talking about with Nicodemus. You can't see the Spirit, which He likened to the wind, but you do see His effects.[27] When the wind blows, tree leaves move. When the Spirit blows other things move as well.

In my unending quest for wisdom, it turned out that the "word of wisdom" was a miracle of God that developed special meaning for me. All the gifts of the Spirit are exceedingly important when springing from faith, hope, and love, but the supernatural bestowal of the word of wisdom is to be cherished.

The word of wisdom, as I indicated in chapter 6 when talking about wisdom in a broader sense, is a glimpse into the future regarding a specific event or truth. It is an unveiling.

Many people think prophecy is futuristic, and it often is. But not always. Prophecy specifically is "forth-telling"—speaking forth the Word of God. Quite often it deals with the present, or perhaps even the past.

I was praying one day early in 1969, and the Lord spoke plainly to my inner man: "Communisim will collapse in the Soviet Union, but then they will be the most dangerous. Fidel Castro will fall in Cuba. There will be a great opportunity for the gospel. The stock market will crash. Only the securities of your government will be safe."

By 1992 I can surely say that Communism has fallen in the Soviet Union, and in the former Eastern Bloc there has been the greatest opportunity for the gospel in the history of mankind. Fidel Castro has not yet fallen, but rumors have it that he has been negotiating an exile in Spain. In 1969 there was a market crash as there was in 1974, but I believe the big one has not yet happened and may soon be upon us. Whatever happens, in this it is clear that God speaks today to those who will listen so that they may prepare His people for what is to come.

PASSING ON THE BLESSING

Part of my motivation for taking the time and effort to produce my newsletter, *Pat Robertson's Perspective,* for "700 Club" members is to transmit to the people of the kingdom the insights the Lord has given me concerning these matters. And the Lord has steadily increased this miraculous manifestation in my life and in ways more directly affecting the ministry than just the performance of the stock market.

One day some years later, at a prayer meeting regarding a then upcoming telethon in which we needed to raise the funds to meet the budget of our expanding outreach, the Lord spoke a word of wisdom as part of a prophecy. He responded to our concern about the burden we carried if we were to fulfill the mission He had given us.

I was speaking in prophecy about the presence of the Lord in what we were doing, and then the word of wisdom came regarding the telethon several days thence: "It will be so marvelous that you will not believe that it is happening. And yet this is going to happen before your eyes, and when it does happen, do not give credit to yourself, to your program people, to your computer operators, or to any of the things you have done. But give Me credit because I am telling you now that I am going to do it. And when it's over, you will see it and you will know who did it."

Of course, the word was fulfilled and we dramatically exceeded our goal. He met our need and the need of the people we were ministering to.

And we could give no one else the credit. Despite the difficulty of the circumstances, we were in God's will and He was with us. According to the pattern revealed by the prophet Isaiah, He had proclaimed the "new things" He was doing, even before they sprang forth.[28]

Probably the most frequent occurrence of the miraculous in my life has involved the word of knowledge, touching on physical or emotional healing or other interventions by the Lord in the lives of people. Such a word quite simply reveals information the natural mind would not know about a condition or a circumstance in which God is acting. And there have been memorable times when, quite unwittingly on my part, the "word of knowledge" has actually been an unveiling of something that was to occur in the future—a "word of wisdom."

For example, a woman in California was watching "The 700 Club" while sitting in a great deal of discomfort from a broken ankle encased in a cast. She heard me say on the air, "There's a woman in a cast. She has broken her ankle, and God is healing her."

The woman immediately knew, in a burst of faith in her spirit, that those words had been spoken for her. She rose from the chair, removed the cast, and, with increasing confidence, began to put weight on the broken foot and then to jump on it. The ankle bone had been healed.

The thing she did not know was that she had been watching a program taped a week earlier and shown in her area at that time. Further checking uncovered that I had actually spoken the words about her ankle before it had been broken. In a word of wisdom, I had spoken about something that was yet to occur. The Lord has caused this to happen many times over the years in my ministry.

He wants each of us to reach up into the invisible world and allow Him to perform miracles through us in the visible world. He will do it without limits of time or circumstances. He waits for us to practice the principles He has set forth in Scripture.

THE UNIVERSITY MIRACLE

One of the most miraculous moves in my life, covering numerous laws of the kingdom and spanning several years, involved the establishment of our CBN headquarters, a graduate university (Regent University), and a lovely hotel and conference center.

I had wanted to buy five acres in the city of Virginia Beach, which was burgeoning at that time, as a possible headquarters site. The owner of the land, however, refused to sell a portion of the 143-acre tract.

But the situation changed the day I was sitting in the coffee shop of the Grand Hotel in Anaheim, California. Invited to a conference at the Melodyland Christian Center, I had arrived late for the opening luncheon and was eating alone. When my meal arrived, I bowed my head to say grace—and the Lord began to speak to me about the site three thousand miles away. People around me in the busy shop must have thought I was terribly grateful for the simple cantaloupe and cottage cheese before me, for I remained in prayer for a long time.

"I want you to buy the land," the Lord said. "Buy it all," He said. "I want you to build a school there for My glory, as well as the headquarters building you need."

I had not thought of a school before. True, we desperately needed a headquarters building. But did we need 143 acres? When I returned to Virginia, I called the banker holding the major mortgage on the property and told him I wanted to buy the entire site and build a school on it. "Praise the Lord!" he exclaimed.

I hadn't been able to get anywhere with my small thinking about five acres, but suddenly I had acquired what God had directed—an interstate site worth $2.9 million, with a gift of $550,000 in equity, nothing down, no principal payments for two years, and the balance of the mortgage at 8 percent simple interest payable over twenty-three years.

The terms could hardly have been more favorable! Furthermore, the Lord wasn't finished. He later enabled us to acquire more than five hundred additional acres at prices that today seem nothing short of miraculous. The magnificent center standing on that property today is eloquent testimony to the power of God and the operation of the Law of Miracles. Although I didn't know it at the time, the story had begun long before my California dialogue with the Lord. I eventually learned the following facts.

First, seven years before our acquisition of the site for the center, an Assembly of God minister had seen and shared with a friend of mine a vision of an international center on that same land. It would be a center reaching out to the world with the gospel. It would have students and dormitories, among other things, and would serve missionaries from around the world.

Second, at a point just ten miles from the site I had purchased, the first permanent English settlers in America had planted a cross on the sandy shore and claimed the land for God's glory and for the spread of the gospel. After 370 years, the ultramodern television facility with world-wide capabilities began to fulfill their dreams.

But that was not the only tie to those English settlers. I learned that a college had been part of their vision. Indeed, they had planned Henrico College as a school to teach the gospel and train young men and women for Christian service, hoping to reach the world through education. The plans for the college did not succeed. But the settlers believed the vision would last, as revealed in an introduction to a sermon pertaining to the overall settlement activity: "This work is of God and will therefore stand. It may be hindered, but it cannot be overthrown." They expected their descendants to rise to the challenge.

Unknown to me at the time we bought the land, I am a collateral descendant of the man of God who led the first settlers in prayer in 1607, and a direct descendant of the surgeon who arrived in 1619 at Jamestown with those who were to build Henrico College.

TRUST AND NEVER DOUBT

The miracle has enlarged beyond my dreams in 1975, when God said to buy and build. Regent University has a graduate population today of

1,450 students representing all 50 United States and 40 foreign nations. Our distinguished law school continues to grow at an incredible rate, and recently enrolled 121 first-year students. Registration is up more than 50 percent in the law school this year over the previous year, and interest is growing.

Associated with the law school now is our American Center for Law and Justice, headed by two of America's most outstanding lawyers, Keith Fournier and Jay Sekulow. Jay Sekulow has gained an international reputation for his success in defending cases involving Christian values and constitutional principles at the highest levels, including victories before the United States Supreme Court.

In addition to degree programs leading to the juris doctor degree, the master's degree, and the doctor of philosophy in communications, Regent University is now offering programs leading to the master of business administration, master of education, master of divinity, and a master of arts in biblical studies.

Clearly, this university is a miracle of God. God had a plan. If miracles were required to fulfill it, then He performed miracles—all according to the laws of His kingdom.

The Bible teaches that when Jesus Christ comes back to earth to rule His millennial kingdom, prophecy will cease, the gifts of knowledge and tongues will cease, and visions will cease because we will be in the presence of the living Lord.

We will not need those things at that time because Christ will reveal all things to us. He is Alpha and Omega, the beginning and the end. Things that are imperfect will be done away with, and we will see the essence of perfection revealed in Jesus Christ Himself.

Until that time, however, we need His life and His spiritual weapons. He has charged us to occupy until He comes again, and He has empowered us to do just that, because we need His miracle power today more than ever.

16

The Law of Dominion

I WAS PRAYING and fasting some years ago, seeking to understand God's purpose more fully. I heard His voice, level and conversational, "What do I desire for man?"

A bit surprised, I replied, "I don't know, Lord. You know." Then the Lord directed me to open my Bible. "Look at Genesis, and you will see," He said.

Genesis is one of the longest books in the Bible, but I opened it at the beginning. As I read along, my eyes fell on this passage:

> And God said, Let us make man in our image, after our likeness: and *let them have dominion* over the fish of the sea, and over the fowl of the air, and over the cattle, and over all the earth, and over every creeping thing that creepeth upon the earth. So God created man.[1]

"Let them have dominion." My eyes went over it several times. Then I knew the Lord's purpose. He wanted man to have dominion—then and now.

It was very clear. This was a kingdom law. God wants man to have authority over the earth. He wants him to rule the way he was created to rule. You cannot help but juxtapose this desire of God with today's reality. The thousands of letters that pour into CBN, the pages of the newspapers, the screens of our television sets reveal anything but a people maintaining authority over their environment.

Christians especially show the symptoms of a defeated people. Many are sick, depressed, needy. They live in fear and confusion. Where, observers fairly ask, is the conquering army sung about in the great church hymns? Where is the blessing promised in the Bible from beginning to end? Was Jesus wrong when He said, "I will build my church; and the gates of hell shall not prevail against it"?[2]

No, Jesus was not wrong. Hell will not prevail. But we are seeing an Old Testament warning lived out among the people of God, and indeed all mankind: "My people perish for want of knowledge."[3] Men haven't been taught the Law of Dominion and the other principles of the kingdom. That is why they are miserable.

But they can change immediately.

AS IN THE BEGINNING

Almighty God wants us to recapture the dominion man held in the beginning. He has gone to great lengths to make that possible, sending His own Son as the second Adam to restore what was lost in Eden.

Remember, at the time of creation, man exercised authority, under God's sovereignty, over everything. He was God's surrogate, His steward or regent.

The Genesis account uses two colorful words to describe this. One, *radah* , we translate as "dominion." Man was to have dominion. The word means to "rule over" or "tread down," as with grapes. It comes from a Hebrew root meaning "spread out" or "prostrate." The picture we get from it is one of all the creation spread out before man, whose dominion would extend wherever his feet trod.

The other word, *kabash*, is translated as "subdue." Man was told to subdue the earth. The root means "to trample under foot," as one would do when washing dirty clothes. Therefore, in *kabash* we have in part the concept of separating good from evil by force.

With the first word, God gives man the authority to govern all that is willing to be governed. With the second, He grants man authority over the untamed and the rebellious. In both instances, God gave man a sweeping and total mandate of dominion over this planet and everything in it.

But stewardship requires responsibility. And implicit in the grant was a requirement that man order the planet according to God's will and for God's purposes. This was a grant of freedom, not of license. As subsequent history proved, God's intention was that His world be governed and subdued by those who themselves were governed by God. But man, as we know, did not want to remain under God's sovereignty. He wanted to be *like God* without having anyone to tell him what to do.

The progression toward the Fall is enlightening. First, note that God, after giving man dominion over the fish, the fowl, the cattle, and all the earth, specified that this authority extended to "every creeping thing that creepeth upon the earth."[4] Man specifically had dominion over serpents.

Then, we ask, what happened when Eve was faced with a challenge by the serpent? She faltered and allowed the serpent to convince her that God's grant of sovereignty was faulty. She refused to exercise her authority, and, worse than that, the serpent took authority over and manipulated her. Worse yet, with that first erosion, mankind allowed virtually all of his dominion to slip away.

It was the Law of Use in operation: Refuse to use what you have been given and you will lose it. Since that time, Satan has been exercising a type of dominion over human beings, deceiving them, destroying them.

God wants man to repossess that original dominion. He is ready to cause the Law of Use to work in our favor, if we will but begin to exercise what has been given.

A SHIFT OF ALLEGIANCE

We need to understand that God did not actually take the dominion away from man. He simply took away man's access to Him because of sin. Man still had dominion, but he lost the relationship and understanding necessary to exercise it properly. From there, the condition deteriorated as man voluntarily gave himself to the dominion of others.

As a result, man has for ages been neglecting and even misusing that which he was told to rule and subdue. He has, in effect, raped the creation rather than take care of it. He has lost the humility and discipline to exercise dominion as God intended. He has exercised it arrogantly, or not at all. He hasn't been a servant of the creation—the animals, the oceans and rivers and streams, the forests, the mountains, the resources. He has violated the Law of Responsibility.

It is clear that God is saying, "I gave man dominion over the earth, but he lost it. Now I desire mature sons and daughters who will in My name exercise dominion over the earth and will subdue Satan, the unruly, and the rebellious. Take back My world from those who would loot it and abuse it. Rule as I would rule."

Included in God's grant of dominion to man was sovereignty over flowers, vegetables, and fruit. The mandate was all-inclusive: "Behold, I have given you every plant yielding seed that is on the surface of all the earth, and every tree which has fruit yielding seed; it shall be food for you."[5]

In one of the tragic ironies of all history, the Fall meant not only that man became a slave of Satan and his own base passions, but also that a sizable portion of mankind would become slaves of flowers, vegetables, and fruit. We have learned that those three can be cruel taskmasters.

According to the statistics published by David Barrett and Todd M. Johnson in 1990, there are more than 650 million men and women worldwide, and a skyrocketing number of children, addicted to the tobacco plant. Of this number, there were 2.6 million tobacco-related deaths in 1990 alone. In addition, there are more than 170 million alcoholics worldwide—victims of corn, barley, rye, and grapes—with at least 20 million in the United States.

These products are involved in more than 70 percent of the fifty-five thousand accident-related deaths on American highways each year. What a fearful toll these addictive stimulants take on human strength, creativity, and happiness.

Yet even more insidious is the weed, *cannabis*—called grass, pot, or marijuana—which has sucked a staggering number of young people into deeper and more destructive addictions over the past three decades. Along with formulated drugs, such as amphetamines, and street drugs, such as crack, crystal, cocaine, heroin, and others—each in some way a corrupted derivative of a plant or natural product—addictive substances are destroying the brains and the futures of entire generations of Americans.

As I reported in more detail in my book, *The New Millenium*, U.S. Justice Department statistics show that 58.5 percent of Americans between the ages of twenty-six and thirty-four have used marijuana and nearly 25 percent have used cocaine. For many these easy-to-get drugs are considered "gateway" drugs to even harder and more dangerous substances. We shudder at the fortunes that change hands and the crimes that are committed by those under the dominion of the coca plant and the opium poppy. The number of people convicted of drug possession in this country doubled in the decade of the 1980s, and the number convicted for manufacturing drugs increased 180 percent.

The drug industry in North and South America is larger than the entire United States automobile industry and apparently more profitable. The alcohol industry rakes in more than $65 billion each year in the United States alone. Despite a growing public reaction against smoking, the tobacco industry gathers in billions more per year. So valuable is cigarette brand awareness that the trade name "Marlboro" and the companion cowboy were recently calculated to be worth $39 billion, more than any other trade name in the world. Of the 50 million deaths worldwide each year, fully fifty thousand are the result of "second-hand smoke"—that is, breathing the smoke exhaled by another person.

The evidence shows that well over half of America's staggering $738 billion medical bill can be attributed to illnesses induced by slavery to these items—vegetables, flowers, and fruit. Yet the statistics only reveal a part of man's slavery. The losses in terms of trials forced on the hearts and souls of these people, and on their mental, physical, and spiritual stability, are incalculable.

But almost every attempt to set people free from these forms of slavery is met with derision. It does not matter that they lead to death, disability, and degradation. Those living outside the kingdom clutch their "pleasures" to their bosoms as if they were holy and sacred rights.

A FALSE CONSENSUS

You see, when man broke free of God's authority, he lost control of himself. Without a clear relationship with God, he became unable to see where he was going, and he soon became captive of what the Bible calls "the world, the flesh, and the devil." His own fears, his animal drives, his lusts drove him. The devil, a malevolent power, played upon his base desires to seduce and entrap him. Then, as the human race grew, each man became a slave of mob psychology—the tyranny of the warped consensus of a sinful world.

Before the world can be freed from bondage, man must be made free from himself. This is why Jesus told the Jews of His day: "If you abide in My word, then you are truly disciples of Mine; and you shall know the truth, and the truth shall make you free."[6]

Again, the writer of the letter to the Hebrews, speaking of the effect of the death of Jesus for mankind, said: "that through death He might render powerless him who had the power of death, that is, the devil; and might deliver *those who through fear of death were subject to slavery all their lives.*"[7]

When man, through Jesus, reasserts God's dominion over himself, then he is capable of reasserting his God-given dominion over everything else. That is the way everything on earth will be freed from the cycle of despair, cruelty, bondage, and death.

I furthermore believe the Lord would have man subdue the natural forces in the universe. Jesus, who was our example as well as our Redeemer, did this, as we have discussed in earlier chapters.

Without in any way advocating fanaticism, I believe God would enable man, under His sovereignty, to deal successfully with the conditions that threaten the world with catastrophic earthquakes. Scripture makes plain that God uses natural disasters as judgment upon mankind, but I am convinced that were man to turn from his wicked ways and seek the Lord, he would be able to take dominion over the faults in the earth's structure and render them harmless. For the words of Jesus spoken to the tumultuous waters of Galilee still echo down through history with great power and authority: "Peace, be still."[8]

Similarly, man, taking his rightful place under God, would subdue the causes of drought and famine. World hunger would cease.

DOMINION THEOLOGY

The Law of Dominion should not be confused with the teachings of what is sometimes called "dominion theology" or "reconstructionism." Reconstructionists believe that through the discipline and authority of the church and the empowerment of Christ, Christians will ultimately reclaim the earth as the kingdom of God and bring peace and unity to all mankind. It is the idea that man, through his own efforts, is going to reconstruct the fallen earth and bring in the millennial kingdom.

While there are elements of this belief which are biblical, in general this view is mistaken. It is a fairly extreme interpretation of the Scriptures, and that is not at all what I want to imply in this chapter.

We have more authority now than any of us dreamed possible, but I do not believe that man, through his efforts, is going to bring the world back to a time of Edenic innocence. The millennial kingdom will not come until Jesus Himself does it, but that does not mean that we should not strive in His name. The great commission says, "Go therefore and make disciples of all the nations, baptizing them in the name of the Father and of the Son and of the Holy Spirit, teaching them to observe all things that I have commanded you; and lo, I am with you always, even to the end of the age."[9]

When I was writing *The New World Order,* God revealed to me in the most palpable way that the biblical prophecies concerning the coming kingdom, given by the prophets Isaiah and Micah, are to be taken absolutely literally. The Law of the Lord is going to go forth from Jerusalem. All the people are going to say, "Let us go to Jerusalem, for there is the Law of the Lord, and we will walk in His ways." I have been privileged to live that out. When I travel abroad now, men and women at all levels of society, from heads of state to taxi drivers, are saying to me,

"Teach us the Law of the Lord." The Bible proclaimed the people would cry out, "Teach us that we might walk in His ways."

A high official in Romania came up to CBN Vice-President for Development Michael Little and said: "Look, I am an atheist; I don't believe in God or Jesus Christ, and I don't believe in the Bible. But I know that if we are going to build a just society in Romania, we have to build it on the Bible."

He said, "We want your Bible on our national television in Romania." So, consequently, today CBN programming is teaching the Bible in animated Bible stores over Romanian television Monday through Friday at 7:30 P.M., throughout that entire nation. Not only that, the Romanians are inviting teachers of religion to come into their schools to instruct them in the Law of the Lord.

IN SEARCH OF WISDOM

This same scenario is being repeated all across Eastern Europe, in Africa, and in many other Third World nations. The kings, presidents, and government officials are saying, "What is the ideal society?" "What is a Bible-based society?" "How do you organize and manage an orderly society?" They want to learn God's Law.

We broadcast a report from Russia on CBN News in the summer of 1991 in which a young woman who had grown up under communism made a challenging comment. She said, "When we look at America, we see prosperity, comfort, success, and relative peace. When we look at Russia, we see poverty, despair, unhappiness, and strife. So we ask ourselves, what is the main difference between Russia and America? and the answer is, in America you have God; in Russia, we have no God. So now we are changing. We want to know about God. We want to know about the Bible. We want to know Jesus Christ."

If indeed all men would walk according to His Law, it would be a whole new world we would be living in, but obviously they are not. The idea that we are going to bring in the millennium by ourselves is, in my estimation, false theology.

GOD'S FELLOW WORKERS

The concept of man's dominion over the created order is too much for us to comprehend unless we get a secure grip on the fact that the Lord thinks of us as fellow workers with Him in the development and operation of His kingdom.

Mark, in his Gospel, tells how the disciples went out after Christ's ascension and "preached everywhere, while the Lord *worked with them.*"[10]

Paul, in his first letter to the Corinthians, reminded them that it was perfectly proper for both him and Apollos to be ministering to them. "We are God's *fellow-workers,*"[11] he said.

Later, in a passage describing Christians as "ambassadors for Christ" to whom God has committed the message of reconciliation, he spoke of "*working together* with Him."[12]

You see, the Bible's view is that God, in a mystery too great for us to fathom, has chosen to use men to carry the truth around the world. To accomplish this, He had to give them authority.

In addition, the Bible speaks of that time when God's kingdom and His Christ will visibly rule on earth. "If we endure," Paul wrote, pointing to the Law of Perseverance, "we shall also *reign with Him.*"[13] That will involve exceptional authority. God wants us to prepare for it.

We see this exemplified in the accounts of the Lord's sending His disciples out to minister: "Jesus called the twelve apostles together and gave them *power* and *authority* over all demons and the ability to heal sickness. He sent the apostles out to tell about God's kingdom and to heal the sick."[14]

Obviously, in the Lord's mind authority went hand in hand with the proclamation of the kingdom. Authority authenticated the kingdom. How would it be possible to say there was a kingdom of God that was to supplant the kingdom of Satan unless it carried power and authority?

Those two words, "power" and "authority," have a significance of their own, too. First, the passage says, the Lord gave them "power," which is translated from the Greek word *dunamis.* It means "resident power." Dynamite, for example, has that kind of power. Christians who have the Holy Spirit operating in their lives also have it. It is the power to perform miracles.

But the Lord also gave them "authority." This is translated from the Greek word *exousia.* It, too, carries with it the idea of force and power, specifically in the sense of authority like that of a magistrate or potentate.

KINGDOM AUTHORITY

Quite simply, Jesus gave them power to perform miracles and authority to use that power over the devil and all creation. At another time, speaking to seventy people who had gone out to minister, Jesus said: "Listen, I have given you power to walk on snakes and scorpions, *power that is greater than the enemy has.*"[15]

With that, He was referring directly back to the Fall, for serpents are a remembrance not only of the deception in the Garden of Eden, but also of the curse that followed. Serpents and men have been at enmity ever since God said the seed of Eve would one day bruise the head of the serpent,[16] pointing to the triumph of Christ over the devil and his works.

So, in giving His followers such authority, Jesus was indeed saying, "I reestablish your authority over the one who robbed you of it in the garden. You can reassert your dominion."

Our problem in the twentieth century, as we perish for lack of knowledge, is that it does us no good to have this authority if we don't exercise it correctly. And most of us don't.

Yet we have tried so hard in many cases to take seriously the words Jesus spoke to His people before ascending to heaven to sit at the right hand of His Father. We must examine those words closely and with understanding: "And Jesus came up and spoke to them, saying, '*All authority* has been given to Me in heaven and on earth. Go therefore . . .'"[17]

In the long and moving prayer Jesus spoke in the hearing of the disciples just a few hours before His arrest and trial, he prayed to the Father saying "I [have] accomplished the work which Thou hast given Me to do."[18] He had destroyed "the works of the devil,"[19] which especially included the robbery performed in the Garden of Eden. He, the King of the kingdom, had "all authority."

"Therefore," He declared, "go!"

His people could move out to accomplish their worldwide task because He had restored man's dominion under God.

SATAN'S STRATEGY

Satan, although defeated, is alive today, of course, and is as dangerous as we allow him to be. His primary weapon is deceit, and he uses it to prevent Christians from exercising the authority that is truly theirs in this world.

First, of course, he tries to entice us into sin, which can cloud or obstruct our view of the Lord and His will and, untended, can separate us from God.

He also tries to lead us into another form of sin, through unbelief. He tries to make us feel unworthy of the grace in which we stand. If he gets the upper hand in this, then we neglect the authority and the power given to us. They fall into disuse and, ultimately, vanish like the mist. The dominion that has been so awfully and awesomely won for us serves no purpose if it is not exercised.

We must combat this with all our strength and all our alertness. We must not be deceived.

We should recognize that we, in fact, *are* unworthy but that through the Lord Jesus we become worthy in the sight of God. We are sinners but, like Paul, who described himself as chief and foremost among sinners,[20] we "can do all things through Him who strengthens" us.[21]

Too many times, people fall into the devil's trap of believing that we can somehow earn our dominion. If we fall for that, we will never feel worthy, and we will never use the dominion given us. And we will never overcome the crises in the world.

If Satan can keep us in a state of timidity, discouragement, or embarrassment, he will nullify our authority and delay the manifestation of the kingdom of God on earth. I have been amazed in recent years by the success of this very simple maneuver. He has rendered Christians ever so slightly embarrassed about being Christians. The world, for example, sees nothing wrong with a person carrying a copy of *Playboy* or *Penthouse* magazine around under his arm on the street, in the bus or subway. The same with a bottle of whiskey or a carton of cigarettes, with all of its life-threatening ingredients. Yet vast numbers of Christians have been intimidated about carrying a Bible on the street or bus or subway. They're afraid of being categorized as religious freaks, or perhaps old-fashioned and out-of-step with the world. They are nervous about being discovered in prayer or other attitudes perceived as different. As for authority—whether it be over Satan or over the natural order—their timidity is overwhelming.

And yet, as we have noted before, the Bible says, "God has not given us a spirit of timidity, but of power and love and discipline."[22]

Neither Satan nor the world has the authority nor the power to limit or impede the Lord's people. They are flying directly in the face of God's desire. He wants us to assure our rightful authority and to hasten the coming of the kingdom on earth. Jesus emphasized this when He said: "And this *gospel of the kingdom* shall be preached in the whole world for a witness to all the nations, and then the end shall come."[23]

You see, there are many signs of the times that we can watch for, but this one is most critical. The gospel of the kingdom in all its fullness and power, with all its authority, is to be carried to every nation. Timidity must vanish. There will be "signs and wonders"[24]—miracles and other evidences of the kingdom.

The Law of Dominion, properly exercised, will guarantee that.

IT MUST BE VOICED

In practical terms, the Law of Dominion works much like the Law of Miracles. It depends on the spoken word. We are to take authority by voicing it, whether it involves the devil or any part of the creation.

We should not argue with Satan. We merely tell him that he has to go, that he has no authority, that he must release this person or that situation. Quite bluntly, we say, "In the name of Jesus, I command you to get out of here, Satan!"

Also, reaching the mind of the Lord, we tell the storm to quiet, the crops to flourish, the flood water to recede, the attacking dog to stop. We simply speak the word aloud.

Again, the central point is to "have faith in God."[25] But we do not have to await a directive from Him in ordinary circumstances as to when to exercise the authority, assuming that we are walking in His will and yielded to His sovereignty. For He has already given us general guidelines: "Be fruitful and multiply, and fill the earth, and *subdue it; and rule* over the fish of the sea and over the birds of the sky, and over every living thing that moves on the earth."[26]

This especially covers "every creeping thing that creeps on the earth," symbolizing the one described in Christ's time as "the ruler of this world,"[27] who has now been utterly defeated. Even though we still must struggle against those forces that willingly choose to ally themselves with Satan, that struggle has already been decided.

The apostle Paul described it this way: "For our struggle is not against flesh and blood, but against the rulers, against the powers, against the world forces of this darkness, against the spiritual forces of wickedness in the heavenly places."[28]

But since the authority for winning that struggle has been granted, Paul was confident that Christians will "stand firm" in "the evil day." The instrument for wielding that authority, he said, is the Word of God, which he described as the "sword of the Spirit."[29]

We simply are to speak forth our God-restored authority, preparing for an even more amazing era.

17

The Coming King

JESUS SAID AN astounding thing to His disciples: "You have been chosen to know the secrets about the kingdom of God."[1] For three years, Jesus walked and talked with His disciples, and He taught them the principles of the kingdom in intimate detail. But when He commissioned that first group of twelve and sent them out into the world to spread the good news of salvation, He challenged them to "make *disciples, . . .* baptizing them in the name of the Father and the Son and the Holy Spirit." If you have received that good news and believed it, it follows that you, too, are a disciple, and you have been permitted to know the mysteries of the kingdom.

Why would the Savior of the world want to share His privileged secrets? The reason is simple, but very important. He wants all people to live in that realm right now, to master its principles so they will be ready to share in the culmination of the age—His divine new world order.

UNCOVERING THE MYSTERIES

If you are not a disciple of Jesus, the mysteries of the kingdom are bound to remain clouded and confusing, for "flesh and blood cannot inherit the kingdom of God."[2] You must be born of the Spirit and receive access to that secret kingdom. That can occur this moment, merely by asking Jesus Christ to be your Lord and Savior and to take up a spiritual residence in your heart. For God desires that you not miss out on anything; that is why He has been so patient these thousands of years.[3]

From the beginning of man's history, the Lord has been intent on establishing—through love, not fear—a kingdom of people who will voluntarily live under His sovereignty and enjoy His creation. That is the thrust of His entire revelation made in what we call the Holy Bible. He is building a kingdom. And a new, major step in that building shows signs of being at hand. The invisible world may be ready to emerge into full visibility.

One can almost hear Jesus speaking to His church: "Beloved, be ready. I have shown you the laws of My kingdom, the way things truly work. Use them. Live them. They will work for good even now."

There is a new world coming. And we already know ten of its principles!

The Law of Reciprocity teaches the golden rule as the foundation of all personal, national, and international relations.

The Law of Use teaches the key principle of success in life.

The Law of Perseverance teaches that the best in life will only be given to those who struggle and persevere.

The Law of Responsibility teaches that God's increasing blessings bring increased obligations to others.

The Law of Greatness teaches that we achieve true greatness when we love others and serve them selflessly.

The Law of Unity teaches that those who share a common vision can change their world.

The Law of Fidelity teaches that true riches will only accrue to those faithful with what God has entrusted to them.

The Law of Change teaches that God's spiritual kingdom requires continuous change in the old structures of this world.

The Law of Miracles teaches that in the secret kingdom nothing is impossible.

The Law of Dominion teaches that God intends man to reign over this earth as His steward.

Having been explicitly stated in Scripture, these principles are God-breathed. They will change the world as we know it and prepare the way for the coming new world, even speeding its arrival. They, and they alone, can calm the crises choking the world and thwart the imminent slide into chaos and dictatorship of the right or the left. They pose a realistic alternative.

THE OUTLOOK

So on the foundation of these laws and the words of the prophets, here is what we can expect to happen in the days, months, and years ahead.

The nation of Israel is God's prophetic time clock. Having been regathered from the countries of the world, Israel, a unified nation living in relative security, will be invaded by a confederation from the north and the east. The prophet Ezekiel described this force as massive, coming like a storm, a cloud covering the land. He identified elements of it as "Gog of the land of Magog, the prince of Rosh, Meshech, and Tubal," joined by "Persia, Ethiopia, and Put," along with "Gomer," "Beth-togarmah from the remote parts of the north," and "many peoples."[4]

Various people have been viewed as Gog and Magog throughout history—the Goths, the Cretans, the Scythians—but the land described by Ezekiel would be directly to the north. Among the present-day nations that have been suggested by biblical scholars as allies to this confederation are Ethiopia, Iran (as Persia), Somalia, and Libya (as Put). The Muslim republics that formerly comprised the southern region of the old Soviet Union may possibly be included.

It is noteworthy that, at this writing, there is mounting tension and strife in all those regions. Conflicts with and between renegade Arab leaders, of course, continue to make headlines; however, there is also a dangerous rise in fierceness, fear, and famine, stretching from Somalia and Ethiopia to the northern frontiers of the Middle East.

People have asked me quite often over the past year, "What is the significance of Saddam Hussein and the 1991 Persian Gulf War?" I have to say that I have the distinct impression that the war with Iraq was the necessary prelude to that bigger confrontation yet to come.

By that I mean that there will come a time when the nations will unite to pressure Israel to conform to the dictates of the so-called new world order. In the disturbances in Iraq, Syria, Lebanon, and Turkey today we are seeing the early symptoms of that process.

In Jeremiah 23, the prophet makes it clear that instead of saying, "Blessed be the Lord God of Israel who brought His people out of the land of Egypt," the people will cry out, "Blessed by the Lord God of Israel who brought his people out of the land of the north." In sheer numbers, the current exodus from Russia is much greater than the original exodus from Egypt. That this should happen now cannot be accidental.

I believe the settlement of those Russian and European Jews is critical to the fulfillment of prophecy. Personally, I always like to cooperate with prophecy, not fight it! If God has a purpose—as He certainly does in Israel—we don't want to be seen as opposing it. Now that the United States is offering Israel loan guarantees for $10 billion, the process will be accelerated.

THE TEMPLE RESTORED

One of the clear signs given by Scripture that would signal the beginning of the "time of troubles" is the rebuilding of the ancient temple in Jerusalem. Until 1948, the very idea of a Jewish homeland seemed impossible; until 1967, the idea of a restored Jerusalem seemed impossible; and until 1991, the idea of a reconstructed temple seemed impossible. But each of these steps has now been taken, and it is clear that the prophets were revealing God's perfect truth, not holy metaphors.

As additional evidence, today archaeologists are unearthing the foundations of the ancient temple in Jerusalem. They now know that the actual site of the Hebrew temple is, in fact, the one at the foot of the Dome of the Rock. The Muslims are not resisting the excavations because the Jewish site does not immediately affect their mosque, but the foundation stones, the pavement, and even the massive columns of the temple are being uncovered. This is an enormously important sign to students of biblical prophecy.

Discovery of the ancient Hebrew temple after thousands of years is just one more indication that the march of world events is right on schedule. And if the uncovering and rebuilding of the temple takes place according to the Scriptures—which of course it will—then this may be a confirmation that what is happening today in Russia and the Confederation of Independent States is, indeed, just a temporary stage.

It may also be that when that land is finally reunited and the critical social issues are resolved to some degree there will be a movement to take up arms against the nation of Israel, perhaps through the provocation of the belligerent Arab nations surrounding her—such as Syria, Iran, and Iraq, and now the former Muslim republics of the Soviet Union.

These events have great consequence in light of Ezekiel 38. For years, like many students of the Bible, I thought that the references in the prophetic writings to the nations of the North referred only to the Soviet Union. Now I have begun to believe it is more likely the Muslim republics—such as Kazakhistan, Tadzikhistan, Uzbekistan, and Azerbaijan. Should these nations align with Iran and Iraq to form a coalition against Israel, and should the Confederation somehow arm, support, finance, or even join them in that effort, this would be a perfect fulfillment of the prophecy.

At this moment we can see that the growing number of Russian refugees inside Israel could well become a factor in some sort of dispute. As I pointed out in chapter 15, I knew that the Soviet Union would collapse; as far-fetched as that idea seemed at the time, it proved to be true. Their destruction did not take place because they invaded Israel, but it was the first step toward breaking loose the Muslim republics who could quite possibly form an unholy alliance—and possibly a new estate—against the Jews.

IMMINENT STRUGGLE

The Palestinian issue continues to incite bitter strife. At issue is some sort of autonomy for the Arabs living within Israel, for which a satisfactory compromise may well be possible. However, from the United Nations to the PLO, public figures are demanding that Israel turn over the West Bank region and the Gaza Strip to Arab rule. On that volatile issue there is no room for compromise.

If the Israelis were ever forced to surrender sovereignty over the provinces of Judea and Samaria, which are very important parts of the Holy Land, that would surely set off a bitter struggle. We must not forget that the land of Palestine was given to the Jews by divine decree. America and its leaders stand against God's purpose in these matters at their peril.

Nevertheless, the globalist thrust is against Israel, has been, and always will be. When the northern forces move against Israel and its "unwalled villages"—"to capture spoil and to seize plunder"—questions will be raised by people identified as "Sheba, and Dedan, and the merchants of Tarshish, with all its villages [or young lions]."[5] Ezekiel did not say that these people would resist the invaders, but merely ask, "Why have you come here?"[6]

These questioners can probably be pinpointed as Yemen, Saudi Arabia, and the United States, which was once settled by people who could be identified as Tarshish merchants. Tarshish was probably a Phoenician settlement in Spain, near Cadiz, that sent ships to Ireland, then to England, and on to the New World—their passengers traveling all over what was to become the United States of America. *If* there is a reference in the Bible to America, that would seem to be it.

Whether these questioners will assist Israel is unclear. Regardless, God, who is even in control of the invading horde from the north, will intervene in Israel's behalf with a great shaking—earthquakes, volcanic activity, fire, confusion, and even fighting among the allied invaders. He also speaks of fire falling upon Magog, the homeland of the leaders of the force, and upon "those who inhabit the coastlands in safety." This could, of course, be a vision of a nuclear holocaust. But it may also be the direct, miraculous intervention of God, for the prophecy says the following very pointedly: "And My holy name I shall make known in the midst of My people Israel; and I shall not let My holy name be profaned anymore. And *the nations will know that I am the* LORD, *the Holy One in Israel.*"[7]

According to Ezekiel, this will be followed by seven years of Israeli ascendance as the nation grows strong in the Middle East and increases in knowledge of the Lord, climaxed by a nationwide outpouring of the Holy Spirit.

WORDS OF REVELATION

At the same time, the Book of Revelation appears to point to a successor kingdom to the Roman Empire that could roughly parallel the current European Community.[8] It is a ten-nation confederation that has an eleventh nation added, apparently along with a merger of two of the nations, and that league could then be a forerunner of what the apostle John called the Antichrist. Presumably this group will make a treaty with Israel and then turn on her and begin to oppress her.

The leader of this confederation will be a spiritual being who will become a counterfeit Christ and draw men's allegiance. Exploiting confused, chaotic conditions, he will turn the league into a dictatorship, thus poising two kingdoms—the kingdom of God and the counterfeit kingdom—for climactic conflict.

Revelation points to another development that will be instrumental in this period. A system of buying and selling that utilizes individual marks will make possible the economic control of the world's population. The tremendous explosions in computer technology have made this feasible. Even now in Brussels, the headquarters of the European Economic Community, a giant computer system—an interbank transfer system— makes it possible to give every person in the world a number and allocate credits and debits on the basis of that number. I understand that the technology now exists and has been successfully tested to allow an identification device of some type, including a tiny microchip, to be implanted under the skin of the hand. This is nothing short of a fulfillment of prophecy which, only a few years ago, seemed improbable if not impossible.

Banks will institute debit cards, with the capacity to debit accounts instantly, and eliminate the need for exchange of currency. Today many companies and government agencies are using so-called smart cards, which contain a remarkably powerful magnetic strip capable of adjusting debit and credit balances as the card is scanned at the point of sale. The next logical step is to control buying and selling through a similar device in one's hand, as indicated in Revelation.[9]

Whatever the technological possibilities, we should keep in mind that the "forehead" signifies volition or will, and the "hand" signifies action. People will submit their wills and their actions to the Antichrist system, with or without the implanted smart cards.

Thus, one scenario seems capable of fulfillment at almost any time: A major war erupts in the Middle East, with the armies of the northern nations leading the assault upon Israel. That force is destroyed; a catastrophic upheaval results, in which oil supplies to Europe and elsewhere are cut off. Europe is thrown into economic shambles, setting the stage for the sudden rise of a charismatic and resourceful dictator to move swiftly to establish his new economic order.

THE RETURN OF MESSIAH

In the meantime, the kingdom of God will move forward, its future never in doubt. Those who choose to live by its rules will do so and be continuously prepared for that time in history when Jesus Christ will return to earth. The Bible says that He will come back to destroy this new political leader and his "kingdom," setting up in its place a reign of peace and justice forever.[10] At that moment, the invisible kingdom will become a visible one. The secret kingdom will be a secret no longer. And the world—the principalities and powers and the angelic host—will see the way God intended for His universe and His society to function.

We need to understand that God will not abandon His world. He has from the beginning been concerned about the historic record and about His own justification. He does not act arbitrarily. It is as though He will send Jesus, then gather His archangels, the angels, the entire heavenly host and say, "Look, this is the way the world would have worked had man not sinned. This is what I desired." God does not have to justify Himself. He merely does it because He is a God of love and order and justice.

But that will not be the end. It might almost be called a transition period, between the earth as it has been and the ultimate plan of God, in which evil and opposition to the Lord will finally be removed and paradise established.

The Bible says this transition period will cover a thousand years, hence the name "Millennium."[11] In it Christ will reign and there will be peace. He will hold everything together and His greatness will be manifest for all the world to see. He will be revealed in the fullness of what the Scripture has been proclaiming for centuries: He is altogether righteous and perfect; there is no failing in Him; His wisdom is absolute.

Seven hundred years before the birth of Jesus Christ, the prophet Isaiah wrote:

> For a child will be born to us, a son will be given
>   to us;
> And the government will rest on His shoulders;
> And His name will be called Wonderful
>   Counselor, Mighty God,
>   Eternal Father, Prince of Peace.
> There will be no end to the increase of His
>   government or of peace,
> On the throne of David and over his kingdom,
> To establish it and to uphold it with justice and
>   righteousness
> From then on and forevermore.
> The zeal of the LORD of hosts will accomplish
>   this.[12]

Speculation will not be necessary. The beauty of the Lord will be evident to all, as is described in the vision of John:

> And I saw heaven opened; and behold, a white horse, and He who sat upon it is called Faithful and True; and in righteousness He judges and wages war. And His eyes are a flame of fire, and upon His head are many diadems; and He has a name written upon Him which no one knows except Himself. And He is clothed with a robe dipped in blood; and His name is called The Word of God. And the armies which are in heaven, clothed in fine linen, white and clean, were following Him on white horses. And from His mouth comes a sharp sword, so that with it He may smite the nations; and He will rule them with a rod of iron; and He treads the wine press of the fierce wrath of God, the Almighty. And on His robe and on His thigh He has a name written, "KING OF KINGS, AND LORD OF LORDS."[13]

The laws of the kingdom will prevail, and His people will govern with Him. Food, water, and energy will be ample. No longer will trillions of dollars be spent on weaponry. It will go for parks and forests, for scientific advances as yet beyond imagination.

But if His people are to govern with Him under these circumstances, they need answers to several big questions. How do you run a just government? How do you run a world? Which principles work and which do not?

That is why Jesus spoke so often about the kingdom. He let His apostles teach about the church. He, the King, spoke of the kingdom and how it works. He wants us to master these principles so we will be able to serve with Him properly.

Remember, those who are great now will become the least, and those who are least will become great.[14] He will take the little people, His kingdom saints, and exalt them to positions of power. The wealthy, the arrogant, the oppressors—they will be diminished. Their authority will go to the saints, "the fullness of Him who fills all in all."[15]

THE REMOVAL OF EVIL

The Bible says that at the end of the transition period, Satan will be allowed to lead a revolt of those who have still refrained from voluntarily accepting the rule of Christ. Then, after a relatively short period, the Lord will remove Satan (along with all evil and opposition) and bring forth "a new heaven and a new earth."[16] This will be the ultimate and eternal kingdom.

Jesus spoke at some length about the removal of evil in a story that has come to be known as the parable of the tares.[17] It tells of a man who sowed good wheat seed in his field, but at night someone sowed tares—false wheat, weeds—in the same field. Both the wheat and the tares grew, and when the landowner was questioned, he said, "An enemy has done this!"[18] But he wouldn't allow his workers to root up the tares for fear of what damage would be done to the wheat. "Let them both grow," he said, "and at the time of harvest I'll tell the reapers to put the wheat in the barn but to gather the tares for burning."

Later, when Jesus was alone with His disciples, they asked Him the meaning of the parable.

> And He answered and said, "The one who sows the good seed is the Son of Man, and the field is the world; and as for the good seed, these are the sons of the kingdom; and the tares are the sons of the evil one; and the enemy who sowed them is the devil, and the harvest is the end of the age [the consummation]; and the reapers are angels. Therefore just as the tares are gathered up and burned with fire, so shall it be at the end of the age [the consummation]. The Son of Man will send forth His angels, and *they will gather out of His kingdom all stumbling blocks, and those who commit lawlessness*, and will cast them into the furnace of fire; in that place there shall be weeping and gnashing of teeth. THEN THE RIGHTEOUS WILL SHINE FORTH AS THE SUN in the kingdom of their Father.[19]

Everything that is offensive will be removed from the kingdom of God, not by men or the church or military might, but by the angels. They will know the righteous from the evil, and they will know how to act.

At that point, the "sons of the kingdom" will be the only ones left, basking in the light of the Lord, living in ultimate reality and perfection.

Jesus reinforced this understanding for His disciples, following the parable of the tares with one about fish, for several of His close followers were fishermen. He compared the kingdom of heaven to a dragnet cast into the sea to gather fish of every kind. When it was hauled in, the good fish were sorted into containers, but the bad were thrown away. The explanation was the same as before: "So it will be at the end of the age [the consummation]; the angels shall come forth, and take out the wicked from among the righteous."[20]

At this moment, our minds cannot comprehend the perfection that will exist then. We can't even speak about it. Our ideas and words are still too limited.

But think of this: What would it be like if all the energies of men and all creation were founded 100 percent on love? Or consider it in reverse: What if there were not a single trace of hatred anywhere?

That is the world God created for us. No pride, no greed, no fear, no crime, no war, no disease, no hunger, no shortages.

THE FINAL STEP

The Bible speaks of a step in this progressive unfolding of God's perfect plan that would appear to come after all the other phases. It sets forth magnificently the unity and harmony of the Godhead and the ultimate unity and harmony of all creation.

The apostle Paul spoke of it in a complex passage on the sequences of the resurrection of the dead. The point we should see in our context is illuminated clearly:

> For as in Adam all die, so also in Christ all shall be made alive. But each in his own order: Christ the first fruits, after that those who are Christ's at His coming, *then comes the end, when He delivers up the kingdom to the God and Father*, when He has abolished all rule and all authority and power. For He must reign until He has put all His enemies under His feet. The last enemy that will be abolished is death. For He has put all things in subjection under His feet. But when He says, "All things are put in subjection," it is evident that He is excepted who put all things in subjection to Him. And when all things are subjected to Him, then the Son Himself also will be subjected to the One who subjected all things to Him, that God may be all in all.[21]

Again, these plans exceed our capacity for thought. Jesus, the Son and King, in whom all things will be summed up and united in the fullness of time,[22] will present everything to His Father for all eternity.

WHAT WILL MEN DO?

So, then, here we stand. What will men do? Will they continue to ignore the principles governing the way the world works? Or will they learn from the secret kingdom?

I appeal to people everywhere to lay hold of the truths of our world—the Bible's insights into the way it works—and to put them into action. There is still time.

• Give and it will be given to you. This principle will not fail. We simply must begin to execute it—individuals, families, companies, nations. Imagine what our times would be like if we treated others the way we wanted to be treated.

• Take what you already have and put it to use. Don't wait until you have everything you want. Use what you have. Multiply it exponentially, consistently, persistently. The wonders of the world will explode into fullness.

• Do not give up. Persevere. Endure. Keep on asking, keep on seeking, keep on knocking. The world will keep on responding.

• Be diligent to fulfill the responsibility required of you. If God and men have entrusted talent, possessions, money, or fame to you, they expect a certain level of performance. Don't let them down. If you do, you may lose everything.

• Resist society's inducements to success and greatness and dare to become a servant, even childlike. True leadership and greatness will follow. The one who serves will become the leader.

• Reject the dissension and negativism of the world. Choose harmony and unity at every level of life—unity centered on the will of God. Mankind flowing in unity will accomplish marvelous results in all endeavors.

• Be humble enough, yet bold enough, to expect and to do miracles fulfilling the purpose of the Lord. Once and for all, become aware of the power of your speech as you walk humbly and obediently.

• Be faithful in the calling with which you have been entrusted; for whoever is faithful in a few things will be entrusted with even greater things.

• As a follower of the Son of God, be prepared to be an agent of change, but don't frustrate yourself trying to put new wine in old skins. Watch God create new structures to fulfill His plans for you, assume the authority, power, and dominion that God intends for men to exercise over the rest of creation. Recapture that which prevailed in the Garden of Eden before the Fall. Move with power and authority.

• Obviously, there are other laws of the kingdom that the Lord wants us to learn, and He will reveal them if we seek Him. But we can, and should—indeed, we must—begin to adhere to those that are now plain before us.

True, "the axe is already laid at the root of the trees,"[23] as John the Baptist warned nearly two thousand years ago, and those things running contrary to God's purpose will be cut down. The process has presumably already begun. But all is not lost. God's plans will not be circumvented. Yet the movement to ultimate fulfillment need not be one of terror and agony. The crises of the world can be relieved. Just in themselves, the laws of the kingdom can accomplish that. The world can be a far better place as it moves toward fulfillment.

His laws will bring blessing by themselves, but at some point, however, the laws of the kingdom outside of the kingdom will not be enough. A choice will have to be made regarding the kingdom itself. For one day there will be a final shaking by God; then only the kingdom will survive.[24]

So, why wait? Why separate the truths contained in the laws of the kingdom from allegiance to the King? Choose Him this moment. It can be all yours right now!

"Don't fear, little flock, because your Father wants to give you the kingdom."[25]

Notes

Introduction

1. Compare Matt. 15:13 KJV.
2. Matt. 3:2.
3. Matt. 26:46.
4. Matt. 4:17.
5. Acts 1:3 NCV.
6. Luke 4:43 NCV, emphasis added.
7. Luke 17:21.

Chapter 1 • *The Visible World*

1. T. S. Eliot, "The Waste Land," 1932.
2. Isa. 59:10–12 NKJV.
3. Isa. 57:21 NKJV.
4. Francis A. Schaeffer, *A Christian Manifesto* (Chicago: Crossway, 1981), 24, 26.

Chapter 2 • *The Invisible World*

1. Mark 1:15 NKJV.
2. Matt. 10:7.
3. Matt. 6:31–34 NKJV.
4. Mark 4:22–23 NKJV.
5. Matt. 6:33.
6. Matt. 4:17.
7. 1 Sam. 10:25 KJV.
8. 2 Kings 6:16.
9. Rom. 8:19.
10. Matt. 16:28.
11. Matt. 17:2–6, 8.
12. Mark 10:27.
13. John 5:19.
14. Matt. 8:26.
15. Mark 11:14 NCV.
16. Mark 11:17 NCV.
17. Mark 11:22 NCV.
18. See Rev. 4:2.
19. Gen. 1:3.

20. Eph. 3:20.
21. Mark 11:23–24.
22. 1 Cor. 3:9.
23. Matt. 3:2.
24. Matt. 12:25.
25. Matt. 6:33.
26. See Rev. 20:4.
27. Matt. 3:3.
28. Isa. 11:9.
29. Isa. 2:4.

Chapter 3 • *Seeing and Entering*

1. John 1:30.
2. John 1:34.
3. See Matt. 7:29.
4. See Matt. 16:16.
5. See John 3:1–21.
6. John 3:3, emphasis added.
7. John 3:4.
8. John 3:5, emphasis added.
9. See John 4:24.
10. See Gen. 2:17.
11. See John 3:6.
12. See John 1:12–13.
13. See Genesis 1–2.
14. John 3:7–16.
15. John 19:38–42.
16. 1 Cor. 2:12–13, emphasis added.
17. Matt. 28:18–20, emphasis added.
18. See 1 Cor. 2:14.
19. Matt. 18:3.
20. Luke 12:32.
21. John 4:23–24, emphasis added.
22. John 14:6 NCV, emphasis added.
23. Matt. 7:21, emphasis added.
24. John 18:33–37 TLB, emphasis added in last two sentences.
25. John 8:26, 31–32, emphasis added.
26. Ezek. 36:26–27, emphasis added.
27. John 14:17.
28. John 8:44 NCV.
29. Rev. 21:27 KJV.
30. Rev. 21:8 KJV.
31. See Col. 1:16.

Chapter 4 • *How God's Kingdom Works*

1. See Matt. 13:11.
2. See Matt. 13:3–8.
3. See Matt. 14:16–21.
4. Luke 2:52, emphasis added.
5. Mark 1:10–11 NKJV; also see Luke 3:22.
6. See Eph. 2:8–18.
7. See Heb. 4:14–16.
8. Eph. 2:4–7, emphasis added.
9. See Num. 6:24–25.
10. Jer. 23:18.
11. Mark 11:23–24 NKJV.
12. Gen. 1:3.
13. See Genesis 1.
14. See John 1:3.
15. See Gen. 1:2.
16. Mark 11:24 NCV.
17. 1 Cor. 2:16.
18. 2 Tim. 1:7.
19. Ezek. 37:4.
20. Ezek. 37:7–10, emphasis added.
21. Isa. 55:11.
22. Ps. 37:4–5 NKJV.
23. Heb. 11:1–3, 6 NKJV.
24. Heb. 11:1 TLB, emphasis added.
25. Rom. 10:17 KJV.
26. James 1:6–8.
27. Prov. 3:5–6 NKJV.
28. See Matt. 17:20.
29. 1 John 5:14, 15.
30. Mark 8:36–37, NKJV.
31. Prov. 13:2.
32. Phil. 4:13.
33. See Prov. 23:7 KJV.
34. See Ps. 51:6.
35. Matt. 12:50 NCV.
36. Gal. 5:22–23.
37. Matt. 18:19–20 NCV.
38. 1 Pet. 4:1–2 NKJV.
39. 3 John 1:2 NKJV.
40. Deut. 28:11–14 NKJV.
41. Deut. 28:15 NKJV.
42. Luke 6:38 NKJV.

43. Ps. 37:23–24 KJV, emphasis added.
44. Ps. 37:33.

Chapter 5 • *Progressive Happiness*

1. See Exod. 3:14.
2. See Judg. 6:24.
3. See Exod. 17:15.
4. See Gen. 22:14.
5. See Matt. 5:3–12.
6. Luke 18:13–14 KJV.
7. See 2 Cor. 7:10 KJV.
8. Ps. 51:17.
9. 2 Pet. 2:6–8 KJV and NASB.
10. See Gen. 19:1–26.
11. Matt. 24:38–39.
12. Jer. 31:13.
13. See Num. 12:3 KJV.
14. 2 Tim. 1:7, emphasis added.
15. Matt. 11:12.
16. See Rom. 5:17.
17. See Gal. 4:4–7; 2 Pet. 1:3–4.
18. 1 Cor. 6:9–10.
19. Acts 1:8.
20. Matt. 5:6 KJV.
21. Luke 11:9.
22. Matt. 6:24.
23. See Rev. 19:16.
24. See Rom. 8:17.
25. See Rom. 5:1.
26. 2 Cor. 5:18–20 NCV.
27. Luke 2:14 KJV.
28. Matt. 5:10–11.
29. 1 Pet. 4:14, emphasis added.
30. See John 3:19.
31. See 2 Cor. 2:15–16.
32. See Acts 8:3.

Chapter 6 • *Upside Down*

1. James 4:6 KJV, emphasis added.
2. Phil. 2:8.
3. Phil. 2:9, emphasis added.
4. Prov. 22:4.
5. Prov. 16:18.

6. See Jer. 29:13–14.
7. 2 Chron. 1:7.
8. 1 Kings 3:7.
9. 2 Chron. 1:10.
10. 2 Chron. 1:11–12.
11. Matt. 6:33.
12. Prov. 9:10.
13. 1 Cor. 13:13 NCV.
14. See Eph. 2:8.
15. Rom. 5:1–4, emphasis added.
16. Rom. 5:5.
17. See Ps. 37:9.
18. See John 1:5.
19. See Rom. 12:21.
20. Matt. 5:41 NCV.
21. See Rom. 12:20.
22. 1 Cor. 13:4–8.
23. Matt. 5:14 NCV.

Chapter 7 • *The Law of Reciprocity*

1. Luke 6:38.
2. Luke 6:31.
3. Luke 6:36–38.
4. Matt. 22:39, see also Lev. 19:18.
5. Luke 6:38 KJV.
6. Luke 6:38.
7. Matt. 6:33 NKJV.
8. Matt. 7:1.
9. Luke 6:38 NCV.
10. Mal. 3:7–10, emphasis added.
11. Mal. 3:10 TLB.
12. 2 Cor. 9:6–8, 11.
13. 1 Chron. 29:12, 14.
14. Ps. 24:1 KJV.
15. Luke 6:38 NCV.
16. Ps. 37:25.
17. Ps. 37:10–11.
18. E.g., Exodus 21–22; Lev. 18:24, 20:1–27, 21:9.
19. James 4:7 NCV.

Chapter 8 • *The Law of Use*

1. Matt. 25:14–15.
2. Matt. 25:26–27, 30.

3. Matt. 25:29.
4. Matt. 13:31–32 NCV.
5. Mark 4:26–29 NCV.
6. Matt. 4:8–9.
7. See John 12:31; 14:30.
8. Deut. 23:19.
9. Deut. 15:6, emphasis added.
10. Lev. 25:4.
11. Lev. 25:8–10, emphasis added.
12. Exod. 25:9, emphasis added.

Chapter 9 • The Law of Perseverance

1. Col. 1:16 NKJV.
2. 2 Cor. 4:18 NKJV.
3. Phil. 4:13 NKJV.
4. Rom. 8:37 NKJV.
5. Phil. 4:6–7 NKJV.
6. John 10:10 NKJV.
7. Matt. 7:7–11.
8. Matt. 11:12.
9. Luke 18:1–8.
10. Luke 11:5–8.
11. Acts 14:22.
12. 1 Kings 19:4.
13. See 1 Cor. 10:13 NCV.

Chapter 10 • The Law of Responsibility

1. Luke 12:48 KJV.
2. See Luke 12:46–48.
3. James 3:1.
4. 1 Tim. 3:1–7 NCV.
5. See 1 Tim. 3:10.
6. Mark 4:11.
7. Rom. 1:14.
8. John 14:6.
9. 1 Tim. 3:15.
10. Matt. 28:18–20.
11. See Matt. 16:18.
12. Euripides, *Alcymene*, c. 485–406 B.C.
13. Sophocles, *Ajax*, c. 495–405 B.C.
14. Luke 12:47.
15. George Gilder, *Wealth and Poverty* (New York: Bantam, 1982), pp. 30–31 ff.
16. Mark 11:22.

17. Isa. 58:1–11 TLB.
18. Isa. 58:1–2 TLB.
19. See James 1:22–25.
20. Isa. 58:3–4 TLB, emphasis added.
21. Isa. 58:6 TLB, emphasis added.
22. Isa. 58:7 TLB.
23. Isa. 58:8–9 TLB.
24. Isa. 58:10–11 TLB, emphasis added.

Chapter 11 · *The Law of Greatness*

1. Matt. 18:2–4 NCV, emphasis added.
2. Luke 22:25–27, emphasis added.
3. See Gen. 1:28.
4. Matt. 23:11 (paraphrased).
5. Matt. 23:12, emphasis added.
6. Prov. 22:4.
7. See Luke 14:28.

Chapter 12 • *The Law of Unity*

1. Gen. 1:26, emphasis added.
2. See Gen. 3:5.
3. Gen. 3:22–23, emphasis added.
4. Matt. 6:10, emphasis added.
5. Matt. 18:19–20, emphasis added.
6. See Deut. 32:30.
7. Acts 1:14, emphasis added.
8. See Acts 11:26.
9. Acts 13:1–3 NCV.
10. See Acts 13:1, 9.
11. See Acts 4:33, 36.
12. John 17:23.
13. Gen. 11:1.
14. See Gen. 11:4.
15. Gen. 11:6–8, emphasis added.
16. See Rev. 14:8.
17. See James 1:6–8.
18. James 1:6 NCV.
19. See Rom. 4:13–21.
20. Ps. 57:7 KJV.
21. Luke 10:38–42.
22. See Matt. 6:24.
23. See Eph. 5:25.
24. Eccles. 9:10 (paraphrased).

25. Matt. 12:25.
26. Prov. 11:29.
27. James 1:8.
28. 1 Cor. 12:4–7, emphasis added.
29. John 17:20–23.

Chapter 13 • *The Law of Fidelity*

1. Luke 16:10–12 NIV.
2. Rev. 22:15 NIV.
3. Luke 16:11 NCV.
4. Luke 12:47 NCV.
5. 2 Cor. 5:10, see also Rom. 14:10.
6. See Neh. 8:10.
7. Matt. 25:21 NKJV.

Chapter 14 • *The Law of Change*

1. Eccles. 1:9 NIV.
2. Mal. 3:6 KJV.
3. See 1 Kings 8:47.
4. Ps. 121:4.
5. Isa. 34:4.
6. See Luke 5:36–38.
7. Matt. 9:17 NIV.
8. 2 Cor. 3:17.
9. See Isa. 6:8.
10. Luke 3:3 NIV.
11. Rom. 12:2 NCV.
12. 1 Kings 19:4 KJV.
13. 1 Kings 18–19.
14. 1 Cor. 5:17.

Chapter 15 • *The Law of Miracles*

1. See John 14:12.
2. Matt. 8:10.
3. Mark 11:22.
4. See Numbers 13–14.
5. See 1 Sam. 14:1–15.
6. Rom. 4:20–21 KJV.
7. Mark 10:27 NCV.
8. See Mark 4:39.
9. See Mark 5:38–42, Luke 7:11–16; John 11:43.
10. See Mark 9:25.

11. See Matt. 8:3.
12. See Matt. 8:13.
13. Mark 9:29 NCV.
14. John 11:43.
15. See 1 Thess. 5:17.
16. Exod. 20:7.
17. See Acts 2:4.
18. See Luke 24:49.
19. Mark 11:25–26 (many manuscripts do not contain verse 26).
20. 1 John 1:7 NCV.
21. See Matt. 22:37–40.
22. Matt. 18:21–22.
23. Matt. 18:32–35.
24. See 1 Corinthians 12–14.
25. 1 Cor. 12:7.
26. 1 Cor. 12:8–10, emphasis added.
27. See John 3:8.
28. See Isa. 42:9.

Chapter 16 • *The Law of Dominion*

1. Gen. 1:26–27 KJV.
2. Matt. 16:18 KJV.
3. Hos. 4:6 JB.
4. Gen. 1:26 KJV.
5. Gen. 1:29.
6. John 8:31–32.
7. Heb. 2:14–15, emphasis added.
8. Mark 4:39 KJV.
9. Matt. 28:19–20 NKJV.
10. Mark 16:20, emphasis added.
11. 1 Cor. 3:9, emphasis added.
12. 2 Cor. 5:20; 6:1, emphasis added.
13. 2 Tim. 2:12, emphsis added.
14. Luke 9:1–2 NCV, emphasis added.
15. Luke 10:19 NCV, emphasis added.
16. See Gen. 3:15.
17. Matt. 28:18–19, emphasis added.
18. John 17:4.
19. 1 John 3:8.
20. See 1 Tim. 1:15.
21. Phil. 4:13.
22. 2 Tim. 1:7.
23. Matt. 24:14, emphasis added.
24. Rom. 15:19.
25. Mark 11:22.

26. Gen. 1:28, emphasis added.
27. John 12:31.
28. Eph. 6:12.
29. Eph. 6:13, 17.

Chapter 17 • *The Coming King*

1. Luke 8:10 NCV.
2. 1 Cor. 15:50.
3. See 2 Pet. 3:9.
4. See Ezek. 38:2, 5–6, 9.
5. Ezek. 38:11–12.
6. Ezek. 38:13 (paraphrased)
7. Ezek. 39:7, emphasis added.
8. See Rev. 17:9–14.
9. Rev. 13:16–17.
10. See Revelation 19.
11. See Rev. 20:2, 4, 7.
12. Isa. 9:6–7.
13. Rev. 19:11–16.
14. See Luke 9:48.
15. Eph. 1:23.
16. Rev. 21:1.
17. See Matt. 13:24–43.
18. Matt. 13:28.
19. Matt. 13:37–43, emphasis added.
20. Matt. 13:49.
21. 1 Cor. 15:22–28, emphasis added.
22. See Eph. 1:9–10.
23. Matt. 3:10.
24. See Heb. 12:25–29.
25. Luke 12:32 NCV.